UNTIED KINGDOM

A Global History of the End of Britain

Stuart Ward

CAMBRIDGE
UNIVERSITY PRESS

University Printing House, Cambridge CB2 8BS, United Kingdom

One Liberty Plaza, 20th Floor, New York, NY 10006, USA

477 Williamstown Road, Port Melbourne, VIC 3207, Australia

314–321, 3rd Floor, Plot 3, Splendor Forum, Jasola District Centre,
New Delhi – 110025, India

103 Penang Road, #05–06/07, Visioncrest Commercial, Singapore 238467

Cambridge University Press is part of the University of Cambridge.

It furthers the University's mission by disseminating knowledge in the pursuit of
education, learning, and research at the highest international levels of excellence.

www.cambridge.org
Information on this title: www.cambridge.org/9781107145993
DOI: 10.1017/9781316536322

© Stuart Ward 2023

First published 2023

Printed in the United Kingdom by TJ Books Limited, Padstow Cornwall

A catalogue record for this publication is available from the British Library.

ISBN 978-1-107-14599-3 Hardback

Contents

Figures

INTRODUCTION

In the second act of Mike Bartlett's 'future history' play *King Charles III*, an exasperated Prince Harry absconds from Buckingham Palace after a row with his newly crowned father. He drifts anonymously through London's side streets in search of a midnight snack where he encounters Paul, a kebab vendor at a kerbside rotisserie, and the pair fall into a conversation about the troubled state of the nation. 'It's like this meat here, all pulled together' ventures Paul, gesturing to the rotating spit – constantly turning and churning but becoming 'smaller all the time' with each slice of the chef's blade. With long carving motions he prepares a shawarma for the incognito Prince, which brings him to the nub of the problem: 'When does Britain get so cut down, that it's not Britain anymore?'[1] The question is allowed to linger, unanswered – as though speaking for itself. In essentials, it is the same question that sets the agenda for this book.

Invoking the 'end of Britain' can seem like an exercise in gratuitous coat-trailing, inviting controversy before a single page is turned. But historians and political pundits have been confidently predicting Britain's expiry date for more than half a century, ever since the first wave of support for separatist political parties in Scotland and Wales in the late 1960s. Speculation about the long-term viability of the Union acquired the weight of scholarly ballast with the publication of *The Break-Up of Britain* – Tom Nairn's influential elegy from 1977 – and has become standard journalistic fare ever since.[2] Though the early momentum stalled with the defeat of the 1979 devolution referendums, Welsh historian Gwyn Williams could nevertheless pronounce shortly afterwards that Britain had 'begun its long march out of history'.[3] In a similar vein, Linda Colley's landmark 1992 study, *Britons: Forging the Nation*, was animated by a sense that 'so many of the components of Britishness' had faded and 'a substantial rethinking of what it means to be British' could no longer be avoided.[4]

Since that time, a surfeit of opinion polls and social surveys have probed the strength of British sentiment, compared with English, Scottish, Welsh or Northern Irish attachments, with results tilting ever-more decisively towards sub-national loyalties.[5] The urge to keep repeating the same question – with ever-growing frequency – became a fixture of British political life from the time of the devolution settlement of 1997, and was refashioned as a binding political instrument during the close-run Scottish Independence vote of 2014 (with polls conducted ever since adding a question about whether voters are inclined to revisit the proposition). Viable nations with a stable body politic do not, as a rule, feel compelled continually to gauge the depth of shared feeling (vis-à-vis the strength of not-so-shared feeling). Any social entity – whether it be a trade union, tennis club or a nation-state – that habitually asks its members whether they would not prefer to be part of something else can hardly be said to have longevity on its side. Over time, there is a sense in which the polling itself has merged into a ritualized tolling of the death knell.

To contemplate Britain's quietus, then, is by no means a preposterous or even a particularly original proposition. But this book is different. It is not in the mould of the 'end of Britain tomes' that appeared in quick succession with the inauguration of the Scottish and Welsh assemblies at the turn of the millennium.[6] Nor does it offer a searing critique of the shortcomings of the unitary British state, or mount a case for the self-determination of its constituent parts.[7] Nor, for that matter, does it add to the vast weight of political commentary on the internal political dynamics of devolutionary pressures since the 1970s, assessing the remarkable upswing in the recent fortunes of the Scottish National Party, Sinn Féin and Plaid Cymru.[8] These are all distinct and necessary approaches that remain crucial to informed contemporary debate. But they also proceed from the same unexamined premise: that the affective ties uniting the Kingdom have frayed to the point where they can longer be taken for granted.

Untied Kingdom addresses this underlying problem, asking questions about the changing historical contingencies of being British and the deeper ruptures over time that have brought matters to such a precarious impasse; not a detailed accounting of 'devolution' per se, but a wider history of what Alvin Jackson terms the 'emotional or spiritual deficit in the Union'.[9] The surprising swing towards 'yes Scotland' in the 2014 independence referendum was widely attributed to the serial missteps of the 'no' campaign, as recriminations redounded on its dearth of charisma, relentless negativity and conspicuous failure to provide an emotional dimension to the Unionist cause. But the lack of passion and verve was not simply the fault of Unionism's 'bloodless advocates'. As Janan Ganesh noted at the time, 'big things do not happen for small reasons ... the trigger for such large events may be fiddly and particular ... but the ultimate cause is deep and structural'. The scapegoating of the campaign overlooked a more intractable problem: that the Union's binding moral compact had been steadily unravelling for decades, unable to recover from the mortal blow of Britain's post-war imperial retreat.[10]

THE IMPERIAL DISAPPEARING ACT: GLOBAL PROJECTIONS

'With the end of Empire and the fading of uniting wartime memory, Britishness has receded as something felt in the pulse, a hot, urgent value, and retreated into official abstraction.'[11] Andrew Marr is only the most recent in a long line of influential voices to discern a link between the historical burden of imperial decline and the slow depletion of shared British sentiment since the Second World War. Speculation about a possible connection between the two can be traced as far back as the origins of decolonization itself. Virtually all the early prophets of the 1970s gave prominence to the end of empire as the crucial precursor event that opened the devolutionary floodgates, and over the years, historians of remarkably diverse leanings from Linda Colley herself to J. G. A. Pocock, Raphael Samuel, Krishan Kumar and Norman Davies have thrown their intellectual weight behind it.[12] To this day, the empire routinely resurfaces to make sense of the diminishing returns of being British, not least in the context of the fault lines exposed by the Brexit crisis.[13]

Yet for all its presumptive explanatory power, the end of empire tends to be framed as an abstract tipping point, with little sense of its real-life interactions or everyday consequences. It appears as a remote backdrop – self-contained and largely self-explanatory – that need not delay matters or divert attention from the main act. As such, its allegedly corrosive properties are habitually glossed over, reducible to the 'disappearance of the project which for so long had defined Britishness and British institutions' – a conspicuous absence rather than a vital interface.[14] This has sustained a range of positions that attribute an extraordinary dynamism to an unexamined subject, as though the empire's mere 'disappearance' were causation itself. A crude logic of subtraction (take out the empire and the edifice crumbles) has taken the place of fine-grained analysis – exemplified by David Marquand's pithy formula: 'Shorn of empire, "Britain" had no meaning . . . it is by definition impossible for Britain as such to be post-imperial'.[15] When the answer literally defines the problem, why probe the matter further?

This book sets out to take seriously the proposition that being British was always heavily entangled in overseas projections, affecting peoples in disparate parts of the globe who came variously into contact with its expanding perimeter. Understanding its protracted demise therefore requires a similarly wide-angled lens. A global history of the end of Britain is not simply about embracing a more diverse or 'inclusive' story, even if it does admit a wider cast of historical actors. More importantly, it addresses the problem in its proper dimensions, working from the premise that *not* approaching the matter in this way simply misses – and misconstrues – too much. If social identities are inherently relational, arising out of intricate patterns of material and cultural exchange connecting peoples across wide distances, then focusing solely on the 'British of Britain' can provide only a partial and incomplete perspective. By incorporating the fate of Britishness in the many corners of the world where it has long since ceased to command any popular allegiance, the diminishing strength of unitary sentiment in the contemporary United Kingdom emerges in a whole new light.

What follows therefore is an attempt to redraw the boundaries of the subject itself – the end of Britain rendered as a series of global ruptures with profound consequences for metropolitan and 'overseas' constituents alike. Charles Dilke's nineteenth-century imagining of a 'Greater Britain' furnishes the principal navigating instrument, retooled for present purposes to override its white racial affiliations and admit a wider assortment of peoples and cultures into its purview.[16] Dilke himself was an unapologetic, dyed-in-the-wool Victorian racist. But the skewed moral compass so typical of his generation can shed valuable light on how his conception of a globally linked fraternity of British peoples ultimately fared. The exaltation of 'the British race' was to be Britain's undoing, and in this sense the otherwise embarrassingly obsolete cadence of Greater Britain can be rendered fit for purpose. It can also contribute to an alternative reading of decolonization, looking beyond the political and ideological implosion of empire to consider the diminished resonance of Britain-in-the-world, affecting an extended chain of communities located variously 'offshore'.

Approaching the subject in this way means jettisoning several key misconceptions and red herrings. Anyone familiar with the long and intricate history of constitutional devolution in the UK will recognize the futility of formulating a direct cause-and-effect relationship. As several critics have pointed out, the centrifugal forces pulling the 'Four Nations' apart emerged either too soon (the Home Rule crises of the late Victorian era) or too late (the post-Thatcher surge of devolutionary pressure) to establish any neat correlation with the end of empire.[17] Similarly, the well-worn paradigm of 'internal colonialism', positing Scotland and Wales as

4

England's 'last colonies' still awaiting emancipation, tends to oversimply a far more complex reality and is best pushed to one side.[18] Readers in search of validation for such reveries are advised to look elsewhere.

If meaningful connections are to be made, a more circuitous route is needed, relinquishing hard and fast distinctions between 'the British' and the wider world they inhabited and assimilated to an expansive view of themselves. This is not a book where the empire is something that 'happens' to Britain, but one that traces how the United Kingdom and its overseas affiliates all became swept up in the global dislocations of imperial decline. The end of empire was no mere trigger but an integral component of the 'Break-up of Britain' – as fundamental as the ongoing political ructions over Scottish independence or the Northern Ireland border. Though the ultimate fate of the Union cannot yet be known, there are valuable insights to be gleaned from viewing its current travails in a much wider perspective, as merely the latest in a long line of civic ruptures in a world where being British has ceased to resonate as a unifying proposition.

It is emphatically a work of history, focused primarily on the four crucial decades from the late 1940s to the early 1980s when the external props of empire faltered, and the expansive properties of Britishness were de-sentimentalized. If 'the ultimate cause' of Britain's demise 'is deep and structural', it is to be found – it will be argued here – in the progressive rollback of its imaginative frontiers. For many, indeed most of the contexts to be explored here, the 'end of Britain' is no idle prediction but a simple, unadorned fact of everyday life – from Kenya to Australia, Zimbabwe, Canada, Jamaica, New Zealand, India, Pakistan, Hong Kong, Singapore, South Africa, Barbados and even (in a somewhat different vein) the Falkland Islands and Gibraltar. As such, it is by no means premature to render the matter as 'history'. Nor can residual British sentiment in the United Kingdom – still capable of stirring genuine, albeit highly ambivalent feelings – be said to have emerged unaffected from the complex fragmentations of empire's end. Here, too, there is a history to be told, even if its full implications remain to be seen.

'THINGS FALL APART': THE ARGUMENT OF THIS BOOK

Among the many repercussions of the Brexit vote of June 2016 was the renewed currency of worldly aspirations among its chief advocates – specifically, the idea of restoring 'Global Britain' as a worthy and desirable national goal. Initially intended as a makeshift substitute for EU membership, over time it also became a means of checking separatist momentum in Scotland, Wales and Northern Ireland. The promise of reactivating a 'world role' could be contrasted favourably with the narrower preoccupations of devolutionary politics, tapping into memories of a time when Britain seemed to count for so much more. But for all its historical resonances, it is the fundamental novelty of Global Britain – the need to spell it out so baldly in such unprecedented circumstances – that exposes the outworn logic of the idea of Britain itself. If Global Britain needed to be rediscovered to resist the tide of national fragmentation, what does that say about the historical connections between the two?

Marquand's premise that 'the British state was, by definition, a global state; and the British people, by definition, was a global people' provides an invaluable starting point, but it remains poorly conceptualized.[19] British identities did not simply evolve in tandem with historical patterns of outward expansion and imperial conquest; they were themselves largely conditioned by overseas enterprise, responding to the need for a serviceable shorthand to encompass new and unfamiliar social realities. From the early seventeenth century, schemes for overseas colonization were tentatively couched in the aspirational language of Britain and Britons. By the mid-eighteenth century, with the consolidation of maritime commerce and incessant global warfare with France, the idea of a British people operating beyond the conventional bounds of geography had become increasingly commonplace. The massive outpouring of migrants in the nineteenth century lent critical mass to an emergent global civic idea, forging a shared identity and corporate purpose, not only among the diverse accumulations of migrants themselves (sourced from every corner of the United Kingdom), but also from a wider assortment of peoples drawn by all manner of complex motivations – physical coercion, material advantage and the lure of British constitutional liberties.

The point is not to impose some spurious uniformity on the intricately layered possibilities for being British but the very opposite – to embrace the sheer diversity of peoples and cultures that became bundled together under such an open-ended category. There can be no easy definitions or simple historical consensus about the many variations of Britishness throughout the lifespan of the empire, but equally there can be no doubt about the effects of imperial decline on the intricate patchwork of affinities forged throughout the world in Britain's name. It is the sheer capaciousness of the subject – geographically, ideologically, sentimentally – that holds the key. Much of what follows engages with long-standing variations, vexations and outright contradictions deeply embedded in a 'greater' conception of

Britain harking back hundreds of years, unable to withstand the unique pressures brought to bear in the post-war world.

'Things fall apart; the centre cannot hold', runs Yeats's well-worn aphorism, but when it comes to accounting for the end of Britain the centre–periphery axis only gets us so far. If British identities emerged out of a wider confluence of peoples and patterns of exchange, their recessional in the second half of the twentieth century also needs to be recounted as a collective experience. To be sure, a crucial piece of the puzzle is the diminished capacity of the United Kingdom to fulfil the role of an imperial hub, having shouldered the burden of two world wars and a crippling economic depression. The challenge of imperial overstretch was nothing new in itself, but the effects of a sustained period of global conflict placed intolerable restraints on what John Darwin terms the 'British world-system'.[20] With a severely reduced capacity to invest overseas, service the heavy requirements of imperial defence and provide the manufacturing clout to sustain traditional patterns of intra-empire and Commonwealth trade, Britain entered the post-war world as a depleted force. This, combined with the unprecedented demand to invest the country's residual resources in rebuilding projects at home (attending to the social as much as the physical infrastructure), set the putative imperial centre down a path of irreconcilable differences with British subjects overseas. Latent conflicts of interest that had permeated empire–Commonwealth networks for generations became endemic in these years, unpicking the many pre-existing flaws in the Greater British fabric.

But there were other factors in play that cannot simply be ascribed to a Gibbonesque 'decline and fall'. The mid-twentieth century marked a decisive moment when 'modern globalization encountered the forces of decolonization' – radically altering the terms of exchange of raw materials for industrial goods between colonies and metropoles.[21] Global demand for manufactures encouraged deeper patterns of economic integration between exporters of finished consumer goods, undermining the economic rationale of colonial systems of commercial allegiance. This coincided with a period of innovation in international civic norms and global governance, with a profusion of multinational organizations and regional blocs that cut across older cultural alignments, marginalizing sub-systems of world order founded on shared British constitutional custom. The global ideological struggle of the Cold War compounded these developments, adding a further dimension to the general climate of adversity for colonialism worldwide. Taken together, the historical conditions that had cultivated and consolidated an imperial culture of Britishness were called into question, profoundly impacting the signifiers of 'greatness' and putting on notice the lazy equivalence of territorial purview with national prestige.

But these factors were slow to reveal themselves and, at least initially, British-derived models provided a certain inspiration for the emerging configurations of global order, particularly in the interwar years where hopes were entertained that the British Commonwealth might provide a template for a 'world Commonwealth'. Despite the influence of J. C. Smuts and other key Commonwealth figures in drafting the UN Charter, however, it soon transpired that a new 'culture of internationalism' geared towards global scales of political organization would throw down a challenge to the comparatively naive conception of a worldwide continuum of interdependent British peoples. 'Globalism offered an alternative to empire', as one history of this pivotal period affirms, drastically curbing the potential of the Commonwealth as a conduit of Greater British sentiment.[22] The most visible sign was the 'Independence Day' spectacle of Union Jacks hauled down in every corner of the globe and replaced by alternative markers of national esteem. But the political success of anti-colonial nationalism tended to overshadow a far broader complex of 'worldmaking' initiatives that experimented with 'political forms beyond and below the nation-state', striving for equality, human dignity and a new international order.[23] The sheer range and proliferation of new moral worlds on offer – Marxist, pan-African, 'non-aligned', or simply humanitarian – would call into question the durability of 'British worlds' anchored in English constitutional liberties.

These global realignments also undercut British identities in far more direct ways. After an extended wartime and interwar hiatus, a renewed era of hypermobility was inaugurated in the early 1950s with British subjects around the world once again asserting their rights (and enhanced means) to move freely to and from Britain, now enshrined in the extraordinarily wide provisions of the British Nationality Act of 1948.[24] This coincided with a mid-century communications revolution that brought dramatic improvements in audio and visual broadcasting technologies, drawing peoples separated by vast distances into more tightly integrated patterns of virtual proximity. These developments might have been expected to consolidate and perhaps even intensify transoceanic networks of Britishness, forging deeper social interactions and breaking down long-distance barriers to familiarity. And to be sure, these possibilities were anticipated and eagerly exploited by way of assisted emigration schemes and enhanced collaboration at what appears (in retrospect) as 'the high point of Britannic broadcasting cooperation'.[25] But over time, and particularly a time when wider British allegiances were subject to intense material and ideological strain, the very opposite tendency began to emerge.

It was a prime example of 'the politics of recognition' – Charles Taylor's conceptualization of 'how much an original identity needs and is vulnerable to the recognition given or withheld by significant others' – played out over immense distances. Self-styled 'British' communities in all parts of the world would be confronted with the jarring 'misrecognition' that arises whenever peoples and cultures presumed to be bound by protocols of mutual regard are suddenly struck by their glaring absence (and find themselves questioning and reformulating their affinities accordingly). Taylor stressed the fundamentally dialogical character of identity-formation – the constantly evolving modes of self-expression 'through interaction with others who matter to us'. The question of 'who mattered' would expose the finer distinctions of being British in the decades after 1945, when a whole range of localized inflections were drawn into closer physical and moral proximity, and hence unprecedented scrutiny.[26]

Stuart Hall drew on Taylor's term to describe the metropolitan encounter of the 'Windrush' generation of West Indian arrivals in the 1950s, who found themselves constantly reminded of the limits of imperial Britishness ('Who are these people? Where are they from? What language do they speak? ... Could someone ever be black and British?'). 'Misrecognition' was coupled with a pronounced 'misremembering' on the part of their hosts, such that Caribbean 'histories, and their long historical entanglements with Britain, disappeared from daily consciousness'. But Hall also saw that the enmity could cut both ways, observing how working-class whites and West Indian migrants 'grew to misrecognize each other as the main cause of their misfortune'.[27] These dynamics did not appear overnight, but marked an acceleration of interwar trends where newly arrived migrants, students and intellectuals from all parts of the empire converged around an incipient counter-political culture centred on London in particular.[28] The effects were compounded throughout the post-war world wherever and whenever competing British sensibilities produced similar shocks of mutual misrecognition.

Often, the extreme measures employed to preserve Britain's global coordinates only accentuated the problem, particularly when it came to combatting colonial insurgencies. It is sometimes overlooked that the decades of decolonization marked a late surge of imperial consolidation, with rising rates of British emigration and even higher rates of military deployments overseas – increasing the likelihood of violent clashes with anti-colonial resistance movements. The same technological innovations that enabled Britain to intensify its military deployments – from Kenya to Malaya, Cyprus, Aden and elsewhere – also brought the grim realities of conflict closer to home. As Erik Linstrum's work so lucidly shows, 'the networks of imperial modernity' not only made 'atrocities possible' but also brought people into ever-more vivid contact with their unnerving implications.[29] The effect was to undermine confidence in overextended frontiers, polarizing attitudes about the morality and the fundamental necessity of British interventions abroad and exposing divisions in the very communities that British power was meant to defend.

Indeed, the fault lines of misrecognition multiplied in these years to expose latent divisions among the 'old' or 'white' Commonwealth. Long-standing embarrassments such as the 'White Australia' immigration policy or the practice of racial segregation in South Africa produced echoes of older liberal and humanitarian misgivings, now lumbered with an immediacy and intensity by technology's triumph over distance. Even the increased frequency of intergovernmental conferences (though presented as the pinnacle of Commonwealth fellow-feeling) brought the disruptive potential of physical proximity to the fore. From the late 1940s, each gathering of Commonwealth prime ministers furnished a fresh volley of recriminations as the certainties of white solidarity faltered. Here, too, an element of misremembering played a part, affecting influential opinion in each of the old settler societies – particularly among an emergent post-war generation bent on relinquishing the imperial baggage of Britishness by promoting new, more self-sufficient conceptions couched increasingly in terms of 'national identity'. It was not simply a case of 'de-dominionization' – decoupling the white empire from outmoded affections for the motherland – but also a process of internal discord, as once-normative British sensibilities fractured internally across social, ideological and generational lines.[30]

The retrenchment of imperial interests and the attendant patterns of misrecognition became self-reinforcing, not least because the idea of Britain drew so heavily on long-distance projections. As the system faltered in one part of the world, others could not avoid being affected (where they were not directly embroiled) – as witnessed, for example, by the spontaneous scramble for new citizenship laws throughout the Commonwealth when Canada unilaterally downgraded British subjecthood in 1946. Being British was not something that could prosper in the absence of significant others (real or imagined) equally invested in other parts of the world. When white Rhodesians finally renounced the British connection in 1965 while striking the defiant pose of loyalty's last true bastion, they were to discover that going it alone was hardly tenable as a 'British' proposition. Northern Irish loyalists similarly began to feel the pinch towards the end of the 1960s, by then no longer securely linked in a global chain of offshore British enclaves. Meanwhile Scottish and Welsh nationalists, instinctively sensing an opportunity in a British world in disarray, managed to secure a permanent foothold in Westminster by the late 1960s. These were halting, and generally hesitant procedures – more a case of creeping obsolescence than mass redundancy – but the signs of a deeper corrosion were unmistakable.

Richard Bourke sees in this a 'paradigmatic process in British history' affecting what he terms 'the fate of allegiance under conditions of imperial retrenchment'. Because British overseas expansion encompassed so many distinct, quasi-autonomous communities in continuous dialogue, he argues, it also produced a situation in which the 'resulting societies were free to cultivate independent systems of expectation' – with the potential to generate extreme levels of friction whenever such expectations were not met. But it also contained the possibility of insulating British domestic politics from perceived crises and upheavals abroad, by the simple expedient of disavowing overseas obligations whenever they threatened civil disruption at home. An empire so capable of 'liberating itself from its own imperial loyalists' placed offshore compatriots in an intolerable bind, obliged to cultivate shared British sentiments as a means of accessing metropolitan resources, but painfully aware that their interests might be subordinated or even sacrificed for the sake of 'domestic constitutional order'.[31] With each flashpoint in the chapters that follow, it will become clearer how the emotional stakes were additionally charged by the implicit knowledge that the bonds of Greater Britain were inherently unreliable.

Much of Bourke's inspiration came from the leading intellectual historian, J. G. A. Pocock – a disaffected New Zealander who had his own complicated investments in 'the fate of allegiance' at empire's end. Rather than stress the self-preserving instincts of a unified metropolitan core, however, Pocock raised a far more radical prospect. 'We all at least claim to dislike balkanization', he told an audience in his hometown of Christchurch in May 1973, 'and I doubt if the most resolutely nationalist among us could say that the disappearance of all meaning from the term "Britain" would do nothing at all to his sense of identity'.[32] Yet the end of Britain was precisely what Pocock apprehended, partly the consequence of entrenched English indifference towards Scottish and Welsh sensibilities; and partly the folly (as he saw it) of sinking British sovereignty into the European Common Market – a move that only four months earlier had severely dented the morale of 'tangential' British identities such as his own.[33] He added a third ingredient, the recent outbreak of a new wave of violent 'Troubles' in Northern Ireland, to raise truly momentous possibilities:

> With communal war resumed in Ireland and a daily cost in lives being paid for the desire of one of the 'British' peoples to remain 'British' as they understand the term, it is not inconceivable that future historians may find themselves writing of a 'Unionist' or even a 'British' period in the history of the peoples inhabiting the Atlantic archipelago, and locating it between a date in the thirteenth, the seventeenth or the nineteenth centuries and a date in the twentieth or the twenty-first.

Pocock characterized Protestant Ulster in the very terms that he would later describe the American colonists of the eighteenth century – as a disenchanted people who 'ceased being "British" when they could not be "British" as they understood the term'.[34] But the scales of mutual affection were never quite so one-sided, nor was the United Kingdom the only political unit prepared to reject the claims of fellow Britons to evade unwanted moral implications. It will be argued here that multiple actors, divergent interests, and conflicting assumptions all contributed to the steady erosion of shared affinities. To be British, it seemed, was to be on the wrong side of history.

Significantly, Pocock identified a special proclivity among *the English* to profess 'no more than an obligatory sense of identity' with any of the neighbouring peoples of their island group.[35] That is to say, Bourke's 'generic feature of British *imperial* history' could apply equally to the internal dynamics of the Union.[36] A penchant for keeping offshore compatriots at arm's length could also account for why Scottish, Irish and (to a lesser extent) Welsh peoples were never fully integrated into the unitary British state, and were permitted to maintain considerable territorial and cultural integrity. Elijah Gould has taken this idea further, arguing that the potential for disruption from Celtic neighbours was the main reason why 'Britain's internal boundaries have proved so resilient and why the nation superimposed over those divisions remains, in some ways, more virtual than real'.[37] In this scheme of things, the 'Four Nations' had always served as a constitutional fire break.

Here we arrive at the crux of the problem: an inherently expansive Britishness, constantly adapting and shape shifting in dialogue with wide horizons while ever ready to jettison overly burdensome liabilities, would eventually run out of appendages to prune. Save for the Falkland Islands or Gibraltar – both strong candidates for future retrenchment – from what other unruly hinterland might Britain's mythical constitutional order be saved, if not the residual irritant of its own internal divisions? We are left with the unanswered question so shrewdly put to the fictional Prince Harry: 'When does Britain get so cut down, that it's not Britain anymore? ... If you take enough layers away what have you got left, underneath, know what I mean?'[38]

ORGANIZATION, STRUCTURE AND SOURCES

Such a wide-ranging agenda does not lend itself to a seamless narrative or exhaustive coverage. Instead, *Untied Kingdom* draws together a number of interlocking threads with a view to demonstrating how global currents were channelled through localized encounters, each unfolding according to their own internal logic, but nevertheless intersecting with wider scales and contexts in direct and indirect ways.[39] Each chapter addresses a particular social, political, cultural or institutional prism through which Britishness was imagined, experienced, disputed and ultimately (if ambivalently) discarded at different times and in diverse locales in the decades after 1945. Collectively, they traverse a wide selection of settings and themes, from the semantic confusion that became attached to the term 'British' in the wake of Indian independence, to the startling political breakthrough of Scottish and Welsh separatism two decades later. Though much of the action unfolds 'overseas', it does so in tandem with contemporaneous developments in the United Kingdom: the social and political consequences of diminished 'global reach'; the widely observed weight of national decline; the renewed emphasis on sub-national affinities as the presumptive benefits of being British were called into question; the extraordinary return of communal violence in Northern Ireland as the support posts of a wider British world faded from view. Tracing these latter developments as distinctively 'domestic' facets of imperial decline is not to posit a simple cause-and-effect connection, but to shed light on the parallel manifestations of the same fundamental phenomenon – in all its manifold iterations and implications.

Part I is concerned with the overseas projections of imperial identity – the long 'Prelude' that produced the material and ideological conditions for imagining Britishness on a global scale. Chapter 1 considers how imperial expansion from the early seventeenth century created the need to make sense of highly fluid movements of people in radically new social formations. The language of Britishness could be employed across enormous distances, but the resultant heterogeneity also engendered fault lines that would later pose formidable problems. Chapter 2 enlarges on the meaning of 'Greater Britain' on the eve of the Great War, asking what kind of intercommunal network was enlivened by the conception of the British as a 'world' people. Contemporaries furnished a wide spectrum of answers, and it is by comparing the extremes of variation from Vancouver to Ulster to Punjab that the underlying patterns of mutual misrecognition start to emerge. Chapter 3 completes the foundations by considering the paradoxical effects of two world wars, at once harnessing an unprecedentedly vast emotional and material reservoir in the service of a common cause while at the same time ushering in a new era of 'internationalism' that would ultimately strip the British world-system of its effectiveness and fundamental rationale.

Part II proceeds to the main argument. Entitled 'Registers', it is structured not according to strict chronology or national 'case' surveys but in terms of the many sub-systems of meaning that conveyed the idea of Britain around the world (and back again). Like all social imaginaries, Britishness was not a fixed object or undifferentiated 'identity'. It is more usefully approached as an unusually broad spectrum of possibilities for people to make claims on British selfhood according to their own individual or collective needs. To be British was to be part of a wider conversation, comprising any number of symbolic and linguistic registers that mediated its imaginative properties. Each register contained common-sense assumptions that were interdependent and mutually reinforcing, but they can also be separated out and examined as distinct vocabularies of Britishness that lend much-needed analytical purchase to an otherwise unwieldy subject. Not only did these registers come under unprecedented strain in the decades after 1945, but they also became key sites of contestation as rival protagonists (individuals, interest groups, community organizations, government operatives and political representatives) sought to access their powers of signification and control their meaning.

Unpacking the registers of Britishness also furnishes access to the terms of endearment that became so volatile and unpredictable in these years. Six consecutive chapters each document a 'little death' of Britain-in-the-world from the 1940s to the 1970s – beginning with the fundamental issue of language (Chapter 4). The narrowing semantic range of imperial Britishness was epitomized by India's request for admission into the postwar Commonwealth as the first member to adopt a republican constitution. Resolving this dilemma placed the adjective 'British' under intense scrutiny, pressing the 'British Commonwealth' to the limit of its capacity to bind an increasingly atomized membership. Subsequent chapters deal with similarly

14

strained registers, including the idea of 'home' as a metaphor for trans-oceanic belonging (Chapter 5); the contradictions of British subjecthood at a time of renewed global mobility (Chapter 6); the faltering foundations of British constitutional liberties in the face of new universal norms (Chapter 7); the moral economy of globally produced British goods as older imperial patterns of commercial exchange unravelled (Chapter 8); and the fraying tenets of a flawed system of global British justice (Chapter 9). Each chapter is anchored in a specific time and place that highlights the importance of local contingencies, while drawing on parallels elsewhere to illuminate the broader dynamics and the sheer scale of the disruptions.

Finally, Part III turns to the major repercussions, not least for the United Kingdom. The opening chapter considers the loss of confidence in Britain's far horizons, which became a major post-war preoccupation as the moral axioms of 'global reach' faltered (Chapter 10). This was closely intertwined with the culture of 'declinism' that took hold from the late 1950s, principally affecting the political and literary culture of England yet also reproduced in strikingly similar ways elsewhere (Chapter 11). Three successive chapters attend variously to the 'Four Nations' – the newly racialized inflections of post-imperial Englishness (Chapter 12); the distinctly 'offshore' resonances of the Northern Ireland 'Troubles' (Chapter 13); and the effects of global decolonization on the changing fortunes of national separatism in Scotland and Wales (Chapter 14). The final chapter ties these issues to the many pathways out of empire, and the often-hesitant process of civic reinvention and readjustment as popular energies were redirected to post-imperial modes of belonging (Chapter 15). This, too, brought patterns of social division and public dispute that were replicated (and modified) across multiple contexts and settings – most recently exemplified by the latter-day controversies over the UK constitution.

It is striking how often people actually noticed the rapid depreciation of their material and emotional investments in being British, particularly when they found themselves at loggerheads with presumptive compatriots elsewhere. These moments of self-awareness furnish a rich trove of original source material that makes up the empirical ballast for each chapter. Though not principally a study of political thought, perspectives are included from the realm of party politics, political rhetoric and the exertions of public moralists. Though falling well short of a history of intergovernmental relations, official archives in many of the countries concerned have also been consulted for specific purposes. Legal and constitutional material also furnishes crucial insights at key junctures (though a precise study of this dimension would require more dedicated treatment), as does evidence from civil society and the many organizations that were in some way invested in Britain's global coordinates. Icons and symbols of 'social self-worship' are additionally incorporated, along with indicators of the changing tenor of public feeling, from news media to opinion polling to electoral politics.[40]

Collecting this material has entailed a journey across continents to those many parts of the world where the events under scrutiny took place, from the Central Highlands of Kenya to the shore of Vancouver's Burrard Inlet; the Hong Kong Public Library to Carmarthen's Guild Hall Square; the narrow confines of Gibraltar's laneways to the elongated sweep of Queensland's sugar belt; memorials to the empire's vanguard in the Eastern Cape to its victims at Jallianwallah Bagh; manicured 'English' gardens in Christchurch to elaborate murals in Derry's Bogside; the former industrial 'brownfields' of Scotland's Clyde Valley to the fertile farmlands of Mashonaland East to name but a few staging posts along the way. The main purpose in covering so much ground has been to access relevant libraries, archives and manuscript collections to piece together a highly dispersed documentary record – testimony to the fragmentation of the subject itself. But experiencing first-hand the extraordinarily diverse historical geography of imperial Britishness, now consigned largely to the distant past, was itself a revealing exercise. By traversing such a diversity of settings with a single object in mind, something of the broader architecture of the book began to fall into place.

Attending to such an eclectic surfeit of material could never be an exercise in scientific precision. What emerges is not a neat historical proposition that can be proven by a single set of documents or reduced to a unifying theory. It is more a matter of fresh historical perspective garnered from multiple vantage points, illuminating discrete crunch moments in a wider narrative arc. No single instalment clinches the argument but taken together, they stake out a broad set of coordinates from which distinct patterns can be discerned. Sceptics scouring these pages for glaring omissions will not go unrewarded, but what is lost in the way of comprehensive coverage will, it is to be hoped, be compensated by finer-grained exemplification.

Understanding how Britain 'ended' ultimately requires attention to how people subjectively responded to the confused and conflicting processes that undermined their wider British allegiances. Each chapter therefore opens with a portrait-in-miniature – the view from a tight-knit group or representative individual grappling with some aspect of the larger theme.

These cameos serve as periodic reminders of how broader patterns of material and ideological change impacted upon those immediately affected. They range from household names (celebrities, prime ministers, royalty) to ordinary citizens now largely forgotten (to the extent they were ever noticed), all of whom became caught up in the intractable identity politics of empire's end.

PART I

PROLOGUE

1

OFFSHORE FORMATIONS: THE UNBEARABLE BANDWIDTH OF BEING BRITISH

John Strachey was one of the first to make the connection in autumn 1962. The prolific author and MP for Dundee West was not himself Scottish, but he had represented the famed capital of Britain's 'jute empire' in the House of Commons for the best part of two decades, virtually assured of his seat in a safe Labour constituency. Even before he entered parliament in 1945, the sinews of commerce binding Dundee's mills to Calcutta's 'jute wallahs' had endured years of severe strain, squeezed by Bengali competitors and the consistent refusal of the British Government to impose tariff relief. Lamented as the 'Cinderella of the Textile Industries', Dundee jute went into steep decline under Strachey's tenure, as employment levels plummeted and local expertise was outsourced to independent India. It was an analogue of the end of empire itself, drawn out in successive waves from the 1940s to the 1970s, denting the morale of the local community and raising questions about their future. Although the linkages were intricate and often hidden from view, Dundee's story also exposed deep structural flaws beneath the surface tension of a unitary Britishness. As one penetrating account concludes, 'the layering and intertwining of Scottish and British identities was beginning to come apart' under the weight of the empire's dwindling returns.[1]

Shortly before his untimely death in July 1963, Strachey himself began to experience vague apprehensions about a rift in the national fabric. 'Writing my books', he confided to fellow Scottish Labour MP Tam Dalyell, 'I have had to reflect deeply on what happens to countries when they divest themselves of colonies and dominions . . . Now that the empire is vanishing, we must prevent the "Balkanisation of Britain" at all costs.'[2] Dalyell had recently survived an unexpected challenge in his West Lothian constituency from the political novice Billy Wolfe, who came from obscurity in June 1962 to galvanize nearly a quarter of the popular vote behind the Scottish National Party. A movement that had barely registered in public life over nearly three decades of fruitless endeavour seemed suddenly to be emerging as a viable electoral force. Strachey himself never had to contend with an SNP challenger in Dundee, and he would not live long enough to find out whether Wolfe's success was a flash in the pan or the harbinger of things to come. But within ten years of his truncated tenure as the local MP, the one-time 'juteopolis' on the River Tay would count among the principal strongholds of a separatist agenda emerging across Scotland.[3]

The spectre of 'balkanization' was an uncharacteristic prognosis coming from John Strachey, who only a few years earlier had offered a far more sanguine view in a major 1959 study, *The End of Empire*. Flagged on the dustjacket as 'the first book to face up to the situation in which Britain finds herself as the result of the voluntary dissolution of her Empire', the emphasis was squarely on the sunlit uplands in store for a country that had suddenly and beneficially been transformed into a 'post-imperial society'.[4] Himself the descendant of a long line of imperial consuls (including his great grandfather Henry, private secretary to Lord Clive), Strachey had shunned his conservative and aristocratic roots at an early age in favour of a lifelong dedication to Marxism. But he drew extensively on the family hoard of imperial papers and memorabilia to reach the decidedly un-Marxist conclusion that the empire was never principally forged for the sake of accumulating wealth; nor (as a consequence) did it ever enjoy any broad-based popular endorsement.[5]

These cardinal rules explained why Britain had managed to avoid becoming 'impoverished by the loss of her empire' – a sure sign that it had always been the plaything of a redundant aristocracy more in search of moral uplift than financial returns.[6] For the vast majority of the population, the empire had brought few rewards and even fewer reasons to lift their gaze from overwhelmingly domestic day-to-day concerns. The traditions of liberal and left-wing anti-imperialism, though never deep-rooted, had penetrated 'just deep enough' to nurture a certain critical distance, ensuring that most people could 'escape from the national fixation upon empire' when the time came.[7] The imperial mission could thus be expected to fade gracefully from view without disrupting the material prospects or emotional disposition of the British as a nation. Indeed, it was this fortuitous detachment that furnished a viable way forward, insulating the country from the ill effects of imperial depreciation.

John Strachey can thus be credited among the very first to articulate, not just one but two seemingly antithetical positions that would acquire enormous influence in subsequent years: that Britain met the challenge of decolonization with an in-built resistance to its corrosive potential; and that the self-same challenge posed a clear and present danger to the integrity of the Union itself. Significantly, only the former proposition was vetted for publication, confidently elaborated over 350 densely argued pages – with the latter sentiments buried diffidently between the lines. Strachey's abiding question 'What are the British to do with themselves now that they have lost their Empire?' was no idle curiosity but a matter in which 'the morale, the spirit, the mental health even, of all of us in Britain are deeply involved'. No less than 'the whole tone of our national life' somehow hinged on the presumed traumas of imperial decline – the 'moral and psychological shock,' the sense of 'personal loss – almost of amputation,' the 'depressing' cumulative effect of 'the hauling down of the Union Jack in yet another part of the world,' – rendered 'all the more difficult to deal with because it is essentially irrational'.[8] It was a curious way of mounting an argument about the *immaterial* consequences of empire's end. Indeed, the high stakes that impelled him to devote an entire book to the subject somehow never squared with his conviction that, ultimately, there were no real grounds for concern. Though outwardly convinced that Britain's painless imperial retreat would long remain 'an irresistible subject of self-congratulation', his sense of inner foreboding was never entirely expelled.[9]

Unsurprisingly, it was the more upbeat version that gained early traction, with the consensus among historians in the 1960s and 1970s overwhelmingly endorsing Strachey's claim that the British had never really been 'imperially-minded' (Beloff); that the empire had 'little or no meaning to working-class life and society' (Price); and that the 'great British public viewed the dissolution of their Empire with disinterest. They thought it was a bit of a joke' (Morris).[10] A. J. P. Taylor went out of his way to excise the empire entirely from his 1965 volume for the *Oxford History of England* with the uncomplicated formula 'The British Empire declined, the position of the people improved', and others generally followed suit.[11] Surveying the after-effects of Britain's imperial endgame, Peter Calvocoressi offered perhaps the most concise statement of the prevailing orthodoxy in 1978: 'The loss of empire has not, one opines, cut deep; and the reason is that having an empire did not cut deep either ... Loss of empire was loss of purpose and perspective, temporarily, for a few.'[12] But in all of these accounts, behind the moral and intellectual certainty lingered something of Strachey's equivocation.

Recent studies have continued to stress the marginal imprint of imperial decline, albeit with new inflexions and more elaborate lines of inquiry.[13] Far from reading decolonization as the beginning of a protracted 'balkanization', David Edgerton forcefully depicts the post-war years as a period of unprecedented national consolidation that flourished through to the early 1980s, surpassing anything before or indeed since – a development he largely puts down to the unsentimental retrenchment of overseas encumbrances.[14] Likening the United Kingdom to countless other 'new nations which arose from the dissolution of the one empire', he rejects any suggestion that the period was marked by the prolonged effects of 'residual imperialism' or 'misplaced nostalgia for empire'.[15] This was a time when 'nation trumped empire and Commonwealth' across multiple political, economic and institutional indictors, when 'Imperialism was a fringe activity confined to private spaces' and when the contours of a 'new British nation' emerged fully into view that 'increasingly knew only itself'.[16] In his haste to consign empire to the historical margins, however, Edgerton nevertheless manages to invest its passing with uniquely transformative properties. If abandoning the imperial mission 'went hand in hand' with the emergence of a new, more clearly delineated British nationalism, one might have thought those *hand-in-hand* interactions worthy of closer scrutiny.[17]

This account takes a different view of those critical decades after 1945, building on the efforts of historians over many years who have argued that the social and cultural sinews of decolonization in post-war Britain were highly significant – albeit uneven, ambivalent and frequently unacknowledged.[18] The inward effects of imperial decline cannot easily be quantified in zero sum terms; nor can they simply be gleaned from opinion polls, popular questionnaires or contemporary inquiries like Strachey's – for the simple reason that the persistent questioning was itself a recurring symptom of the problem.[19] Defending Britain's imperial remit undoubtedly became deeply unfashionable, perhaps even 'a joke', especially in the wake of the 1956 Suez crisis. But leaving it at that fails to capture the full measure of the embattled empire's enduring social and political significance.

Enlarging on this means recasting the question in a different light. Decades of historical debate about the empire's metropolitan 'impact' have brought largely inconclusive returns, primarily because the issue has been so narrowly framed – disaggregating 'the British' from a presumptive external agency penetrating their social formation at various intervals (with the dispute hinging on the meaning and magnitude of the intrusions). It will be argued here that the end of empire did indeed raise formidable challenges to the durability of a unitary Britishness – ushering in something broadly akin to Strachey's 'Balkanisation'. But the registers of impending rupture appeared in a language, imagery and symbolism that transcended the physical confines of the United Kingdom.

Embarking on a world history of the end of Britain means rethinking Britishness as a global category of analysis, working from that fundamental premise to unlock the dynamics of its protracted unravelling. This chapter sets out to make good on that foundational claim, tracing the historical evolution of British sensibilities from the outside-in – starting with the earliest offshore formations of Jacobean colonization, through the 'settler revolution' of the Victorian era to the high diction of 'Greater Britain' at the turn of the twentieth century. The point is not to argue that imperial reach was the sole, exclusive or even the most obvious constitutive element in the eyes of contemporaries, but to make a case for the indispensable quality of a certain bandwidth in making Britishness an attractive, rewarding and necessary proposition.

'THE MAINE CONTINENT I CALL BRITANNIA': TRANSATLANTIC CROSSINGS

If John Strachey was the first to grapple with these issues from the perspective of empire's end, it was another Strachey (and another ancestor) who some 350 years earlier penned one of the first histories of overseas expansion under the banner of a nascent Britishness. In 1612 William Strachey (7th great grandfather of the MP for Dundee West) compiled *The Historie of Travaile into Virginia Britannia* – a dramatic eyewitness account of 'the landes, countries, and territories of this parte of America which we call ours'.[20] Conceived as an 'imperfect defence' against 'the many mouthes of ignorance and slaunder' that had condemned the colonization of the Chesapeake Bay as 'unnationall and unlawfull', it was an early example of the enlargement of England's moral world to encompass the exploits of His Majesty's subjects overseas.

It was also an early example of substituting *Britannia* for England as the proper designation of that world – echoing the Jacobean fashion for *Great Brittaine* following the 1603 dynastic Union of the Scottish and English Crowns. Chroniclers and poets eagerly curried favour with James I and VI by indulging a formula only very few would have recognized – or found particularly meaningful. Books such as Robert Johnson's *Nova Britannia* extolled the plantations of Jamestown in a new idiom vying for semantic purchase, while others hailed a 'Virgin or Maiden Britaine' which, given time, could become 'the farm of Britain, as Sicily was of Rome'.[21] Samuel Purchas commended the Virginian enterprise in 1613 as 'the foundation of a *New Britanian* Common-wealth', much as Michael Drayton's 1606 ode 'To the Virginian Voyage' appealed to the imaginations of able-bodied colonists worthy of their 'Countries name'.[22] But it was not the name of England he summoned:

> Britans, you stay too long,
> Quickly aboord bestow you,
> And with a merry gale
> Swell your stretch'd sayle,
> With vowes as strong,
> As the winds that blow you.[23]

Very little of this actually took root in the civic language of the seventeenth century, however. King James's vision of a 'perfect union of laws and persons' transcending ancient rivalries failed to impress his English and Scottish courtiers, engendering a chorus of 'crossings, long disputations, strange questions, and nothing done'. He was obliged ultimately to relent in the face of the very jealousies and divisions he had hoped to reconcile, though not without misgivings ('I knew mine own end but not others fears').[24] His 'British' nomenclature nevertheless continued to enjoy a modest currency, often employed by his 'most strenuous opponents' in the hope that by giving lip-service to the name they might 'destroy any hope of the reality'.[25]

It nevertheless remains significant that the New World seemed an obvious – and in many ways more politically expedient – place to project a novel conception of Britishness as the epitome of an aspirational new 'common-wealth'. David Armitage makes the point that 'Britannia' would have been instantly recognizable to contemporaries as a classical represen-tation of 'a new world waiting to be discovered . . . Britons would be the new Romans, carrying civility to the Barbarians'.[26] Talk of a 'maidan Britaine' conjured a place that was enticingly exotic but also reassuringly familiar, perfectly pitched to coax waverers into committing 'in purse or person' to the Virginian enterprise.[27] William Strachey made a point of dividing the settlement between the 'low country' from the mouth of the Chesapeake up to the fall line of the James River (which he dubbed 'Virginia') and the vast and 'as yet undiscovered' reaches above the falls that beckoned the virtuous and the bold: 'the maine continent I call Britannia'. As if to assimilate the landscape to the British sensibilities of a new dynasty, he deemed the partition no 'lesse proper, or more impertinent' than the physical division of Britain between England, Scotland and Wales.[28]

'Britannia' never stuck as a catch-all for the vast North American hin-terland, and it would be more than a hundred years before the idea of a 'British' empire, or even a British people, began to edge its way into popular consciousness. It was a drawn-out process, not because the language of Britishness was unavailable but because its semantic range was captive to the very ancient resonances that made it such a tempting analogue for the promise of the New World.[29] To the extent that 'Britons' were to be found in the seventeenth century, they were generally located closer to home – but 'offshore' nevertheless – in the Jacobean plantations of Ulster where the newcomers referred to themselves variously as 'British families', 'British tenants' and 'British undertakers' of '*Brittish* birth and descent'.[30] It was a loose-fitting term, designed to knit peoples drawn from different backgrounds into new networks of mutual obligation and trust transplanted to unfamiliar settings.

Meanwhile, English colonization in America remained just that – English – and the colonists themselves were content to go by that name (the term 'Americans' referring exclusively to the Indigenous peoples inhabiting the waterways of the Atlantic coast). Their experiences nevertheless foreshadowed a fundamental dilemma arising out of the circumstances of colonial overextension that would acquire larger importance in later years: the 'seeming impossibility of sustaining any true community in the face of sheer distance'.[31] Malcolm Gaskill identifies a pronounced 'yearning for transoceanic continuity and intimacy' among the English inhabitants of seventeenth-century America, ever-anxious to vouch fealty to their sovereign and fellow subjects to ward off the constant impress of 'feelings of estrangement'.[32] But paradoxically, they also quickly became accustomed to relatively slight interference from metropolitan lawmakers and thus jealously guarded their political autonomy.[33] Devising terms of endearment that could reconcile these competing registers of cultural and political affiliation presented a puzzle that defied easy resolution, sowing the seeds of future discontent.

The process of forging a more popular British sensibility that could accommodate (without ever superseding) regional and sub-national attachments is conventionally ascribed to the religious wars of the eighteenth century – a period when the scale and efficiency of the British fiscal-military state underwent rapid transformation.[34] The Revolutionary Settlement of the late seventeenth century not only entrenched the Protestant succession, but also enshrined the English Constitution as the 'sacred symbol' of certain rights and liberties that would furnish the bedrock of pan-British sentiment for generations to come.[35] Here, too, however, the results were often patchy and inconclusive. The 1707 Union of England and Scotland produced no shortage of sceptics who doubted the viability of the arrangement ('a firmer Union of policy with less union of affection has hardly been known in the whole world', remarked Daniel Defoe famously in 1713) and this was reflected in early Scottish demands for the new British state to be dissolved.[36] The Union came about at a time of sharp divergence between English and Scottish sentiments, and had to be rammed through 'inspyt of the inclinatione of the people' (in the words of one Scottish nobleman). Trenchant opposition to the Treaty endured for decades, ensuring the survival of a distinct and durable Scottish political culture.[37] Queen Anne herself appealed to subjects of both nations to 'act with all possible respect and kindness to one another, that so it may appear to all the world they have hearts disposed to become one people'.[38] Keeping up appearances seemed the next best thing until a more genuine amity presented itself – which the Jacobite wars would delay for several decades.

Nevertheless, from roughly the second quarter of the eighteenth century, the emergence of shared British allegiances can be readily discerned. In Linda Colley's classic account, it was the combined effects of warding off the dreaded bogey of Catholicism, defending hard-won constitutional liberties against a belligerent French absolutism, and building a mercantile empire out of myriad transactions with racialized 'others' that gradually drew the English, Scottish, Welsh and (albeit marginally) the Irish into closer circles of intimacy. What had previously amounted to little more than a convenient dynastic contrivance was thus sentimentalized through the persuasive force of shared religious prejudice, a common foe, and converging material and strategic interests.[39] Colley placed decisive weight on exogenous developments in the world at large, powerfully moulding the outlook and temper of an incipient British solidarity.

Yet paradoxically, her account has often been interpreted in strikingly insular terms, attending only to the narrow band of peoples 'forged' within the territorial unit of the United Kingdom. This is partly because Colley herself focused squarely on England, Scotland and Wales (even the Irish were a bridge too far on account of their Catholicism), describing a people compelled 'to look anxiously and inquiringly inwards' in the face of external threats that 'impressed them with the belief that they were different from those beyond their shores'. The fact that Britain was an island served not only as a defensive moat but also as a mental demarcation line, 'keeping Britons enclosed and together' and reinforcing the 'profound sense in which its inhabitants saw themselves, particularly in times of emergency, as a people apart'.[40]

But on closer inspection, a much wider social formation clearly shaped Colley's entire approach, fanning outwards in the guise of merchants, soldiers and settlers uprooted and reconstituted in remote settings (displacing countless others into the bargain). Disruption on such an unprecedented scale could never foster stable, water-tight social categories, but it did produce dynamic patterns of response and new forms of language to encompass a web of relations at once intimate yet highly dispersed. Colley's evidence clearly suggests that these global instrumentalities and the 'Britons' they engendered could not easily be disentangled, whether it be the simple testimony of hymns such as 'Rule Britannia' that celebrated 'Britain's supremacy offshore', the sheer spread of imperial commerce that enabled Britain to fight on such a global scale, or the proliferation of 'patriotic societies' whose activities invariably extended to the other side of the Atlantic.[41] Colley introduced readers to a rich cast of eighteenth-century characters for whom, like the engineer James Watt, 'winning access to a wider stage of endeavour . . . broadened his patriotism'.[42] The empire, she conceded, had 'always been emphatically British' (at no time was it customarily termed an *English* empire) – while others have underlined how the empire 'acquired its "British" identity earlier and with fewer reservations than many of the domestic institutions of the newly unified state'.[43]

Colley was at pains to point out that being British 'never obliterated other, older attachments' to England, Scotland and Wales. To that list should be added the Thirteen Colonies, the plantations of Ireland and the white ruling class of Britain's slave colonies in the Caribbean – each with their own distinctive stake in the British amalgam, but equally anchored in local networks and parochial loyalties. Colin Kidd characterizes this heterogeneity in terms of the 'failure of almost three centuries of Anglo-Scottish union to generate a comprehensively "British" conception of national identity'. British patriotism, he argues, was modern, fragile and 'unable to tap deeper roots of national consciousness' – better understood as 'Anglo-British' given the heavy reliance on myths of English constitutional progress. It was a 'retarded formation' that failed 'to fuse into a British whiggism' formed from the sum of its sub-national components in the spirit of 'full blown' romantic nationalism.[44]

But treating Britishness as a historical aberration – a flawed variant of something it evidently was not – risks misconstruing the fundamental nature of the beast. Far from falling short of expectations, it served precisely the function and the unique set of demands foisted upon it: to structure and mediate relations between diverse and highly variegated communities, each with their own traditions of local autonomy (or the vague aspiration thereof). Being British was the answer to the question of unity in diversity for a heterogenous patchwork, each owing an uncompromising fealty to a particular place but nevertheless sharing material interests and wider cultural sympathies that imposed real obligations of practical assistance and mutual regard. This was not nationalism according to the strict Gellnerian principle that 'the political and the national unit should be congruent' but a looser arrangement that permitted variously interacting, historically inter-linked peoples and polities to co-exist and make claims on each other's loyalties, without 'full blown' amalgamation.[45]

Which is not to suggest that Britishness constituted a perfectly primed system, or the optimal framework for international organization that would arouse such uncritical veneration among its advocates in the nineteenth and twentieth centuries. Its very amenity to multiple perspectives lent it a slippery quality that could denote vastly different things. Though an abiding reverence for constitutional liberty provided the sheet anchor, wide discrepancies remained about how its benefits should be bestowed (and upon whom), just as regional variations in the designated in-group (and hence out-group) produced marked fluctuations of emphasis and meaning. It is unlikely, for example, that religious conformity loomed as large for settler populations as for metropolitan Britons, enabling the Irish increasingly if ambivalently to buy into the empire's bounty overseas; while the proximity of presumptive 'savages' was clearly more significant in shap-ing the outlook of frontier Britishness.[46]

Moreover, despite the binding element of shared commerce that sus-tained mutually beneficial ties of fellow-feeling (so that 'the whole Body of the People of *Great Britain* may be considered either as the Customers to, or the Manufacturers for each other' as one 1757 observer enthused) the vast expanse of physical separation inevitably produced sharp conflicts of mater-ial interest.[47] Added to this were the social cleavages of metropole and periphery, where rigid gradations of social rank were crudely grafted onto the scales of distance. In a century when the manners and etiquette of polite society filtered down through the English class system, colonial Americans, Scots and especially the Irish could be relegated to the margins as vulgar outcasts (even as they busied themselves emulating metropolitan mores). Jack Greene has documented the 'ubiquitous language of alterity' that proliferated in the wake of the Seven Years War, arising from widespread feelings of 'revulsion against the behaviors exhibited by many groups of British peoples overseas' – initially in the Caribbean and American colonies, but also increasingly in relation to the arbitrary despotism of the East India Company 'operating beyond the line of European civility'.[48]

A predisposition to regard offshore compatriots as somehow less than equals did not pass unnoticed by the settlers themselves. Benjamin Franklin had the opportunity to observe this at close quarters during his long years of service as a colonial agent in London, taking great exception to the depiction of Americans as 'the lowest of Mankind and almost of a different Species from the English of Britain'.[49] When in 1774 the constitutional reformer Granville Sharp advocated a 'true constitutional mode of connecting British dominions that are otherwise separated by nature', he neatly condensed the problem of British self-representation to its fundamentals – the maintenance of cultural unity and commercial stability among peoples 'whose interest might perhaps be as widely different' from each other 'as their situation upon the face of the globe is distant'.[50]

In other words, the cultivation of Britain's boundless realm of liberty and commerce generated as much conflict as consensus at a time of heightened public engagement with the meaning and morality of overseas conquest.[51] It was at the edge of empire that new allegiances were improvised in radically new surroundings and incorporated imperfectly into changing social, political and religious alignments emanating from the metropole, in a process that resembled less a coherent imperial enterprise and more an exercise in 'piecemeal, contingent, uncertain' experimentation.[52] The taxation crises of the 1760s and 1770s that culminated in the American War of Independence were but the outward signs of mounting internal pressure on an idea straining to encompass an improbably vast sweep. Fundamentally, the American colonists 'always strove to be Britons' until the striving itself became the problem – producing an intense moment of collective disenchantment.[53] It was not a coherent, fully formed American patriotism that fired the emotional fuse of 1776 but the aggrieved bewilderment of a community 'profoundly confused' by the shifting determinants of imperial identity.[54]

P. J. Marshall once termed the ensuing crisis 'the war of Britishnesses' – the inelegant cadence capturing something of the disorder and chaos that engulfed everyone involved. Although the eighteenth-century British 'aspired to be a world-wide people', experience would reveal in no uncertain terms 'how difficult such aspirations would be to fulfil'. The weight of contingency and the discrepancies of time and place ultimately served to bolster the underlying parochialism at the heart of pan-British feeling. Americans may have protested that they were being 'deprived of their Britishness', but they, too, were on a distinct and divergent historical trajectory which was only accentuated by the outbreak of hostilities.[55] The patterns of enmity also criss-crossed continental fault lines, with substantial reservoirs of sympathy for the colonists to be found among English dissenters (some of whom heaped blame on autocratic Scots, bent on a 'quarrel with English liberty').[56] Likewise, the polarizing passions and factional antagonism that blighted the Thirteen Colonies would produce lasting trauma, not least for those who found themselves on the wrong side of the argument. Transatlantic Britishness may have succumbed to overburdened expectations, but as Maya Jasanoff's work has shown, the consequences of these broken affinities were painfully real for the tens of thousands of loyalist refugees disbanded to every corner of Britain's residual territorial remit.[57]

THE 'SETTLER REVOLUTION' AT THE PIVOT OF GLOBAL MODERNITY

With the rift that transformed North American settlers 'from fellow-nationals to foreigners', the emotional purchase of a consolidated Britishness might have fallen by the wayside as the need for a wider, globally integrated vocabulary receded.[58] The resounding victory over France in the Revolutionary and Napoleonic Wars might equally have rendered unitary sentiments obsolete, neutralizing the main external driver and signalling a resumption of mutually exclusive 'Four Nations' loyalties within a composite monarchy. But the wider consequences of the surrender of the American colonies militated against this. The humiliating defeat at the hands of offshore compatriots did not – contrary to public expectation and widespread propaganda – prove to be a destabilizing experience for the United Kingdom, largely due to the 'counter-revolution' of the sovereign power of crown and parliament that immediately ensued. Upon relinquishing the claim to the American colonies, calls were raised for the full incorporation of Ireland into the Union to pre-empt any similar bid for effective autonomy on the part of the Anglo-Irish elite. The subsequent rebellion of 1798 put an end to the equivocation, ushering in the 1801 Act of Union to create a new United Kingdom of Great Britain and Ireland.[59] The loss of America also led to a deliberate tightening of parliamentary control over Britain's expanding holdings in Asia, reigning in the unchecked fiefdom of the East India Company. Meanwhile, new colonizing ventures took root in Upper Canada and New South Wales in the immediate aftermath of American Independence. The challenge of how to make sense of a plurality of peoples had not gone away.[60]

If all-out warfare between Britain and its European trading rivals had been the crucible of pan-British solidarity in the 1700s, it was the relative absence of naval conflict in the aftermath of Napoleon's comprehensive defeat that favoured the persistence of British identities in the century that followed. The cessation of hostilities not only left Britain unchallenged as the dominant maritime power, but also produced the ideal conditions for unleashing a relentless onslaught of white settlers onto vulnerable Indigenous populations the world over. Fitfully at first, new colonial bridge-heads were established in Asia, Africa and the Pacific while older zones of settlement in the Americas (including the relinquished frontier of the United States) were rapidly consolidated. Material and technological advantages accumulated over the previous century provided the initial spark, heralding a new age of modernity powered by steam, rail, rapid communications, urban industrialization, specialized labour and extended lines of credit. Above all, these crucial decades witnessed a dramatic widening of the geographic scope of social and political organization. In an era when 'people's horizons of desire changed', their categories of community and collective selfhood were enlarged upon accordingly, not in steady, continuous increments but as part of a fitful and often fraught dialogue conducted over vast distances.[61]

The magnitude of this 'settler revolution' (comprising some eight million departures from British ports in the second half of the nineteenth century) was not only without precedent but also unmatched by European rivals, amounting to what James Belich terms an 'Anglo divergence' that is too often taken for granted.[62] As Britain's strategic purview widened from the early nineteenth century to encompass bases in Malta (1802), Cape Town (1806), Singapore (1819) and Aden (1839), a parallel wave of aggressive human enterprise buttressed and broadened older settlements or founded new ones; not in the guise of the new-world nations now familiar today, but as a scattering of isolated enclaves that mushroomed in quick succession – Port Phillip, Moreton Bay and Port Adelaide in 'New South Wales'; Canterbury, Otago, Port Nicholson and New Plymouth in New Zealand; Albany, Kat River and British Kaffraria along the Eastern Cape; and at opposite ends of Canada's north-west, from the Red River Settlement to Vancouver Island. By the mid-1850s, for example, a mere 50,000 settlers in New Zealand had established seven elected governments – a sign of the rapid proliferation of new polities intent on securing their constitutional 'birth-right' in unfamiliar settings.[63] British governments, for their part, recognizing that imperial rule would need to tread lightly in the shadow of the American revolution, proved more willing to concede responsible government on the principle that 'untying the knot would only strengthen the rope'.[64] Indeed, the proliferation of new polities gave new meaning to the foundational myth of constitutional progress – upheld as proof positive that expansion overseas fostered the beneficial spread of British liberties.

Meanwhile, the settler revolution became normalized and deeply internalized even for the vast majority who elected to stay at home – or were simply content to migrate internally within the British Isles. The distinction between 'emigration' and relocation to other parts of the United Kingdom soon became blurred by the belief that Britain had successfully replicated itself overseas.[65] In this way, as John Darwin suggests, the 'geographical space within which people in the British Isles could imagine their lives' was dramatically transformed.[66] This applied especially to recently 'emancipated' Irish Catholics, for whom it became increasingly plausible to buy into a looser and more flexible imperial Britishness that could accommodate their own colonial ambitions without absorbing their distinctive culture.[67] It remained a contingent, even precarious arrangement, but one that millions of Catholic emigrants – bound for the United Kingdom as well as further afield – were able to leverage to their advantage.

Each new outcrop of settlers relied on a combination of ruthless trammelling of prior Indigenous entitlements (where they were not extinguished outright) and the ready exploitation of economic, cultural and social links arcing back to their place of origin. In addition to capital, labour and raw materials, these networks mobilized what Belich terms 'the cultural vectors of the system': news, books, music, fashions, folklore, material culture, clergy and a steadily growing stream of mail, consolidating kinship networks, institutional linkages and projecting imperial Britishness as 'an extended circle of transoceanic trust'.[68] The Industrial Revolution had fuelled an explosion in long-distance transactions throughout the United Kingdom, based on heightened levels of confidence between remote contracting parties that rested largely on the 'reputational mechanisms' of social, cultural and institutional norms.[69] Gary Magee and Andrew Thompson credit these same informal civil codes with breaking down barriers to long-distance enterprise overseas, ensuring contracts were honoured and narrowing the 'psychic distance' between the sourcing of goods and their intended marketplace. 'Co-ethnic networks' were thus crucial to shoring up confidence in Britain's precariously overextended supply lines, facilitating transfers of capital, goods, labour and developing a long-range transport and communications capacity.[70] The weight of shared language and cultural practices also raised awareness of distinctive racial attributes that settlers avidly cultivated, not merely out of an innate sense of superiority, but also as a tacit guarantee for their creditors.

In other words, visceral racial prejudice was not just the incidental by-product of settler intrusions, flaring up at the forward zone of violent contact with Indigenous peoples. It was the very precondition of genocidal practices designed to entrench a reliably white British kinsfolk. Put simply, the perception that colonial frontiers had been cleared for unimpeded white occupation was good for business. But it was a perception plagued by constant evidence to the contrary as Indigenous peoples mounted campaigns of resistance to colonial incursions – particularly at the violent perimeters of the Eastern Cape and New South Wales from the 1830s (with later convulsions to follow from New Zealand to Saskatchewan to Natal).[71] Settlers also had to contend with humanitarian and abolitionist sentiment in Britain that lobbied actively against the exterminatory logic of an expanding frontier. In an echo of eighteenth-century prejudices, settler enclaves were often depicted as having strayed from the fundamental principles of Protestant liberalism – a wayward offshoot of 'aberrant Britons'.[72] Resentments multiplied at these unwanted impediments to 'progress', prompting many settlers to 'close ranks and to forge an unprecedentedly clear and embattled political identity'.[73] The *Sydney Morning Herald* rallied to their support, decrying the 'kind-hearted' liberals who reserved all their pity for 'devastating and murdering savages'. In this view, frontier violence was merely a necessary last resort for hardy pioneers 'plagued by the blacks' and bewildered by 'the unprotected manner in which the whole population had been left to fight their own battles'.[74]

The perils of exile fail to take in the full scale or significance, however. These early intruders may have felt like vulnerable outcasts, cut off from the comforts of a familiar world left behind, but their frame of reference was avowedly global in their dogged pursuit of colonial commodities across newly integrated transoceanic networks. This was not 'transplanted Britishness' in the sense of a migratory people unpacking their prior allegiances in 'virgin' territory, but a dynamic and dangerous environment where settlers actively devised new inflections of British selfhood to ensure the moral and material backing of the home front. As Alan Lester suggests, out of this new global modernity emerged a whole new chapter in the long-standing 'struggles over the nature of Britishness itself' – now with an even more rapacious and racially exclusive edge.[75]

The mid-point of the nineteenth century furnished the definitive paradox of Britain's expanding imaginative frontiers. On the one hand, the combined effects of Catholic emancipation (1829), the first Reform Act (1832) and the abolition of slavery throughout the British empire (1833) nurtured a unique reverence for constitutional liberty as the peculiar genius of Britain and Britons – popularized by T. B. Macaulay's hymn to the Williamite Settlement in his five-volume *History of England* (1848–61). But at the same time, the moving settler frontier brought unapologetically illiberal sentiments to the fore. Catherine Hall describes the decades from the 1850s as 'a time when racial thinking in the metropole hardened', displacing an earlier, emphasis on Aboriginal 'protection' and heralding 'a different political culture, a more defensive relationship to the world outside, a bleaker view of racial others'.[76] It was a view that proliferated with the military setbacks of the Crimean War and the widely disseminated horrors of colonial rebellion from Lucknow to Morant Bay, providing a ready platform for key figures such as the eminent historian Thomas Carlyle (who tied England's genius for liberty to the superior vigour of 'the Anglo-Saxon race') and the nonconformist preacher George Dawson (for whom 'the doctrine of race' ensured that 'the square large-headed man does ever rule the world').[77] But the accentuation of racial difference (and the assumption that the darker-skinned races must give way to the lighter) continued to rest uneasily with residual undercurrents of universalism in English jurisprudence, stirring much older misgivings that imperial despotism might expose a more primitive polity at its heart – perhaps even the 're-barbarization of Britain' (as the veteran critic of empire, Herbert Spencer, elaborately cautioned).[78] Contemporaries could freely indulge the myth of an empire of liberty dispensing the benefits of material prosperity and global order, but 'only on the condition that the violence that undergirded colonial economic structures was ideologically contained'.[79]

One particularly acute source of disquiet was the bloody reprisals meted out in the aftermath of the Jamaican uprising of 1865, because it distilled precisely the liberal paradox of enforcing the rule of law by flagrantly authoritarian means. Lurid tales of the insurgents' violent assault on the symbols of white authority led the *Pall Mall Gazette* to conclude that 'two races originally and essentially different in type and character, and in utterly different stages of civilization, cannot live together on terms of absolute legal and social equality'.[80] Equally, however, the wholesale government repression and summary executions of hundreds of Black Jamaicans – including their elected House of Assembly Representative, George William Gordon – caused a momentary disturbance in the white liberal conscience. Race was the congenital flaw, producing deep 'tectonic stresses' in a transoceanic Britishness caught between 'global imperial ambition and bedrock moral and legal sensibilities'.[81] For all the hand-wringing about civic entitlements denied to subject peoples, however, many British liberals simply side-stepped the anomaly. Macaulay's conceit was to insist that 'we are trying ... to give a good government to a people whom we cannot give a free government ... to engraft on despotism those blessings which are the natural fruits of liberty'.[82] Equally commonplace was the contention that darker races were assured the fruits of liberty, but only after an unspecified period of 'tutelage'.[83] But above all, liberals resorted to the expedient that British rights were not rights at all, but a matter of character and 'moral worth'. In this way, the merits and just deserts of those deemed racially inferior could be dismissed with 'an almost sarcastic brusqueness', as Jennifer Pitts observes, 'too obvious to require justification'.[84]

Such insouciance collided head-on with a rising clamour among non-white subjects themselves, insisting on their rightful stake in the bounty of constitutional freedoms. Episodes such as the Morant Bay reprisals brought wider perspectives into the public sphere, as Jamaican dissidents mounted fervent appeals in the name of 'Britain and British rule' that not only challenged the evident hypocrisy of white liberalism but also contained meanings that were often starkly at variance with metropolitan assumptions. Priyamvada Gopal makes the crucial point that liberals in England 'were rather more used to calling for the benevolent deployment of humanitarianism towards the "weaker races" than having the claims of common humanity articulated as a *demand*'. These radical Black voices from the Caribbean – augmented by early moves among Indigenous peoples to petition their grievances directly to Queen Victoria – pushed for a more racially inclusive conception of the moral and legal world of British constitutionalism. Although ultimate success invariably eluded them, 'it was black insurgency that made space for the construction of a radical "us" that crossed both racial lines and the boundary between colony and metropole'.[85] Metropolitan conservatives and liberals alike would contrive all manner of reasons why these claims could not be acknowledged in practice. But significantly, the theoretical possibility of a colour-blind Britishness could not easily be dismissed out of hand.

ILL-FITTING LABELS: THE IMPERFECTIONS OF 'GREATER BRITAIN'

The 'doctrine of race' emerged in lockstep with the phenomenon of mass nationalism as a way of knitting mobile, rapidly urbanizing communities of language, culture, commerce and ethnicity into broader, more aggregated units. But despite decades of argument and counter-argument, social and political theorists have never arrived at any workable consensus as to whether the roots of nationalism grew out of much older, pre-modern dynastic and kinship ties, or whether it was a thoroughly modern phenomenon, crafted out of the material forces that created the very preconditions for communities imagined on such a comprehensive scale.[86] There can be little doubt, however, that the historical emergence of British identities conforms more closely to the latter scenario – as a creative response to the search for political and social stability in a dynamic global setting. The early experimentation with transatlantic modes of British selfhood in the eighteenth century can be viewed in retrospect as a dress rehearsal for the far more complex spread of British sensibilities that emerged in its long aftermath.

It would be during the second half of the nineteenth century that the idea of being British came into its own – not as a species of *nationalism* per se (with a view to binding Britons of the world into a unified polity) but as an elaboration on the problem of unity within diversity that had eluded previous generations. Even as the civic culture of settler colonialism lauded the British connection (frequently judged by contemporaries as 'more British than the British themselves'), the proliferation of new legislatures compounded the problem of preserving local autonomy within a wider, shared patrimony.[87] Significantly, the settler colonies steadfastly resisted the barrage of schemes for imperial federation that circulated in the decades down to the Great War, defending their hard-won legislative gains with a determination matched only by the reluctance of the Imperial Parliament at Westminster to become more closely bound to such a wide assortment of colonial offshoots.[88] Henry Parkes of New South Wales could revel in the fact that 'the population of Australia is more purely British than any other outside of the shores of Britain' (perhaps even 'more loyal than England herself'), while passionately advancing the case for federating the antipodean colonies as 'the *British* States of Australia'.[89] But asked to consider *Imperial* federation, his ardour quickly dimmed: 'I am opposed to it. I have no hesitation in telling you that . . . Imperial federation is a fanciful dream' that could hardly 'be broached by sane men'.[90] Even among avid supporters of a federated empire the issue was never clear-cut. One contemporary noted how Canadian politicians would 'talk enthusiastically about Imperial Federation in the abstract' provided it was clearly understood that 'no serious practical action is to be taken towards that end'.[91]

The Home Rule debates that dominated the metropolitan political agenda towards the end of the nineteenth century also tacitly conceived of Britishness as a web of distinct but interlocking sovereignties. When Irish Home Ruler John Redmond received a lukewarm reception in Australia and New Zealand in 1883, he asked a Melbourne audience why they were not willing to concede to Ireland constitutional arrangements which they themselves 'acknowledge is the source and the cause of their own prosperity and their own loyalty'.[92] Home rulers of the more moderate Parnellite–

Redmond stripe went out of their way to affirm their allegiance to a wider unity – with the settler colonies serving as a kind of guarantor for their devolved sovereignty scheme for the United Kingdom. It was 'Unionism' that was the problem, not Britishness per se (though their opponents did not necessarily see it that way, nor indeed all of their supporters). Though Home Rule was ultimately defeated three times (twice in the House of Lords and finally in the tumult of the 'Ulster Crisis' of 1912–14), it is significant that it came much closer to fruition than the ill-fated proposals to federate the British peoples of the empire as a whole.

This delicate balance of centrifugal and centripetal tendencies has invited no end of confusion as to how British modes of group consciousness ought to be conceptualized. Paradoxically, Britishness borrowed freely from the raw materials of nationalism for its categories of inclusion and exclusion – shared language, culture, religion, history, ethnicity and civic ideals, all duly romanticized and mythologized – while at the same time resisting the principal object of nationalist strivings: a sovereign claim to a clearly delineated territory. To be British was to inhabit a moving frontier comprising a patchwork of peoples who never seriously demanded or developed an integrated, transoceanic popular sovereignty. Indeed, if the modern nation – in Benedict Anderson's classic formulation – was 'imagined as both limited and sovereign', then the indistinct, indeterminate, intercommunal space occupied by imperial Britishness was presumably something else.[93]

This is borne out by the protracted rummaging around for a suitable label among nineteenth-century pundits. 'Anglo-Saxonism' was the preferred designation of Thomas Carlyle and other influential mid-century figures – a term that continued to circulate down to the First World War, often with a view to knitting the United States into a global fraternity of white English-speakers.[94] J. A. Froude fashioned the term 'Oceana' to convey a sense that 'the people at home and the people in the colonies are one people' – only this time incorporating the white planter oligarchy in the British West Indies.[95] The idea of a British 'Commonwealth' also made its first appearance in the 1880s, touted by Lord Rosebery in the Adelaide Town Hall as the reason why none of Britain's settler colonies need ever contemplate 'leaving the empire' in the name of petty nationalism, 'because the Empire is a commonwealth of nations'.[96]

Most prominent of all in these years was the idea of 'Greater Britain' – coined by the young radical liberal Charles Wentworth Dilke as he 'followed England round the world' on a two-year voyage traversing the major hubs of the settler empire (again, including the United States) in 1866–7. Writing

Figure 1.1 A young Charles Dilke, taken a few years after his circumnavigation of 'Greater Britain'. Source: Hulton Archive/Getty Images.

up his experiences upon his return, he ventured an elaborate conception 'of the grandeur of the race, already girdling the earth, which it is destined, perhaps, eventually to overspread'.[97] Though his term was eagerly taken up and widely disseminated by contemporaries, it neither furnished a clear definition nor even a reliable guide as to the peoples and places that were meant to be included. Dilke had elected to write a travelogue rather than a political treatise, allowing greater licence to squeeze all manner of experience into his chosen remit, while summarily excluding others. He was willing, for example, to contemplate a symbolic merger of the destinies of 'Americans and Britishers', defying the logic of 1776 to incorporate the former into the wider fellowship of the latter (an aspect that many of his emulators simply chose to ignore). At the same time he was strangely dismissive of English Canada, which he dealt with perfunctorily in a single chapter that plaintively debunked their self-serving 'loyalty', all the while insisting that 'we are no more fellow-countrymen of the Canadians than of the Americans of the North or West'.[98] Above all, he was ambivalent about British India, which he seemed to include in his itinerary only for the purpose of removing it from consideration. 'England in the East is not the England that we know', he maintained, deploying the classic Burkean stigmatization of a 'mysterious Oriental despotism, ruling a sixth of the human race, nominally for the natives' own good, and certainly for no one else's'.[99]

Meanwhile, the most revered oracle of them all, the Regius Professor of Modern History at Cambridge University, J. R. Seeley, co-opted Dilke's term in *The Expansion of England* (1883), hailing the 'ethnological unity' among 'those tens of millions of Englishmen who live outside of the British Islands', their very prosperity affirming that 'England did in some sense go with them across the sea'.[100] Seeley devoted a similarly large portion of his magnum opus to justifying his reasons for excluding India, explaining that:

> the enormous Indian population does not make part of Greater Britain in the same sense as those tens of millions of Englishmen who live outside of the British Islands. The latter are of our own blood, and are therefore united to us by the strongest tie. The former are of alien race and religion, and are bound to us only by the tie of conquest.[101]

Blood, race, Englishmen, Greater Britain. What these axioms fundamentally shared was an unwavering devotion to some version of 'race patriotism' and a remarkable inattention to conceptual rigour. Dilke in particular lauded the 'British race', the 'English race' or simply 'our race' interchangeably, with an astonishing indifference to the finer distinctions, while Seeley elided 'England' and 'Britain' on virtually every page.

Historians have fared no better in devising a consistent, consensual conceptualization for the British-at-large, becoming frequently bogged down on the utility (or otherwise) of 'British World' paradigms.[102] But rather than treat the terminological looseness as an impediment to analytical precision, it is more useful to consider how it was hard-wired into the idea of Britain itself, and hence of cardinal importance to understanding the circumstances of its eventual undoing. For contemporaries who cleaved to an expansive Britishness, the profusion of terms was part of the mystery and romance – containing the promise of transcendence from one state to another. It also constituted a strategy of constructive (if unacknowledged) ambiguity, advancing a sense of the people that would know no bounds. Dilke made a point of proffering a 'conception, *however imperfect*' of Greater

Britain, and it was precisely the imperfections that enabled it to travel so far (literally in Dilke's case, whose entire voyage was an exercise in containing 'the constant slippages of difference').[103] Such was his cavalier attitude to language that at one point, reflecting on the preponderance of industrious Scots he encountered on his travels, he even considered it 'strange, indeed, that Scotland has not become the name for the United Kingdom' – a sardonic flourish, perhaps, but one that also implied that 'Britain' had much larger, unspecified work to do.

These imperfections not only gave metropolitan imaginings an unusually wide berth, but also allowed considerable scope for offshore vocabularies of Britishness to proliferate on their own terms. The meaning of Greater Britain was never the exclusive preserve of metropolitan sooth-sayers (influential as they undoubtedly were) but was augmented and offset by any number of inflections circulating elsewhere. In one sense this was acknowledged and even embraced by Dilke in his overriding emphasis on the vagaries of 'climate, soil, manners of life' – all of which had progressively 'modified the blood' to produce a variety of divergent 'types'.[104] But the discrepancies were more complex and the world he described far more heterogenous than the reveries of race patriotism allowed.

Among the millions who departed British ports were countless contin-ental Europeans headed in every direction who found ways of accommodat-ing their specific aspirations and distinctive outlook in destinations otherwise drenched in the overt veneration of anglophone whiteness. Substantial ethnic and religious minorities in Canada and South Africa that predated British incursions cannot be overlooked, nor the sojourners from South Asia, East Asia and the Pacific who overcame formal and infor-mal racial barriers to movement in the empire (or alternatively, were actively recruited for the purpose through a variety of indentured labour schemes). Indigenous peoples engaged in all manner of dynamic inter-actions with their respective intruders, at times (but by no means always) developing their 'own strains of Loyalist ideology' attuned to their specific needs.[105] Experience would show that Indigenous, religious and ethnic minorities – despite strenuous efforts to confine them to the margins – could, in certain circumstances, be incorporated into British civic networks on qualified terms of access (necessitating subtle modifications in the parameters of belonging itself).[106] Because of this, and an almost unlimited assortment of permutations, race patriotism acquired a range of distinct local emphases, each with their own provincial prejudices and sensibilities. The unitary language of Britishness and its fragmented reality were never in perfect alignment – one key reason, perhaps, for the staunch absolutism of its outward forms of civic ritual and public ceremony.

It was largely because Britishness acquired so many regional tonalities that the compulsive blurring of England and Britain did not pass unnoticed. Many, but by no means all Canadians would have adhered to W. L. Morton's caveat: 'British we were, but English in the sense of southern English we never were.'[107] The former was presumed to be malleable, the latter less so. The complaint was even more frequently heard among Scots, Welsh and Irish emigrants who formed their own Caledonian, Welsh and Hibernian societies in the colonies to underline the distinction.[108] Objections could equally be raised by avowed 'Little Englanders' in the Home Counties, such as the radical jurist Frederic Harrison who abhorred 'the silly, unhistoric, and bombastic term "Briton" supplanting the ancient and grand name of "Englishman"', vowing that he would 'let no Scot, no Australian, no Rhodesian, swagger me out of that name'. Significantly, he detected insidious *offshore* influences as the main driver of British sensibilities. For good measure, he added that 'an empire, to which its own subjects cannot agree to a given national name, is not in a sound and abiding state'.[109]

Perhaps. But it is more likely that it was an ingenious way of managing difference, not only the distinctions of English/British but also a far wider profusion of loose talk including (again imperfectly) the endemic contradictions of race. As Duncan Bell has argued, in contrast to an early generation of scholarship that conceived of Britishness in terms of 'a binary coding of difference in relation to an exotic "Other"', closer examination of late Victorian British theorists of Greater Britain suggest they 'were concerned as much (and sometimes more) with the projection and sustenance of a coherent sense of Britishness throughout the settler communities'.[110] But they did not always stop at the settler colonies. The forms of language they deployed inscribed a capaciousness that pushed the boundaries to the widest possible extent (leaving open – often unwittingly – the theoretical possibility of encompassing non-white subjects), while retaining a retracting mechanism that could curb access where required.

Only in one sense can any consistent pattern be discerned in the tangle of England/Britain in these works, encoded in Seeley's almost throwaway reference to an 'England steadily expanding into Greater Britain'.[111] Dilke said something not dissimilar in his characteristically fulsome proclamation: 'That which raises us above the provincialism of citizenship of little England is our citizenship of the greater Saxondom which includes all that is best and wisest in the world.' Leaving aside the intrusion of yet another nebulous category, the implication seems clear enough: it all started with England, a fully imagined, thoroughly historicized place with limited (and potentially limiting) physical frontiers, *expanding into* a more elevated, indeterminate and unbounded self. It was this, Dilke argued, that secured 'our real preservation from the insularity we deprecate', alleviating the dreaded 'curse of small island countries, the dwarfing of mind which would otherwise make us Guernsey a little magnified'.[112] The point where England merged into Britain was where the mystique and majesty resided. Girth equalled grandeur; England begat Britain and moved effortlessly around the world within its beneficent, elongated compass. What this clearly implied was first – as Darwin observes of Seeley – 'that the opportunity, power, and prestige brought by empire reinforced the appeal of a composite "British" nationality in the Home Islands themselves', keeping the insidious threat of provincialism firmly in check.[113] And second, that the idea of Britain – more so than England – was heavily freighted with the imagined properties of global reach, and hence more vulnerable to the perils of imperial decline.

Into the twentieth century, and particularly in the decades after 1945, this elaborate complex came comprehensively unstuck, not just in the many dominions and dependencies that cultivated some version of British selfhood but also belatedly in the United Kingdom itself. Seeley had always assumed that Greater Britain rested on three pillars – 'community of race, community of religion, community of interest' – arguing that the first two were not only sufficient in themselves, but would also ensure the long-term survival of a unity 'of a more vital kind', even if at some point in the future the community of interest should wane.[114] In this he was evidently quite wrong in 1883, and would be proven all the more so in the decades after 1945.

In order to grasp fully the interconnections, John Strachey's 'Balkanisation of Britain' needs to be approached as just one facet of a much wider phenomenon, unfolding globally within the shared, albeit intricately layered context of empire's end. Objections might be raised that the 'Four Nations' of the United Kingdom represent an entirely special case, subject to their own internal rhythms and temporalities that not only diverged from the rest of the imploding empire but also persist into the present day, with unresolved legacies that continue to dominate headlines in Scotland and Northern Ireland in particular. But the same could be said of any or all of the contexts to be examined here, no two of which conformed to some 'default' pattern or were affected equally by the serial crises and flashpoints that punctured confidence in a capacious Britishness. As for continuities, it will be argued that Britain is far from the only place where Britishness remains unfinished business.

Recounting such complex interactions and their myriad implications poses any number of challenges. If readers will permit one last Strachey, it was the cousin (once removed) of the MP for Dundee West, Lytton Strachey, who once wrote of the Victorian era that its history 'will never be written: we know too much about it'. By that he meant that the sheer deluge of extant sources defied the capacity of any lone historian to read and absorb – let alone relate to others 'by the direct method of a scrupulous narration'. A task of such magnitude, he said, necessitated 'a subtler strategy', advancing on the subject 'in unexpected places' to prise open multiple entry points and cast a 'revealing searchlight into obscure recesses, hitherto undivined'.[115] Much the same might be said of the terrain to be traversed in what follows, where there can be no pretence of turning every stone. The End of Britain resists linear treatment, much like the early formation of British identities because it proceeded along so many criss-crossing trajectories, temporalities and dispersed geographies.

If the essence of the British problem was affective overstretch, then the scale of the historian's task carries similar risks. Lytton Strachey's advice was to 'row out over that great ocean of material, and lower down into it, here and there, a little bucket which will bring up to the light of day some characteristic specimen, from those far depths, to be examined with a careful curiosity'.[116] Writing exactly a century later, James Vernon similarly recommended a micro-historical approach to what he termed the 'worlding of Britain', as one of the best avenues to address 'global processes without losing sight of the locales and individuals through which they are lived and shaped'.[117] That is broadly the advice that is followed here; as the only satisfying way of capturing the many registers of dialogue among a plurality of peoples, each with their own varying stake in being British. The chapters that follow are not 'micro-histories' in the narrow sense – they attend frequently to the cracks-in-between contexts, and the unintended consequences engendered elsewhere. They are rather snapshots in time, illuminating key moments when the unbearable bandwidth of being British was stretched beyond the limits of plausibility.

2

THE LIMITS OF LOCATION: GREATER BRITAIN

Like many colonial-era port cities, Vancouver was built with its back to the water. The original 'Gastown' settlement faced resolutely inward from Burrard Inlet onto Maple Tree Square, shielded from the surrounding tidal flats by a strip of dockyards, sawmills, canneries and warehouses lining the waterfront. Famed for its saloons and low-rent lodgings for sailors and sojourners after weeks on end at sea, the demand for ocean views was hardly at a premium. On the contrary, the town offered a welcome refuge from the low-lying, distinctly swampy ambience of the shoreline. The effect was complete with the arrival of the Canadian Pacific Railway in 1887, the dockside trestle and terminus posing a firm barrier between land and sea, reorienting the townsfolk towards their vast hinterland.[1]

Vancouver would turn doggedly inward on 23 May 1914, when the SS *Komagata Maru* passed through the narrows guarding the inlet with its cargo of aspiring settlers, ready to disembark. If ever a place were accustomed to new arrivals, it was surely this booming frontier entrepôt on the eve of the Great War. In the space of barely two decades, the population had experienced a tenfold explosion from a paltry 13,700 in the early 1890s to some 115,000 by 1914 – easily outstripping the capital, Victoria, as the largest urban centre in British Columbia. Just how 'British' is revealed by the migrant influx, where new arrivals from England, Ireland, Scotland and Wales (plus a smattering of Australians, New Zealanders and South Africans) accounted for some 40 per cent of the increase (the bulk of the remainder coming mainly from other parts of English-speaking Canada and the United States).[2] Surveying the magnitude of the change in 1908, an item in *Westward Ho! Magazine* considered the 'possibilities in store' for this natural 'home for the British emigrant':

> possibilities in short as a greater Britain on the Pacific, where British arts and institutions will expand under fresh impetus, 'where the British flag will forever fly, where British laws and justice will be respected and

enforced, and where British men and women will be bred equal to the best traditions of the race'.[3]

By 1914, one in three Vancouverites was British- or Irish-born, wielding a disproportionate civic influence in business and politics that would endure for generations.[4] In a population where less than 15 per cent were actually born in British Columbia, a consciousness of the community's itinerant composition was ever-present, fostering a culture of boosterism that eagerly sought out fresh arrivals (one business organization styling itself 'The Hundred Thousand Club' had to change its name after reaching its goal in less than five years).[5] Migrants were inherently welcome as a raw index of prosperity and ready reassurance for those already settled that they had made a shrewd move.

But not these migrants. No sooner had the *Komagata Maru* dropped anchor a few hundred yards offshore than its passengers were refused permission to land. On board was not the typical consignment of aspirational white faces turned out in their Sunday best, but a party of 376 male Sikhs hailing originally from Punjab who had set out from Hong Kong in

Figure 2.1 The passengers of the *Komagata Maru* alongside Gurdit Singh (in grey suit) and his son Balwant on the morning of their arrival in Vancouver, 23 May 1914. Source: Danvis Collection/Alamy Stock Photo.

April before taking on additional passengers in Shanghai, Moji and Yokahama. From its first appearance at William Head on the southern tip of Vancouver Island, the Glasgow-built and Japanese-owned steamer was intercepted by journalists eager to secure an early scoop. It was here that Baba Gurdit Singh announced his name to the world – the fifty-five-year-old instigator from Amritsar who had personally chartered the *Komagata Maru*, overcoming any number of obstacles strewn in his path. Resplendent in his white turban and matching white beard, he now declaimed through an interpreter: 'We are British citizens and we consider we have a right to visit any part of the Empire.'[6]

On the same day that the *Komagata Maru* cleared customs and proceeded to an icy reception in Vancouver, a controversy of altogether different dimensions came to a head in the House of Commons in London, where debate commenced on the third reading of the Government of Ireland Act, 1914 (also known as the Third Home Rule Bill). Just as Gurdit Singh sought answers to the anomalies of British subjecthood, so too Home Rule was intended to resolve years of controversy about Ireland's disputed British credentials. Two previous bids to re-establish an Irish parliament in Dublin (while continuing the practice of returning Irish MPs to Westminster in a devolved sovereignty experiment) had collapsed acrimoniously in 1886 and 1893 under the weight of fierce Irish Protestant opposition and the support of their parliamentary allies. The prospects of this third attempt were no less hazardous; indeed, the Liberal prime minister H. H. Asquith courted destruction in his efforts to secure a workable compromise between John Redmond's Irish Parliamentary Party, who had been given a cast-iron promise of Home Rule as the price of propping up the Liberal government, and a Conservative and Unionist opposition staunchly opposed to the move. As with the *Komagata Maru*, the outbreak of war in August 1914 would intervene to deflect attention and energies elsewhere, obscuring the memory of how close British parliamentary democracy came to complete collapse in the spring and summer of that year.

Over a period of three months from May to July 1914, these two episodes played out at opposite ends of the empire, dramatizing latent divisions over the rights and entitlements conferred by British liberties and igniting passions that threatened the order and stability of the empire itself. Each entailed an audacious challenge to parliamentary supremacy on the part of aggrieved minorities determined to take matters into their own hands, raising fundamental questions about the complex, even confused configurations of British selfhood. But in no sense did contemporaries view the two moments in tandem. It was not simply a matter of distance, or the evident disparities of moral, political or indeed practical significance. At a more fundamental level, the discontents of white Ulster Protestants at the heart of the Union were accorded an order of magnitude far outweighing those of itinerant Sikhs at the edge of empire, whose claims were widely regarded as little more than a species of mischief.

Almost a century earlier, the administrators of colonial New South Wales devised a resonant term for these mental demarcations – the 'limits of location' – referring to the perimeter of the original nineteen counties where free settlers could take up land (known alternatively by the early convicts simply as being 'inside'). It was partly a means of wresting control over a 'boundary-pushing society', but also a way of rendering Indigenous peoples invisible.[7] Asserting authority in this way enabled settlers to 'come to terms with new spaces and distances', surveying the extent of their effective conquest and consigning unwelcome interlopers to the world 'outside'.[8] But it was also a counter-intuitive practice for an expansive mindset that vaunted blurred boundaries and indeterminate frontiers. The extended horizon of British constitutional liberties that signalled limitless 'possibilities in store' for a 'greater Britain on the Pacific' rested uneasily with the logic of racialized barriers to free movement across the seas. Under the weight of these competing tensions, as Catherine Hall observes, the 'map constantly shifted, the categories faltered' according to ever-changing circumstances that exerted constant pressure on the mental coordinates.[9]

It is here that Gurdit Singh's enterprise signalled new and potentially turbulent tidings on the eve of the Great War. The problem with the *Komagata Maru* was not the crossing of physical boundaries per se, in an era that had seen abundant movements of South Asian merchants and labourers (many of them indentured) to the Caribbean, South Africa, East Africa, the South Pacific, East Asia and beyond. Rather, it was about the prerogative to determine and direct those movements, and the interests they ultimately served.[10] Likewise, the Ulster crisis – for all the intricacies of the constitutional issues at its heart – was fundamentally about asserting authority; the right to stake out the limits of location and secure the position of those deemed to reside within. When Charles Dilke spoke of 'imperfections' in the fabric of Greater Britain, neither Ulster Protestants nor Punjabi Sikhs were at the forefront of his thinking. But it was precisely these unintended consequences that exposed the deeper contradictions in his grand scheme. A liberal conception of Greater Britain at once expansive yet avowedly exclusive could not easily be contained within a strictly racialized purview – a dilemma that posed serial challenges to its emotional reach and popular resonance. In this sense, Dilke's term can usefully be reclaimed to probe the entangled fate of Britishness abroad and the real time travails of the United Kingdom.

'QUITE CONTRARY TO NATURE': CROSSING FROM EAST TO WEST

Gurdit Singh had every reason to anticipate difficulties making landfall in Vancouver in May 1914. The prior experience of countless of his compatriots who over more than a century had charted a passage out of India (not least to 'the heart of empire' in metropolitan Britain) served as ample forewarning of the likely obstacles.[11] In British Columbia in particular, inward migration from India, China and especially Japan had inflamed tempers since the turn of the century, and although the numbers were miniscule compared with the torrent of white arrivals, it became a matter of 'passionate and unalterable conviction' among local community organizations and provincial politicians.[12] It was also the source of regular friction with both the national government in Ottawa and imperial authorities in London – the former due to uncertainty over whether Canada had the authority to enforce an entry ban; the latter out of concern for the repercussions elsewhere if an outright colour bar were imposed. Similar tensions had arisen over restrictive immigration practices in Natal, New Zealand and the newly federated Commonwealth of Australia, where objections from London hinged largely on the need to avoid undue offence to the Japanese, with whom Britain had entered into a naval defence pact in 1902. But migration from South Asia was all the more vexed due to the shared legal category of British subjecthood. Winston Churchill flagged the anomaly in 1908:

> Is it possible for any Government with a scrap of respect for honest dealing between man and man to embark on a policy of deliberately squeezing out the native of India ... ? Most of all we ask is such a policy possible to the Government which bears sway over three hundred millions of our Indian Empire?[13]

British Columbia's answer was an emphatic 'yes', and after repeated attempts by the Provincial Legislature to pass restrictive measures were struck out by the federal government and the courts (occasionally at the behest of the Colonial Office in London), local resentments finally came to a head. The Vancouver race riot that erupted over two days in

September 1907 was a spontaneous outburst of unedifying racial enmity. Enraged at the impending arrival of some 900 Indian migrants on the SS *Monteagle*, several thousand white citizens descended on Asian businesses and clashed violently with local Asian residents. It was the moment that finally forced the federal government's hand in tightening the entry rules – mainly out of concern that unless remedial action were taken, 'British Columbians might forget that they are British' (in the words of one government informant close to the scene) and succumb to secessionist sentiment already brewing in the community.[14]

Future prime minister W. L. Mackenzie King was assigned the delicate balancing act of quelling local passions without jeopardizing imperial loyalties. After failing to persuade the British Government in India to lend assistance by imposing restrictions on departures, he devised an arrangement whereby South Asian migrants at Pacific ports would only be admitted if they proceeded directly from their country of origin 'by a continuous journey' and on a single ticket. With no steamship company operating directly between India and Canada, it became a simple matter to render oceanic migration from the British Raj effectively impossible. King congratulated himself on avoiding legislation 'either in India or Canada which might appear to reflect on fellow British subjects in another part of the Empire'. Indeed 'nothing could be more unfortunate' he ventured in all sincerity, if it were to appear that Canada was 'not deeply sensible of the obligation which citizenship within the empire entails'.[15] Despite, or perhaps because of the imperative of racial exclusion, it remained a matter of great symbolic import to uphold the theoretical possibility of Greater Britain as a continuous, unimpeded journey in the spirit of Charles Dilke.

There matters might have rested but for the determination of Vancouver's five-thousand-strong Sikh community to challenge the arbitrary impediments to free movement by encouraging relatives at home to try to beat the ban. They drew encouragement from an October 1913 decision of the British Columbia Supreme Court to allow a group of fifty-six Indians to disembark in Victoria due to inconsistencies between the wording of the legislation and the precise regulations that deemed the (necessary) break in their journey legitimate grounds for exclusion. Although the Canadian Government quickly closed the loophole, rumours abounded that the Canadian courts provided a way around the restrictions.[16]

This accounts for how Gurdit Singh was able to charter, equip and recruit several hundred paying passengers in Hong Kong for such a high-risk venture in spring 1914, and why he announced to awaiting pressmen his determination 'to make this a test case'. If entry were refused on account of the 'continuous journey' requirement, he insisted, the matter would 'not end here'. He was equally apprised of the wider political complex that made the mere attempt to enter British Columbia a source of acute embarrassment for British authorities in India and London, and was not averse to talking up the magnitude of the stakes: 'What is done with this shipload of my people will determine whether we shall have peace in all parts of the Empire.' His conviction that 'no power on earth can stop us in Vancouver' rested on a precarious balance of misplaced confidence in Canadian courts and a genuine belief in British rights and entitlements that ought not to be denied.[17]

The passengers of the *Komagata Maru* would be left to languish for two enervating months on Burrard Inlet in appalling conditions, before finally being escorted back into the Pacific by the Royal Canadian Navy on 23 July. Their arrival presaged a prolonged stand-off, where the initial stalling tactics of immigration officials (in the hope that Gurdit Singh's creditors would lose patience and insist on the vessel's departure) soon gave way to various forms of inhumane coercion. Contact of any kind with the 'Shore Committee' of local Sikh supporters was refused, unsupervised access to legal counsel was denied, and critical supplies of food and water were unscrupulously controlled to puncture the newcomers' resolve.

Meanwhile, white community groups became increasingly restive, their leaders issuing bellicose resolutions on behalf of a citizenry described as 'intensely imperialistic'.[18] Even the British Army service records of many of the passengers failed to garner sympathy – on the contrary, rumours of 'trained soldiers' on board only heightened concerns that 'they will put up a strenuous fight'.[19] The objection of distinguished geologist Henri-Marc Ami mirrored the general tenor of public indignation. In presuming to arrive 'by way of the Pacific Ocean these good people go quite contrary to nature' he propounded; that is to say, 'the natural way the sun travels' from East to West. If only they had followed the 'orthodox way of procedure', they could have earned a deeper appreciation of the civilizing steps 'taken by generations past in their Westerly advance' – and all the 'trouble and trials to all concerned' would have been avoided.[20] In short, it was an inversion of the temporal, spatial and indeed natural order, authorized by the imperatives of race.

As garbage piled up on the deck of the *Komagata Maru* and hopes of a successful legal challenge faded, the passengers conveyed their desperate plight in a series of urgent missives to the governor-general: 'Sent many telegrams unanswered ... being shut in ship from 4 months becoming sick no good food water and exercise dying decide immediately.'[21] Tensions also escalated between provincial and federal authorities, with the belligerence of local immigration agents countermanded by Robert Borden's Conservative government in Ottawa, anxious to avoid an international 'incident' at all costs. The Viceroy of India also weighed in with a curt reminder by cable: 'While vessel is on British waters of course very desirable to avoid use of force which would have extremely bad effect in Punjab.'[22]

Nevertheless, a bungled raid on the vessel was attempted under cover of darkness on the weekend of 18–19 July (only to be repelled by a shower of heavy objects hurled indiscriminately from the decks of the *Komagata Maru*). In a further escalation, the Mayor of Vancouver called out the militia on 21 July while the Naval cruiser *Rainbow* (one of only two ships in service in the fledgling Canadian Navy) was ordered to Burrard Inlet to train its guns on the hapless steamer in a blatant show of intimidation.[23] It was then that Vancouverites turned out in numbers, crowding the wharves along Burrard Inlet while others took to the water in pleasure craft of every description as the action unfolded. 'Immense crowds constantly on waterfront', cabled

Figure 2.2 The *Komagata Maru* (left) on Vancouver's Burrard Inlet, flanked by the Canadian naval cruiser HMCS *Rainbow* and assorted pleasure craft two days before the vessel's expulsion on 23 July 1914. Source: 914 Collection/Alamy Stock Photo.

Borden's personal representative, urging an 'immediate solution' to address the frenzied air of public expectation.[24] From his shipboard vantage point, Gurdit Singh looked on despondently as 'thousands flocked' to 'watch the destruction of 360 almost starved to death Indians'.[25] But the anticipated showdown never materialized. That same afternoon, a resigned plume of black smoke issued from the vessel's smokestack as it began preparations for departure, with all but twenty of its inbound passengers still on board.[26]

By then, the fate of the passengers had been determined by the British Columbian Court of Appeal, where lawyers for the appellants had mounted a full-throated challenge to Canada's right to refuse entry to British subjects. Although counsel conceded that the exclusion of overseas 'aliens' clearly fell within the Canadian Government's legitimate jurisdiction, there had been 'no case yet tried ... where the question of a British subject's right to come into Canada' had been properly tested. Arguing that the entire matter was not one of 'immigration' at all, but a blatant case of deprivation of liberty, it was submitted that the passengers had passed out of federal jurisdiction from the moment they crossed the three-mile shore limit, at which point they entered British Columbian jurisdiction where provincial civil liberty laws trumped any federal government regulation pertaining to aliens. The court emphatically disagreed, ruling that such an interpretation would give itinerant British subjects the possibility of picking and choosing jurisdictions. The matter of 'domicile' was deemed crucial to civil status, and thus a British subject could 'not leave India and come to British Columbia' and upon entering the three-mile limit claim to be 'clothed within the attributes of a citizen of Canada'.[27]

It was a landmark decision, bringing legal precision where a studied ambiguity had long prevailed. As Renisa Mawani has shown, by inscribing 'vertical geographies' and imposing 'variegated conceptions of British subject-hood', the court had made a ruling on the taproot of Britishness itself, fusing 'racial power' to the 'very foundation and architecture of imperial rule'.[28] In this way, one of Dilke's many 'imperfections' was subjected to unsought scrutiny. Not that British Columbians (or for that matter the passengers of SS *Komagata Maru*) needed an Appeal Court ruling to point out these 'common-sense' racial disparities. Indeed, for all its legal significance, the departure of the *Komagata Maru* provoked none of the anticipated civil unrest, either in Vancouver or Punjab.[29] The failed challenge to Canada's immigration laws merely affirmed what Marilyn Lake and Henry Reynolds have termed 'the global colour line' – the pervasive barriers partitioning a racially ordered world, governed by everyday habits of mind and forms of racial knowledge that 'animated white men's countries and their strategies of exclusion'.[30]

It was Gurdit Singh's audacity in chartering a ship to exploit the evident anomalies that brought matters to a head. If Britannia 'ruled the waves', by what authority did a Sikh merchant with minimal maritime experience presume to avail himself of the promise of the open sea? In forcing his antagonists to reject his assertion of equality so baldly, and at such close quarters, he dramatically 'ruptured Britain's claim to temporal and spatial uniformity', laying bare the limits of location.[31] Although it hardly registered among the crowds thronging the wharves of Vancouver, his efforts to expose the flawed logic of an expansive Britishness would have longer-term implications in the years ahead.

'WHEN IS A BRITISH SUBJECT?': BEYOND BURRARD INLET

When the *Komagata Maru* retraced its route back into the Pacific, it also passed out of history for more than half a century; swept aside by the outbreak of war in Europe less than a fortnight later, and subsequently marginalized as a fleeting anecdote of purely local historical interest. Only with the fading verities of empire and Britishness was the story recovered, first tentatively in the mid-1970s but acquiring ever-greater prominence into the twenty-first century. Documentary films, theatre productions, radio plays, exhibitions and a commemorative monument on Vancouver's waterfront brought added prominence, while official apologies from the British Columbian Legislature (2008) and Liberal prime minister Justin Trudeau (2016) set the seal on its emblematic status. By 2012, Ali Kazimi could confidently describe it as 'one of the most infamous "incidents" in Canadian history'.[32] Yet it remains emblematic of a specifically Canadian and an avowedly immigrant experience, rarely broached outside of either context. Despite recent efforts to tease out transnational connections and oceanic perspectives, the episode is largely absent from conventional accounts of anti-colonial resistance and global decolonization – and remains entirely peripheral to the history of embattled Britishness in the twentieth century.[33]

It was during the height of the stand-off in 1914 that the *New York Times* reduced the matter to its essentials in a piece called: 'When is a British Subject?' – a question that resonated far more widely than the shores of Burrard Inlet.[34] Distorted echoes ricocheted around the British world, reverberating all the way to the symbolic and legislative hub – the House of Commons in London. When the Third Home Rule Bill was first tabled in April 1912, more than half a million Ulster Unionists gave their own unequivocal answer by signing the Ulster Covenant – a solemn pledge to 'stand by one another in defending ... our cherished position of equal citizenship in the United Kingdom'. Led by the redoubtable Dublin barrister and Unionist MP Sir Edward Carson, their determination embraced the possibility of resorting to unconstitutional means in the event of a separate Irish Parliament 'being forced upon us'. While objections to Home Rule were vehemently held among Protestants throughout Ireland, the position of Ulster was unique due to the concentration of six of the original 'plantation counties', comprising a local majority of Protestants who abhorred the prospect of submission to the preponderance of Catholics in the South. Foreshadowing a populist politics that would proliferate into the twentieth century and beyond, they fashioned the principle that the properly constituted, democratically elected assembly at Westminster remained subordinate to some ethereal conception of the people whose interests it was duty-bound to serve. Should that duty be dishonoured, the will of the parliamentary majority could legitimately be defied.

Such sentiments were emboldened by the prevailing atmosphere of political and moral crisis, fuelled by a succession of emotionally pent-up loyalist rallies staged throughout the country on an unprecedented scale.[35] On the morning of the very first of these at the Balmoral showgrounds in Belfast on 11 April 1912, *The Times* ran a highly tendentious leader posing as a measured assessment of 'the exceptional gravity of the occasion'. While 'enlightened Liberalism' might 'smile at the belief and passions of the Ulster Protestants', and 'make light of the deep-rooted convictions' at the core of the dispute, it was 'useless to argue that they are mistaken. They have reasons, never answered yet, for believing that they are not mistaken'.[36] The empire's unofficial poet laureate, Rudyard Kipling, penned 'Ulster 1912' for the occasion – impugning the deceit and disloyalty of Ulster's Catholic and Liberal political enemies. The central quatrain neatly distilled the core grievance:

> Before an Empire's eyes
> The traitor claims his price
> What need of further lies
> We are the sacrifice

Irony was the galvanizing weapon of an avowedly British constituency, spurned by the ancient seat of British democracy itself. To underline their intent, the 'Ulster Volunteer Force' was established in January 1913 with more than 100,000 recruits pledging to take up arms against their own government if necessary. Such openly seditious activity from an excitable minority would not have posed such intractable difficulties for the Asquith government were it not for the abundant reservoir of sympathy within the ranks of the British Army, as doubts rapidly accumulated about the resolve of British troops in the event of an armed clash with Ulster militiamen. These apprehensions were confirmed in March 1914 when a poorly planned pre-mobilization elicited the refusal of the vast majority of duty officers stationed at the main British Army base in Kildare to initiate military operations against Ulster. Though no explicit orders were ever refused, the 'Curragh Mutiny' issued a powerful statement of dubious principle (duly leaked to the press) and robbed a humiliated Asquith of crucial political leverage against the conspirators.[37]

More crucial in strengthening Ulster's subversive resolve, however, was the astonishing contempt of parliament displayed by the Leader of the Conservative and Unionist Opposition, Andrew Bonar Law. From the moment of his surprise selection as Party leader at the end of 1911, he rallied to Ulster's cause with a single-minded conviction entirely in keeping with his Ulster Presbyterian roots. According to his first biographer, Ulster was one of the few issues he 'cared intensely about', arousing passions bordering on 'violence' which were 'in no way artificial or affected. On that topic, he meant every word he said.'[38] It was equally clear to contemporaries that the defence of Ulster was his all-consuming concern, more so than any wider commitment to Unionism as a constitutional principle.[39] Bonar Law staked out his position at a major Unionist gathering at Blenheim Palace in July 1912, deriding the Asquith government as a 'Revolutionary Committee' and insisting that his party would not be 'bound by the restraints which would influence us in an ordinary constitutional struggle'. He then famously elaborated in terms highly unusual for someone aspiring to lead the world's oldest democracy:

> I said the other day in the House of Commons and I repeat here that there are things stronger than Parliamentary majorities . . . I say so now, with the full sense of the responsibility which attaches to my position, that if the attempt be made under present conditions, I can imagine no length of resistance to which Ulster can go in which I should not be prepared to support them, and in which, in my belief, they would not be supported by the overwhelming majority of the British people.[40]

For good measure he added that the Liberals would be 'lighting the fires of civil war' if they pressed ahead with their plans.[41] As Thomas Bartlett rightly points out, 'altogether less militant statements from O'Connell, Parnell and Dillon in previous years had led to their swift incarceration: but Bonar Law would face no such penalty'.[42] Moreover, there is every indication that the

Conservative leader lent his silent blessing to illegal gun-running activities at Larne, covertly arming the Ulster Volunteer Force and turning an already-volatile situation into a powder keg.[43]

Taking his cue from Kipling, Bonar Law stressed that the struggle was not Ulster's alone but encompassed the fate of the entire empire. At the Balmoral rally, speaking before a ninety-foot-high flagstaff sporting the largest Union Jack ever woven, he assured his audience that although the government had attempted to 'shut you off from the help of the British people', it was a manoeuvre that was bound to fail. Summoning a much wider unity, he assured them that help would come, and when the struggle was finally won 'men will say to you ... you have saved yourselves by your exertions and you will save the Empire by your example'.[44] In thus mobilizing a conception of the British people spanning the globe, the Conservative leader embodied what Bill Schwarz terms 'a startling historical paradox' – on the one hand speaking for 'militants for the greater empire', while at the same time identifying the 'encroaching enemy as the imperial British state'.[45] Bonar Law

Figure 2.3 Conservative and Unionist Party Leader Andrew Bonar Law (right) with Ulster Unionist Leader and founder of the paramilitary Ulster Volunteer Force Edward Carson in London, 1 August 1915. Source: Hulton Archive/Getty Images.

seemed unperturbed by the anomaly, providing an early glimpse into 'the fate of allegiance under conditions of imperial retrenchment'; the fundamental dynamics of which would later be replicated throughout the post-war British world.[46]

But there was a more immediate, contemporary parallel – albeit an unlikely one and certainly unacknowledged – far removed from Ulster on the waters of Vancouver's Burrard Inlet. The 376 Punjabis claiming the right of entry into British Columbia gave no inkling of any wider commonalities in their desperate telegrams to the governor-general and may have been wholly unaware of the contemporaneous struggle lurching towards disaster more than four thousand miles away. Yet their plight presents an oblique analogue to the Covenanters' demand that their Britishness be recognized and reciprocated. The contexts could not have been more dissimilar nor the moral implications more dissonant. But much as Bonar Law declared of his Protestant compatriots, here too were 'men whose only crime is that they refuse to be driven out of our community and be deprived of the privilege of British citizenship'.[47]

Andrew Bonar Law was himself Canadian – by no means an idle detail, yet it is routinely overlooked in assessments of his pivotal role in the Ulster crisis of 1912–14.[48] Born in New Brunswick in 1858, the youngest son of the Rev. James Law, an Ulster Presbyterian minister who served the rural population of Kingston (now Rexton) for some thirty-two years, it was at the age of twelve that he migrated to Scotland with one of his returning aunts. But he retained an enduring identification with his Canadian origins (among his few intimates were Canadian premier Robert Borden and fellow New Brunswicker, Lord Beaverbrook); one contemporary describing his South Kensington home as 'the natural product of Scotch-Canadianism – no swank, no posing, no pomp'.[49] During a wartime parliamentary debate on the insidious threat posed by naturalized Germans, Bonar Law gave himself as an example of someone who, in a hypothetical war between Britain and Canada, 'would fight for Canada against the land of his adoption'.[50] More to the point, he readily joined his colonial affinities to the imperative of 'saving' Ulster, emphasizing the Canadian connection in his first major speech as party leader in Leeds at the end of 1911:

> Ladies and gentlemen, as you probably know, most of you, I was born in Canada [Cheers]. I spent the early years of my life there. Among the many disqualifications for the position which I now hold – and no one feels them more strongly than myself – that is not a disqualification [Cheers]. It is an advantage [Cheers]. For 25 years the determination to maintain the

integrity of the United Kingdom has given a name to our party. We are the Unionist party [Hear, hear]. But ours is now a larger Union ... It is for us to maintain, and we shall maintain, in spite of the lowering clouds which now threaten us, the integrity of the United Kingdom. But it is for us also, it is for the men of this generation, to guard the vital Union of the British Empire.[51]

Evidently for Bonar Law, there was no question of picking and choosing jurisdictions – no burden of Canadian 'domicile' weighing on his civil status. And hence nothing to prevent him boarding a ship bound for Britain and, upon entering the three-mile limit, claiming to be 'clothed within the attributes of a citizen' – or offering himself as the nation's first citizen. Here, sailing contrary to the 'way the sun travels' counted as no 'disqualification'. But the fact that he even paused to consider the possibility suggests a certain unease – as though some unmarked boundary had indeed been surreptitiously crossed. In turning it to his 'advantage' he was likely preaching to the converted (the spontaneous cheers suggest as much). To this day, he is routinely referred to as the 'only British Prime Minister born overseas' or alternatively 'born in Canada' – rather than the only *Canadian* ever elected as UK prime minister.[52] The cardinal point is that he was 'British-born', wherever that happened to be; a habit of mind inherited from former times, but one which was conspicuously unavailable to the passengers of the *Komagata Maru*.

Two discrete episodes, two wholly unrelated flashpoints, neverthe-less converge to shed light on a common problem: the one, a boatload of unwanted outsiders trying to break into the limits of location; the other, a belligerent minority aggressively mobilizing to prevent their country being moved out. The shared element of ambiguity about the benefits of being British (intersecting, as chance would have it, at Canadian ocean crossings) casts them fleetingly into the same frame. In both instances the British government equivocated in the face of pressure from a volatile, self-designating in-group, while remaining anxious to avoid the political embarrassment (and attendant civil strife) of alienating those deemed 'borderline'. Whatever natural inclination there might have been to align openly with racial and religious 'kin' was rendered politically fraught by nearly two centuries of dissembling at the edges of British identity. Taken together, they represent the extremes of inward and outward tensions tearing at the fabric of Greater Britain at the threshold of the twentieth century.

WHO OR WHAT WAS GREATER BRITAIN?

We might reasonably assume that there was little mutual sympathy between Ulster Protestants and Punjabi Sikhs – to the extent that they acknowledged each other's claims at all (and sure enough, the Vancouver County Loyal Orange Order passed a resolution 'commending' the blockade of the *Komagata Maru* and 'seeking the total expulsion of all Oriental immigration into this Dominion').[53] Placing the two in any kind of analytical proximity or alignment might seem a tendentious ploy – asking more of the historical record than it can plausibly deliver, or worse, a glib exercise in false moral equivalence. But it is precisely the moral asymmetries and the sheer unlikelihood of mutual resonances that raises questions about the social composition and geographical sweep of Greater Britain. It is not a matter of whether the two episodes were objectively similar but of how such disparate sensibilities – in no way allied one to another – came to rely on the same social categories to bolster their claims. This requires closer attention to the underlying properties of Greater Britain – not just in the eyes of contemporaries but also the unintended consequences arising out of its key formative contexts.

Historians have generally taken Greater Britain at face value – proceeding from what contemporaries themselves had to say about their widening horizons and interpreting their words within the political, strategic, technological and ideological setting of late nineteenth-century imperialism. There was, as we have seen, no shortage of pundits elaborately heralding the arrival of Greater Britain in terms that left little doubt about their intentions. What they clearly had in mind was an unprecedentedly wide, but emphatically closed circle, available only to the exclusive cohort answering to J. R. Seeley's famous description of a 'homogeneous people, one in blood, language, religion, and laws, but dispersed over a boundless space'. Charles Dilke was similarly preoccupied with the 'English-speaking, white-inhabited, and self-governed lands' of the British empire – a diverse sweep of migrant communities where 'in essentials, the race was always one'.[54] Greater Britain was unambiguously reserved for English-speaking white people in all their assorted particulars, and virtually no one among the diverse milieu of proselytizers ever seems to have said otherwise.[55] But for the purpose of grasping the fragility of global scales of British selfhood, there is every reason to consider widening its conceptual remit.

Duncan Bell's *The Idea of Greater Britain* (2007) is the indispensable guide to Dilke's influential term, tracing its inflections and permutations among the many Victorian pundits for whom 'the British national "self" was thought to extend across the planet'.[56] The significance of these public moralists lies, not merely in popularizing a new civic vernacular, but more importantly in promoting the kind of 'political and cultural consciousness necessary for a true global community'. It was as much about a cognitive shift in the 'spatiotemporal dimensions of the world itself', enabled by new, epoch-making technologies – principally steam and telegraphy – that altered the 'material structures of social and political life'.[57] Bell also disentangles the extraordinary 'slippage of terms' that characterized the genre – starting with the term 'Greater Britain' itself, frequently substituted with any number of proximate synonyms. The disparities grew even starker when it came to rendering the promise of a global polity as practical politics.[58] All manner of ill-fated federal schemes jostled for attention, each contending with more moderate proposals for looser forms of intergovernmental cooperation – opposed, in turn, by those insisting that Greater Britain had already reached peak functionality through the existing, informal linkages and channels (and that any burdensome constitutional 'machinery' would only jeopardize its future). For all the rhetorical jousting, few ever declared themselves sworn opponents of Greater Britain. The intrinsic ambiguity of the term allowed it to circulate virtually unchallenged as a pleasing idiom for addressing the plural in the singular. But in its capaciousness, Greater Britain also harboured an auto-destruct mechanism of which contemporaries were more nervously aware than they generally let on. If the new 'spatiotemporal' scales of global political consciousness were to be so unreservedly welcomed, how were unwelcome outsiders to be kept out?

To delve further requires a closer look at how Greater Britain resonated under conditions of active deployment – as distinct from the formal or 'theoretical' iterations promoted by armchair imperialists. It was through the intricacies of operationalization that the 'slippage of terms' generated moments of extreme contingency, to the point of jeopardizing the integrity and viability of the very thing itself. Greater Britain could inspire widely varying degrees of political commitment – not just on the question of constitutional reform but also in relation to state-sponsored migration schemes, proposals for customs and tariff unions, and the particularly vexed question of cooperation in naval defence.[59] It was these material issues that translated the rhetoric of Greater Britain into practical politics, but in so doing they also produced no end of bitter disagreement.

The political struggle over Irish Home Rule exemplified the difficulty. On the one hand, powerful voices such as Seeley's insisted on the 'strong natural bonds of race *and religion* ... practically dissolved by distance', without which there could be no discernibly 'British' global polity. But the conviction that religion was absolutely central was far from unanimous. Bell's exhaustive trawl through the contemporary sources leads him to conclude that 'the relationship between religion and visions of Greater Britain was a complex one'; that there was 'no single religious position' and that 'people of all denominations (as well as those of none)' ardently supported some version of allegiance to the whole.[60] Indeed, it was this ambiguity that permitted Greater Britain the widest possible amplitude. But in no way did this prevent Ulster Unionism from mobilizing its supporters around the principle of religious exclusion when the issue came to a head, equating Protestantism with 'loyalism' and portraying Catholicism as 'England's oldest foe' (as Kipling would have it). Both sides of the dispute anchored their claims in the wider fraternity of Greater Britain, arguing that the future of the entire empire was at stake – thereby ensuring that the political schism of 1912–14 was reproduced in Toronto, Melbourne, Wellington and elsewhere. It was the tacit awareness of the 'slippages' that furnished so much emotional leverage; the implicit knowledge that rival and indeed mutually antagonistic allegiances could draw on the same civic vocabulary. For all the insistent rhetoric that 'the race was always one', Greater Britain was a two-edged sword, equally efficient as a means of sowing discord.

Two key formative contexts ensured that the seemingly straightforward protocols of 'race patriotism' could produce divisions among the very constituency of exalted white Britons. First, it is evident that Greater Britain in its late nineteenth-century iterations arose out of fundamentally defensive instincts – responding to anxieties generated by the same technological innovations that had made a global continuum of Britons imaginable in the first place. Fierce competitors for commercial and naval supremacy emerged in these decades, equally determined to harness the tools of modernity to their material interests and challenge the stability and supremacy of Britain's overstretched assets. Concern centred initially on Russia but turned increasingly towards rapidly industrializing Germany and even the United States (despite the latter's occasional inclusion in the brotherhood of Anglo-Saxonism). Here, the language of race was used interchangeably with nationality, such that racial or ethnic pride could be deployed in contradistinction to European rivals (or South African 'Boers') as much as it furnished a signifier of whiteness.

At some point prior to the Great War, the balance tipped towards the irreducible alterity of 'alien races' and the idiom of whiteness was accentuated accordingly – a point difficult to determine with precision because threat perception in the empire was never uniform. The settler colonies were at the forefront in sounding the alarm against an 'awakening Asia' – stirred initially by jealousies on the colonial gold fields but later dramatized by fears and phobias of Chinese and Japanese militarization. By the turn of the century, Australia's 'great national ideal', according to the union leader W. G. Spence, was 'purity of race and the preservation of Greater Britain for the Anglo-Saxon stock'.[61] In Natal, meanwhile, Indians were becoming despised as 'the real canker eating into the community' and, with the grant of responsible government in 1893, the principle of 'race unity' was cited as grounds for restricting the franchise and curbing South Asian immigration.[62] But in Ontario, Quebec and the Canadian Maritimes, anxieties about either group – East Asian or South Asian – rarely reached the same fever pitch, much to the constant infuriation of British Columbians.

Such disparities were partly a function of physical proximity, producing no end of confusion about where to draw the line of exclusion (and the preferred means of enforcement). When the Australian colonies in the 1880s strenuously lobbied the Liberal colonial secretary, Lord Derby, to annex large portions of the Pacific to allay their invasion anxieties, the response was one of incredulity. 'I tried a little mild sarcasm', Derby confided to his diary, 'asking them whether they did not want a whole planet to themselves . . . but I found the matter too serious for joking: they could not think themselves safe in a country as big as Europe if Italy or Germany had a harbour within three of four days steaming of their shores.'[63] When the British later conceded the northeast portion of New Guinea to Germany ('Kaiser Wilhelm's Land') in 1886, the exasperation of Victorian premier James Service was 'boundless' (by his own lights) – engendering a 'bitterness' towards Britain that would 'not die out in this generation'.[64]

The uneven proximity of threat perception merged with a second key context that curbed the otherwise hard, racial edges of Greater Britain. Already by the mid-nineteenth century, with the abolition of slavery and the experimentation with responsible self-government in the settler colonies, the accent on liberty had become an entrenched feature of imperial self-congratulation – particularly the ideal of an empire of free labour.[65] It was an ironic juxtaposition, at a time when the *illiberal* empire of conquest was rapidly consolidated with the incorporation of India under the British Crown (symbolized by Victoria's elevation to the title of 'Empress of India') and the subsequent 'scramble' for colonial territory in East, West and Central Africa. The idea of Greater Britain was part of a wider preoccupation with disaggregating the two, thereby insulating the 'liberal, inclusive, popular arrangement' from the more 'despotic or absolutist' alternative.[66]

Seeley made the distinction clear in his refusal to incorporate India in his design, claiming that Greater Britain was 'not in the ordinary sense an Empire at all' – whereas the arrangements in India were 'really an Empire and an Oriental Empire' at that, scarred through the ages by tyrannies of every description of which British despotism was merely the latest. 'We cannot', he averred, 'on looking more closely into the phenomenon, reconcile ourselves to it.'[67] These were not heresies whispered in dark recesses but discussed openly as a profound anomaly at the heart of the British constitution. Sir Alfred Milner made no secret of the discrepancy between 'the Two Empires', insisting that 'we can only fraternize with those with whom we have something in common, morally or spiritually speaking – in other words a community of race, language, civilization, history, tradition and ideals which form the basis of the link between Great Britain and the Dominions', as distinct from 'the other, the Dependent Empire'.[68] He lamented that the very terms 'Empire' and 'Imperial' were 'in some respects unfortunate' due to their connotations of 'domination, ascendancy, the rule of a superior state over vassal states' when in reality it was all about nurturing a 'common civilization' in an 'organic union'.[69] Attending to the disparity seemed all the more pressing at a time when Britain's own democratic institutions were undergoing radical reform, compounding the age-old dilemmas of the British as a 'free-though-conquering people'.[70] More fundamentally, evading the stigma of despotism was also a matter of defying the historical laws of decline and fall. An aspirational empire of fellow British feeling need not – as contemporaries constantly emphasized – be conceived as an 'empire' at all, but a unique social experiment destined to 'escape the fate of Rome'.[71]

The combined effects of divergent threat perception and the liberal hankerings of 'public moralists' account for the curious diffidence among the high priests of Greater Britain when it came to imposing *absolute* limits on the limits of location. Their relentless promotion of the 'community of race' was matched by a surprising reticence about the place of Indigenous peoples or other non-British elements within the settlement colonies, and as Bell observes: 'when discussion did arise it was frequently perfunctory and evasive'.[72] Seeley made the revealing remark that, just as the Anglo-Saxon unity of the mother country could accommodate a fair smattering of 'Celtic language and Celtic blood', so too, throughout Greater Britain 'a good many French and Dutch and a good many Caffres and Maoris may be admitted without marring the ethnological unity of the whole'.[73] It was Seeley's way of squaring the evident heterogeneity of the settlement colonies with an idealized racial vision of Britain in the world, without disturbing the underlying tenets of a liberal empire. But the evasiveness exposed the fault lines of potential fragmentation, particularly when arrayed against the race absolutism of settler–colonial legislatures.

The evasiveness was all the more conspicuous when the liberal conscience was prodded by the activities of someone like the young M. K. Gandhi in Natal, who in the 1890s demanded to know how a policy of racial exclusion could be squared with 'the best British traditions' – foreshadowing Gurdit Singh by nearly two decades. The activities of the Natal Indian Congress challenged the verities of Greater Britain at their most vulnerable pressure point – the conviction that 'any British subject . . . is entitled to vote irrespective of caste, colour or creed'.[74] As someone who genuinely believed that the empire rested not 'on material but on spiritual foundations', and who saw 'something fine in the ideas of the British Constitution', Gandhi framed the issue as a moral challenge: 'Tear away those ideals and you tear away my loyalty to that Constitution; keep those ideals and I am ever a bondman.'[75] The response of the *Natal Mercury* exemplified the brazenness of white hypocrisy, venturing that 'the British subject theory from an abstract point of view may sound all very well, but . . . '. And to be sure, this self-serving relativism was replicated throughout the settler empire, resonating all the way to British Columbia. As Lake and Reynolds have shown, the concerted efforts of the Natal Congress and other protest groups in exposing the anomalies only emboldened many settlers to be even more trenchantly racist, accelerating the processes whereby the settler colonies increasingly came 'to define themselves as "white men's countries"'.[76]

But the hesitations should not be overlooked – indeed, they are everywhere to be seen if only we pause to consider them. Even a tireless advocate of 'white's only' entry laws such as Australia's Henry Parkes – himself a committed Chartist from the hearth of radical nonconformity in the English Midlands – could not completely shake the dictates of the 'reverential cult surrounding the constitution'.[77] In a debate on the imposition of Chinese restrictions in the New South Wales Parliament in 1881, he felt bound to preface his remarks with a revealing caveat: 'I am willing to admit that legislation of this kind is undesireable. I am as anxious as any can be that we should maintain the boast that whoever steps upon our shore shall find an asylum of freedom here.' More to the point, his passionate case for hard and fast racial barriers met deep pockets of principled opposition both in the New South Wales legislature and the local press, condemning Parkes's harsh measures as 'unnecessary, unfair and "un-British"'.[78] Here, the 'iconic importance' of liberal constitutional norms as signifiers of 'national status and civilizational affectations' ran headlong into the counter-imperatives of racial authority and ethnic purity.[79] That the dissenting voices ultimately lost out to the more absolutist strains of race patriotism should not diminish their significance, especially with regard to the matter that concerns us here – the protracted unravelling of the Greater British ideal in the longer term.

These apprehensions were arguably most acute in metropolitan Britain, where the problem not only touched upon the philosophical axioms of a liberal empire, but also raised the risk of provoking political volatility in the colonial empire should racial exclusion become visibly and overtly obnoxious. Colonial Secretary Joseph Chamberlain tried to explain the position to the colonial premiers gathered for the occasion of Victoria's Diamond Jubilee in 1897:

> We quite sympathize with the determination of the white inhabitants of these colonies which are in comparatively close proximity to millions and hundreds of millions of Asiatics that there shall not be an influx of people alien in civilization, alien in religion, alien in customs, whose influx, moreover, would most seriously interfere with the legitimate rights of the existing labour population ... but we ask you also to bear in mind the traditions of the Empire, which makes no distinction in favour of, or against race or colour; and to exclude by reason of their colour or by reason of their race, all Her Majesty's Indian subjects, or even all Asiatics, would be an act so offensive to those peoples that it would be most painful, I am quite certain, to Her Majesty to have to sanction it.[80]

The upshot was the infamous compromise based on the 'Natal formula', whereby unwanted immigrants were excluded, not formally on the grounds of race but by way of a test of literacy, which could be widened where necessary to include European languages other than English. It satisfied Chamberlain's minimum requirements (as he confided to his staff: 'All we can do is to prevent the exclusion of British subjects') while allowing colonial legislators to boast to their constituents that they had achieved precisely that.[81] It was rapidly adopted by all the settler colonies with the notable exception of British Columbia – hence, Mackenzie King's equally disingenuous 'continuous journey' requirement which served the same (dual) purpose. Significantly, the British Columbian premier Sir Richard McBride wrote to his Queensland counterpart immediately following the departure of the *Komagata Maru* to ascertain his view ('privately and confidentially and in a sense quite unofficially') as to how the Natal formula 'works out in practice'. Though McBride himself entertained doubts on the grounds of the linguistic dexterity of 'Orientals', he 'should be willing to agree to the suggestion if I were fully satisfied that its adoption would be a complete bar'.[82]

The duplicity was remarkably calculated, and historians have understandably viewed the Natal formula as an instance of base political expediency – white chauvinism at its most blatantly insincere. To be sure, the intricate procedures devised to reject 'undesirable' races without explicitly saying so smacked of a blithe indifference to the purely 'theoretical' dictates of British liberty. Nevertheless, insufficient attention has been paid to why such transparent subterfuge seemed unavoidable. The veneration of the British Constitution was a pervasive feature of Victorian civic life, not least – indeed especially – in the colonies of settlement where the myth of 'England's greatest contribution to the world' nurtured deeper, more durable roots in otherwise thinly tilled soil.[83] Kumarasingham makes the crucial point that the effect cut both ways – as the outward projections of Greater Britain flourished, 'so did the culture of constitutional hagiography'.[84]

The extraordinary measures employed by colonial legislatures to circumvent these bedrock convictions were not simply a cynical move to placate the diplomatic wobbles of Whitehall. It was far more likely intended to quell a disturbance from within, assisting those intent on 'looking more closely into the phenomenon' to somehow 'reconcile' themselves to it.[85] After all, there is precious little evidence that anyone else fell for the Natal formula's flimsy pretext. The cherished cause of British liberty was cited in virtually every colonial legislature as a genuine reason for proceeding 'pragmatically', and as grounds for real concern should illiberal urges be permitted too much latitude. It was never enough to turn the tide of racist sentiment, but sufficient to pry open a tiny but significant crack in the hard exterior of race patriotism.

Alfred Milner unwittingly personified the dilemma before a Johannesburg audience in 1903. Apparently forgetting his own strictures about the 'unfortunate' stigma of 'domination', he roundly declared that if 'the white man should rule ... then let us say that plainly and do not let us only say it, but let us justify it'. The frustration was palpable – to be armed with such convictions but unable to square them 'plainly' with a liberal belief system. Five years later he would describe himself to a gathering in Ottawa as a 'British Race Patriot' – all the while abhorring discrimination on the grounds of race. As in Johannesburg, he was at a loss to account for the flawed logic, inviting his listeners instead to consider the unique privilege 'for every white man of British birth, that he can be at home in every state of the Empire from the moment he has set foot in it, though his whole previous life may have been passed at the other end of the earth'.[86]

This was the core conceit targeted by Gurdit Singh in his dramatic gesture of May 1914, laying claim to the same entitlements of 'British birth' that came so effortlessly to Lord Milner. Significantly, his case was argued in the BC Appeal Court, not on the intricacies of immigration law but as a writ of habeas corpus – invoking the mythological authority of the early Plantagenets and Magna Carta. In one sense, his voyage resembles an ironic move – in that he was aware of the likelihood of rejection and charted his voyage in a self-conscious spirit of defiance, citing no less than 'peace in all parts of the Empire' as his fundamental cause. But there was something more – more than a mere symbolic protest or a principled stand, without which he would never have mastered the logistics nor come so close to success (nor, for that matter, been kept in limbo for more than two months by baffled port authorities). At some level, he and his compatriots knew that the 'global colour line' was perforated with doubt, misgivings and perennial disagreement over where the line ought to be drawn. He had spotted a gap, aided by an unmistakable glitch on the moral compass, and was determined to sail through. It is here that Greater Britain takes on a more capacious meaning.

What kind of community did advocates of this vast conglomerate imagine themselves belonging to? What cast of mind compelled Gurdit Singh to set out for Vancouver, secure in the knowledge that the destination was rightly his? What was 'the thing' that was 'stronger than Parliamentary majorities' in the eyes of a Bonar Law? Contemporary opinion was divided between those who were emphatic that Greater Britain qualified as a nation (many insisting that it was the only entity that so qualified as 'you can not have two nations in one nation'); and those who were equally convinced that imperial nationhood could only be couched in the plural.[87] The young English journalist Richard Jebb became a prominent advocate of the latter view following a world tour in Dilke's footsteps at the turn of the century, where he found that such 'phrases as "the Expansion of England" or "Greater Britain"' could no longer be squared with the reality of 'separate national aspirations'.[88] But he, too, failed in his efforts to deliver semantic coherence with his alternative conception of a 'Britannic Alliance'.[89] The vast majority were content to leave the matter hovering somewhere in between, buoyed by the hazy conviction that 'Britannic-ness' embodied an 'organic' conception of the people that drew strength from the fact that it defied easy categorization. The celebrated author, John Buchan, famously described it in 1906 as 'a spirit, an attitude of mind, an unconquerable hope ... the wider patriotism which conceives of our people as a race and not as a chance community'.[90] It was a deliberate fudge, elevating conceptual looseness to a metaphysical virtue.

If nations can be constituted from diverse materials with multiple objects in view, there may be scope for regarding Greater Britain as a rogue variant, summoning a species of nationhood for atypical and largely indeterminate ends.[91] As we have seen, it traded in much the same currency (history, language, ethnicity and a shared sovereign if not sovereignty); found expression in similar kinds of civic objects (monuments, anniversaries, folklore, rites and rituals); all adhering variously to a coherent credo of civic and constitutional ideals. Buchan was no doubt correct to assert that it was 'not a chance community', in the sense of some diffuse cultural association celebrating customs, lore and language with no conception of a shared polity whatsoever – like the Caledonian and Hibernian societies that mushroomed throughout the empire in memory of a distant home. For all its elusive contours, Britishness imposed morally binding obligations with a real capability to harness material and political capital to shared purposes – or at least, the heavily overfreighted anticipation of shared purpose.

But the evident detachment from the demand for popular sovereignty invested Greater Britain with an unusually subversive potential, not least in its elastic conception of the people that transcended the governing writ of any given legislature. This indistinct mass could – in the right circumstances – be called on to defy the will of parliament, including the Imperial Parliament at Westminster if necessary. Such a possibility was already implicit (and frequently explicit) in the case for separate statehood among the self-governing dominions, where legislative autonomy was seen as a guarantor of 'British' freedoms in the face of the unpredictable whims of metropolitan political expediency.[92] Popular vigilance in the service of such higher ideals disrupted the otherwise harmonious rhetoric of blood, honour and 'race patriotism', furnishing what Bill Schwarz has termed the 'lineaments of an ethnic populism'.[93] Just as Dilke's advocacy of Greater Britain displayed a spectacular 'disregard for the scope of British sovereignty', so too his term became imbued with the possibility that race might take precedence over fealty to sovereign parliaments.[94] This 'global Anglo-British ethnic compact' could be mobilized in defence of the empire against South African Boers, Sudanese 'Dervishes' or the combined forces of the European Central Powers; but it could also be turned against the imperial state to preserve a 'pure' conception of the British people from 'the depredations of the politicians'.[95] Such were the matters that weighed 'stronger than Parliamentary majorities'.

But they were not the sole or exclusive preserve of a specifically ethnic populism. Or not quite. Just as the myth of British liberty lauded universal principles that lent a hard-to-refute legitimacy to the claims of non-white subjects, so too the latter could challenge the authority of the legislature in the name of a more capacious Britishness. More than a decade after his ill-fated enterprise, Gurdit Singh was unrepentant when he sat down to record his 'life-history in connection with the voyage':

> We were poor Indians seeking to enter Canada to earn our livelihood and we thought we had every right to enter there as India as well as Canada were under the British Crown. When even the slum dweller of London could freely move to India as well as Canada why should not we? We are insulted, we are dishonoured we are disgraced in all parts of the wourld [*sic*] because *we have no Government* that will feel for indignities inflicted on us.[96]

Here was a radically modified conception of the people versus parliament – asserting the right to disobey laws that deprived his compatriots of British 'status' both at home and abroad, leaving them 'ill-used' with 'no claim to be treated as human beings'. Despite the ruling of the Appeal Court, he insisted, 'we never admitted and never would that we were in the wrong in resisting Canada's unlawful orders'. In mounting a challenge to expose 'the utter hollowness of the equality-cult' of imperial Britishness, he brought on a confrontation that would 'for ever blacken the History of Canada' and 'show the blackguardy of Great Britain'.[97] In ways not wholly dissimilar to Bonar Law, he appealed to a 'higher law than that sanctioned by mere institutions of the state'.[98] Both protagonists, each straining against the limits of location, would have successors in the years ahead; not least in the decades after 1945 when their rival British worlds would spectacularly collide.

3

'BRITISH WITH A SMALL "B": THE IMPRESS OF INTERNATIONALISM

The summer of 1941 finds Leslie Howard half-dozing on a sunlit bench near Trafalgar Square, puffing nonchalantly on a pipe with the brim of his hat drawn down over his eyes. The legendary English star of *Pygmalion* and *Gone with the Wind* has recently returned from Hollywood to contribute to the war effort, and will shortly be called on to do his bit in unanticipated ways. His afternoon rest is stirred by the sound of an elderly woman draped in a fox stole and plumed hat accosting three uniformed soldiers. 'Do tell me', she implores them breathlessly, 'Are you boys from the Empire? I just had to come up to you to tell you how wonderful we think you are. Coming all those thousands of miles to answer the Motherland's call to arms. Splendid fellows!' The three respond awkwardly as she bustles on, ill at ease with her heavy-handed gratitude. It is then that Howard affects a rescue, rising from his bench to offer the boys a pint in a nearby Regent Street pub. Relieved to be spared the motherland's affections, all three – Australian, New Zealander and Canadian – follow his lead towards Piccadilly.

The moment was wholly contrived, staged for a fifteen-minute Ministry of Information short film, *From the Four Corners*, with Howard playing a mythologized version of himself. In the next scene he presents four brimming beer mugs to the thirsty troops, and their reactions to the 'well-meaning lady' spill forth. 'That's a lot of hooey', spouts Private Johnston from Vancouver, and Corporal Atkinson of Sydney concurs: 'Too many people over here have got the wrong idea.' Each recites his individual path to enlistment, with Private Gilbert from New Zealand insisting that none of them were in any sense 'called' to arms. Howard wholly sympathizes, assuring them: 'You're absolutely right, you're your own masters', in no way beholden to any other country's bidding. But he presses the issue nevertheless, for the mystery still remains; indeed, the 'one thing you haven't explained: exactly why you came?' If it was not the reflex of blind fealty, how was he to account for 'why you left your girl, you your farm and you your career?' Brushing aside platitudes about 'kicking Hitler in the pants' and 'seeing the old country', he tries out a theory of his own. 'I'll tell you what it is, you're all idealists, practical idealists if that softens the blow.' Their evident bewilderment spurs him to his feet: 'I'm going to take you fellows somewhere. I think I can show you what I mean.'

In the final act they arrive at the top of the dome of St Paul's, looking out upon Britain's 'ancient foundations and most worthy liberty' as Howard surveys the scene. He points out monuments to kings and queens past; namechecks the Pacific exploits of legendary English navigators; gestures upriver to Runnymede, source of the 'elementary principles of British justice all over the Commonwealth'; and beholds the Houses of Parliament at Westminster, 'the mother of them all'. 'You see', he affirms, 'there's something here for all of us ... all part of London, and part of ourselves.' The three exemplars of colonial manhood have now assumed a more solemn bearing, peering earnestly into the middle distance as their host delivers one last homily:

> Once [the city] ended here just where we're standing, then as it put out a tentative street here, a casual row of houses there, so our fathers' minds crept along with it, their ideas of justice and tolerance and the rights of man, taking shape in the sunlight and in the smoke, sometimes standing still, sometimes even slipping back, but slowly broadening with the centuries. Some of those ideas are written in the constitutions of the Commonwealth; and some are unwritten, we just try to carry them in our hearts, and in our minds ... your fathers carried them to the end of the earth.[1]

Here was Greater Britain with a wartime twist – shorn of the once-obligatory worship of 'the British race' (though the four white faces still conveyed the visual grammar of old). Gone, too, was the insistence on a single, continuous nation, fanning out from the imperial hearth. Such certainties had seemingly become absurd, the preserve of retired colonels and old spinsters – like the one whose tactless tribute brought them so fortuitously together. But it was Greater Britain all the same, powered by the same metaphors – 'putting out', 'taking shape', 'carried' forth, and of course 'broadening' out across the continents; the slow perfection of 'ancient liberties' leavened by the outward carriage; the temporal and spatial trajectories seemingly indistinguishable.

By 1941, the exigencies of war and the demands of rallying resources from every part of the globe had focused the propaganda effort on promoting a progressive empire 'with a tolerant, liberal Britain at its centre acting against racial prejudice' – hence the accent on shared rights, laws and liberties.[2] Harnessing the energies and resources of diverse colonies,

dominions and dependencies meant that the rhetoric of colonial subordination had to be downplayed – a point that Howard's film was at pains to
emphasize. It was a disingenuous ploy; the leading man's commanding
presence in every frame clearly conveyed that not all were equally in charge.

But even before the war, there had been indications that some of the
conviction was leaching out of the idea of Greater Britain as 'one people',
while a new myth of steadily 'maturing' colonial nations bound in
a partnership of equals had steadily gained ground. 'Race patriotism',
though by no means obsolete, was couched increasingly in euphemistic
terms (or rendered obliquely, as in the glaring absence of non-white troops
in Howard's family circle). It was not a case of widespread popular rejection
of imperial loyalty or a collective turning away from racialized conceptions
of identity. More significant were the sweeping changes in the international
system that emerged out of the Great War, geared increasingly towards
more tightly organized, multilateral structures anchored in new institutional frameworks. The Paris Peace Conference of 1919 and the high
hopes for the new League of Nations as a supreme arbiter of international
conflict had ushered in a new era of 'foreign affairs' – across a broadly
constituted matrix of sovereign nation-states. In this new setting, the ambiguities of a loosely defined assembly of blood 'relatives' was always going to
be an awkward fit. The interwar experiments with transnational governmen-
talities signalled a new 'sentiment of internationalism' that profoundly
shaped conceptions of peacetime order – notwithstanding the disorderly
outcomes of the late 1930s.[3] Interwar internationalism emphasized wider
human commonalities and an incipient global civil society, but it also
enhanced the significance of the nation-state 'as a defining, order-creating
unit'.[4] In this scheme of things, the 'organic' conception of the linkages
between variously (and vaguely) sovereign 'British' peoples, sustained by
a cacophony of familial and bodily metaphors, came to occupy an indeterminate – and ultimately untenable – space between the national and the
international.

The most immediate casualty was the term 'Greater Britain' itself, which
fell rapidly into disuse. Oswald Mosley's attempt to retool it as a rallying cry
for his Union of British Fascists with the publication of *The Greater Britain* in
1932 assured its rapid demise thereafter. But as James Belich maintains,
'Greater Britain was not just a failed idea.'[5] Works such as Seeley's *Expansion
of England* would continue to be reprinted into the 1950s.[6] The lack of
support for elaborate and unrealistic schemes of federal union may have
put paid to the idea of an imperial super-state, but there remained ample
scope for redirecting the core 'intuitive, emotional, and symbolic' energies

that had always loomed large in the Greater British imaginary.[7] Throughout the interwar years, the effort to define and contain the ever-elusive spirit binding a plurality of peoples continued, producing new conceptualizations and a slew of semantic innovation.

Among the more inventive was the Australian historian W. K. Hancock who, borrowing an idea from one of his English colleagues, described himself as 'British with a small "b"'. Reflecting on his childhood days when he would gaze at the map on the wall, 'measure up all the vast territories coloured red, and say to myself: "All this belongs to us"', Hancock had come to recognize that 'British possessions' were 'no longer "possessions" of Britain in any sense at all'. Rather than exit the imperial fold entirely, however, the self-governing colonies had forged a pathway 'out of the British Empire' and 'into the British Commonwealth, that new and growing association of independent – and *inter*dependent – nations'. Extolling the virtue of balancing 'the two *necessities*', he urged the importance of finding 'a method by which they can live their own individual lives and at the same time share a common life with each other'. Writing from Birmingham in 1941 – just as *From the Four Corners* was educating cinema audiences about the new dispensation – he elaborated in terms worthy of Leslie Howard himself:

> I know that there still exists the kind of man who thinks of the British Empire as something which is British with a large B – something which is the peculiar glory and the peculiar possession of 'the British race'. But 'the British race' is a minority in the British Empire. If we wish to be true to our past achievements and future destiny, we must look forward to the day when Indians and Africans, too, are able to assume their full share in the privileges and burdens of the Commonwealth's freedom. Our political institutions and ideas are rooted in the history of Great Britain; but we are a diverse family of many kindreds and languages . . . our Commonwealth is *british* – with a small b.[8]

It was an early iteration of what would later become the 'new Commonwealth' (stripped ultimately of any 'b' whatsoever) in a bid to square the iniquities of the colonial past with some semblance of a shared future. Hancock seemed well aware that he was ahead of his time – that the 'British race' persisted as a potent ideal, not easily reconciled with the new social and political formations emerging in the international system. But he seemed not to recognize the inherent contradiction of emptying his 'british' convictions of racial authority entirely. His small 'b' prescription stemmed from the same 'vision of moral order' that had moved earlier generations to conjure a unified race offering 'stability and leadership, benevolently but firmly, to a chaotic world'.[9] It remained the white man's prerogative to distinguish order from chaos, and it was therefore far from clear how non-white subjects could assume 'their full share in the privileges and burdens' without disrupting the historical axioms of Britishness itself. In this sense, Hancock had touched upon a key fault line that would produce any number of tremors at war's end.

This chapter concludes the opening section by exploring three key indicators of Britishness with a 'small b' in the interwar years, looking first at the realm of political and constitutional innovation in a transformed international setting. The focus then moves to the terrain of Greater British economic cooperation in the first half of the twentieth century that produced a range of imaginative attempts to make good on Hancock's 'two necessities'. In the final instalment we return to the empire of civic and constitutional entitlements, only this time as they were perceived and deployed by Indigenous activists for essentially anti-colonial ends – a prelude to the wholesale rejection of British modes of self-representation among Indigenous peoples in the post-war years.

In each instance, the interwar period can be seen as a time of ironic consolidation – ironic in the sense that the push to elaborate an ideally calibrated British world only succeeded in exposing further the glaring design flaws. John Darwin's work has shown how the World Crisis of 1939–45 fatally undermined the material and strategic props of the 'British world-system'. But it also left much to be undone in the realm of colliding sentiments, as the two 'b's of Britishness entered the post-war world.

'THE STATUS PUSH': FROM GREATER BRITAIN TO BRITISH COMMONWEALTH

Both Howard and Hancock presumed that their ideal polity was steeped in time immemorial, matured by the years and perfected by the rites of relocation overseas. But their comparatively liberal conception of a 'British Commonwealth' was barely fifteen years old at the time, having only officially been endorsed at the 1926 Imperial Conference after years of exhaustive debate. Its evolution as something distinct from 'the Empire' was a protracted affair, emerging out of a succession of colonial conferences at the turn of the century.

These periodic gatherings of the colonial political elite were fraught with what might now be termed 'status anxiety', so much so that devising a terminology befitting the honour and rank of the attendees became a regular item on conference agendas. It was agreed at the 1907 meeting, for example, to change the name from 'Colonial' to 'Imperial' conference at the behest of the Canadian prime minister, Wilfred Laurier, who felt the designation 'colonial' implied an inferior standing.[10] Agreement was also reached in these years on 'self-governing Dominions beyond the seas' as the operative collective noun, elevating white settler societies a notch higher than mere 'colonies' on the imperial ledger. The concept of 'Dominion status' was always inherently vague (Laurier himself described it as 'a general term which covers many words which it is not possible to define otherwise'), not least because it addressed an emotional as much as a constitutional need.[11] But it nevertheless formed the basis of a parallel imperial lexicon that would raise as many problems as it solved.

According to H. Duncan Hall's monumental study, by the time of the 1911 Imperial Conference 'the Empire had taken on the attributes of Commonwealth; though it still lacked that name'.[12] It would be during the First World War that reformers associated with the Round Table group (most prominently Lionel Curtis and Alfred Zimmern) actively began promoting the use of 'Commonwealth' as part of their search for an ideal form of imperial association. Zimmern first used the expression 'British Commonwealth of Nations' in an article in March 1914, inspired by the example of classical Athens (as expounded in his 1911 treatise *The Greek Commonwealth*).[13] Curtis, too, had 'reached the point of seeing that that part of the world under the British Crown was not, or ought not to be, an Empire, and for months I cudgelled my brains as to some alternative form'.[14] For him, 'Commonwealth' implied, not the diminution of colonial ties but quite the opposite: a more perfect form of imperial union.

It was ultimately the capacity of 'Commonwealth' to signal the very opposite – the distinctiveness and autonomy of its constituents rather than their 'perfect' totality – that would cement its place in the political lexicon. South Africa's Jan Smuts was the chief advocate, adapting Zimmern's term in a widely circulated 1917 pamphlet, *The British Commonwealth of Nations*, where he sought to erase any doubt about the separate political status of the dominions.[15] 'I think the very expression "Empire" misleading', he argued, 'because it makes people think as if we were one entity, one unity . . . we are a system of nations, a community of states and of nations far greater than any Empire that has ever existed.'[16]

This was the paradox of the Great War, at once the culmination of long-conditioned expectations that Greater Britain would pull together in the face of shared exigencies, marshalling an extraordinary arsenal of material and human capital from across the globe, but also the occasion for urgent reflection on the efficacy of a partnership based on obligations that were as ill-defined as they were obscurely regulated. In the early stages of the conflict, the dominions were largely content (with the exception of the Union of South Africa) to contribute colossal amounts of money and manpower to the cause without expecting much in the way of a direct say over grand strategy. They did, however, insist on deploying their troops as distinctive national armies rather than allow them to serve in melded 'Greater British' units. This was to bring its own source of political pressure as the war dragged on and the enormity of the casualties hit home. Canadian premier Robert Borden was the first to feel the pinch, demanding greater involvement in coordinating the war effort following the disastrous losses of 1916. The Imperial War Cabinet, convened in spring 1917, was the imperfect response to the practical dilemmas of coordinating strategy, and while it never really functioned as the name implied, it was to shape future expectations of separate dominion representation when it came to negotiating a viable peace.

The Great War also accentuated the problem of who counted as 'Greater Britons'. In India, the Lucknow Pact of December 1916 brought the Indian National Congress and the Muslim League into closer concert, presenting a common front through the activities of the Home Rule Leagues to demand urgent constitutional reforms as a fair price for India's indispensable wartime contribution. Their efforts forced a series of concessions from Edwin Montagu's India Office, though mainly in the form of vague promises projected into an indeterminate future (described with excruciating caution by Montagu himself as 'a decided step forward on a road leading at no distant period' to some unspecified form of 'responsible government').[17] Meanwhile, the unresolved crisis over Home Rule in Ireland spiralled completely out of control, as John Redmond's dream of Irish dominionhood was progressively overwhelmed in the troubled aftermath of the 1916 Easter Rising. The spectacular political rise of Sinn Féin's more radical demand for complete Irish independence soon swept the moderate platform of the Irish Parliamentary Party to one side – amid bitter recriminations about Britain's alleged 'betrayal' of Ireland's one-time destiny 'as a self-governing part of the Empire'.[18]

These interlocking pressure points combined to bring the 'British Commonwealth' increasingly into vogue. It appeared prominently, for example, in the Anglo-Irish Treaty of 1921 that carved out a separate Irish Free State, underlining 'the common citizenship of Ireland with Great Britain and her adherence to and membership of the group of nations forming the British Commonwealth of Nations'. Michael Collins regarded this as something of a personal triumph (as the chief Irish negotiator), boasting to a sceptical Irish Assembly: 'For the first time in an official document, we have got rid of the word Empire.'[19] Meanwhile in London, his British counterparts would present the exact same text as a testament to stability, continuity and the preservation of a British family of nations. From the outset, the Commonwealth was pressed into service to reconcile tensions produced by an eclectic set of relationships that inevitably meant different things to different people – a characteristic it shared with its semantic predecessors. That Ireland rapidly descended into a bitterly fought civil war suggested that it was not a particularly auspicious start.

Above all it was the enunciation of Woodrow Wilson's Fourteen Points and the elevation of national self-determination as the basis of an emergent international order that underlined the need to clarify the status of Commonwealth membership. The founding Covenant of the League of Nations was attended by considerable fanfare, displayed prominently in the first chapter of the Treaty of Versailles with twenty-six carefully crafted Articles solemnly assented to by thirty-two signatory nations. The contrast with the unstructured informality of an ill-defined congregation of British peoples could not have been more striking. It was always assumed from the British perspective that the two entities were in some sense intertwined, with the League to be guided by the Commonwealth's inspirational moral example. Saul Dubow notes the striking overlap between key personnel who were heavily involved in the emerging conception of the Commonwealth who also had a major hand in the League – General Smuts the most prominent among them.[20] It was at the 1921 Imperial Conference that Smuts outlined the connection as he conceived it, describing the League's Covenant as 'specially sacred to the British Empire':

> The method of understanding instead of violence, of free co-operation, of consultation and conference in all great difficulties which we have found so fruitful in our Empire system, is the method which the League attempts to apply to the affairs of the world. Let us, in the British Empire, back it for all it is worth. It may well prove, for international relations, the way out of the present morass. It may become the foundation of a new international system which will render armaments unnecessary, and give the world at large the blessings which we enjoy in our lesser League of Nations in the Empire.[21]

The problem with this was the mirror it held up to Smuts's cherished British precedent. His conception of a 'lesser League' unwittingly conceded the Commonwealth's residual status, falling somehow short of the full international equality conferred by participation in the wider arena. In seeking to affect a translation of the long-standing ideals and precepts of Greater Britain, Smuts cast a probing light into the latter's unexplored shortcomings.

Though short-lived, the League of Nations would ultimately have the more profound influence over its presumptive tutor as the machinery and practice of the new internationalism took shape in the 1920s – displacing the grand alliances of the pre-war era in a newly inaugurated 'international realm'.[22] Though never itself a model of perfection, the League nevertheless forced fundamental questions on the 1921 Imperial Conference, with several delegates lamenting the lack of formal protocols and bureaucratic structures that were becoming so familiar in Geneva. New Zealand's W. C. Massey made the revealing observation that 'we do not even know what to call ourselves, and there is a great deal in a name'.[23] The practice of scheduling interwar imperial conferences immediately after the conclusion of League Assembly meetings (permitting dominion leaders to attend both), further accentuated the contrast – and the silent procedures whereby the Commonwealth assumed a subsidiary role.

Even more fundamental was the inability of the five dominion governments to formulate a common response, not least when it came to striking a balance between autonomy and solidarity. The governments of South Africa and the Irish Free State harboured powerful republican aspirations that inclined them towards a looser form of association, while Australia and New Zealand (at the other extreme) were generally loathe to countenance derogations from the principle of unbreakable unity. Canada hovered somewhere vaguely in between with its own intense domestic political divisions (not least due to the outlier of Quebec). These dynamics were played out over a series of combative imperial conferences in the 1920s, with various actors and interests vying to encapsulate the Commonwealth mystique in a form of words acceptable to all. Canada's W. L. Mackenzie King underscored the challenge of finding sufficient common ground among a 'British community of nations . . . scattered over the globe' and hobbled by the 'absence of precedent for the experiment in co-operation which members are working out'.[24]

The November 1926 'Committee on Inter-Imperial Relations', chaired by Lord Balfour with dominion representation at prime ministerial level, was to mark an entirely new departure for Greater British nomenclature, tackling the anomalies over two exacting weeks of painstaking drafting.[25] For the most part, it was an exercise in holding out against J. B. M. Herzog's full-frontal attempt to trumpet the complete 'freedom and autonomy' of all five members – as not just 'absolutely independent of each other as

Governments', but also enjoying unimpeded sovereignty over their wider moral obligations as self-governing peoples. 'We are not a secret society', implored the South African premier, and it was therefore the duty of all assembled 'to have the uncertainty immediately removed' and make it 'abundantly clear just where the Dominions stand as over against Great Britain'.[26] Abundant clarity would prove conspicuously elusive, however, and a twelve-page compromise was eventually produced – wholly lacking in the elegant simplicity of the League Covenant. It included a formula 'of almost theological intricacy' to describe the nature of the modern Commonwealth (the relevant passage highlighted in italics so as not to become lost in the barrage of words).[27] Henceforth, Charles Dilke's imaginative flourish of the 1860s would be known collectively as '*autonomous communities within the British Empire, equal in status, in no way subordinate one to another in any aspect of their domestic or external affairs, though united by a common allegiance to the Crown, and freely associated as members of the British Commonwealth of Nations*'.[28]

Herzog would later claim that he had slain the dragon of the unitary 'Empire State', though this was already a straw man long before 1926.[29] It was more a matter of what Irish delegate Kevin O'Higgins termed 'the status push', drawing a much sharper distinction between the self-governing 'British Commonwealth' and the 'British Empire'. Significantly, the Balfour Committee also agreed to inform the League of Nations that the reference to 'British Empire' in the League Covenant would henceforth refer only to Britain and 'all parts of the British Empire which are not separate members of the League' – bearing witness to the shadow of the new internationalism as the real motive for change.[30] But it was a cognitive more than a constitutional step, attended by considerable hesitation and containing very little that had not been said before.[31] All of the dominion governments had difficult balancing acts to perform, each with powerful 'loyalist' segments within their own constituencies that needed to be placated.

It was only a small logical step to the passing of the Statute of Westminster in 1931, removing the last vestiges of imperial interference in the dominion legislatures and thus giving statutory form to the principles of the Balfour formula. But here, too, the inconsistencies multiplied due to the reluctance of Australia and New Zealand to ratify their newfound legislative independence in their own parliaments – putting the matter quietly to one side for more than a decade.[32] Their apprehensions were rooted partly in the strategic vulnerability of two Pacific outposts at the furthest remove from the protection of the Royal Navy, and hence unusually wedded to the psychological guarantees conferred by imperial unity. But it was also a matter of underlying unease – shared by many in Canada and indeed the United Kingdom itself – at the erosion of the 'instinctive', and hence unwritten precepts of Greater British solidarity. The English constitution was widely assumed to be innately superior to the 'overly intellectual and intrinsically fragile' paper instruments of continental Europeans.[33] 'The letter killeth', reflected Australia's Robert Menzies years later, 'but the spirit giveth life'.[34] The very requirement of 'drafting' – the bureaucratic paraphernalia that was so integral to the new culture of internationalism – seemed somehow antithetical to the organic British ideal.

The most intractable element of the interwar 'status push' was the matter of India, where progress towards the unspecified promises of the 1917 Montagu Declaration proceeded at a glacial pace into the 1920s. The offer of 'responsible government ... as an integral part of the Empire' was made at a time when the British Commonwealth lacked the weight of verbiage that it subsequently acquired, and Montagu's formula was presumably crafted with much greater flexibility in mind. The term 'responsible government' had originally been inserted in place of 'self-government' to keep Indian expectations low, and British authorities were at pains to remind Congress leaders that the term was not intended to concede the same standing as the other five dominions.[35] But by the time Lord Irwin saw fit to clarify matters in 1929, affirming that what Montagu had contemplated was indeed 'the attainment of Dominion status', the fundamentals of dominionhood had been significantly altered.

Thus, an extraordinarily fluid situation arose in which some (but not all) of the self-governing dominions (mindful of the enhanced international prestige invested in the League of Nations), sought to have their own international status semantically enhanced, which in turn brought inflationary pressures to Indian demands for the same constitutional status. At the same time, sharp divisions of opinion emerged in Britain between a parliamentary majority willing to take their chances on a form of words for India that would provide real constitutional progress and the conviction among a vociferous group of Conservatives that 'never in the wildest of dreams' should India enjoy the standing of the Balfour formula. Neither persuasion was in any way prepared to relinquish the essentials of the idea of 'British India'.[36] Congress meanwhile grew impatient with British dissembling, cooled on the idea of dominion status almost in the moment it was offered, and revised their goal in January 1930 to no less than *Purna Swaraj* (complete sovereignty). Shortly afterwards the first of the civil disobedience campaigns of the 1930s was inaugurated.

This marked the culmination of long-standing discrepancies in the ideological projection of a British Raj. On the one hand, 'an insistence on India's difference' had effectively barred entry into the charmed circle of Greater Britain. But as Thomas Metcalf points out, this co-existed with an underlying sense of India's similarity that British authorities 'could never entirely repudiate', necessitating a shared vocabulary of British constitutional progress and the nervous contemplation of a 'brown Dominion' joining the British fold.[37] General Dyer's brutal assault on humanity at Amritsar in April 1919 represented the opposite side of the coin, looking back to the racialized horrors of the 1857 'Mutiny', the memories of which were never far from the surface.[38] At stake was the problem of racial authority and the fearful consequences of 'letting go'. Relinquishing Britain's 'grip' was to become a pervasive metaphor for decolonization in the years ahead, distilling the anxieties of the white man's standing *in extremis*, and pointing to deeper, more disturbing psychological undercurrents at work.

It is easy to look back on the interwar Commonwealth and see signs of an organization pulling inexorably apart. But this was not generally how it appeared to contemporaries. The incessant tweaking of the organizational structure (replete with a new vocabulary in tune with the new protocols of international order) reflected a determination that the wartime success of imperial cooperation should be assiduously maintained. The rapid resumption of pre-war emigration levels to the dominions suggests that at the level of popular awareness, 'there was no mood of imperial fatalism' in these years.[39] Nor among its adversaries in India and elsewhere could it be supposed that British hegemony would come to an end any time soon. For all the finer distinctions drawn by the Balfour committee, the popular salience of Britishness as an unbounded domain under a divisible Crown remained largely undiminished.

A COMMON (BRITISH) MARKET?

If the political conundrums of the interwar years taxed the spirit of mutual accommodation in the transition to 'small "b" Britishness', the economic prospects for living 'individual lives' while sharing 'a common life with each other' were no less intricate. But this did not deter the architects of economic union who, from roughly the turn of the century, sought to capitalize on the emotional dividend of empire trade goods by devising formal structures for buying and selling within the family circle. Joseph Chamberlain's ill-fated proposal for an imperial *Zollverein* (described by one fervent supporter as the inspiration of a statesman 'fallen under a spell which all of us who know Greater Britain at first hand must feel, sooner or later') represented the first major challenge to the hitherto unassailable doctrine of free trade.[40]

These schemes emerged at a time when economic activity across the British world had expanded at phenomenal rates that cannot simply be explained by market forces. Britain's global economic performance in these years was 'embedded in complex cultural matrices' which not only became heavily skewed towards the empire's settler societies, but also laid bare the preferments of kinship that determined the flow of goods and services.[41] Over the seventy-year period from 1870 to the Second World War, the empire's share of British exports rose from 26 to 41 per cent, with the settler societies of Australia, Canada, New Zealand and South Africa taking a markedly disproportionate share. 'Greater' British consumers allocated vastly greater portions of their per capita incomes to British products than their Western European or even US counterparts – a burgeoning trend that would only begin to subside in the 1960s.[42] Gary Magee and Andrew Thompson attribute this largely to 'the ethnic and cultural ties that bound settlers emotionally, financially and spiritually to "home"'. Commodities, they argue, took on a 'symbolic value from the environment in which they were produced' thereby conditioning consumption habits such that 'tastes, expectations and values were readily familiar, communicable and compre-hensible to manufacturers back in Britain'.[43]

Similarly, colonial staples flowed back to Britain from the settler empire at an accelerating rate during these years, supplying nearly half of Britain's total food intake by 1938. Canadian wheat and timber, New Zealand butter and lamb, and Australian beef and processed fruits were among the commodities shipped in unprecedented quantities to a 'home' market that accounted for the lion's share of export income in each of the self-governing dominions.[44] This was partly due to vastly improved transport networks and efficient production techniques, but again there was the enabling factor of kinship networks – 'a kind of transnational social capital that lubricated and buttressed economic interaction', thereby lowering the transaction costs of large-scale bulk commodity exchange across formidable distances.[45] The settler economies habitually tailored their products to metropolitan demand but they were also in a position to alter consumer behaviour, facilitating among other things a boom in metropolitan meat consumption through the wholesale des-patch of frozen lamb and beef products that people could more readily afford.[46]

The revolution in refrigerated shipping in the 1880s would equally transform the settler colonial landscape, greatly enlarging the scope for small-scale pastoral production.[47] For British shoppers, notoriously wary of 'foreign' culinary offerings, there was a certain reassurance in purchasing 'British' farm produce from overseas (marketed variously as 'New Zealand Lamb – British to the Backbone'; 'Canadian milk ... from the cattle of the finest British stock'; and 'Kangaroo butter: an all-British product').[48] These networks were also thought to diminish the food security risk that was sometimes cited as a reason to avoid overreliance on 'foreign' suppliers. Trust, reciprocity and the 'distortions of time and space' were thus the constituent elements of an ever-expanding emporium of Greater British consumer goods.[49]

Free traders strenuously resisted the push for imperial tariff reform, seeking to protect British industries from higher costs and uphold the twin cause of cheap food and frictionless trade – itself 'a moral project' of individual freedom, civic-mindedness, international trust and civil-ized markets.[50] Despite repeated demands from the self-governing dominions for preferential tariff rates (many of whom had already extended preferential treatment to British manufacturers from the mid-1890s), the mother country resolutely declined to reciprocate.[51] Not that they lacked supporters in England – Rudyard Kipling's ode of gratitude, *Our Lady of the Snows*, for example, was inspired by the unpromising material of Canada's 1897 preferential tariff. Nevertheless, the Liberal landslide at the 1906 general election, campaigning on the 'cheap loaf' as the symbol of liberty itself, seemed to settle the issue decisively in favour of free trade. Some historians tend to discount the sentimental tug of empire goods during free trade's long ascendancy, stressing that imperial preference 'was in a crucial respect not an orthodoxy but a challenge to it. It was always a plan, a project, more than a reality.'[52] To be sure, Greater Britain was in no sense watertight or supremely efficient. Like any economic system geared to 'patriotic consumption' it had to contend with rival sensibilities that curbed its sway over consumer choice. But while free traders managed to delay the establishment of a fully sanctioned imperial tariff system for many years, this in no way prevented British producers from exploiting distinct cultural advantages in settler colonial markets.[53]

More to the point, although roundly defeated in the tariff debates at the turn of the century, imperial sentiment was able to perform a remarkable comeback when the material conditions altered drastically during the Great War – with debates about trade regulation, resource management, and food security assuming renewed prominence. The ever-present threat of wartime disruptions to supply led to the resurrection of elaborate plans for imperial economic integration – described by W. K. Hancock as an 'emotional torrent' that overwhelmed the pre-war axioms about open markets.[54] The conviction rapidly took hold that mobilizing the empire's economic power to win the war was only a job half-done – it needed urgently to be placed on a permanent footing to secure the peace. Speeches, pamphlets and publications called repeatedly for 'a self-supporting empire', a 'self-contained empire for defence and subsistence', 'an economic unit', a 'pure British policy' and a 'policy of self-preservation'. 'The Empire as a whole' became a ubiquitous refrain among economic planners demanding 'the development of their natural wealth towards a definite and recognized object'.[55] Although the war would never entirely obliterate the older divisions between free trade and imperial tariff reform, it was during these years, as Frank Trentmann has shown, that 'established truths lost their authority, a search for new principles began'.[56]

In April 1919, the Lloyd George coalition government finally relented in extending tariff preferences to empire tea, coffee, sugar, dried fruit and tobacco (while stopping short of the more politically sensitive duties on food). Although only limited in scope, these measures were nevertheless widely viewed as a significant break with the past.[57] More ambitious were the various forms of consumer-oriented campaigns to promote empire goods that sprang up in the 1920s. The British Women's Patriotic League led the way with the establishment of the first 'Empire shopping week' in 1923 to coincide with Empire Day. Dominated by well-heeled and avowedly Conservative ladies, the League soon diversified its activities to include empire pageants, empire dinners, lantern lectures and travelling cinema vans to promote the 'Buy British' cause (comprising colonial as well as locally produced goods).[58] Their work was reinforced by the more middle-class Women's Unionist Organisation which organized empire cake competitions, issued empire cook books and lobbied retailers and government for clear labelling of empire produce.[59] These campaigns were aimed squarely at British housewives; a strategy lauded by the husband of one of its leading lights:

> The Empire Week movement was a woman's movement, for women were the principal shoppers and they could create a demand for Empire goods by seeing that those they dealt with kept them. Imperial preference was of two kinds: there was the preference of tariffs, which was a political matter ... and there was the preference of sentiment which we could extend to the Dominions in spite of any Government.[60]

Women's activism was fundamental to fostering this 'preference of sentiment' (the female counterpart to the male domain of preferential tariffs)
enlarging the scope of maternal affection to encompass a globally dispersed
imperial family. Trentmann likens the movement to 'a mother putting the
needs of her children and her husband before her own', ensuring that
consumers were given the opportunity to 'express imperial care'.[61] No less
than the royal family was enlisted to bolster these inclinations, letting it be
known that the royal Christmas dinner for 1926 would consist solely of
produce sourced from the empire. A campaign to emulate the king's own
'empire Christmas pudding' became something of a consumer sensation,
popularized by an official recipe (by the king's own chef) featuring an
intricate assortment of empire ingredients. As *The Times* enthused, 'it
could not fail to touch the imagination of every British family', even if
cramming the whole empire into a single pudding proved to be more
politically fraught than anticipated.[62] It remained a potent symbol of imperial civic activism in the interwar years – far more so than the forensic diction
of the Balfour formula – extolling the moral imperatives through the
purchasing power of the discerning consumer.

The 'preference of sentiment' also drew official support at the British
Empire Exhibition at Wembley in 1924, where visitors were encouraged to
bestow favour on the acres of imperial produce on display. The star turn at
the Canadian pavilion was a life-sized sculpture of the Prince of Wales
(alongside his favourite Canadian horse) fashioned from three thousand
pounds of Canadian butter. Rarely had the commodification of imperial
fealty taken such tangible form, replete with a cold storage display case
replicating the prince's private ranch in Alberta.[63] Not to be outdone, the
New Zealand pavilion featured its own butter-hewn effigies including a life-
size cow and a typical farmhouse, epitomizing 'the Dominion's claim that
she is the dairy farm of the Empire'.[64] Here, too, an underlying friction
could be discerned between the organic display of imperial oneness and the
wider 'sentiment of internationalism' that was beginning to redirect civic
energies elsewhere. Canada's Mackenzie King privately viewed the Wembley
event as an 'imperialist scheme – of the "safe" variety' which he could
happily lend his endorsement. But in his public utterances, he could not
resist pointing to the wider international context in terms reminiscent of
General Smuts, describing Wembley as 'the physical expression of a union
such as the world has never seen before' – indeed, no less than 'a League of
Nations, functioning with hardly any friction, and suggesting the possibility
of the larger League which is the vision of lovers of peace and good-will
among all the nations of the world'.[65]

Figure 3.1 The Prince of Wales exhibit at the British Empire Exhibition, Wembley Park, showing a model of the prince and his horse fashioned from three thousand pounds of Canadian butter, London, 1925. Source: Library and Archives Canada/Department of Supply and Services, fonds/PSA-75995.

It was on the strength of Wembley's success that an official Empire Marketing Board was established shortly afterwards to placate the dominion governments' impatience with the slow progress towards preferential tariffs. Rather than enforce consumer choice by the selective imposition of import duties, the aim was to entice British consumers away from 'foreign' purchases through an elaborate series of poster hoardings. Devising the slogan 'Buy Empire Goods – Ask, is it British?', the campaign bundled together a vast array of peoples and products as natural extensions of Britain itself (with the Irish Free State pointedly refusing to employ the slogan whenever Irish produce appeared).[66] Again, the empire-as-extended-family metaphor was pressed into service, trumpeting the twin benefits of filial loyalty and mutual economic assistance.[67]

Though intended to promote the interests of the whole empire, however, the scheme was heavily skewed towards the fields and pastures of Australia, Canada, New Zealand and South Africa. Felicity Barnes emphasizes the distinct 'idea of dominionhood' that emerged from the visual depictions of the Empire Marketing Board, which stressed the settler empire's fundamental similarity to Britain.[68] In that sense, it was the economic equivalent of 'small "b" Britishness', distinguishing the settler societies from the dependent empire through their depiction as limitless farmlands serving the needs of metropolitan consumers. Native flora and fauna appeared only rarely, while Indigenous peoples were completely hidden from view in a sequence of bountiful landscapes, thinly populated by flourishing livestock and sturdy white men. Images of factories and urban production were reserved exclusively for metropolitan Britain, often juxtaposed with dominion pastures to stress the symbiotic exchange of UK manufactures for empire farm produce.[69] The abiding message was proximity, plenty and a unique propinquity – in short, the moral economy of Greater Britain, reduced to a visual language that could more easily be rendered than constitutional formula.[70]

It was not until 1932 that the British government, largely due to the financial exigencies of the Great Depression, finally succumbed to demands for a comprehensive empire tariff system at the imperial economic conference in Ottawa. At the head of the New Zealand delegation, J. G. Coates opened proceedings with a rousing statement of intent: 'It is instinctive in our people that, in adversity, we should seek not merely our own self-preservation but also the preservation and advancement of other members of the family of British nations.'[71] Behind the scenes, however, lurked a more sordid exercise in self-interested horse-trading, likened by one account to 'the kind of family squabble that might result from intestate death'.[72] Nevertheless, the myth of greater British fraternity seemed to have triumphed over its adversaries at a time when intra-empire trading had grown exponentially to its greatest extent.

But its path to pre-eminence reveals two innate flaws that would render it highly vulnerable to future adversity. First, as we have seen, the system was skewed along racial and kinship lines that fractured the much-vaunted 'unity' of the empire. 'Caring for imperial producers meant helping white farmers in Canada and Kenya, not Indian peasants or Caribbean sugar cane workers' – with the commodities themselves (butter, wheat, apples, pears, beef, mutton and lamb) indelibly associated with white prosperity.[73] Well might W. K. Hancock have looked '*forward* to the day when Indians and Africans, too, are able to assume their full share' in a new 'british' Commonwealth, given the persistent hold of white racial solidarity.

Second, it bears emphasizing that the triumph of imperial trading in the early 1930s came relatively late in the day, surmounting formidable political obstacles that never really went away. Imperial preference was a belated innovation, a novelty that lasted barely three decades amid the rival attractions of an incipient internationalism. Advocates of empire trade went to considerable lengths to conceal this inconvenient truth, with one especially fanciful Empire Marketing Board poster trumpeting the immortal lines of the sixteenth-century seafarer Sir Hugh Willoughby: 'So that hereby not only commoditie may ensue both to them and us but also an indissoluble and perpetual league of friendship' – backdating the cause by nearly four centuries.[74] It was the commercial counterpart to Leslie Howard's ode to Britain's 'ancient foundations and most worthy liberty'. But while reading the ancient scrolls may have bestowed a reassuring primordial quality (replete with the archaic spelling of 'commoditie'), it could not erase the uneven progress and highly contingent fulfilment of the empire's economic promise. The disruptive potential of a global economy was already emerging into view.

'THE RIGHT TO BE LOYAL BRITISHERS': THE MORAL WORLDS OF INDIGENOUS PROTEST

September 1937. In a dilapidated duplex in Melbourne's inner-West, William Cooper compiles a petition of over 1,800 signatories to King George VI, calling for Aboriginal representation in the Australian Federal Parliament. At seventy-six years of age, the Yorta Yorta stockman from the Echuca district in northern Victoria has only recently turned his hand to indefatigable protest, staging a succession of public meetings and demonstrations, lobbying the press and composing an uninterrupted stream of letters to local, state, federal and international authorities. Two years previously he founded the Australian Aborigines' League, the first Indigenous rights movement to restrict full membership to those 'possessing some degree of Aboriginal blood'.[75] The petition, humbly addressed to 'the King's Most Excellent Majesty' is unique in garnering signatures from across five of Australia's six states and the Northern Territory – the first document of its kind to claim representation of the 'Aboriginal inhabitants of the Continent of Australia'. Asserting that it was 'not only a moral duty, but also a strict injunction' that Australia's earliest settlers should have 'adequately cared for' the original inhabitants, the petitioners call on the king 'to intervene on our behalf' in order to 'prevent the extinction of the Aboriginal race'.[76] The logic of appealing to a sovereign at the opposite ends of the earth requires little elaboration: 'If we cannot get full justice in Australia we must ask the King. Some tell us that the King has no power now in these things, but we shall try anyway.'[77]

Cooper's demand for Indigenous equality under the law, with equal rights and equal access to work, education and material prosperity rests awkwardly with latter-day notions of Indigenous selfhood – not least his pithy formulation: 'We ask the right to be fully British.' He took every opportunity to emphasize that the 'ultimate object of the League' was 'to secure their uplift to the full culture of the British race' – the just reward for a people 'British to the core and loyal to a man' who were among 'the first to offer for enlistment' in the Great War to 'protect the British Empire'. As he bluntly told a Melbourne journalist in 1937: 'We want to get up to the same standard as the whites', and it was precisely the theme of aboriginal 'uplift' that would define his activities throughout the 1930s.[78]

Cooper's speeches and writings were infused with claims under the 'British Flag' to 'British justice', 'British principle', 'British nationality', 'British sentiment', 'British citizenship', 'British Fair Play' and, above all, 'the privileges of British subjects'. He had no qualms describing Indigenous Australians as 'a population not merely European in culture but British in sentiment and loyalty' who were asking for no more than 'the right to be loyal Britishers, sharing with their white brethren the privileges and responsibilities of citizenship'. In a personal appeal to Prime Minister Joseph Lyons, he framed the entire problem of Indigenous disadvantage as a matter of upholding 'the dignity of the British Empire'. Just as the 'conquering power of Rome' had once 'lifted the British to culture and civilisation', so too Aboriginal Australians were entitled to 'that same uplift. Are we unreasonable?'[79]

Cooper's reliance on imperial civic standards can be easily misconstrued as a longing for ethnic or cultural absorption; a species of false consciousness, awaiting the remedies of post-war decolonization. But he went out of his way to rule out such fallacies. He explicitly rejected the notion that 'the dark man admits the superiority of the White and desires incorporation in that race' as 'most decidedly wrong ... We are dark complexioned and do not wish to be otherwise.'[80] As Tim Rowse suggests, Cooper 'did not confine the category "British" to white people; he meant people of a standard of civilization, regardless of race'.[81] Though it never occurred to him to render the term with the figurative 'small "b"', there is reason to believe that he would have appreciated the distinction.[82]

Indeed, Cooper's tireless advocacy on behalf of what he termed 'British Australian Aborigines' afforded a means of appealing to a set of social, material and moral standards that transcended the inhibiting confines of racial prejudice. When it came to morality, dignity and what he termed 'real humanity', Cooper could even assert that 'the Aboriginal is more British often than the white'. In other words, the language of Britishness furnished a ready foil for the inhumane treatment visited upon Aboriginal people for generations – serving as a proxy for universal norms at a time when human rights rhetoric was barely in its infancy. It is striking how frequently Cooper coupled his 'right to be fully British' with 'the recognition of our full humanity' – a core demand that ran consistently through his campaign.[83] 'Believing the British Empire to stand for justice, order, freedom and good Government' (as he prefaced one of his many entreaties), Cooper saw in the Crown the promise of principled arbitration – a source of redress outside the racial strictures governing the everyday lot of Aboriginal Australians.[84]

In pursuing his grievances in these terms, Cooper was by no means eccentric or even particularly unique.[85] The practice of petitioning the king had older roots in the nineteenth-century symbolism of Queen Victoria as the bestower of rights and the 'strong belief among indigenous peoples in New Zealand, South Africa and other British colonies in the Queen's bounty'.[86] Victoria occupied a unique place in Indigenous oral tradition due to the conviction that she was personally implicated in historic agreements between Indigenous peoples and the British Crown, and hence morally accountable.[87] The veneration of Victoria similarly furnished a key component of West Indian political activism in the nineteenth century on account of her perceived association with the abolition of slavery.[88] The connection was particularly resonant for New Zealand Maori, not least given the prominence of 'KO WIKITORIA te Kuini' ('Her Majesty Queen Victoria') in the 1840 Treaty of Waitangi, in whose name the Maori had been guaranteed a whole gamut of protections – their property, peace, good order and 'all the Rights and Privileges of British Subjects'. Victoria's name furnished both 'a common sense of membership in empire and alienation from it' – a 'moral compass' as Michael Belgrave terms it, against which settler degradations could be measured and redress urgently sought.[89]

But even as Indigenous claim-making acquired the cadence of British constitutionalism, the incipient internationalism of the interwar years furnished a powerful counterpoint. Two fleeting examples – both deemed wholly inconsequential at the time – can be seen in retrospect as harbingers of things to come. In 1917, Levi General assumed the chieftainship of the Cayuga – one of Canada's 'Six Nations' of Iroquois – adopting the hereditary title 'Deskaheh'. In 1921 he embarked on the well-worn route to Britain to petition King George V about injustices suffered by his people. He was denied an audience by Winston Churchill, then serving as colonial secretary, who predictably advised that the complaint be lodged with the Canadian Government. What subsequently transpired represented a radical departure from custom. After painstaking preparation, Deskaheh left Canada once again in July 1923, this time bound for the League of Nations in Geneva where he had been granted a fresh opportunity to press his case. He would spend the best part of a year in Switzerland, stopping over in London en route to issue the following declaration of intent:

> I go because your Imperial Government refused my plea, for protection of my people as of right against subjugation by Canada. The Canadian 'Indian Office' took that refusal to mean that it could do as it wished with us . . . If we have no special claim on British justice . . . as we believed we had, we who live to-day have a special right at Geneva.[90]

Deskaheh did not elaborate on the nature of the 'special right' invested in the League, nor how he anticipated any effective remedy. In any case he held no illusions about his prospects: 'I am going to Geneva, and I suppose many stones have been placed in my path. But I must go there.'[91]

The following year in April 1924, the Maori spiritual leader T. W. Ratana departed from Wellington with an extended entourage of singers, dancers and musicians set to perform at the British Empire Exhibition in Wembley. But his mission was primarily political. Armed with a petition bearing 34,000 Maori signatures, a Bible and a copy of the Treaty of Waitangi, he vowed to shake the hand of King George V and place the evidence before him. 'I will ask him, "This is the Treaty you have made. What do you think of it?" He will not be able to deny it.'[92] Over a period of several months in London his repeated efforts to make direct contact with the king were rudely rebuffed (including a letter stuffed into the pocket of an unsuspecting Prince of Wales at a St James's Palace garden party). Upon receiving word that his gifts (and the letter) had been returned, Ratana was unable to contain his dismay: 'On this day I have led the morehu across the seas of the world to . . . see our father and present to him the cries of his children for justice, as I stand at this door that is closed to us, you see before you an orphan, I have no home here.'[93] Little over a month later, he followed directly in the footsteps of his Iroquois counterpart and entered the main chamber of the League of Nations building in Geneva, depositing the Waitangi Treaty together with a huia feather and a kiwi cloak with the League's Indigenous representative. It was a purely symbolic gesture, however. Having been informed by League officials that he should refer his

Figure 3.2 Deskaheh in Geneva, 1923. Source: Bibliothèque de Genève.

grievances to the New Zealand Government, Ratana only succeeded in gaining admission by way of a sightseeing tour.[94]

Neither Deskaheh nor Ratana achieved anything of substance at the League of Nations, but the real significance is that it occurred to them to try. The abrupt realization that they had 'no special claim on British justice' – or in Ratana's evocative phrase, 'no home here' – was the necessary jolt to seek alternative pathways to justice; new ways of orienting their demands that might enhance their inherent dignity and humanity in the eyes of an impartial arbiter. That they chose to seek redress in Geneva underlines the force of the League of Nations 'as an agent of geopolitical transformation' in the interwar world, embodying a symbolism more powerful than its practical success in brokering international stability.[95] As Ravi de Costa has shown, the actions of Deskaheh and Ratana signalled an audacious new departure, redirecting their grievances 'to a post-imperial international authority, one assumed to govern a moral world in which there was a dignified place for sovereign indigenous nations'.[96]

De Costa's concept of 'moral worlds' is particularly useful in unlocking the meaning of Indigenous adherence to imperially ordained norms. British constitutional modes of petitioning were not simply about appealing to a higher legal authority, but also a means of drawing the petitioner and the authority into a 'shared moral order', relying on 'an enlarged vision of morality in order to justify their specific claims'. Indigenous claims to Britishness rested on the belief that it constituted a normative system of rights that enshrined a higher morality than the closed circle of settler racism – one in which they themselves could claim inclusion as 'full human subjects'. Ratana's experience of becoming an 'orphan' in London in 1924 reveals the depth of the personal and emotional investments this entailed. Although it would take decades to materialize, de Costa points to a direct relationship between the unravelling of imperial civic and moral structures and the advent of a 'transcendent moral order' in which Indigenous claims would later find an entirely new foothold. As 'the growing coherence of universal norms began to provide a new basis of connection between political identity and authority', he suggests, Indigenous peoples around the world would promptly jettison the moral baggage of Britishness.[97]

These fleeting encounters exemplied W. K. Hancock's 'small "b" Britishness', aspiring towards a 'diverse family of many kindreds and languages' all sharing equally in 'the privileges and burdens of the Commonwealth's freedom'.[98] But they also underlined its severe limitations. Such was the long ascendancy of race in the hierarchy of Greater Britain that it could not easily be cast to one side. Just as the advent of internationalism cast doubt on the credibility of an 'organic' British Commonwealth, so too, entirely new avenues were emerging for the pursuit of racial justice outside of the British fold.

◆

These changes were slow to fully materialize, however. In April 1946, a private members bill was passed in the Canadian House of Commons to effect a change to the name of the 1 July National Holiday from 'Dominion Day' to 'Canada Day'. Prime Minister Mackenzie King had given the Bill his tacit support, noting with satisfaction in his diary that the Bill formed 'part of what has been achieved in rounding out Canada in the years of my administration'.[99] His choice of metaphor was deliberately subtle;

95

'rounding out' referred, not to some radical overhaul, brazenly repudiating the colonial stigma of dominion status, but a more delicate matter of steady, judicious refinement. The delicacy lay in triangulating the unique tensions of a people and polity caught between *three stools* – the national, the imperial, and the international. The prime minister's role (as he saw it) was merely that of an overseer – enlarging upon innate forces at work in a world becoming increasingly attuned to the 'sentiment of internationalism'.

Mackenzie King badly misjudged the temper of opinion in April 1946, however. The proposal to drop 'dominion' invited a spontaneous chorus of contempt from the English-speaking press, interpreting the move as a Quebec-inspired assault on Canada's British heritage.[100] Scorn was abundantly poured on the 'ultra-nationalists' for 'confusing love of Canada with dislike of everything British', amid dire predictions that the next to go would be the Union Jack and *God Save the King*.[101] The *Hamilton Spectator* decried the substitution of 'dominion' for 'a term without meaning, without tradition or force' (the offending term being 'Canada'); while the *Vancouver Sun* voiced astonishment that 'a great and historic designation is close to oblivion'.[102] The *Family Herald* turned its ire on the advocates of a name-change, whose 'inferiority complex is so deep that they are afraid of their own history'.[103] Meanwhile, Mackenzie King's supporters hit back, accusing the 'super-imperialists' of harbouring deep resentment 'of the fact of Canada's national status'. They were 'colonials still', pining for their 'Britannic world kingdom'.[104] Taken aback by the furore, the prime minister allowed the bill to be quashed in the Senate and it would be more than thirty-five years (and twenty subsequent attempts), before the redundant 'dominion' would receive its quietus with the formal name change of October 1982.

Remarkably, neither side in this unusually bad-tempered debate imagined that the issue carried any legal or practical significance. It was wholly a matter of Canada's honour and standing in a changing world, allowing tempers to flare at comparatively little material cost to anyone involved. This was 'identity politics' long before the term was coined, serving as a reminder of what is sometimes overlooked by historians of twentieth-century internationalism: its uneven resonance and highly fragmented appeal. The flawed promise of the League of Nations, the collapse of the painstakingly constructed institutional edifice of the interwar years, the procedures suspended, careers cut short, all undoubtedly furnished the crucial backdrop to the restoration of global order in the post-Second World War era, signalling (further) dim portents for a world conceived as an unbroken chain of British peoples. But this did not translate into any spontaneous or broad-based shift in popular sentiment. What seemed 'a lot of hooey' to Vancouver's Private Johnston in 1941 had no shortage of adherents in 1946, enough to warrant extreme caution on the part of the Canadian government.

Much the same can be said of the effects of the Second World War more generally. There can be no doubt that in retrospect the devastating implications for the British world-system were everywhere to be seen, so much so that it is hard to refute John Darwin's powerfully argued thesis that the 'Eurasian revolution' of 1938–42 effectively 'destroyed almost all of the global preconditions on which the British system had depended since the 1830s'. Specifically, the grim upshot of strategic and military defeat – with the fall of France in 1940 followed soon after by the debacle of Singapore – rendered 'effectively bankrupt' the unique combination of geo-strategic advantages that had long underpinned Britain's global standing.[105] The collapse of the European balance of power on which British naval supremacy rested, coinciding with the rapid incursions of a ruthless military rival in East Asia, left the British bereft of the means to defend their global positions. By the middle of 1942 all but 'the faintest hope of restoring the *status quo ante*' had slipped beyond their grasp.[106] Indeed, such were the crushing implications that the spoils of victory over the Axis powers in 1945 were to prove largely illusory. The post-war recovery was merely a 'short-lived remission' for a British world rapidly reaching its endpoint. 'It only remained to acknowledge its passing.'[107]

Darwin's concluding words offer oblique testimony to the unfinished business of Greater Britain. Wartime exigencies may have shattered the material and strategic props, but 'acknowledgement' would be another matter entirely. To be sure, contemporaries did not gloss the calamity in the Far East, particularly those at the receiving end of the Japanese onslaught. The sudden implosion of the expatriate world of the Malayan Peninsula, for example, where the sight of 'lorries streaming south' ahead of the Japanese advance 'carrying personal effects such as carpets, rattan chairs, golf clubs, tennis rackets and even canaries in cages' spoke its own irrefutable language of British retrenchment.[108] In Singapore, where less than five years earlier the coronation of George VI had elicited 'elaborate performances of Britishness' in the form of parades, fireworks and pageantry embracing all faiths and ethnicities, the emphasis soon shifted 'to public devotion to Japan'.[109] Meanwhile the 'China Britons' of the Treaty Ports, whose British world was abolished by decree on 11 January 1943, were left to forge new lives in or out of China, 'refashioning themselves as they could'.[110]

Figure 3.3 Refugees from the evacuation of British Malaya at Ipoh Station in Perak, en route to Singapore, February 1942. Source: D and S Photography Archives/Alamy Stock Photo.

But for those only indirectly apprised of the scale and human cost of the strategic setback, the implications would take much longer to sink in. In March 1942, prompted by Britain's disastrous capitulation in the Far East, the Conservative MP Sir David Gammans poured out his anguish in a letter to *The Times*:

> When the Union Jack was lowered on Fort Canning, in Singapore, on that Sunday morning it marked the sudden and dramatic end of an epoch in our Colonial Empire. I hope the Colonial Office realizes it. What the Colonial Office now needs is a dynamic leadership which will create an entirely new conception of our responsibilities of trusteeship, a conception of common citizenship and common ideals which will inspire the people of our Colonial Empire as well as ourselves. The fall of Singapore is either the end of our Colonial Empire or the beginning of a new chapter which can be even more honourable and glorious than the past.[111]

Having identified the tell-tale signs of a calamitous downfall, Gammans refused to grasp the full implications. For him, it was ultimately no more than a passing 'chapter', leaving open a path to 'glory' and 'honour' in a refashioned, revalidated empire of the future. In his refusal to embrace the logic of defeat, he was by no means an isolated figure. Churchill himself was purportedly 'stupefied' by the surrender of Singapore; his Secretary of State for India, Leo Amery, stunned by the evident 'loss of the white man's prestige' – yet neither made any serious effort to revise their bedrock assumptions. As Max Beloff reflected decades later, 'the British Empire, loved or reviled, was as much a part of the order of things as the moon or the stars ... How then envisage its disappearance?'[112] For the most part, contemporaries chose not to try too hard. No attempt was made to turn Singapore into a Dunkirk-style 'heroic failure' nor, as Richard Toye notes, did the battle itself ever find a firm place in British commemorative culture.[113] Within weeks of the surrender at Fort Canning, *The Times* gave voice to nascent rumblings about a colonial system 'too long and too deeply rooted in the traditions of a bygone age', but the emphasis was overwhelmingly on the need for renewal rather than relinquishment.[114]

In Australia, the repercussions pressed closer to home, with Britain's poor showing against the Japanese sparking bitter recriminations about Churchill's 'inexcusable betrayal', amid urgent reflection on the efficacy of relying so heavily on imperial defence guarantees. But as with Canada's rear-guard defence of Dominion Day, there was little appetite in 1942 to face up to the full significance, with wartime prime minister John Curtin – even as he 'looked to America' to shore up Australia's northern flank – voicing a stern resolve to continue defending his country 'as a citadel for the British-speaking race'.[115] It was an unorthodox turn of phrase, with a decidedly nervous edge – as though aligning Greater Britain with a 'British' language might somehow firm up otherwise shaky ground. It conjured something of Leslie Howard's mythical foursome standing watch from the dome of St Paul's.

The fall of Singapore was the canary in the coalmine, issuing early portents of an altogether more protracted affair. It marked the culmination of long-standing tensions that were hard-wired into Dilke's Greater British imaginary – specifically, the failure to reconcile universal aspirations with the persistent hold of the British race (with an unmistakably upper case 'B'). But its demise as a global civic idea would take much longer to materialize. In Part Two, we turn to the multiple registers of 'thwarted Britishness' in the decades after 1945, starting with the 'British-speaking' properties of the language itself.[116]

PART II

REGISTERS

4

'WE MUSTN'T USE THE WORD "EMPIRE"': THE BRITISH NAME

Addressing an outdoor rally at the February 1950 general election, Winston Churchill was in full rhetorical flight, extolling the virtues of Britain's post-war empire before pausing to correct himself. 'We mustn't use the word "empire", it's naughty', he cautioned. Amid muffled laughter from the crowd his mood turned a shade darker: 'Soon they'll tell us we mustn't use the word "British."'[1] Churchill had alighted upon the semantics of decolonization; the shape-shifting of words he had long revered and the unwelcome intrusions of a new lexicon. As it happens, 'empire' was by no means a political outcast in 1950 (it was uttered 542 times in parliament in that year alone) but Churchill had nevertheless caught the drift of a rapidly turning tide. The tumultuous events surrounding the transfer of power in India three years earlier clearly marked a watershed, consigning 'empire' slowly but surely to cold storage.[2] Even more troubling for Churchill was an entirely new development signalled the previous year when Jawaharlal Nehru insisted on jettisoning the adjective 'British' from the Commonwealth of Nations as a precondition of Indian membership. The effects of this were harder to discern, though ultimately more sweeping in their implications. In a world that could no longer be labelled 'British', the very idea of Britain as Churchill and his generation conceived it was called into question.

On the face of it, tweaking the idiom of empire was something the British themselves tightly controlled. Having emerged victorious from two world wars, it was the good fortune of Britain's political elite that they found themselves in a position to 'adjust the language of world empire to the new ideological requirements' of the post-war world.[3] The post-war Labour Government of Clement Attlee responded to the rising tenor of anti-colonialism with a spate of measures to place the empire on a more legitimate footing, with the emphasis on equality, development and a new progressive vocabulary.[4] In the years from 1945 to 1961, Britain's ruling establishment weighed its words like never before, as government officials engaged in a deliberate and often painstaking overhaul of imperial nomenclature, relegating older terms such as 'dominion', 'empire' and 'imperial' while nudging newer, less obviously tainted alternatives to the fore. In particular, the evolution of the 'British Empire' via 'British Commonwealth' into the 'Commonwealth of Nations' became a key strategy for managing domestic expectations and international perceptions as Britain's post-war standing steadily waned.

All too often, historians have taken this process for granted, as though relabelling the empire were the natural corollary to its inevitable demise. But if 'the reputations of empires were rhetorically constructed' through politically charged and often highly emotive forms of language, the changing inflexions of imperial words were equally intrinsic to perceptions of imperial decline.[5] Language was frequently the crux of the matter, crystallizing changing attitudes while deflecting outdated and unwanted nuances.[6] As the empire evolved into a new multi-racial organization, finding the right form of words became all the more paramount, reshaping the contours of the conversation across a wide social spectrum from politics to the media, diplomacy, education and everyday speech. Moreover, the shifts were never entirely voluntary, but were to a greater or lesser extent foisted on a bureaucratic machine struggling to absorb multiple outward pressures and conflicting internal priorities. This was anticipated as early as 1950 by prominent anti-colonial critic R. Palme Dutt, who put the matter frankly: 'Since the older term "Empire" has begun to stink in the nostrils of mankind and become a term of abuse, a euphemism had to be found by the more mealy-mouthed apologists of imperialism.'[7]

When government officials turned their hand to devising new terms, they assured themselves that they were merely 'correcting misunderstandings' about the empire – a useful shorthand for combatting ideological adversaries at home and abroad. Yet crucially, these tussles were not confined to the corridors of Whitehall and Westminster, but fanned out across a far broader rhetorical terrain, as contending groups grappled to invest changing concepts with their own preferred meanings.[8] Refitting the imperial lexicon could materially alter the terms of endearment, undermining the capacity to bind a global British entity around shared values and mutual obligations.[9] India's objection to the adjective 'British' brought matters to a head, embroiling a worldwide cast of actors in a protracted argument with voices from Britain, Canada, Pakistan, Australia, Ceylon, South Africa and New Zealand all claiming a crucial stake in the outcome.

Britishness had always performed the dual function of encompassing the peoples of the 'British Isles' (give or take the Irish), as well as evoking the outward projection of their culture, language, ambition and authority around the world. Disaggregating the two was rarely something contemporaries consciously contemplated (though neologisms such as the now-defunct 'Britisher' were occasionally deployed to distinguish the British-in-the-world from their stay-at-home counterparts). Broadly speaking, the effect was to evoke a universal experience, whether in terms of a continuum of British 'peoples', 'principles', 'culture', 'race', 'justice', 'commerce', 'forces', 'interests', or simply the visual language of schoolroom maps streaked with patches of red. This chapter examines how that intricate nexus unravelled, and how stripping Britain of its worldly connotations struck at the heart of an imperial language system. The banishment of 'British' from the Commonwealth lexicon furnishes unusually vivid testimony, as multiple claimants and conflicting priorities converged on the question of Commonwealth naming rights – marking a tipping point in the contraction of the idea of Britain itself.

THE SEMANTIC ANAESTHETIC

On 20 February 1947, almost five years to the day after Britain's capitulation in the Far East, Prime Minister Clement Attlee announced the appointment of Rear-Admiral Louis Mountbatten of Burma to serve as the last viceroy of India. Mountbatten had personally received the Japanese surrender in Singapore in September 1945 and now, with the roles soon to be reversed, his new assignment was to devise a 'dignified' solution to the problem of Indian independence. The war years had transformed the Indian political landscape following the decision of the Indian National Congress to decline a qualified offer of independence (on condition of wartime cooperation), electing instead to pass their famous 'Quit India' resolution of August 1942. This would play in their favour when the Congress leadership was released from prison in 1945 and applied themselves to negotiating an amicable settlement with their former captors.

Burdened with intolerable war debts and heightened political expectations for domestic welfare reform, the new Labour Government reluctantly reached the conclusion that Britain no longer had the will or the resources to resist Indian demands for a rapid transition to full independence. With few levers at their disposal, the Cabinet agreed on New Year's Eve 1946 to bring nearly two hundred years of British administration in India to a close. In so doing, however, ministers stressed that the decision should 'not appear to be forced upon us by our weakness nor to be the first step in the dissolution of the Empire'. The aim was to package independence as a great and noble gesture; indeed, 'the logical conclusion, which we welcomed, of a policy followed by successive Governments for many years'.[10] It was in this spirit that Mountbatten was sent out as the last of his kind, with a deadline for departure set for June 1948.

It was during Mountbatten's tenure that the semantics of imperial retreat became elevated to the point where they were virtually indistinguishable from the terms of independence itself. It was no longer a question of whether Britain should give way to a self-governing India, but what the handover should be called, with a variety of possibilities vying for attention – from 'devolution' (borrowed from the 'home rule' debates in Ireland and Scotland before the Great War) to 'decolonization' (from interwar German usage) to 'de-imperialization' (which never caught on) – all prefix-laden terms which somehow implied a reversal or setback.[11] These were all bypassed in favour of the 'transfer of power', a more dynamic construction that suggested forward momentum guided by a benevolent hand. Mountbatten himself was particularly attuned to the rhetorical nuances and would soon devote his energies to the minutiae of cultivating the right form of words.[12]

The viceroy's official instructions were to secure a passage to an independent India 'if possible within the British Commonwealth' – a prospect which became something of a personal obsession. Fundamentally, Mountbatten aimed at the same constructive ambiguity that had attended the wordplay of the interwar Commonwealth, assimilating India into the intricacies of the 1926 Balfour formula.[13] If the transfer of power could be achieved, not as a complete repudiation of empire but within the pre-existing constitutional and lexical conventions of the British Commonwealth, it would be an invaluable concession to continuity. It marked the beginning of what John Darwin has termed the 'anesthetising rhetoric' of the Commonwealth; the 'indispensable painkiller' for the ailments of imperial decline.[14]

But if 'dominion status' had proven so difficult to pin down in the 1920s, its chances of marshalling a consensus in post-war India seemed all the more remote. The key figure with whom the British were obliged to negotiate the terms of the handover harboured long-standing aversions to the mere mention of the term. Like many educated Indians of his generation, Jawaharlal Nehru 'had his roots in two countries', the product of years of early exposure to a British social system that instilled in him 'the prejudices of Harrow and Cambridge' (as he declared from the dock at his first trial in 1922). Years of social conditioning had taught him to look 'upon the world almost from an Englishman's standpoint'; so much so that upon his return to India he was 'as much prejudiced in favour of England and the English as it was possible for an Indian to be'.[15] Decades later, on a return visit to Harrow in May 1960, he again reflected on how his school years contributed to 'a certain association of friendship and fellowship between your country and my country, in the Commonwealth'.[16]

But this never seems to have endeared Nehru to the promise of dominionhood. Throughout the 1920s he clashed openly with the Congress leadership (including his own father, Molital) about the symbolic enticements periodically dangled by the British, and complained bitterly to Gandhi in January 1928 that the 'very idea' of dominion status 'suffocates and strangles me'.[17] It was precisely his intimacy with the ways of the English, his keen grasp of the intricacies of imperial language that caused him to bristle instinctively – just as he came to regard any constitutional arrangement that fell short of *Purna Swaraj* as a betrayal of India's spiritual destiny. Two decades and six lengthy prison spells later, his view remained unchanged, spelling out his antipathy in *The Discovery of India* (1946). 'This particular type of so-called internationalism is only an extension of a narrow British nationalism', he observed, 'which could not have appealed to us even if the logical consequences of Anglo-Indian history had not utterly rooted out its possibility from our minds.'[18]

Nehru was nevertheless ultimately persuaded that Commonwealth membership could be made compatible with Indian independence, and he was even prepared to accept 'dominion' status under the Crown as a temporary measure – primarily due to the need for a period of continuity and stability until a new Republican constitution could be drafted.[19] There were also the difficult security requirements of the handover period to consider, specifically the need to retain the stabilizing influence of thousands of British officers (all sworn to serve under the Crown and unlikely to continue in the absence of that personal bond). The prospect of the immediate mass departure of British service personnel was therefore a powerful argument for a more graduated transition to republicanism.[20] But above all, Nehru was swayed by the seeming inevitability of partition, and particularly the prospect of Pakistan remaining inside the Commonwealth after India's departure. The Muslim League did not share the long-standing antipathy of Congress towards dominion status – a factor that Mountbatten was eager to exploit – and it required little imagination to envisage a situation that would play greatly to Pakistan's political advantage in the event of armed conflict between the two new states. There are even subtle indications that Nehru hoped to reunite India around a shared dominion status once the unworkability of partition had become apparent.[21] In sum, it was a 'combination of fear and necessity' that brought

Congress around to the idea of dominion status as a short-term measure, buying time to secure the smoothest possible transition.[22]

In considering a solution along these lines, however, Congress leaders were adamant that the semantics would need to be attended to – a point they repeatedly impressed on Mountbatten. Nehru at all times insisted that the king should lose the title 'Emperor of India' and that something was needed to soften the controversial edge of 'dominion' status. While he had no objection to the use of the term in legal documents, a 'better term' for public consumption would have to be devised.[23] When Mountbatten and Nehru finally held substantive discussions at the viceregal residence in Simla on 10 May 1947, it was quickly agreed to bring forward the target date for the transfer of power by almost a year on the basis of dominion status but 'without the offending phraseology' of the term itself.[24]

Recognizing the difficulty for Congress of embracing a form of words they had so roundly and publicly rejected, Mountbatten creatively proffered 'Free Nation of the Commonwealth' as an alternative – to which Nehru voiced guarded approval.[25] The viceroy conceded that 'empire' and 'dominion' would have to go, as he toyed with a revised formula: 'A Member of the *British* Commonwealth (or Association) of Free Nations'. Though insisting that 'it was the substance of the future relationship and not words, which mattered', he seemed clearly to press his luck with the addition of such a loaded adjective.[26] Mountbatten misjudged Nehru's temper in this regard, who had made it abundantly clear that he saw the continuation of the Crown in India as a purely interim measure.[27] But this did not deter the viceroy from sending hyperbolic cables to Whitehall heralding 'the greatest opportunity ever offered to the Empire', and entertaining hopes that a variation on dominion status 'might prove to be acceptable as a permanent arrangement' – the ideal soft landing for the retrenchment of British India.[28]

The misunderstandings multiplied when Mountbatten's missive set off a chain reaction to fast-track 'a larger though looser' conception of the Commonwealth 'which will enable us to bring in new members without losing the old'. With Indian independence brought forward to August 1947, the Whitehall machine went into overdrive to find 'some form of association other than "Dominion status" in which independent states can maintain the British connection'.[29] The prime minister moved quickly to convene a special Cabinet committee charged with devising a 'new formula' in the light of clear indications that 'the phrase if not the content of "Dominion Status" is not now attractive'.[30] What all this overlooked was the evident cross-purposes of the main protagonists. Nehru's insistence on erasing the rhetorical remnants of the 'British connection' was seen in Whitehall as the ideal means of preserving it.

The other members of the Commonwealth were kept wholly in the dark about these deliberations. On the very day that Attlee embarked on his search for a 'new formula', an incoming letter from South Africa's Jan Smuts urged him to reconsider the 'inglorious ending' of the British Raj.[31] Meanwhile, Australia's Prime Minister Ben Chifley repeatedly stressed the need to draw the Commonwealth closer together around those members who 'fully represent the British tradition and outlook' (even employing at one point the unique coinage of his predecessor, John Curtin: the 'British-speaking race').[32] Nor had any clear consensus emerged in Whitehall about the price that was worth paying to secure India's adherence to Crown and Commonwealth, with one highly equivocal assessment of February 1947 compiling a list of pros and cons that clearly tilted towards the latter. Given the Congress leadership's 'life-long and rooted hostility to British rule', it seemed hard to envision how India could be anything other than 'an unreliable and largely non-cooperative element' within the Commonwealth, perhaps even 'more of an embarrassment than an asset' with the potential for weakening and impairing relationships among the existing members.[33]

For the rest of his life, Mountbatten would never tire of boasting that in August 1947 he secured independence with honour.[34] Measured against his own unambitious criteria of divesting responsibility at minimal material and symbolic cost, he had every reason to feel satisfied. The overwhelming verdict of the British press was that Mountbatten had pulled off something of a minor miracle, with Fleet Street headlines heralding the 'Power Transferred at Midnight' (*The Telegraph*), 'Farewell and Hail' (*The Guardian*) and 'Lord Mountbatten on a Friendly Parting' (*The Times*). The 'fulfilment of the British mission' was the overriding message, with frequent resort to T. B. Macaulay's adage that it would be 'the proudest day in English history' when Indians were ready to govern themselves.[35] The *Daily Mail* credited the departing viceroy with achieving 'in less than five months what others for more than a decade had sought in vain to do' – all on the strength of 'his own remarkable powers of personality'.[36] Harold Nicolson plumbed the irony in his diary: 'I am sure that Dickie has done marvellously . . . But it is curious that we should regard as a hero the man who liquidates the Empire which other heroes such as Clive, Warren Hastings and Napier won for us. Very odd indeed.'[37]

But it was not a matter of what 'Dickie had done', so much as the successful management of expectations by way of studied semantic fudging.

While India's newfound 'dominion' status was widely lauded in public commentary, the British government pressed home its advantage by consigning the term itself to historical oblivion. With a hopeful eye to finding some permanent basis to keep India in the Commonwealth, it was decreed that the word 'dominion' henceforth should be eliminated from all official discourse. The name of the Dominions Office in Whitehall was duly and discreetly changed to the 'Commonwealth Relations Office', and the foreign secretary, Ernest Bevin, advised all overseas missions that it was now 'desirable' to modify all communications accordingly. 'So far as is practicable', he urged, 'references to "the Dominions" or "Dominion Governments" as collective terms should be avoided. Phrases such as "other members of the British Commonwealth" or "other British Commonwealth Governments" should be employed instead.'[38] It was the first of several semantic innovations aimed at prolonging the life of the post-war empire.

TO BE OR NOT TO BE BRITISH

Even before the 15 August deadline for Indian independence, the Attlee Government had begun tentatively to consider whether the adjective 'British' might equally have to be sacrificed in the name of retaining the 'British connection'. It was the prime minister himself who first mooted the idea in a specially convened Cabinet committee of June 1947, where he anticipated the need to meet the Indian Government's inevitable objections. He ventured the alternative 'The Associated States of the Commonwealth' but was politely rebuffed by his Cabinet colleagues who insisted that 'whatever form of words might be decided upon, it would be essential to retain the word "British"'.[39] Other possibilities were floated (from 'The Commonwealth of British and Asian Peoples' to the 'Commonwealth of British and Associated Nations'), but the clunky combinations only accentuated the impasse.[40]

The following year, Attlee broached the issue directly with Nehru in a personal letter of 11 March 1948. 'The British Commonwealth of Nations is now in effect the Commonwealth of British and Asiatic nations', he ventured. 'It may well be that the title should be changed.' Conceding that 'we are in this country rather insensitive to the content of names and cheerfully keep on titles that have come down to us from the past', he offered an assurance that his government was 'far from under-rating the importance of names'.[41] Nehru would not be drawn to express an opinion either way, but in a private note to India's high commissioner in London,

Krishna Menon, he acknowledged that it was 'hardly possible for us to continue as a Dominion of the British Commonwealth', which would 'be fiercely opposed by various elements in India' and might even split the Congress Party.[42] Menon fundamentally agreed, but was also at pains to preserve something of the special intimacy of the British connection. He thought it would be worth absorbing a degree of criticism and 'perhaps some ridicule' to maintain the sense of a 'family arrangement' with Britain and the Commonwealth – reaping the benefits of 'the organic nature of the relationship' rather than stressing the cold, distant ties of foreign treaties. While it would not be possible to speak openly of a 'family arrangement', nor advisable politically to persist with the existing 'British' nomenclature, he was nevertheless open to some suitably ambiguous alternative that might be to India's advantage.[43]

That the matter was handled so delicately is a measure of its sensitivity. At the October 1948 Commonwealth Prime Ministers' Conference it was decided not to place nomenclature on the agenda at all. A closed circle of British ministers and senior advisers chose instead to address the matter behind the scenes in informal discussions with select Commonwealth leaders. This was partly a reflection of the enlarged format that included a record eight prime ministers; the founding 'old' members now joined by Nehru from India, Liaquat Ali Khan of Pakistan and Ceylon's D. S. Senanayake all attending for the first time.[44] It was also the first meeting since 1923 where no Irish delegation attended, due to the sudden announcement by Taoiseach John A. Costello of his country's intention to withdraw – on account of having recently severed the last remaining links with the Crown. This came shortly after the announcement that Burma would become independent as a Republic, and hence be obliged to exit the Commonwealth as well.[45] Attlee may well have feared a rush for the exit were he to throw open the question of naming protocols in the main conference sessions.

A far more substantive discussion about renaming the Commonwealth seems to have occurred at the bedside of the convalescent W. L. Mackenzie King at London's Dorchester Hotel. Unable to attend the conference due to ill health, the Canadian prime minister was nevertheless favourably disposed to making it easier for India to retain its membership, particularly at a time of escalating Cold War tensions when the Commonwealth would 'need all the friends they can have'.[46] He therefore turned his mind to devising a substitute name that would 'keep free of the words "Empire" and "British"', coming up with the 'Commonwealth of Free Nations' which he tried out on Nehru during a visit of 10 October – evidently making a favourable impression.[47] King George VI also called in at the Dorchester, apparently fully briefed about the naming dilemma which had raised acute difficulties for palace staff in drafting his ceremonial address to the visiting prime ministers at Buckingham Palace (under strict instructions to avoid 'any use of the words "British" or "Dominion"').[48]

The Australian delegation was highly suspicious of these informal conversations, particularly a series of meetings at Mountbatten's home midway through the conference involving Nehru and senior UK Cabinet ministers to discuss matters about which Australia was 'not consulted in any way'.[49] The Australian foreign minister H. V. Evatt (deputizing for Prime Minister Ben Chifley) held passionate views about the fundamentally British and monarchical essence of the Commonwealth bond, and was far less disposed than Mackenzie King to make symbolic concessions for the sake of a wider unity. It was presumably for this reason that his views on the naming issue were never directly sought. Instead, an attempt was made to dispense quietly with 'British' usage without provoking Evatt or his New Zealand counterpart, the Scottish-born Peter Fraser. The drafters of the final conference communiqué managed to avoid any reference to the 'British' Commonwealth whatsoever – quite a feat given the sixteen separate mentions of the organization in the communiqué text (and in striking contrast to previous years).

This was immediately seized upon by the press as marking a deliberate new departure, a view actively propagated by one unnamed 'spokesman' for the Commonwealth Relations Office who affirmed that 'the change was deliberate ... the prefix "British" has been dropped'. Other officials were more circumspect, issuing press guidance that the wording merely reflected 'the spirit governing the meetings' or 'the continuation of a trend'.[50] Either way, it was clearly no accident, eliciting reactions in all parts of the Commonwealth. The *Hindustan Times* warmly welcomed the refreshing change and the accompanying signs of a 'new concept of Commonwealth' emerging,[51] while the secretary general of the Indian External Affairs Ministry, Sir G. S. Bajpai, minuted approvingly:

> It is significant that, for the first time, the final public statement regarding the work of the Conference omits the word 'British' from the phrase 'Commonwealth of Nations'. This is doubtless a concession [deleted: consolation] to the sentiments of members of the Commonwealth like India, apart from being a recognition of the fact that the Community of Nations is no longer British in tradition, civilisation and race.[52]

Much as the Conference organizers had feared, however, reactions in other parts of the Commonwealth were unusually hostile. The overwhelming consensus in New Zealand was that too high a price was being paid for retaining India's membership in the Commonwealth, with the *Auckland Star* insisting that 'nobody can prevent us calling ourselves British . . . we cannot conceive that any country is a full member of the British Commonwealth which does not give full allegiance to the British Crown'.[53] The UK high commissioner in Wellington had been taken completely by surprise, and duly despatched a reminder that 'one could hardly remain in New Zealand for any length of time without becoming aware of the existence of quite strong feelings on this subject'. Throughout the country, opposition to dropping 'British' was virtually universal, the more so since the issue had now become a matter of public controversy. 'The new nomenclature', he concluded, 'will be unpopular in New Zealand and she will be slow to bow to the inevitable'.[54]

In Australia, too, the *Melbourne Sun* ran with the indignant headline 'Are We British?', while Opposition Leader Robert Menzies objected that the prime ministers' meeting had no constitutional authority to execute a name change without the consent of the member parliaments.[55] A Gallup poll revealed that 73 per cent of Australians preferred the term 'British Commonwealth', with only 15 per cent prepared to countenance a change of nomenclature.[56] Evatt sought to lower the temperature, insisting that all the 'fuss and bother' had simply been caused by an 'erroneous communiqué', and that there was no substance whatsoever (as far as he was concerned) to reports of a name change.[57] He pressed the point home in a nationwide radio broadcast:

> There has been a great deal of loose talk about the omission of the word 'British'. The name 'British' doesn't mean that every nation in the group is British in race, because they are not. But it does mean that there is a central feature of the Commonwealth deriving from Britain and the tradition of Britain, and that means to Australia the most intimate relationship of all – with the King. So it is the British Commonwealth.[58]

Opinion in South Africa was divided between the pro-government Afrikaner press, on the one hand, which welcomed any sign of the 'British Empire Disintegrating' (to quote one headline in *Volksblad*), and the English-speaking press on the other, ever-vigilant against even the slightest indications of a drift towards republicanism. South Africa's new prime minister, the nationalist D. F. Malan, rejoiced openly that 'by dropping the word "British"' the conference had affirmed 'the British peoples love of freedom', strongly implying that another link in the chain of imperialism had been broken.[59] The *Rand Daily Mail* objected in the strongest terms in an editorial headed by an empty set of scare quotes (as in: " "). Any or all of the five words in 'the British Commonwealth of Nations', it was argued, could 'offend the susceptibilities of some section in some member State' (including 'of' with its possessive overtones, or the absolutist slant of 'the'). 'If a job is to be done at all', therefore, 'it should be done thoroughly' by way of wholesale expurgation, leaving only the quotation marks 'which should be acceptable to everybody'.[60] A light-hearted view, perhaps, but one clearly laced with moral indignation.

In Britain, too, Opposition Leader Winston Churchill issued a withering denunciation in parliament, reciting a litany of objections ranging from the dwindling moral capital of the word 'empire' to the tendency to dispense with the term 'dominion', before turning to the name of the Commonwealth itself:

> Apparently the Socialist Government wish to direct us into channels where these words will be heard no more, or as little as possible. The style and title which we are to give to our worldwide associations of States and communities must not contain anything that recalls past tradition. It must contain nothing that embodies pride of race or country; it must contain nothing that could be deemed controversial, nothing that could offend the weakest of the weaker brethren in our slowly-formed association throughout the globe ... The word 'Empire' is to be suppressed. 'Dominion', for some strange reason, is judged peccant and unwholesome, and now, on the morrow of our greatest victory and service to mankind, we come to the elimination of the word 'British' which was so lately held in the highest honour in many lands.

Churchill clearly grasped how 'pride of race' was inscribed in lexical forms. Nehru in particular was a key target, whom he charged with seeking all the political and material benefits of Commonwealth membership without committing to 'the slightest obligation or even to any symbolic or sentimental gesture or token in return'. By allowing him to injure Britain's pride at every turn, the government had only succeeded in damaging the spiritual bonds that linked the older (white) Commonwealth members. How could anyone, he demanded, be 'inspired to lay down their lives for the common cause in the hour of mortal danger when that common cause and association cannot be expressed in words which carry any intelligible meaning to any human being'. Echoing Menzies' concerns about the lack of constitutional authority to effect such a change, he proposed that until the matter was properly resolved there should be agreement on a compromise for-mula: the 'British Empire and Commonwealth of Nations'. By displacing the adjective to the other side of 'Empire', Churchill hoped to preserve something of conventional usage until 'the Government have made up their minds what we are to be called or are to call ourselves'.[61]

What the Attlee Government had naively hoped to stage-manage as a gradual transition had turned predictably sour. Not even the entire Cabinet had been informed of the strategy, and Commonwealth Secretary Philip Noel-Baker was duly called on to explain himself:

> Although ['British'] had not in fact been a deliberate omission, it was true that, in informal conversations with several Commonwealth Prime Ministers, the suggestion had been put forward that it might be useful to establish, without any formal change, the convention of describing the Commonwealth as 'the Commonwealth of Nations' instead of the 'British Commonwealth of Nations'. The object of this informal change would be to foster the impression that the Commonwealth was wide enough to include nations which, by reason of their race and history, could not feel that they were 'British' nations.[62]

This only compounded matters. Despite issuing a formal denial of any deliberate omission of the word 'British', the Commonwealth Relations Office nevertheless prepared advice for all overseas diplomatic missions to the effect that 'it would be useful' if all staff could be habituated to referring to the organization as 'the Commonwealth of Nations', without necessitat-ing any controversial announcement of a formal nomenclature change. While this should not rule out every conceivable mention of the word 'British', it should be used prudently and with diminishing frequency.[63] In this way, the entire exercise became cloaked in subterfuge, with Heads of Mission advised not to release the new advice for general distribution, but instead to 'bring it to the notice' of their most senior people before locking it away in the office safe – so as to maintain maximum secrecy and prevent the contents falling 'into the hands of the press'.[64]

Unsurprisingly, within twenty-four hours the whole absurd state of affairs had been duly leaked, furnishing the sensationalist front-page splash of the *Daily Express*. 'Britain Bans British':

> Secret Instructions have been issued to British Ministers and senior civil servants to shun the words 'British' and 'Dominion' in references to the Empire if it is thought that anyone who does not like the words might object. The words are to be played down, it is explained, to avoid any suggestion of inferiority on the part of other Governments in the

Commonwealth. In future the great Dominions are to be described in official documents as 'Fully self-governing countries of the Commonwealth'.[65]

The source of the leak was never found, but the effects were highly damaging given the government's repeated denials. Noel-Baker was incensed at the incompetence of his departmental officials and confessed to Attlee: 'I am afraid that we may be faced with questions from some other Commonwealth countries, and perhaps, with controversy here. The question of using the word "British" has become a live one'.[66]

'A PECULIARLY BRITISH RESULT': THE LONDON DECLARATION, 1949

When the Commonwealth prime ministers reassembled in London barely half a year later, matters had come to a head. India was now only months away from finalizing its Republican Constitution, while the objections of Australia and New Zealand to a Commonwealth without a unifying British element remained undimmed. Prime Minister Attlee had exhausted his powers of persuasion in a bid to win Nehru over to the benefits of the link with the Crown, at one point even suggesting that if the English could tolerate monarchs of Angevin, Welsh, Scottish, Dutch and German origin for centuries, it was a small matter for India to embrace the Windsors.[67] Needless to say, Nehru was unmoved by these 'surprisingly naive' arguments, and the problem of overcoming India's refusal to acknowledge allegiance to the king would dominate proceedings, largely overshadowing the question of whether the Commonwealth should be bracketed with 'British'.[68]

The two issues were inextricably linked, however, with little prospect of compromise from either side. British diplomats in Delhi advised that Nehru would resist any outcome that smacked of subservience to the British sovereign.[69] Moreover, a Congress Party resolution of December 1948 had rejected outright any notion of a two-tiered Commonwealth (with a 'British' Crown core and 'outer' republican fringe). In a letter to all provincial premiers in the lead-up to the Conference, Nehru issued a firm assurance that whatever arrangement he might strike with the other member states, it would 'no longer be called the British Commonwealth'.[70]

Meanwhile New Zealand's Peter Fraser had come to the conclusion that 'it would be better to lose India than for our British peoples to lose faith in the reality and integrity of their Commonwealth'.[71] This was not just his own personal conviction, but came with the firm backing of the New Zealand diplomatic corps and the vast majority of press and public opinion.[72] The opposition National Party raised the stakes even higher on the eve of the conference, describing republican membership of the Commonwealth as an 'unthinkable future' that would 'never be tolerated by the people of this dominion. With us, Empire is an instinct. Loyalty to the Crown, almost a religion.'[73] Dismayed to learn that Louis St Laurent would not be attending in person, Fraser urged the new Canadian prime minister to consider the dire consequences of complacency: 'Are we', he pleaded, 'to end up with a form of words covering an arrangement which is entirely nebulous?'[74]

In South Africa, Jan Smuts (now in opposition after the 1948 election) also cautioned against any measure that might impair the 'outlook and objective shared by peoples of common origin, if not entirely British then at any rate Northern European'.[75] Obliged to hedge on the matter of Britishness for obvious domestic political reasons, his statement only compounded the complexity. Meanwhile the Australian position seemed to have hardened, with Dr Evatt divulging to *The Times* only a month prior to the conference that 'the elements of kingship, kinship and practical comradeship are all of supreme significance'.[76] Privately, he told his British counterparts that the retention of the word 'British' remained essential in this regard. Nehru's response was to dismiss Evatt's views as 'simple and childlike'; the idea of 'kingship and kinship' could simply have 'no meaning for India', nor for that matter the 'idea of calling the Commonwealth "British"'.[77] Ahead of the conference he shared with senior British and Canadian ministers a personal 'memorandum on points of agreement', including his determination to 'redescribe and retitle' the Commonwealth – pressing for Mackenzie King's suggestion of a 'Commonwealth of Free Nations'.[78]

The week of deliberations in London in April 1949 failed to achieve any real reconciliation of these passionately held views. There was, however, a significant breakthrough as far as the status of the king was concerned. Although the prime ministers each made a vigorous display of high principle at the outset (Fraser's opening words were 'New Zealand was colonised by people of British stock and ... would not tolerate any dilution of [their] loyalties'), all were eventually swayed by the greater good of holding the Commonwealth together. After several days of semantic scrabble, it was agreed to restyle the king as 'the symbol of the free association of its independent member nations and as such the Head of the Commonwealth'; a designation that preserved some semblance of common purpose, while allowing each member to make of it whatever they pleased.[79]

But the drafters were to be stymied in their efforts to resolve the 'British' problem. When the matter arose on 25 April, Nehru elaborated his case in full, arguing that the adjective 'had ceased to be factually accurate' and was widely regarded as connoting 'some form of political subordination'. While he understood and respected the Australian and New Zealand attachment to the term, it would not be possible in the future to speak of the 'British Commonwealth' in India and it would be necessary for him to be able to say publicly that the correct term was 'The Commonwealth of Nations'. In reply, Chifley and Fraser pointed to the political controversy that had erupted in the wake of the 1948 Conference, making it equally necessary for them to be able to point to the correctness of British usage. How to square this with India's express condition that the term be discontinued permitted no easy solution. The only concession Nehru could offer was the

Figure 4.1 Commonwealth prime ministers assembled for the imperial conference, 21 April 1949. From left to right: D. S. Senanayake (Ceylon), Lester B. Pearson (Canadian minister for external affairs), Liaquat Ali Khan (Pakistan), King George VI, Clement Attlee (Britain), Ben Chifley (Australia), D. F. Malan (South Africa), Peter Fraser (New Zealand) and Jawaharlal Nehru (India). Source: Hulton Royals Collection/Getty Images.

possibility that the offending adjective might still be used 'elsewhere', and that there might be 'some variation of practice in this matter'.

This, ultimately, was as much as the prime ministers could agree on; to make no formal announcement of a name change but allow each member to choose for themselves. Although a tolerable means of avoiding the issue, it nevertheless raised (yet again) the problem of finding a felicitous form of words for the final conference communiqué. Here, a compromise of sorts was reached. Nehru waived his objections in the opening sentence which 'referred to the existing situation', while insisting that the concluding lines should contain his own preferred formula, pointing implicitly towards the future.[80] By this tortuous route, a text was crafted to suit all rhetorical persuasions:

> The Governments of the United Kingdom, Canada, Australia, New Zealand, South Africa, India, Pakistan and Ceylon whose countries are united as members of *the British Commonwealth of Nations* and owe a common allegiance to the Crown, which is also the symbol of their free association, have considered the impending constitutional change of India. The Government of India have informed the other governments of the Commonwealth of the intention of the Indian people that under the new constitution which is about to be adopted India shall become a sovereign independent republic. The Government of India have, however, declared and affirmed India's desire to continue her full membership of *the Commonwealth of Nations* and her acceptance of the King as the symbol of the free association of its independent member nations, and as such the Head of the Commonwealth.[81]

Subsequently dubbed the 'London Declaration', it left the matter of nomenclature in a state of lexical limbo. Nehru could triumphantly telegram his senior Cabinet colleagues: 'Phrase "British" is ... to be dropped hereafter', but he could not claim any kind of consensus.[82] That something so fundamental as the name of the organization could be left to personal taste was unprecedented in international affairs, and constitutional experts were quick to call out the anomaly. Prominent among them was Ivor Jennings, who issued a stern warning in a letter to *The Times* that 'terminology gives rise to political disputes as easily as conflicts of interest' if they are not properly addressed. He recommended that an international panel be appointed to resolve the confusion once and for all – a suggestion that fell on deaf ears.[83] The king himself was informed that 'the title British for the Commonwealth has been left optional', and his senior palace staff did their utmost to accommodate this in his closing conference address. Drawing on both names in different parts of the speech, the king congratulated the prime ministers on finding a solution 'that is a striking example of the elasticity of our system'.[84] Privately, though, Sir Alan Lascelles reflected from Buckingham Palace:

> My own attitude to the whole thing is rather that of a man who has to undergo a surgical operation. Nobody in his senses wants to have an operation, but when it becomes inevitable it is a great blessing to get through it as cheaply as possible, and with the hope that one's future health may be benefited thereby.[85]

Prime Minister Attlee was widely applauded for his skill and patience in holding India to the Commonwealth, although he too came in for criticism for allowing the semantic uncertainty to continue unchecked. Observing that India had chosen to remain within the Commonwealth, but not the 'British' Commonwealth, the *Daily Mail*, asked plaintively: 'What does all this mean? We do not know, and we doubt if anyone else does – including those who prepared the statement. How can they?'[86] *The Guardian* was more sanguine, concluding that it was ultimately the best possible solution 'to keep both names and to use them according to taste and circumstance'.[87]

In Australia, the Chifley government was bitterly divided. 'Sickening!' was the verdict of Foreign Minister Evatt, hand-scrawled across a London despatch extolling Chifley's virtues as a negotiator.[88] That the prime minister had reneged on two crucial points of vital importance to Australia – the aspect of 'personal loyalty' to the sovereign and 'the importance of the name of Britain' – remained a source of lasting personal resentment.[89] Press commentary ranged from the high umbrage of the Melbourne *Argus* (condemning the 'face-saving formula' struck from 'the principle of trying to have it both ways') to the cautious endorsement of the *Sydney Morning Herald* (welcoming the agreement – without a trace of irony – as a compromise 'typically British in the best traditional sense').[90] The opposition indicted Chifley for 'putting the British Commonwealth into liquidation', even as the prime minister continued to use the older formula in his spirited defence of the London Declaration.[91] Meanwhile in South Africa, Jan Smuts could not 'forbear expressing my misgivings' about the submergence of the Commonwealth's 'true character . . . in a mist of misleading verbiage'.[92] And in Canada, the *Ottawa Journal* indulged in some contorted verbiage of its own, affirming on the one hand that 'so many of us are British and the word "British" is dear to our heart' while at the same time dismissing the name-change as an irrelevance: '"British" is just a word . . . Let [it] slip from the formal designation. We'll most of us remain loyal to it in spirit.'[93]

Back in Britain, Attlee was soon challenged in the House of Commons but refused to concede that there had been 'agreement to adopt or exclude any one of these terms'. Nor was he prepared to state his own personal preference: 'Opinions differ in different parts of the British Empire and Commonwealth on this matter, and I think it better to allow people to use the expression they like best.'[94] It was a hopeless state of affairs for the Commonwealth Relations Office, now saddled with a deluge of enquiries about correct official usage. As the deputy under secretary wearily replied to one such query, the entire matter had caused 'much head-scratching and all, I regret, without result ... I am afraid you were being too charitable in expecting that we had found an ideal solution'.[95]

The awkwardness was palpable at a parliamentary committee meeting in Ottawa, where the new foreign minister, Lester Pearson, was subjected to a sustained grilling by members of the Canadian opposition. The verbatim transcript reveals something of Pearson's personal discomfort, and the incredulity of his questioners:

MR FLEMING: May I ask if the title was discussed at the meeting?

MR PEARSON: Yes, it was.

MR FLEMING: Then how far do you feel free to indicate to us the discussion that was had?

MR PEARSON: I feel that I have to be a little careful ... the new dominions from the sub-continent of India ... have not the same links of tradition and race and lineage antecedence as say New Zealand and Australia have with the United Kingdom, and which, indeed, Canada has with the United Kingdom. [They] are not British in that sense, do not feel British in that sense. Doctor Malan, the Prime Minister of South Africa ... does not feel British in that sense. Their attitude towards the use of the word British is obviously not the same as that of the Prime Minister of New Zealand who certainly does feel British in that sense.

MR GREEN: The position in that respect is that each member of the Commonwealth ...

MR PEARSON: The position is that each nation can use whatever expression it cares to use. It can use British Commonwealth, or Commonwealth of Nations and possibly in even any one nation of the commonwealth, people can use any expression they like ...

MR FLEMING: Is it fair to say that when the matter was discussed no conclusion was reached, and it is just sitting there?

MR PEARSON: No formal conclusion of any kind was reached. There was a discussion and a peculiarly British result.[96]

MR GREEN: I hope you are not going to change the name of British Columbia to Columbia.

MR PEARSON: If we did, we should call it Columbia, Gem of the Pacific.

When Pearson arrived in Delhi a few months later for the inauguration of the Republic, he spoke with surprising frankness at a press conference: 'We have had the British Empire, we have had the British Commonwealth of Nations and we are now initiating a new Commonwealth of Nations. Some of us can call it British if we want to, but it is in a sense, a new commonwealth.'[97]

Amid the confusion, diplomatic staff at the UK High Commission in Ottawa saw a potential windfall, asking whether, 'if we are no longer to use "British" as a term of general Commonwealth application, the inhabitants and the Government of Britain might once again be allowed to call themselves British?'[98] Although only a fleeting thought bubble, it suggested that British officials were themselves growing weary of overstretched expectations, or were at least prepared to reconsider their own self-designation in the transition from empire to Commonwealth. But the prospect of winding the clock back to some imagined baseline – with the presumptive core 'once again allowed to call themselves British' – was nowhere near as straightforward as it seemed. It threw into sharp relief the underlying question posed by Nehru's flat disavowal of a British world: what was left of Britain, stripped of its wider semantic remit?

'AMBIGUOUS ALBION': REPATRIATING BRITISHNESS

It would be more than a decade before the idea of repatriating the British moniker was revisited. Throughout the 1950s it remained official government practice to avoid referring to 'British' and 'Britain' when speaking only about Great Britain in a Commonwealth context and to rely instead on the 'United Kingdom' or 'UK'. This was mainly out of respect for residual Commonwealth sensitivities, but it also had the advantage of avoiding misunderstandings over the status of Northern Ireland (as well as ensuring close alphabetical proximity to the United States and the USSR in seating arrangements at international conferences).

But in November 1960, the Macmillan government took steps to relinquish all 'Greater' British connotations entirely, reopening the question of reserving 'British' for purely 'UK' purposes. The rationale was twofold: first, the creeping obsolescence of a British world had engendered doubts as to whether the term still served any wider purpose; and second, the 'United Kingdom' seemed inadequate to the task, unusually cumbersome as an adjective and lacking a serviceable collective noun. The Whitehall machine thus went into nomenclature mode once more. But with memories of the unresolved rhetorical struggles of 1948–9 still fresh, it was feared that the other Commonwealth governments might strongly disapprove. It was there-fore decided to consult with UK high commissioners in Australia, Canada, New Zealand, South Africa and India.[99]

The response from all posts was cautious but encouraging. From Pretoria, Sir John Maud was positively relieved 'to get away from the verbal gymnastics we sometimes have had to perform in order to make ourselves use "United Kingdom" where inclination and popular usage combine to make "British" the natural adjective'.[100] It was in any case not unusual for South Africans themselves to use 'Britain' and 'British' interchangeably with the United Kingdom. Though Maud could offer no guarantee that controversy could be completely avoided, a political backlash seemed unlikely. But his reasoning suggested that he himself had missed the point of the change entirely: 'Our friends here', he felt sure, would not feel it carried 'the implication that South Africans were no longer "British"'.[101]

His counterpart in Canberra, Bill Oliver, reminded Whitehall of the enduring appeal of the 'double sense' of British to mean 'a number of things not confined to Britain' which needed to be taken heed of.[102] Similarly from New Zealand, the advice was handle with care, betraying considerable misgivings among senior British officials themselves. 'This country rightly thinks of itself as British', urged Francis Cumming-Bruce, although he did not think objections would be raised provided the change was sensitively implemented.[103] Joe Garner in Ottawa was more sanguine, noting that although Canadians were once 'immensely proud' of their Britishness, 'the position has changed here and ... today, with some excep-tions, there would be no general objection to the use of the term "British" to apply to the people of Great Britain'. Yet even he found, in conducting an informal poll of his own office, that the diplomatic personnel were entirely in favour whereas a clear majority of the locally engaged staff (i.e. Canadians) were overwhelmingly against.[104]

Determined to press ahead, Commonwealth Secretary Duncan Sandys submitted a compelling case against the continued use of 'United Kingdom' to the Cabinet in March 1961:

> This soulless, official designation is totally lacking in popular appeal and inspires no emotions of affection or loyalty. In the years before the war, when it was still permissible to talk of 'the British Empire' or the 'British Commonwealth', it was rightly felt that our member countries might resent it, if we arrogated to ourselves the term 'British' which was common to

them all. But since then the whole character of the Commonwealth has changed. The new members, such as India, Ceylon and Ghana, have never regarded themselves as British. Meanwhile the Canadians, Australians and New Zealanders, although as proud as ever of their British ancestry and of their links with the 'old country', have now developed individual nationalities of their own. Thus there is no longer any good reason why we should continue to handicap ourselves with the present unsympathetic nomenclature.[105]

The intention was not to change the legal status of 'The United Kingdom of Great Britain and Northern Ireland', which would continue to be used for signing treaties (and favourable seating arrangements at summits).[106] Rather it was about everyday usage, speeches, conversation, correspondence, letterheads and the brass plates on High Commission gates. The Cabinet was quick to approve the measure, but progress was impeded by an eleventh-hour intervention from the Cabinet secretary, Sir Norman Brook, who elaborated his misgivings personally and insistently to the prime minister: 'Are we sure that we shall not give offence to Australia and New Zealand, and perhaps to Canada, if we arrogate the term "British" to ourselves alone?'[107] Recalling the acute difficulties of the late 1940s, he anticipated further ructions among those 'who still like to think of themselves as "British" and would not be best pleased if we appropriated this epithet to ourselves'.[108] Particularly noteworthy was Brook's assertion that 'the organisation as a whole is still formally known as "The British Commonwealth of Nations" – though it is true that in common parlance we have felt obliged to drop the adjective "British" to refer to the "Commonwealth" out of deference to the feelings of Indians and others'.[109] This was only partially true, as Brook himself must surely have known. Such was his equivocation that he concluded his missive by referring to Britain as 'the islands in which we live'.[110] That someone at such a senior tier of government could harbour doubts about the name of the country he served suggests a uniquely vexed state of affairs.

It was enough to make Macmillan blink, deciding that the entire matter 'had better be looked at again'.[111] As a precautionary measure he ordered that personal messages be despatched to the prime ministers of Australia, Canada and New Zealand with a view to securing their blessing.[112] No such courtesy was extended to South Africa, having exited the Commonwealth in March 1961, nor the African, Asian or Caribbean members whom it never occured to anyone to ask. It transpired that none of the governments consulted could find any reasonable grounds for complaint, and all quickly gave their assent. But it was an undeniably absurd situation. 'Every country has the sovereign right to decide what it will call itself', reasoned Canadian officials, seemingly puzzled as to why such an elementary proposition had been put to them in the first place.[113] It was but one of many anomalies of a concept still captive to offshore resonances.

The change was finally approved in September 1961 and implemented 'quietly and unobtrusively' (shrouded as ever in a culture of secrecy).[114] British media coverage was therefore sporadic and remarkably belated, often relying on reports originating from Canada and Australia. It would not be until the end of October that *The Times* announced '"Cold UK" becomes British' – and a further three months before *The Economist* picked up the story, warmly applauding the arrival of 'Ambiguous Albion' and the demise of 'Yewkai':[115]

> One of the few things that are always changing about this country is the name by which different people call it; another change is taking place behind the scenes at the moment ... although, perhaps to placate the old Commonwealth hands (who are attached to the Yewkai in the same way as fifth-generation Australians, New Zealanders and English-speaking Canadians are attached to Home), great discretion, even secrecy, is being maintained about the fact that the change is being made. In the CRO's institutions abroad, we can now reveal, Britain this country are [*sic*] to be; High Commissioners are to be British and perhaps bold and brave as well. The decision is a sensible one: for its success, we should like to wish its sponsor the best of United Kingdom luck.[116]

Covertly and without fanfare, the last lexical vestige of Greater Britain was officially laid to rest. Ironically, the one place where it generated a ripple of dissent was the British High Commission in India, in a series of despatches extolling the merits of the United Kingdom. 'We are going to have a bit of a business making this transition', explained High Commissioner Sir Paul Gore-Booth, because English-speaking Indians were 'now firmly wedded to "UK" which they use as an almost affectionate title for post-imperialist Britain'.[117] According to these lights, the 'UK' was 'not altogether a soulless term' in India – it had become widely associated 'with the new, friendly attitude to our country' which had developed since 1947. 'Britain', by contrast, still had 'something of an imperialist ring', whereas UK brought 'the sense of one country in a Commonwealth of equals and has less of the association of a ruling power'.[118] Thus, by a twist of logic, the one Commonwealth country that had refused any wider application of 'British' in 1949 was feared most likely to baulk at its downsized designation in 1961. Undoubtedly, a lingering imperial stigma was associated with the language of Britishness in India, much as it remained the source of its residual appeal in Australia and New Zealand. But in any event, no official objection was forthcoming from the Indian Government, even if the transition was to prove slower in India than in other Commonwealth countries.[119]

In this way, a process that had brought thunderous condemnation from Churchill in the Commons thirteen years earlier was carried to completion with only residual voices raised in protest. To the extent that it was commented on at all, press reactions ranged from the resigned shrug of *The Times*, to the playful irony of the *Vancouver Sun* in an editorial titled, 'the British name':

> First to go was the term British Empire. Then we dropped the British from the British Commonwealth ... Is the famous old name fading from history's pages? Fortunately, no. It has been readopted – by the British themselves ... It is a reflection, probably, of the changing nature of the Commonwealth that national names are now well enough established that the original owners of the British name can take it back again.[120]

It was an easy and alluring assumption – that Harold Macmillan had merely reverted to the status quo ante, reconnecting the 'famous old' adjective with its original meaning after a few centuries out on loan. But it cannot stand up to scrutiny. The weight of decades of imperial inflexion, of greater British innovation (much of it originating in the colonies and dominions themselves) precluded any simple resurrection of a pre-imperial essence. The persistent tinkering between 1947 and 1961 was not a restorative move so much as a subtle reinvention. In claiming exclusive rights to their scaled-back British brand, the British Government unwittingly crafted something new, something relatively untried, unpredictable, perhaps even unviable. Just as 'UK' was condemned for lacking popular appeal and inspiring 'no warmth or affection', so too a Britishness stripped of its 'greater' resonance faced similar adversity – not immediately but over the longer term, as the implications of its semantic retreat slowly took hold.[121] No doubt the recalibrations of the 1960s helped to reconcile the political elite and the people they governed to a more modest conception of their place in the world. But they could not guarantee a limitless future for a downsized conception of Britishness itself.

On the eve of Indian independence in 1947, veteran colonial administrator Leo Amery consoled Winston Churchill on the unhappy trends in world affairs. 'We can only hope', he ventured, 'that, somehow or other, the

126

Britannic orbit will remain a reality in this parlous world even if, to assume the worst, Indian politicians are unwise enough to wish to break the formal link'.[122] His turn of phrase – the 'Britannic orbit' – went to the heart of the matter. Although India ultimately chose to remain within the Commonwealth, it would do so on terms that eroded the very 'orbital' connotations their membership was intended to preserve. The rhetorical price proved far greater than Mountbatten or Attlee could ever have envisaged. Just as terms such as 'empire' and 'dominion' were progressively squeezed out, so too, Britishness itself was quietly decoupled from its global dispensation. An idea which had once encompassed a vast semantic field (long before Charles Dilke first coined 'Greater Britain' in the 1860s) was thus retooled for a post-imperial world. The implications of stripping the Commonwealth of its custodial adjective were most immediate in those parts of the world where its writ no longer ran. But it would also have complicated repercussions for the 'Four Nations' of the United Kingdom.

The effect was by no means sudden or straightforward. Countless individuals, interest groups and organizations, both in Britain and elsewhere, would tenaciously adhere to older expressions and usage into the 1950s, 1960s and in some cases beyond. By its very nature, it is impossible to pinpoint precisely when it became no longer plausible to project the language and imagery of Britishness onto a broader canvas. But the pattern of official rhetoric and the calculated decisions to modernize imperial language furnishes rare insights into how these intricate processes played out. What distinguishes official rhetoric from other forms of speech is the proximity to an immediate political context, raising the stakes and inviting open critique and contestation. It should therefore be understood, not as some inert indicator of societal change but rather one of its key drivers.

Churchill himself was acutely aware of this. Throughout the remainder of his career, he never ceased to point out how insidious slippages of the tongue were eroding his cherished British world. As he complained to the king in July 1942, all parties concerned 'had already been *talked into* giving up India'. It was the changing tenor of the conversation that had 'contributed to make their minds up that our rule in India is wrong & always has been wrong for India'.[123] Nor were these misgivings solely the preserve of the Conservative side of politics. For all the semantic innovation of the Attlee years, it was at all times attended by an extraordinary hesitation and political dissembling. Attlee himself was all too familiar with the perils of nomenclature as a galvanizing force, devising the revealing rule of thumb: 'In dealing with the Dominions ... the more we avoid precise definitions, the better.'[124]

The trouble for Attlee was that precise definitions had become the order of the day – with a recurring cycle of Commonwealth prime ministers' conferences acquiring the machinery and protocols of international diplomacy. Though there was nothing intrinsically new about the delicate wordplay of Commonwealth relations in the post-war years (coming on the heels of the tortuous procedures of the interwar years) the point had clearly arrived where constructive ambiguity would no longer do. The profoundly altered political and ideological context of the post-war empire, with a radically reshuffled membership bringing much wider scope for dissent and general discord, made the mere fact of holding meetings potentially fraught with semantic controversy. Or as Mackenzie King lamented in his diary from the Dorchester in October 1948, 'the real mischief of Conferences' was that they led 'to questions being asked which it is difficult to answer'.[125]

5

HOMES AWAY FROM HOME: THE HOUSES OF WINDSOR

In April 1947, Princess Elizabeth delivered her 21st birthday broadcast from South Africa on the BBC World Service; a coming-of-age ritual that attracted an unprecedented global audience. Addressing 'all the peoples of the British Commonwealth and Empire, wherever they live, whatever race they come from, and whatever language they speak', her words were carefully crafted to draw a special circle of intimacy: 'As I speak to you today from Cape Town, I am six thousand miles from the country where I was born. But I am certainly not six thousand miles from home.' Here, at the post-war apogee of 'Britannic broadcasting', was a world unbounded by physical barriers in the mould of Seeley and Dilke.[1] It was an ingenious way of refashioning the romance of empire for a new era, evoking a vast extended family simultaneously tuning in to their sovereign-in-waiting. Capacious in its reach, it also struck a reassuring note of fealty, fellowship and fireside amity.

The theme of the 'Royals at home' had been a mainstay of media coverage of the 1947 Royal Tour of South Africa. Veteran *Daily Mail* correspondent G. Ward Price likened the setting to 'the closest possible overseas reproduction of English provincial life', surmising that the 'average Englishman', when 'asked where he feels most at home in the Empire, says South Africa'.[2] The royals themselves seemed to revel in the comparison, with Princess Margaret sharing her enchantment in a letter to Queen Mary: 'I can't tell you how extraordinary it was, but we all had the feeling that we were in a kind of England overseas.' That these impressions were more rhetorical than real seemed evident enough to her older sister, whose private thoughts turned to a more limited conception of home: 'I felt sad when I realised that I would not spend my coming of age at home, but now I think that it forms a very happy link with South Africa.'[3] The high diction of empire injected an element of civic duty, cementing links with distant domains and blurring the edges of Britain's frontiers. This, she declared on her birthday, was 'the great privilege belonging to our place in the world-wide Commonwealth – that there are homes ready to welcome us in every continent of the earth'.

Figure 5.1 Princess Elizabeth broadcasts to a global audience from the gardens of Government House in Cape Town on the occasion of her 21st birthday, 21 April 1947. Source: Hulton Royals Collection/Getty Images.

Within months of the broadcast, her thoughts were literally set in stone when the princess was gifted a home of her own in the foothills of Mt Kenya. Sagana Lodge was one of the more elaborate wedding presents bestowed on Elizabeth and Prince Philip in November 1947. Despite an official edict discouraging undue extravagance at a time of post-war scarcity, the Kenyan Colonial Government could not resist the opportunity to devise something uniquely personal.[4] Although it has long-since entered into royal folklore that the princess was in residence at Sagana at the time of George VI's death in February 1952, surprisingly little is known about the circumstances that made her a homeowner in this improbable part of the world. Decades of hindsight seem in no way to have denaturalized the setting, nor raised questions about the sheer audacity of establishing a royal residence in East Africa at the tipping point of post-war decolonization. Frequently overlooked is the (in)security of tenure that prompted Kenya's white settler community to enlist the mystique of royalty to shore up their tenuous land claims. It will be argued here that the gift marked a pivotal moment in the global projection of Britishness, at once affirming the salience of 'home' as a synonym for Greater Britain, while at the same time exposing its endemic flaws.

What made the idea of home so serviceable was its profusion of meanings. For centuries, it had become common currency among British settlers the world over as an everyday reminder of the spiritual connection to the old world. For recent arrivals, the term could be employed literally to invoke a personal connection to a specific place of origin. Over time and with the passing of the generations, however, it acquired a more generalized symbolic capital, laden with emotional baggage. In Anthony Trollope's 1867 maxim: 'It is . . . to those who live farthest away from home, to those who find the greatest difficulty in visiting home, that the word conveys the sweetest idea.' This was the lot of the transplanted Briton; those for whom 'home is across the blue waters, in the little northern island . . . from which circumstances, and the necessity of living, have banished him'.[5] As early as the 1760s, the colonial governor of Massachusetts Bay remarked on the 'almost mechanical affection' among even the most unsentimental of His Majesty's subjects for a place 'which they conceive under no other sense, nor call by any other name, than that of *home*'.[6]

For all its reassuring intent, however, the flipside of 'Home' was perennial displacement. Ranajit Guha underlines the everyday irony of forging a sense of belonging out of alien territory; hence, the tenacious hold of 'a place far away' that could alleviate the 'indefinite and pervasive anxiety about being lost in the empire'.[7] An anonymous Hong Kong colonist conceded in 1934 that it was 'because we are separated from our home standards by so much distance that we see only the main outlines of them and these are what we hold on to. They are our landmarks without which we should lose our bearings.' In this scheme of things, the meaning of everyday habits and symbolic gestures acquired unsettling undertones: 'This is why we hear God Save the King so frequently: it is to assure ourselves on every occasion that we are still British and no accident of geography can affect the matter.'[8] Alison Blunt terms this the 'spatial politics of home': the distinctly colonial resonances of a metaphor that at once 'miniaturizes and occasionally intensifies' emotional investments scattered around the globe.[9] Far more than a nostalgic cliché, it underscored the added potency of imagining home 'at a distance of forced exile or voluntary roaming'.[10]

In these settings, home could signal a pervasive, if not always acknowledged disorientation. Those who actually made the return journey were often struck by the unfamiliarity of 'home' (without necessarily denting their convictions) while others found their expectations confirmed by years of cultural conditioning.[11] In 1935, for example, Australia's Robert Menzies kept a diary of his first visit to Britain, reflecting on the unique sense of anticipation among 'those who go "home" to a land they have never seen'.[12] The ambivalence was not confined to returning settlers but also permeated the mixed race 'Anglo-Indian' community of South Asia; the feeling compounded by the ever-present reminders of racial exclusion.[13] Nor was home always deployed as a unifying concept. In New Zealand in the interwar years, recent immigrants from Britain were branded with the mildly pejorative nickname 'homies', reinforcing the familial bonds with Britain while at the same time placing its inhabitants at one remove.[14] Home was never a simple shorthand for a seamless continuum of British peoples, but a means of reconciling wide divergences in outlook, temperament and material conditions with an ever-shifting imperial compact.

Consequently, it acquired added force in times of adversity.[15] In Kenya in the 1950s, the idea of home as the epitome of a transcendent British family remained very much in vogue, indeed increasingly so as the pace of decolonization quickened and the battleground moved into the hearths and homes of its beleaguered constituents. By the time the royal couple took possession of Sagana Lodge in February 1952, the violent incursions of Kikuyu dissidents had arrived on their doorstep – literally so, as the forests of the Mt Kenya foothills became one of the key recruiting areas for the dreaded 'Mau Mau' insurgency. Throughout the early years of bloodshed, familiar depictions of the settler home appeared graphically in British newspapers and newsreels in the gruesome aftermath of Mau Mau farm invasions. The violation of British notions of ordered domesticity became a potent means of mobilizing empathy for the embattled settler community of Kenya, widely depicted as ordinary Britons abroad in need of extraordinary relief measures.

Needless to say, the deteriorating security situation did not augur well for the royal household, and as the Kenyan crisis wore on into the 1950s, the queen's highland residence would remain 'neglected and empty' for more than a decade.[16] The intersecting story of Sagana Lodge, the monarchy and the domestic horror of Mau Mau provides a unique window into the eclipse of Greater Britain in Africa's settler heartland, revealing the limits of home as an enduring symbol of Britain's spurious place in Africa. As the crackdown on the insurgency grew increasingly brutal and arbitrary, the British public's unbridled support for their Kenyan kinsfolk began to unravel.

Accordingly, home became incongruous – *unheimlich* in its jarring familiarity – and an emblem of thwarted Britishness.

THE GIFT: NOVEMBER 1947

Sagana Lodge, the only official royal residence ever established outside the United Kingdom, was designed and built over a period of three years from 1948 to 1950. Now the rural retreat of the president of Kenya, the house is tucked high into the Mt Kenya foothills on a meandering route that runs off the main highway between Nyeri and Nanyuki, the nerve centre of what was once famed and romanticized as Kenya's 'White Highlands'. In Elizabeth's day, the road was unsealed and shrouded in thick forest, the lodge itself perched on a rise overlooking the rapids of the Sagana River. Even today it is remote from tourist itineraries, devoid of signposts and ideally suited as a place of refuge (it was always meant to be difficult to find). Few vehicles venture along the narrow turns that wind towards the unadorned entrance, and a surly reception awaits those who venture too close.

It was the British governor of Kenya, Sir Philip Mitchell, who fell upon the idea of bestowing a remote mountain cottage on the royal couple to celebrate their forthcoming nuptials.[17] The official engagement of July 1947 came only three months after the royal family's African sojourn, with memories still fresh of the saturated press coverage. There is therefore every reason to assume that the gift was inspired directly by Princess Elizabeth's own 'homecoming' reflections in her Cape Town broadcast. It was during a meeting of his Executive Council that Mitchell unveiled the idea that 'the presentation should be made to HRH Princess Elizabeth of a camp or Lodge to be built in the National Park, to be named "Princess Elizabeth Camp"'.[18] He subsequently flew to London to ascertain the princess's pleasure and seek the king's permission – on the understanding that the gift implied 'no obligation to come out' on a regular basis.[19]

But it was not merely the happenstance of Elizabeth's Cape Town speech that inspired the governor to embark on such a novel undertaking. Nearing the end of a career spanning forty years of uninterrupted service, Mitchell was greatly exercised by the adverse prospects for European colonial rule the world over and in Africa in particular – given the recent acceleration of the timetable for Indian independence. In a lengthy despatch to Colonial Secretary Arthur Creech-Jones in May 1947, he expounded at length on the crisis of confidence that was insidiously undermining the entire empire project. 'British imperialism', he lamented, once an 'expression of faith and purpose' had become a widespread term of abuse. Above all he detected a 'growing loss of confidence in the permanence of British sponsored institutions' overseas, which greatly hampered colonial administrators in carrying out their weighty task. He urged his political superiors to summon all due 'fortitude and tenacity of purpose' and to recognize that 'Colonial responsibilities are not a disreputable inheritance from a not very respectable past, but an honourable task of the greatest importance and significance'.[20] In a public address at Nakuru the following year, he was even more forthright: 'This is a British country ... Kenya and its people are forever British.'[21] Only by assuming 'the will to exercise authority' and eschewing any 'apologetic or defensive attitude' could the British work towards a 'restored and reinvigorated belief in ourselves'.[22]

What better way of restoring that self-belief than erecting a royal residence in the empire's African interior? Throughout the early design

Figure 5.2 Sagana Lodge, the Kenyan Colonial Government's wedding gift to the royal couple in 1947, situated in the Nyeri district of the Central Highlands, pictured just prior to their arrival in February 1952. Source: Universal Images Group Editorial/Getty Images.

and planning phase, the emphasis was on simplicity – aimed at producing something raw and rugged in the spirit of Mitchell's initial concept of a royal 'camp'. As far as decorum would allow, the royals should be placed in an unmistakably colonial setting in the guise of hardy pioneers. The proposal subsequently went through several iterations under a variety of labels – from the original 'Princess Elizabeth Camp' to Princess Lodge, Forest Lodge and the Royal Hunting Lodge before finally settling on 'Sagana Lodge' to evoke the surrounding river landscape. Two core requirements remained paramount: that the home should be constructed from local materials in the style of an early settler's dwelling; and that there should be ready access to wild game. It would take the best part of three years to find a suitable location, construct the buildings and complete the extensive landscaping. The result was a relatively modest home built of local cedar logs on a stone foundation with a shingle roof, posing a striking contrast to Balmoral in its frontier simplicity and romantic log-cabin ambience. As far as can be ascertained, the cost was borne by the Kenyan Colonial Government although budgetary details are not to be found among the scant documentation available.[23]

As the lodge neared completion towards the end of 1950, Governor Mitchell tentatively probed the possibility of luring the royal couple out for an official handover. His initial overtures were dismissed out of hand by senior palace officials, who could only concede that their majesties 'hoped' to take possession of the lodge at 'some time or other'; but the idea of them making a flying visit to Kenya in the foreseeable future was 'so remote as to be almost a certain loser'.[24] The Colonial Office strongly advised Mitchell to refrain from issuing any formal invitation or otherwise raise public expectations, and to content himself with sending the princess a selection of high-quality photographs. Mitchell duly complied but found it hard to suppress his irritation: 'You will appreciate that the present has got to be presented some time or other and the people out here will expect to be told that it has been presented in this way.'[25]

It was around this time that a landmark study of the culture of gift-giving was published by the leading French sociologist Marcel Mauss (translated into English four years later as *The Gift*) in which he argued that there could be no such thing as a 'free gift' because 'in reality they are given and reciprocated obligatorily'.[26] It was the evident lack of any sense of reciprocal obligation on the part of Buckingham Palace that stoked Governor Mitchell's ire. Clearly, the wedding present was pregnant with expectation, not in the sense of material reward so much as a licence to tap into the aura of royalty for essentially self-interested purposes. At a time of violent upheavals in Madagascar and drawn-out colonial wars in French Indochina and Dutch Indonesia, Europe's embattled imperial project brought unwelcome tidings for those heavily invested in its survival. That these wider ructions played directly on the minds of Kenyan settlers is evident from the *East African Standard*'s editorial on the occasion of Elizabeth and Philip's wedding day on 20 November 1947:

> In a generation which is seeing the conception of Empire change character and which finds that Empire assailed in peace by troubles as serious as ever beset it in war, the one constant factor is the British Royal Family, its position unchallenged, its hold on the affections of the people more firm than ever, its existence the dynastic symbol which gives meaning and purpose to the conception of a Family of Nations.[27]

To the extent that the gift had a reciprocal nature, it was about reinforcing this 'one constant factor'. Though rarely spelt out in such bald terms, the establishment of a royal household in Kenya's settler stronghold brought a much-needed dose of dynastic staying power: an 'unchallenged' presence, at once emotionally reassuring and politically empowering. Above all, the wedding gift was designed to harness the unrivalled capacity of the younger generation of royals to stir the 'affections of the people', thereby sealing the all-important emotional bond with metropolitan Britain. Securing a return on the investment, however, required that the new tenants put in an appearance – ideally at regular intervals. For all its ingenious conception, Sagana Lodge risked backfiring should the house remain conspicuously unoccupied for too long.

THE VISIT: FEBRUARY 1952

It would be a further two years before room could be found in the royal itinerary for the princess and the duke to take possession of Sagana Lodge – en route to their abortive tour of Australia and New Zealand in February 1952. The seven-day stopover was divided into two parts, with official duties reserved for the first weekend in Nairobi, followed by an informal retreat to the royal couple's new highland home. Nairobi rolled out the full fanfare of a royal tour, with an elaborate welcome reception, garden parties for local worthies, a hospital visit, an inspection of the regiment and a game drive into nearby Nairobi National Park. The bunting-lined streets swelled with onlookers seeking the best vantage point to catch a glimpse of the royal motorcade. The *East African Standard* described how the royals could observe 'the story of a British colony in the making' in the roadside architecture as they journeyed into town, from the 'mouldering corrugated iron shacks' of the earliest settlers to the bustle of iron and steel in the city centre:

> Here for the Princess and the Duke to see is what remains of the conditions in which men and women pioneered a new land and enjoyed full and wonderful and satisfying lives. The buildings in which they worked and lived, tawdry and mean now but once the pride of achievement, are still there in numbers. Emerging from them, built upon them, is the promise of a new modern capital city made in faith, the latest symbol of a great tradition.[28]

The theme of homemaking remained at the forefront of the entire visit. The highlight was the official presentation of the wedding gift at a luncheon party at the New Stanley Hotel, where the princess was presented with a wrought iron key and embossed title deed with a decidedly medieval touch; the wax seal, vellum parchment, extravagant calligraphy and archaic language belying the sheer novelty of the occasion. As if to underline the theme of permanence, the deed itself was published in a full-page insert in the *East African Standard*, announcing that Kenya's land tenure laws had been set aside so as to grant the royals unalienable rights in perpetuity.[29] Much was made of the princess's official words of gratitude, and the spontaneous cheer when she expressed her hope that she and the duke would come back to the house often.[30] In local reports 'hope' was quickly transposed to a 'promise', such was the weight of expectation on a young couple destined – or so it seemed to their hosts – to become familiar faces in the district.[31]

The second half of the tour, scheduled over four days from Sunday 3 February, was ostensibly 'informal' to allow the royal couple to travel north to Nyeri and relax in the surrounds of their new home. Although no official engagements were scheduled, a busy programme awaited them nonetheless. Pursued by a scrum of local and international pressmen, the princess and the duke engaged in an array of activities designed to portray them as any other pioneer couple in the 'White Highlands'. On their first night they attended evensong at the Anglican church at Naromoru – a squat, buttressed stone edifice that would not have looked out of place in an English market town. The following afternoon they attended a polo chukka between Nyeri and Nanyuki, where the duke took turns playing for either side while the princess filmed proceedings from the clubhouse amid gaping stares from the local rural gentry. And most famously, they spent a night at the

nearby Treetops Hotel, viewing and filming the nocturnal game that fre-
quented the adjacent watering hole.

Their four-day sojourn in the highlands was an exercise in carefully
staged ambiguity, depicted alternately as a long-awaited homecoming
and a celebrity visit from overseas. Much was made in press commentary
of the style and setting of the lodge itself, bearing 'many features typical
of Kenya pioneer homes'.[32] 'For a few days', remarked the *Daily Express*,
the royal couple would 'live as cottagers' – clearly with a view to
assimilating the royals into the local surrounds. Glasgow's *Evening
News* similarly rejoiced in the fact that 'the Princess and Duke will live
far from the bustle and panoply of a Royal visit. They will live as an
ordinary Kenya couple.'[33] The contrast with the formal trappings of
monarchy was a constant reference point, as in the *Daily Graphic*'s
observation: 'Built of cedarwood and stone, with a shingle roof, typical
of many country homes in Kenya, it is a far cry from the palatial
residences associated with the Royal family.'[34] The *East African
Standard* spelt out the desired effect:

> Until they leave the Colony on Thursday they will stay in their home on the
> foothills of Mt Kenya, quietly and privately, just like any other residents in
> the country. They will be able to enjoy the pleasures of their garden, the
> comfort of a log fire in the evening, a tussle with the trout in the pools of the
> Sagana before breakfast ... That is how the people of Kenya would like
> them to enjoy the gift they gave the Princess and the Duke. That is the kind
> of simple and care-free happiness they hoped they would have in the simple
> home in the forest.[35]

They also clearly hoped to telegraph the glad tidings of order, stability
and undisputed sovereignty as far and wide as possible. In that sense,
the royal couple furnished ample recompense for their hosts'
generosity.

Equally prevalent was the depiction of Kenya as an extension of Greater
Britain. For all the rustic pioneer ambience, readers were constantly
reminded of the uncanny resemblance to 'the simplicity of an English
cottage home'. The Nyeri Polo Club was described as 'a rough wooden
pavilion such as you find on village cricket greens'.[36] *Home Chat* magazine
extended the comparison to the wider landscape and scenery: 'Much of
Kenya resembles our own English countryside, but the low white buildings,
the rolling plantations of sugar, coffee and tea, the great cedar woods and
the ostrich farms will remind the Princess that she is still in Africa.'[37] The
conflation of English and African essences – the familiar with a touch of the

exotic – was epitomized by Britain's oldest weekly women's magazine, *The Lady*:

> Princess Lodge is a bungalow in an old-world English garden of rose trees and dahlias, a few yards from a well-stocked trout stream. And yet it is in the heart of the highlands of Kenya in East Africa . . . The town of Nyeri, where the Princess has her East African home, has an equable climate where you can wear ordinary English cotton frocks in the summer and light tailored suits in the winter although it is only twenty miles from the Equator.

Modern-day visitors to the Nyeri district would struggle to recognize the propinquity of old England, devoid as it is of any real physical resemblance. But in 1952, sheer necessity lent the comparison a certain plausibility. The easy, mutual accommodation between English and African elements was crucial to naturalizing Elizabeth's – and by extension the entire settler community's – tenuous claim to belonging. Depicting Nyeri as an exotic homeland combined the enduring certainties of the old world with the requisite dose of romance and wonder. African fauna furnished the key ingredient, with one report describing a recent invasion of the couple's home by a startled leopard (somehow locking itself in a bathroom) and a baboon that helped itself to several volumes in the royal library.[38] In this scheme of things, Elizabeth's rural English idyll was disturbed only by 'the cries of birds in the woods and the distant rumble of herds of elephants as they crash their way through the undergrowth'.[39]

That this was not merely an English but a British fantasy can be gleaned from Scottish accounts of the visit. Not to be outdone by Fleet Street, the Aberdeen *Press and Journal* emphasized Elizabeth's Scottish maternal heritage and her husband's Edinburgh dukedom in proclaiming: 'What could be more in accord than that Princess Elizabeth should own a residence in the Highlands? The fact that these Highlands are situated in Kenya, and not in Scotland, seems almost immaterial from a social point of view, because so large a number of Scotland's sons and daughters are also situated in Kenya.' Again, it was the 'antics of the monkeys' and the 'occasional hungry leopard in the moonlight' that served to 'remind one that it is Africa', but the overriding projection of a Greater Britain provided the dominant register: 'No doubt the many kilts to be seen, and the jigs, reels and Strathspeys to be danced during the festivities held in their honour will make them feel more than ever at home.'[40]

The obsession with the royals' comfort and convenience – that they should feel 'at home' – was far more than a matter of everyday hospitality. It was symptomatic of deeper anxieties about the legitimacy of settler colonialism at a time of quickening anti-colonial convulsions. Indications of Britain's dwindling imperial resolve cast a shadow on Elizabeth and Philip's African sojourn in ways that had not affected the royal tour of South Africa only five years earlier. On the very day of their arrival, for example, the *East African Standard* published a prominent piece by Lord Beaverbrook entitled 'Do you care if we lose the empire?', effectively calling on loyal Britons the world over to rally to the defence of their besieged belief system.[41] Numerous press reports registered a sense that the settler colonial order itself was becoming vaguely anachronistic, often with nostalgic references to the white Kenyan oligarchy as 'the last of its kind'.[42]

As if to counter this, older folkloric elements of muscular pioneers taming rugged territory were toned down to make way for a new emphasis on domestic order. Elizabeth's womanly stamp in the family home was constantly fore-grounded, with the duke playing more of a background role than perhaps even he was accustomed. This was particularly prominent at the official turning-of-the-key ceremony at the lodge on Sunday 3 February, where press photo-graphers eagerly snapped the solitary princess entering her humble abode (assisted only by the governor who stepped in when the key jammed), while her husband was kept well out of shot. Press correspondents waxed freely about 'Princess Lodge', the 'Princess at her Kenya Home', 'Princess's Highland Home in Kenya', 'This is the Princess's home on the equator' and 'This is the house that Kenya built for a Princess', as though it were a birthday rather than a wedding present.[43] Elizabeth's feminine role as homemaker became central to framing the lodge as a shared symbol of a British way of life – the sovereign-mother moving in, echoing earlier, nineteenth-century depictions of women as the symbol of 'the domestic, social and moral value legitimating imperial rule'.[44] One English press correspondent explained the comfort this brought to a white community displaced from their original homes:

> The Kenyan's love for Britain is measureless; the moment he arrives back in the colony after a leave in the Old Country he begins to economise and save up for his next leave, which may be two, or three or five years ahead. Not to go home for a leave is unthinkable. So you can imagine the real joy these people are experiencing just now, when, symbolically through a Royal couple, Britain herself is paying them a visit.[45]

These impulses were duly relayed back to Britain, reinforcing the message that Kenya was still safe for colonization. The East Africa Office in London experienced record levels of interest from prospective new settlers during the week of the royal visit, and was 'inundated' by press correspondents seeking background information on the colony.[46]

Figure 5.3 Princess Elizabeth takes possession of her Kenyan home on Sunday 3 February 1952, assisted by the British governor of Kenya, Sir Philip Mitchell. Source: Hulton Archive/Getty Images.

The surest sign that the Royal tenure spoke principally to these wider British affinities can be seen in the almost complete absence of African peoples from the itinerary. Even allowing for the settlers' political and social dominance at the time, the absence of an Indigenous ceremonial component is striking – compared with the 1947 royal tour of South Africa, for example, or Elizabeth's later visit to Australia and New Zealand in 1953–4. Although she was greeted on the tarmac in Nairobi by a three-year-old African boy, 'Prince Charles Bin Salim' (born on the same day as his royal namesake) and despite formal introductions to 'local personalities' and 'native notabilities' at Nairobi garden parties (none of whom were sufficiently notable to be named in press captions), no provision was made for Elizabeth and Philip to meet any Kikuyu in their new neighbourhood.[47]

Moreover, this was rarely remarked upon by visiting journalists, seemingly obsessed with the image of royalty as the pinnacle of a white British family. One notable exception was Arthur Brittenden, correspondent of the left-leaning *News Chronicle* who remarked on the 'thousands of Africans' who waited nearly four hours at a roadside vantage point to watch the royal convoy pass through to Treetops, only to be ushered aside by police when thirty white women made a late appearance for front-row viewing. In a similar vein, his report on the Monday afternoon polo match stressed how Kikuyu spectators were confined to the far end of the ground, with only Europeans permitted near the clubhouse. Enquiring about this to a club official he was frankly told: 'Of course it is not that we don't want them ... these chaps who come to watch the polo are among the best types of African, you know ... But we have got to be careful, you understand. We don't want to risk bad-hats getting round the club house.'[48]

The shocking news of the death of King George VI, which percolated through the community on the afternoon and evening of Wednesday 6 February, had the immediate effect of cutting short the royal visit by a day. The press corps magnified the moment as somehow emblematic of the special bond forged with a princess 'so near to home'.[49] Several overlapping narratives proliferated as the royals staged their hurried return to England. Suddenly African perspectives were given prominence, with several reports depicting crowds of crestfallen Kikuyu lining the roadside murmuring 'Shauri mbya kabishe' ('very worst affair').[50] Many accounts stressed the fact that the princess was camped up a tree at the time of her father's death (though she would not learn of his fate until she had returned to Sagana Lodge the following day); the jungle ambience furnishing a fitting backdrop for an imperial succession.[51] Most prominent of all was the story of the new queen's courage and stoicism in the face of the staggering news, replete with some extraordinary embellishments. The *Daily Mirror* relayed whispered scenes in the royals' private quarters at Sagana, with the duke tasked with the burden of 'whispering it on' to his wife: 'For an instant the Princess stood quite still. Then, she turned her back and hands to her face burst into tears.'[52] It was a complete fabrication, fuelled by the tremendous public appetite for the intimate details of the household drama.

The new queen's homeward journey seemed particularly ripe for reflection on the global reach of the British monarchy. The first destination was the small settlement of Nanyuki – an hour's drive north of Nyeri – where an aircraft was waiting to spirit the royal couple out of Kenya. The town had been richly decorated for her anticipated arrival the following day, which made for some poignant contrasts. 'I have just returned from the most moving and historical sight I suppose I shall ever see', wrote one local resident to her sister in Somerset, 'our new young Queen, with her husband at her side, driving slowly through the gaily decorated and beflagged main street of little Nanyuki to board a plane for ... their return home'.[53] From this humble, small-town ambience the press eagerly traced the royal progress back to Britain via a change of aircraft in Uganda, with the *Evening Standard* taking in the full panorama of romance and pathos:

> In their anxious attendance on her arrival millions of people travelled with the Queen in their imagination – over Kenya, Uganda, the Sudan and Libya; across the Mediterranean, over Naples, Rome and the cloud-piercing Alpine peaks ... The drama of the journey home has demonstrated also the closeness to the Homeland of all those Colonial territories of the Empire which the airlines link. Since the King's death, messages have been coming so fast from the Colonies that it has required a special staff at the Colonial Office to deal with them ... from tribes, clubs, racial, political and national organisations, in the four corners of the world. The Queen, as her car bore her through the sympathetic murmur of the crowds to Nanyuki airfield was not, it seems, so far from home after all.[54]

This completed the arc from Elizabeth's Cape Town essay to her procurement of a Kenyan dwelling on the eve of her succession. The symbolism of the first British monarch 'to make her initial entry into her country by airplane' signalled a new age when 'British strength will inevitably move from this island to the wide Empire of which our homeland is the heart'. Even prior to landing she had already been proclaimed 'Queen of this Realm and of all Her other Realms and Territories' – 'a neat way', as David Edgerton observes, 'to avoid specifying what her realms actually were'.[55]

In the wake of her return journey, the question was widely posed: whether the queen must 'continue to be permanently resident in London?' Suggestions were raised from as far afield as Australia about the possible procurement of royal residences in other parts of the globe – an idea that received ringing endorsement from the *Sunday Express*:

> All over the Empire our peoples are beginning to say that the Monarch who is the constitutional ruler of all of them should consider dwelling among each of them in turn. The presentation of the Sagana Lodge, in Kenya, to the Queen marked the new trend of thought ... What a tremendous change for the new Queen to inaugurate.[56]

As far as Her Majesty's loyal white subjects in Kenya were concerned, the importance of regular future visits remained paramount. There was inevitable rejoicing when her parting words to the local district commissioner in Nyeri were made public: 'Even though things are different now, we will be back.'[57] She followed this up days later with a personal message to the Kenyan people, thanking them for their many kindnesses and above all for the gift of the lodge 'which surpassed our keenest expectations, and to which we greatly hope to return'. The governor dutifully replied: 'It is the earnest hope of every one of your Majesty's loyal subjects in Kenya that they may have the great happiness of other visits.'[58]

HORRORS OF HEARTH AND HOME: MAU MAU

The royal family was destined never to return to the home so painstakingly prepared for them in the Mt Kenya foothills. Though their legal tenure would persist for a further eleven years, the two solitary evenings in February 1952 (separated by a night in a tree house) were to be the sum total of their occupancy. The failure of Sagana Lodge to live up to its overfreighted expectations seems spectacular in retrospect, yet the reasons are not difficult to discern. The year 1952 would bring the first deadly portents that Britain's colonial tenure in Kenya would shortly be overwhelmed, the tide of events transforming the image of the 'White Highlands' from an English haven into something worthy of Conrad.[59]

The name 'Mau Mau' has become so synonymous with the brutal pattern of Kikuyu resistance and ruthless counter-insurgency in Kenya's independence struggle that it can be difficult to capture its extraordinary intricacy and complexity.[60] Long-standing Kikuyu land grievances had simmered for decades, exacerbated by mounting post-war tensions within Kikuyu society caused by the displacement of tenant farmers and a rise in urban militancy. Mau Mau emerged in the late 1940s as an offshoot of the comparatively moderate Kenyan African Union (KAU), whose practice of administering oaths to elite members was taken up by more militant elements and adapted for the purposes of mass mobilization among the urban poor of Nairobi.[61] By 1950, reports of enforced oathing and intimidation of farm workers had begun to spread throughout the rural districts of Mt Kenya and the Rift Valley. The first large-scale oathing ceremonies were reported in Nyeri in August 1950, although the initial complaints from settlers arose solely from the disruptions to their labour force. The colonial government promptly banned the 'Mau Mau society' and the south Nyeri district became known to the authorities as an area of 'notably belligerent militancy'.[62] From the outset the problem was officially regarded as one of 'bad apples' from the Nairobi slums infiltrating rural areas. Colonial officials spoke of a 'sullen, subversive, anti-government and anti-European feeling' disturbing the karma of otherwise contented, prosperous Kikuyu communities.[63]

By the time of the royal visit in February 1952, these disturbances were already entering a new and bloodier phase. It was only days before Elizabeth and Philip's arrival in 1952 that brewing resentments erupted into open violence between militant and moderate Kikuyu.[64] Eleven cases of arson against government 'headmen', courtroom clerks and others suspected of assisting the police were reported in Nyeri over a period of six nights in late January. Although nobody at this stage was killed, the burning of 'loyalist' homes represented a significant escalation in the pattern of violence and intimidation. The following month, European farms were targeted for the first time when several thousand acres of grazing land were set ablaze in the nearby Nanyuki district.[65] Yet this unnerving backdrop was almost entirely absent from the exhaustive media coverage of the new royal neighbours. It would be several months before Mau Mau posed a threat of direct physical violence to settler families, and the entire matter was therefore treated as an irrelevance as far as the pageantry of the royal progress was concerned.

But it did elicit at least one offhand comment from press correspondent Dudley Hawkins, who revealed the existence of 'a secret society, the Mau Mau', with 'vile ceremonies' and deadly oaths that aimed at 'the complete removal of European methods and influence'. His indifference to the proximity of the danger seems remarkable in retrospect:

> At Sagana Lodge, the Royal visitors will be far removed from these trouble-makers, who prefer the back streets of Nairobi and the fastness of the forests to the farmlands of Nyeri. And if they do hear the drums beating at night, it will be in praise of the fairness of the daughter of Kingi Georgi and extolling the virtues and prowess of her tall Bwana (husband).[66]

Over the ensuing months, attitudes soon changed when a spate of murders targeted loyalist Kikuyu 'headmen' in Nyeri, with further killings of police informers and crown witnesses in neighbouring districts. Nyeri witnessed a killing spree against loyalist Kikuyu in August 1952, resulting in the imposition of a night-time curfew and the despatch of a fresh detachment of police.[67] Attacks on European farms continued in the Nanyuki area, mainly affecting farm buildings and livestock (causing far greater alarm among the settler community than the rising toll of government-employed Africans).[68] In October, the polo club where the duke and princess had rubbed shoulders with the local white elite was burned to the ground by Mau Mau insurgents.[69] That same month, the arrival in Nairobi of new governor Sir Evelyn Baring was quickly followed by the assassination of the paramount loyalist Kikuyu chief Waruhiu wa Kunga on the outskirts of the capital. A state of emergency was hastily declared that would continue for the remainder of the decade. In these circumstances, talk of a follow-up royal visit to Sagana Lodge was entirely out of the question. Within the space of only a year, the tranquillity of the queen's forest home would be disturbed, not by the romantic rumble of elephant herds but the relentless sorties of RAF Lincoln bombers, determined to flush out the insurgents from their mountain hideouts.[70]

But the idea of home continued to provide the emotional lodestone of the escalating crisis, particularly towards the end of 1952 when Mau Mau violence turned sporadically on the settlers themselves. The first European to fall prey was the semi-recluse Eric Bowker, hacked to death in his bath on a remote farm only a week after the emergency was declared on 27 October. A month later a middle-aged couple taking tea in their sitting room were attacked with pangas on a property near Thompson's Falls. This was soon followed by the murder of two settlers in the Wanjohi Valley, Dick Bingley and Charles Fergusson, who had just sat down for their evening meal in pyjamas and dressing gowns. It was these intricate details of domestic order – the bath, the tea set, the bloodied night robe – that featured prominently in press reports, abhorring the inherent disorder of blade-wielding Africans turning the tables on their colonial masters.[71] Widely circulated stories of household betrayal, in which African servants were often found to have been secretly 'oathed' to Mau Mau, fuelled a pervasive dread among rural whites. As Graham Greene famously quipped, for the settler who had 'established that peculiarly English dream of "a home from home" . . . it was as though Jeeves had taken to the jungle'.[72] It was an inversion of the natural scheme of things, laying bare the vulnerability of the domestic inner sanctum – an image freely deployed by the *East African Standard* to convey the settlers' innermost fears: 'The home, gathered together so laboriously through good seas and bad over a long period of years, may be found smashed to matchwood and fragments of glass and crockery.'[73]

It was also the home front that furnished the emergency's first tale of stoic settler fortitude. On 3 January 1953, with the panic over the Bingley–Fergusson killings still palpable, two elderly white Nyeri women, Kitty Hesselberger and Dorothy Raynes-Simpson, were besieged in their home by half a dozen or more night-time assailants. Alerted by the nervous demeanour of their domestic servant, the women transformed their sitting room into a makeshift redoubt and grimly awaited their attackers. When the assault came, it was beaten back by successive volleys of shotgun fire that left three Kikuyu dead and a fourth badly wounded. The two women were promptly hailed as the standard bearers of settler grit and courage; their fighting spirit in the sitting room epitomizing the sanctity of domestic space. It was in many respects a reprise of stirring tales from the Sepoy uprising in Lucknow almost a hundred years earlier, which had also stressed the vulnerability of white women defending their homes.[74] Similarly in Kenya these horrors of hearth and home would become central to settler perceptions of the insurgency, buttressing their determination to keep the home safe for white civilization.

Such framing was not merely for settler consumption but became crucial for mobilizing empathy among white Britons the world over. Domestic objects could be depicted in such a way as to signal an 'expanded boundary of the self', tying embattled settlers into an elaborate system of moral obligation and mutual regard.[75] As Wendy Webster has shown, English newspapers in particular conveyed details of warm domestic interiors with 'the comfort of good books and nice things', 'Christmas cards arranged on the mantelpiece' and 'plucky white British women, staying on despite the danger'.[76] A particular fetish was the armed frontierswoman in slacks with a holster on her hip, whom the *Daily Express* likened to British soldiers dropped behind enemy lines in the Second World War. The appeal to metropolitan sensibilities was none too subtle: 'Britain! ... Today give your hearts to the women of Kenya. They are surrounded by menace but they do not budge.'[77] In these and countless other ways, the enormity of the situation was routinely and graphically conveyed to British audiences in the gruesome aftermath of Mau Mau visitations – a familiar world rent asunder by base depravity. Just as the landscape of Sagana Lodge had been likened to the Scottish Highlands or an English village green, so too the homes of Mau Mau victims were domesticated for British readers through depictions of the 'lovely, English-looking garden', or the 'little corner of Somerset in the foothills of the Aberdare mountains'.[78] The Colonial Office went out of its way to emphasize women, home fronts and well-tended English lawns, anxious to deflect media attention from the violent excesses of counter-insurgency while at the same time urging the necessity of harsh retaliatory measures.[79]

Such was the overwhelming media focus on these isolated attacks that it bears recalling that settlers were but a tiny minority of the overall casualties of the insurgency. Daniel Branch estimates that more than 90 per cent of the officially acknowledged death toll were Kikuyu (many of whom fell victim to fellow Kikuyu), while the severity of Mau Mau violence tended to be at its most indiscriminate and unrestrained between rival Kikuyu adversaries. The massacre of nearly one hundred villagers on Lari Ridge in March 1953 (and the brutal reprisals that followed) were described by one influential observer as the 'definitive horror' of the Mau Mau experience.[80] The moderate Kikuyu reformer, Harry Thuku, wondered 'why it is that when loyal Africans are killed by Mau Mau there are no questions in the House of Commons?'[81]

It was black on white violence that absorbed the attention of major news outlets and shaped the political response.[82] Months before Mau Mau began invading settler homes, London press agencies were already predicting a wholesale massacre of Kenya's rural whites.[83] Elspeth Huxley's fictionalized account, *A Thing to Love* (1954), revolved around a Mau Mau plot to annihilate the entire settler population (on that most sacred of homely rituals, Christmas Day).[84] Visiting parliamentary delegations throughout the early 1950s were informed that the 'ultimate massacre of the European population of the Colony' remained the abiding obsession of the Mau Mau movement.[85] That these apocalyptic visions never materialized (a total of thirty-four settlers were murdered during the seven years of the emergency) somehow eluded the media's attention, such was the 'pathological atmosphere' that enveloped the crisis in its early stages.[86] The symbolic power of Mau Mau farm invasions lay not in their quantity but their quality: their capacity to breed fear at the emotional hub of settler colonialism and galvanize panic by way of response.

Of all the reported Mau Mau 'outrages', the one that most effectively harnessed the symbolism of the settler home was the brutal murder of the Ruck family in the Kinangop region on 24 January 1953. Here too, the violence was perpetrated at night (its victims again in nightdress) with the collusion of a Kikuyu employee who lured Roger Ruck from the house to assist with a concocted emergency. Ruck was promptly overwhelmed by the blades of his attackers, his agonized screams summoning a loyal African farm hand who was also cut down. At some point, his wife Esme emerged from the house with a shotgun, but she had no time to discharge her weapon. All three were left lying mutilated in the yard as the perpetrators proceeded to ransack the house for supplies, which lead them to the double bolted bedroom door of six-year-old Michael Ruck – setting the scene for what would become the definitive popular symbol of Mau Mau savagery. Newspapers declined to publish the grisly photos of the blond boy slain in his bed, but images were widely circulated of his room in disarray – the blood-stained linen, the toy train tracks scattered across the floor furnishing a vivid portrait of white domestic harmony defiled.[87] Esme Ruck's final, anguished letters to her mother were syndicated to the press, providing a further window into a familiar world ruthlessly rent asunder.[88]

The Ruck case distilled in a single episode the pervasive symbolism of decent white Britons under siege. As a healthy, resourceful, good-looking young family who played an active role in the local community, they were the kind of people in whom 'the future of white settler society was embodied'.[89] As one contemporary account noted, 'if the country had wished to portray itself in the most favourable light, the Rucks would have been the family unit to portray on the posters'.[90] And in a sense, this was to be their fate in death. Mrs Ruck's medical work with the local Kikuyu in the clinic she ran on the farm enhanced the image of selfless dedication to a cause larger than themselves. Contemporary newsreels of their Nairobi funeral described them simply as 'a British family brutally murdered by the Mau Mau'.[91] The sustained media focus on one family diverted attention from the murders of two other families only a few months later – one Italian, the other from the Seychelles – neither of which generated anything like the same horror and indignation. It was the peculiarly racial, and specifically British, conception of a community in dire peril that furnished the Ruck murders with heightened significance. David Anderson describes it as the one incident that channelled 'the full range and fury of the settler community' in the early months of the crisis by virtue of the complexion of the victims themselves – 'an established, vigorous white family ... of British stock'.[92]

Much the same can be said of the emotional reaction in Britain where the Rucks made front page news, at once sensationalizing and familiarizing the murders. Once again it was 'that English-looking lawn' that brought the scene closer to home, amplified by the fact that Esme Ruck was the niece of Lord Hankey – the one-time doyen of Whitehall – thus tying her tragedy into local networks of preferment and esteem.[93] The *Daily Mail*'s front-page editorial drew attention to the contagion emanating from within – the handiwork of home-grown 'left-wing intellectuals' whose corrosive influence had 'penetrated' the Kenyan highlands and 'persuaded the natives they are being "exploited"'. The final column of the report was headed by a single, all-embracing term, highlighted in bold face: 'British'.[94] No elaboration was needed to convey what was ultimately at stake.

HANDING OVER THE KEYS: THE LIMITS OF EMPATHY

While these reports underscored a deeper convergence between metropolitan and settler loyalties, they would exert an increasingly intolerable strain as the human and material costs of the counter-insurgency mounted. For all the ready sympathy for the suffering of individual families, the depiction of home comforts in a forbidding setting ultimately had the effect of placing the settler community at one remove. Over time, a certain distancing can be discerned, never fully articulated and in no sense displacing the more commonplace expression of racialized empathy. Settler demands for more aggressive and indiscriminate action against the Kikuyu would strike an increasingly discordant note with liberal opinion in Britain. Emergency regulations such as the practice of 'collective punishment' on entire villages and the extraordinary range of offences that qualified for the death penalty seemed wholly out of proportion to the threat posed. The improbably high number of insurgents shot while 'attempting to escape' raised concerns among key sections of metropolitan opinion about the atrocities perpetrated in Britain's name. Clinical experts in Britain also voiced objections to the portrayal of Mau Mau as a collective psychosis, pointing instead to the experience of 'deprivation or oppression' at the root of the crisis.[95]

For all the revelations in recent scholarship about the shocking severity of the crackdown, there was plenty on show for the 1950s newspaper-reading public amid murmured allegations of torture, summary executions and arbitrary justice. As Erik Linstrum argues, although public engagement with these darker implications was 'uneven, fragmented and sporadic', there can be no doubt that harsh measures of repression 'inevitably reverberated in the metropole one way or another' via the inner-workings of multiple interlocking 'circles of knowing'.[96] Highly publicized visits to Kenya by left-wing MPs such as Fenner Brockway in 1952 and Barbara Castle in 1955 helped to raise awareness of the consequences of siding wholesale with Kenyan settlers. Though their efforts were frequently dismissed as 'the lunatic fringe of the extreme left', they nevertheless fed into wider circulations of rumour, speculation and official denials that the defence of the realm in Kenya was not proceeding as planned.[97]

Joanna Lewis's study of mass circulation tabloids has brought to light the extent of metropolitan criticism of the methods and mindset of the counter-insurgency – especially in the pages of the *Daily Mirror*. One especially prominent voice was the liberal correspondent James Cameron, whose early dispatches from Kenya in late 1952 confronted readers with the damaging effects on Britain's reputation, inspiring one *Mirror* editorial to proclaim: 'What are we doing in Africa? What are we doing in Kenya? In our unhappy, furious folly, what are we doing to ourselves?'[98] It was the 'self-corrupting' dimension of the Kenyan quagmire – its capacity to tarnish the idea of Britain itself – that invested it with a special urgency to key sections of the British public. 'We have another stake in the country, our good name',

Cameron averred in his 'Open letter' to Sir Evelyn Baring published on 12 December, calling on the governor to 'let the settlers howl . . . We shall be for you, and there are more of us than there are of them.'[99] It was both a foretaste of a widening rift in metropolitan sympathies, as well as a throwback to the 'Burkean qualms' of the eighteenth century about the empire's corrosive effects on the national character – ever liable to sully Britain's 'good name'.[100]

To be sure, the *Daily Mirror* was a minority voice in 1952 – albeit one with the highest circulation figures in the country – and there remained a pronounced gap 'between what reporters knew, and what they communicated to the public'.[101] Many news outlets continued to preach solidarity with fellow Britons overseas, conveying the moral stakes of Mau Mau in terms that aligned largely with settler interests.[102] But crucially, these sentiments had to contend with the steady accumulation of doubt, as evidence of so-called 'excesses' on the part of settlers and the security forces piled up. Journalists typically erred on the side of understatement, anxious not to be seen to be 'taking sides' or compromising their professional detachment.[103] In December 1953, for example, *The Times* cautioned that while 'all the sternness in the world is admirable' there was no excuse for fostering the atmosphere 'of an afternoon's shoot or pig-sticking match'.[104] The slow drip of allegations was sufficiently damaging to monopolize all of the creative energies of the British and Kenyan propaganda agencies in their efforts to reverse the tide of 'public alarm' (as the Colonial Office termed it).[105]

Even those charged with carrying out the systematic repression of Kikuyu dissent could find themselves questioning their loyalties, particularly as the settlers grew increasingly reckless in their demands for wholesale repression. Upon taking charge of the counter-insurgency campaign in June 1953, General 'Bobbie' Erskine recorded his first impressions of Kenya: 'A sunny land for shady people.' Over time, and as he grew more familiar with settler attitudes and behaviour, his contempt bristled. 'I hate the guts of them all', he confided to his wife in January 1954, 'they are all middle-class sluts'.[106] Churchill himself was uncomfortable with the Kenyan judicial system's frequent recourse to the gallows, recognizing the danger that settler justice might diminish Britain's standing in the world.[107] While he sympathized privately with the settlers' predicament, he pointedly declined to issue any public message of support.[108]

There is also every indication that the muted suspicion cut both ways. For the settlers, too, episodes such as the Ruck murders could elicit loud cries of dismay and disgust at the failure of the 'home country' to recognize their plight. At times this was directed specifically at left-wing and liberal opinion, deemed especially prone to side with 'the terrorists' whenever it suited a queasy conscience. But more commonly it was the entire British body politic that was presumed to be inherently suspect, either by dint of ignorance or treachery. A meeting of the East African Women's League to address the Ruck crisis in Nairobi agreed unanimously that 'one of our chief enemies at the moment is uninformed opinion in England'. Members were urged to write to British newspapers or to bring 'the true facts to England' when journeying 'home'.[109] Mrs Ruck herself had put the case candidly only days before her death, writing privately of her despair at 'the crack-pots in England' who imposed easy moral categories on a complex reality: 'One's got to be a thug to earn their sympathy.'[110] Spontaneous settler meetings throughout the highlands frequently generated as much enmity towards the mother country as the Mau Mau insurgents themselves. A journalist attending one such gathering noted how they were 'only the outward democratic evidence of the stresses and strains going on inside the minds of a free British community exasperated by events and . . . by what they regard as the lack of understanding of their situation among the people of Britain given to a country for which they have done so much'.[111]

The furore over the Ruck murders culminated in an angry demonstration outside Government House in Nairobi on 26 January 1953, where protesters demanded 'swift and decisive action' (implying varying degrees of violent repression) to apprehend the perpetrators (variously identified as Mau Mau, local tenant farmers or the entire Kikuyu population). As the unruly crowd surged towards the main entrance, the ten-foot cedar doors were barricaded from the inside while a cordon of Askaris was hurriedly assembled to prevent a breach of security. The use of African police to guard the entrance to the governor's home provoked an instantaneous uproar: 'There, there, they've given the house over to the f——g n——s, the bloody bastards', cried one particularly unhinged woman who captured, in a single stream of invective, the raw racial investments at stake. In the idiom of settler grievance, 'giving over the house' was tantamount to the wholesale abdication of white authority – a feeling that only intensified when the Sultan of Zanzibar, who had been staying as a guest at Government House, emerged on the balcony to survey the scene, prompting a 'tremendous roar' of further abuse.[112] The entire spectacle exposed the pathology of Black encroachments on the white man's domain – further evidence (as far as the settlers were concerned) of Britain's divided sympathies. It was only when Governor Baring relented to demands that the Askaris be removed that the uproar was finally quelled.

Particularly revealing was the heartfelt rendition of *God Save the Queen* that erupted from the white mob as a mark of their anger and disgust. Michael Blundell – the leader of the self-styled 'liberal' faction in the colonial legislature – recalled how settlers made a habit of bursting into spontaneous hymns of loyalty to the sovereign whenever they 'were about to indulge in some desperate action to demonstrate their contempt for the Colonial Office'.[113] One press report from a communal gathering in the highlands explained the phenomenon thus:

> On occasions when Kenya settlers feel they may be called on to consider, or even to say, things that strain their deep-seated, traditional loyalty, they always start with the National Anthem. It has happened before: it may even happen again. The conscience is eased and by some apparently illogical process, loyalty is strengthened.[114]

Here, the royal connection, so solemnly sealed by Her Majesty's visit twelve months earlier, had taken on a new meaning for white Kenyans. The queen's status as a local resident permitted a subtle inversion of centre and periphery, with the settlers assuming the mantle of Her Majesty's true subjects; their rituals of loyalty doubling as an indictment of the duplicity emanating from 'home'.

In truth, the tensions and contradictions of Kenyan Britishness were not simply the product of irreconcilable differences between settler and metropolitan opinion, although this was one formidable fault line. The 1950s also witnessed major realignments in Kikuyu loyalties, largely due to the extraordinarily repressive measures that saw thousands of innocent men swept up in the infamous 'pipeline' system.[115] The term 'loyalist' in Kikuyu society is an ill-fitting one, implying passionate, even militantly 'British' sensibilities akin to the loyalists of the American Revolution or the Northern Irish 'Troubles'. Kikuyu loyalism was rooted in local community dynamics, not to be conflated with the civic language of Indigenous protest in the older settler colonies harking back to the Victorian era.[116] Here, to be a loyalist was about negotiating complex webs of material and social accommodation with the colonial state – a more recent coinage arising out of the peculiar social tensions of the interwar and post-war era.[117] Nevertheless, as these alignments continued to unravel into the 1950s, a major plank of the settlers' claim to British entitlements was progressively undermined. KAU leader Jomo Kenyatta frequently co-opted the 'home' metaphor for the liberation struggle, explaining wryly to his trial judge Ransley Thacker in January 1952: 'I think if you woke up one morning and if someone had come to your house and said the house belonged to him, you would want to know by what arrangement.'[118]

Among settlers too, the constant carping and recriminations against the mother country were not the sole story of their alienation from the British fold. Substantial segments of settler opinion remained acutely aware of their dependence on metropolitan goodwill and strove to maintain some semblance of pan-British solidarity even as the underlying sense of common purpose imploded. Visiting correspondents reported instances of individual settlers voicing private regret at the more strident public utterances of 'extremists', hoping that the latter 'would not find their way into the newspapers – especially those in Britain though they were afraid they would'.[119] The public disturbances at Government House were openly condemned by some, with one particularly outspoken critic condemning the lawlessness as the very antithesis of Britishness: 'This is a British Colony, and it is expected that the high ideals and principles of the British Way of Life should flow from the British people in this country.'[120] Throughout the 1950s, various liberal policy initiatives cast about for a local version of multi-racialism that might somehow accommodate the survivalist anxieties of the hard-line settler majority. In other words, the stresses and strains of the emergency also prized open internal divisions within the settlers' own distinctive brand of British selfhood – between the fervour of 'race patriotism' and the veneration of bedrock liberties bestowed by the English constitution.

Nor back in Britain can any neat generalizations be employed, where attitudes towards Kenyan settlers continued to fluctuate on a scale from resolute sympathy to outright revulsion – with a substantial measure of indifference in between. These divisions provided the dramatic tension for several 'Mau Mau' feature films in the mid-1950s, with the sanctuary of the settler home providing the central motif. These productions strove to have it both ways: investing heavily in the emotional turmoil of serial outrages against wholesome white families, while taking great umbrage at the arbitrary retribution meted out by way of response. The opening scene of *Simba* (1955) depicted a white, pyjama-clad man falling prey to a random assault by a machete-wielding Kikuyu, headlining the domestic horror story.[121] But the film was equally at pains to condemn brutal acts of reprisal, and to present the entire conflict in terms of an intractable moral dilemma. Foregrounding the contemporary liberal conundrum was virtually guaranteed to garner laudable reviews from the Fleet Street press because it rendered the conflict 'in a way they could most easily understand, and without any direct criticism of British policy or actions'.[122] As Michael Paris notes, *Simba* (like its contemporaries *Safari* and *Something of Value*) raised no overt critique of British settlers' claim to belonging; on the contrary, the heroine played by Virginia McKenna opens her account with the familiar entreaty 'Africa is my home.'[123]

Mau Mau was ultimately defeated by the slow grind of 'Operation Anvil' – relentless, arbitrary and on a scale unprecedented – but it came at the cost of a parallel war of attrition for metropolitan sympathy. The changing political and moral slant of broadcasting, newsreels and particularly the popular press in the late 1950s points to a subtle shift away from earlier imperatives to defend the settler hearth and home as a natural extension of Britain itself. The trajectory was never uniform, with many prominent individuals and pressure groups continuing to lobby for the Kenyan settlers well into the 1960s. But the cumulative effect of repeated affronts to 'British' standards was to de-sentimentalize the connection between Britain and the settler empire. By 1959, even among relatively conservative media outlets, the belief had taken hold that 'where colonial rule had to confront a belligerent African nationalism was no place for an Englishman to be'.[124] It required no great additional leap of the imagination to accept what had seemed unthinkable to the generation of Sir Philip Mitchell only a decade earlier – the prospect of an independent Kenya.

———————◆———————

Kenyan independence in December 1963 produced the anomaly of a British population numbering in the tens of thousands suddenly resident in a foreign country – prompting a twofold response from the British Government. A 1964 amendment to the British Nationality Act ensured that those 'belonging' to the United Kingdom could automatically reclaim their status as British subjects should it be forfeited by the citizenship requirements of the new state – a privilege reserved almost exclusively for white settlers, only a fraction of whom chose Kenyan citizenship in any case. In a similar vein, the government pledged itself to the 'million acre scheme' to aid settlers in selling up their farms for redistribution to Indigenous landholders, allowing them to relocate back to Britain or, more commonly, elsewhere in the residual British world. On the eve of Kenya's independence celebrations, the *East African Standard* recorded the 'inevitable sadness for some of those people of British stock who made their homes in the Kenya of years ago which they regarded as a piece of England abroad'.[125] What had once seemed so simple, even self-explanatory in Princess Elizabeth's coming-of-age broadcast in 1947 was now a delicate problem to be solved.

Emblematic of these abandoned claims was the fate of Sagana Lodge itself. In June 1963, Buckingham Palace was informed of the Kenyan leadership's wishes, supported by the Colonial Office, that Kenya should achieve independence as a republic – raising immediate concerns about the upkeep of a royal lodge in a non-monarchical jurisdiction.[126] A responsibility that had hitherto fallen on the colonial government could hardly be foisted on an independent Kenya poised to relinquish its ties to the Crown.[127] Added to this was the extreme unlikelihood that the queen would find it practically or politically possible to put the lodge to any regular, or even occasional use. The conditions that only sixteen years previously had produced a royal residence in a Kenyan mountain forest had irreversibly been transformed.

In August 1963, palace officials contacted Kenya's last governor, Sir Malcolm MacDonald, requesting that he sound out the incoming Kenyan prime minister (and later president), Jomo Kenyatta, about the possibility of handing the lodge back to the people of Kenya as an official independence 'gift' from the queen.[128] MacDonald duly arranged a confidential meeting, and explained to Kenyatta that the queen had naturally hoped to occupy the house on a more regular basis. But 'the affairs of the world give her ... so little rest or leisure that this pleasant dream has had no chance to come true'. Kenyatta initially expressed some reluctance at the suggestion, as it was widely understood that the lodge was Her Majesty's own cherished private property. But he also saw the potential of Sagana Lodge as a presidential retreat for hosting visiting dignitaries, and soon relented.[129]

Thus, the royal family's one and only official residence outside the United Kingdom was handed back to a man once condemned (and wrongly incarcerated) as the ringleader of Mau Mau terrorism – an ironic outcome for a place intended to keep such encroachments at bay. For all its intended overtones – open, capacious, enduring – the house was ultimately a crude territorial claim that could not withstand the scrutiny of a decolonizing world. Though a special request was sent to Buckingham Palace inviting the queen to attend the 12 December 1963 independence ceremony 'owing to the circumstances touching Sagana Lodge', no exception was made to the convention of sending a royal proxy – lest the stigma of imperial capitulation attach itself to the sovereign herself. Instead, it was the man once kept out of shot at the lodge's inauguration, the Duke of Edinburgh, who finally took centre stage.[130]

The idea that the royal family might become a 'peripatetic Monarchy' with official residences in multiple realms remained a residual fantasy throughout the 1950s and 1960s. Neville Shute's 1953 novel *In the Wet* – published to coincide with the coronation – posited a dystopian Britain of the future ruined by socialism and austerity, no longer safe for a royal family who were duly spirited to Australia where the true essence of Britishness lived on.[131] In the 1960s, the British High Commission in Canada repeatedly

Figure 5.4 The Duke of Edinburgh celebrates Kenyan independence with Jomo Kenyatta, December 1963. Source: Hulton Archive/Getty Images.

lobbied Whitehall to facilitate an official Canadian royal residence to counteract mounting public indifference and early murmurings of republican sentiment.[132] And in 1968, a similar obsession of Australia's high commissioner in London resulted in the selection of a sheep station, 'Bolaro', in the New South Wales Southern Highlands as a prospective royal household in the antipodes (and one which evidently met with the satisfaction of the Duke of Edinburgh). But in each instance the idea appealed more to the imagination than to practical politics, floundering on the intricacies of who should foot the bill.[133]

Today, Sagana Lodge is almost entirely forgotten as a remnant of Queen Elizabeth's personal stake in Britain's overextended frontiers. Although royal jubilees routinely recalled (with unconcealed relish) the African origins of her reign, it was invariably the jungle setting of Treetops Hotel that came to mind, more so than the heavily guarded house on the Chaka-Sagana Road.[134] If collective memory is fundamentally about group durability, this strain of forgetfulness seems entirely in keeping with the post-independence exodus of the Kenyan settler community – those for whom a royal residential keepsake was intended to bring comfort. Their own former homes, many now abandoned, have today become a peculiar source of fascination, nostalgia and more than a twinge of regret for visitors guided into Kenya's Central Highlands on specialized tours. The defining template of Juliet Barnes's *The Ghosts of Happy Valley* (2013) is the 'indefinable mystique' that hangs over the dilapidated houses of a vanished settler clique who departed in droves in the 1960s, seeking a new purchase on British belonging.[135]

Their literary spokesperson, the novelist Elspeth Huxley, lost no time composing an elegy for the spiritually dispossessed. *A Man from Nowhere* (1964) recounts the exploits of a fictionalized Kenyan settler who returns to England with the all-consuming desire to murder the secretary of state for colonial affairs. Securing lodgings as a farm hand on the minister's country estate (and seducing his daughter in the process), he waits patiently for an opportunity to strike. Here, at the domestic hearth so emblematic of settler grievances, retribution seems certain for an embattled white enclave that 'rose in glory, burst in pride, fell in futility and ended in ignominy, forgotten and expunged'.[136] But disenchantment on such a bewildered scale permits no easy resolution. The minister survives the attempt on his life; his guilt unredeemed for crimes 'left floating in the void'.[137]

6

IMPERIAL WELCOME: THE BRITISH SUBJECT

When Learie Constantine booked a room in London in summer 1943, fate would have him choose the Imperial Hotel. The celebrated Trinidadian cricketer had taken time out from his wartime duties in Lancashire to captain a West Indian test team at Lords and reserved a four-night stay at the Russell Square establishment. The Imperial in those days was no modest affair. The soaring towers, green copper mansard roof and intricately gilded facade cluttered with marble statues and terra cotta gargoyles all signalled a certain cut above. The plush interiors, designed by the same architect who had fitted out RMS *Titanic*, boasted a lavishly decorated 'Wintergarden' tea room situated above 'the finest Turkish baths in the world'. Some inkling of the 'imperial' theme could be gleaned from the five tower bells, each inscribed with the words 'Australia', 'Canada', 'New Zealand', 'India' and 'The United Kingdom' – though ominously, no mention of the Caribbean. 'We may well laugh at such exuberance', noted the doyen of post-war British architecture, Nikolaus Pevsner, describing the turn-of-the-century design as a 'vicious mixture' of art nouveau gothic and tudor.[1]

Vicious also readily describes the reception the Imperial had in store for its prominent West Indian guest, who arrived in the early evening of 30 July accompanied by his wife Norma and sixteen-year-old daughter Gloria. Having acquired their keys and occupied their room, the family was suddenly informed by the duty manager that they would not be permitted to stay. Her reasoning was as abrupt as it was deeply insulting: 'We won't have n———s in this hotel.' She repeated the slur several times, one witness later recalling 'the offensive way she used the word'. By way of elaboration she pointed to the presence of several hundred American service personnel who could not be expected to tolerate such an impertinence. Margaret O'Sullivan was no rogue receptionist but a highly valued employee of some thirty-eight years' service with every reason to feel sure of her ground. Constantine initially refused to budge. He had received advance assurance that the hotel did not practice a 'colour bar' and could see no reason why American 'aliens' should 'have any preference at the hotel over a British

Figure 6.1 The original Imperial Hotel on Great Russell Street in its interwar heyday. Source: Hulton Archive/Getty Images.

subject'. But the management would hear none of it, ushering him to the distinctly less opulent Bedford Hotel, several doors down.[2]

Learie Constantine was far from the first West Indian to be refused lodgings in London. Virtually every prominent Caribbean figure who sojourned in England during the interwar years had a similar tale to tell, from the 'Harlem Renaissance' writer Claude McKay to the anti-colonial activist George Padmore to the founder of the League of Coloured Peoples, Harold Moody.[3] On the very day Constantine's story hit the headlines, a West London magistrate berated three Canadian soldiers for their drunken and disorderly attempt to evict two West Indians from a hotel in Hammersmith. 'These coloured people are British subjects and are serving and doing their bit', admonished the judge. 'It is the whole basis on which our civilisation and our Empire rest.'[4] Constantine himself spoke out about everyday casual racism, how 'digs' were always notoriously difficult to find – recalling one particularly humiliating rejection at a Brighton hotel that had left him unable to sleep or eat for days.[5] So commonplace was his ejection from the Imperial that the hotel's proprietor, a Mr Harold Walduck, was entirely nonplussed by the sudden barrage of media interest. 'Ninety-nine people out of a hundred share the prejudice against staying in a hotel with coloured people', he remonstrated. 'There is not a colour bar. We prefer to cater to white people.'[6] In his disarming frankness, Walduck distilled the doublethink of imperial subjecthood – an all-inclusive category at Britain's entry ports, but riven with raw, unrepentant racial barriers when it came to moving in.

What distinguished Constantine's experience from countless others was partly his sporting celebrity (and hence, attendant publicity) and partly the glaring discrepancy with the spirit of wartime cooperation (at a time when Caribbean servicemen were making a crucial contribution). 'This war is supposed to be a war against the Herrenvolk theory', objected Harold Moody, 'but this incident is very much like a demonstration of the theory.'[7] But above all, the episode was noteworthy for the fact that Constantine decided to file a suit against the Imperial Hotel, which was heard in the High Court the following year. Even more remarkable was his resounding victory in the case, resulting in a five-pound fine for breach of contract and a withering judicial censure for both the hotel and the 'lamentable figure' of its duty manager.[8]

The notoriety was such that the wartime home secretary, Herbert Morrison, was pressed to issue an apology of sorts in the House of Commons. 'If in this case there has been failure to accord to a British subject in this country the full equality of status and treatment to which he is entitled', he ventured cautiously, 'I would assure him that any such failure is deeply deplored and strongly condemned by responsible public opinion throughout the United Kingdom.'[9] Press coverage universally sided with the plaintiff, including one newspaper that indignantly called on Mr Walduck to 'change the name of his hotel'.[10] The cartoonist David Low savaged the proprietor in the *Evening Standard* with a depiction of Colonel Blimp frantically debarring a dapper West Indian at the entrance of the 'British Empire Hotel'. 'Gad, Sir, we can't have a coloured man <u>here</u>!' the overwrought Blimp exclaims, 'It would take the minds of the resident stinkers off their

Figure 6.2 David Low satirized Learie Constantine's racial rebuff at the Imperial Hotel in the *Evening Standard*, 7 September 1943. Source: dmg media licensing, supplied by British Cartoon Archive, University of Kent.

struggle for the ideals of the British family of free and equal peoples.' Lest the irony was somehow lost, the image bore the simple caption: 'Imperial Welcome'.[11]

The Constantine case sits awkwardly in the history of race relations in Britain; at once a vivid illustration of the stubborn prejudice long-endured by West Indian and other non-white colonial subjects, but also a harbinger of change; a sign of an apparent readiness bordering on anxiety to condemn the scourge of 'racialism' and embrace the principle of equality for all under the British flag. A snap poll in London by Mass Observation found that public opinion was 'very vigorously' in sympathy with Constantine, amid suggestions that he should be invited to lunch with the royal family at Buckingham Palace.[12] Such resolute support was rarely as unbridled as it seemed, however. Many of his well-wishers placed far greater weight on his status as an elite cricketer and all-round 'respectable chap' than any deeper commitment to a colour-blind Britain.[13] Although the Colonial Office agonized over the adverse effects on wartime morale (even to the point of considering legislative action against racial discrimination in hotels), it was clearly the embarrassing publicity rather than the principle that mattered. As one briefing paper conceded: 'We are not so concerned about the admission of coloured persons into hotels as the prevention of insults. If hotel keepers wish to keep these people out of their hotels they can easily do so in some other way than by referring to their colour.'[14] Likewise, when Constantine sought to air his experience on the BBC, it was deemed 'too controversial' for a prime-time radio slot. In rejecting his offer to appear on the popular interview series *Postcript* and rescheduling him for a weekday, the director of BBC talks wondered why he had not tapped audience sympathies by expounding on 'some of the joys of first-class cricket'. He added for good measure: 'You will remember that the object of that series is to stress unity rather than diversity.'[15]

This was the core conceit of British subjecthood at the threshold of the post-war world. The exigencies of wartime survival and the need to galvanize a unified imperial effort brought a new sensitivity about 'colour prejudice' both in Britain and throughout the empire. At the same time, the imperative of keeping the empire intact placed clear limits on metropolitan receptiveness to colonial controversies and racial injustice. These conflicting priorities became entangled in virtually every sphere of imperial governance in the post-war world, from colonial welfare to economic development, constitutional reform and combatting insurgency in Africa, South-East Asia and the Middle East. But they presented a particularly intricate set of problems in the realm of citizenship and nationality, where drawing the boundaries of British subjecthood greatly exercised the minds of post-war legislators.

The British Nationality Act of 1948 was the Attlee government's response to the problem of unity in diversity. The new statutory instrument not only reflected long-standing assumptions about the British people as a unique fellowship scattered around the globe, but also accorded official recognition of the legal equality of all British subjects, regardless of colour, gender or creed. In thus reaffirming the entry rights of citizens of the empire and commonwealth, the 1948 Act devised the new category of 'Citizen of the United Kingdom and Colonies' – enshrining a civic Britishness that transcended conventional ethnic, linguistic or territorial markers. Rarely, if ever, had the boundaries between metropolitan Britain and its wider imperial purview been so studiously blurred. According to

Labour's Home Secretary James Chuter Ede, the new nationality provisions enabled a 'great, loyal confederation of people' to continue thriving as 'a living, growing organism'.[16]

Yet no sooner was this expansive vision enacted than it began to fracture under the weight of its flawed promise. The immediate fault lines began to appear even before the Act received royal assent, as British subjects from the colonial empire availed themselves of the opportunity to remake their lives in Britain. There was never any direct causal relationship between the new nationality laws and the increase in new arrivals from the colonies and Commonwealth. Migration was not at the forefront of thinking about nationality, nor were the migrants themselves motivated by legislative changes so much as their own material plight and personal aspirations. But their journeys were nevertheless predicated on global networks of British belonging. This was particularly so in the case of the West Indies, where for generations the civic language and rituals of Britishness had served as a conduit of rights, respectability and civic identity.[17] For these transatlantic voyagers, the journey was not only about social and economic opportunity but also about a deeper set of assumptions that was essentially a localized, Caribbean imprint of Greater Britain.

The 'imperial welcome' that awaited the tens of thousands of West Indian newcomers is often depicted as a clash between the modernizing impulse of a new global mobility and a dogged, insular British racism.[18] While this was abundantly in evidence, there were other cross-currents in play – arguably more profound in their longer-term effects. The sheer necessity of defining a serviceable British citizenship was itself a watershed, requiring an element of precision where Dilkean 'imperfections' had previously prevailed. It marked a head-on collision between older, abstract projections of an unbounded self, collapsing racial and cultural difference (in theory) in a global civic continuum, and the disaggregating logic of decolonization that stressed separate national entities and independent futures. These new demarcation lines would radically reshape the terms of nationality and citizenship throughout the empire, not least in Britain itself. Historians have long assumed that the impress of imperial decline went hand in glove with post-war West Indian demands for inclusion and acceptance as British subjects; indeed, that the political struggles over racial equality 'exposed another front of decolonization – the Empire at home'.[19] This seems incontestable, but there was a flipside that is rarely explored. While West Indian claims on British belonging undoubtedly brought the end of empire onto Britain's doorstep, the wider aspirations of decolonization also served as a repudiation of the global civic networks on which those claims ultimately were founded.

Much as we saw with the fate of a common 'British' nomenclature for the post-war Commonwealth, so too the search for mutually satisfying categories of shared citizenship would encounter deep and influential pockets of resistance – from Canada to South Asia, Eire, Southern Africa and ultimately throughout the United Kingdom. The diminishing purchase of Britishness abroad is rarely factored into the history of UK immigration restriction, yet it was one of the key registers within which arguments for erecting barriers acquired an air of inevitability and hence political potency. By the early 1960s, the Macmillan government was prepared to take steps once deemed unthinkable to revoke the entry rights of offshore British subjects – not only West Indians but colonial and Commonwealth citizens *tout court* (albeit on unequal terms). The result was a profound overhaul of the laws governing the free movement of peoples around the former empire, effecting a radical curtailment of the scale and reach of British subjecthood.

'HOW COME ENGLAND DID NOT KNOW ME?'
CARIBBEAN BRITONS

The disembarkation of HMT *Empire Windrush* at London's Tilbury docks on 22 June 1948 is so emblazoned onto popular historical consciousness that its meaning and significance are often taken for granted. It comes to us virtually ready made with a rich visual archive; the hopeful arrivals in their Sunday best, the returning wartime recruits, aspirational young scholars raised on a diet of Dickens and Thackeray, able-bodied workers in search of a better deal in the 'mother country'. Such is their familiarity that the images have become blurred by their iconic depiction. The dockside figure of Trinidadian calypso sensation 'Lord Kitchener' serenading Pathé News with his impromptu rendering of 'London Is the Place for Me' appears to capture the wide-eyed expectation of the so-called 'Windrush generation', their claim to belonging as uncomplicated as the twenty-eight pound passage to Britain itself. The subsequent experience of social alienation and material hardship – the pervasive racism, the institutional barriers to opportunity and consequent disillusionment – has come to occupy a special niche in British popular culture. Novels, films, documentaries, television series, oral histories, radio programmes and successive 'Windrush' anniversaries have shaped these experiences into a pathos of unrequited Britishness.[20] In the words of Andrea Levy's fictionalized protagonist Gilbert Joseph in *Small*

Island (2004): 'Let me ask the Mother Country just this one simple question: how come England did not know me?'[21]

Such has been the emphasis on the *Empire Windrush* that objections are sometimes raised to its definitive status as the wellspring of multi-racial Britain. It is said that Windrush presents a 'deficient and myopic accounting', which not only disavows the long history of Britain's Black population reaching back five centuries, but also screens out the significant African and Asian presence alongside the new arrivals from the West Indies.[22] The relentless focus on a single ship as emblematic of an entire 'generation' is also said to reduce the sojourners to a 'homogenized and unreal mass', effacing the very history of hypermobility their presence is meant to evoke.[23] Contemporary press reports were typically brief and cursory, suggesting something fleeting and ephemeral rather than epoch-making, with little to indicate that the vessel would later provide the touchstone of multicultural Britain.[24] Certainly, the government officials charged with processing the passenger list were confident that the episode was 'not likely to be repeated' – and for a time these expectations were borne out by the arrival statistics, which declined to a mere 'trickle' until well into the 1950s.[25]

But for the purposes of tracing the myriad connections between the end of empire and the downsizing of British subjecthood, the Windrush moment remains cardinal. The significance of the newcomers lies not in their overfreighted arrival per se (in this they were by no means pioneers) but in the anomalies of imperial belonging that their passage brought to light. As Learie Constantine and countless others could readily attest, the discrepancies between the theory and practice of universal subjecthood were as old as the empire itself.[26] But it was the unprecedented scale and, more crucially, the timing of the encounter marked by the appearance of 492 West Indians at the mouth of the Thames in June 1948 that prompted patterns of public and political response out of all proportion to their numerical significance.

Understanding the social and political conditions that fashioned Black West Indian conceptions of Britishness was once a neglected area of study, certainly when compared with the former colonies of white settlement. Stephen Howe notes the long-standing habit of treating West Indian affirmations of British identity 'as a simple mistake, a dream from which there was, on exposure to attitudes in Britain itself, a rude awakening'.[27] But despite the monopolistic claims of white settlers, imperial Britishness could mean 'different things to different people all over the world', and was never the exclusive preserve of any single constituency.[28] The abolition of slavery in the 1830s was a crucial formative context in the West Indies, where the public celebration of emancipation from the plantation-owners became enmeshed with the veneration of Queen Victoria (who was often seen as having personally bestowed freedom on her enslaved West Indian subjects).[29] From the mid-nineteenth century, West Indian affirmations of Britishness became associated with campaigns for political empowerment and racial equality, with advocates of reform anchoring their arguments in British rights and liberties flowing from membership of an imperial body politic. On issues ranging from land redistribution to wage reform to political representation, vocal exclamations of British 'loyalty' provided a compelling means of claim-making.[30] Though success remained elusive, it was the persistent denials of civil liberties that both crystallized and amplified West Indian demands for active participation in shaping the meaning of British subjecthood. Or as Lara Putnam avers: 'if a good portion of the men who ran the empire presumed "British subjects of colour" to be categorically excluded from citizenship, a good portion of those subjects never doubted that citizenship was theirs'.[31]

What portion, precisely, and how deeply it permeated the many regional and social substrata of a highly dispersed and richly diversified Caribbean population is difficult to discern. In her detailed study of the civic rites of West Indian Britishness, Anne Spry Rush is notably circumspect, limiting her scope to the realm of what she terms 'middle class respectability' – more a matter of socio-economic advancement than political activism, its significance largely confined to educated, status conscious, urban-based, 'white-collar' West Indians. Rush justifies this in straightforward terms: 'Caribbean peoples who were trying to get ahead in their colonial society were more likely to be exposed to pro-British propaganda for longer periods of time.'[32] Thus she catalogues a steady stream of loyalist British sentiment in education curricula, public broadcasting, Empire Day celebrations and the official pageantry of royal jubilees that invited West Indians into a world of 'shared values' with their fellow subjects overseas.

Yet for all the emphasis on patterns of imperial 'exposure', Rush is also at pains to point out that middle-class West Indians were not simply brainwashed into being British but were themselves actively engaged in its social formation, harnessing imperial networks of belonging to their own circumstances and for their own ends.[33] Kennetta Hammond Perry similarly argues that the idea of Britain as a 'Mother Country' was 'strategically *selected* and appropriated by colonial subjects to make claims to political rights, economic aid, and access to routes of social mobility'.[34] Indeed, if historians are agreed on one thing, it is that Caribbean Britishness 'was not merely *imposed* but actively fashioned and worked for', and that this process was 'neither mutually exclusive nor fundamentally contradictory' with more local (or indeed pan-African) identifications and affinities.[35]

But while West Indians had no difficulty reconciling their Britishness with other cultural affiliations, the middle-class embrace of a shared British respectability inevitably accentuated internal social divisions. Marcus Garvey once observed how Black Jamaicans at the base of the social structure were 'trampled on by all the shades above', and this surely contributed to wide discrepancies in access to, and identification with, the benefits of being British.[36] In his famous account of the sinews of empire in Trinidad, C. L. R. James described his grandfather's pathway out of poverty to a prestigious position 'normally held by white men' on a sugar estate:

> This meant that my grandfather had raised himself above the mass of poverty, dirt, ignorance and vice which in those far-off days surrounded the islands of black lower-middle class respectability like a sea ever threatening to engulf them ... The need for distance ... was compounded of self-defence and fear. My grandfather went to church every Sunday morning at eleven o'clock wearing in the broiling sun a frock-coat, striped trousers and top-hat, with his walking stick in hand, surrounded by his family, the underwear of the women crackling with starch. Respectability was not an ideal, it was an armour.[37]

West Indian Britishness was a fragmented affair, combining in varying degrees elements of cultural appropriation, rights advocacy, social mobility and a tenacious hold on respectability. In this respect, it bore vague similarities with equally complex identity formations in Australia, New Zealand, Canada and elsewhere in the imperial world where local contexts also profoundly skewed and fractured the social and ideological bent of being British, with class affinities signalling distinct shades of British identification. But in one crucial respect the West Indian example clearly stood out on its own – namely the question of race and the possibility of a mutually resonant Black Britishness. Racial bars to mobility within the empire were one obvious register of difference, where the stridency and stringency of immigration restrictions in the settler colonies stemmed from the conviction that to be Black was to be anything but British. To underline the point, white spokesmen in the dominions routinely invoked their blatantly discriminatory entry rules in the name of preserving the 'British character' of their societies.[38]

Even more fundamental was the disconnect between West Indian expectations and the racial assumptions that permeated metropolitan Britain. Virtually all of the leading advocates of Greater Britain in the late nineteenth century tended to bypass the Caribbean entirely (or include only the descendants of the white planter oligarchy in their remit). Charles Dilke himself was quite clear in delimiting his concept to 'the English-speaking, white inhabited, and self-governed lands' of the empire, and others tended to follow suit.[39] Although J. R. Seeley's 1883 magnum opus included the West Indies as one of the four 'great groups of territory' that comprised the 'expansion of England' (the others being Australasia, Canada and the Cape), he nevertheless defined these as areas inhabited 'either chiefly or to a large extent by Englishmen'.[40] Though devoting a large portion of his study to explaining why India could never be counted among this 'ethnographic unity', he could not even accord West Indians the dignity of reasoned grounds for exclusion.[41] In predicting that 'in not much more than half a century' the combined population of the British at home and 'beyond the sea . . . will be much more than 100 millions', he referred solely and exclusively to a scattered legion of white subjects.[42] Some sixty years later in 1946, Winston Churchill offered a strikingly similar vision: 'Do not suppose that half a century from now you will not see 70 or 80 millions of Britons spread about the world united in defense of our traditions, and our way of life.'[43] Again, the arithmetic clearly omitted non-white subjects from the equation.

Of all the early high priests of Greater Britain, only J. A. Froude gave the Caribbean more than a second glance, devoting an entire volume to *The English in the West Indies* (1888). But as the title clearly intimated, his purpose was to assimilate the West Indian islands into the Anglo-Saxon world he lauded so lavishly in *Oceana* two years earlier. Just as the settler colonies were 'part of ourselves', so too the British West Indies could only prosper if the racially inferior Black population of 'docile, good-tempered, excellent and faithful servants' were properly subsumed within the Greater British orbit.[44] 'Those beautiful West Indian islands were intended to be homes for the overflowing numbers of our own race', he lamented, 'and the few that have gone there have been crowded out by the blacks.' He recognized that the proportion of the white population could no longer be substantially increased, but insisted it was not too late to restore a sense of mutual responsibility and common cause between the 'English planters' and 'their countrymen at home'. If only England could 'let it be known' that '[she] regards the West Indies as essentially one with herself', the white oligarchs would 'resume their natural position, and respect and order will come back' – to the benefit of all, not least the disenfranchised Black majority:

> Out of the now half-organic fragments will yet be formed one living Imperial power, with a new era of beneficence and usefulness to

mankind. The English people are spread far and wide. The sea is their dominion and their land is the finest portion of the globe.[45]

Such grandiloquence could easily be dismissed as the idle hankerings of a gentleman entering his seventies, but it was shortly after the book was published that Froude was offered the Regius Chair of Modern History at Oxford University. His authoritative bearing underscored the distance between English and Black West Indian notions of shared British sub-jecthood. Nevertheless, it was an authority consumed by doubt about its longer-term prospects. As Catherine Hall points out, Froude visited the Caribbean at a time of widespread talk of a self-governing West Indian federation; the crucial context for his appeal for the restoration of England's influence and his conviction that 'the only true West Indian was a white West Indian'.[46]

Froude's racial arrogance provided the spur for the Black Trinidadian schoolmaster John Jacob Thomas to pen his immortal rebuttal: *Froudacity: West Indian Fables by James Anthony Froude* (1889) – excoriating Froude's 'ghastly imaginings' that savoured 'only too much of the slave pen and the auction block'. It is rightly regarded as a formative work of West Indian intellectual self-determination.[47] Thomas was particularly attuned to the insidious effects of language, not least Froude's use of the pronoun 'us' as a proxy for white planter interests:

> His US, between whom and the negro subjects of Great Britain the gulf of colour lies, comprises, as he himself owns, an outnumbered ... and not over-creditable little clique of Anglo-Saxon lineage ... He invokes the whole prestige of the Anglo-Saxon race in favour of the untenable pretensions of a few *blasés* of that race, and that to the social and political detriment of tens of thousands of black fellow-subjects.[48]

Thomas was not alone in seeking to expose the 'gulf of colour'. The Barbadian Liberal N. Darnell Davis raised similar objections in *Mr Froude's Negrophobia* (1888), likening the regius professor's actual knowledge of the West Indies to that of a 'Cook's Tourist'.[49] In the interwar years, the Grenadian editor T. A. Marryshow drew on Thomas's metaphor to deplore the 'wide and unbridgeable gulf' between the theory and actuality of shared subjecthood, which inevitably appeared whenever a West Indian sought to 'put his claim to the test'.[50] It was not the theory these critics objected to but the intrusions of everyday racism that distorted the prism. Or as Theodore Koditschek argues, they were 'no less concerned about the place of the West Indies in Greater Britain than was Froude'; it was the latter's exclusively white vision of greater British patriotism that rankled.[51]

For all his cricketing prowess, Learie Constantine was not exempt from these procedures – indeed, his virtues were often extolled in the most baldly racial terms. The leading interwar cricket writer Neville Cardus drew on the literary conventions of high imperial adventure to describe a 'savage' player possessed by a 'fury of primitive onslaught', 'violently destructive . . . a panther on the kill, sinuous, stealthy, strong but unburdened. The batmanship of the jungle.' Readers were left in no doubt that here was no specimen of Greater Britain:

> When we see Constantine bowl or bat or field, we know he is not an English player, not an Australian player, not a South African player. We know that his cuts and drives, his whirling fast balls, his leaping and clutchings and dartings – we know they are the consequences of impulses born in the blood, a blood heated by the sun and influenced by an environment and a way of life much more natural than ours; impulses not common to the psychology of the over-civilised places of the earth. His cricket is racial.[52]

Like Froude's 'us', Cardus placed Constantine outside the circle of the 'we' who 'knows'. Despite generations of West Indian declarations of,

Figure 6.3 Learie Constantine on the eve of the Second World War, 10 May 1939. Source: Hulton Archive/Getty Images.

171

and indeed insistence upon, a stake in British networks of belonging, very little of this seems to have sunk in back in Britain.[53] For all Constantine's skill and success on the playing field, his grasp of imperial idiom and the intricacies of English social norms, his 'blood' placed him at one remove.

These same blinkers go a long way to explaining why the symbol of *Empire Windrush* is so routinely misrepresented as the opening of a new dialogue rather than the culmination of a much older one.[54] 'Welcome sons of Empire' was the *Evening Standard*'s extravagant greeting, displaying the gaping fascination that might have been reserved for visitors from another galaxy.[55] This was the view from the metropole that persists to this day, framing the moment as a point of rupture and stamping the migrants with an indelible novelty. 'Written out of the story', as Stuart Hall recalled, 'forgotten, disavowed, misrecognized – were the prolonged historical entanglements between the Caribbean and Britain.'[56]

The contrast with contemporary reporting in the West Indies could not have been starker. Here, the weight of decades of experience brought a ready awareness of the continuities – and a note of trepidation. The *Barbados Advocate* acknowledged 'a certain amount of racial friction' surrounding the approaching vessel and called for 'careful handling and much thought if West Indians are not to be made to feel that they are the unwanted members of the British Empire'.[57] The London correspondent of the Jamaican *Daily Gleaner* sounded a warning against 'such a large body of men' converging on the imperial capital at once: 'Speaking as a West Indian ... I would like to express the hope that nothing of the kind will be repeated under similar conditions.'[58] Meanwhile the *Trinidad Guardian* seemed even more perturbed, declaring that 'the whole affair should be a warning to people in the West Indies that they cannot expect to go to the Mother Country whenever the whim takes them'.[59] Such extreme caution stemmed from a much longer tradition, drawing on an intrinsic understanding of the racial contingencies of West Indian Britishness. The Black Trinidadian clergyman M. E. Farquhar predicted 'difficulties as complicated as they are far reaching' as he reflected on the profound changes since the days when Britain was a 'closed book' to all but the tiniest minority of migrants:

> The visits of West Indian cricketers to England; two great wars, furnishing the opportunity of acquaintance with England to a comparatively large number of West Indians, together with a marked rise in the economic level

of the middle classes, have combined to alter the conception of this remoteness. Now people can talk casually about going to England as they would not have done 25 years ago even with respect to going to a place like Barbados . . . It is when these diverse facts are related together that this mass emigration assumes its proper symbol and threatens a portent.[60]

Farquhar seemed to suggest that it was only the fortuitous isolation of West Indians from the object of their British loyalties that had insulated the bonds of empire from the strain of racial difference. Now that this 'remoteness' had been breached, a new era of mutual suspicion and discord could be apprehended.

There is also ample evidence that the voyagers themselves were under no illusion about their likely reception in England. According to one passenger's testimony, rumours circulated on board that a British warship shadowing the *Empire Windrush* 'might blow us out of the water' in the mid-Atlantic 'because there was some people didn't want black people coming to England'.[61] The first journalists to board the ship at Tilbury eagerly reported the 'first question' on the migrants' lips: 'What do British people think of our coming here?' (which the *Daily Gleaner* co-opted for its front-page splash the following day). One cohort of new arrivals baulked at their designation as 'refugees' in a London morning newspaper: '"Refugee" is wrong', they insisted, 'We are British and give our support to the Mother Country of all that is British.'[62] Even prior to disembarkation, these presumptive 'pioneers' were faithfully rehearsing the taut structures of a long and turbulent encounter.

To return to Gilbert Joseph's query, 'How come England did not know me?', the answer lies in the congenital flaws in the fabric of imperial subjecthood itself. By 1948, 'men and women in the British Caribbean had been grappling explicitly with these tensions for a full generation'. While many would later record their personal shock, alienation and apparently sudden realization that their Britishness was not reciprocated, such reactions were deeply embedded in a much longer history where unrequited loyalty was part and parcel of West Indian claims to British belonging.[63] In short, West Indians had long since developed their own vernacular of imperial citizenship 'as an ideal continually betrayed'.[64] What was truly pioneering about the Windrush moment is that the conversation had relocated to the heart of metropolitan Britain.

'OUR PROUD BOAST': SUBJECTHOOD VERSUS NATIONALITY

On the very morning that the passengers of *Empire Windrush* filed down the gangplank at Tilbury, *The Times* published a leader headed 'Citizenship and Nationality' – not by way of commentary on the newcomers from the

Caribbean (for whom no column space was allocated at all), but to herald the dramatic scenes in the House of Lords the day before when the second reading of the British Nationality Act was blocked by an outspoken majority.[65] The new legislation had been introduced to reconcile the changing trends in the modern Commonwealth with the time-honoured principle of uniform status for all of His Majesty's British subjects. But dissent in the Lords stemmed from suspicion that the Act would have precisely the opposite effect, inaugurating a precariously fragmented and multi-tiered imperial citizenry. As Lord Altrincham remonstrated:

> We on these benches would lament any tendency to differentiate between different types of British subject in the United Kingdom. Hitherto, it has been our proud boast that all British subjects have equal rights in the United Kingdom. Whatever you may say at the outset, if you create a distinctive citizenship it is bound to set up a tendency towards differentiation ... This Empire has always been an untidy Empire, and I think that is the chief reason why it still exists. Let us not rely too much on logic, for I verily believe that that would spell the decadence and demise of our greatest asset—namely, the practical political wisdom of our race.[66]

Altrincham fixed on the two interlocking problems that would define the terms of debate about British nationality policy in the years ahead – the existence of multiple communities of Britishness and the imperative of packaging this 'untidy' assembly as a unitary empire. The dilemma was whether acknowledging diversity would come at the cost of unity – whether the 'proud boast' of a common British subjecthood could accommodate an assortment of permutations without bringing the entire edifice down. Even when the Lords finally approved the amended Bill, there remained an uneasy feeling that the Rubicon had been crossed. As future Tory home secretary David Maxwell Fyfe cautioned in the Commons, 'inevitably, such differentiation will creep in. We must maintain our great metropolitan tradition of hospitality to everyone from every part of our Empire'.[67] Remarkably, not a word of this wide-ranging debate touched upon the several hundred Windrush West Indians presently enjoying the government's hospitality in a wartime shelter, thirty metres beneath Clapham Common.[68]

The impetus behind the 1948 Nationality Act came not from any domestic demand for greater precision in the designation of British subjecthood but from events on the other side of the Atlantic in the Canadian legislature, where the government of W. L. Mackenzie King had introduced a Nationality Bill two years earlier that radically upended the basis of imperial belonging. Prior to this, the so-called 'Common Code' had bestowed British subjecthood on all souls residing within the empire as their primary nationality, uniting them in common allegiance to the sovereign.[69] But in 1946 the Canadians introduced the concept of Canadian citizenship as the principal means of binding the individual to the Canadian state. British subjecthood was retained, but it became a secondary category that stemmed from the fact of being Canadian, rather than the other way around.[70] The Canadian Government's motives are often put down to a new post-war national assertiveness, and it is certainly the case that Mackenzie King prided himself on enhancing Canada's international profile.[71] But he viewed this not in terms of a brazen repudiation but as part of a more delicate process of recalibrating Canada's ties to Britain and the Commonwealth. The delicacy lay in finding an appropriate balance between local attachments and the wider British fraternity to which many English-speaking Canadians (including Mackenzie King himself) remained devoted. He was also politically wary of newly assertive French–Canadian sentiment (symbolized by the wartime emergence of the Bloc Populaire in Quebec), which made no secret of its antipathy to loyalist totems – hence the political value of reforms that toned down the significance of the British connection.[72] The passage of the Canadian Citizenship Act through parliament was anything but smooth, sparking a long and particularly heated parliamentary debate that dragged on for several weeks – with Conservative opposition members unable to suppress their indignation at the way that English Canadians were being asked 'to forfeit a generous measure of their birthright'.[73] The future leader of the Canadian Tories, the Saskatchewan lawyer John G. Diefenbaker, pointed to the wider repercussions of separate citizenship 'which may well strike at the unity of British citizenship everywhere within this empire'.[74]

Thus, while the House of Lords agonized over the perils of distinguishing between various categories of British subjecthood, those very distinctions were already being drawn in other Commonwealth parliaments. And much as Diefenbaker had prophesied, the lines of demarcation could not be contained within a single legislature. In the words of UK Cabinet secretary Norman Brook, the Canadians had 'driven a coach through the "common code" of British nationality', leaving it to other parliaments to decide whether to follow suit.[75] In Britain, the Attlee government tried to have it both ways – following the Canadians' lead in devising a more circumscribed citizenship, while at the same time trying to preserve as much as possible of the pre-1948 system of universal subjecthood. These were the broad objectives of the 1948 British Nationality Act (BNA), but they posed one intractable problem: if the United Kingdom were to embrace the Canadian model of a designated, localized citizenship as the 'gateway' to British subjecthood, how should the denizens of the United Kingdom be categorized? And what of the dependent colonial empire, many of whom had no legislature in which a separate citizenship might be enacted?

One possible solution was to create distinct and separate citizenships for all of the constituent parts of the empire, including the United Kingdom (a method favoured by the Home and Foreign Offices), but this was opposed by the Colonial Office out of concern that it would only embolden the forces of anti-colonial subversion. With India soon to become independent and insurgencies brewing in Palestine and Malaya, the idea of creating separate citizenries for the dozens of remaining colonies would hand a powerful galvanizing weapon to the empire's enemies.[76] Ultimately it was this view that held sway, and the cumbersome category of 'Citizenship of the United Kingdom and Colonies' (CUKC) was duly cobbled together. As Kathleen Paul observes, the logic was straightforward: 'If the colonials were to continue to regard themselves as British, they must share a single nationality with the United Kingdom.'[77] Responding to objections that such a conception was a 'violation of geography and common sense', the government emphasized that the CUKC category was merely the legal pathway to the more crucial element of British subjecthood – the universal rights and privileges of which remained completely unchanged. Such was the stress on continuity that the Colonial Office even considered adopting 'Citizen of Greater Britain' in place of the more cumbersome 'United Kingdom and Colonies' – an odd choice, given the deliberate exclusion of non-white subjects from virtually all previous iterations of the term. But the idea was cast aside due to its 'outmoded "land of Hope and Glory" flavour' – revealing the extent to which the old Dilkean formula was already losing traction in the post-war world.[78]

Such was the tortured reasoning behind the reaffirmation of nominal civic equality and the theoretical freedom of entry at Britain's ports for 800 million subjects around the globe. Yet remarkably, no one at the time seems to have viewed the provisions of the 1948 BNA as a precursor to mass inward migration – indeed many advocates of the Bill spoke more in terms of its 'symbolic' value in tightening the imperial circle than any anticipated practical implications. As Labour's Lord Chancellor (Jowitt) explained, it was not the 'material advantages' conferred by an all-pervading British nationality. 'It is, if you like, rather mystical ... It is the mark which differentiates the family from mere friends'.[79] But family are notorious for turning up unannounced and historians have subsequently marvelled at the cognitive dissonance, describing the BNA variously as hopelessly naive, wilfully disingenuous, 'starkly myopic', or simply too charitable in its dispensations.[80] With the benefit of hindsight, any or all of these labels might readily apply, but legislators were effectively blind-sided by historically low levels of inward colonial migration to Britain which tended to fix their assumptions about the future. Randall Hansen sees no reason to attribute a 'lack of political prescience' in the collective failure to recognize what now seems obvious: the intrinsic connection between citizenship rights and potentially large-scale movements of people.[81]

Other Commonwealth governments soon followed suit in determining their respective citizenship requirements, and it was here that the cracks widened. In Australia and New Zealand, the position was almost identical to the one taken over the official name of the Commonwealth – that these were British countries with no particular need to dwell on the finer distinctions.[82] One opinion poll revealed that 65 per cent of Australians wished to retain their official British nationality, rather than complicate matters with a separate Australian citizenship, and officials in the Immigration Ministry found that they had to 'rack their brains' for good reasons to carry out the change.[83] When legislation was finally and reluctantly introduced into the Australian Parliament in November 1948 the Chifley Labor government was extremely guarded about its significance, dubbing it the 'British Nationality and Australian Citizenship Act'. The exact same wording was used in New Zealand, with the responsible minister going out of his way to stress that 'we did not seek this freedom for ourselves'. While Canada 'no doubt had her good reasons' to elevate Canadian citizenship, for New Zealand there could be no doubt whatsoever that '"British nationality" comes first, and "New Zealand Citizenship" second'.[84] This did little to ward off criticism from the opposition benches in both countries. The normally dour deputy leader of the Australian Country Party Jack McEwen could 'imagine no greater disaster to the entire human race than any step which is calculated further to dismember the British peoples'.[85] His Liberal Party counterpart pleaded for Australia's exemption from the entire scheme on the grounds that it was all very well for Canada or South Africa or India to demand separate status 'because those countries have racial problems, but it is not understandable in Australia which is essentially British'.[86] This was to raise the very distinctions that were deemed so objectionable. If Australia was 'essentially British', it followed that other Commonwealth countries were somehow less so, or not at all – a possibility that poked holes in the organic unity that the new legislation was intended to uphold.

In South Africa, the new pathway to British subjecthood proved to be particularly short-lived. The election of the nationalists under D. F. Malan in June 1948 – the same month as the BNA's passage through Westminster – presented a timely opportunity to harness the concept of South African Citizenship to wider Afrikaner political aspirations. Thus, the Act that came into force in September the following year omitted any reference to British subjecthood, or indeed any common status whatsoever. Instead it provided for a system of *reciprocal* citizenship arrangements with other Commonwealth countries – clearly a downgrading of the common code for South African purposes, creating the legal anomaly that South African citizens were deemed British subjects in UK law but denied that status in their own. The new government insisted that there could no longer be talk of a common allegiance to the king with India's admission to the Commonwealth as a republic, and hence no shared subjecthood.[87] This was partly about fulfilling cherished nationalist goals harking back to the South African War, but it also had a pre-emptive dimension. At a time when a newly energized generation of Black intellectuals were beginning to talk of citizenship as a right to be assertively claimed, the nationalists were also keen to close ranks domestically by devising citizenship requirements that would enable them to manipulate the electoral role – first by delaying the voting rights of newly arrived British migrants, second by removing 'coloured' voters from the role altogether and third (to the extent they ever entertained it as a remote possibility) forestalling the franchise for Africans indefinitely.[88] It was the first of many confrontations with the white English-speaking minority who complained loudly that nothing 'could do more than this loss to break the formal ties that still link us to our kinsmen all over the world'.[89] As the *Manchester Guardian* reported, the South African Citizenship Bill was bound to be 'another step in the direction of making Great Britain a foreign country'.[90]

The inconsistencies multiplied in the case of Ireland, whose citizens had been in a state of constitutional limbo ever since the 1935 Irish Citizenship Act, when the Free State government had unilaterally revoked all prior claims to British subjecthood. Nevertheless, successive British governments had continued to admit Irish workers (and recruit them for wartime service) as though their British subjecthood were unaffected. As the new post-war system began to take shape, Eamon de Valera deliberately raised the stakes. 'We are not British subjects', he impressed on an audience in Waterford in 1946, 'and it is an impertinence to call us such ... We are today an independent republic, we acknowledge no sovereignty except that of our own people.'[91] The compromise eventually enacted in the BNA was to bestow the *rights* but not the *status* of British subjecthood on Irish citizens, thereby preserving a ready source of labour without the offending British categorization. Further provisions were made for any Irish citizen who, for personal (and no doubt political) reasons, wished to remain a British subject.[92] But the majority of the population were henceforth classed as neither subjects nor aliens, but an indistinct category hovering precariously between the two.[93]

Equally opposed to British subject status was newly independent India, and thus further permutations were inserted into the BNA to forestall possible objections. The citizenship issue became entangled in the whole conundrum of India's membership of the Commonwealth and for a time there was serious consideration of upgrading the concept of 'Commonwealth citizenship' to become the key binding ingredient (in place of the common allegiance to the Throne). Although strongly favoured by Jawaharlal Nehru, Krishna Menon and other leading Congress figures, the idea of a universal Commonwealth citizenry failed to find favour with the Australian and Canadian governments, anxious as ever about the likely consequences for their restrictive immigration regimes.[94] But while never gaining any formal status in terms of a shared code of rights and privileges, the term nevertheless found its way into the opening passages of the BNA:

> Any person having the status aforesaid may be known either as a British subject or as a Commonwealth citizen; and accordingly in this Act and in any other enactment or instrument whatever, whether passed or made before or after the commencement of this Act, the expression 'British subject' and the expression 'Commonwealth citizen' shall have the same meaning.[95]

This tortuously worded passage was inserted solely, as Whitehall officials later conceded, 'in order to make the new scheme more palatable to Indians' by effectively rendering the two categories indistinct. Only British subjecthood had an established meaning in UK law, however, whereas the wholly unfamiliar 'Commonwealth Citizen' was at best a statutory synonym. Thus, the passage merely allowed that Indians (or anyone else) 'may be known' as Commonwealth citizens, but this in no way diminished their status as common law British subjects.[96]

Unsurprisingly, therefore, the interchangeable terminology brought no end of confusion and misunderstanding between the British and Indian Governments. One particular source of friction was the form of words used for immigration notices at British ports, which typically invited

Indians to join the queue for 'British subjects'. The mere mention that Indian sojourners to Britain could be so described was enough to spark loud cries of dissent in the Indian press and parliament, often directed at the Indian Government for failing to deliver on the promise of independence. British diplomats in Delhi pressed their counterparts in Whitehall to show greater sensitivity, but the Commonwealth Relations Office confessed to 'a certain amount of reluctance here in the United Kingdom to drop the term "British subject"' – not least on account of the Indian Government's own lack of enthusiasm for promoting 'Commonwealth citizenship' (which was not even inserted in their own Citizenship Act of 1955).[97] On one occasion when a junior Home Office minister lumped Indians into the category of British subjects in a House of Commons speech, Prime Minister Nehru came under intense domestic political pressure to register an official protest. With evident reluctance, he rose in parliament to clarify the position as he saw it, noting that the Home Office's formulation 'was not correct of course ... Obviously so ... Nobody in the wide world who has any knowledge of the facts considers any Indian as a British subject.' His absolute certainty elicited a smug rebuttal from UK officials in Delhi, who decided it was 'best to ignore his remarks, far from the truth though they were'.[98]

Thus, from the simple desire of the Canadian legislature to distinguish between their own citizens and other British subjects around the world, a plethora of permutations had emerged – from the cumbersome designation of Citizen of the United Kingdom and Colonies, to the South African concept of reciprocal citizenship, the Indian predilection for Commonwealth Citizenship, the Irish opt-out for neither/nor status and the Australasian preference for no permutations at all. Here was a British subjecthood straining to contain the atomizing force of national self-definition, all stirred by the political and ideological currents of decolonization.

Inevitably, these same pressures were soon brought to bear in the United Kingdom. As the value of an expansive British subjecthood became diminished in the eyes of others, so too, successive British governments began questioning the advisability of an 'open door' policy (the currency of the phrase itself indicative of changing mentalities). From the early 1950s, Home Office officials began to examine ways of removing the right of abode from West Indians and South Asians without foisting themselves on their own petard of universal subjecthood. Any scheme to exclude certain categories of British subject without applying the same measures to the white descendants of the settler empire risked tarnishing further the standing and utility of the Commonwealth. Or in the crude formulation of Churchill's private secretary, David Hunt: 'The minute we said we've got to keep these black chaps out, the whole Commonwealth lark would have been blown up.'[99] Although Hunt was reminiscing from a remove of nearly forty years, his choice of idiom evoked the mindset of the 1950s. The Commonwealth 'lark' – implying a strong element of subterfuge and sleight of hand – was losing the lustre of Lord Altrincham's 'proud boast' of 1948, producing a pervasive citizenship limbo.

CHANGING THE SUBJECT: THE ROAD TO EXCLUSION

Throughout the 1950s, successive Tory governments continued to voice a commitment to free entry for all British subjects, whatever might have been said behind closed doors. In the meantime, public speculation about Britain's 'colour bar', its underlying causes and possible remedies, spawned a plethora of books, research projects, government studies and frequent television and radio broadcasts. In some accounts, such as Learie Constantine's *Colour Bar* (1954), the issue was framed as a self-evident fact of contemporary British life, while in others it was posed as an open question (as in the 1955 BBC television documentary *Has Britain a Colour Bar?*).[100] The persistent questioning tended to affirm the proposition, as pressure mounted for legislative action to curb what was increasingly touted as the root cause – the unchecked entry of non-white Commonwealth migrants.

The racial violence that broke out in Nottingham in late summer 1958 marked a clear shift in the momentum for change. What started as a pub brawl in the St Ann's district on 23 August escalated rapidly into a night-long spree, with more than a thousand white rioters engaging in indiscriminate attacks on West Indians. A week later the focus shifted to London's Notting Hill, with hundreds of white antagonists besieging a terrace in Blenheim Crescent inhabited by West Indians. Over four consecutive nights, reports of random beatings, petrol bombs, iron bars, racial chants and razor-wielding 'Teddy Boys' swelled the columns of the morning papers.[101] Instantly dubbed Britain's 'race riots', the violence attracted worldwide media attention and invited comparisons with the racial animosities of Alabama, Arkansas and South Africa. Newspapers throughout Europe, Africa and North America registered genuine bewilderment that such enmities could erupt in a country normally depicted as a paragon of tolerance and racial inclusiveness.[102] Coping with the barrage of inquiries from overseas missions, the Foreign Office conceded that the riots had 'cast an unwelcome blot on the conscience of Britain'.[103]

In the West Indies, too, the attacks were viewed in the mainstream media as running completely counter to everything 'Britain' stood for – so much so that several newspapers went out of their way to play down their significance. The *Barbados Advocate* urged that 'Notting Hill is not Little Rock ... not one Englishman or Englishwoman in a thousand has anything but contempt for the provocateurs', while the *Daily Gleaner* issued an appeal to 'Take it Easy', reassuring readers that the troublemakers were 'drawn from the riff raff' of England.[104] Jamaican premier Norman Manley also viewed Britain's racial strife as fundamentally out of character for a people who had 'always led the world in tolerance and decency', but he nevertheless felt compelled to announce his immediate departure for London to investigate the matter personally. Press reports depicted a statesman returning 'to the very hearth' of the liberal principles that sustained him: 'It is an encouraging and poetic concept, his going back to Britain to plead for the safeguarding of British tolerance.'[105] Not for the first time, a West Indian was cast in the role of the mother country's liberal conscience, offering lessons in the capaciousness of true British selfhood.

Figure 6.4 Jamaica's Chief Minister Norman Manley at Notting Hill in September 1958 on a personal mission to investigate the conditions that produced the race riots in the late summer of that year. Source: Hulton Archive/Getty Images.

Reactions in Britain verged on the schizophrenic, with the riots depicted variously as the isolated excesses of an unrepresentative underclass and a harbinger of more troubling trends requiring urgent political action. Press reports were quick to apportion blame to the unprovoked aggression of white Englishmen, but equally quick to dismiss them as the very dregs of society – 'inherently deviant and categorically un-British'.[106] A leader in *The Economist* placed the perpetrators far beyond the pale as 'The Nazis of Notting Hill' – deflecting blame rather than plumbing any deeper causation.[107] Much of the debate turned on the correct choice of words. Did the 'disturbances' constitute a 'riot'? Were the underlying grievances 'racial' or was race merely a rallying point for everyday (and hence more morally valid) grievances over 'jobs', 'housing' and 'women'?[108] Such dilatory procedures tended to discount the significance of race entirely, yet they could pivot effortlessly to grave tidings and future foreboding – often in the same breath. 'Clearly, racial hatred is not typical of the British people', remarked the *Daily Express*, before concluding ominously: 'This could just be the beginning ... something horrible has come to Britain.'[109] The *Daily Mirror* seemed equally confused, on the one hand conceding the indelible shame of 'every decent person in this country' and soberly praising the loyal, law abiding, hard-working West Indian community, while on the other hand succumbing to rank sensationalism:

> The Mirror is probably more guilty than any other British newspaper in assuming that it **couldn't happen here**. It has. The events of the past few days have brought our smug satisfaction to an abrupt end. Let's cut out the moralising. Here is the Daily Mirror's plan for ACTION NOW: 1. Commonwealth Citizens – whatever the colour of their skin – should not be allowed to enter Britain as immigrants unless they have a job AND a home to come to ...

The full list comprised four demands, the first three entailing immediate curbs on the number of West Indians in Britain (with a distant fourth calling for heavy sentencing for the white 'hooligans' at the heart of the trouble). Despite targeting 'IGNORANCE' as the source of the unrest, the *Mirror*'s coverage flaunted that very quality in abundance, fanning popular fears and prejudices while calling on the home secretary to overhaul Britain's immigration laws before it was too late: 'Mr Butler, You Can't Sit on a Riot'. It was a blatant exercise in having it both ways, combatting racial prejudice by calling for curbs on the admission of non-white subjects.[110]

Nottingham and Notting Hill saturated the news cycle over a period of several weeks, to become a national and eventually a global event. The sheer concentration of media attention produced a scramble for quick diagnoses and easy remedies that generated its own momentum, seemingly affecting every shade of opinion. Much was made of an editorial in *The Times* on 4 September ironically titled 'A Family of Nations', which roundly asserted that 'the laws governing the presence of coloured persons in Britain need an enlightened but firm overhaul'. It was no use dismissing the riots as insignificant – 'official Britain' had already 'closed its eyes' for too long, compounding the escalating panic. Though stopping short of making specific demands, there was no mistaking the broader implications: 'The time has come to admit that there is a colour problem in our midst. It would be wrong to exaggerate it. It would be disastrous to appear to give way in the face of violence. But to ignore the existence of the problem altogether is to invite disaster.'[111] Here, the authority of Britain's oldest and most respected newspaper was brought to bear, in a show of sobriety and 'balance' clearly meant to strike a contrast with tabloid sensationalism. But the message was fundamentally the same.

When Prime Minister Macmillan finally issued a statement on 4 September, he was predictably circumspect, cautioning that 'the significance of the incidents should not be exaggerated at home or overseas'. Adopting the reluctant pose of a man whose hands were tied, he conceded that the government had 'for some time' been considering its position on the 'time-honoured practice' of admitting British subjects from overseas in the light of mounting public agitation. While he would not reach any hasty decision without 'careful consideration', the whole thrust of the statement worked to reassure an anxious white constituency that something was being done.[112] It would take another two years to overcome deep ministerial divisions over the hallowed principle of free movement, but by the close of the decade the task for the Home Office had become clear: 'to construct a case that could be used to justify a recommendation for immigration control'.[113]

To the extent that historians have argued over the precise pattern of causation from the 1958 riots to the passage of the 1962 Commonwealth Immigrants Act, it has generally hinged on the relative importance of the popular will versus administrative expediency – whether public opinion fundamentally shaped, or was shaped by, the growing appetite for change in elite governing circles.[114] Yet there was far more to the radical overhaul of the system than purely domestic political considerations. The vocal calls for reform (and their equally vocal denunciations) resonated at a time when Britain's global purview encountered multiple setbacks. Macmillan's 'Wind of Change' tour in 1960, the massacres in Sharpeville, Nyasaland and

Kenya's Hola Camp, the quagmire of the Congo, the escalating tragedy of French Algeria and South Africa's controversial exit from the Commonwealth all contributed to an image of colonial Africa spinning out of Europe's orbit. With each successive crisis, the imperative and indeed the plausibility of preserving Britain's good name at the head of a worldwide congregation of British peoples was progressively eroded; just as the likelihood that the 'new Commonwealth' would furnish a vehicle for British aspirations abroad grew increasingly remote. As decolonization gathered an air of inevitability, the rationale behind preserving a universal British subjecthood became vulnerable to enemies from without as well as within. In ways that never occurred to the drafters of the British Nationality Act, it became permissible to contemplate harsh measures to curb Commonwealth free movement.

THE 'LOYALTY OF COMMON SENSE': DOWNGRADING THE BRITISH CONNECTION

These currents cut both ways. Just as other Commonwealth countries devised citizenship laws that enhanced the distinctions between them, so too West Indian identities became progressively dislodged from wider British templates. Only months prior to the violent outbreaks at Nottingham and Notting Hill, a five-day celebratory pageant in Trinidad inaugurated a new West Indies Federation, comprising ten former British colonies of varying size and economic strength. It marked the culmination of more than two decades of emancipatory politics, initially sparked by widespread labour unrest in the turbulent 1930s – a time when Norman Manley heralded the arrival of a new generation of leaders who had 'seen through and rejected all the false imperial philosophies of the scribes of the empire builders'. Acknowledging that it 'must seem sacrilege to many', he offered a new vision of Jamaican loyalty in 1938:

> This country has a destiny of its own separate and distinct from the destiny of any other country. Our first and paramount duty is to work for, and to be loyal to, that destiny. That destiny is bound up as a practical and necessary fact with the destiny of the British Empire of which we are part. And since that empire is still the depository of ideals which admit the rights of subject peoples we may be glad of the connection. That is the loyalty of common sense.[115]

This was to find constitutional expression two decades later with the creation of the West Indies Federation – not a complete repudiation of the wider networks of British belonging but nevertheless a clear downgrading of their significance. The imperative of repudiating the historical legacy of slavery was among the principal elements binding these otherwise disparate island communities together, and in that sense the official rhetoric of 'taking our place among the free nations of the world' was inextricable from the parallel aim of 'liquidating once and for all every vestige of colonialism'.[116] These aspirations were dramatized in Derek Walcott's official production for the 1958 federal pageant, *Drums and Colours* – a redemptive journey through the iniquities of the colonial past, heralding a new era of equal opportunity and mutual respect.[117] Devising the official name of the new federal union also became an exercise in diminishing imperial sources of political legitimacy. At the eleventh hour, the 'British Caribbean Federation' was judiciously altered simply to 'The West Indies' – with the express purpose of putting Britain back in its place.[118]

More than fifty years ago, Samuel J. Hurwitz noted how the West Indian Islands 'seen at close range' had precious little in common, 'but viewed from the distance of England, where West Indian nationalism was incubated, there was a similarity in the peoples and conditions of the British Caribbean which seemed to make more for unity than separation'.[119] Enlarging on George Lamming's oft-quoted aphorism that 'most West Indians of my generation were born in England', historians frequently point to the crucial role of British-based West Indians in developing the federal idea – perhaps more so than any grass-roots federalism in the Caribbean itself.[120] This was partly a matter of familiarity wrought by proximity – as one 1950s voyager recalled, 'when the ship rock and rolled, and the spaghetti spread itself within the white wine and we got tangled, everybody spoke'.[121] But it was also a response to the encounter with Britain itself – of being lumped together as unwanted 'coloureds', enduring similar patterns of hardship and social exclusion that were all the more harrowing for being unanticipated. Or in Bill Schwarz's formulation, 'an accumulation of individual experiences was worked into a collective story of mythic properties', unleashing an 'array of perplexed, painful musings of the unhomeliness of the imagined homeland'.[122]

When Donald Hinds published *Journey to an Illusion* in 1966, he condensed these disparate 'musings' into a coherent portrait of a people 'struck dumb' by the shock of misrecognition.[123] Hinds had arrived from Jamaica in 1955, raised on a diet of English classics and the genteel offerings of Gainsborough Studios, but was immediately unsettled by the everyday markers of racial difference. He cited the 1958 riots in Nottingham and Notting Hill as a key catalyst for self-examination. But it was especially the racially motivated murder of the Antiguan carpenter Kelso Cochrane in May 1959 that called his British affinities into question. 'After Cochrane's death', he recalled in an interview fifty years later, 'we had to rethink everything; we had to revise our faith in the Union Jack.'[124] It was then that Hinds began to write for the *West Indian Gazette and Afro-Asian Caribbean News*, a Brixton-based monthly established in spring 1958 by the radical Trinidadian exile Claudia Jones. At a time when West Indian aspirations for equal treatment as British subjects were routinely punctured, the *Gazette* offered a creative outlet for a generation relying increasingly on their own cultural resources.[125] Hinds recalled how it was in this 'climate of expectations dashed' that the first London Carnival was launched in 1959, partly as a response to the Notting Hill disturbances but also as an expression of an emergent Caribbean consciousness.[126] 'A pride in being West Indian is undoubtedly at the root of this unity', announced Jones in the 1959 souvenir program, 'a pride that has its origins in the drama of nascent nationhood.'[127]

Journey to an Illusion combined the author's personal experience with a compilation of memoirs from his fellow migrants: 'those of us colonial born and bred, who did not understand the meaning of imperialism, who moved towards the mirage'.[128] George Lamming's influence is evident throughout, not least his famous depiction of the passage to Britain as a 'journey to an expectation'.[129] But where Lamming wrote of a 'perplexing', 'enigmatic' encounter with England as the 'gaiety of reprieve which we felt on our departure ... gave way to apprehension', for Hinds it was a case of wholesale disenchantment: the 'myth of the Mother Country' exploded. Each eyewitness installment recorded a moment when the scales fell from the newcomers' eyes; indeed, one of his interviewees declared himself 'grateful to the English. Grateful for rejecting me in order to discover myself.'[130] Hinds became convinced that the accumulated myths of Greater Britain – the entitlements conferred by the possession of a British passport, the shared history and cultural inheritance that placed them 'on a par with the Englishman' – had been 'swallowed hook, line and sinker by West Indians'. It was only 'as things got tougher and tougher' in Britain that the 'migrants began to believe less and less in the validity' of their British birthright. If coming to Britain was the 'climax' of a journey begun in childhood, he surmised, the 'denouement' soon followed: the 'sudden realization that all the years of coaching could offer little to his being at home in Britain'.[131]

Viewed from this perspective, the process of disentangling West Indians from wider networks of British belonging was not simply a matter of rioting

Teddy Boys, *Daily Mail* letter-writers and Whitehall mandarins grasping for a politically expedient means of restricting Commonwealth immigration. Throughout this period of globally rewired coordinates, West Indians were more than mere objects of British 'policy', unceremoniously excluded in a flurry of legislative zeal. They were themselves fully immersed in their own identity formation, fashioning new understandings of West-Indianness, Britishness and the evolving spaces in between. In Sam Selvon's landmark literary depiction, *The Lonely Londoners* (1956), the setting is neither 'England' nor 'Great Britain' but *old Brit'n* – a place inhabited by West Indian personalities, perspectives and a pervasive dislocation. 'No place at all', ponders the hard-luck protagonist Moses, 'neither forward nor backward' – but nevertheless a space where West Indians could imagine themselves anew.[132]

When the clamp on Commonwealth migration finally came in 1962, it was surprisingly not by way of an amendment to the 1948 British Nationality Act. Instead, an entirely new instrument was devised – the Commonwealth Immigrants Act – tabled in November 1961 and passed into law six months later. This had the political advantage of stemming the rate of new arrivals without opening the whole gamut of issues pertaining to nationality and subjecthood throughout the Commonwealth. In this way, the Macmillan government achieved the remarkable feat of stripping British subjecthood of its worldly entitlements without making any mention of the British subject, the British citizen, or indeed the adjective 'British' whatsoever. To be sure, they were still looking to have it both ways, maintaining the spurious distinction between inclusive nationality laws and restrictive immigration practices. But in changing the subject to 'Commonwealth Immigrants', the boundless reach of Britishness – so assiduously buttressed since 1948 – lapsed quietly into obscurity. It would be another twenty years before UK nationality laws would be amended to recognize the hard distinctions between the British of Britain and their offshore counterparts foreshadowed by the 1962 measures.[133] Thus for a time, universal subjecthood would continue to be honoured in theory, but from 1 July 1962 it was no longer possible for British subjects from the colonies and Commonwealth to exercise the most basic right of citizenship – to move without restraint within the sovereign space conferred by their nationality.[134] In the words of the civil rights advocate Cedric Thornberry, the 1948 British Nationality Act could now be viewed in its true light – 'as a last maternal clutching at a family fragmenting in face of pressures from within and without'.[135]

To deflect accusations of racial discrimination, the new restrictions were imposed across the board to all Commonwealth countries, but an intricate voucher system was devised to allow more favourable terms of entry for the white denizens of the 'old' dominions. As Home Secretary Rab Butler privately enthused, the 'great merit' of the Act was that although its provisions were drafted in non-discriminatory terms, 'its restrictive effect is intended to, and would in fact, operate on coloured people almost exclusively'.[136] The New Zealand Government was confidentially assured that although the restrictions 'would in form apply to all "British" subjects entering the United Kingdom', their effects would be 'limited to those who give rise to social tensions' – or putting euphemism to one side, there would be 'no restriction on the entry of white applicants'.[137] Such covert discrimination only heightened suspicion about the racial motivations behind the legislation, and in any event failed to placate objections in Australia and New Zealand where the mere inconvenience of applying for an entry voucher was widely condemned as an affront to their British credentials. The Australian Government (still practising the most racially exclusive immigration policy ever devised) lobbied British ministers behind the scenes to think harder about the impact of the new regulations on 'the traditionally loyal "old" white Dominions people'.[138] The *Sydney Morning Herald* was less circumspect, mounting the puerile protest: 'We are, or thought we were, the same people – simply the British overseas. Now, it seems, we are not.'[139]

The announcement was unpopular throughout the West Indies where the restrictions were intended to bite hard and where population and employment pressures were especially acute. The prime minister of the West Indies Federation, Sir Grantley Adams, issued a 'special protest' that was read out in the House of Commons by an indignant Labour leader, Hugh Gaitskell; his grievances ranging from the lack of any prior consultation (despite countless prior assurances) to the insulting exemption for citizens of the Irish Republic who would continue to move freely into the UK. This, perhaps more than anything else, exposed the sham of colour blindness – the point when the 'whole despicable plot' was revealed, as one newspaper disclaimed.[140] Britain had 'fallen on evil days', declared Adams, when the government of the day could 'descend to the stage of keeping British subjects from Britain. Their ancestors were above that sort of thing.'[141] He made arrangements to fly to Britain at once to press his case personally with the Macmillan Government, issuing an official statement calling on 'all Britishers of goodwill to do everything that lies in their power' to stop the Bill.[142] To awaiting journalists at Heathrow airport he declared that 'the British have lost their heads. They are doing things to us they should never do'; while in private consultation with Harold Macmillan later that day he complained that the people of the West Indies 'felt that they were being deprived of their status as citizens of the United Kingdom and Colonies and classed halfway towards aliens'.[143]

Adams's fundamental grievance was condensed in one of his more widely quoted utterances: 'We are as British as a person from Somerset, Devon or Cornwall.'[144] In November 1961, however, such sentiments fell conspicuously on deaf ears – notably in Britain where he was politely ignored, but even in the West Indies where press coverage seemed generally more resigned to the changes.[145] The *Barbados Advocate* noted the historic passing of 'a policy that goes back to 1608' when James I declared himself 'one entire king over all his subjects in whichsoever of his dominions they were born'. But there was little dissent from the verdict of the Barbadian Labour minister: 'We have got to accept these restrictions and hope for the best.'[146] Grantley Adams would not be the last West Indian leader to return empty-handed from negotiations with the British Government, but he would be the last to assert such unqualified equivalence between West Indians and their fellow citizens in the United Kingdom. In future, the emphasis would shift to more compelling arguments arising from the legacies and iniquities of colonialism and slavery – more so than the outmoded identity politics of Greater Britain.[147]

The London visit capped off a bad year for the West Indian prime minister, which also saw the unravelling of the West Indies Federation that he had served for the entire duration of its four-year existence. Three months earlier in September, the strained relations between the larger and smaller member-states had culminated in the Jamaican people's vote to break away from the federation, followed by Trinidad shortly afterwards. The departure of the two economic powerhouses reduced the federal ideal to an economically unviable scattering of smaller islands, and the entire project was ultimately dissolved on the very date originally slated for full independence: 31 May 1962. But the fundamental cause of the federation's demise was the emergent strength of national feeling in its constituent parts, virtually all of which had achieved full internal self-government since the initial strides towards federation in the late 1940s. As Elisabeth Wallace argues, 'the more authority they attained in their own islands the less willing they became to share or lose it'.[148] It is striking how the Windrush era of free migration from the Caribbean to Britain coincided almost exactly with the lifespan of the West Indies Federation, from the first federal conferences of the late 1940s to the wind-up of the federal legislature barely a month after the passage of the Commonwealth Immigrants Act in 1962.[149] In a sense, both conceptions were swept aside by the updraft of national self-determination that worked against the logic of wider loyalties – whether spanning the anglophone Caribbean or the even wider embrace of Greater Britain.

It has become a mainstay of contemporary British history that post-war migration from the colonies and Commonwealth marked a pivotal moment: that the 'reversal of the colonial encounter' mounted a major challenge to prevailing assumptions about race, community and civic identity in the United Kingdom. It is said that the immigration debates of this era 'could not be wholly separated from discussions of what it now meant to be British', that metropolitan attitudes 'collided head-on' with the newcomers' own 'distinct self-understandings and preconceptions about Britain' and that the attendant tensions and anxieties 'made race central to questions about home'.[150] Some accounts emphasize a consequent 'racialization of national identity' – a moment when 'a consciousness of being white intensified for a significant number of indigenous Britons'.[151] Others suggest the very opposite: that these encounters 'effectively destabilized racially exclusive boundaries of Britishness', serving 'to forge a historically informed, racially inclusive definition of British citizenship'.[152] In virtually all accounts the West Indian migrant assumes particular prominence as a transformative figure, challenging the metropole with the conviction 'that Blackness could be British and Britishness could be Black'.[153] In this scheme of things, as Bill Schwarz contends, 'West Indians who crossed the seas and travelled to the mother country found themselves, against all expectations, living on the unofficial front-line of this larger struggle for decolonization.'[154]

This larger setting of post-war decolonization is equally critical for understanding the eclipse of an expansive, global British subjecthood, affecting all of the empire's subjects in varying degrees and spawning new, more circumscribed definitions of citizenship that disrupted older, more fluid allegiances. Though the changes were implemented haphazardly, with local contingencies producing any number of permutations, the broader shift towards diminished reliance on Britishness as a global marker of civic identity is unmistakable. West Indian claimants to British belonging were themselves transformed in the process. When Harold Moody campaigned for equal rights in interwar Britain, his claims had been steeped in a 'spiritual, cultural, and mental equality … with every other member of the British Empire'; his fundamental aim 'to embody the term "British citizen" with some meaning and some reality as far as we are concerned'.[155] Less than three decades later this reasoning could no longer sustain a compelling case, neither for a substantial body of opinion in the United Kingdom nor, crucially, in the changing climate of the Caribbean itself. For all the 'reordered boundaries' of domestic British politics, these changes were part of a worldwide reordering of loyalties and affinities in which the very idea of Britain was in rapid retreat.[156] Accounting for this requires attention, not only to the intimate histories of individual and collective migrant experiences in Britain, but also to the broader eclipse of Britishness as a meaningful category of nationality and citizenship in a decolonizing world.

This in no way diminished the demand for racial equality among the hundreds of thousands of West Indian and other Commonwealth migrant communities who had remade their lives in Britain (or indeed the many more still to come). But in a world where Commonwealth citizenship no longer conferred an automatic right of abode in Britain, the terms of the debate were fundamentally transformed. With the infamous Smethwick election campaign of 1964 around the corner, and further immigration restrictions looming in the shadow of Powellism, these were early days in the struggle to fashion new, more inclusive categories of belonging in post-imperial Britain. Black could emphatically still be British (and vice versa) but by and large the relevance of a globally dispersed British subjecthood fell by the wayside – to be replaced by a more inward-looking focus on civil rights, 'race relations' and the challenge of domestic racial injustice.[157]

The shift was signalled by the first intimations of 'multi-racialism' (later to be rebranded multiculturalism) in the political vernacular of the 1960s – a potentially more inclusive social contract, certainly one less immediately anchored in the historical conditions of colonialism. The watershed was the Labour Party's controversial decision not to repeal the Commonwealth Immigrants Act and reinstate unrestricted entry for all British subjects upon its return to power in 1964. Aware of the widespread disappointment and indeed disgust among many of its supporters, the Wilson government sought atonement by redirecting its energies towards anti-discrimination legislation – addressing the rights and needs of the existing migrant population rather than resurrecting the hopes of offshore aspirants. Although the 1965 Race Relations Act is often dismissed as a 'whimper of a law', not least in its failure to include housing and employment in its remit, it nevertheless marked a new departure in disaggregating 'race relations' from immigration policy in a radically circumscribed civic nation.[158]

And by outlawing any form of racial discrimination in a public place, including '*any hotel*', the Act addressed a familiar and long-standing grievance of many a West Indian sojourner.[159] When the first Race Relations

Board was appointed on 17 February 1966, it was entirely fitting that Learie Constantine (now Sir Learie) was invited to serve on its inaugural panel of three members.[160] In its first year alone, the board would sit in judgement on 327 complaints, including twelve involving hotels – no doubt stirring memories of Sir Learie's humiliating experience nearly a quarter of a century earlier. Within a few months of his appointment the decaying structure of the Imperial Hotel in Russell Square once again stood condemned – this time by the issue of a demolition order from the Greater London Council. Years of managerial neglect and a changing clientele had reduced the Imperial to a parody of its former grandeur – derided by 'Carry-On' screen icon Kenneth Williams as fit 'only for a grubby Spanish holiday resort'. Plans for a refurbishment were abandoned when flaws in the foundations exposed the futility of the endeavour. The surveyors decreed that 'the whole frame was so structurally unsound that there was no possibility of saving it [even] if a preservation order had been placed on the building' – a fitting epitaph for the equally weathered frame of Greater British subjecthood.[161]

7

THE WIND CHANGES: HUMAN RIGHTS AFTER SMUTS

In the latter months of 1946, a premonition of English-speaking whites stranded on an epic scale came to the South African historian Arthur Keppel-Jones. A direct descendant of the immortalized 1820 settlers, the Rhodes scholar and long-time anti-racism campaigner promptly put pen to paper. Composed at 'a feverish pace' over three short weeks, his futuristic dystopia *When Smuts Goes* was 'a study in historical extrapolation' – conjuring a history of South Africa from the vantage point of the year 2015.[1] Part allegory and part science-fiction, Keppel-Jones retrospectively foretold the rise of Afrikaner nationalism under the fictionalized demagogue Obadja Bult. The nationalist victory at the 1952 election (sweeping every province but Natal) presaged an ever-darkening descent into one-party dictatorship, punctuated by a raft of repressive laws abolishing the oath of allegiance to the king, stripping the Union Jack from public ceremonies and outlawing English as an official language. The proclamation of a South African Republic in 1966 set the seal on a ruthless Afrikaner insurgency, consigning a despairing minority of anglophone whites to political purgatory. With breakneck speed it had become 'obvious to those who had not known it before that South Africa was lost to the British Commonwealth', setting the scene for the wholesale emigration of white English-speakers in search of a more liberal dispensation and the familiar comforts of home. The 'Second Great Trek' marked their spontaneous flight, bound for Australia, New Zealand and other settler societies 'inhabited and ruled by their own people'.[2] An initially modest flow of emigrants into Rhodesia soon turned into a 'tidal wave', virtually emptying South Africa of its loyal British contingent by the early 1970s.[3]

As though reading his own runes, Keppel-Jones would gather up his family a decade later and relocate to Kingston, Ontario for the remainder of his long years. Aged fifty, he was still young enough to establish a new life teaching history at Queen's University, and as he recalled decades later in his eighties: 'My spirit had emigrated from South Africa long before my body.' For all the unexpected accolades for *When Smuts Goes*, the intervening years had brought more of his fantasy to fruition than he cared to endure, starting with the defeat of Field Marshall Smuts to D. F. Malan's nationalists in 1948 (four years earlier than his grim forecast had anticipated). Although initially throwing his energies into averting 'the disaster that was overtaking the country', the subsequent elections of 1953 and 1958 only further entrenched the dominance of 'the Nats' against the enfeebled heirs of Smuts's United Party. He soon lost confidence in the bogus liberalism of the latter, and found increasingly that 'the politics of the period pushed me in the direction of my British roots, and to an emphasis on the liberating aspect of British culture'.[4] When it finally came, his departure was a rare confluence of fiction and fate, emulating that of his literary creation, George Rodwield – the Cape Town schoolmaster who struck out for Rhodesia in 1959 (the same year as the author's own meticulously planned escape):

> As his train passed over the Karoo, where he had lived as a child ... something in him responded to the distant lines of stony hills, *spitskop* and *tafelberg*, and bushes like the tufts on a bushman's head. The very names of sidings and stations – Paardevlei, Behrshoek, Houtkraal – were music to his ears. Yet his allegiance to the King and his affection for England and her past – his past – were a part of him, too; and these had won.[5]

Keppel-Jones's parable brought to light a facet of settler-colonialism frequently shielded from view – the repressed memory of emigration. In common with virtually all British settler societies, English South African folklore celebrated the taming of new territory far more than the romance of the outward voyage – it was the land, not the sea that was the object of their strivings. Screening out the moment of arrival also had the salutary effect of downplaying violent histories of invasion and dispossession, allowing prior Indigenous occupation to slip easily from public view.

When Smuts Goes signalled a sharp break with tradition in this regard, dwelling on the intricacies of large-scale emigration in elaborate detail. Railway timetables, shipping berths, emigration agents, property auctions, asset sales, border camps and exhaustive population tables all served to heighten the tension, signalling a tacit intimacy with prior displacement. Faced with an existential threat to their way of life, it seemed perfectly logical and indeed inevitable that a transplanted people would emigrate once more, not by way of return to their point of origin (a path Keppel-Jones barely contemplated) but further afield to more reliably British new worlds. In thus dramatizing the privations of dis-encampment and spiritual escape, he stirred dim memories of earlier ruptures – highlighting the inherent transience at the heart of 'Greater Britonism'.[6] For all his prescience in raising the alarm for English cultural and political dominance in South Africa, he could not relinquish his faith in the immutability of a British world elsewhere.

Remarkably, these reveries of tragi-heroic flight were prompted, not by the insistent claims of a resurgent Black activism but by the obdurate chauvinism of a rival cohort of whites. Like most of his contemporaries, Keppel-Jones failed to register the post-war emergence of a new generation of Black intellectuals and activists pressing for wholesale changes to the pursuit of racial justice. These were pivotal years in the struggle against white domination, marking the early careers of Walter Sisulu, Oliver Tambo, Nelson Mandela and other key figures in the newly founded ANC Youth League.[7] From the perspective of Keppel-Jones, however, Afrikaner nationalists seemed the more urgent threat to South Africa's British moorings with their age-old historical grievances and enduring anti-British resentments. Indigenous resistance appeared only belatedly in his imagined timeline of events; a scourge of Zulu violence erupting long after the Englishman's departure (staged as the inevitable comeuppance for the Afrikaners' stubborn racial belligerence). In this scheme of things, Britain's stabilizing liberal influence was the indispensable bulwark holding both sides in check – Black insurgency and white extremism alike.

Yet beneath the antipathy for Afrikaner fanaticism lurked a more subliminal dread, distilled into three highly charged words. *When Smuts Goes* portended more than a mere change of government or the passing of a political titan. For decades, the figure of Smuts had been synonymous with the liberal credentials of the British empire itself, combining the imperative of white rule with the civilizing benefits of the link with England.[8] Lauded variously around the world as 'the demigod of British imperialists', 'the greatest African that had yet appeared' and 'the most considerable person in Greater Britain', Smuts enjoyed unrivalled prestige as the quintessential imperial statesman – the embodiment of 'England's destiny overseas'.[9] His Cape Afrikaner origins only cemented his authority, underlining the power of redemption and the opportunity 'to redirect and expand local nationalisms into a wider sense of belonging'.[10] Combining the 'moral truth of the frontier' with the 'force-field of English ethnicity', this was 'Britishness without the centring of Britain'.[11] Smuts not only coined the notion of a 'British Commonwealth of Nations' but also came to personify its idealized global fraternity. To contemplate his demise was thus to question the durability of an entire way of life – the life of Greater Britain, so intrinsic to Smuts's sense of racial order.

Within months of Keppel-Jones's departure for Canada, his forebodings soon materialized with the arrival of the first serving British prime minister ever to visit South Africa. Harold Macmillan's disembarkation at Cape Town's Duncan Dock in January 1960 was greeted by bunting-lined streets, cheering crowds and festive tidings that concealed the sombre message he would soon deliver to the whites-only South African Parliament: 'The Wind of Change is blowing through this continent and, whether we like it or not, this growth of national consciousness is a political fact.' Macmillan's historic pronouncement foreshadowed the final act of the liquidation of the British empire in ways that even he never fully grasped. Widely acclaimed for confronting white intransigence head-on, his deft turn of phrase soon became synonymous with the eclipse of colonialism and the promise of self-determination the world over.[12]

But as shorthand for the fundamental impetus behind Africa's shifting power-balance, Macmillan's aphorism is deficient in almost every respect. His Cape Town speech cited a 'growth of national consciousness' as the galvanizing force – one of the 'constant facts of political life' since the fall of the Roman Empire now making its presence felt in Africa. Its underlying causes were 'to be found in the achievements of western civilisation', sowing the benefits of the same 'processes which gave birth to the nation states of Europe'. Just as Keppel-Jones had failed to detect the disruptive potential of African dissent, so too Macmillan misconstrued decolonization as the latest instalment of an age-old clash of rival nationalisms, attributing African grievances to the dissemination of Europe's peculiar genius for political organization. His presumption has been widely and rightly debunked, but only relatively recently has his core premise – a colonial world transformed by a derivative nationalism – come in for questioning.[13]

Colonial nationalism per se was not the prime mover in 1960, nor was it the defining feature of post-war decolonization routinely depicted in conventional historical accounts.[14] Far more significant was the surge of *international* consciousness: the advent of newly conceptualized moral worlds couched in the language of universal rights and the primacy of human dignity. In the decade or so after 1945, a uniquely opportune climate for humanitarian and anti-colonial claim-making was forged – not least for the empire's First Peoples. All over the world, settler communities were confronted with insistent demands to redress the injustices flowing from the pioneering intrusions of their forebears, challenging their foundational myths and raising nagging questions about their security of tenure.

Colonies of settlement that for generations had been collectively known as the 'White Commonwealth', marked out for eternal habitation by peoples whose legitimacy and staying power had seemed beyond question, now grappled with Indigenous claims to equal entitlements according to newly fashioned universal norms.

Though this was never Macmillan's purpose in crafting his words in Cape Town, their real significance lies in the fact that he had no choice but to utter them. The odium of South African racial practices had rarely troubled any of his predecessors, shielded behind the Commonwealth principle of 'non-intervention' in the domestic affairs of other members. But just over a decade after the 1948 Universal Declaration of Human Rights, in a world increasingly turning to the rhythms of a new multilateralism, Macmillan could ill-afford to remain silent on one of the burning issues of the day. For all his emphasis on a combustible new spirit of nationalism, the wind of change foreshadowed an incipient internationalism that encroached on the belief systems of British old worlds as it ushered in the new. For the minority of white, professedly 'liberal', English-speaking South Africans, bent on combatting Afrikaner political dominance, the advent of Indigenous demands rooted in universal rights would ultimately pose the more severe test to Smuts's legacy.

SOUTH AFRICA'S 'LANGUAGES OF LOYALISM'

South Africa presents an especially complex and tangled field for tracing the lineaments of Greater Britain, as the 'least thoroughly anglicized and undoubtedly the most troublesome' of the white dominions.[15] Doubts about South Africa's potential as an integral component were as old as British colonization itself (Charles Dilke himself was unconvinced due to the 'double difficulty' of the heavy preponderance of Afrikaner and African peoples). Unlike Australia and New Zealand where 'British race' affinities were openly revered, in South Africa such sentiments were comparatively subdued due to the requirements of reconciling 'Briton and Boer' in the wake of the South African War.[16] But this did not consign Britishness to the civic margins. The absence of an official culture of British boosterism produced fertile ground for a great variety of offshoots to proliferate – what Andrew Thompson terms the many 'languages of loyalism', fanning out across the country's myriad social, regional and ethnic divides, each selecting elements of British civic culture that served their specific needs.[17] These sub-varieties were never self-contained but remained in constant dialogue, drawing their emotional power not only from the avowedly anti-

British strains of Afrikaner nationalism, but also from the knowledge that others – even bitter rivals – could claim access to the same civic entitlements. In this highly fluid setting, as Saul Dubow maintains, 'the problem with Britishness was not its absence or its weakness so much as the fissile multiplicity of forms that it took'.[18]

Among South Africa's Indigenous peoples, the registers of loyalty multiplied with an array of religious, ethnic and language groups all seeking a purchase on British constitutional liberties – with the memory of Queen Victoria again symbolizing the original 'font of freedoms and rights'.[19] This was partly a matter of the sheer pervasiveness of imperial ritual and British political symbolism that was virtually impossible for dissident groups to circumvent. As the South African sociologist Bernard Magubane surmised, British domination 'was to saturate society and its values to the extent that they would become common sense for people under its sway'.[20] Yet others have cautioned against reading loyalist and monarchical sentiment in an African context 'as an overzealous, gratuitous, almost pathological affirmation of imperialism'.[21] A succession of royal tours in the nineteenth and twentieth centuries provided a ready platform for ever-more elaborate displays of monarchical fealty, but they also presented ample opportunities 'for masking and ventilating less than loyal feelings'.[22] In her study of the 1925 African tour of the Prince of Wales, Hilary Sapire identifies a unique combination of sincere emotional attachments to king and empire, coupled with a more pragmatic strategy for alleviating the conditions of white domination. Unqualified expressions of African loyalty could be compared favourably with 'narrow and selfish settler loyalty' that distorted '"true" British imperial values', but they also furnished a 'defence against the charge of subversion' – as exemplified by Charlotte Maxeke, the founder of the Bantu Women's League who prefaced her trenchant critique of racial injustice with the simple formula: 'I am a British subject, and I am very pleased to owe allegiance to the flag, so I trust no-one will misconstrue my motives.'[23]

The early leaders of the African National Congress (founded in 1912 as the South African Native National Congress) were drawn typically from among aspirational, mission-educated Africans with devoutly Christian and Cape liberal leanings – often portrayed as 'an essentially middle class elite much enthralled with things British'.[24] The inaugural president, John Dube, routinely buttressed his case against segregation with wider appeals to 'England's duty' and the 'white man's burden', while the first secretary-general, Solomon Plaatje, was a great admirer of the English literary canon, completing the first translation of Shakespeare into an African language.[25]

His successor, Saul Msane, the veteran of repeated attempts to take African grievances to the heart of the empire, implored delegates at a 1918 Congress meeting to be 'inflexibly loyal to their Supreme Chief, His Majesty the King'.[26] Peter Limb has explored the 'many signifiers of Britishness' in the early ANC: their organizational structure based on the bicameral system of Westminster (with an Upper House for chiefs); their official delegations and petitions invariably dispatched to London; their speeches and writings, heavily inflected with the ideals of British freedoms and justice; and their campaign materials adorned with the Union Jack.[27]

These outward trappings became all the more conspicuous as the rights and entitlements of non-white subjects were cast aside by the racist provisions of the Act of Union of 1910. Prior to the Bill's enactment in 1909, a self-styled 'Delegation of the Representatives of the Coloured and Native British Subjects Resident in the British Dominions of South Africa' journeyed to London to protest against the insidious effects of 'nativization'. To be categorized as 'natives' was to be denied political and civil rights, hence the imperative of petitioning specifically as 'Black Britons'.[28] Ten years later, another delegation arriving in London at war's end to influence the terms of the peace was similarly at pains to resist relegation to the inferiority of separate status: 'We have come not to ask for independence, but for an admission into British citizenship as British subjects so that we may also enjoy the free institutions which are the foundations and pillars of this magnificent Commonwealth.'[29]

Seeking amends for historic wrongs was thus founded on the principle of equality for all within the British fold – which is not to say that the early ANC was incapable of perceiving Britain's abundant shortcomings. The yawning gap between theory and practice became a constant refrain in the interwar years – the more avowedly 'loyal' their credentials, the more effectively they dramatized the gap. Already within the first year of his presidency, John Dube had privately conceded that 'going to England seems to me hopeless' in the light of the evident failure of a number of delegations that had 'returned without success'.[30] ANC support for the British war effort in 1914 was similarly hedged with 'regret that the settlement of our just grievances has been ignored'.[31] 'Are We the King's Subjects?', demanded the ANC weekly paper *Abanthu-Batho* in 1919, when the 'rights of the native population were not only ignored, but were turned upside down with the King's consent'.[32] Plaatje's own fastidiously restrained line of critique could not disguise his subversive intent: 'We would put it to all concerned for the honour and perpetuity of British dominion in South Africa, can the Empire afford to tamper with and alienate [our] affections?'[33] Though acutely aware of how far Britain fell short of its moral obligations, ANC aspirations nevertheless rested squarely on British conceptions of rights, entitlements and public morality – through a succession of impassioned appeals (and serial disappointments) that continued right up to the Second World War.

To account for why they persisted for so long, it is worth revisiting the interwar crusade of the Australian Aboriginal activist William Cooper, discussed in Chapter 3: 'If we cannot get full justice . . . we must ask the King.'[34] By this he meant that Indigenous peoples in settler societies had literally nowhere else to turn – no alternative source of transcendent authority for pressing their legitimate grievances. At a time when 'rights were defined as much by residual bonds of loyalty to the British Commonwealth or Crown as by membership of a new self-governing state', there existed no obvious national or transnational body to which Indigenous dissidents might conceivably appeal.[35] Plaatje conceded in a 1919 interview: 'the only people from whom we have any sympathy and support are the International Socialists, and, unfortunately, they are an insignificant minority'.[36] This seemingly throwaway remark clearly suggests that Indigenous advocates were not blind to the possibility of seeking redress elsewhere, according to alternative precepts of natural justice within a wider internationalist framework, but the options were severely curtailed. It would take years of bitter perseverance before Indigenous rights agendas were decoupled from British norms. As Adom Getachew has shown, it was only after having 'tried out various strategies to secure participation and equal inclusion within imperial frameworks' that anti-colonial activists finally settled on 'rejecting them altogether'.[37]

The subtlety of the switch can be seen in the contrasting pronouncements of the ANC leadership at mid-century. In 1938, shortly before assuming the ANC presidency, A. B. Xuma issued a vow of loyalty to the king and empire in terms fully aligned with the idealized moral world of Greater Britain, a world 'based on justice and fair play for all His Majesty's subjects irrespective of race and colour'.[38] Four years later, with planning for the post-war world already set in train by the 1941 Atlantic Charter, Xuma embarked on a major reorganization of the ANC with a view to preparing Africans to plead their case 'before the international court of human justice'.[39] It was an early portent of a more radical substitution of imperial totems for the inherent rights and entitlements invested in humanity itself. While the empire and the crown continued to provide a realm within which rights could be enshrined and remedies sought, they were shortly to be superseded by the new spirit of internationalism emerging from the embers of global conflict. In the space of less than two decades, ANC demands for inclusion in the civic bounty of British selfhood (like William Cooper's claim to the 'right to be fully British') would fall completely into disuse.[40] To understand why, and to appreciate how the shifting strategies of Black advocacy would affect the 'liberating aspect of British culture' for the likes of Keppel Jones, it is crucial to consider the disruptions of the post-war world that presented new opportunities for reconfiguring Indigenous protest, while at the same time challenging the moral axioms of the British settler state.[41]

'THE INHERENT DIGNITY ... OF THE HUMAN PERSON': NEGOTIATING UNIVERSALITY

Contrary to widely disseminated myth, the aftermath of the Second World War did not spontaneously usher in a new order of universal norms, global justice and human rights for all. The 1941 Atlantic Charter – in which Churchill and Roosevelt pledged themselves to a future where 'all the men in all the lands may live out their lives in freedom from fear and want' – is often hailed as the 'defining, inaugural moment' of the human rights era.[42] From Dumbarton Oaks to the San Francisco Conference and the celebrated UN Charter of 1945, these signposts are frequently invoked to mark the inexorable path to the 1948 Universal Declaration of Human Rights, with its forceful assertion of 'the inherent dignity and of the equal and inalienable rights of all members of the human family'. The reality, however, is more complex and fragmented. Though these new legal instruments undoubtedly reflected the aspirations of a restless era, recasting the language of individual rights in a new idiom, their effect on the primacy of sovereign nation states (and their colonial empires) would take years to evolve. Upholding the '*inherent* dignity and worth of the human person' – the central tenet of the 1948 Universal Declaration – would raise complex questions and interminable debates about the precise meaning, applicability and even desirability of universal norms.

The 1947 South African tour of the British royal family came right at the intersection of these cross-currents – marking the apogee of empire as a system of civic rights and moral obligations. George VI, Queen Elizabeth and their daughters Elizabeth and Margaret were greeted by rapturous crowds throughout their journey stretching over two months and more than five thousand miles. In addition to the predictable hordes of flag-waving English-speaking whites, the tour drew in a consistently large contingent of non-white South Africans of every description. Abundant anecdotal evidence suggests that the event marked 'a uniquely jubilant moment' for otherwise disenfranchised peoples who continued to look to the sovereign as the source of civic entitlements, seemingly oblivious to the new-fangled abstractions emerging from San Francisco and New York.[43] Upon their arrival in Zululand on 19 March 1947, the royal entourage was officially hailed by future ANC president Chief Albert Luthuli in the tradition of isiZulu praise poetry: 'Just as when the lion roars, all nature is hushed, as when Your Majesty speaks to us we will listen to Your Majesty in silent awe, knowing that only wisdom will come from your lips.'[44] It was a direct carry-over from the deference of the interwar years, played out repeatedly as the royals wound their way through the country on the specially fitted 'White Train'. The ANC Youth League's *Inkundla Ya Bantu* would describe the entire spectacle as 'a cause for great rejoicing among many Africans who still viewed the British sovereign as their ultimate protector'.[45]

'Still' is the operative word – emitting a faint signal of impending rupture. Although the visit succeeded for the first time in bringing the mystique of royalty into closer proximity with non-white subjects, it also threw the region's deep racial iniquities into sharp relief in an official programme 'soaked in segregation'.[46] No effort was spared to avoid placing the king and his family in a mixed-race setting, with an endless round of banquets, balls and garden parties carefully corralled into separate communal gatherings. No provision was made for the royals to meet the leadership of the African or Indian Congresses, and indeed a fierce internal debate erupted in the ANC over a resolution calling for a complete boycott of the tour. The wording of the resolution objected to 'the barbarous policy' of denying 'elementary rights to Africans', not least 'in view of the fact that these injustices are perpetrated and maintained in the name of His Majesty, King George VI'.[47] The boycott failed to achieve majority support, but the mere suggestion that 'elementary rights' were being withheld in the king's name posed a subtle inversion of the paradigm. Once lauded as the ultimate bestower of rights, the sovereign now found himself cast as chief perpetrator of wrongs – judged by the standards of incipient new norms enshrined in universal principles.

How new and how universal are both matters of contention among historians, who remain sharply divided over the provenance of human rights as a force for social and political change in the mid-twentieth century. It was once axiomatic that the universal 'rights of man' were forged in the great revolutions of the late eighteenth century, evolving fitfully but inexorably ('cascading' in the view of one influential account) towards the new vistas of the post-Second World War era and beyond.[48] But this view has come under assault from the rival contention that human rights as we know them today are entirely novel – indeed, barely a few decades old. In Samuel Moyn's influential critique, rhetorical odes to inherent rights reaching back to the time of Thomas Paine almost never made the conceptual leap to become genuinely universal, untethered from the legitimating and control-ling sanction of popular sovereignty – at least not until comparatively recently. According to this view, the eighteenth-century notion that individ-uals were the bearers of rights remained unambiguously embedded within 'the authority of the state, not invoked to transcend it'.[49] It was only the misguided idealism of 'historians of an invigorating and well-intentioned American liberalism', eager to construct a deeper legitimating myth for contemporary rights agendas, that blurred the lines between the modern conception of human rights and the romanticized world of enlightenment humanitarianism.[50]

Moyn's critique applies equally to the fabled leap forward in the 1940s where he insists that human rights were 'peripheral' in framing the post-war international order. He further dismisses the later struggles over decolon-ization in the 1950s and 1960s – devoting an entire chapter to 'Why Anticolonialism Wasn't a Human Rights Movement'. Central to his argu-ment is the 'clear and fundamental difference' between an older, more conventional conception of rights firmly predicated on belonging to a circumscribed political community and the latter-day emergence of 'human rights', distinguished by their potential to 'contradict the sovereign nation-state from above and outside rather than serve as its foundation'.[51] To the extent that there was a 'rights of man' movement prior to the 1970s, it was the story of 'liberal nationalism, which sought to secure the rights of citizens resolutely in the national framework'. Here, Moyn's argument merges with Brian Simpson, Reza Afshari and others, who regard the surge of post-war anti-colonialism as a 'single issue struggle' with the pri-mary aim of *enhancing* the power of the post-colonial state over the individ-ual – rather than the other way around.[52] The collective rights invoked by struggles over colonial emancipation and self-determination afforded no guarantee of individual freedoms, as witnessed by a slew of post-colonial despotisms 'blighted by human rights violations' in the 1960s.[53] Hence, those who have anchored the evolution of universal rights in the global post-war struggles over race and empire are guilty of a fundamental category error: 'There was a truncated principle that decolonization universalized. But it was that of collective liberation, not human rights.'[54] For Moyn, we need look no earlier than the 1970s for the arrival of a genuinely universal rights moment that had to await 'the collapse of prior universalistic schemes' (ranging from European imperialism to international socialism, anti-colonialism and, indeed, anti-communism in wake of Vietnam) and the 'construction of human rights as a persuasive alternative to them'.[55]

Ranged against this is the equally forceful view that the post-1945 struggles over European colonialism and the advent of universal human rights were in fact profoundly intertwined. While sharing Moyn's scepticism about continuities with the political philosophers of the Enlightenment, Steven Jensen is unconvinced by his 'Big Bang' approach to a human rights phenomenon that only belatedly emerged in the 1970s, 'seemingly from nowhere'.[56] Greater attention is needed, he argues, to the post-war wave of decolonization that 'transformed the normative backdrop upon which human rights were projected on the world stage from the 1940s and the decades that followed'.[57] The advent of new international fora, new legal instruments and above all a new political language were crucial to merging human rights with the wider field of international diplomacy. The language may have been ill-defined and the instruments imperfect but it is precisely this that constitutes the core historical dynamic of human rights in the post-war world – 'the simultaneous coexistence of proclamation and denial'.[58] Far from being a 'single issue struggle', anti-colonial movements were perpetually locked in a tug-of-war between the more limited goal of national self-determination and the loftier ideals of individual rights and freedoms – a crucial dimension that needs to be factored into longer term historical outcomes, rather than summarily dismissed as an irrelevant dead-end. The point is not to erect monuments to the triumph of universal norms, but to capture 'the complex and contradictory constellation of outcomes that followed decolonization' – a process that 'both advanced and obstructed the progress of international human rights'.[59]

While such debates are intrinsically fascinating, the effects of polarization have brought their own distortions. The question of *when* human rights secured their mythical 'breakthrough' (a term employed by virtually all the major combatants, none of whom adequately explain it) has tended to overshadow the more pertinent issue of *where*, and to what ends.[60] The global optics and the fixation on world systems has raised the stakes to an all or nothing duel – out of all proportion to the dimensions of the problem.[61] Virtually all are agreed that universal rights occupied the minds of certain individuals from roughly the early 1940s (even Moyn concedes that 'there really were some who hoped to place rights above the nation-state in World War II's aftermath').[62] What, then, to make of their efforts? Undeniably, advocates of universal rights in the post-war era were to encounter formidable obstacles, skewing debates in the direction of outcomes that provided scant protection for individual rights from the incursions of the state. But it is surely a stretch to conclude that these actors and their ideals were historically insignificant (or that historians who linger too long in their company are mired in romantic anachronisms).

Further, as Frederick Cooper contends, the clash of rival schools has also tended to reduce the entire debate to 'only two analytic fields, one national, the other universal', thus overlooking 'what lies in the middle ... namely, empire'.[63] He might have added the difficult terrain occupied by Indigenous rights activists in settler colonies who had comparatively little scope to imagine (let alone carry out) a fully fledged campaign for national self-determination (or even 'collective liberation') and who are invariably left out of the 'sovereignty versus rights' equation.[64] The post-war era raised thorny questions about whether 'a rights-bearing community' should be national, imperial or universal – all the more so for Indigenous rights campaigners long accustomed to the fixed moral coordinates of a benevolent sovereign.[65] For these activists, the enlarged scope for pitching claims outside of the rigidities of national and indeed imperial frameworks invested human rights with far greater attractions than perhaps for anyone else. Even more so than anti-colonial nationalists who struggled to balance the competing claims of individual entitlements and collective statehood, Indigenous rights campaigners engaged vigorously – and at a comparatively early stage – with the problem of 'negotiating universality'.[66]

'THE NEW WIND BLOWING THROUGH THE WORLD': THE SOUTH AFRICAN CASE

South Africa presents the most tangible instance of universal rights penetrating the post-war political scene, with profound implications for the disappearing moral world of Greater Britain. Here, there is no need to wait until the 1970s to discern a putative human rights 'breakthrough', nor is it necessary to delay matters until the tipping point of African decolonization in the early 1960s. Robin Blackburn's verdict is unequivocal: from the very outset, the struggle against apartheid 'was an icon of the anti-imperialist movement and surely had an absolute claim to the banner of human rights'.[67] Even the most dedicated debunkers of a 1940s 'New Deal for the World' concede that in South Africa 'human rights made inroads as a strategic language ... more than anywhere else'.[68]

Universal norms impinged on post-war South Africa on at least three interlocking levels. First, their rhetorical influence was everywhere to be seen, with the prime movers of the Indian and African Congresses eager to tap into the subversive potential of the Atlantic Charter. This was most clearly symbolized by the ANC's adaptation of the charter's provisions 'to our own conditions' in their December 1943 statement: *Africans' Claims in South Africa*. Here, the imprint of wider aspirations encompassing 'justice and fairplay for all human beings' was unambiguous, including the demand that 'the Atlantic Charter must apply to the whole British Empire, the USA and to all the nations of the world and their subject peoples'.[69] Nor was there any doubt about the energizing potential for global redress: 'We want the Government of the United Nations to know and act in the light of our own interpretation of the "Atlantic Charter" to which they are signatories.'[70] Ideals of 'human justice' and 'human decency' had 'aroused hopes and fired the imagination of all peoples', not least among 'Africans and other Non-Europeans' who would 'not be excluded from the rights and privileges which other groups hope to enjoy in the post-war world'. The statement strongly urged that 'the peculiar circumstances' of Indigenous peoples ruled by entrenched communities of 'Europeans' should not be overlooked in the post-war settlement.[71] As Dubow makes clear, the ANC 'genuinely universalised the meaning of freedom set out in the Atlantic Charter', explicitly framing African demands against the prevailing inclination to restrict the Charter's language and liberties to 'white people'.[72]

Whether these initiatives brought immediate success is not the cardinal issue; the aspiration in itself was groundbreaking. The ANC leadership went on to adopt the 'attainment of basic human rights and full citizenship' among their formal list of objectives in March 1947 (at the very time of the royal family's jubilant progress throughout the country).[73] It was a fitting juxtaposition. Events both at home and abroad would ensure that the 1947 tour was the last of its kind; and certainly the last broad-based display of deferential Black loyalty to older emblems of empire and Britishness. In place of the time-honoured ritual of despatching delegations to London, ANC president Xuma took the opportunity of lodging a petition with the newly minted United Nations in 1946 to protest against South Africa's racial policies; the change of venue signalling a whole new grounds for complaint.[74] It was at a UN reception in New York that Xuma encountered Smuts for the first time (quipping to reporters: 'I have had to fly 10,000 miles to meet my prime minister. He talks about us but won't talk to us.')[75] Smuts, for his part, seemed perturbed by the implications of their unlikely meeting place – the consequence, as he saw it, of the ANC's cynical move to manipulate the Atlantic Charter and 'stretch its meaning' to incorporate their own marginal grievances.[76] He reportedly took the ANC leader to one side and murmured: 'Look here, Xuma, these people don't understand us. Let us go back home and sit down together and solve our problems.'[77] But this missed the point entirely. Xuma had deliberately moved the conversation onto a higher moral plane – his 10,000-mile journey serving as dramatic testimony to the wider 'us' he now so urgently sought to address.

This chance encounter in New York raises a second key register of a distinctly South African human rights voice – the remarkable readiness of world opinion to listen. Famously, Smuts had been one of the principal architects of the UN Charter, penning the first draft of its stirring preamble and introducing the concept of human rights into its second paragraph. Inspired by the interwar example of the British Commonwealth as the surest foundation for international cooperation, Smuts 'took the moral mission of empire for granted' in his bid to enlarge on the Commonwealth ideal in a wider international setting.[78] Thus, his conception of human rights (and assorted references to 'the equal rights of men and women and of nations large and small') was never truly universal or individualistic in scope but heavily predicated on the responsibility of 'advanced people to look after the more backward'.[79] The anomaly of one of the world's leading proponents of racial segregation championing 'the sanctity and ultimate value' of humanity did not immediately occur to Smuts himself. In any case, he had reason to assume that the contradictions would never surface thanks to the provisions of Article 2.7 of the UN Charter, which expressly forbade intervention 'in matters which are essentially within the domestic jurisdiction of any state'.

Two ill-timed measures by the post-war South African Government would dramatically expose Smuts to the moral force of his own words. In June 1946, the Asiatic Land Tenure and Indian Representation Act imposed new voting and residence restrictions on South Africa's Asian community, sparking an immediate uproar and inviting passionate criticism on the floor of the UN General Assembly, spearheaded by the interim Government of India (only months shy of independence).[80] Vijaya Lakshmi Pandit – head of the Indian delegation and sister of the incoming prime minister Jawaharlal Nehru – tirelessly argued that the matter was not simply one of domestic jurisdiction but involved the moral obligation of India to attend to the needs of Indians elsewhere in the world who had been denied their civic entitlements.[81] During the same session, Smuts compounded matters by petitioning to have the former League of Nations mandate over South-West Africa incorporated fully into the Union of South Africa. This furnished his detractors with additional means of circumventing the strictures of Article 2.7, unleashing a further volley of protest against South Africa's domestic racial policies. The motion tabled by the Indian delegation culminated in an embarrassing personal defeat for Smuts (by thirty-two votes to fifteen with seven delegations abstaining) – greatly enhancing Nehru's personal stature and establishing his country's reputation as (in his own words) 'a guardian of human rights'.[82] The two-thirds majority caused an immediate sensation, running counter to the expectations of virtually all concerned. But as Mazower notes, the most remarkable aspect of India's public indictment of South Africa was 'the willingness of the assembly to hear it at all'.[83]

The longer-term significance can be inferred from the reaction of Smuts himself, whose private correspondence reveals the depths of his personal humiliation. Although he had already detected a 'strong humanitarian tendency' at the San Francisco Conference the previous year, with repeated demands for 'equal rights all round and other embarrassing proposals so far as we are concerned', he was clearly ill-prepared for the 'avalanche of condemnation' that had 'so suddenly and unexpectedly overwhelmed' the South African delegation in New York.[84] From his suite in the Waldorf Astoria, he wallowed variously in self-pity and future foreboding: 'Colour queers my poor pitch everywhere . . . Doubts like clouds pass over our minds and dim the glory of the day.'[85] But through the fog he clearly perceived the scale and gravity of the challenge ahead: 'I sometimes wonder what our position in years to come will be when the whole world will be against us.'[86] Back in South Africa, he had to endure on the one hand the jeers of the opposition ('Here is the author of the great preamble of the Charter, exposed as a hypocrite and a double-faced time server!') while at the same time grappling with an emboldened African resistance that resorted increasingly to the language and logic of inherent rights. 'We even hear about them', he despaired, 'from our domestic and farm Natives who really have nothing to complain of, but are deeply stirred by all this talk of equality and non-discrimination.'[87] Seemingly at every turn, Smuts had to contend with the reality that 'the Natives want *rights* and not improvements' – and not just rights in their conventional framework. Older notions of 'equal rights' that had long accrued to male subjects of the British empire were 'becoming synonymous with the very different concept of *human rights*, the valency of which was taking on new significance'.[88]

Smuts's personal conundrum points to a third and final gauge of the early inroads of universal rights in their South African setting – the deleterious effect on the outlook of the white minority. Smuts saw how the new universal strain in African rights advocacy had 'just the opposite effect on European mentality', rendering compromise all the more intractable and driving the all-white electorate to even more extreme forms of racial exclusion.[89] In his parting words to Madame Pandit in New York, he allegedly said: 'You have won a hollow victory. This vote will put me out of power in our next elections, but you will have gained nothing.'[90] It is certainly the case that South Africa simply ignored the UN censure; whether it contributed to Smuts's defeat at the hands of the nationalists in 1948 is impossible to determine. But henceforth, South African governments would make no secret of their disdain for the United Nations and the malign effects of universal norms which they saw as an existential threat. The South African UN delegation insisted bluntly that 'there could be no universality in the concept of equality' and continued to display 'unremitting hostility towards civil liberties' in the decades ahead.[91] Indeed, should there be any doubt that human rights 'mattered' in South Africa in the late 1940s, one need only consider the unrelenting ire and invective they elicited from government spokesmen.

In other words, there can be no mistaking the significance of human rights advocacy in South Africa in the immediate post-war years – even if the fundamental precepts were fiercely contested. Patterns of Indigenous protest in Australia, Canada and New Zealand would follow a similar course from the late 1950s, jettisoning older appeals to British moral worlds in favour of new universal norms that presented an opening for claiming 'special rights' as First Peoples – land rights, spiritual rights, Indigenous rights in some form or another – 'rather than the same rights' that settlers enjoyed.[92] This was no 'breakthrough' in the sense of sweeping all opposition aside, nor were human rights the only substitute for British constitutionalism, with pan-African and Marxist alternatives also avidly pursued in these years. What gave human rights special purchase was the all-encompassing nature of the demand, drawing colonized and colonizer into a 'shared moral order' and placing the onus squarely on white authority to account for the blatant denial of equal status as 'full human subjects'.[93] It presented South African whites with a clear choice between making concessions or adopting ever more blatantly illiberal forms of exclusion.

Mazower contends that Smuts ultimately 'defeated himself' in advancing a flawed and outdated conception of 'inherent human dignity' that he was unable to contain or control. But this is only superficially persuasive; the deeper global undercurrents were stronger than the missteps of any single actor.[94] Anticipating Harold Macmillan by more than a decade, Smuts himself attributed his failure to 'the new wind blowing through the world'.[95] Unlike Macmillan, however, he knew that he was contending with something infinitely more subversive than a rival brand of 'nationalism'.

'TENDRILS IN THE AIR': THE ELUSIVE ENGELSSPREKKENDE

If the diminishing moral world of British rights opened new avenues for Black South Africans, its effects were no less significant (though less easily discernible) among English-speaking whites. It was at the very nadir of South Africa's 1946 censure at the United Nations that Arthur Keppel-Jones penned his future projection of an uprooted people. The sudden setback to Smuts's much-vaunted international 'prestige' seemed to tie one man's fate to the prospect of imminent disorder. Afrikaners could respond to the challenge of universalist claim-making by closing ranks behind their own exalted white nationalism. But for English-speakers, the alternatives seemed more elusive. Keppel-Jones roundly criticized the nationalists for exploiting the distinction between *Afrikaner* and *Engelssprekende* – a deliberate ploy, as he saw it, of 'implying that one has a nationality and the other only a language'.[96] But he too struggled to find a serviceable collective noun for the great white hope in which he set so much store; referring to them variously as 'British South Africans', the 'British section', 'British subjects', 'the English', 'South African Loyalists', 'settlers of British stock' or simply those 'attached to the Monarchy and the old British connection'.[97] A once powerful constituency that had long benefitted from the ubiquity of their language and the veneration of British culture now faced the intractable dilemma of plausible self-definition as the frontiers of Greater Britain imploded.[98]

'Tellingly', observes Dubow, it was at this very time that 'the adjectival term *English-speaking South African* came increasingly into vogue'. As the only group in the 'category-obsessed apartheid state' not to be defined along racial or ethnic lines, their status as a mere community of language had the salutary effect of distancing them from the moral stigma of apartheid (without denying them any of its privileges).[99] But the flipside was not just the loss of political power but the erosion of their paradigmatic status. Though lacking the outward trappings of sub-national unity on account of wide regional, political and class distinctions, English-speakers had long enjoyed a presumed ascendancy that became that much harder to sustain in the face of the post-war nationalist challenge and the eclipse of British hegemony worldwide. Keppel-Jones was among the first to give voice to an almost obsessive fear of erasure, publishing a follow-up to *When Smuts Goes* in 1949 where he doubled down on the idle complacency among his *Engelssprekende* compatriots:

> If our purpose is nothing more than to have a good time, enjoying the services of a docile labour force and fighting only for our own privileges, we are of no significance at all. A mere freak of western civilization, we could disappear from the pages of history without being missed.[100]

Loss of purpose was a particular fixation of British liberals at empire's end, affecting a generation who came of age just as their imperially ordered world had begun to unravel. In the United Kingdom this took the form of angry young men grasping for a new purchase on British stature, railing against narrowing horizons, national decline and other perceived ailments of the body politic.[101] Its South African variant could be even more emotionally fraught, conjuring a timid and disoriented people bereft of any defining characteristics whatsoever. Numbering just over a million at the time of the 1948 election, at a stroke they had become the world's only substantial community of white English-speakers lacking the means directly to govern themselves.[102] With the death of Smuts in 1950 and the consolidation of the nationalists' electoral stronghold, this state of affairs soon acquired an air of permanence – compounded by the failure of the United Party to muster any effective opposition. One visiting sociologist from Britain in the mid-1950s remarked on 'a revival of jingoist attitudes as a result of the growing feeling of impotent resentment' among English-speakers, not least the older generation for whom the outlook could seem extraordinarily bleak.[103]

Smuts's former high commissioner in London, George Heaton-Nichols, briefly assumed the mantle of chief spokesman for the more extreme 'loyalist' contingent in predominantly anglophone Natal. As the prospects for securing any kind of domestic political victory grew increasingly dim, he looked to Britain for moral guidance – to the point of secretly lobbying the British government to support a wholesale secessionist movement. In meetings and correspondence with senior UK ministers in 1953, Heaton-Nichols voiced Natal's determination 'to stand alone in order that British interests in South Africa should not disappear ... that after a hundred and fifty years of sacrifice in blood and treasure in maintaining civilization in South Africa the British will not abandon Natal in its hour of need'.[104] While eliciting personal sympathy from senior cabinet figures such as Lord Salisbury (who abhorred 'the idea of deserting the British element in Natal and handing them over to a fanatical anti-British and anti-Native regime') the government ultimately gave the secessionists little encouragement – anxious to avoid the impression of meddling directly in South African affairs.[105] As the realization dawned that no serviceable British solution presented itself, Heaton-Nichols grew increasingly despondent, conceding in a posthumously published memoir that 'the Englishman in South Africa' had 'largely lost his feeling for the roots which originally established him'. It was the bleakest of verdicts for a community 'now seeking tendrils in the air which bear no relation to [their] ancient and historic heritage'.[106]

Others sought urgently to reverse the slide, such as Cape Argus journalist John Bond in his 1956 chronicle *They Were South Africans*. 'An unknown people inhabit South Africa', he ventured – their relative obscurity belying an enduring moral influence 'out of all proportion to their numbers'. He ascribed the fact that 'no history of them has ever been written' to the sheer difficulty of disaggregating the phenomenal impact of their 'restless energy' from South African history as a whole. Again, it was the lapsed universal standing of a people no longer occupying the centre ground that framed his fundamental perspective – imploring readers not to 'take them for granted'.[107] Such apprehensions arose from multiple wellsprings – some more readily acknowledged than others – but never far from the surface was the diminished force of Britain-in-the-world as guarantor of their social and political prestige. Bond's professed aim was 'to redress a balance and restore a lost sense of proportion' – commonplace euphemisms for a lost sense of entitlement.

Remarkably, the new dynamism of Black South African rights advocacy was rarely factored into the equation. The relentless focus on the nationalist government was all-consuming – particularly its determination to strip away the symbolic trappings of the British connection. The enactment of a new Citizenship Bill in 1949 signalled a clean break with British subjecthood (publicly condemned by Keppel-Jones as a violation of the 'ties that still link us to our kinsmen all over the world') but the changes did not stop there.[108] New eligibility rules raised the bar for granting voting rights to British newcomers by several years, direct BBC news broadcasts were summarily shut down (a despised source of pro-British 'propaganda' for nationalists); and judicial appeals to the Privy Council in London were ended the following year. The old compromise of flying two national flags and singing two national anthems was dispensed with in the mid-1950s, bringing an end to the South African careers of the Union Jack and 'God Save the Queen' (though diehards would continue to flaunt both for decades afterwards). No residual symbol of subordination to Britain was overlooked in a comprehensive makeover of the national fabric (including changes to school atlases to ensure that South Africa no longer appeared 'in the same colour as even the most insignificant British possession').[109]

For all the bitterness these measures generated, none of them was sufficient in itself to galvanize a concerted backlash among English speakers. Where opposition finally cohered was around the issue of the South African Constitution, arising out of the nationalists' determination to remove the 'entrenched clauses' guaranteeing the Cape franchise for coloured voters. The nationalists claimed that Cape coloured entitlements were a remnant of British imperial domination (enacted solely for the purpose of denying Afrikaners a parliamentary majority). Hence, the urgent removal of these statutory rights amounted to no less than reclaiming sovereignty over the Constitution itself. In a political and legal drama played out over five years, including two successful challenges in the Appeal Court and a thwarted attempt to alter the Constitution via a joint sitting of parliament, the government finally got its way with the enactment of the 1956 Senate Bill; the bluntest of legislative instruments devised to stack parliament with the requisite numbers to effect constitutional change. Thus framed as a struggle between South African nationalism and British liberalism, the aim of shedding South Africa's British constitutional mantle was geared to the higher purpose of enacting apartheid in its purest form.[110] For Keppel-Jones, ever-ready with a condemnatory column in the Johannesburg *Sunday Times*, the nationalists had finally crossed the line 'that distinguishes democracy from dictatorship'.[111]

Given the age-old veneration of constitutional liberties as the bedrock of British sentiment, it is unsurprising that it was here that English South Africans chose to make their stand. But the struggle over the Constitution was only the surface tension masking a deeper frustration. Fundamentally, English-speakers were coming to grips with the fact that they no longer comprised the principal opposition – a mantle that had been quietly ceded to a proliferation of disenfranchised non-white protest groups. The advent of apartheid had ushered in a pronounced change of tactics among African dissidents, with the new generation of leaders repudiating an older, more cautious emphasis on dialogue and 'moderation'. A key milestone was the ANC Youth League's 'Program of Action' in 1949, urging a coordinated strategy of strikes, boycotts and conspicuous acts of insubordination. At its December 1951 Annual Congress, the ANC renounced its former 'willingness and readiness ... to cooperate with the Government' and embarked instead on a Defiance of Unjust Laws campaign, conveying their intentions in the most uncompromising terms. Henceforth, civil disobedience would be the price of the imposition of arbitrary laws that 'insult and degrade the African people by depriving them of fundamental human rights enjoyed in all democratic communities'.[112] The Defiance campaign was launched in June 1952, deploying passive resistance to flout apartheid strictures in an assortment of public places, amid mass arrests and large-scale imprisonments numbering in the thousands.[113]

214

Throughout this turbulent early phase, demands for universally endowed rights and the imperative of human 'struggle' proliferated, culminating in the 1955 'Congress of the People' – a multi-racial gathering of the African,

Figure 7.1 The famous montage of the defendants in South Africa's Treason Trial taken by ANC photographer Eli Weinberg, December 1956. The image underlined the miscalculation of the South African government in handing their opponents a unique opportunity to convey a common front to amplify their cause. Source: Gamma Keystone/Getty Images.

Indian and Coloured Congresses, trade unions and other groups committed to combatting apartheid; all of whom contributed to the celebrated 'Freedom Charter'. Envisaged as 'the South African people's declaration of human rights', the Charter brought many of the complexities of its UN predecessor to the fore, not least the unresolved disparity between the radical espousal of universal entitlements and their legitimate enforcement.[114] The contrast with the white English-speaking 'opposition' could not have been starker. While the latter waged a lonely and losing battle in the courts in the name of 'constitutional principles', a much wider coalition of African dissidents was busy exposing apartheid's most vulnerable flank – the flagrant insult to humanity itself. A government crackdown the following year led to the arrest of 156 leading activists and an elaborate treason trial, the indictment list reading like a roll-call of anti-apartheid activism in the 1950s. The government's tactics in corralling the fragmented and highly dispersed leadership of anti-apartheid resistance into a single show trial ultimately backfired, lending much-needed coherence and critical mass to their cause. As ANC president Albert Luthuli later recalled, 'I doubt whether we could have devised so effective a method of ensuring cohesion in resistance and of enlarging its embrace.'[115] It was also ideally suited to casting the official parliamentary opposition even further into the shade.

To the extent that white, English-speaking liberals made any significant contributions to combating apartheid in this early period, it was often the work of recent arrivals from Britain, notably expatriate Anglican clergymen such as Michael Scott and Trevor Huddleston. Their appeal to the Christian conscience merged older liberal traditions of anti-slavery humanitarianism with the post-war rhetoric of universal rights to furnish a new subversive edge. Scott had been directly involved in challenging South African racial policies at the United Nations in the 1940s and thus stressed the need for white liberals to commit to 'a wholehearted expression of "solidarity"' with Africans.[116] Mobilizing empathy was the principal emphasis (sharing 'more fully the problems and the pain' as Huddleston termed it) – marking a point of departure from older traditions of Liberal paternalism. In his bestselling *Nought for Your Comfort* (1956), Huddleston explained:

> I believe that because God became Man, therefore human nature in itself has a dignity and a value which is infinite. I believe that this conception necessarily carries with it the idea that the state exists for the individual, not the individual for the state. Any doctrine based on race or colour prejudice and enforced by the state is therefore an affront to human dignity and *ipso facto* an insult to God himself.[117]

216

Human dignity, infinite value, the individual before the state; these were the common currency of universal rights in the post-war world, with the added seal of legitimacy from the Almighty. Huddleston and Scott also had the earthly benefit of a rich network of UK contacts to communicate the human cost of apartheid to the British public, their message of universal solidarity influencing other progressive organizations such as Fenner Brockway's Movement for Colonial Freedom and Canon John Collins's Christian Action. It was the changing temper of metropolitan liberal opinion, increasingly – if fitfully – tuning in to the plight of oppressed Africans, that so unnerved a white English-speaking minority long-habituated to a special claim on British sympathies. As Paul Rich has emphasized, the efforts of metropolitan activists in the 1950s ultimately drove a wedge between British and South African liberal sentiment.[118]

In this and countless other ways, the frequency of appeals to universal norms served to marginalize English-speaking resistance to apartheid – which in any case remained (with only few exceptions) a hesitant and disjointed affair. Any coordinated response was hampered by long-standing ideological, generational and regional divides; compounded by the rules of parliamentary arithmetic that obliged the United Party to attract a proportion of Afrikaner voters to muster a viable government. Any overt defence of British values was therefore unlikely to pay electoral dividends; though this did not always deter the party from campaigning along those very lines, especially in Natal. Extra-parliamentary opposition became caught in a similar bind, such as the short-lived War Veterans Torch Commando – formed in 1951 to guard against nationalist encroachments on the Constitution. Though the emphasis on shared wartime experience – staged in a series of elaborate military-style rallies and parades – lent the organization an implicitly 'loyalist' flavour, it was divided internally on the extent to which it should stress the importance of the British connection (as the guarantor of constitutional safeguards) and even more bitterly split over the admission of non-white members.[119]

Similar cracks emerged in the 'Women's Defence of the Constitution League' (known colloquially as 'the Black Sash'), formed by six white, English-speaking Johannesburg women in 1955 in a bid to stymie the government's draconian Senate Bill. Described as the 'first time in the history of their land' that 'the English-speaking section began to examine its personal political principles', the movement was based not so much on a coherent platform as a collective urge to 'do something' about the unwelcome pace of change under the nationalists.[120] Their message and methods marked an innovation in anti-apartheid protest, organizing silent marches and requiem-like vigils outside public buildings. The overriding message was the moral authority of motherhood and the imperative of a more 'caring' politics. But though united against 'unconstitutional' measures to disenfranchise coloured voters, the members were not so easily persuaded to admit non-white women into their ranks (or even to permit non-white speakers to address their meetings). The question of race was carefully side-stepped by the expedient of restricting admission to those entitled to vote (a disingenuous move, given that voting rights were the main constitutional bone of contention), on the spurious grounds that broadening the racial composition would hand the 'very ammunition' to nationalists that would alienate support in the respectable suburbs. Ultimately, it was never entirely clear whether the Black Sash had been founded as a progressive campaign for racial equality or a reactionary royalist redoubt, geared solely to defending the Crown against a *herrenvolk* Republic. Those prepared to go further to confront the central issue of white supremacy 'found themselves a severely winnowed group' when non-white women were finally admitted in the early 1960s.[121]

Figure 7.2 Members of the Black Sash mount a vigil outside the South African Parliament in Cape Town, 1955, to protest against the apartheid regime's repeated violations of the Constitution. Source: Paul Popper/Popperfoto/Getty Images.

In these circumstances, the remnants of Smuts's United Party fared particularly badly, unable to mount a viable political vision for the whole of South Africa or contain the 'fissile multiplicity' of British sensibilities within its ambit.[122] The result was a debilitating fragmentation, with the more staunchly 'loyal' element breaking away in 1953 to form the Union Federal Party, while in the same year an attempt at multi-racial political cooperation was launched under the banner of the 'Liberal Party', led by the renowned novelist Alan Paton. A further schism occurred at the end of the decade when the liberal remnants of the United Party struck out on their own as the Progressive Party. None of these rival factions had any prospect of winning government. But as Paton himself observed in 1959, the problem was not the fragility of white English-speaking solidarity, so much as a far more endemic weakness in white liberalism: 'It cannot conceive of a co-defence of democratic values made by white and non-white together.'[123] It was an inability to engage with the new universal struggle that formed the backdrop to the internal divisions among liberal-leaning whites in the 1950s. Neither the Torch Commando nor the Black Sash nor any of the English-speaking political parties made genuine common cause with the Congress of the People or the ANC Defiance campaign in the 1950s. Years later, from his new vantage point in Kingston, Ontario, Arthur Keppel-Jones would acknowledge his own personal failure to engage with the Black political struggle, despite years of frenetic anti-nationalist invective in the pages of the *Sunday Times*. He came belatedly to recognize that his 'detachment from direct involvement' in a cause he fundamentally shared 'was a basic weakness of the whole approach'.[124]

'A TREACHEROUS AND UNCHARTED SEA': 1960

The name Sir De Villiers Graaff would be unfamiliar to all but the keenest observers of post-war South African politics. But for a time, he represented the last throw of the dice for a viable successor to Smuts. The descendant of Afrikaner gentry, his British credentials were no less impeccable; a hereditary baronet, Oxford law graduate and veteran of Tobruk, he was awarded an OBE for attempting to escape from a German prisoner of war camp in a cupboard. Always impeccably turned out, he had been hand-picked to take the first dance with Princess Elizabeth at her 21st birthday ball in Cape Town in 1947 (committing the gaffe of forgetting to wear gloves for the occasion). A personal favourite of Smuts, who identified him as a potential future prime minister even prior to entering parliament, he won his Cape Town constituency in the 'apartheid' election of 1948 –

marking the beginning of a twenty-nine-year stint of uninterrupted opposition. Graaff – or 'Div' as he was known to almost everyone – took over the leadership of the United Party at the height of the Senate Bill crisis in 1956, in the hope that he might swing sufficient Afrikaner support behind a more liberal slant on segregation.

The year 1960 began well for Graaff's United Party, warmly embracing Harold Macmillan's February visit and quietly relishing his 'Wind of Change' speech in the Cape Town parliament. The prime minister's words had been carefully weighed, levelling criticism only at 'some aspects of your policies' – thus creating the impression of a partisan intervention aimed solely at the nationalists under Hendrik Verwoerd. Macmillan's entourage recorded the muted elation among United Party members at the parliamentary reception afterwards – 'so jubilant that they thought it best (evidently) to conceal their full feelings and speak only out of the corner of their mouths'.[125] Graaff made a point of personally congratulating the prime minister on the speech, while stopping short of commending it in public.[126] Most accounts – official, press and private correspondence – emphasized the implicit rebuff to Afrikaner nationalism, applauding the way Macmillan's visit had 'put new life into the English-speaking people'.[127] But the view from the British High Commission in Pretoria suggested otherwise:

> The United Party ... have warmly welcomed [the speech] as a blow to the Nationalists, while ignoring the implications for themselves ... some of the English-speaking community, who welcomed it as a personal triumph for the British Prime Minister, may be less enthusiastic when its meaning sinks in.[128]

That meaning soon became apparent as the watershed year 1960 unfolded. On 21 March 1960 the massacre of sixty-two African protesters by government security forces at Sharpeville brought worldwide condemnation of the Verwoerd government, followed soon after by an assassination attempt on Verwoerd himself. In one single act of arbitrary political violence, Sharpeville raised global awareness of the base cruelty and illegitimacy of apartheid while at the same engendering a new spirit of African militancy.[129] Meanwhile, political turmoil in the Belgian Congo degenerated into civil disorder which only stiffened the resolve of South African whites to refuse any concessions to non-white political representation. In Britain, the long-awaited report of the Monckton Commission opened the way for the dissolution of the Central African Federation, delivering a further blow to settler interests in Africa. By the end of the year, some sixteen states had secured independence in Africa (fourteen of them French), prompting disaffected French settlers in Algeria to mobilize against their own government to resist the struggle for independence.

Meanwhile, it was in the 'euphoric atmosphere' of 1960 that the tide of universal rights culminated in the landmark UN Resolution 1514: the Declaration on the Granting of Independence to Colonial Countries and Peoples.[130] Though the drafting process revealed enduring tensions, the final wording of the resolution was unambiguously styled as a reaffirmation of the 1948 Universal Declaration, condemning all forms of 'subjection of peoples to alien subjugation' as a 'denial of fundamental human rights'. Driving the message home for white South Africans, the Nobel Peace Prize that same year was awarded to ANC president Albert Luthuli, his acceptance speech underlining the 'universal striving for human liberty' at the core of the ANC struggle and the indispensable support of world opinion in 'actively upholding the quality of man'.[131] It was a world away from the younger Luthuli's 'silent awe' in the presence of the infinite wisdom of King George VI in 1947 – the substitution of moral worlds was complete.

The year 1960 would also signal the toppling of the Crown itself in South Africa as the nationalists pressed ahead with their cherished ambition of inaugurating a white republic. On the eve of Macmillan's visit, Verwoerd announced that a referendum would be held later that year, providing the all-white electorate with the opportunity to become a 'unified people' under a republican constitution.[132] It was a deliberate attempt to lure English-speakers into the Afrikaner fold with the promise of security in numbers – an appeal to white racial solidarity against the unnerving back-drop of a rapidly decolonizing Africa. Though a significant proportion were ultimately persuaded, the more immediate response among English-speakers was to dig their heels in – spurning Verwoerd's overtures as a blatant attempt to punish them for 'the unforgiveable sin of being British!'[133] The referendum campaign posed an intractable dilemma for De Villiers Graaff, obliged to defend the royalist sensibilities of the majority of his United Party constituents, while equally aware that Afrikaner votes would be required to defeat the republic at the ballot box. It was deemed vital to avoid anything that might hand the government an opportunity 'to depict us draped in Union Jacks', and Graaff therefore deliberately toned down appeals to British kinship on the campaign trail.[134] In one public appearance in East London he even crossed out a passage on the depth of popular feeling for the monarchy, substituting it with a note of caution about pitting the emotional investments of either side against each other. Seemingly missing the whole point of the referendum entirely, Graaff pleaded: 'There will be no profit in weighing sentiment against sentiment.'[135]

Instead, the case against the republic stressed the benefits of Commonwealth membership, which was widely presumed to be in jeopardy should South Africa switch to a republican constitution.[136] The flags of Australia, New Zealand, Canada and the United Kingdom featured prominently at anti-republican rallies, while the banners of 'new' Commonwealth countries such as India, Ghana and the Malayan Federation were conspicuous by their absence. To remove any trace of ambiguity, one 'no' campaign advertisement baldly declared: 'I shall vote anti-republican because I value our close association with the *White* nations of the Commonwealth.'[137] This was partly a matter of material advantage (with more than a third of South African exports protected by Commonwealth trade preferences) but more broadly it invoked a fear of racial isolation in a world where the historical fortunes of settler colonialism seemed to have been put into reverse. It was in any case a version of racial solidarity that was losing traction in the wake of Sharpeville. Once-dependable countries such as Australia and New Zealand began tentatively to withhold their support, anxious to distance their own discriminatory practices from the stigma of systemic racism that apartheid so baldly symbolized.[138]

One campaign poster vividly captured what seemed to be at stake, depicting an elderly white man trudging listlessly towards a barren horizon – above the forbidding slogan: 'It's a long road to walk alone.'[139] It was here that Macmillan's 'wind of change' metaphor was refashioned as a dim portent. The mayor of Pietermaritzburg – a tenacious bastion of loyalist sentiment – feared that relinquishing Crown and Commonwealth would risk sacrificing 'the one anchorage we have in this storm-tossed world'.[140] Naval and meteorological metaphors abounded in loyalist English press coverage, culminating in the *Natal Mercury*'s grim warning on the eve of the 5 October poll: 'Not to vote against the Republic is to help those who would cut us loose from our moorings, and set us adrift in a treacherous and uncharted sea, at the very time that the winds of change are blowing up to hurricane force.'[141] Both the 'yes' and 'no' campaigns sought to exploit the powerful undertow of racial trepidation – the one side offering voters a unified white bastion in a hostile world, the other seeking safety in numbers among the global remnants of Greater Britain.

The result was a narrow victory for Verwoerd's republic by a margin of 52 per cent, with a particularly strong showing in rural areas and the Orange Free State. Equally large majorities for 'no' were returned in the major cities and especially Natal with upwards of 80 per cent of eligible (white) voters steadfastly opposed. This briefly sparked further moves to solicit the British Government's blessing for Natal's secession from the Union – the overtures once again dismissed completely out of hand by British officials as 'utterly unrealistic'.[142] The rebuff came as a particularly rude shock to Douglas Mitchell – the titular head of the anti-republican 'Natal Stand' – who was 'struck by the very plain attitude of the British Government. It was so contrary to what many in Natal believed to be the position: that all we had to say to Britain was that we wanted to be under her wing and she would welcome us back with open arms'.[143] He was similarly spurned by Rhodesia's Roy Welensky at a secret meeting in Salisbury to broach a possible merger of Natal with the Central African Federation.[144] The failure of Greater British solidarity was hard to ignore.

The way was now clear for the inevitable showdown over South Africa's right to remain in the Commonwealth. India's Jawaharlal Nehru was the chief antagonist, pressing South Africa for a string of concessions on racial segregation as the price of readmission. No middle way presented itself, however, and the acrimonious Commonwealth Prime Ministers' Conference of March 1961 culminated in South Africa's abrupt withdrawal. Making a virtue of necessity, Verwoerd depicted the outcome as the final act of purification of South African nationhood – effectively closing off any residual avenue for English-speakers to rally around the redundant pillars of white Britishness. 'They are cheering because we have withdrawn from the world', remarked Mitchell upon Verwoerd's triumphant return from London. 'Will they cheer when the world withdraws from us?'[145] Awaiting the world's judgement seemed all that was left for a United Party now largely devoid of purpose, having squandered their influence over more than a decade of moral equivocation and political marginalization.

Judgement was soon forthcoming from the *Manchester Guardian*, which marked the proclamation of the republic on 31 May with a scathing profile on South Africa's English-speaking white citizens – a people 'for the most part content to allow international anger to fall on the nationalists' while reaping the benefits 'of being part of the dominant white race'. With their absorption into a white republic, it was argued, English speakers would soon find themselves 'held in lower respect among Africans than the Afrikaners'.[146] These barbs inevitably sparked wounded reactions, with the *Cape Times* rejecting the 'hoary half-truths' and 'shrill' tone – asking whether the people of Manchester would 'voluntarily abandon status and wealth to accommodate a great inrush of West Indians'. Others such as Laurence Gandar of the *Rand Daily Mail* were more willing to acknowledge the 'image problem' of English-speakers as overly self-assured, materialistic and pleasure-seeking, vulnerable to criticism for their 'highly conservative racial outlook' and 'easy-going beer and rugby civilization'.[147]

More penetrating were the lessons learned by the leadership of the Black Sash, now reduced to a residual rump following the 1961 decision to admit non-white members.[148] The tumultuous events of 1960 had witnessed mass resignations of upwards of 80 per cent, partly arising from regional divisions over how vehemently the republic should be opposed, but more significantly – as the National Executive conceded in November 1960 – because members generally did 'not want any kind of political change that will entail non-whites having a share of political responsibility'.[149] It was a microcosm of the wider rupture among South African whites, giving rise to an unsparingly bleak diagnosis in the September 1961 newsletter. Ever since the nationalist victory of 1948, it seemed, English-speakers had persistently pursued the wrong cause, confusing the symbols of civic virtue for the substance. Having 'fought stubbornly for its flag, its anthem and all other emblems of the British connection', the community had all too often failed 'to take an equally strong stand on the moral principles that are the true essence of the British tradition, especially in the vital sphere of Black-white relations'. In so doing, the 'English section' (the collective noun as elusive as ever) had all but 'ensured its own decline and eclipse'.[150] It was an astute assessment of the moral chasm between a flawed British symbolism mired in racial prejudice and the hallowed constitutional liberties at the heart of Greater Britonism – the principal fault line of a flawed ideal.

———————◆———————

For the ANC, the proclamation of the republic on 31 May 1961 also marked a major watershed, underlining the futility of seeking accommodation or compromise with a government so clearly determined to wield unfettered control over South Africa's subject peoples. In the weeks leading to the official inauguration ceremony, Nelson Mandela announced a 'stay away' campaign as the first instalment of a 'head-on clash with apartheid'.[151] Emerging from hiding to give his first ever television interview in the early hours of 31 May, he intimated that 'the time has come for us to consider . . . whether the methods which we have applied so far are adequate'. Within two weeks he had co-founded Umkhonto we Sizwe – the armed wing of the ANC – in a calculated resort to violent measures that was not taken lightly; nor without seeking a last-minute accommodation with the United Party leadership.[152]

On 21 May, Mandela had composed a personal two-page letter to Sir De Villiers Graaff, urging him to recognize the sheer ruthlessness of their shared adversary and the gross iniquities of a constitution neither of them had sanctioned. The republic had been welcomed 'by little over half of the white community'; and opposed by every disenfranchised dissident group throughout the country. As 'none of us can draw any satisfaction from this developing crisis', he reasoned, the options had narrowed considerably: 'Stated bluntly, the alternatives appear to be these: talk it out, or shoot it out.' Mandela's preferred solution was to talk it out, by convening an elected National Convention of all races, tasked with drawing up a new constitution that would be acceptable to all. Having secured the agreement of representatives of the Indian and coloured communities, the Liberal and Progressive parties, leading church organizations and influential sections of the English language press, one obvious question remained:

> Where, Sir, does the United Party stand? We have yet to hear from this most important organization – the main organization in fact of anti-Nationalist opinion amongst the European community. Or from you, its leader. If the country's leading statesmen fail to lead at this moment, then the worst is inevitable. It is time for you, Sir, and your party to speak out . . . We in South Africa, and the world outside, expect the answer. Silence at this time enables Dr. Verwoerd to lead us onwards to the brink of disaster . . . On our part, the door to such a discussion has always been open. We have approached you and your party before, and suggested that matters of difference be discussed. To date we have had no reply. Nevertheless we still hold the door open. But the need *now* is not for debate about differences of detail, but for clarity of principle and purpose. For a National Convention of all races? Or against?

Mandela's call to unite 'the overwhelming majority of our people, white, Coloured, Indian and African, for a single purpose' was an invitation to the United Party leader to embrace the moral world of universal human values that had so confounded J. C. Smuts fifteen years earlier. It offered a way out of the entrenched binaries of white racialism, breaking not only with the older comforts of Greater Britonism but also the new fortress of white solidarity on offer from Verwoerd. This was safety in numbers backed, not by the empire but a much wider coalition of liberal internationalism and a newfound singularity of purpose. 'We strongly urge you to speak out now', Mandela reiterated. 'It is only ten days to May 31st.'[153]

Graaff's curt reply came five days later: 'We are not prepared to see the Union parliament abdicate its sovereignty in favour of a so-called National Convention. Nor do we favour adult suffrage for all races, colour and creeds.' For good measure, he strongly condemned Mandela's futile effort 'to force your views upon South Africa'.[154] As a response from the leader of a whites-only political party to a known Black subversive wanted by the police, the contents of Graaff's letter were in no sense surprising. Yet it was a moment wholly unforeseen by Arthur Keppel-Jones in his elaborate projection of dystopian tidings in 1947. Mandela's constitutional convention never materialized, and a more militant path was chosen – closing 'a chapter as far as our methods of political struggle are concerned' and closing the door on what, by his own admission, could have been 'the turning point in our country's history'.[155]

8

PRIDE IN THE GOODS: THE MORAL ECONOMY OF THE COMMON MARKET

Reg Pollard was a rarity among 1960s Australian Labor MPs in that he knew something about farming. According to party folklore, it was while plough-ing his fields in Victoria's Macedon district in 1924 that 'some blokes I knew came up and said that the local member had died and that I ought to give it a go'.[1] A great war veteran, 'soldier settler' and moderately successful grazier, he served as minister for agriculture in the Chifley Labor Government of the late 1940s, playing a key role in securing the terms of trade for Australian commodity exports in the post-war financial system. Narrowly defeated for the party leadership in 1960, he faded rapidly into obscurity, remembered only by the R. T. Pollard Gardens in the Melbourne suburb of Sunshine. But over a political life spanning forty years he applied himself indefatigably to the twin cause of stable markets and fair returns for Australian primary producers, both at home and abroad. It was at the twilight of his career, in response to an entirely new threat to Australia's rural industries, that he rose in the Australian House of Representations in August 1961 to proclaim:

> As with other members of Her Majesty's Opposition, who spring from British stock, I have very great pride in the quality of the goods that the United Kingdom has poured into Australia over many years. We hope that the people of the United Kingdom hold the same sentiments about the goods that we in turn have poured into Britain.[2]

The occasion was Harold Macmillan's widely anticipated announcement only days earlier that the UK Government would embark on negotiations to seek membership of the European Economic Community (EEC) – a move that threatened to disrupt the historically ordained traffic of goods between Britain and Commonwealth countries. Pollard was the obvious choice in the opposition's ranks to speak out against European encroachments in Australia's most critical overseas market. But rather than table the intrica-cies of export quotas, commodity agreements and tariff preferences, he freighted the goods themselves with a meaning and significance far outweighing the commercial imperatives. Here, 'British stock' became entangled in the currency of racial pride and enduring blood ties that bound the white remnants of a British world in a time-honoured pact of mutual assistance. According to this unwritten code, Britain quite literally owed Australia a living.

Pollard was not conjuring some fanciful covenant of his own invention. However naive, his sentiments were in tune with strong residual currents of popular feeling that would hamstring Britain's bid to join the European Common Market in the years ahead. Macmillan himself was dogged by jeers, name-calling and chants of 'shame' from both sides of the House of Commons when he revealed his intentions in the summer of 1961. With remarkable spontaneity, what was ostensibly a matter of securing the most profitable arrangements for UK exporters became heavily overlaid with accounting of a different kind: the ledger of filial loyalty to compatriots overseas.[3] Cartoonists had a field day depicting Britain variously as the neglectful mother, the wayward spouse, the fair-weather friend, while whispers of 'ingratitude' for wartime sacrifices were frequently insinuated.

There was every reason why Commonwealth producers would seek to raise awareness of the urgent threat to their livelihood, but what seems extraordinary in retrospect is the emotional leverage they were able to mobilize – without which, Britain's turn to Europe would have been a far less fractious affair. Fundamental to this were the value judgements bound up in the business of buying and selling. Harold Wilson's famous parliamentary retort to Macmillan – 'We are not entitled to sell our friends and kinsmen down the river for a problematical and marginal advantage of selling washing machines in Dusseldorf' – captured the prevailing mood.[4] Trade was inseparable from the moral economy of Greater Britain; imposing rules of conduct that any self-respecting British government was duty-bound to observe. Yet within a remarkably short space of years a brittle consensus had emerged in British government, business, media and financial circles about the need to sacrifice Commonwealth trade ties as the price of EEC membership – an agonizing reappraisal, frequently overlooked in the wider history of post-war decolonization. Indeed, economic relations generally, so intrinsic to the emergence of a British world-system in the eighteenth and nineteenth centuries, have tended to take a back seat in accounting for its demise in the decades after 1945.[5]

Britain's decision to seek EEC membership would disrupt an already beleaguered Commonwealth trade compact in an era of burgeoning mass consumption. The colonial economic model, in which highly specialized staples tailored to British consumer needs were the mainstay of entire communities throughout the Commonwealth, now had to absorb the added strain of British entry into a trade bloc notorious for protecting its own primary producers. Everyday consumer items with little in the way of obvious emotional ballast – wheat, butter, sugar, lamb and tinned fruits – would play a crucial role in denaturalizing Britain's place in Commonwealth markets and vice versa. To be sure, there was no single commodity that could furnish a 'tea party' moment, and the sheer range of products in jeopardy tended to overwhelm the discerning UK consumer, just as it hampered any concerted response among Commonwealth suppliers. But viewed from the perspective of disparate communities heavily reliant on goods for export to the UK market, the passions and resentments ignited by Britain's European aspirations would become inseparable from the goods themselves.

The role of everyday emotions as drivers of social and political change is now widely acknowledged by historians, with a profusion of new concepts jostling for recognition. 'Emotional communities', 'emotional regimes', or simply 'emotionology' have been variously deployed to lend analytical rigour to processes that can be hard to pin down.[6] Surprisingly, this proclivity for auditing 'affective economies' (Sarah Ahmed's term) is rarely applied to the realm of the economy itself, as though commercial relations can somehow be sealed off from the realm of human sensibility. Some have even disavowed the connection to avoid confusion, insisting that for historians of emotions 'the word "economy" has nothing to do with *the* economy, in a financial and labour sense'.[7] According to this view, taking stock of the emotional economy is an intuitive practice rather than an exercise in balancing the ledger, drawing on 'observable signifiers of emotional expression' to assess 'the emotional presence in public life'.[8] But others have sought to move beyond emotional discourse to consider how 'complex systems of emotional circulation and exchange' involve accumulations of affective capital determined by the dynamics of supply and demand.[9] Viewed in these terms, Reg Pollard's 'pride in the goods' was no mere emotional 'signifier' but a point of exchange in a much wider system of reciprocity that was inextricably linked – at the opposite end of the balance sheet – to the 'shame' showered on Harold Macmillan in the House of Commons.[10] As with so many of the key registers of embattled Britishness in these years, the currency of race remained a crucial arbiter of the market value of wider British obligations.

This chapter situates racial sentiment and the residual mystique of imperial commodities at the heart of the economic turmoil of Britain's courtship of the Common Market from the early 1960s. The allure of

Greater Britain had always rested on a precarious alignment between community sentiment and commercial self-interest; a system of production and consumption governed by shared affinities to generate mutual prosperity. Reg Pollard's forlorn hope that Britain would 'hold the same sentiments' about consumer goods imported from Australia went to the very heart of the problem of sustaining the emotional investments of old in the face of cold, cost-benefit calculations in a decolonizing world. That such appeals to a wider moral economy ultimately failed to prevent the UK from taking the plunge – albeit delayed by a decade of false starts and endemic ill-feeling – suggests that the diminishing returns of greater British goods was a reliable index of an imploding British world.

A MATTER OF PREFERENCE: BRITAIN'S TURN TO EUROPE

On the evening of 24 January 1962, Prime Minister Harold Macmillan delivered a televised address to the nation, imploring viewers to be more positive about Britain's enduring strength and influence in a volatile world – and perhaps to 'do a little bit extra' to uphold the nation's moral authority. But he saw no cause for alarm or defeatism. His choice of words, however, belied his unruffled exterior:

> There's one thing I think people mustn't be frightened about. Some people think that if you enter into one of these alliances or groupings, you will lose your identity. Well of course if you enter into any kind of a contract, a treaty, if you join a club ... you hand over to the common pool something of your own liberty. But that doesn't mean that if we join one of these, that Britain will cease to be Britain or British people to be British.[11]

It was an extraordinary moment; a British prime minister assuring voters that come what may, Britain would still be Britain. Six months into his historic bid for EEC membership, the prime minister had little to show in the way of progress in the entry negotiations, let alone the much-vaunted 'safeguards' he had promised for the interests of UK and Commonwealth farmers. But under mounting political strain from a plethora of anti-Common Market pressure groups, he took the remarkable step of appearing on television to allay rumours about the imminent end of Britain. His reasons for voicing such an explicit disclaimer originated from a widely discussed item that appeared the week before in the *Daily Express* – the sworn enemy of the government's European ambitions. 'Loss of identity is a disturbing condition in an individual', remarked the veteran correspondent René MacColl (himself half French). 'How much worse for a nation!

A nation which – like Britain today – finds itself being elbowed out of its own way of doing things . . . by the hidden persuaders inspired by Bonn, Paris and Rome.'[12]

The early 1960s witnessed a rising tide of apprehension about the downward trend in the nation's fortunes – later dubbed 'declinism' – which tended to influence public perceptions of virtually any new development.[13] Such existential gloom also had its place in the rhetorical armoury of the no less passionate champions of EEC membership in these years, many of whom spoke in terms of the dire need for emergency shock therapy that only Europe – with its economic dynamism and supranational idealism – could provide. For *The Guardian*, it was the near-terminal state of British productivity that presented a simple choice 'between swimming in the main stream and vegetating in a backwater'.[14] The *Daily Mirror* sounded repeated warnings about an impending descent into oblivion, urging readers to view the Common Market as a choice between 'Little Britain or Great Europe?'[15] More reluctant converts such as Whitehall mandarin Edwin Plowden pointed to the abject slide in Britain's global fortunes, permitting only one of two options: 'To look outwards, which must mean some change, or to look inwards, think about our glorious past and decline not only materially and politically but in our whole moral fibre.' Though he desperately wished 'we could become as we were, or even stay as we are', necessity dictated that Britain should 'find an out-let for our undoubted political talents' in a new European adventure.[16] These vague projections of an unsubstantiated dread were never spelt out in economic terms; nor was Britain's business sector particularly prominent in stoking the clamour for the Common Market in 1961.[17] By and large, the forebodings were cultural and political in nature, fuelled by a hard to quantify sense of a nation on the ropes.

Ultimately however, it was the trenchant opponents of Common Market membership who invoked the spectre of Britain's 'disappearance' with a more genuine conviction. For Sir Roy Harrod, professor of international economics at Nuffield College, it was 'the final quietus of Britain . . . We shall have to think up a suitable epitaph.'[18] These premonitions were invariably tied to the dire consequences in store for Commonwealth primary producers at the hands of Common Market protectionism. Little was left to the imagination in the grim prophecy of *Sunday Express* editor John Juror: 'When the Commonwealth is finished, so is Britain. There then is the extent of our peril. It is real and deadly.'[19] A. J. P. Taylor regularly devoted his Sunday newspaper column to variations on this theme, spelling out the logic on New Year's Eve 1961: 'It means the end of the Empire, the end of the

British Commonwealth. We shall cease to be an independent country . . . We shall be back where we started, when Britain was a province of the Roman Empire.'[20]

The frequent intrusion of the adjective 'British' in Commonwealth advocacy was a useful means of blurring the distinction, as though the fate of the two were inextricably linked.[21] Any attempt to disaggregate them, warned the popular historian Arthur Bryant, would be tantamount to the 'permanent and arbitrary division of the English race . . . an act of fratricide, and, I believe, in the long run suicide'.[22] It was a case of the one thing flowing inexorably from another; the collapse of the Commonwealth exposing the inner fragility of Britain itself. Labour Leader Hugh Gaitskell famously bound the destinies of nation and Commonwealth in his forthright rejection of EEC membership at the October 1962 Labour Party Conference. Under the heading 'End of Independence', he proffered the following:

> We must be clear about this: it does mean, if this is the idea, the end of Britain as an independent European state. I make no apology for repeating it. It means the end of a thousand years of history. You may say 'Let it end' but, my goodness, it is a decision that needs a little care and thought. And it does mean the end of the Commonwealth. How can one really seriously suppose that if the mother country, the centre of the Commonwealth, is a province of Europe (which is what federation means) it could continue to exist as the mother country of a series of independent nations? It is sheer nonsense.[23]

In this tangle of extinction and ruin, the transition from Commonwealth primacy to European province represented an inversion of the natural order. Despite more than a decade of decolonization throughout Asia, Africa and the West Indies, the eclipse of Britain as an imperial 'centre' or 'mother' could still seem unprecedented, breaking with a whole millennium of national endeavour.

Macmillan himself was a late convert to the cause of EEC membership, having for years insisted on the sheer incompatibility of a European Customs Union with the system of Commonwealth trade preferences formulated at the Ottawa Conference in the early 1930s.[24] As chancellor of the exchequer in the Eden government, he had monitored the progress of the founding EEC members towards closer economic integration but ruled out any UK participation that would involve swapping Commonwealth preferences for a system of Europe-wide tariffs.[25] From the outset, he went out of his way to elevate Commonwealth ties as 'our first purpose' in any future accommodation with the new Europe, assuring a conference of Commonwealth finance ministers in 1956 that if Britain were ever faced with a choice, 'of course we could not hesitate. We must choose the Commonwealth.'[26] He went even further as prime minister in 1957, stressing the emotional constraints on any narrowly conceived self-interest: 'If there should at any time be a conflict between the calls upon us there is no doubt where we would stand; the Commonwealth comes first in our hearts and in our minds.'[27] For all his frequent insistence that Commonwealth primacy 'goes without saying', however, it remains striking how often he felt obliged to spell it out.[28]

Macmillan's radical change of heart in 1961 has been the subject of endless argument and speculation, but it ultimately boiled down to mounting apprehensions about the slide in Britain's world standing.[29] By the early 1960s, a combination of flagging relative economic performance, uncertainty over the future of the Commonwealth, diminished influence in the ongoing Cold War struggle, and the promise of rejuvenation at the heart of a dynamic new Europe had persuaded the prime minister that EEC membership was the only way of turning the ship around. Coming to office on the heels of the botched Suez Canal invasion of 1956, the task of restoring British prestige became the hallmark of his premiership. He was additionally influenced by South Africa's untidy exit at the Commonwealth Prime Ministers' Conference of March 1961, which had exposed the dearth of common ground among a rapidly diversifying membership. It was shortly afterwards that he determined to face down the inevitable chorus of protest to find a way of becoming part of the European project.

In finally taking the plunge on 31 July 1961, Macmillan was at pains to downplay the potential economic disruption, particularly for Commonwealth countries, claiming gingerly that he was merely entering into negotiations with the EEC to see if mutually workable solutions could be found to protect 'vital Commonwealth interests'. At times, he seemed genuinely to believe that two rival discriminatory trading blocs might be reconciled to the mutual benefit of all. But behind the scenes he freely acknowledged the implications of substituting Commonwealth free entry with a system of 'reverse preferences' for European suppliers.[30] As he privately conceded to his inner circle, it was no longer a question of whether Commonwealth countries should accept the terms of British entry, but how they might 'be *made* to accept' it.[31]

His convictions were bolstered by longer-term trends steadily diminishing the importance of the Commonwealth as a viable economic unit. By the end of the 1950s, the customary pattern of exchanging British manufactures for Commonwealth food and raw materials was clearly of declining economic value. Contrary to wartime expectations that primary producing nations would dictate the future terms of trade, it was largely the exchange of mass consumer goods between manufacturing countries that fuelled the post-war economic boom. Shattered confidence in the security of Britain's sea lanes (the combined effect of German U-boats in two world wars) had also brought intense political pressure to shore up Britain's food supply, prompting a massive expansion in domestic farm production which inevitably displaced Commonwealth suppliers.[32] At the same time, the global imperative of combatting famine, underdevelopment and international communism drove a wave of new agricultural research with the development of high-yielding grains, mechanized production techniques, new irrigation systems, pesticides and other innovations – all of which exerted downward pressure on food prices and imposed limits on the purchasing power of Commonwealth primary producers.[33] In other words, Britain's capacity to absorb Commonwealth farm produce was shrinking while the real opportunities for UK growth lay elsewhere, resulting in a steady decline in inter-Commonwealth trade from a post-war high of 48 per cent (1948) to little more than 20 per cent by 1961.[34] By the mid-1950s, senior voices in the UK Treasury and Board of Trade were already whispering that there was 'little dynamic life left in the Commonwealth preference system'.[35]

Yet it remained only a whisper. Far more powerful was the stubborn persistence of its underlying moral precepts, which nurtured an abundance of wishful thinking. Opinion polls throughout the 1950s continued to show high levels of public support for the Commonwealth as a major political priority and a natural sphere of mutual economic interest.[36] Even the transformation of the Commonwealth in the late 1950s from a white man's club to an expanding, multi-racial organization elicited little in the way of overt reflection on its changing economic character. When the Federation of Commonwealth and British Empire Chambers of Commerce belatedly recognized the moral repugnance of restricting membership to an all-white business constituency, it was agreed in 1959 to include delegates from the 'new' Commonwealth and remove 'British Empire' from the masthead. Last-minute hesitations from the Canadian and New Zealand delegates, however, resulted in the compromise wording: 'the Federation of Commonwealth *and British* Chambers of Commerce'.[37] 'Empire' it seems was dispensable; it was that much harder to relinquish the feeling of being British.

In short, the underlying patterns of global economic divergence proved insufficient to disrupt the depth of feeling about the immutability of

Greater Britain. What Andrew Dilley terms the 'un-imagining of the Commonwealth' required something more; a tremor of sufficient magnitude to strike at the nerve centre of the empire's emotional purchase.[38]

'*UNE CERTAIN SYMPATHIE AMUSÉE*': THE EMOTIONAL AUDIT OF 1962

At the risk of stating the obvious, feeling for Britain in the early 1960s was far from uniform throughout the Commonwealth, with the arrival of a succession of newly decolonized states striking out on their own after years of colonial subjugation. Equally, however, virtually the entire membership retained a stake in the UK market for significant portions of their economic livelihood and could ill afford the loss of preferential treatment or the erection of insurmountable new trade barriers. The emerging details of the EEC's Common Agricultural Policy (CAP) were a particular cause for alarm, signalling an inward-looking, radically protectionist bloc designed to placate powerful European farm lobbies eager to expand into the British market. But the shared material threat to Commonwealth prosperity failed to elicit any concerted political response – with wildly varying assessments of the economic and emotional stakes accentuating deep fissures already emerging at the heart of the organization. Of all of Britain's multiple attempts to gain entry to the EEC, it was the first under Macmillan that administered the severest test of the Commonwealth's devotional mettle. Though proceedings were abruptly called to a halt by Charles de Gaulle's dramatic 'veto' of January 1963, the strained loyalties of this opening bid would leave a lasting imprint on British sympathies the world over.

The uneven Commonwealth response was partly a matter of divergent traditions, but there were also disparate scales of material hardship. New Zealand was by far the most heavily dependent on UK market access, with exports of primary produce (predominantly meat and dairy goods) still accounting for 52.9 per cent of the country's entire export income.[39] Such was the precarious reliance on British goodwill that the government of Keith Holyoake elected to place their 'trust in British assurances', ratcheting up the emotional leverage with occasional reminders that New Zealand was 'Britain's other farm'.[40] The leaders of New Zealand's meat and dairy industries were notably more vociferous, objecting loudly to any arrangement that would entail Britain 'divorcing the Commonwealth to marry into Europe' and leave New Zealand 'tossed out in the snow'.[41]

Australia's Robert Menzies found the whole matter of Britain and Europe deeply disturbing, upending all that he regarded as sacred about the British connection. 'It seems right', he reflected at the 1962 Commonwealth Prime Ministers' Conference, 'to feel a proper, though controlled, emotion in facing these issues'.[42] His appeal for 'control' was a veiled barb aimed at his own deputy prime minister (and leader of the largely rural-based Country Party) Jack McEwen, whose visceral outbursts about 'foreigners' displacing Australian producers in the UK market had ruffled a few too many feathers.[43] McEwen held no qualms about playing the sympathy card, imploring British audiences that Australia had 'cleared jungles, drained swamps, brought out immigrants' and developed 'vast irrigation schemes to take scarce waters hundreds of miles to dry areas' in order to supply British consumers with vast quantities of wheat, dairy produce, sugar, meat and tinned fruits. Drawing on the same imagery that had adorned the interwar hoardings of the Empire Marketing Board, McEwen implied that these Herculean exertions had been undertaken solely for Britain's benefit, warning that 'a feeling, almost of being abandoned, could easily be aroused' if the familiar trade patterns of old were terminated.[44]

John Diefenbaker's Canadian Government was less troubled by the economic consequences for Canadian exporters (the United States having long since usurped Britain as the principal market) but dwelt heavily on the political implications. According to his private secretary, Diefenbaker 'could never quite overcome a sense of mystified grievance' that Macmillan had decided to 'marry into Europe', and harboured suspicions of a plot orchestrated by the United States Government to dislodge Canada's special affinity with Britain.[45] Convinced that Macmillan and President Kennedy were 'engaged in the unilateral planning of the fragmentation of the Commonwealth', he resorted to infantile analogies: 'All the King's horses and all the King's men may never be able to put it together again.'[46] Press opinion diverged across a wide spectrum, with the *Vancouver Sun* voicing contempt for 'this pathetic bleat that we're being deserted by mother Britain', while the arch-conservative *Calgary Herald* admonished the government for its lack of faith in British assurances, insisting that 'there should be no suggestion or accusations that Britain is going "outside the family"'.[47] The government soon found itself caught in a political bind; by hoisting the banner of Commonwealth unity 'the impression was abroad that Canada had given Britain but two alternatives – in or out – and had been anti-British'.[48] Surveying the confusion, the *Ottawa Journal* posed the fundamental question:

> In the matter of wanting to join the Common Market, what is meant by Britain? Not the British people, surely, seeing that according to all the

surveys made, more of the British people are against the Common Market than for it. And this of course makes nonsense of the cry, heard from some in Canada, that when the Canadian Government takes the stand it is taking on the Common Market it is 'opposing Britain'. What the Canadian Government is opposing is a position being taken by Prime Minister Macmillan and his ministers. Which is something different.[49]

Greater clarity was forthcoming from the Government of India, faced with a precarious balance of payments and a looming foreign exchange crisis. Here, the problem of Britain and Europe stirred a very different emotional reflex, equally rooted in the imperial past. For Prime Minister Nehru, the entire project of European unity smacked of an attempt 'to revive Western economic imperialism in a new garb', not least with respect to the Treaty of Rome's provisions for 'associate membership' for former colonial territories on account of their continued dependence on economic ties to Europe. Such arrangements, he feared, would merely restore the conditions of colonial bondage for newly independent states (or risk delaying independence for those in waiting) and he thus made it patently clear that India would not accept such a demeaning outcome. In the words of his finance minister, Morarji Desai, associate status would not be touched 'even with a bargepole'.[50] Responding to Menzies at the 1962 Commonwealth conference, Nehru concurred that the likely terms to be offered to Commonwealth producers were wholly inadequate, but he also made a point of lowering the emotional stakes: 'One gets used to all kinds of things one does not like.'[51]

Similar misgivings were voiced by the newly independent African states, with Ghana's Kwame Nkrumah particularly wary of the EEC's neo-colonial overtones. Any arrangement that reinforced perceptions of Africa as 'a hewer of wood and a drawer of water' would be wholly unwelcome, resembling the fate of former French colonies whose sovereign dignity he regarded as inherently compromised by 'Associate' status.[52] By the same token, Ghana's heavy reliance on the UK market as a source of scarce foreign exchange made it exceedingly difficult to reject the offer of associate membership upon Britain's accession.[53] Nigerian leaders were equally wary, and understandably puzzled as to why, if the EEC was inclined to extend favourable market access to African countries, it should be 'at all relevant' whether Britain were a member or not. The implication was that the whole matter hinged on their status as a former colony, with Britain's right to negotiate on their behalf taken entirely for granted.[54] These were very different moral and emotional priorities – devoid of 'King's horses' and sentimental dues.

Between these extremes were the reactions of West Indian leaders, where an equally heavy reliance on UK market access brought forth impassioned appeals to moral integrity of a different kind. This was no family feud along antipodean lines but an exercise in moral claim-making that largely avoided devotional appeals to British sentiment. Here, it was the shameful legacy of slavery that imposed a special 'responsibility' (sometimes phrased as a 'historic obligation') to minimize the disruption to West Indian livelihoods as the price of EEC entry. Trinidadian premier Eric Williams pointed to Britain's stake in the Caribbean's future as much as its past, imposing a duty to avert an economic fate 'even more hopeless than it seems at present'.[55] The *Barbados Advocate* spoke warily of an impending 'divorce of the West Indies from Britain' while leading figures in the sugar industry objected to Britain 'putting herself first and the colonies last ... giving up her birthright to the other European countries' and subjecting Caribbean interests to the whims of a trading bloc 'who are unlikely to show the same sympathy as Britain herself would'.[56] A powerful residue of distrust enlivened the entire debate, drawing on age-old doubts about the moral certainties of the British connection. 'They're bound to join, whatever we say', was the weary verdict of Jamaica's Alexander Bustamante – all too aware that British honour was unlikely to count for hard currency.[57]

West Indian reactions were compounded by Britain's clampdown on Commonwealth immigration in November 1961; the culmination of years of speculation geared specifically towards curbing the flow of inward migration from the West Indies.[58] Coming so soon on the heels of Macmillan's EEC entry bid, the twin barriers to the movement of people and the importation of goods provoked a passionate outburst from Federal West Indian prime minister Grantley Adams. In a letter to Harold Macmillan in November 1961, he amplified Britain's 'historic responsibility' arising from 'the forceful severance' of generations of enslaved Caribbean peoples from their African homes, and 'the rich trade in bodies and goods on which much of Britain's prosperity has been founded'.[59] For Britain to raise the drawbridge for the sake of commercial gain elsewhere – at an intolerable cost to West Indians – was an unexpected plot twist that seemed to defy all standards of decency. Far from echoing Reg Pollard's 'pride in the goods', here was moral indebtedness drawn to a vastly different scale.

What these reactions suggest is that Macmillan's bid for EEC membership doubled as a prolonged audit of the emotional balance sheet. While virtually all parties harboured residual investments in the unfinished business of empire, the pronounced disparity of feeling exposed multiple fault lines. This was to have two significant repercussions. First, it militated against any coordinated Commonwealth campaign aimed directly at British voters – a scenario that Macmillan was particularly anxious to avoid. And second, it split the domestic opposition to British entry into rival camps arguing from wholly incompatible moral templates – the one advocating racial solidarity with white farmers; the other pressing the case for developing Commonwealth economies still finding their feet – which again largely suited Macmillan's purposes.

Indeed, it is striking how the disparities in the reactions of Commonwealth countries were replicated in the British debate. On the one hand were the various anti-Marketeer movements that proliferated in autumn 1961, for whom it was almost exclusively the white 'dominion' cohort that seemed to matter at all. Drawing on a conception of the Commonwealth stuck fast in the 1920s, they resorted frequently to racialized rhetoric that might have embarrassed all but the most brazen offshore Britisher, with abundant references to British 'blood', 'stock', 'sons' and indeed 'the British race'. Such proclivities were especially prominent in the pages of the *Daily Express* (then the second-highest circulating newspaper in the country) under the avowedly reactionary proprietorship of the Canadian press baron Lord Beaverbrook. As we have seen, A. J. P. Taylor had few qualms about purveying the proprietor's world view in his weekly *Sunday Express* column:

> Call it sentiment, emotion, anything else you like. The fact remains that the nations of the Commonwealth are our brothers and sisters, and that foreign countries are not. The fact is true in the most literal sense. Millions of people in Canada, in Australia and in New Zealand are our relations by blood. When they or their ancestors left this country, they did not cease to be British. They went to the colonies or the Dominions in order to remain British. They took with them an allegiance to our institutions, to our soil, to our common past.[60]

For a publication that railed constantly against the effrontery of Commonwealth leaders from Nehru to Kenyatta to Nkumrah and Makarios (while voicing firm support for white settlers in Africa), devotion to 'the Commonwealth' was highly compartmentalized. A string of Beaverbrook-funded advertisements appeared in all the major UK dailies in summer 1962 featuring wartime hero Field Marshall Montgomery imploring readers: 'I say we must not join Europe … Let the Mother of Nations gather her children about her in obedience to the call of common kindred.' Should a third world war threaten to shatter the hard-won peace, there was 'only one race under Heaven which could stand between the

Western World and utter destruction ... That is the race to which we belong – the British people – united by close ties of blood, speech and religion the world over.'[61] Polling conducted in March 1962 showed that Canada, Australia and New Zealand were the Commonwealth countries which mattered most to the British public, particularly among Conservative voters – a statistic that weighed heavily on the strategic calculations of the Macmillan government.[62]

But Montgomery's ode to 'the expansion of the British race' had lost much of its moral force by the early 1960s, challenged by a new global ethics arising out of post-war humanitarian and developmental agencies. Tehila Sasson argues that by the mid-1960s, 'the question of who got a fair share of the plate became the heart of a new international politics' – a trend already apparent by the time of Britain's first EEC membership bid in 1961.[63] Feelings of profound moral obligation to the independent nations of the new Commonwealth inspired much of the anti-Common Market sentiment emanating from the Labour Party and other left-wing organizations, largely reiterating the objections of Eric Williams and Grantley Adams. Prominent Welsh Labour MP Sir Lynn Ungoed-Thomas put the matter succinctly: 'This is exactly the time when these people most need understanding, encouragement, assistance and friendly help. This is the very time when this Government, with its imperialist conception instead of a Commonwealth conception, chooses to abandon these people.'[64] Similarly, when Hugh Gaitskell urged from the opposition benches that 'there are moral obligations in this', he called to mind not the kinsfolk affluently ensconced in the old Commonwealth but the emerging priorities of the newer members. 'It would be quite outrageous', he insisted, if 'by going into the Common Market, we did things which seriously damaged, for instance, the extreme poverty-stricken West Indies because they lost their preferences in the sugar market'.[65]

Significantly, these same divisions also left an impression on Britain's negotiating counterparts in Brussels, who tended to show far greater concern for the economic plight of the newly independent Commonwealth states of Asia and Africa for whom 'Associate' membership was readily contemplated (ignoring the objections of Nehru and Nkrumah). Although conscious of the 'valeur sentimentale' of the family ties among the rural constituency of the old Commonwealth, the EEC member states saw no reason why these relatively well-off countries should be given special treatment.[66] A major French appraisal of February 1962 asked 'what common ideology unites men of such different nature as Mr. Nkrumah, Archbishop Makarios, and Mr. Menzies', suggesting that the much-vaunted 'moral unity' of the

Commonwealth was merely a British ploy to disguise the absence of any real economic dynamism or political accord. Indeed, much of the 'nostalgia' that drove Britain's fervent advocacy of Commonwealth interests in the EEC negotiations could be discounted as little more than '*une certain sympathie amusée*' – cultivated by a British government caught between two stools. Macmillan was hardly likely 'to sacrifice, in the name of the Commonwealth, the fundamental interests of Great Britain in the face of the dual peril of political isolation and economic stagnation'. That being so, there seemed no reason why France should make things easier by granting meaningful Commonwealth concessions.[67]

Faced with a divided Commonwealth, a domestic opposition at cross purposes, and French unwillingness to make the going easier, Britain's negotiating team – virtually all passionately pro-Common Market – became increasingly prepared to jettison Commonwealth claims to special treatment. It was by no means an overnight conversion but a case of slow, grinding attenuation of esteem over time, as frustration and resentment came increasingly to the surface. Britain's chief negotiator, Edward Heath, conveyed his 'disgust' to Macmillan with 'the ignorance, ill manners and conceit of the Commonwealth', which seemed so unlike the 'courteous and well informed' Europeans to whom he was temperamentally better attuned.[68] Ironically, it was the fabled 'common kindred' of the old Commonwealth that proved the greater irritant. 'These people', Heath complained, could 'hold out against us and put pressure on us' due to their vast reserves of popular goodwill in Britain. Such sentimental leverage was not the case with the Europeans 'and it is not likely to be the case with the Commonwealth much longer if our negotiations in Brussels are unsuccessful'.[69] Even New Zealand was not exempt, disparaged by the senior UK diplomat in Wellington (answering to the imperious eponym of Sir Francis Hovell-Thurlow-Cumming-Bruce) as a country that 'moves more slowly than the speed of events elsewhere requires'. His choice of metaphor revealed an underlying contempt: 'As with one of the smaller dinosaurs having slow moving limbs and a small head, no amount of kicking and pricking or even the risk of destruction will make the animal move much faster than its habit. But we will do all we can here to push it along from behind.'[70] Such extreme condescension stemmed from equally outworn assumptions, but it was also accentuated by the emotional proximity. By forcing hard questions on the terms of endearment, fraternal claims on British sympathies became more trouble than they were worth.

Macmillan took the initiative at the September 1962 Commonwealth Prime Ministers' Conference to lower expectations and impose clear limits on kindred spirit in a coldly competitive world. He recalled wistfully the days when only six prime ministers gathered for imperial conferences, when it was 'fashionable to refer to the Commonwealth as a family'. But with the passage of time and the diversification of membership, it had become more apt to think of the Commonwealth as a group of 'friends and relations who, with different problems in all the various parts of the world, nevertheless hold in common certain beliefs and traditions and retain a continuing interest in and practical concern for each other's welfare'. Avoiding all mention of the once mandatory sense of mutual 'obligation', 'duty', 'commitment' and 'responsibility' (let alone the affinities of 'blood', 'race' and 'organic unity'), his heavily watered-down devotion to 'the fundamental unity of the human race' needed little deciphering.[71] Members of his inner circle warmly congratulated the prime minister afterwards, revelling in a sense that at last 'the boats were burnt and ... the time had come to argue for Common Market entry without inhibitions'.[72] Henceforth, as far as the prime minister was concerned, the sacred bond that only six years earlier had come 'first in our hearts and in our minds' would have no more claim on British sympathies than humanity itself. Macmillan recorded his personal satisfaction in his diary later that evening with an undeniably patrician arrogance: 'It is ironical to hear countries which have abused us for years now beseeching us not to abandon them. The thought that UK might declare herself independent seems so novel as to be quite alarming.'[73]

DISCOUNTED WARES: THE 'EMPIRE OF GOODS' UNRAVELS

The mixed emotions stirred by Britain's European overtures calls to mind Arjun Appadurai's axiom: 'commodities, like persons, have social lives'. Just as economic value hinges on human relationships, he argued, so too the presumed worth of bartered goods arises out of complex community dynamics that structure the terms of trade. As the British empire expanded, enormous cultural significance became attached to otherwise impersonal, bulk-produced items for mass consumption.[74] This was particularly pronounced in the case of commodities shipped in vast quantities to the imperial metropole. As the very bedrock of colonial economies, the social standing of staples for export was all the more resonant for the communities that produced them, forging a shared realm of everyday experience that bound producers and consumers in a wider 'empire of goods'.[75] Equally, trade could play an active part in disrupting imperial scales of kinship and community. T. H. Breen's example of colonial America placed everyday consumer items – cloth, ceramics, paper and, of course, tea – at the fore-front of the American Revolution because the colonists' exposure to an almost identical range of imported goods was crucial to forging viable and enduring relationships transcending colonial borders. Benjamin Franklin grasped the essentials in *The Interest of Great Britain Considered* (1760), where he observed the subtle effects of imported consumer goods on colonial Americans who 'must "know," must "think," and must "care," about the country they chiefly trade with'.[76] It was only when parliament took steps to politicize these goods that 'they took on a radical, new symbolic function', capable of forging a unity of purpose that no ideological programme could have engendered.[77]

It was E. P. Thompson who first proposed the idea of a 'moral economy' working in tandem with the material laws of supply and demand, subtly regulating the terms of exchange according to 'passionately held notions of the common-weal'. Socially generated norms were scarcely visible most of the time, he argued, tending only to 'intrude at moments of disturbance' in the economic order as a kind of cultural corrective.[78] Economic historians have increasingly explored how complex cultural mediations and collective social behaviour influence patterns of commercial exchange. Joel Mokyr describes the emergence of a 'civil economy' of clubs, societies, academies and informal networks in eighteenth-century Britain that enforced a system of moral codes, without which 'the worlds of credit and commerce would have disintegrated rapidly'.[79] Meanwhile, Frank Trentmann has considered how 'moral imaginaries' also affected patterns of imperial consumerism in the interwar years, serving as a prime example of 'a historical stretching of intimate caring relations'.[80] It is not a question of whether the empire was itself an inherently 'moral' enterprise, so much as how it registered in contemporary perceptions of the 'common-weal' – and how it subsequently fared under a particularly severe 'moment of disturbance' as the empire-project unravelled in the 1960s.

It seems surprising, then, that Britain's agonizing decision to seek entry into the EEC – instantly politicizing an extensive assortment of Commonwealth consumer goods – has never been viewed in a similar light. Although there are obvious limits to comparing the early colonial period with the complex commercial rules devised for the twentieth-century Commonwealth, there was nevertheless a shared element of everyday con-sumer items serving as proxies for imperial sentiment. Some (but as we have seen, by no means all) Commonwealth governments wasted little time appealing directly to the British people in a bid to embarrass British politi-cians eager to offload unwanted encumbrances to secure the benefits of an enlarged Common Market. That they could so effortlessly resort to implied obligations of fealty and kindred spirit was the legacy of decades of ingrained attachments that had become imprinted on the goods themselves. Indeed, General de Gaulle himself always expected that some version of the Greater British moral economy would intervene to hobble Macmillan's membership bid in a hail of Commonwealth recriminations. The final resort to a formal French veto in January 1963 only became necessary once it had become clear that Commonwealth sentiment would not perform the task for him. Why, then, was the empire of goods found wanting, both at the time of Macmillan's initial overtures and a decade later when Britain finally secured entry in 1973?

By the early 1960s, the culture of consumption in Britain had been dramatically transformed, no longer conforming to the patterns of the pre-war era. The effects of a belated but burgeoning post-war affluence ushered in a new era when an increasing portion of disposable income was spent on satisfying individual wants rather than needs, with far-reaching consequences for international trade relations.[81] The right of the 'sovereign consumer' to a certain level of prosperity forged a political culture more at ease with material gratification, while consumer awareness became primarily associated with securing production quality and safety standards, voicing 'the concerns of consumers against producers' in place of the 'buy British' activism of former times.[82] Erika Rappaport has charted the rocky path of imperial consumerism through the example of the humble cup of tea, once the 'poster child for the entire empire shopping movement' in the interwar years. In an era when older, industrial-based consumption patterns were giving way to global circulations of an expanding array of consumer goods, tea was subjected to 'a major rebranding effort' to transform old habits 'into a modern, hip, youthful, and cosmopolitan pleasure'.[83] By the mid-1960s, most British consumers 'did not think of the empire when they brewed their tea' – and much the same could be said of the wider array of Commonwealth imports more obviously at risk from EEC competition.[84]

All of which suggests a deeper realignment in the governing assumptions of 'virtuous consumption' in the post-war years.[85] David Thackeray emphasizes the hiatus of the Second World War and its aftermath, when British consumers were 'radically disempowered by shortages, rationing and controls' – placing clear limits on consumer choice. When controls were eventually lifted in the 1950s, 'patriotic buying' had become recast in more narrowly nationalistic terms, largely stripped of its interwar imperial resonances.[86] Similar trends emerged in Commonwealth markets, with a profusion of 'Australian made' and 'Made in Canada' logos (while the

Government of India succeeded in 'nationalizing tea's consuming culture', largely expunging the stigma of service to an imperial master).[87] In the meantime, innovations in the field of market research cast doubt on the efficacy of undifferentiated appeals to mass markets, turning instead to 'segmented marketing' which pitched products according to social, generational and gender differences. Consumers could still be bought by the power of moral persuasion, but the causes that moved them were diverse and perpetually in flux. The launch of the first mass consumer boycott of South African goods in the wake of the Sharpeville massacre in 1960 was a harbinger of changing community attitudes, and although South Africa's departure from the Commonwealth removed it from consideration in the matter of joining the Common Market, the 1960 boycott marked the beginning of a slow attenuation of the 'preference of sentiment' for racialised compatriots abroad.[88]

Thus, for all the arch indignation of the anti-Common Market lobby in the early 1960s, remarkably little effort was made to enlist the patriotic consumer to their cause. Although some mileage was made out of the 'foreign giant looming over breakfast', threatening to 'substitute dear French food for cheap Commonwealth fare', appeals to the welfare of overseas farmers producing specified trade goods were few and far between.[89] Relentless campaigns such as that of the *Daily Express* were waged largely in terms of generalized cultural affinities, placing greater store on a New Zealander's ability to 'distinguish between a no ball and a googly' than any filial loyalty inherent in purchasing their butter.[90] Indeed, pro-EEC papers such as the *Daily Mirror* often had the better of consumer advocacy, stressing the benefits of 'more choice in the shops', lower prices for manufactured goods, better quality and the lure of prosperous countries 'where beer flows like water and money flows like beer'.[91] The BBC's September 1962 special broadcast, *Commonwealth Crisis: Britain and the Old Dominions*, referred only tangentially to the special intimacy between dominion farmers and UK consumers. A year earlier, one-time Suez rebel Angus Maude (returning from three years as editor of the *Sydney Morning Herald*) delivered a broadside against waning consumer diligence on the BBC's home service:

> The British do not really care about Australia, whereas Australians care deeply about Britain . . . They want to hear whether anyone really knows or cares – in terms of hard figures – what is going to happen to their wheat and metals and beef and butter and eggs. It happens to be a matter of life and

death to them. We cannot defend them anymore. We cannot even help them much. But we might at least *care*.[92]

Indeed, to the extent that earlier patterns of imperial consumerism featured at all, they had the inverse effect of downgrading dominion goods in the moral hierarchy. Just as the earlier iconography of the Empire Marketing Board in the interwar years had singled out the bucolic plenty of the settler colonies, so too their perceived (and indeed real) levels of prosperity would set them apart when it came to assessing claims for special treatment in an enlarged Common Market.[93] This was certainly the attitude of the EEC member states (who could not resist pointing out that even hard-pressed New Zealand farmers were 'millionaires compared with the peasants of Calabria'), but it was also implicit in the calculations of UK negotiators in determining what counted as genuine hardship.[94] Unsurprisingly, when the Wilson Labour government relaunched a second (and equally ill-fated) membership bid in 1967, a drastically reduced shopping list of Commonwealth consumer goods was submitted for special treatment (restricted largely to New Zealand lamb and dairy produce and Commonwealth sugar).[95]

By this time, new consumer initiatives such as the Haslemere Group had drawn attention to Britain's 'unique ethical responsibility towards the decolonizing global South', pushing for a 'more capacious restructuring of trade' with an emphasis on primary commodities produced in the developing world, not least in Britain's former colonies.[96] Where once the moral economy had been skewed towards racial affinities, by the 1960s the new imperatives of Commonwealth 'development' and humanitarian aid had tipped the scales towards ensuring minimum living standards – at a time when early precursors of the 'fair trade' movement were forging a 'new global moral geography'.[97] This did not pass unnoticed, nor without a measure of indignation on the part of newspaper editors in Australia and New Zealand who objected to Britain's apparent readiness to 'dump' kinship ties, 'but not the politically dangerous, newer, underdeveloped black Commonwealth countries' as part of the price of EEC entry.[98]

THE 'WAR OF THE TWO SUGARS' REVISITED

This bifurcation of the moral economy has no better illustration than the example of cane sugar. Arguably the original (and certainly archetypal) imperial staple with more than its share of accumulated moral baggage, sugar would prove to be the last and most difficult commodity problem to be solved when Britain finally secured entry to the EEC in the early 1970s. Cultivated over more than three hundred years in British-owned offshore plantations at an unspeakable human cost, it was one of the first commodities to exemplify the intricate networks of empire and Britishness.[99] As such, it also bore the added distinction of having galvanized the world's first consumer boycott in the 1790s. From the early 1800s, cane sugar had to vie with the intrusions of the European-grown beet variety, and thus the prospect of British entry to the Common Market seemed to mark the culmination of the centuries-long 'war of the two sugars'.[100] Right down to the 1960s, cane sugar continued to carry the weight of complex community expectations, particularly in the Caribbean where it remained the principal generator of employment and foreign exchange in Jamaica, Barbados, Belize, Guyana, Trinidad and St Kitts – a situation made even more complex by virtue of multiple sites of cultivation throughout the Commonwealth, with vastly different production conditions and even more diverse historical resonances.

In addition to its crucial role as the major provider in a plantation economy such as Barbados, cane sugar was also the principal means of livelihood for the overwhelmingly white, British-derived settler population of north Queensland. With the expulsion of Melanesian indentured labour in the early 1900s, Queensland had made a virtue of transplanting white labour to the tropics; a feat of colonization symbolized by the veneration of 'white' sugar.[101] When Colonial Secretary Leo Amery visited the coastal 'sugaropolis' of Mackay in 1927, he was handed a commemorative booklet boasting of 'the only tropical country in the world where every class of work, from the highest kind of intellectual effort to the roughest and most arduous kind of manual labour, is practically done by white people'. At the heart of this supposed miracle was an abundant sugar crop produced entirely by white hands that could 'outwork any non-British race in the sugar fields' (a marginal note explaining that 'the term "British" is used to cover all white British nationalities, whether born in Australia or Great Britain').[102] In this scheme of things, the everyday consumption of Queensland sugar 'became a loyal act and a symbolic action' – preserving 'white jobs' in the tropical north while bolstering Australia's northern reaches against potential Asian designs.[103]

Despite their obvious disparities, tropical Queensland and Barbados shared a number of vague similarities, not only as 'monocultures' wholly reliant on a single crop but also in their 'deep need for metropolitan approval' fuelled by nagging doubts that a tropical setting might count against them as fellow Britons.[104] Charles Dilke himself had reported that 'the Queenslanders have not yet solved the problem of the settlement of a tropical country by Englishmen', while Trollope described the heat as a subject of 'extreme delicacy' north of Capricorn.[105] Barbadians, too, felt obliged to compensate for their tropical dispensation by talking up their Britishness. Known from the early nineteenth century by the sobriquet 'Little England', as late as 1961 the island could still be casually described as 'more British than Britain'.[106] The statue of Lord Nelson in Bridgetown's Trafalgar Square – only very recently hauled down – signalled a distant, if distorted echo of Mackay's central grid of Victoria, Gordon, Alfred and Shakespeare streets intersecting with Milton, Peel, Wellington and Nelson.[107]

But there the similarities ended, particularly when a new Conservative government under Edward Heath finally received the green light from de Gaulle's successor, George Pompidou, to make a third application for EEC membership in 1970. Britain's bargaining position was inherently weakened by having twice been spurned by France, which tended to dampen any residual inclination to fight hard for anyone but themselves. In any case, opinion polls indicated that by the early 1970s, only 9 per cent of respondents identified the Commonwealth specifically as a cause for hesitation about joining the EEC.[108] On this occasion it was Heath's close ally and committed 'European', Geoffrey Rippon, who spearheaded Britain's entry bid, striking the debilitated pose of a nation on the ropes. 'A decision not to join', went the government's official case, would entail 'a rejection of an historic opportunity' to reverse the country's fortunes: 'In a single generation we should have renounced an imperial past and rejected a European future.'[109] Rippon himself freely conceded that 'in the process of converting Empire into Commonwealth . . . we have – let us admit it – lost a measure of our national self-confidence'. Echoing the anxieties of the previous decade, he saw in European unity a unique opportunity to 'recover [our] self-respect' rather than sit back and 'worry uneasily whether we still have what it takes, whether our peculiarities of character and talent can survive'.[110] To the extent that he was inclined to issue any 'specific and moral commitment' to third countries, he confined himself exclusively to New Zealand pastoral interests and a limited range of imports from the developing Commonwealth – specifically, the sugar producing countries for whom no alternative market existed.[111]

Caribbean cane growers found themselves largely at the mercy of Britain's dealings with the EEC. In the words of the Barbados *Advocate-News*, it was a case of 'Protect Our Sugar or We Perish'.[112] The president of the Caribbean Cane Farmers' Association could not contain his bewilderment that 'two resounding and humiliating rebuffs by France' had in no way deterred the United Kingdom from 'ITS SINGLE-MINDED OBSESSIVE PURSUIT OF COMMUNITY MEMBERSHIP'.[113] Invariably described as a 'battle' or 'struggle', there was little dissent from the view that 'the sugar boat stands in fear floundering on the shoals of Britain's Common Market negotiations'.[114] Amid copious references to sugar as the 'lifeblood' of the Caribbean economies, it was again widely anticipated that European sugar producers 'will now be sharpening their beet knives' to claim the West Indies' vulnerable share of the UK market.[115] Their champion was Lord 'Jock' Campbell of Eskan, a major estate-owner in Guyana and chairman of the Commonwealth Sugar Exporters Association who had devoted much of his adult life to improving the social and human conditions of West Indian plantations. Not averse to delivering home truths, he frequently impressed upon metropolitan audiences (British and European alike) the ethical stakes of EEC enlargement:

> And remember that as in most of the 'sugar islands': metropolitan countries founded the sugar industries entirely to suit their own economic interests, in virtually uninhabited countries, with imported slave labour. It is surely unthinkable that European countries should now, to suit their own economic interest, condemn these countries to catastrophe by closing their markets to them … For countries and industries developed on slavery, indenture and colonialism there are still many unpaid debts to their peoples.[116]

It was a compelling argument, but it also stirred misgivings about special pleading on the part of West Indian sugar interests which posed a barrier to genuine emancipation. Barbadian prime minister Errol Barrow admonished that 'we are still seeking crumbs from the tables of other people' while Guyana's Cheddi Jagan urged West Indian sugar representatives 'not to adopt the role of beggars'.[117] Evidently, the memories stirred by sugar could cut both ways, its capacity to harbour complex, conflicting sentiments evidently undimmed.

The solution for sugar was thrashed out at a meeting at London's Lancaster House on 2 June 1971 between Rippon and fourteen Commonwealth sugar producers, culminating in a 'firm assurance' of continuing access to the enlarged Common Market for pre-existing quantities of Commonwealth imports. From a West Indian perspective, this was as sure a guarantee as anyone hoped for in the circumstances, and there was broad agreement that 'the delegates could return home assured that they had secured the future of the Commonwealth sugar industry'.[118] But the

Figure 8.1 Protesters in London object to EEC restrictions on importing sugar cane from the Commonwealth, following UK entry into the European Economic Community, 28 March 1973. Source: Hulton Archive/Getty Images.

Lancaster House gathering signalled a major reckoning for the sole Commonwealth sugar producer not invited to attend – Australia, and specifically Queensland sugar, which was deemed too affluent to warrant an extension of the special guarantees on offer. It was not about the economic fortunes of the nine thousand cane farms sprawling the length of the Queensland coast, so much as an assessment of the political repercussions given Australia's broadly favourable economic prospects and the relatively marginal place of sugar in the country's overall foreign earnings. Accordingly, the fact that six out of ten Australians living north of Capricorn remained wholly dependent on sugar production was properly deemed Australia's problem, not Britain's.[119] In the absence of the deplorable legacies of plantation sugar so resonant in the Caribbean, a history of intrepid whites transplanted to the tropics could no longer underwrite bankable claims on British sentiment.

In closing the door on Queensland, Rippon made two political calculations: first, that the EEC would not countenance concessions for rich white sugar growers, and second, that Australia could absorb the political and economic cost. On both counts his judgement proved perfectly sound. Australian attitudes had in any case moved on from the moral indignation of the early 1960s. Editorial opinion at the time suggests that the rapid diversification of Australia's overseas trade had 'made us less anxious, as a nation, about the prospect of British entry' (*Sydney Morning Herald*), particularly now that it had become abundantly clear that 'the sentimental ties no longer contain sufficient economic sustenance' (*The Australian*). Britain had already 'burnt most of her bridges' in two prior membership bids (Hobart's *Mercury*) and even the residual arguments about strengthening the Commonwealth by bolstering Britain's economy had 'a faint air of nostalgia ... we are all looking after ourselves' (*The Age*). Few Australians now seriously believed that Britain could 'be turned from her course', nor did they see any cause for alarm (*Canberra Times*).[120] Earlier appeals to the shared sentiments bound up in exported goods had given way to a blanket of acquiescence.

But the adjustment to a de-sentimentalized trading world was by no means uniform, with stark regional variations according to disparate levels of anticipated hardship. Reactions in North Queensland, still reliant on the same volumes of guaranteed UK sugar consumption as a decade earlier, reveal the remarkable persistence of expectations forged in the moral economy of the pre-war years. From the humblest cane grower to most senior industry executive, the consensus on Queensland sugar was one of impending disaster. 'We'll all be in the soup', said John Pavetto from his cane farm north of Townsville: 'The little blokes like me may be washed up if we lose the British market.'[121] Queensland Sugar Board chairman Sir Alan Summerville protested that 'the great bulk of the British people are against joining the Common Market', while the chairman of the sugar refining giant CSR accused the British of making 'no serious effort' to live up to their obligations.[122] 'Britain did not even bother', echoed the *Townsville Daily Bulletin*, while the *Daily Mercury* voiced disbelief that Queensland could be 'dumped so readily for a deutschmark'.[123] When the UK deputy high commissioner was despatched to Mackay to unruffle feathers, he only compounded matters in a widely reported statement at a local sugar-storage facility: 'Australia is a big girl now. She has developed into a Pacific power and no longer needs to hang on to Mum's European skirts.'[124]

Meanwhile, the redoubtable state premier, Joh Bjelke-Petersen (the bilingual son of a Danish Lutheran pastor), bypassed Australia's formal diplomatic channels entirely, issuing a personal statement in London lambasting Britain's 'out-of-character, and, in effect, callous indifference to the well-being' of Queenslanders, the great majority of whom were 'British people or children or descendants of British people'. Likening the harsh treatment to General de Gaulle's 'non' to British Common Market entry eight years earlier, the premier complained that such a flat rejection was 'just too "European" to be British. It is at variance with the voice of Britain that I have known for so long and grown to respect.'[125] In a campaign better-suited to garnering accolades up and down the state's vast sugar constituency than influencing the terms of British entry, Bjelke-Petersen missed no opportunity to paint a 'frightening and calamitous picture' of the 'complete loss of our sugar income'.[126]

In purely economic terms, these statements were certainly overblown (only 30 per cent of export earnings stood to be affected), but they do convey the human dimension of a community 'deeply wrapped up in sugar' now suddenly 'bracing themselves for adversity'.[127] Under the headline 'Cloud over Cane', the *North Queensland Register* surveyed the skies ablaze for the crushing season, the customary smoke billowing from burning cane fields signalling a brooding portent:

> This year the sugar industry stands under a cloud of a different kind as it plunges into the 'crushing'. This could be far more serious than a weather disturbance. It has appeared as a wisp in previous seasons, but now it gathers, dark and threatening, as a peril to the industry's future. This is the Common Market cloud. It is impossible, when visiting northern sugar towns, not to detect an air of uncertainty about the future ... What will be the effect on whole towns if such a large proportion of the export market disappears through British membership of the European Economic Community?

North Queenslanders had hoped that 'the traditional ties of brotherhood and trade partnership might mean more to Britain than they now appear to mean', but the signs emanating from Europe offered not 'the slightest shred of hope'.[128] Mackay's *Daily Mercury* published an extraordinary requiem for the 'fading glory' of Greater Britain; a historical sweep encompassing Victoria and Albert, Disraeli, Gladstone, Empire Day, Churchill and 'a long line of adventurous explorers and empire builders who saw the strength of dominions and colonies as the greatness of England'. With the final act now 'lamentably close to fulfilment', it would henceforth feel 'strange to us all to regard the United Kingdom as a member of a foreign consortium, a partner in a European alliance that excludes us, a mother who has abandoned her offspring to live with a de facto husband who speaks another language'. There was no mistaking the sense of bewilderment that 'we no longer have inherited priorities', and the residual urge to upbraid 'Britain's desire to shed herself of obligations' to compatriots overseas. This was 1971, and yet the weight of more than two decades of imperial retrenchment could not alleviate the shock 'for people who have grown up in the British tradition', now forced 'to recognise the processes of dissolution in their own empire'.[129]

The circumstances of Britain's tortuous route to EEC membership, drawn out over more than a decade with recurring stumbling blocks along the way, were fundamental to the implosion of the 'empire of goods'. Economic relations were deeply woven into patterns of community sentiment, and the unravelling of the one could not but impact adversely on the other. Some historians have disputed this, pointing to the longer-term trends that doomed Commonwealth trade ties almost from the time of the Imperial Preference deal struck in Ottawa in the early 1930s. According to this gradualist view, Britain's courtship of Europe was merely a superficial manifestation of 'deeper forces' corroding the Commonwealth imaginary and should therefore not be attributed undue importance.[130] But this conflates the largely invisible structures of macro-economic change – which were indeed gradual and systemic – with the political crises and emotional disruptions they periodically engendered, which tended to converge around symbolically charged moments such as Britain's turn to Europe. From the set-piece of Macmillan's opening gambit (and dramatic rebuff), followed by successive attempts to chart a viable pathway to EEC membership, the complexities of Commonwealth economic partnerships were distilled into a single issue that channelled immense quantities of political energy into otherwise obscure recesses.[131] In this sense, gradualist accounts tend to overlook the power of symbolism and sentiment in affecting contemporary perceptions of economic and social change.

For all the manifold reverberations, however, Greater British sentiment ultimately failed to prevent Britain from joining the EEC. 'Patriotic consumption' was no longer the rallying cry it had once been, and the Commonwealth was in any case divided about the imperative of preserving traditional economic ties. The mobilization of humanitarian sentiment had effected an inversion of the moral hierarchies of old, placing the need to ensure adequate terms for the developing Commonwealth over and above the claims of white kinship (even as reactionary elements continued to lament the severing of economic ties with Australia, New Zealand and Canada). The magnitude of shifting priorities should not be overstated, however. The psychological adjustments were only partial and unevenly distributed, while conflicting sentiments would continue to plague Britain's place in Europe for decades.

For a sugar-producing community such as North Queensland, long accustomed to the protocols of white solidarity, the refusal to extend the same exemptions negotiated for the West Indies offers a prime example of the delayed emotional response. Queensland's exclusion from the Lancaster House meeting of June 1971 underscored the bifurcation of the moral economy in which the moribund claims of British race sentiment parted company with the new imperative of redressing (or at least, not compounding) the historical legacies of plantation sugar. Emotional reactions in Queensland and the Caribbean represented either side of the ledger. Though neither white kinship nor post-colonial culpability could secure cast-iron claims on British priorities, it now appeared that the latter was better attuned to the moral imperatives of the 1970s – at least as far as the sugar trade was concerned. Local Queensland press reports persisted with plaintive recriminations, long after the futility of the cause had become embarrassingly obvious. Brisbane's *Courier Mail* served up a particularly tedious sample :

> Australia? What's Australia? It's a forgotten land, my friends. Long newspaper pieces, and TV and radio coverage, review Britain's Common Market entry struggle, dissect in detail the meaning of the terms, and make their forecasts. New Zealand is suddenly big. Mauritius, Samoa, Fiji and even Tonga are significant enough to get a mention somewhere, but Australia – No ... We're out. We're not even minor actors in the play. We don't exist. We don't even get a consolatory pat on the head for being good obedient boys and making no trouble.[132]

Here, at the farthest reaches of a fragmenting empire were the dying convulsions of a discarded belief system. What inflamed the passions was the sense of negation, the feeling that 'we don't exist' – the unsettling residue of sentiments no longer reciprocated. Not for the first time the emotional balance sheet was skewed at the margins where the sense of entitlement ran deeper, and the burden of expectation rested squarely on the goods themselves. North Queensland's thwarted claims on the metropolitan conscience bears out E. P. Thompson's maxim that it is typically 'an outrage to these moral assumptions, quite as much as actual deprivation' that triggers the corrective procedures of the moral economy.[133] Only in this instance, the correction proved wholly ineffective. 'White sugar' conspicuously failed to strike a chord with the UK citizen-consumer in June 1971.

One fleeting exception, the work of a young journalist at Sheffield's *Morning Telegraph* in June 1971, underscores the subtlety of the switch. Instructed by his editor to address the Common Market's impact on the Commonwealth, John Heffernan eschewed 'dry as dust economic terms', electing instead to sample 'a corner of somewhere like Australia and see what happens'. His curiosity alighted on North Queensland, an area that supplied more of Britain's sugar consumption than 'few of us I am ashamed to say' were even aware. Surveying the grievances of the northern sugar growers, he soon found himself peering into a dark and disconcerting future where the civilizing impulse of colonization was put into reverse. 'What I see is a Queensland which has received a tremendous kick from the home country. I see an area which has been carefully nurtured by an assured market in Britain for its main industry becoming a virtual jungle again.' Perhaps it was 'inevitable and right', he reflected, that those parts of the world 'peopled by men and women who came from this country' should henceforth underwrite their own futures. But at the very least their fate deserved 'to be more widely debated'.[134] It was precisely the reaction that Queensland sugar interests had so persistently craved – the assurance of mutual recognition; a belated signal that the old racial reciprocity could still be revived. Clippings were duly dispatched to Brisbane and paraded before the premier as proof that his overtures finally were cutting through. But in truth, it was a conspicuous outlier – a throwback to emotional investments leached of their former conviction. This was not pride in the goods but a half-turn of the head, surveying the remnants of a lapsed vocation.

9

UNCOMMON LAW: THE REACH OF BRITISH JUSTICE

Africa Unity Square in the heart of Zimbabwe's capital Harare is ringed with reminders of a troubled British past: Meikles Hotel to the south, the old *Rhodesia Herald* office to the east and the colonial-era parliament nestled alongside St Mary's Anglican Cathedral on the northern flank. It marks the site where the 'Pioneer Column' sponsored by Cecil Rhodes first hoisted the flag on 12 September 1890. Formerly 'Cecil Square' (not after Rhodes himself but the British prime minister presiding at the time, Robert Cecil), it is vaguely reminiscent of a Bloomsbury garden uprooted to warmer climes.[1] To this day, its criss-crossed avenues of pathways, fountains and jacaranda trees are configured in the pattern of a Union Jack.

On 7 March 1968, this one-time oasis of empire loyalism became the scene of an unseemly affray. At 9 am, a group of white Rhodesian women strode onto the lawn opposite the parliament to mount a silent protest. After a solemn wreath-laying ceremony, they took turns in groups of three to hoist placards bearing the words 'In Memory of Rhodesian Humanity', 'In Memory of Rhodesian Justice' and 'In Memory of Rhodesian Law'. Any political gathering of more than three individuals would have infringed Rhodesia's stringent anti-demonstration laws; hence the careful separation of the trio of placard-bearers from a dozen or so supporters reclining in the nearby shade.[2] No voices were raised, nor any attempt made to draw a crowd with rousing rhetoric – the atmosphere more akin to a requiem service than a political rally. Just before lunchtime, a police presence assigned to check any subversive intent was quietly withdrawn as the protesters continued their vigil amid occasional taunts from pedestrians and passing motorists.

At precisely 2.15 pm the mood abruptly changed when a white Rhodesian man in his twenties burst angrily onto the scene. 'Why do you support murderers?' he demanded, before seizing a nearby garden hose and dousing the entire party. One local press photographer captured the unnamed intruder as he wrenched a placard from an elderly white lady in elbow-length gloves, knocking her to the ground. He was joined by another malcontent who tore up the remaining placards and kicked away the wreaths, all the while egged on by a gathering crowd. 'Give it to them, give it to them' one woman cheerily exhorted, while others hastily constructed a new banner from the fragments pronouncing: 'Thank God for Law & Order & Ian: Forward Rhodesia'.[3] For the editor of the *Rhodesia Herald* it was 'the ugliest incident' the Rhodesian capital of Salisbury had seen for a long time, 'cowardly and brutal'.[4]

The cause of the uproar was the events of the previous day, when two young African dissidents, James Dhlamini and Victor Mlambo, were sent to the gallows by the rebel Rhodesian Government of Ian Smith. As members of the so-called 'Crocodile Gang' they had been convicted in 1964 of participating in the ambush and murder of a passing white motorist; the inaugural act of political violence by the Zimbabwean African National Union (ZANU). But their fate also had the distinction of becoming a test case for the reach of British justice in the renegade colony. Smith's Rhodesian Front had famously issued its Unilateral Declaration of Independence (UDI) in November 1965 in open defiance of the British Government, while remaining avowedly loyal to Her Majesty and, by extension, the British people. The belief that white Rhodesia embodied the true essence of a British way of life that had been forfeited by pusillanimous governments in the United Kingdom was fundamental to popular understandings of UDI, not only among Smith's constituents but also across substantial swathes of white opinion throughout the Commonwealth where popular sympathy for the Rhodesian cause ran high.

On the eve of their execution, Dhlamini and Mlambo's defence team had decided to test Rhodesian loyalties by seeking leave to appeal to the Privy Council in London – in a direct challenge to a Rhodesian judiciary that had spent more than two years in a state of limbo, continuing to serve the outlawed Rhodesian state while drawing legitimacy from the nominal sovereignty of Queen Elizabeth II. The case raised even more complex issues when the queen herself intervened at the eleventh hour to commute the sentences to life imprisonment. The 'hanging case' (as it became known) effectively called the bluff of Rhodesian claims to upholding the lonely mantle of British justice in a continent run rampant with post-colonial despots. The Rhodesian Appellate Court's decision to defy the queen and let the defendants hang would spark a major international outcry echoing from UN Secretary-General U Thant to Indira Gandhi to Pope Paul VI. British diplomats in Nairobi and Addis Ababa were pelted with rocks and rotten vegetables and an attempt to blow-up the British High Commission in Lusaka was narrowly averted.[5] In Britain, it sparked violent clashes between police and student demonstrators outside Rhodesia House on the Strand, while *The Guardian* called on the British Government to waste no time in invading Rhodesia.[6] Beneath the tumult, the hangings would mark a parting of the ways between white Rhodesians and their British 'kith and kin' more profound and lasting than the moment of UDI itself.

Among the core tenets of Britain's much-vaunted 'global reach' was the belief in a shared tradition of British justice inherited from the Common Law. This was not just about maintaining order, but also a matter of ensuring that far-flung investments with slow-maturing returns would be protected by shared legal custom. 'Lawyers prospered mightily in the British Empire', Chris Bayly once observed, the immediate beneficiaries of buoyant land speculation as vast new tracts were summarily confiscated.[7] The imperative of legal certainty was inseparable from settler incursions, bringing a stabilizing element to an otherwise disorderly and hazardous enterprise.[8] Though administered by way of separate judicial systems in widely disparate jurisdictions, the law nevertheless furnished a potent symbol of continuity through the force of shared judicial principles and procedures, joint-channels of appeal and a common source of legitimacy in the British Crown. In theory, non-white British subjects were entitled to the same legal rights and protections, but this rarely squared with the social reality of frontier settings where 'the insecurity of whites had always been the central premiss of public law'.[9] Criminal court proceedings – especially between settler and Indigenous protagonists – always had the potential to expose profound 'dissonances within the ranks of colonizers', disrupting the crucial affective ties to metropolitan Britain. As Martin Wiener underlines, the uneven ramifications of frontier justice served to amplify and dramatize 'deep clashes of ideology about Britishness and the rights of Britons'.[10]

In Rhodesia in the 1960s, the system was turned on its head as the resort to British legal norms and especially Privy Council appeals became a source of acute *uncertainty* for the increasingly isolated white minority. Axioms that could no longer be relied on to underwrite white authority were swiftly discarded in favour of a much cruder conception of 'law and order' founded on naked force. The fracas on the lawns of Cecil Square in March 1968 was a local variant of a much wider ideological ferment at a time when the verities of offshore Britishness were swiftly unravelling. In mourning the passing of 'Rhodesian Justice', the outnumbered protesters signalled a profound breach with wider British legal entitlements and liberties that were fundamental to their own self-identification as British Rhodesians in a wider circle of belonging. If the 'moral imagination' of Greater Britain 'fundamentally was a legal imagination', it becomes crucial to consider the legal imperfections that came catastrophically to the fore at empire's end.[11] This chapter takes the hanging case as the crucible of broken allegiances in these critical early years of the Rhodesian crisis, fatally undermining the common law as the sheet anchor of a global British justice.

'CLOCODIEL GROUP ON ACTION': THE CRIME, JULY 1964

It was almost four years earlier, on a lonely stretch of road in the remote south-eastern borderlands of Manicaland, that James Dhlamini and Victor Mlambo took part in the events that would later seal their fate. At sunset on 4 July 1964, a local factory hand by the name of Petrus Johannes Andries Oberholtzer (Andrea to his friends) was driving home towards Melsetter (present-day Chimanimani) in his Volkswagen kombi with his wife Johanna and three-year-old daughter Elizabeth, the youngest of his seven children. Suddenly they were forced to pull up at a row of small boulders strewn in their path as a makeshift roadblock. What subsequently transpired is subject to conflicting witness testimony, but a few undisputed facts can be reliably discerned. Oberholtzer got out and busied himself removing the obstacles when four African men appeared by the roadside. A fierce confrontation ensued which resulted in Oberholtzer receiving sixteen stab wounds and four fractures to his skull. He struggled back to the vehicle and ploughed his way through the barrier, managing another 250 yards before slumping over the wheel and rolling the kombi into a roadside ditch. The attackers arrived in pursuit, smashing the windscreen and pouring petrol into the breach. Repeated attempts to set the vehicle on fire were thwarted by Elizabeth Oberholtzer, desperately blowing out the incoming matches as she lay wedged under the frame of her burly husband.[12] Suddenly the lights of another car appeared and the attackers fled, leaving mother and daughter relatively unscathed. The less fortunate Andrea Oberholtzer, however, was pronounced dead at the scene.

The following morning police found two notes left by the attackers scribbled in red ink on green notepaper – photostats of which are preserved in the CID file in the Zimbabwean archives.[13] One reads:

> 'Clocodiel group on action. We shall kill all whites if they don't want to give back our country. Confrontation'.

The other similarly states:

> 'Confrintation Smith Bossop Crocodiel Group will soon kill all Whites. R. I. Hokoyo'.

'Bossop' was a corruption of the Afrikaans term 'passop', meaning 'watch out' or 'beware', but nothing in the file reveals the meaning of 'R. I. Hokoyo'.[14] The reference to Smith, however, is clear enough: Ian Smith, who only twelve weeks earlier had deposed Winston Field as prime minister of Southern Rhodesia, was on a collision course with a new militant strain of African resistance.

The notes leave no doubt that Oberholtzer's death was more than a case of random thuggery. However poorly planned and haphazardly executed, the attack was a deliberate act of political violence, arguably the first of its kind in what would become the brutal Rhodesian bush war of the 1960s and 1970s.[15] The four attackers were all members of ZANU, which had been formed the previous year by the Rev Ndabaningi Sithole as a breakaway movement from Joshua Nkomo's Zimbabwe African People's Union (ZAPU). Sithole, together with Robert Mugabe, Herbert Chitepo and other emergent dissidents, had grown frustrated at ZAPU's non-violent platform, electing to adopt a new policy of all-out 'Confrontation' at their inaugural May 1964 party conference. Sithole personally conducted a reconnaissance of the Melsetter region in early June to identify potential targets and establish a local support network.[16]

Figure 9.1 The Reverend Ndabaningi Sithole announces the creation of the Zimbabwe African National Union (ZANU) at a press conference in Salisbury in Southern Rhodesia (later the Zimbabwean capital, Harare), 12 August 1963. Source: Hulton Archive/Getty Images.

The men recruited to inaugurate the new policy were young party members originally from Rhodesia but resident in newly independent Zambia where they received political guidance and rudimentary training. Their leader was William Ndangana, deputy secretary of ZANU's Youth League, assisted by Dhlamini, Mlambo, and another young dissident named Master Tresha. A fifth member, Amos Kademaunga, accompanied the group to Rhodesia but absconded before the Oberholtzer attack (later giving extensive testimony to the police that would greatly assist the capture and conviction of Dhlamini and Mlambo).[17] The group was hastily assembled in Zambia only days before their exploits; they had no access to firearms and were expected to carry out their task with whatever implements they could muster. On 24 June 1964 they were smuggled from Zambia to Sithole's home in Salisbury, and five days later relocated to Umtali to purchase supplies and four knives. They then proceeded south to the Melsetter district, chosen because the dense scrub and mountainous terrain provided ample scope to move undetected, and established a hidden base for their activities in the bush near Nyanyadzi (described as an abandoned 'Hyena's lair' in the police report).[18] It was here that they adopted the codename 'Crocodile Confrontation Group', the menacing overtones barely disguising the ad hoc amateurism of the whole enterprise. Among the reading matter allegedly found in their suitcases was a copy of Enid Blyton's 1943 children's classic *Five Go Adventuring Again*.[19]

By the time of their arrival, Sithole had been arrested on charges of sedition and was standing trial in Umtali, yet such was his extensive local network that he was able to issue instructions during adjournments in the hearing.[20] The group's mission was to launch a petrol bomb attack on the police station at Nyanyadzi and then to set up roadblocks in various parts of the district for the purpose of killing an undisclosed number of ordinary whites.[21] The entire plan, the support network and the resources at their disposal were deficient in almost every respect (Ndangana had to use his own underpants to fashion wicks for the petrol bombs) and the group's achievements ultimately fell well short of their aims.[22] The assault on the police station was thwarted by the vigilance of on-duty officers while an attempt the following night to blockade the Chikwizi Bridge ten kilometres to the south was also aborted when the group mistakenly attacked a carload of Africans (none of whom were harmed). But it was here the attackers left the first of their distinctive notes, proclaiming: 'A clever white man shall go before he looses [sic] his life. Clocodiel Group wants all whets [sic] to go back to their own homes in UK, SA and USA, Bassop, Confrintation [sic] ... a white man is divel [sic].'[23]

The 4 July attack on Andrea Oberholtzer was thus the group's first and only successful action, after which they parted company in pairs. Ndangana and Master Tresha managed to find their way back to Salisbury and then onward to safety in Zambia, where their local ZANU colleagues in Kitwe held a party to toast their triumph.[24] Mlambo and Dhlamini fled in the opposite direction towards Mozambique, assisted by Watch Mlambo, Victor's uncle and headman of a village located a few miles across the border. Dhlamini carried a debilitating knee injury from childhood which greatly hindered their progress, but they managed to reach the relative safety of Portuguese jurisdiction by 15 July.

From here they might have vanished completely into obscurity, but for a tip-off by a local informant that reached Chipinga police station on 20 July. At 8 pm that evening, Constable Paul Naish, having just returned from a three-day patrol in search of the fugitives, was promptly ordered back into the border region together with two African officers, Tapera and Alexius. Armed with a .303 rifle, a revolver and a twelve-bore shotgun, but without the benefit of torchlight (having flattened the batteries over the previous two nights), they left their vehicle at the border and set off into the night on foot, guided through the mountainous terrain by their informant. The Portuguese border post raised no objections to their entry, but the stormy weather conditions made the going exceedingly difficult. After a three-hour hike through dense forest, lashing rain and a belting wind, they came upon an isolated hut in a clearing dimly lit by firelight. At 2 am the officers stormed in to find three figures huddled under a rug on the earthen floor. They were promptly 'kicked into life' – dazed, exhausted and completely petrified. As Naish recalls, 'I put two holes through the wall with the .303, an act of warning that escape was not an option. One of them had looked furtively at the open door, so that put an end to that.' The fugitives flatly denied their identities, but their blood-spattered clothing and Dhlamini's pronounced limp were impossible to conceal. The officers handcuffed the three men together – Dhlamini, Mlambo and a third who had come to warn them of the approaching officers – and marched them through the quagmire that threaded back down the mountain into Rhodesia. The captives frequently lost their footing along the way, dragging each other repeatedly into the mud, but at no stage did they make any show of resistance or flight, as though resigned to their fate.[25] For Dhlamini and Mlambo, it would be their last trek through open country. Arriving at Chipinga at sunrise, the exhausted pair, 'wet and bedraggled' were clapped in leg-irons and formally placed in custody, never to be released.[26] Over the next few days they each signed statements clearly implicating themselves in the Oberholtzer attack.[27]

At their trial in December they retracted these confessions, claiming that they had been made under duress. 'What I said I said because I was afraid', pleaded James to the trial judge, while Victor was more explicit, claiming he had been 'frightened and tortured' into confessing his guilt.[28] Both alleged that the dried blood on their clothing was not Oberholtzer's but their own, courtesy of a beating administered by the arresting officers.[29] They now pleaded that they were unwitting accessories to Ndangana's wholly spontaneous crime. 'I did not wish to reach the point of murder', Mlambo insisted, 'The point which I wanted was only roadblocking. Murder was done by someone, not myself.' Dhlamini mounted a similar defence: 'I want to say I did not kill him', he said. 'The only thing I did to help was to put the stones, and I threw stones. That is all I did.'[30] The trial judge dismissed outright the suggestion they had been assaulted by police and was equally disdainful of the claim that they had been arrested outside of the jurisdiction of Rhodesian law enforcement. On the strength of Mrs Oberholtzer's testimony, both defendants were convicted of 'attempting to set fire to a person with inflammable liquid', a capital offence under Rhodesia's state of emergency provisions.[31] It was for this, alone, that they were sentenced to hang. An 'alternative charge' for murder was never put to trial as the death penalty had already been handed down for the easier conviction; nevertheless, the two would henceforth be invariably described as 'brutal and savage murderers'.[32] For the next three years they languished on death row together with scores of other offenders and quickly disappeared from public view. By the time of their trial both ZANU and ZAPU had been declared illegal organizations and their leaders – Sithole, Mugabe, Nkomo – had all begun long jail sentences.

Given the significance their case would later assume, it is extraordinary how little is known of James Dhlamini and Victor Mlambo.[33] Even their coconspirators – interviewed years later – could provide little in the way of personal detail, having only met them for the first time on the eve of the operation.[34] Nor were the Rhodesian police particularly concerned with mapping their past, their family upbringing and influences, or their pathway to radicalization. The CID file contains a photo of Victor in happier times, smartly attired in a white shirt, bowtie and sunglasses, stating (incorrectly) that he was aged between 19 and 20 years, standing five and a half feet tall with a medium build and a mark on his left shin.[35] He hailed from the Melsetter district but had grown up in Marandellas, leaving school at the age of sixteen to work on his father's African purchase farm before moving

Figure 9.2 The only known image of James Dhlamini (left) and Victor Mlambo shortly after their capture by Rhodesian police, July 1964.

to Northern Rhodesia in 1959. For James Dhlamini there is neither mug shot nor physical description, nor any clue as to his personality, motives or political convictions; only a mention that he was employed at the 'Luxury Tea Room' in Kitwe, Zambia. Indeed, there was some dispute at the trial over whether he had reached eighteen years of age (the threshold for the death penalty) but as the court was unable to locate his parents it was left to the judge to determine his age at nineteen.[36] The only known photograph of the defendants (Figure 9.2), taken shortly after their capture, is a study of nervous trepidation – Dhlamini's hands clasped grimly to his face, Mlambo's furrowed brow fixed despondently on the camera.

One slim shard of personal testimony survives in the CID file, indeed the only item flowing directly from the fugitives' own hand. While on the run, Dhlamini had penned a few hurried notes intended for ZANU comrades in Zambia which he subsequently tore up and discarded. The scraps were later pieced together by police from their abandoned campsite, furnishing a different perspective on the depraved killers routinely depicted in the press. 'Dear Brother', begins the first missive, 'I am on a very critical position, police is looking for us in a bad way. If you heard of white man who died at Umtali no answer here.' In the second he elaborates: 'We did the job though we facing a dangerous corner. But we shall try to escap [*sic*] if we will be found you will not see me.' He urged his friends to 'greet every ZANU man' and concluded both notes with 'ZANU here is 99½ per cent'.[37] Whatever was intended by this cryptic formula, it seems clear that the writer was committed to his political cause and unrepentant about the consequences of 'confrontation'. Equally, his words disclose a very human predicament, a fragmentary window into their desperate plight.

OUTLAWS: THE LANGUAGE OF LEGITIMACY

Historians of Britain's imperial endgame in Africa have emphasized the symbolic capital of politically motivated killing, whether officially sanctioned executions of convicted African insurgents or the premeditated attacks of dissident groups on unsuspecting white settlers.[38] The Oberholtzer murder carries the distinction of igniting passions on both sides – the initial wave of white revulsion at the random cruelty of the crime later matched, indeed surpassed, by worldwide liberal outrage at the punishment meted out to the perpetrators. Oberholtzer was the first white Southern Rhodesian to be killed by knife-wielding subversives, just as Dhlamini and Mlambo were the first executions in the wake of UDI, thereby amplifying community reactions across all shades of opinion. Comparisons can be drawn with the death of white mother-of-two Lilian Burton at the hands of anti-colonial dissidents in the Northern Rhodesian settlement of Ndola in May 1960, which elicited a sustained chorus of settler demands for the heavy-handed enforcement of 'law and order' and the removal of the 'albatross' of Colonial Office control. Likewise, the dubious conviction and execution of three of her suspected killers in 1961 galvanized African nationalists in their demand for an independent Zambia. Walima T. Kalusa notes how Burton's death not only aggravated the polarization between Africans and Europeans but also 'deepened political fissures within each of these nationalisms, pitting conservative white settlers against white liberals and moderate black nationalists against black radicals'.[39] Much the same could be said of the afterlife of the Oberholtzer murder, where the vocal response was not simply a reflection of embedded community attitudes, but a heightened state of awareness that sharpened existing divisions and produced new ones. Both murders bear out the maxim that 'the dead enliven the politics of the living'.[40]

What was at stake in the killing of Oberholtzer and the subsequent executions was not only the imperative of law and order, but also the mantle of lawfulness itself, which became central to the question of Rhodesian political legitimacy in the years ahead. One white man's grisly fate (and the telling and retelling of its macabre details) not only focused the white community's attention on the issue of public safety, but also became a platform for demonstrating where the law properly resided. Although the *Umtali Post* described the attack as 'the first European fatality in Southern Rhodesia's road terrorism', the initial tendency was to downplay the attackers' dissident motives.[41] Dhlamini and Mlambo were depicted as common criminals rather than political insurgents (let alone combatants in an armed conflict) and the entire case was treated as a purely police matter with virtually no direct involvement of the Rhodesian security forces.[42] Although they styled themselves the 'Crocodile Group', this was often rendered as 'gang' in police, press and trial reports, with its more overt connotations of banditry.

Yet within days of the incident, the Rhodesian Army produced a paper entitled 'A Flexible Response to the Terrorist Threat', implying something far more subversive in the offing.[43] Similarly, when the Rhodesian Front outlawed ZANU and declared a state of emergency in the Highlands district of Salisbury in August 1964, the Melsetter murder was highlighted as part of the wider context for the government crackdown.[44] Thus the case sat awkwardly between criminal and seditious intent, portraying Rhodesia as an orderly country with an efficient law enforcement system, while justifying extreme measures to counter the threat of African militancy. It was significant that the Rhodesian Front minister charged with the task of repressing political dissent, Desmond Lardner-Burke, bore the title of 'Minister for Law and Order' (rather than 'Attorney General' or 'Justice Minister' more common to British usage). He drew on an obscure Thomas Jefferson quote to advance his core moral conviction: that 'the law of necessity, of self-preservation, of saving our country are a higher obligation' than the strict observance of the written law. Indeed, he insisted that 'when there is any chaos it is impossible to apply the rule of law'.[45]

It remains one of the many ironies of the Rhodesian crisis that this obsession with combatting lawlessness would culminate in a singular act of audacious illegality on 11 November 1965. The Smith government's UDI had long been anticipated after months and indeed years of failed talks with successive British governments who refused to yield on the principle of 'unimpeded progress towards majority rule'. Yet it still came as a shock to many when the moment finally arrived. The Rhodesian Front's liberal opponents immediately reached for the normative language of British justice, causing a momentary uproar in the Rhodesian parliament on 25 November when Independent MP Dr Ahrn Palley called on the speaker to suspend the illegal gathering. He was unceremoniously ejected by the sergeant at arms amid muffled cries of 'I will not obey any order which to me is illegal ... I accept no ruling from this House ... I leave this House ... Long Live the Queen!'[46] The Churches were virtually unanimous in denouncing the government's actions, though generally relying on moral rather than legal imperatives. 'I believe what has been done is wrong', was the simple verdict of the Anglican bishop of Mashonaland, Cecil Anderson, before cautiously adding: 'I do not impose my beliefs on you.'[47] Already the lines were blurring between the inchoate realm of 'belief' and the certitude of the law.

In Britain, the House of Commons was unanimous in condemning the Rhodesian Front's 'unlawful' actions, while Labour prime minister Harold Wilson catalogued the list of economic sanctions to be imposed to rein in these 'lawbreaking men'.[48] In a televised speech later that evening, he explained that the Rhodesian Cabinet had placed themselves 'beyond the pale of world society' and pledged to bring the people of Rhodesia 'back to their true allegiance, back to the rule of law, back to their true destiny in the family of nations'.[49] Earlier in the day, in one of his more futile gestures, Wilson asserted full jurisdiction over Rhodesia, exercising authority through special Orders of Council to be implemented by the Rhodesian governor, Sir Humphrey Gibbs. An English-born, Eton-educated Rhodesian farmer with a dedication to his post and a quiet resolve, Gibbs would remain holed up for several years in the stately surrounds of Salisbury's Government House with his phone lines cut and his chauffeur-driven Rolls Royce confiscated. Instructed by Wilson to dismiss the entire Rhodesian Cabinet from office, the effect of his first intervention in the Rhodesian crisis proved entirely negligible.[50] But he was rewarded for his effort a week later with the conferral of a Knight Commander of the Royal Victorian Order (KCVO).

Crucially, neither Wilson nor Gibbs had the means to impose their will. Already a month earlier, the prime minister had ruled out the use of the British armed forces in the event of a white rebellion, ostensibly on the basis of military advice that an invasion was logistically unfeasible but more probably to avoid the damaging political fallout from instructing 'United Kingdom soldiers to go to Rhodesia and kill Britishers'.[51] With his options thus curtailed, Wilson implored Governor Gibbs to remain in harness but notably refrained from asking him to arrest the Smith ministry. Rhodesian service chiefs could not guarantee the obedience of their senior officers in the event of a conflict of loyalties, and the fact that the police commissioner, F. E. 'Slash' Barfoot, was solidly pro-Smith rendered pointless any attempt to round up the rebels.[52] Gibbs's own press statement underlined his impotence, calling on his fellow Rhodesians to 'refrain from all acts which would further the objectives of the illegal authorities' but qualifying this by affirming 'the duty of all citizens to maintain law and order . . . and to carry on with their normal tasks'.[53] How the citizenry were supposed to uphold the law under an illegal regime was left to their own imagination. Wilson issued similarly confused instructions to Rhodesian civil servants not to leave their posts, but to avoid assisting the rebel government in any way.[54] Although there were a few resignations of senior civil servants, most Rhodesians returned to their jobs and to business as usual. It was an uncanny prelude to the situation that would arise in Northern Ireland only four years later where, by Wilson's own admission, he found himself 'exercising responsibility without power'.[55]

Meanwhile in London, Rhodesia House on the Strand was allowed to continue operating as a quasi-diplomatic mission, ostensibly due to the legal difficulties in effecting a seizure of the building. The UK attorney general, Sir Elwyn Jones, advised that since 'our case against Smith and his associates is based on legality' care should be taken to avoid any hint of unlawful acquisition on the part of Her Majesty's government.[56] Thus a scaled down consular staff was allowed to remain, while the Rhodesian high commissioner, Brigadier Andrew Skeen, was politely ejected from the country 'as though he were an envoy of a sovereign state possessing diplomatic immunity, rather than the treacherously criminal agent of a rebellious regime'.[57] Arriving in the opposite direction, Rhodesia's entrant in the Miss World pageant to be held in London that month was officially cleared to compete after a hastily convened meeting of the judges. 'Miss Rhodesia', twenty-two-year-old 'honey blonde' Lesley Bunting (measuring in at 37–25–37 according to drooling press reports) informed an eagerly awaiting scrum of male reporters: 'I am an Ian Smith girl all the way, but I hope nothing like politics will be mixed up in a thing like a beauty contest.'[58] In these and other less blatant ways, a degree of normality was conferred on the rebellious state which would help win waverers over to Smith's side.

By far the most intractable dilemma was that confronting the Rhodesian judiciary, virtually all of whom were educated in Britain and sworn to uphold the principles of British justice. More to the point, the hallowed convention of judicial independence meant that Rhodesian judges were formally appointed by the governor and drew their authority and legitimacy directly from the Crown. In the weeks leading up to UDI, senior members of the Rhodesian High Court had urged Chief Justice Sir Hugh Beadle to issue a warning that a unilateral break with Britain would be an illegal act. Beadle demurred, however, ostensibly on the grounds of keeping the judiciary out of politics but also harbouring divided loyalties of his own.[59] It was therefore an open question how individual judges would respond to the new remit after 11 November. The result was the most brittle of compromises whereby the judges agreed to continue to perform their duties in the interests of averting social chaos, without acknowledging the legitimacy of UDI.[60] They were encouraged in this by the UK attorney-general who, while describing Smith's actions in the Commons as 'treasonable', went on to add: 'nothing I have said ... affects the complete independence of the judiciary of Rhodesia or the duty of all lawyers in Rhodesia to play their part in upholding the rule of law'.[61]

By this tortuous logic, Smith's rebel Cabinet was recognized as the de facto but in no sense *de jure* government of the country, a hopelessly ambiguous formula for judicial certainty. To compound matters, the judges vowed to dispense justice according to the 1961 Constitution (which had been approved by Westminster with Royal assent) rather than the new UDI constitution which formed the basis of the Rhodesian executive's governing writ. As a show of solidarity with his sovereign, Chief Justice Beadle moved into Government House with Gibbs, serving as his main constitutional advisor and dining companion for the next several years. Extraordinarily, Smith's Rhodesian Front went along with this arrangement, allowing Gibbs to remain in Government House (understaffed and at his own expense, with his police guard withdrawn from the gates) in the hope that he might prove useful in reaching a future settlement with the British Government.[62]

What the Rhodesian Front lacked in legal legitimacy, it made up for in the sheer strength of popular feeling among embittered whites – drawing on long-standing resentment directed at the perceived duplicity of successive British governments. The whole tenor of Rhodesian defiance was built on the conviction that it was they who preserved the best of Britishness in the face of a United Kingdom Government that had repeatedly sold out its own people. The collapse of the Federation of Rhodesia and Nyasaland in 1963 loomed large on the list of grievances, not least the Macmillan government's capitulation to African demands for the secession of Nyasaland and Northern Rhodesia. Rubbing salt into the wound was the same government's refusal to confer similar rights of independence on white-dominated Southern Rhodesia until such time as constitutional guarantees of progress to majority rule could be agreed upon. Despite repeated attempts to appeal over the government's head to the kinship and common sense of the British people, the Rhodesian political elite were shocked to find themselves isolated and marginalized in the wake of the federation debacle – yet unshaken in their belief that ordinary British folk were fundamentally on their side.[63]

These sentiments came prominently to the fore in the wording of the Unilateral Declaration of Independence in November 1965: the Rhodesian people, having 'demonstrated their Loyalty to the Crown and their kith and kin', and witnessing 'all that they have cherished about to be shattered on the rocks of expediency' could no longer acquiesce in Britain 'persisting in maintaining an unwarrantable jurisdiction over Rhodesia'. This in no way derogated from the special bond of kinship with the British people – on the contrary these were 'the people with whom we have the closest affinity, both in our way of life and in our conception of justice and civilisation'.[64] The Rhodesian Front saw itself as a reservoir of British grit and resolve that had long since been squandered at home, with Smith frequently comparing his lot to that of his wartime hero, Winston Churchill. Indeed, if Churchill had still been alive, ventured Smith (only nine months after his hero's epic funeral in London), he would have emigrated to Rhodesia because 'all those admirable qualities and characteristics of the British that we believed in, loved and preached to our children, no longer exist in Britain'.[65] This accounts for his otherwise incongruous decision that 'whatever else other countries may have done or may yet do, it is our intention that the Union Jack will continue to fly over Rhodesia and the National Anthem continue to be sung'.[66] In this conception, Rhodesia was Byzantium to Britain's Rome.

Byzantine also readily describes rebel Rhodesia's emotionally fraught attachment to the British monarchy. The symbol of Her Majesty the Queen became a crucial element in squaring the overt lawlessness of UDI with some semblance of popular legitimacy. The Rhodesian Declaration of Independence concluded with the words 'God Save the Queen' (evidently without irony) and images were widely circulated of the Cabinet signing the document before a portrait of the young Elizabeth II in full regalia. Smith even had the audacity to write to Buckingham Palace requesting that the newly appointed head of state, the diminutive Rhodesian Front power broker Clifford Dupont, should be afforded the viceregal title of 'governor-general'. Her Majesty predictably declined and Dupont had to settle for the decidedly un-regal 'Officer Administering the Government', evoking the no-man's-land the Rhodesians had sallied into – too loyal to embrace republican conventions, but well beyond the bounds of the royal blessing.[67] In his first official appearance in his new capacity – an address to the annual dinner of the Central African Deep Sea Angling Society – Dupont stared straight into the void. 'I do not think my stories are suitable', he confessed to his audience of land-locked fishermen, 'because I am told that from now on I have to be dignified, and I am not allowed to be political so, what is there to talk about?' The man who only three years earlier had defiantly pronounced: 'We can and will halt the wind of change', was forced to concede: 'I could not think of anything appropriate to say.'[68]

The anomaly of the co-existence of two rival viceroys in Salisbury's sedate, country town setting was bound to tear at the fabric of Rhodesian loyalties. Wary that the rebel regime might seize possession of Government House, Gibbs was effectively a prisoner within its gates for nearly four years, only venturing out on Friday evenings for a game of snooker at the Salisbury Club. Dupont had managed to commandeer Gibbs's official Rolls Royce in which he was regularly seen riding around town but had to content himself with 'Governor's Lodge' as his official residence – the more modest home of the former governor of Southern Rhodesia, barely a mile from Gibbs's stately manor. Himself a keen snooker player, Dupont gave the Salisbury Club a wide berth on Friday evenings so as to avoid crossing paths with his alter ego.[69] This stand-off would continue for several years, reaching the peak of absurdity at the annual duel for the hearts and minds of white Rhodesians on the occasion of the official queen's birthday.

The second Saturday in June had long been marked by a public holiday in honour of the sovereign, but divisions emerged over precisely where and how the queen's subjects should register their fealty in an era of open defiance of the British government. Gibbs quickly saw the opportunity to put Government House to good use, throwing open the gates to the public to sign the visitor's book and take tea on the lawn. Not to be outdone, Dupont hosted a similar event at his own residence the same day, mingling among the faithful over tea and biscuits. The Union Jack fluttered proudly over both gatherings and the two hosts naturally sought to make political capital out of the crowds thronging to their respective gardens. As Dupont recalled:

> In spite of the widespread distrust of the British Government, the whole country had remained completely loyal to the person of Her Majesty the Queen ... Nearly a thousand invitations were issued and well over seven hundred people attended. By 11.30, when the reception started, guests were still queuing down the entire length of the drive and for about two hundred metres along the road outside the grounds.[70]

Both sides had a vested interest in massaging the figures, but Gibbs seems to have had a clear crowd advantage, judging from the official censorship of the *Rhodesian Herald*'s reportage for 1966. The diary of Gibbs's comptroller,

John Pestell, underlines the political messages that were implicit in attendance at one or the other event:

> A beautiful sunny day, and some 2100 people signed the book and there were letters with 600 signatures ... there is no doubt that it gives terrific encouragement to T[heir] E[xellencie]s to continue in their most difficult role. There is some political significance in this of course, as only people who are loyal to Her Majesty and want a settlement would sign the book.[71]

The architects of UDI may have modelled themselves on the American revolutionaries, but even they could not have envisaged such a distorted echo of duelling tea parties – bearing out the Marxist dictum that history repeats itself 'first as tragedy, second as farce'. Whereas Dupont imagined that his handsome turnout reflected 'widespread distrust of the British Government', the Gibbs gathering was seen as a symbol of popular desire for a settlement with Harold Wilson. Some individuals managed to contrive a visit to *both* events (the distance could be scampered on foot in fifteen minutes) much to the chagrin of the governor who kept close tabs on 'waverers'.[72] For both sides, the person of the queen remained indispensable to upholding their purported stand for justice in the face of lawlessness.

IN-LAWS: THE MOBILIZATION OF EMPATHY

If white Rhodesians had an 'almost infinite capacity for self-deception' about the righteousness of their cause, their confidence was crucially buoyed by a continuous stream of global white reaction that could be relied on to buttress their claims.[73] Although Smith is often depicted as an insular figure, indifferent to 'world opinion', he was acutely attuned to the moral and political leverage afforded by substantial reservoirs of greater British sympathy. Indeed, one of his key arguments for seizing independence in 1965 was the need to act while 'massive support' could still be counted on abroad, particularly in the UK.[74] These well-wishers might not have occupied crucial positions in the ruling establishment (indeed they often spoke from relatively marginalized positions) but this only enhanced the conviction that white Rhodesians represented a silent moral majority – fellow Britons abandoned to their unhappy fate.

The South African province of Natal was by far the most reliable source of support, on account of the obvious echoes of their own earlier struggle to remain within the British fold in the face of Afrikaner domination.[75] Smith's in-laws were a respectable English-speaking Natalian family, and his wife Janet's highly publicized visits to her sister's home in Durban painted a reassuring portrait of deeper family affinities that transcended Rhodesia's quarrel with Britain. The *Natal Witness* was a particularly staunch ally, frequently drawing parallels with the lot of white English-speaking South Africans. It was a case of should white Rhodesia fail, 'what then can lay in store for us?'[76] Thus, the northern neighbour could be extolled as a reliable British redoubt in the heart of Africa, a feeling by no means confined to older, conservative segments of the community. In the early days of UDI, student activists in Durban were seen climbing a tower at the University of Natal and unfolding a banner that simply read, 'Rhodesia'.[77]

Elsewhere, support was more measured, couched in terms of a more generalized empathy for the plight of the Rhodesian people rather than an explicit endorsement of UDI. For Australia's Robert Menzies, Rhodesia would be his last international crisis before retiring as prime minister in January 1966, and one which posed 'a horrible problem, in which my sympathy and my realism find themselves in conflict'.[78] In a marathon weekend Cabinet meeting in November 1965, the Australian Government reluctantly came around to supporting Wilson on economic sanctions, but there was clearly no appetite for condemnatory rhetoric. Military action of any sort was deemed 'repugnant', while concerns were raised that economic sanctions might provoke a public backlash.[79] The prevailing view around the cabinet table was that Australia had been 'swimming with the tide' on the winds of change for too long at the expense of their 'white brethren' in Africa.[80] Menzies demonstrably refused to take part in the Commonwealth Prime Ministers' Meeting hastily convened in Lagos in January 1966 to address the Rhodesian crisis – a move that was widely (and rightly) regarded as a show of tacit sympathy for Smith and a remarkable (for Menzies) vote of no confidence in the legitimacy of the Commonwealth.[81] In the weeks and months ahead, the Australian Government's sole decision on Rhodesia was to allow the forthcoming cricket tour of southern Africa to go ahead as planned. Thus on 7 November 1966 (just days before Rhodesia celebrated its first year of independence) Australian test skipper Bobby Simpson steered his side to an eight wicket victory in Salisbury over a team representing an outlawed rebel regime.[82]

Menzies' governing coalition partner, the Australian Country Party, was even more torn by the Rhodesian crisis. With an overwhelmingly rural constituency, the party rank and file were at a loss to understand the government's imposition of sanctions on Rhodesian farmers and lobbied heavily to have them lifted. The New South Wales Annual Party Conference passed a resolution deploring the government's 'despicable and cowardly' action in supporting Harold Wilson's 'infamous betrayal of British sovereignty'. Queensland Party trustees were particularly outspoken, calling on Federal Party Leader and Deputy Prime Minister Jack McEwen to 'refrain from humiliat[ing] our kith and kin', before promptly passing a resolution of their own that left no room for the imagination: 'That this Council deplores the present persecution of Rhodesia by the Socialist Government of Britain, and asks the Federal Government to abandon sanctions imposed against our British cousins.'[83] McEwen responded with a disarmingly frank press statement which did little to mollify the membership:

> The very circumstances of our own origin inevitably engender sympathy for the settlers of British blood in Rhodesia. At the same time our own belief in democracy and our constant professions of this belief make it inevitable that we should be conscious of the need that the African population should be assured of progressive development ... To act on the argument which many here have used would amount to taking the side of the white man against the black. However deep our personal sympathies may be for Rhodesian settlers, this course would be one of deadly national danger for Australia.[84]

It was an open tug-of-war between the heart and the head, between the persistent call of racial sentiment and the principles of parliamentary democracy that were no less constitutive of Greater Britonism – harking back to the original 'imperfections' of Dilke and Seeley. When the two collided – as they so often did in these years – the result was an unedifying fragmentation.

Australian press coverage followed suit, with the respectable dailies virtually unanimous in opposing UDI as a constitutional abhorrence. But the emphasis was placed squarely on the foolhardiness of Smith's venture, its 'stupidity', 'intransigence', 'maladroit' and 'short-sighted' nature, rather than any inherently malign or obnoxious intent.[85] Far more trenchant language was reserved for the African leaders demanding military intervention, variously labelled 'malicious', 'lunatic', 'militant' and 'clamouring firebrands' whose 'tumult and shouting' came at the expense of urgently needed 'reason', 'restraint' and 'calm'.[86] The *Melbourne Herald* freely indulged the inclination to side with fellow whites in a lead-article timorously titled, 'They must feel that they have a lot worth saving'. The facing column – by 'women's page' editor Isabel Carter, just returned from Salisbury – depicted a 'bustling', 'peaceful' city of modern amenities, tranquil streets, 'fine shops', contented Africans, all 'bathed in a purple glow of Jacaranda blossom'.[87]

Even more explicit comfort and support emanated from New Zealand, where the *Auckland Star* neatly summarized the position: 'For a British country like New Zealand, the Rhodesian crisis poses painful problems.'[88] Senior government ministers aired their Rhodesian sympathies in no uncertain terms, such as Labour minister Tom Shand who was in no doubt that 'if military force was used in Rhodesia the majority of New Zealanders would want to support their own flesh and blood'.[89] Meanwhile, letters to the National Party government of Keith Holyoake reportedly streamed in at a rate of ten to one in support of Smith. Among the reasons given were: 'Great Anglo-Saxon peoples of the world should support each other' and 'our duty first and foremost is to our kith and kin in Rhodesia'.[90] The Wellington *Sunday Times* chimed in with a piece indignantly titled 'Come off it!':

> History will record few instances of such gutless bullying as the spectacle of tiny Rhodesia, with its 217,000 whites, being belted by the nations of almost the entire world because its legally-elected government wants to run its own affairs. The tide of sympathy is beginning to run the other way as more and more people like the New Zealanders, with their feelings for the underdog, say: 'Aw, come off it! Be your age! Give Smith a fair go!'[91]

The few newspapers that came out unambiguously against Smith, such as the *Otago Daily Times* and the *Christchurch Star*, conceded that the UDI crisis had given 'New Zealand a rare glimpse of itself as a country riddled with prejudice and bedevilled by insularity.'[92] Smith himself sought to consolidate the resolve of his Kiwi kinsfolk by publishing a 'personal telegram' in the *New Zealand Truth*:

> We both believe in the British way of life . . . [which] means a hundred-and-one things that are good and decent and bear no relation to the cheap sneers about 'Colonial exploiters' and so on . . . wherever we came together, we found that we were pretty much the same kind of people. It could hardly be otherwise for not only were we of the same blood – we came from pretty much the same kind of countries . . . it is our belief that if Rhodesia had been peopled by New Zealanders, you would have adhered to precisely the same solution as we have.[93]

By far the most crucial lifeline of support was to be found in the United Kingdom where, for all the official condemnation of the 'unlawful' regime, informal channels of sympathy were to be found in abundance. For years, UK officials in Salisbury had voiced concern about the way white Rhodesians 'delude themselves that British public opinion is fundamentally on their side: *if it could only find expression*.[94] This was part-fantasy, but it also drew on a reservoir of genuine sympathy that lingered at the political margins.

Among those prepared to broach the matter openly, Lord Salisbury was the undisputed champion, making a series of widely publicized statements in the House of Lords which left no doubt about where Britain's sympathies ought properly to lie. The one-time Tory powerbroker and former dominions secretary under Churchill roundly condemned sanctions as a 'supine repudiation ... of the British way of life in Central Africa', returning repeatedly to the theme of Britain's betrayal of 'ordinary decent British men and women, people very like ourselves'.[95] His sentiments were echoed in the Commons by a coterie of 'Monday Club' members, often defying the whip to give voice to a troubled white conscience. Edward Heath thus had to tread a fine line as Conservative Opposition Leader, reminding Wilson that Rhodesians were of British descent and that no such people 'whether they were acting legally or not would knuckle down to crude threats'.[96] Remembrance Day Sunday in 1965 became a potent outlet for these feelings, with the Anglo-Rhodesian Society (presided over by Salisbury himself) staging an unofficial afternoon ceremony at the Cenotaph following the traditional morning service. The empire-touting *Daily Express* contrasted the emotionally arid morning ceremony reserved for 'politicians, ambassadors, generals and civil servants' with the 'full-blooded cheers' for Rhodesian war veterans in the afternoon; a less well-drilled but by implication more genuine and spontaneous manifestation of Britain's better instincts.[97]

To be sure, the overwhelming bulk of British reportage, political commentary and official pronouncements made no attempt to conceal their contempt for the Rhodesian Front, often presenting a dim view of white Rhodesians more generally. The BBC's *Panorama* devoted its 22 March 1966 programme to a close-up on Rhodesia's white minority depicting them in wholly unflattering terms (resulting in Ian Smith imposing a blanket ban on BBC broadcasting in Rhodesia).[98] The press recycled long-standing settler stereotypes to vilify a country of spoilt, nouveau riche opportunists with good wages, low taxes, smart cars, swimming pools and an abundance of cheap African labour to service their every indulgence. Yet Smith's consistently bad press only reinforced the conviction among his metropolitan supporters that the true voice of white solidarity was being officially silenced.

As a consequence, many looked for alternative outlets to vent their feelings, writing emotionally pent-up letters to their local MP or relevant government ministers to record their indignation. Lord Salisbury's papers at Hatfield House contain a formidable horde of such correspondence from around the world, comprising a unique cachet of recrimination and regret directed not only at the dire predicament of Rhodesia but also spilling over into the scourge of socialist decadence in Britain itself – the fate of the two seemingly intertwined. Here the grievances multiplied, with letter-writers complaining variously that the vast majority of British people were being ignored; that Britain had become a callow, decaying shadow of its former self (with blame apportioned variously to immigration and the 'wind of change'); and that humble, ordinary Rhodesians were being thwarted in their gallant attempt to keep the British flame burning abroad.[99] What gave this form of protest particular poignancy was the conviction that 'hour by hour, thousands of others, friends and neighbours, were doing the same' – drawing succour from an imagined world of significant others. For those who felt marginalized by mainstream politics, here was an opportunity to give voice to what was 'otherwise unspeakable in public'.[100]

Many writers from Rhodesia took the additional step of renouncing their British identities. A Mrs H. M. Bailey from Bulawayo reflected on years of feeling homesick for 'the land of my birth – Britain', but not any more: 'All those thoughts are gone . . . You have no idea how sick with revulsion we EX-BRITISHERS feel.'[101] Across the border in South Africa, a former magistrate remonstrated: 'I am British, with British passport fought for Britain, have defended her round the world from hostile critics, and have voted for Tory. But I am finished with this gutter politics of all parties in decadent, dying Britain.'[102] It was a defiant act of misrecognition in reverse, rescinding the outward trappings of Britishness so that some inner moral fibre might be preserved. 'I was English . . . and I was very patriotic', wrote one veteran of the Royal Women's Navy Squadron: 'Now, to me, England is not England any more. She is dishonourable & dishonest. I firmly believe that we, here, are England now.'[103] In this, too, they were joined by metropolitan sympathizers, with writers from England wishing that their 'apologies for being English could reach the Rhodesian people'. Some even seemed prepared to relinquish their British identity 'and at the earliest opportunity ask Rhodesia if she will take me in under her nationality'.[104] Grace Boddington of Kent tapped the familiar theme of shared wartime exploits to convey the depth of feeling: 'It is a bitter thought that my own Government plans to do something that Hitler couldn't, and I worked in London during the Blitz. What have we come to that a Government minister even talks about sending Englishmen to kill Englishmen?'[105]

The letters to Lord Salisbury were overwhelmingly and effusively appreciative of his public stand, with precious few dissenters. Conversely, when Wilson's solicitor-general, Dingle Foot, resigned his post in August 1967 in protest against the government's failure to bring Smith to heel, his postbag swelled with a torrent of abuse. The letter-writing public were particularly incensed by his remark in a BBC radio interview that the time had come for Britain to aid Rhodesia's 'resistance fighters' since 'after all, they and we are on the same side'.[106] Mail from all parts of England voiced unalloyed 'contempt', 'disgust', 'nausea' and 'resentment', including a number of entreaties to the ex-minister to emigrate and join the cause he so treacherously espoused (one writer addressing him as 'Guerrilla Foot', another simply as 'Dirty Dingle'). One gentleman 'was left wondering if you possessed any of the attributes of a decent Englishman', while the more intemperate expressed an urge to administer various and elaborately devised punishments by way of retribution. A woman from Tunbridge Wells caught the gist of the collective indignation: 'Would you be so good as not to presume that the majority of the British people have the instincts of murderers such as you appear to possess . . . You may be the sort of person who is willing for his kinsfolk to be murdered. I can assure you that the majority of the electors in this country are appalled at such an idea.'[107] Attributing criminality to the Wilson government as the real wrong-doers was a deliberate counter-strategy, aligning the scales of justice with the moral imperatives of race.

The significance of Smith's support network lay not in its numerical strength or even its capacity to sway the Wilson government so much as its role in blurring the boundaries of British justice and moral rectitude. Just as the Rhodesian Front drew legitimacy from Britain's perceived duplicity, so too their supporters around the world sought solace in the comforts of kinship as a way around the legal technicalities, fostering deep scepticism about the supposed 'illegality' of the Rhodesian Government. One prominent Smith ally in the House of Lords, Lord Coleraine, reacted particularly strongly against the use of the term 'rebellion' to describe UDI: 'Rebellion is an ugly word and an ugly thing. I know of one thing uglier, and that was when a people surrendered under threat of force its conviction, its tradition and its heritage.'[108] In this way, talk of legality became a proxy for British racial and cultural patrimony. Fleet Street columnist Peregrine Worsthorne underlined the racial imperatives in play at the height of the 'Kenyan Asians' passport crisis of March 1968: 'They are no more British citizens than Ian Smith is a genuine British traitor.'[109]

The persistent querying of whether white Britons could truly, 'genuinely' be in the wrong only strengthened the resolve of the Rhodesian Front, offering welcome reassurance that 'British justice' would ultimately prevail.

Clifford Dupont was emboldened to declare that vindication was near to hand in a broadcast of 22 February 1966:

> There is tangible evidence of sympathy and support not only in South Africa but also in other countries such as America, New Zealand, Australia and France, where many people are now beginning to recognise the justice of the stand we have taken in Africa. In other words our struggle is at last being seen in its true perspective. This is growing and will grow until its final conclusion of world recognition of independent Rhodesia and world acceptance of its Government, not only as the 'de facto' but also as the 'de jure' political administration.[110]

Although historians generally refer to rebel Rhodesia as an inherently besieged polity, battered on all sides by sanctions, UN resolutions and worldwide condemnation, it bears emphasizing the ready supply of encouragement and kindred spirit from an extensive global ring of white sympathy; the fragmented but defiant residue of Greater Britain.

NAILING THE COLOURS: THE ROYAL REPRIEVE

On the morning of Wednesday 6 March 1968, a middle-aged African couple and their daughter stood at the white-walled entrance of Salisbury Central Prison, having spent the night in a car borrowed for the journey from their farm several hours away in Marandellas. At 8.40 am, the bulky blue wooden gates creaked open and a prison officer emerged into the morning glare to inform them: 'You will not see your boy again.' The family of Victor Mlambo had received less than a day's notice that their son, his accomplice James Dhlamini and a third condemned prisoner named Duly Shadreck (convicted of an unrelated offence) were due to be executed that morning. Throughout the night they had made repeated requests for one last opportunity to spend time with their condemned son and brother. At this final rebuff, Victor's forty-six-year-old mother Janet let out a cry of maternal anguish and collapsed to the ground.

Less than an hour later at 9.30 am, the waiting crowd of around sixty people, more than half of them journalists, stood back as a Rhodesian police superintendent stepped out to nail a typewritten notice on the gates. He appeared nervous, cursing the impenetrable hardwood as he fumbled with the hammer. 'This time Smithy's really done it', murmured an onlooker as heads strained to read the writing on the wall – official confirmation that the executions had been carried out. Victor's father, Nthaniso Mlambo, spoke grimly with reporters while his distraught wife and daughter comforted each other in the nearby shade. He explained that his son was a quiet boy who had never voiced any political beliefs or convictions, although he was aware that two years prior to his arrest he had become involved with a dissident group. 'I accept that my son killed the Boer farmer', he conceded, 'but I think he was misled into believing it was his duty to do so.'[111] No one arrived to mourn the death of James Dhlamini – nor did press reports seem to notice. By contrast, a fraying Union Jack hanging limply over the prison gates was duly recorded by virtually every correspondent at the scene.

The executions of Victor Mlambo and James Dhlamini had been in abeyance for more than three years, due to the uncharacteristic caution of the Rhodesian Front government in bringing forward cases that might challenge the legality of their governing writ. It was far from certain whether the judiciary would give legal force to the signature of the 'Officer Administering the Government' when normally the assent of the governor was required for execution warrants. It was one thing for Dupont to challenge Governor Gibbs over a tea party, but quite another to usurp his power over life and death. Two years into UDI, however, pressure had mounted among Smith's hardliners demanding an end to the ambiguity at a time of brewing armed insurgency. 'Law and Order' Minister Lardner-Burke therefore announced on 31 August 1967 that the convicted Oberholtzer killers would be the first on a list of more than eighty condemned prisoners to go to the gallows.[112]

News of the hangings sparked a worldwide backlash that was swift and unrelenting. The Organisation of African Unity (OAU) called for Smith's 'immediate arrest and handing over for trial', while students in Karachi marched through the streets with banners reading 'Hang Smith'. The UN Decolonization Committee deplored Britain's failure to prevent the killings and held a minute's silence in honour of 'the victims'. A similar gesture was observed in the Indian parliament in Delhi, where Prime Minister Indira Gandhi declared that the time had come to arm and equip Rhodesia's 'freedom fighters'. In Guyana flags flew at half-mast and Prime Minister Forbes Burnham paid tribute to Dhlamini and Mlambo as 'the martyrs and heroes of the Coloured world'. And in England, student representatives of ZAPU, the ANC and Mozambique's Frelimo led a torchlight procession through the streets of Oxford before laying wreaths at the local war memorial to 'those who have fallen in the liberation struggle'. More ominously, acting head of ZAPU, James Chikerema, told television viewers in Zambia that he was unable to say what his organization would do about the hangings 'but blood is going to be shed'.[113]

The House of Commons was the scene of a particularly impassioned debate, the tone set by Harold Wilson's widely publicized remark that 'some of the people' he had been dealing with in Salisbury were 'essentially evil'. Although the opposition fell in with the government in condemning the hangings, it was Labour members who provided the rhetorical fire. Member for Smethwick, Andrew Faulds, decried the hangings as 'judicial murder' and demanded that 'proper retribution be exacted ... not excluding the death penalty' for every individual involved – starting with the hangman all the way up to Dupont. His fellow backbencher, Anne Kerr, voiced incredulity that in a week when the House was voting on two billion pounds in military expenditure it was 'incapable of putting down a revolt in a colony, the white population of which is the size of Croydon's'. Meanwhile, the Conservative's Peter Hapstell drew rapturous acclaim in dredging up an old Boer War maxim from Winston Churchill: 'Grass grows quickly over the battlefield. Over the scaffold – never.' Liberal leader Jeremy Thorpe invoked the same imagery to excoriate Ian Smith as a leader who had 'chosen the gallows as the symbol of his self-assertion'.[114]

That same day, the Strand became the site of a drawn-out clash between police and around 300 student demonstrators waving placards imploring Wilson to 'Stop These Murders Now' and 'Jail Smith'. Like their counterparts in Salisbury's Cecil Square, they placed a wreath at the entrance to Rhodesia House mourning the death of 'The Rule of Law'. Among the demonstrators were twenty sitting MPs, most of them Labour but also including the recently elected Welsh nationalist MP Gwynfor Evans who had recently entered parliament to further the cause of freedom for an independent Wales.[115] Newspapers the following day drew attention to the cynical posting of the only West Indian constable serving in London at that time – PC Norwell Gumbs – to stand guard at the entrance of Rhodesia House. Scotland Yard issued an embarrassed disclaimer that his placement was 'just a coincidence', while PC Gumbs himself disavowed any interest in politics: 'It's just part of the job.'[116]

Clearly, for all the latent sympathy in Britain for rebel Rhodesia's cause there was a formidable counterweight that could rally spontaneously at a moment's notice. With the Salisbury hangings there was the compounding factor that Britain had only very recently abolished capital punishment – indeed within days of Smith's UDI declaration in 1965 – in a drawn out and heated political drama.[117] Rhodesia's stubborn persistence with the practice of executing its miscreants further distanced its inhabitants from the more liberal precepts of morality and justice prevailing in Britain. As one *Times* editorial lamented, 'Mr Smith could have reprieved the men had he wanted.

Figure 9.3 Police struggling with demonstrators protesting against the execution of James Dhlamini and Victor Mlambo outside Rhodesia House on the Strand, 3 March 1968. Source: Keystone Press/Alamy Stock Photo.

Instead he has had them done to death.' That Mlambo and Dhlamini's interminable wait on death row had not 'wrung a particle of mercy' from the Rhodesian Front bore witness to the callous hypocrisy of an organization 'who proclaim their Britishness' only when it suited them.[118]

But it was the legal reasoning of the Rhodesian High Court, and particularly that of its chief justice, Sir Hugh Beadle, that effectively dismembered Rhodesia from any residual legal or constitutional tie to the mother country. Rhodesian born and Oxford educated on a Rhodes scholarship, Beadle was morally and legally torn by the strain of UDI. Described by one correspondent as a 'small and gingery man with a bristling moustache', he was as much at home in bush-hat and shorts on the veldt hunting big game as he was enrobed on the bench. Contemporary accounts often contrasted his 'bantam-like' physical stature with the weighty moral task that had befallen him.[119] For more than two years he had resided at Government House with Governor Gibbs and had given every indication throughout of unswerving loyalty to his sovereign. But as UDI dragged into its third year, the anomaly of upholding the law in an illegal regime was beginning to reveal cracks in the judicial firmament more generally – and Gibbs's moral fibre in particular.

The case was decided in the Appellate Division of the Rhodesian High Court in a series of judgements between 29 February and 4 March 1968. The court had to make a ruling on three separate issues, and it would fall to Beadle to write the judgement in each instance. First was the matter of the validity of Dupont's signature on the execution warrant. Here the chief justice followed a decision from the previous month, which held that a de facto government needed to be able to carry out all the responsibilities that fell within the ambit of the 1961 Constitution, whatever its *de jure* credentials. If the Smith government were to be permitted to govern at all, then the officer administering the government must be able to perform all the acts that the governor had performed, including the administration of capital punishment. Thus, despite the enormity of the stakes, the execution warrants could be upheld as de facto law without necessarily bestowing legitimacy on the government.[120]

The second matter related to the defendants' application for a stay of execution while leave was sought to appeal to the Privy Council, a right fully enshrined in the 1961 Constitution but revoked under the unlawful UDI constitution of 1965. Law and Order Minister Lardner-Burke opened proceedings by taking the extraordinary step of filing an affidavit to the effect that the Rhodesian Government would under no circumstances pay heed to any judgement of any court outside of Rhodesia. More ominously, the government would 'forbid and prevent' any officer of the law from 'doing any act or taking any step which would assist or enable' such an appeal. This was the judicial high noon of UDI, where the court was asked not only to adjudicate on the discrepancies between the lawful 1961 Constitution and its usurper from 1965, but also to reckon with the implied threat of government intervention should the judgement not fall in its favour. It was here that the requirements of the courtroom collided with the blurred logic and creative ambiguity of a 'loyal rebellion'. A judiciary that had served two masters for more than two years was finally called on to make a ruling one way or the other; either white Rhodesia was an integral component of an organic chain of global British justice, or it was a rogue entity, openly defying British sovereignty along with the spiritual and cultural belief system that sustained it.

Beadle's response was anything but a model of judicial fortitude. Rather than face down Lardner-Burke and allow a Privy Council hearing, he ruled instead that there was simply no point in doing so. Although acknowledging the judicial right of appeal, Beadle was satisfied that it would be 'of no value ... no benefit' because even if the Privy Council found in the appellants' favour, the government would still go ahead and execute them. It was a bizarre finding which boiled down to the fact that Lardner-Burke and his Rhodesian Front colleagues 'mean what they say'. Or as the chief justice elaborated, 'no matter what the judgement of the Privy Council might be and, *even if it were reinforced by an order of this court*, it is perfectly clear the present Government would ignore it'. To find otherwise would 'only raise the hopes' of the condemned men 'when there is no cause for hope' and would thus be tantamount to 'an act of gratuitous cruelty'.[121]

The judgement not only flew in the face of judicial independence but also scaled new heights of legal absurdity, all the more remarkable coming from a knight of the realm who himself was a privy councillor. Unsurprisingly, he came in for withering criticism both at home and abroad. Two Rhodesian high court judges (neither of whom sat on the case) openly voiced their dissent, one of whom quit his post in disgust at the absence of any coherent legal reasoning.[122] In the United Kingdom, Lord Hailsham decried the 'travesty of justice' and castigated Lardner-Burke's affidavit as 'a clear case of contempt of court'. Dingle Foot also underlined the stark political basis of the decision: 'The court was being defied by the executive. The three judges uttered not a word of protest.'[123]

With a Privy Council appeal thus out of reach, the defence team was left with only one option: a direct petition for mercy to Queen Elizabeth II. It was in fact Harold Wilson and Commonwealth Secretary George Thomson who fell upon the idea at an urgently convened meeting at Downing Street on the evening of 1 March.[124] The following morning the defence team were advised to lodge a petition with the palace and later that day, Thomson advised the queen (as per his constitutional role) to commute the sentences to life imprisonment. Although mercy pleas for all three condemned prisoners received royal assent, it was only Dhlamini and Mlambo who sought to test Her Majesty's writ in the Rhodesian High Court (Duly Shadreck's counsel having deemed it tactically wiser – unwisely as it turned out – to appeal directly for mercy to Clifford Dupont).

The hearing the following Monday morning was relatively brief. The counsel for the condemned men argued that while the queen normally delegated her prerogative of mercy to the governor, this did not entirely divest her of the prerogative which she could freely dispense in a case such as this. Beadle flatly rejected this argument, claiming that the 1961 Constitution clearly vested the power of mercy in the governor on the advice of his Rhodesian ministers, and that this had effectively 'divested the Crown in the United Kingdom of this power'. Her Majesty could thus only exercise mercy on the advice of her Rhodesian ministers, not her United Kingdom ministers. Throughout the judgement he persisted in referring to the 'right of the United Kingdom Government' (as distinct from the queen) to exercise the prerogative of mercy and at one point boiled the problem down to 'the right of the United Kingdom Government to govern in Rhodesia today'. Framed in those terms, the appeal was bound to be thrown out. Beadle concluded his judgement with the sombre verdict: 'Her Majesty has no power in this matter' – all the while deploring the fact that her name had been dragged into the case to begin with.[125]

Thus, in three discrete judicial steps Beadle's court removed all remaining obstacles to the executions and in so doing removed himself from the favour of Governor Gibbs. When pressed by Gibbs to explain his wayward judicial reasoning, Beadle made the revealing comment that he 'had to offer some protection to officials who would be ordered to carry out the executions'.[126] In other words, his abiding concern was to shore up the legal position of the hangmen rather than the hanged in the event that 'judicial murder' charges might later be brought (should the Smith regime collapse at some future date).[127] In these circumstances, Gibbs clearly could not allow a chief justice so openly in defiance of the queen to remain under his roof and he therefore instructed Beadle to pack his bags at once. It was a signal moment; the parting of the ways between the Crown and the judiciary after years of awkward cohabitation. 'I shall always remember that final handshake!' Gibbs would ruefully recall years later.[128] The *Cape Times* depicted Beadle's hurried departure from Government House in ramshackle terms, chauffeured off 'in a police Wolseley packed with bags, guns, fishing rods and other effects'.[129]

The hanging case marked a watershed, signalling the end of the road for white Rhodesia's British credentials. The *Sunday Telegraph*'s leader was simply titled 'Goodbye Smith', while the headline of the *Daily Express* (hardly known for forward thinking on colonialism) underlined the signifance:

> The split is now unwritten but complete: historians can take the time from the instant the trap dropped beneath the feet of these brutal Africans . . . as far as the people of this once very loyal Colony are concerned the break between Britain and Rhodesia became final and irrevocable at 9am today.[130]

The House of Commons loudly applauded Dingle Foot's statement that there could 'be no valid or honourable agreement with this gang of criminals'. Others referred to the 'closing of the door', and the ex-communication of the Rhodesian Front 'outside of civilised behaviour'.[131] Wilson informed the Cabinet that Smith had 'effectively slammed the door' (although he himself would continue in vain to look for ways of prying it open for the remainder of his premiership).[132] Others such as Enoch Powell preferred to close the chapter on Rhodesia and seal it shut, pointing to the abject failure of Britain's judicial authority abroad: 'The independence of Rhodesia is something stronger than the law', he averred grimly. 'It is fact'.[133]

Similar conclusions were drawn on the streets of Salisbury, where the correspondent for the *Daily Express,* John Monks, 'could not find a single Rhodesian today who was against the hanging of these savage killers. No one I spoke to believed there was now any chance of continued negotiations with Britain. Few cared.'[134] In the district where Oberholtzer was killed, the local press inveighed against the 'slap in the face from the Royal hand', decrying the queen's intervention as 'the final straw which will turn "loyal rebels" into real rebels'.[135] Far from heralding the death of 'British justice', the hangings were hailed for their salutary cleansing effect, inaugurating a new era of 'Rhodesian' justice. As the *Umtali Post* rejoiced: 'Rhodesian justice is not dead but three savage killers are very dead – and rightly so.'[136] The sense of a community shedding its British affinities under the weight of a contentious courtroom drama was palpable.

Similarly, when Smith finally appeared on television to address the nation nearly three weeks later, there was an unmistakable change of posture. He described the recent 'attempt to interfere with the maintenance of law and order in Rhodesia' as 'one of the most despicable acts ever committed by a Government of Great Britain', made all the more odious by the fact that it was carried out covertly 'behind the skirts of their Queen'. It is inconceivable that Smith would have invoked Her Majesty's name in such vulgar terms prior to this episode, but even more significant was the substitution of 'our' queen for 'theirs'. He informed his listeners that any personal doubts he had once held about Rhodesia becoming a republic had been 'wiped out completely by the antics of Harold Wilson and his Socialist Government'.[137]

One viewer, ensconced in Government House and more isolated than ever before, switched off his television and turned to his astonished staff. 'I thought Smith looked particularly evil', murmured outgoing governor Humphrey Gibbs.[138]

◆

The tumult of March 1968 focused the minds of Smith, Dupont and the Rhodesian Front government on the efficacy of persisting with the charade of sovereignty in Britain's name. The legal nexus that had buttressed white authority for generations had been dramatically severed, calling into question the whole paraphernalia of Britishness itself. Within a matter of days,

Dupont told Godfrey Winn from the *Daily Mail* that 'the Republic virtually came into being' with the High Court's ruling in the hanging case, and it would not be long before the full implications emerged.[139] Dupont's 'speech from the throne' to officially open parliament in May was edited to remove the words 'in her Majesty's name'.[140] In April the queen's birthday was officially defrocked as a public holiday, ostensibly because allowing the nation 'to relax in the enjoyment of a public holiday ... would be quite inappropriate while this country is involved with terrorists on our northern frontier and members of our Security Forces are risking life and limb'.[141] At a stroke, the annual battle of the tea caddies came to an abrupt end. Later that year on 10 August the High Court passed a judgement that recognized what was already implicit in the hanging case – internal *de jure* status for the Smith government.[142]

Figure 9.4 Rhodesia's 'Officer Administering the Government', Clifford Dupont, signs a new republican constitution bill under the watchful eye of Rhodesian Front prime minister Ian Smith, 8 December 1969. Source: Hulton Archive/Getty Images.

It was also in August of that year that the government unveiled the design of an independent Rhodesian flag to replace both the colonial blue ensign and the Union Jack. With its two green bars flanking a white centre panel emblazoned with the Rhodesian coat of arms, it struck many as an uncanny replica of the Nigerian flag. It was in any case a world away from its predecessor. Some residual regret was aired that the Union Jack had not been incorporated into the design, with the *Rhodesia Herald* lamenting that it would have been a 'fitting acknowledgement of this country's British heritage and of the oft-mentioned determination to uphold and maintain the standards of conduct which made Britain great – whether or not these standards are considered to exist in Britain today'.[143] But by and large the new flag was embraced by the embattled white minority as a matter of necessity. The official unfurling took place on 11 November 1968, recently enshrined as 'Independence Day' at a ceremony on Salisbury's Jameson Ave attended by a packed audience (literally crowding the rooftops) in the presence of a bronze-cast Cecil Rhodes surveying the scene from his pedestal on the main thoroughfare. He seemed an unlikely substitute for royalty, rocking casually on his heels, both hands firmly thrust in the pockets of a loosely fitting suit. Conspicuously, no anthem was played as the old flag was lowered and the new held aloft in eerie silence – followed by a round of applause.[144] Later that afternoon, the Union Jack that had flown over Cecil Square since the arrival of the pioneer column in 1890 was permanently hauled down by two African constables. It was widely thought to be 'the last Union Jack to fly officially in Africa'.[145]

Except that it wasn't. Ten blocks to the north of Cecil Square, Humphrey Gibbs continued to fly the Union Jack over Government House for a further eight months. But even he was forced to reconsider his position when Smith announced that a referendum would be held on 20 June 1969 to vote on a new republican constitution. Gibbs appeared on television to inform viewers that he would ask the queen to release him from his duties and return to his farm in the event of a 'yes' vote. His appeal does not seem to have affected the outcome either way, with a poorly organized and under-resourced 'no' campaign conspicuously avoiding any mention of the governor, or indeed the tarnished image of the queen herself. Bereft of a credible strategy to save the Rhodesian Crown, the dissenters ran with the oxymoronic slogan: 'Be Positive, Vote No'.[146] The outcome was an overwhelming endorsement of Smith and all he now stood for, with upwards of 82 per cent of the (eligible, overwhelmingly white) electorate voting to dispense with Her Majesty. At Hatfield House in England, this was too much even for Lord Salisbury, who 'as a life-long and convinced

Monarchist' felt bound to resign as president of the Anglo-Rhodesian Society.[147]

For Humphrey Gibbs, too, it was a signal defeat. Two weeks later, he returned from a late afternoon walk with his black labrador to perform his final duty as governor of Rhodesia. Standing to attention on the lawn of Government House, dog trustily at his side, he watched mournfully as the Union Jack was lowered for the last time. Shortly afterwards, he and his wife departed the house that had held them captive for three and a half years.[148] The date was symbolic: 4 July 1969, some 193 years after the American Declaration of Independence – but also five years to the day since the murder of Andrea Oberholtzer by four young African insurgents, two of whom paid the ultimate price for their actions. Rarely had a single act of political violence brought such lasting implications, effecting a rupture in the fabled reach of British justice.

PART III

REPERCUSSIONS

10

EAST AND WEST OF SUEZ: RECEDING FRONTIERS

On an autumn evening in 1951, Peter Fleming – adventurer, travel writer, decorated naval officer – was emerging from a theatre in London's West End when a fleeting exchange caught his ear. 'Henry's bringing a friend of his who is just back from Rangoon', murmured a passer-by to her male companion. 'Do come if you can.' The words immediately struck him as faintly curious, even a little odd. As he wandered into the night mulling over their meaning, he began to grasp the significance: 'In England today, a man who has just come back from Rangoon is a rare and a potentially interesting phenomenon, a purveyor of exotic information, a sort of little austerity lion.'

Fleming lost no time penning a short piece for *The Spectator*, taking the 'Man from Rangoon' as the personification of Britain's changing outlook. In only a few short years, he marvelled, the mental geography of the British people had been completely reconfigured. Whereas once the intricate imperial networks that had 'linked these islands with remote parts of our planet' were entirely taken for granted, now the prospects for pursuing 'enterprising things' in 'far-flung' realms had become drastically curtailed. 'Remote, romantic place names' that were once 'domesticated in English households' and 'pasted into snapshot albums' – from Simla to Tientsin to Rangoon itself – had been placed out of bounds, beyond the imaginative reach of ordinary folk. Worse still, the new barriers and embargoes had become widely accepted as 'an almost axiomatic feature of the world we live in', the inevitable upshot of 'the contraction of our Empire on the one hand and our incomes on the other'. Though the opportunity for overseas adventure had never been available to all, Fleming was sure that 'even if we had no contact with it as individuals, it did, I think, perceptibly flavour the background of our national life'. He found the new mental maps of the 1950s wholly discouraging:

> The horizons of the British have been sharply contracted ... no longer dotted with a dependable network of Government Houses and Residencies

and dark bungalows, hill-stations and cantonments, between which residents and visitors formerly drifted almost without effort ... it must be true that, generally speaking, the British at the moment are more out of touch with the rest of the world than they have been for several generations.

To underline the point, Fleming recounted his wartime experience of recapturing the Andaman Islands from the Japanese, describing a fellow naval officer who asked wearily whether 'these blasted islands' were worth the effort. 'Of course they are', retorted another, 'only place I ever made a century.' For Fleming, it was these myriad triumphs-in-miniature in the most improbable places that wedded the British to their wide territorial remit. The diminished scope for such exploits served as mournful testimony to the country's lost latitude. 'Our horizons have shrunk', he reiterated, 'and look like continuing to shrink.'[1]

Within three months, the antidote for Fleming's malaise had been hammered out in a Jamaican bungalow belonging to his less glamorous, considerably less wealthy, and (at the time) far less famous younger brother Ian. *Casino Royale*, published in April 1953, introduced British readers to Commander James Bond, the suave, handsome, ruthlessly efficient agent of Her Majesty's Secret Intelligence Service.[2] An initially lukewarm publisher (Jonathan Cape) thought the younger Fleming's work 'not up to scratch', but resolved to publish it anyway 'because he's Peter's brother'.[3]

Thus, the iconic, triple-digit '007' was unleashed onto a surprisingly receptive public, selling out the first two editions in less than two months. No mere paragon of selfless service to his country, Bond was endowed with a mystery and cunning that gave him an unpredictable and insubordinate edge, custom-made for a predominantly male readership impatient with the slide in the nation's fortunes. With the empire dissolving and Cold War rivalries relegating Britain to a subsidiary role, Bond's covert escapades in exotic locales bucked the trend, bringing ready reassurance that a touch of British class still counted for something.[4] His ability to affect an outcome through the sheer force of character was a salutary reminder that the nation's dwindling material resources need not render its manhood moribund. For a country still emerging from the indignities of post-war rationing, Bond was himself an 'austerity lion' of sorts. But the quality that really galvanized his mass appeal was a certain compass. In a rapidly dawning jet age, Bond moved effortlessly across borders, shuttling between Europe and the United States, the Caribbean, Africa and the Middle East, unencumbered by diplomatic niceties or the dictates of national sovereignty. Not for him the confinements of 1950s Britain.

The careers of both Flemings had been profoundly shaped by the British naval establishment, and their instincts and attitudes resonated widely in contemporary debates about Britain's strategic outlook. For a century or more, the imperative of 'sea power' had mapped out the contours of a world conceived as an extension of Britain's blurred boundaries. Ruling the waves, the never-setting sun, the 'wider still and wider' bounds of a nation 'throned amid the billows'; these everyday aphorisms are often discounted by historians as little more than quaint reminders of a fleeting hubris.[5] But they were the commonplace register of an attitude and outlook that deeply penetrated the social world of mid-twentieth-century Britain, nurturing the belief that the country's vocation must be played out on a broad canvas. Half a century earlier, the Foreign Office mandarin Sir Eyre Crowe had reflected on the 'immutable' geographic conditions of a nation 'whose existence and survival as an independent community are inseparably bound up with the possession of preponderant sea power'. His words summoned a mindset that would endure for decades:

> No one now disputes it. Sea power is more potent than land power, because it is as pervading as the element in which it moves and has its being. Its formidable character makes itself felt the more directly that a maritime State is, in the literal sense of the word, the neighbour of every country accessible by sea.[6]

In this formulation, a 'British presence' around the globe was an existential creed, as essential as the water molecules on which it was borne. Little wonder that Commander Bond was a naval man.

By the 1950s, the burden of shouldering an extensive array of overseas bases and tactical deployments was becoming increasingly intolerable. The perennial goal of preserving Britain's 'global reach' (axiomatic, yet conspicuously ill-defined) not only posed a heavy drain on the balance of payments (and hence Britain's ever-vulnerable gold and dollar reserves), but also diverted scarce resources, manpower and technical expertise from the production of high-quality merchandise to help pay Britain's way in the world. But despite these obvious material realities, successive British governments, their service chiefs and the wider 'defence community' of strategic analysts, academics, and journalists found it exceedingly difficult to contemplate even the most glaringly urgent reductions. Though sound assessments of the 'national interest' always seemed ready to hand to justify overstretched defence deployments, Britain's vast network of security commitments remained an unshakeable end in itself. Cold calculations of strategic priorities could never be entirely insulated from the alluring tug of a belief system inherited from former, more exalted times.

There can be no better gauge of a people's imaginative frontiers than the territory they feel duty-bound to fight for – not least in times of reluctant retrenchment. The progressive rollback of Britain's defence posture in the post-war world is in many respects a familiar tale; one of steadily diminishing capacity, as economic and geo-strategic impediments curtailed Britain's military effectiveness overseas.[7] But it is also a story of a profound collective mental and moral paralysis, symbolized by a sand-blown port on the northern shore of the Red Sea. *El Suweis* not only lent its name to the 1956 crisis that revealed the limits of Britain's world-power aspirations, but also became the strategic and psychological fallback for the traumatic retreat from the Far East in the late 1960s. Historians continue to debate whether the 1956 Suez crisis really devastated popular morale to the extent that is routinely claimed. It is argued here that the deeper impact of Suez can be traced through its dissonant resonances around the globe, puncturing not only the prestige of Anthony Eden's enfeebled government, but also the feasibility of a world conceived in terms of Britain's ubiquitous 'presence'. For the challenge it posed to the governing assumptions about extended horizons and elastic frontiers, Suez exemplifies the post-war constraints on the idea of Britain itself.

In 1950, the Cambridge political philosopher Peter Laslett ventured that 'the peace of the world depends ... on the Englishman being able to reconcile himself to a continuous diminution of the consequence of his country. This can only be done if he can learn to separate his personal prestige from the prestige of his nation state.'[8] He might have added that it depended on disentangling 'his country' from its wider overseas projections. Laslett's forecast was undoubtedly overblown (the 'peace of the world' surely hinged on one or two more weighty variables in 1950) but his notion of a 'continuous diminution of consequence' neatly captured the dilemma of a nation that, quite literally, was losing ground. James Bond and the infantile grievances of his author's elder brother were uniquely ill-suited to disaggregating the personal prestige of 'the Englishman' from his diminished international standing. But they fared no better than Eden and his inner circle whose equally unhelpful hankerings brought their country into disrepute, sowing endemic suspicion and mistrust throughout a world they so keenly sought to hold.

'READY TO ENCOMPASS THE EARTH':
ELIZABETHAN PRELUDE

Peter Fleming was by no means alone in lamenting Britain's narrowing horizons in the early 1950s. One reliable source of woe was the surge of returning colonial administrators who railed against the defeatism of a country they no longer recognized. Old 'India hands' such as Sir Olaf Caroe could be especially despondent. The former governor of the north-west frontier province composed a personal memoir after a thirty-year absence, observing that 'the very look of Englishmen and Scotsmen has altered, and the old values on the surface at least, seem dying and even dead'.[9] Other accounts were more wistful, such as the Flemingesque 'Impressions of a Dubai Post' penned by A. J. M. Craig, one of the last of Her Majesty's servants to bear the time-worn mantle of 'Political Agent' in the Middle East. Reflecting on a time when such epithets themselves were imbued with 'a remoteness in time and place', Craig cast his mind back to a succession of colonial 'Residents', 'Collectors' and 'District Commissioners' – 'those originals on whom the sun used never to set, the final, executive blood vessel in the network of arteries that stretched out, long, efficient and complex, from the distant heart of empire'. But there could be no denying their imminent demise: 'The ghosts of dead colleagues rise up: in the club at Mandalay, saddling their horses in Peshawar, har-anguing the tribes in the Kalahari. And the nostalgia grows with the aware-ness that one is very nearly the last of that very long line.'[10]

Someone who was more attuned than most to reconfigured frontiers was Cyril Radcliffe, returning to Britain in autumn 1947 having completed the exacting task of drawing the lines of partition between India and Pakistan. Convinced that the British imagination had 'remained untouched' by the momentous events of Indian independence, he aired his thoughts in a major BBC broadcast surveying 'the five continents in which British soldiers lie buried'. The mere mention of overseas military sacrifice lent his words an elegiac quality. 'We have been such wanderers that the mud of every country is on our shoes', he intoned. 'In all recorded history up to the present no people has ever mixed its dust with the dust of the wide world.'[11] In this view, Britain's long history of holding the 'thin red line' retained a spiritual quality that transcended the political and material spoils of war, lingering long after the British had departed.[12]

The death of the ailing King George VI in early 1952 and the accession of his eldest daughter brought a brief phase of misplaced optimism, buoyed by the promise of a 'Second Elizabethan Age'. The coronation in June the following year was an elaborate display of the young queen's boundless royal writ, replete with the visual spectacle of troops and regiments from all parts of the world. The fortuitous coincidence of the 'conquest' of Mt Everest by Edmund Hillary and Tenzing Norgay, relayed to the world on the very morning of the coronation, triggered a sustained volley of journalistic hubris. *The Times* heralded a 'Coronation gift for the Queen' while other headlines trumpeted Her Majesty's 'crowning glory' in the Himalayas and the 'brilliant jewel in the Queen's diadem'. Hillary and Tenzing were routinely compared with Raleigh and Drake, while the BBC likened their triumph to a daring military feat. Another 'far horizon' had been conquered.[13] Although the new queen herself sought to play down the comparison with her Tudor namesake, she did allow that 'there is at least one significant resemblance between her age and mine. For her Kingdom, small though it may have been ... was great in spirit and well endowed with men who were ready to encompass the earth.'[14]

The Conservative governments of Winston Churchill and Anthony Eden contained more than their share of ministers caught between the despondent misgivings of a lost vocation and the recharged optimism of the new Elizabethans. Senior Cabinet figures such as Lord Salisbury, Lord Swinton, Oliver Lyttleton and Alan Lennox-Boyd were as prone to rue the receding tide of Britain's fortunes as to work tirelessly to arrest the trend. Foreign and Colonial Office officials voiced concern that their political masters were stranded between two modes of thought, lapsing frequently into 'Edwardian' assumptions about a coercive capacity 'which we no longer possess'.[15] Lyttleton himself confessed that some of his colleagues were 'still to the right of Rudyard Kipling', having completely failed to observe the 'march of time' and appreciate 'that dominion over pine and palm had given way to new axioms of government by consent'.[16] He seemed to be describing his own inner Jekyll and Hyde as the minister charged with prosecuting costly colonial counter-insurgency campaigns on two fronts in Kenya and Malaya, who recalled seeing the 'horned shadow of the Devil himself' in the deeds of Kenya's Mau Mau insurgents.[17]

Churchill and Eden were conspicuously caught between two worlds – hamstrung by the dictates of Britain's drastically reduced economic capacity yet continually setting goals and measuring success by pre-war standards. Churchill's pronounced time lag in coming to terms with Indian independence remained almost a source of personal pride, and while he in no way sought to reverse any of the decolonizing measures of his Labour predecessor, he freely aired his frustration at being unable to do so. He concluded his final Cabinet meeting in April 1955 with a solemn plea that Britain should weave 'more closely the threads which bound together the countries of the Commonwealth' – or, as he himself 'still preferred to call it, the Empire'.[18]

Eden's perspective was more nuanced, not least as a considerably younger figure whose prior experience was almost exclusively in dealing with Europe and the United States. He was not normally to be found among the imperial rear-guard of the Conservative Party, either in opposition or government, and rarely indulged in Churchillian resistance to the transition from empire to Commonwealth. Yet he, too, harboured a conception of Britain that transcended its immediate British or European context, remarking on more than one occasion that a casual rummage through the postbag of 'any English village' would reveal the extent and intricacy of the imperial and Commonwealth attachments of the British people.[19]

Particularly revealing was his first major Cabinet submission as foreign secretary on 'British Overseas Obligations' in 1952, prepared in response to the Treasury's urgent appeal for expenditure reductions to ease the incessant pressure on sterling. Although he breezily conceded that Britain's existing military bases and burdens were 'beyond the resources of this country to meet', he nevertheless refused to contemplate abandoning any major obligation, citing a range of strategic imperatives from the risk of creating a Cold War 'vacuum' to the attendant weakening of the Commonwealth. Ultimately, though, his case rested on intangibles – the priceless commodities of 'prestige' and 'grip', the loss of which would be 'incalculable' and certainly 'wholly out of proportion to financial saving'. Improvising the maxim 'once the prestige of a country has started to slide there is no knowing where it will stop', he furnished no charts or figures to back his convictions, acting instead on assumptions that were impervious to arithmetic. His refusal to give ground, to contemplate any relinquishing of the nation's tenacious 'grip', ultimately boiled down to what he termed the 'unalterable marrow' of British life.[20]

The net effect of these competing pressures – between the starkly material and the airily ethereal – was a debilitating inertia. 'Keeping change within the bounds' became the guiding principle of the Churchill and Eden governments, witnessed by the fact that not a single Colonial Office territory achieved independence during their combined tenure.[21] But they still had to grapple with persistent challenges to the greater British mindset. Beyond the armed struggles of the Malayan jungle and the Kenyan highlands, pressure points emerged at multiple strategic junctures. In South Africa, the nationalist government of D. F. Malan demanded the return of the Simon's Town Naval base on the Cape of Good Hope (operated and financed by the Royal Navy since the 1790s) as part of a more general push to purge South Africa of its outward British trappings. Despite the diminished strategic importance of the base, Churchill was loath to 'contemplate any transaction which would be presented as yet another surrender'.[22] A further incursion into Britain's sphere of influence arose in September 1951 when the Australian and New Zealand governments entered into a security pact with the United States. On the face of it, the ANZUS Treaty seemed ideally suited to easing Britain's overstretched defence commitments, but Churchill made no secret of his displeasure at not having been invited to join.[23]

But the most formidable challenge – tactically, politically and emotionally – emerged out of the swirling political tensions of the Middle East and especially in Egypt. The successive withdrawals from India and Palestine in the 1940s had not only magnified the significance of Britain's residual foothold in the region, but also rendered it more vulnerable to the perils of strategic overstretch. In October 1951, after years of inconclusive talks, Egyptian prime minister Mustafa el-Nahas promptly abrogated the 1936 treaty that regulated Britain's rights to its bases along the Suez Canal. Amid violent anti-British riots in Cairo and skirmishing between British and Egyptian forces, a new era of intrigue, enmity and instability had begun. Eden's initial gambit was to propose handing over the Suez bases to the Egyptians, leaving only a modest troop presence on the understanding that British forces would be free to return in times of necessity. 'The plain fact is', he told Churchill prophetically, 'that we are no longer in a position to impose our will on Egypt, regardless of the cost in men, money and international goodwill.'[24] This was a difficult argument for Churchill and large swathes of his party to swallow but before any progress could be made, matters were complicated in July 1952 when the Egyptian court of King Farouk was toppled in an army coup staged by the 'Revolutionary Command Council', led by General Muhammad Naguib and Lieutenant Colonel Gamal Abdel Nasser. The key components of the Suez crisis had fallen into place.[25]

Suez occupied a special place in the wider imperial vista, one that evoked heightened passions and an acute resistance to change. Straddling the east–west divide, the passage from the eastern Mediterranean to the Red Sea had long been imbued with an aura of transcendence. The narrow, floodlit waterway represented a 'suspension between two states of being' – between a timeless, alluring East, beckoning the intrepid and enterprising, and the accelerated modernity of the West, the apparent triumph of European ingenuity over the physical barrier of Asia.[26] As E. M. Forster's narrator observed in *A Passage to India*: 'Somewhere about Suez there is always a social change: the arrangements of Asia weaken and those of Europe begin to be felt.'[27] Malcolm Muggeridge witnessed the 'strange transformation' in his fellow passengers on the outward voyage in the 1920s, as 'more or less ordinary middle- or lower-middle class English' became 'more assertive ... more la-di-da' as the vessel neared the eastern Mediterranean. 'By Port Said the change was complete.'[28] Suez symbolized both a great civilizing achievement as well as a crossroads between civilizations. In Somerset Maugham's *East of Suez* from 1922, the juncture was dramatized by a hapless British desk officer brought to his destruction by the beguiling charms of a mixed-race Eurasian woman.[29] These 'accretions of meaning' in literary and traveller accounts gathered persuasive force as generations of sojourners recorded their impressions, each lending further weight to the canal's symbolic capital. As Elleke Boehmer's contends, Suez was not just a key strategic waterway but more crucially a storehouse of imperial memory, mediating the passage to Greater Britain.[30]

In keeping with this, Eden himself described the canal as 'the swing-door of the British Empire, which has got to keep continually revolving' – never pausing to question the urgency of an armed guard at the entrance.[31] Britain's stated objectives in the Middle East – a forward position for resisting Soviet designs, a guarantee of Persian Gulf oil supplies, a critical hub for regional influence – were indistinguishable from the interests of any or all of the Western European democracies, but none felt the same compulsion to secure these aims by way of a massive physical presence.[32] Nor, by the early 1950s, could Whitehall agree on an objective assessment of the pros and cons. One Foreign Office Cabinet submission warned that maintaining the British garrison against Egyptian wishes would leave the troops 'wholly absorbed in coping with a situation their very presence creates', while another FO minute urged that it was 'useless to maintain troops simply to be shot at'.[33] At the other extreme were frequent and distinctly airy assertions that 'if we lose Egypt, we shall lose the rest of the Arab World'.[34] In this view, a physical presence 'to be shot at' was of no small value. Lord Salisbury spelt out the logic in a personal minute to Churchill during the 1951 crisis over the nationalization of British oil interests in Persia:

> For while our people are actually there, it is always open to us to send in troops ... to protect British lives. But once they have left, we could only re-enter to protect British property, which is not at all the same thing from the international point of view.[35]

Clearly, getting 'mud on our shoes' as Cyril Radcliffe had rhapsodized was the indispensable component. The point is not that Britain's material interests in the region were wholly illusory, or merely a cynical cloak for antiquated colonial hankerings. Rather, as Albert Hourani has argued, calculations of national interest were never fully liberated from the lingering and often unspoken fixations of the past that carried their 'own force, tending to distort the ways in which interests were pursued'.[36]

The upshot of Eden's protracted talks with the Egyptian military regime was an agreement of July 1954 to completely evacuate the canal base by summer 1956, in return for an assurance that it could still be used by Britain to defend Turkey or the Arab states from attack.[37] By this stage, General Naguib had himself been deposed by Nasser, who was positioning himself as the popular symbol of Arab freedom and hence a natural antagonist of the British. The decision to abandon Suez was instantly condemned from the cross-benches of the House of Lords by the one-time doyen of imperial defence (and Suez Canal company director) Lord Hankey:

> Until yesterday we used to say: 'From East to West the tested chain holds fast; the well-forged link rings true'. I fear that after to-day we cannot say that with the same conviction as in the past.[38]

He had evidently failed to notice the good many 'links in the chain' that had already given way since the Second World War. This same suspended disbelief permeated the Tory backbench, where the decision to evacuate the canal became virulently unpopular. Indeed, the new treaty with Egypt marked the advent of the so-called 'Suez group' led by Charles Waterhouse and Julian Amery. Initially numbering roughly forty members, this highly vocal faction embodied everything that rankled about Britain's diminishing 'reach' – a veritable phalanx of 'Rangoon men' whose influence was bolstered by powerful sympathizers including Churchill himself. It was clear from their histrionics in the Commons and fierce backroom lobbying that the issue in no way turned on whether Britain's material objectives in the Middle East could be met by an amicable deal with the Egyptian government. At a more fundamental level the resentments were fuelled by passions that were not open to examination. 'This is not a sell-out' denounced Waterhouse, 'it is a give-away. Instead of having a physical control of a great base, instead of having troops on the major waterway of the world, we have got this piece of paper in our hands.'[39] For the Suez group, it was Munich all over again – a humiliating climbdown and a feeble substitute for the reassuring presence of 'troops on the waterway'. It was but a lightly modernized version of 'the old Greater Britain concept' in which the very survival of the nation still hinged on its expansive properties.[40] In Enoch Powell's formulation, an 'empire of positions' would have to be maintained even as the 'empire of governing peoples' gave way.[41]

Meanwhile, the Labour opposition had little difficulty in stigmatizing the 'semi-hysteria' and 'old imperialist outlook' of the Suez group's parliamentary antics. Even within the Conservative ranks their views and tactics were controversial (at one point prompting the formation of a notably less-galvanized 'anti-Suez group').[42] But for all their detractors, the Suez group would become increasingly influential as the crisis in the region escalated and their numbers swelled; such was the potent blend of material weakness, strategic challenge and emotional intrigue that formed the backdrop to the events of 1956. Historians have been remarkably forgiving in their assessment of a crisis stoked by the ardour of an anachronistic, even delusional element within the political class of the 1950s (wholly unreconciled to the 'continuous diminution of the consequence' of their country). Peter Hennessy is not alone in shying away from harsh judgement, pleading that 'only so much adjustment of personal mental maps, as well as the wider geography of Britain's power, can be expected even from those whose minds tended towards the tougher end of the spectrum'.[43] That may be so, but even by the standards of their own contemporaries, the reveries and resentments that lined the pathway to Suez were, in the words of Labour's Harold Davies, a 'gargantuan atavism'.[44]

'WE, THE BRITISH': 1956

In April 1956, the BBC broadcast the first in a six-part series of programmes ominously titled *We the British, Are We in Decline?* narrated by the Labour Party's Christopher Mayhew. The 'We' in the title clearly referred to 'the British' of Britain, but Mayhew's appearance beside a spinning globe suggested a wider set of coordinates. 'Is it seriously true that we're going downhill as a nation?', he ventured grimly. 'Has Britain kept the symbols of greatness but not the substance?' Much of the programme was devoted to Britain's waning military preponderance in the world, where the deployment of troops in disparate locales – from Kenya to Cyprus, British Guyana and Malaya – signalled a deeper malaise. As Mayhew conceded: 'Our troops run forward, but British rule is on the defensive ... the mere fact of fighting sets back our prestige in world affairs, is attacked as Colonialism by our enemies.'[45]

But it was not the 'mere fact' of fighting so much as the perception that the fight was progressively being lost through a succession of drawn out, indecisive guerrilla-style campaigns that rested uneasily with the wartime mythology of clearly drawn battle lines, bold advances and stiff resolve in the face of enemy onslaughts. Nor could Britain's presumptive superiority easily be squared with the often-inconclusive results in the field. BBC audience research recorded widespread public dissatisfaction about the many 'trouble spots' around the world 'and the fact that every little nation seems to think it can cock a snook at us'.[46] Although Mayhew urged his audience 'not to think that we've something to blame ourselves for' he fed them ample material to do just that, insisting that 'decline' had become a fact of contemporary British life. For all the intangible 'moral influence' of the modern Commonwealth, there was 'no substitute for the direct rule of one sixth of the world's population which we had in 1900'.[47] The programme broached openly – but in no way resolved – the anomaly of defending a ubiquitous 'presence' in remote, scattered settings increasingly out of sync with Britain's global standing in the 1950s.

These were the fault lines that only three months later would produce the political drama of Nasser's so-called 'seizure' of the Suez Canal on 26 July 1956. It is a common misconception (one prevalent both at the time and since) that Nasser executed a bold land-grab, evicting the prior owner-occupants from their age-old slice of the Middle East. Thus, he

Figure 10.1 The Egyptian president, Gamal Abdel Nasser, announced the nationalization of the Suez Canal to a crowd of 250,000 people during a celebration of the fourth anniversary of the 1952 revolution, 26 July 1956. Source: Gamma Keystone/Getty Images.

became 'Grabber Nasser' in the *Daily Mirror*'s reportage, and countless other news outlets eagerly followed suit.[48] Yet by 1956, Egyptian sovereignty over the Suez Canal was not in dispute; it was Nasser's nationalization of the Anglo-French company that had administered the canal for nearly a century that was the bone of contention. Indeed, for all their outspoken indignation, Eden's Cabinet privately recognized that Nasser's action 'amounted to no more than a decision to buy out the shareholders'.[49]

The distinction quickly became blurred, however, not least because virtually all the major antagonists had an interest in distorting the significance of what had transpired. The fact that the Egyptians had moved with unseemly haste, little more than a month after the departure of the last of the British garrison, enhanced the feeling that Britain had been deprived of a major territorial asset – which Nasser's triumphalist rhetoric did little to dispel. Thus, in British as well as French eyes it seemed a deliberate provocation and both governments became quickly obsessed with the idea of ejecting the Egyptians from the canal by force and bringing about 'regime change' in Cairo. They were restrained, however, by the attitude of the US administration of Dwight D. Eisenhower – no admirer of Nasser, but in an election year the president remained adamant that the British and French should cool their heels.[50]

The infamously foolhardy 'collusion' with Israel, whereby the latter agreed to attack Egyptian territory in the Sinai on the understanding that Britain and France would immediately 'intervene' to separate the warring parties, was the culmination of an emotional as much as a strategic build-up. For years afterwards, rumours circulated that Eden's foreign secretary, Selwyn Lloyd, had sported a false moustache en route to the Parisian suburb of Sèvres where the agreement was concocted in the strictest secrecy – conveying something of the cloak-and-dagger intrigue.[51] The UK Army chief of staff was advised of the plan in a dilapidated hut in Malta, later describing his impressions as 'really almost like a James Bond sort of set up'.[52] But unlike the airtight secrecy of fictional espionage, the chances of keeping the 'Sèvres Protocol' out of the public domain were slim at best. That such reckless naivety could have taken hold in the most senior ranks of government bears witness to the pervasive cultural factors that were constantly in play.

The rest of the story is a matter of public record. Israel launched its unprovoked invasion of Egypt on 29 October. On cue, Britain and France issued an ultimatum to both parties to withdraw ten miles from the canal zone within 12 hours, or risk Anglo-French military intervention. When Egypt predictably failed to comply, the combined assault of 79,000 British and French service personnel was ordered to proceed. Over the ensuing days, the Egyptian air force would be decimated by the RAF (exposing further the sham of impartiality), with the loss of three thousand Egyptian soldiers and an additional one thousand civilian deaths. The British and French sustained around a hundred casualties, with some twenty-three British servicemen paying with their lives for Eden's folly.[53] But within a matter of days, the adverse reaction of the international money markets, combined with a withering censure in the United Nations, forced the British to agree to humiliating ceasefire terms and an ignominious withdrawal, leaving the French high and dry with no choice but to follow suit. Eden's health quickly collapsed, further compounding the sense of a major national calamity with 'few parallels in the long gallery of military imbecility'.[54] If 'We, the British' had seemed on the brink of decline in April 1956, this surely was the real thing.

Figure 10.2a and 10.2b Largely because it was deemed a strategic fiasco, the sheer physical destruction of the Anglo-French Suez invasion is routinely overlooked in historical accounts: (a) an Arab boy surveys the ruins of a Port Said street as a British tank approaches; (b) displaced Egyptian civilians walking through the rubble of bombed streets, November 1956. Source: (a) Bettmann/Getty Images; (b) Hulton Archive/Getty Images.

Figure 10.2a and 10.2b (cont.)

Raking through the embers of Suez, historians have placed an inordin-
ate amount of weight on Eden's volatile state of mind and his precarious
health (the result of a gall bladder operation in 1953 that went horribly
awry) – working from the premise that a gamble as reckless as Suez could
only have been contemplated by a leader who had taken leave of his senses
or was so high on Benzedrine and other stimulants as to be in no fit state to
govern.[55] Ronald Hyam goes so far as to pour scorn on any attempt to find
deeper structural causes, contending that 'the records demonstrate beyond
all doubt' that the course of events was chiefly dictated by the 'severe
decline' in Eden's temperament and ill-health in October 1956. In what
might be termed the 'deranged man' view of history, Suez can thus be

written off as an 'aberration' (as David Edgerton would have it) – 'essentially the work of an insecure and unwell Prime Minister'.[56]

But this view misses too much. The Suez intervention was not Eden's own personal delirium but a tangled weave of deal-brokering between three sovereign nations. His most senior Cabinet colleagues willingly egged him on, in particular the man who would ultimately go on to govern for a further seven years. There is no suggestion that Harold Macmillan was suffering from a delusional mental state (even though as chancellor it was his miscalculation of the impact on sterling that hurt Eden the most) nor the permanent secretary of the Foreign Office, Sir Ivone Kirkpatrick, who famously described Eden as 'the only man in England who wanted the nation to survive'.[57] The brinkmanship of the Suez group was rewarded with a flood of fresh recruits, its membership swelling from forty to over a hundred backbenchers, while one of its leading lights, Julian Amery (Macmillan's son-in-law) was involved in a mind-boggling matrix of intrigue against Nasser through his links to MI6 and ground operatives working to overthrow the Egyptian president in Cairo.[58] This latter-day *Boys' Own* network was intrinsic to the culture of the right wing of the Conservative Party, gathering momentum through a succession of perceived 'scuttles' from India, through Palestine, Persia and now Suez – the moment when the dam burst.[59] Eden effectively threw in his lot with the Suez group in autumn 1956 because he was running out of ways to uphold Britain's global self-projection by more conventional means. That is not to deny that he was prone to tantrums, fevers and a visceral dislike of Nasser. But more revealing is the deeper culture of entitlement, prestige and worldly expectations that produced Eden's personal phantoms.

It also bears recalling that for much of the crisis, Eden had the better of press and public opinion. Particularly during the months-long build-up there was widespread agreement that 'something must be done' to divert Nasser from his devious ends. This may have been chiefly a matter of Eden's skilful handling of Fleet Street – rather than a direct cipher of popular sentiment – but it nevertheless points to a wider groundswell of belligerency in the face of the perceived threat to Britain's world standing.[60] Headlines such as 'It's GREAT Britain again' (*Daily Sketch*), 'Resisting the Aggressor' (*The Times*) and 'How good it is to hear the British Lion's roar' (*Daily Telegraph*) hardly evoked an isolated prime minister out of touch with the electorate (let alone his senses).[61] Even at the very nadir in the government's fortunes when the invasion was called off, the *Daily Mail* somehow salvaged an upbeat headline: 'Cease Fire: Canal Ours. Objective Achieved'.[62] As one of Eden's more diffident Cabinet supporters Rab Butler reflected years later, 'deep-seated emotions affecting liberal-minded people ... coalesced only too easily with less generous sentiments, the residues of illiberal resentment at the loss of Empire'.[63] In short, there are firm grounds for assuming that Eden was buoyed by a broad, if shaky consensus and that the crisis itself was 'very much a collective enterprise'.[64]

But if Eden's Suez gamble was anchored in a deeper, more pervasive set of anxieties and convictions, what was their wellspring? Much has been made of the long shadow of 'appeasement', and the lessons of the 1930s that dominated contemporary press commentary. But the world was awash with despotic regimes in 1956 and Nasser had merely exercised his sovereign entitlement to nationalize a key strategic asset. Invocations of appeasement were more about presumed frailties in Britain's own national fibre, conjuring half-forgotten mistakes of the past never to be repeated rather than some clearly adumbrated *casus belli*. Although no doubt sincerely felt, the rallying cry of 'Munich' was never the crux of the matter. Nor can the mood be attributed to some deep-seated, if unacknowledged longing for the wholesale restoration of the British empire. Too much had transpired, too many milestones towards the new Commonwealth had been passed to caricature 1956 as a belated imperial muster.[65] Eden went out of his way to explain to President Eisenhower that the Suez operation was 'not part of a harking back to the old colonial and occupational concepts. We are most anxious to avoid this impression.'[66] And to the extent that he ever fully understood his own actions, it is clear that he had no desire to take back responsibility for the running of Egypt.

But the undimmed allure of global reach still coloured the Eden government's words and deeds in autumn 1956; the outward projection of Britain's global quintessence and the unshakable conviction that the nation's survival depended on holding forward positions. To that extent, the unreconciled upshot of imperial retrenchment was the decisive factor. Only this can explain the Eden government's assertion (entirely contrary to Foreign Office legal advice) that armed intervention could be justified by the principle of *self-defence*.[67] Whether it was Lord Home's dire warning that 'we are finished if the Middle East goes', Julian Amery's assertion that 'our life is at stake', Macmillan's urging that 'we must [humiliate Nasser] quickly, or we shall ourselves be ruined', or indeed Eden's own appeal to President Eisenhower that 'it would be an ignoble end to our long history if we tamely accepted to perish by degrees', the sense of an existential threat was as palpable as it now seems implausible.[68] Eisenhower could not suppress his disbelief at Eden's talk of 'the end of history', replying gingerly (as in: 'permit me to suggest') that Eden was making rather more of Nasser than the man warranted.[69] But the president was not privy to the tortured logic and involuntary reflexes of empire's end. For the key British protagonists, the thought of being pared back to their own island fortress seemed tantamount to the end of Britain itself.

COMMONWEALTH DISCORD AND THE 'BRITISH THING'

This is also borne out by Eden's attempts to knit the Suez Canal into Britain's own historic fabric. In his first public broadcast addressing the crisis in August 1956, he sought to bring the matter closer to home:

> The Suez Canal is a name familiar to everyone. You, or some member of your family perhaps, have served there, or maybe one of you or more have helped to defend the canal in one or other of the two great wars. For Britain the Canal has always been the main artery to and from the Commonwealth, bringing us the supplies we and they need . . . and what Colonel Nasser has just done, is to seize it for his own ends.[70]

Perhaps anticipating an audience sceptical of the significance of such a remote asset, Eden deliberately struck a note of intimacy: of Suez as a natural extension of the family domain, invoking the shared history of wartime endeavour. The organic image of the 'artery' also underscored Suez as a 'matter of life and death' (as he termed it later in the speech) and an indispensable lifeline to Commonwealth kith and kin. It was an absurd proposition. The percentage of his listeners who had direct personal experience of Suez could only have been miniscule, but the mere mention of 'two great wars' and the defence of the realm was enough to confer a hazy credibility.

As the crisis escalated, it was this presumptive link in a worldwide familial chain that was increasingly called into question. Suez erupted at a time of relative calm within the Commonwealth, between the awkward wrangling over India's republican membership in the late 1940s and the bitter recriminations to come over South Africa's membership in the early 1960s. It also represented the first real test of the much-vaunted 'new Commonwealth' as a vehicle for British influence in world affairs. Only days before Nasser's move on Suez, the Commonwealth prime ministers had assembled in London for one of their periodic conferences, where the Suez Canal did not even figure on the agenda. But within a matter of months, the entire organization fractured along multiple fault lines as its members adopted deeply antagonistic positions. The embarrassing spectacle of a Commonwealth in disarray only hastened the fragmentation, undermining the sense of 'proprietorial pride' in Britain in particular.[71] It

Figure 10.3 Patrons at a pub in Wandsworth gather to watch Prime Minister Anthony Eden's television broadcast on the Suez Canal situation, 10 August 1956. Source: Bettmann/Getty Images.

was not just that the British Government found itself so starkly at odds with other member states, but also that attempts to bring the moral authority of the Commonwealth to bear so conspicuously failed. For each of its members, the crisis raised difficult questions about their identification with and obligations towards Britain, and hence their own stake in a rapidly receding British world.

For Australia under the arch-conservative Robert Menzies the position was clear. 'It is apparently not fashionable to speak of prestige', he declared in a BBC television broadcast in August 1956. 'Yet the fact remains that world peace and the efficacy of the United Nations Charter alike require that the British Commonwealth and, in particular, its greatest and most experienced member, the United Kingdom, should retain power, prestige, and moral influence.'[72] Thus, Menzies went out of his way to assist Eden, even to the point of leading an ill-fated mission to Cairo in September to mediate a solution. Although his activities attracted due criticism from the Labor opposition and elements within the Australian External Affairs Department, the broader public response was conditioned by an overwhelming pro-British sentiment and a 'special category of contempt' for Egyptians stemming from memories of Australian troop placements in Cairo in both world wars.[73] To the extent that Menzies paid a political price, it was largely on account of his vain (and ineffective) performance as a world statesman rather than any sense that he was supporting the wrong side. The outbreak of hostilities was greeted with general approval in the Australian press, diverging only on the question of means rather than ends. Thus while Sydney's *Daily Telegraph* revelled in Britain's unilateral show of force ('This is more like the old Britannia'), the verdict of its chief competitor, the *Sydney Morning Herald*, was to support 'what Britain had done' but to 'wish it had found a less devious way of doing it'.[74] Though few would have echoed Menzies' fawning assurance to Eden ('You must never entertain any doubts about the British quality of this country'), there was relatively little dissent about the importance of upholding global British 'prestige'.[75]

Broadly similar instincts determined the official response in New Zealand, where conservative Prime Minister Sidney Holland loudly applauded Britain's determination to resist Nasser. 'I believe that is the mood of the people of New Zealand', he assured parliament at the outset: 'Where Britain stands, we stand; where she goes, we go, in good times and bad.'[76] Yet the matter was complicated by the presence of New Zealand's recently purchased (and aptly named) cruiser *Royalist* as part of the Royal Navy's Mediterranean fleet (shortly due to depart for the South Pacific). Thus, the Holland Government was not only expected to support Britain's actions politically, but also militarily as an active partner in the naval strike force should armed intervention become necessary. Eden not only emphasized the 'strong political and stabilising effect' of the New Zealand cruiser, but also raised concerns that a decision to withdraw *Royalist* from active service might be 'misconstrued' as a lack of solidarity with Britain.[77] In a country almost unreasoningly sympathetic to all-things-British (Holland routinely referred to Britain as 'Home' in his correspondence with ministerial staff), this came close to emotional blackmail.[78] Eden not only grossly misled the New Zealand Government about the strategic importance of *Royalist* (falsely claiming that its anti-aircraft capability was indispensable) but also repeatedly evaded the New Zealanders' requests for more detail about the scope and nature of the action contemplated – to the point of declining to reveal the cruiser's precise location.[79]

Thus, while Eden's dealings with other Commonwealth leaders over Suez might charitably be termed 'unforthcoming', in the case of New Zealand it can only be regarded as the most wilful deceit. In effect, he sought to embroil New Zealand in the tripartite collusion against Egypt without the courtesy of an invitation to Sèvres. The prospect of taking direct part as a belligerent in the crisis reduced the New Zealand Cabinet to a state of near paralysis, loathe to shrink from such a signal test of their British loyalty but under heavy pressure from their legal and diplomatic advisers (who regarded any direct military involvement as 'international suicide') to do just that.[80] In the end they chose the most timorous option available: to allow *Royalist* to remain in the Mediterranean (and so avoid the stigma of visibly breaking ranks) while refusing permission to engage the ship directly in hostilities. Holland's tortured reply to Eden was hedged with the ritual platitudes of Greater Britain ('There is no need for me to stress New Zealand's strong ties of blood and Empire and our traditional attitude of standing by Britain in her difficulties') but the import of his message was clear. Despite the 'distressing predicament of wishing to stand by the United Kingdom, however great our misgivings on the wisdom of the present course of action', there could be no question of 'direct involvement in a war with Egypt'.[81] Asked by journalists afterwards whether he would care to repeat his earlier 'where Britain stands, we stand' motto, the prime minister responded with a curt 'no comment'.[82] The following week he disappeared on a four-day fishing trip to remote Lake Taupo – out of reach of telephone contact and about as far as he could possibly remove himself from where Britain stood. Meanwhile, the skipper of *Royalist*, Captain Peter Phipps, reluctantly disengaged from the fleet, noting ruefully in his log that the ship's withdrawal 'was a bitter disappointment and the reaction throughout the ship was savage resentment'.[83]

In what was becoming a recurring pattern, the South Asian Commonwealth took a very different view, roundly condemning the Suez intervention and laying the blame almost solely at the feet of Britain. In Pakistan, angry demonstrations erupted outside British missions in Lahore, Peshawar and Karachi (where the UK high commissioner kept a souvenir rock that sailed through his office window), while in 'East' Pakistan (as it was then known) the British Information Service in Dacca was burned to the ground. As Canadian diplomats reported, no French consular offices were subjected to any such treatment: 'Sir Anthony Eden in particular was represented as the villain of the piece.'[84] In a virulent editorial headed 'Hitler reborn', the Muslim League's English-language newspaper *Dawn* concluded: 'So this is the second "Elizabethan age" of which so much was talked about when Britain's young Queen ascended the throne!'[85] The disproportionate blame accorded to Britain suggested a weight of moral expectation far exceeding the standards applied to mere 'foreigners' such as the French.

India's Jawaharlal Nehru relayed similar misgivings in his many public statements. Although he duly reproached all three aggressors for committing a 'grosser case of naked aggression' than anything he had previously witnessed, he singled out the British for failing to live up to their own liberal ideals and trammelling over the 'close and friendly relations' with India. 'Because of this', he declaimed, 'my sorrow and distress are all the greater.'[86] In a private note to Eden he voiced his 'deepest regret' that Britain 'with her record of liberal policies' should have become party to an action that so flagrantly stirred the 'memories of colonialism'.[87] Over the ensuing months, Nehru would occasionally pour out his frustrations in his personal correspondence with his sister, Vijaya Lakshmi (then serving as Indian high commissioner in London):

> I am afraid that the British people have undergone a considerable transformation. They have lost their old balance. The process has been a gradual one, but the Suez crisis and what followed has upset their mental equilibrium completely. I am sorry. What we see in England today and especially in the Press there is some kind of perverted thinking backed by passion and preconceived notions.[88]

Needless to say, no such analysis of the 'mental equilibrium' of the French was forthcoming, either from Nehru or indeed the many other diagnosticians of Britain's collective neurosis. Although Guy Mollet and his Cabinet came in for abundant criticism, they were widely assumed to be behaving as one might naturally expect – with customary French arrogance and self-regard.[89] Only the British, it seemed, had breached the mythical standards of liberal restraint.

India's principled stand was to have a powerful influence on the Canadian government – perhaps the most intriguing of all Commonwealth protagonists in the Suez story. Liberal prime minister Louis St Laurent took something of a back seat to his external affairs minister, Lester Pearson, who would later be awarded the Nobel Peace Prize for his Suez exertions. The laws of geography dictated that Canada's vital interests were not bound up in the passage of goods and raw materials through the canal, and so Pearson became principally concerned with upholding the legitimacy of the United Nations and preserving the integrity and long-term viability of the Commonwealth.

Neither objective could be served by following Australia's and New Zealand's obsequious line, and thus an unprecedented breach between Ottawa and London became inevitable. St Laurent conveyed his displeasure to Eden even more acerbically than Nehru, detailing the many 'distressing', 'regrettable' and 'deplorable' consequences of Britain's actions and flatly rejecting the premise that either the Israeli attack or the Anglo-French response were legally or morally justified. Above all he made clear his resentment at being informed of the fiasco in his morning newspaper. Although Canada would work constructively towards amicable solutions, he signed off with an indignant flourish: 'I would not wish to leave you with the impression that as seen from here the situation appears other than tragic.'[90]

These exchanges can be seen in retrospect as marking the emergence of a radically reconfigured post-war Commonwealth. The Canadian high commissioner in New Delhi, Escott Reid, hammered away in his dispatches to Ottawa about the need for a new approach, asking whether the time had come 'for Canada to move away from the concept of a Commonwealth divided between the old and the new members, with all that that connotes?' He sketched out the bald realities of India's alienation from much of what the Commonwealth stood for, and the need for Canada to take a lead in steering a new course:

> Mr Nehru's faith in the judgement and integrity of the British Government has been shattered. There will be no short or easy healing of the breach . . . it is necessary that Mr Nehru be led gradually to form a new picture in his mind of the Commonwealth, not as a wheel with London at the hub, but as a complicated criss-cross pattern of relationships between the various capitals of the Commonwealth . . . In the period of readjustment in Mr Nehru's thinking about the Commonwealth, a special responsibility will devolve on Canada. Mr Nehru has no great respect for the Prime Ministers of Australia and New Zealand. He indeed contemplates their speeches and actions with a certain wry amusement. Even before Suez, he was inclined to think that Mr Menzies and Mr Holland were fit subjects for a Victorian museum. The way in which they both rallied to the defence of what he considers the treacherous aggression of Great Britain against Egypt has certainly not improved his opinion of them. Mr Nehru's relations with the Prime Minister of South Africa are correct but, of course, cold. This leaves Canada as the only white or 'old' member of the Commonwealth towards which Mr Nehru has friendly feelings.[91]

Reid's assessment was fundamentally self-serving, containing many of the old assumptions about the primacy conferred by Canada's 'white or "old"' status. But it was nevertheless wildly at variance with the world role nurtured by Eden and his supporters; one in which spheres of prestige and influence emanated outwards from Britain's shores through a series of strategic checkpoints of which Suez was the keystone. In this sense, the crisis clearly marked a psychological watershed, widely remarked on at the time. For Labour's John Strachey it proved 'once and for all' that expunging the adjective 'British' from Commonwealth nomenclature in 1949 had 'been no empty form, but had expressed the reality that Britain was becoming simply one member' of a multi-polar organization.[92]

But these undercurrents did not merely pose problems for Britain. In Canada too, Suez constituted 'a significant juncture in the dissolution of English-speaking Canada's self-representation as a British nation'.[93] The St Laurent government came under sustained attack from the opposition and wide sections of the English-speaking press for its failure to observe Canada's customary pro-British stance, with many viewing the crisis as part of a deeper Liberal conspiracy to strip Canada of its British heritage. Others detected a shameless kowtowing to Washington in the demeaning garb of a 'United States chore boy'.[94] Few took up a neutral pose, with the *Edmonton Journal* (at one extreme) accusing St Laurent of treating 'the complex and confusing Suez crisis as a magnificent opportunity to finish the job and break the Commonwealth altogether', and the *Toronto Daily Star* (at the other) congratulating the government for having 'the courage to put principles before sentiment' rather than following Canada's 'feeling for Britain'.[95] José Igartua's survey of some twenty-six English language dailies reveals an even split between wholesale support for the government's high-minded stand and scathing indictment of its betrayal of the mother country. But even the anti-Suez element tended to complain about a betrayal of British instincts, advocating a higher loyalty to the sacred principles of constitutional liberty (often aligning themselves with dissenting voices in the United Kingdom to reinforce their case).[96] This was broadly how Pearson himself viewed his breach with Britain over Suez in his own private post-mortem of the crisis, drafted on the basis of extensive and intimate conversations with senior British Cabinet figures. Though he readily deduced that France had certainly colluded with Israel over the invasion of Egypt, he could not bring himself to admit, despite abundant evidence to the contrary, that the British had in any way acted in bad faith.[97]

The overall effect of English-Canada's reckoning with its British conscience in 1956 is hard to pin down, such were the extremes of political and popular reaction. At the height of the crisis, the Conservative foreign affairs spokesman Howard Green called for a 'government which will not knife Canada's best friends in the back'.[98] Within six months, his wish was granted when he himself became Canada's new external affairs minister following a massive 8 per cent swing at the June 1957 election that bundled St Laurent out of office and installed the Conservatives under John G. Diefenbaker. Some have attributed the election result to a concerted voter backlash over Suez, and it might even be argued that the 1956 crisis was the occasion, not for the rollback of Canadian Britishness but its reinvigoration. Yet that somehow fails to ring true to the deeper flaws in a civic consensus that had been fraying at the edges for decades.

Contemporaries also found it difficult to assess the consequences of Suez with any precision. 'Disintegration' was the theme of an editorial in the *Ottawa Journal* in the immediate aftermath, grasping for some deeper meaning beneath the confusion and clamour: 'This was disintegration, not of the British Empire, but of the British "thing", that mysterious prestige which has arisen vaguely from Britain's being so long associated with so much that the world has been proud to call its best.'[99] The evident fumbling for an appropriate form of words spoke to the elusive nature of the object coming unstuck – a nebulous amalgam of thought, feeling and vague aspiration, now losing its capacity to cohere around a shared ideal.

'EDEN'S OTHER ISLAND': THE BALANCE SHEET OF SUEZ

In mid-summer 1956, only days prior to Nasser's takeover, a Royal Navy troopship passed through the Suez Canal, bound for Korea. Years later, Second Lieutenant John Wells waxed lyrical about the journey:

> From Southampton, we went down through the Bay of Biscay, and stopped at Gibraltar, with the Union Jack flying. We then went across the Mediterranean without stopping, and through the Suez Canal, just before the Suez crisis, and the next stop was Aden, with the Union Jack flying. Then we went to Colombo, with the Union Jack flying; then we went to Singapore, with the Union Jack flying; Hong Kong, the same; and we just didn't stop where there wasn't a British presence. And it just seemed perfectly natural.[100]

How quickly did this 'perfectly natural' vista fade from view? What role did the humiliation of Suez play in exploding the myth of Britain's ubiquitous 'presence' on the map? Historians have drawn remarkably divergent conclusions about the deeper social and political import of Suez. Peter Hennessy's is the more conventional view, maintaining that the latter months of 1956 'really do merit the over-used description of a "turning point". For almost everything that could have been in flux *was* in flux.' He marshals testimony from a wide range of contemporaries who recalled the stark realization that things 'wouldn't be the same' after Eden's dramatic denouement.[101] It is surely no coincidence that J. R. Seeley's 1883 classic, *The Expansion of England*, finally went out of print in 1956 – steeped as it was in the jaded conception of Greater Britain that Suez had so rudely punctured.

Yet much of this is informed by hindsight. For those who lived through it, the impact of Suez was uneven and fragmented, and it would take considerable time – possibly decades – for the 'lessons' to sink in.[102] Even trenchant critics such as the 'angry young men' (and women) of Tom Maschler's Suez-inspired volume *Declaration* (1957) could combine abundant scorn for the imperial delusions of the Eden government with reveries of their own about rebooting Britain's global prestige.[103] Tony Benn's remedy for a disillusioned generation was the cause of anti-colonialism itself, which would take them 'outside of themselves' and thus forestall the 'wildly frustrated and defeatist and bitter and apathetic' fate of relegation to the status of a 'little Denmark'. In a turn of phrase worthy of Peter Fleming himself, he called for 'a widening of Britain's horizons so that we can get satisfaction from the achievements of others'.[104]

Many did, in fact, take the opportunity to get 'outside of themselves' – either by way of 'staying on' in technical and advisory roles after independence, or by enlisting in one of the many overseas development charities that mushroomed in these years. This partly reflected a wider international fashion for volunteer aid work but there were also distinctively British variations on the theme. Voluntary Service Overseas (VSO), for example, was founded in 1958 for the express purpose of providing a new outlet for Britain's youth at a time when National Service was being phased out and the opportunities for colonial service were drastically curtailed. Widely celebrated as the 'new heroes of a post-imperial age', the young VSO recruits were meant to experience the kind of hard physical and psychological challenges that seemed no longer available in an affluent, welfare state.[105] Into the 1960s, emigration rates from the United Kingdom skyrocketed – particularly to Australia and Canada – supported by a variety of assisted passage schemes that persisted long after the formal liquidation of empire.[106] Viewed in this light, Peter Fleming's evocation of a people 'more out of touch with the rest of the world than they have been for several generations' surely counts as a gross mischaracterization. His lament for lost horizons was not meant to be taken literally, however. It was more about loss of authority and a greatly diminished capacity to control events beyond Britain's receding frontiers – which the acid test of Suez had so starkly exposed.

For the prime minister at the centre of it all, broken and discredited in his post-Suez recuperation, one final irony lay in store – not in Canada, Australia, or South Asia but in the small Caribbean town of Oracabessa on Jamaica's verdant north-east coast. It was here on 18 November 1956 that a telegram

318

arrived from London: 'Three important friends arrive November twenty-second for three weeks visit STOP Please ... get extra staff prepare house STOP Clean yard and drive STOP.' The sender was Ian Fleming, now on his fifth Bond novel in less than four years, anxiously preparing his winter writing retreat 'Goldeneye' for Eden's impending convalescence. Fleming's wife Ann was an old friend of Clarissa Eden (the godmother of the Flemings' only son Caspar), and the previous autumn the Flemings had paid the prime ministerial couple a visit at Chequers. So, when doctors ordered the overwrought Eden to take an extended break from 10 Downing Street to relieve the strain on his health, Oracabessa seemed a natural choice. Arrangements were finalized through Fleming's secretary (with the improbably Bond-esque name, Una Trueblood) and an imposing white Cadillac was put at the prime minister's disposal by Jamaica's chief minister, Norman Manley. But apart from the occasional visit from the British governor and Fleming's neighbour, Noël Coward (himself an avowed Suez 'hawk'), the couple spent three weeks in total seclusion. 'Everything here more wonderful than we expected. A thousand thanks' cabled Clarissa to her suitably gratified hosts.[107]

Figure 10.4 Spy novelist Ian Fleming in February 1964 on the beach at his Jamaica home 'Goldeneye', which he offered to his ailing friend, Prime Minister Anthony Eden, in November 1956. Source: Hulton Archive/Getty Images.

This fortuitous collision of disparate worlds – high politics and pulp fiction – may seem arbitrary, even trivial; and of little value to the historian.[108] But there was nothing arbitrary about the intricate social and political web of 1950s Britain. This was the 'world of the magic circle', the meshwork of personal and professional intimacy at the helm of post-war Britain, comprising a privileged matrix of patronage bound up in shared tastes, assumptions, social background and extended horizons.[109] The British press certainly had little difficulty in placing a Tory prime minister in Fleming's fantasy world, indulging in the easy naturalization of the West Indian setting. 'Eden reaches Eden' trumpeted the *Daily Mail*, positively revelling in the 'whitewashed bungalow', the 'sheltering palms' and 'away from it all' ambience. In a series of despatches, readers were invited to join the *Mail*'s correspondent on an 'escapist mission' that would not only bring welcome respite to the war-weary prime minister but also 'take you away too' on a 'passport from the crises and November Britain'. 'Eden's other island' was the whimsical byline for each daily instalment, regaling readers with the prime minister's taxing schedule of swimming, fishing and sunbathing on the beach, punctuated by 'hearty' breakfasts and ample helpings of 'lobster baked in the shell'.[110] Goldeneye, much like the Bond novels themselves, combined a 'reassuring conservatism' with a hint of dangerous sensuality; or as Fleming himself termed it, a 'certain disciplined exoticism'.[111] Despite the body blow to Britain's global reach in 1956, Eden's own mental horizons seemed neither shaken nor stirred; the inimitable Rangoon man.

Behind the scenes, however, distinct rumblings could be heard in the party and parliament that the timing and coordinates of Eden's tropical hideaway were somehow a bit off. 'Why, if he was only tired, did he have to go to Jamaica?', was the 'whispered question' that lingered in Eden's absence.[112] His senior Foreign Office adviser, Evelyn Shuckburgh, thought the Jamaican jaunt incredibly ill-judged, indeed 'the most extraordinary feature of the whole thing . . . The captain leaves the sinking ship which he has steered personally onto the rocks.'[113] One particularly wry headline upon Eden's return in mid-December underscored the anomaly: 'Prime Minister visits Britain'.[114] Three weeks later he relinquished the premiership, 'a sacrificial figure for the nation's illusions'.[115]

––––––––––◆––––––––––

In other words, Suez raised a gamut of questions that 'hung in the air', in David Marquand's pungent phrase, 'like birds of prey'.[116] The final run-down of Britain's overseas military commitments would be played out in the shadow of Suez, but over a longer timescale and according to factors that remained largely unforeseen in 1956. John Darwin sees in this something of a conundrum: Suez may have ushered in an alternative view of the world, 'no longer "Great", no longer imperial', yet there remained a dogged recidivism among the political classes that screened out inconvenient truths, clinging to the 'extraordinary faith that, with its sails duly trimmed, Britain must remain a world power'.[117] It fell to the Labour Government of Harold Wilson to grapple with the final throes of Britain's outpost mentality in the 1960s, and Wilson himself to issue the last-ditch boast in June 1965 that 'Britain's frontiers are on the Himalayas'.[118] Such absurdities could only make sense in a country long accustomed to projecting its borders far ahead of itself; a habit that had become distinctly antiquated long before Labour assumed office.

It was during the Wilson years that a new slogan entered the political lexicon: 'East of Suez', now cast as Britain's indispensable new 'role'; one that was widely presumed (largely because the phrase was pilfered from Kipling) to have deep historical resonances.[119] In reality, it was a latter-day improvisation cobbled together from the offcuts of empire – the outposts of the old Indian Raj in the Persian Gulf and Malaya that lingered long after the main game had been lost.[120] The 'East of Suez' policy flowed directly from the debacle of 1956; at once a flawed attempt to invest obsolete 'interests' with contemporary meaning and a hazy euphemism for empire at a time when the imperial tag had become taboo.

No sooner had Wilson popularized the term than he unwittingly 'made it a matter of intense scrutiny and debate', at a time when the economic burden of maintaining a global defence posture had become intolerable.[121] The writing was already on the wall with the February 1966 Defence White Paper – an attempt to reinforce the rhetoric of Britain's 'world role' while making drastic reductions to naval expenditure to shore up an embattled pound. It soon proved woefully inadequate for either purpose. The fateful decision to cancel Britain's aircraft carrier programme was particularly heavy with symbolism, rendering obsolete any meaningful long-range British defence capacity. It prompted the dramatic resignation of First Sea Lord Admiral David Luce, as well as Minister for the Navy Christopher Mayhew, unable to accept a policy that permitted 'only an in-between posture east of Suez'.[122] Exactly ten years after his BBC television special *We the British, Are We in Decline?*, Mayhew seemed to have found his answer.

Right down to the moment when Wilson was forced to abandon entirely Britain's defence posture East of Suez in January 1968, the waterway linking the Mediterranean and the Red Sea retained a residual capacity to order

Britain's world. To be sure, British governments of all shades have continued ever since to place a high premium on global 'influence' and 'prestige' and seek to play a prominent role in international affairs.[123] But the one-time axiom of maintaining a 'British presence' at multiple staging posts around the world soon fell into disuse – a development that can be traced with reasonable precision to the last retrenchments East of Suez in the late 1960s. Philip Larkin marked the occasion with 'Homage to a Government' (1969), the middle stanza conveying something of the grudging resignation:

> It's hard to say who wanted it to happen,
> But now it's been decided nobody minds.
> The places are a long way off, not here,
> Which is all right, and from what we hear
> The soldiers there only made trouble happen.
> Next year we shall be easier in our minds.[124]

Peace of mind, however, was harder to come by. In late summer 1971, John Osborne staged a new play at London's Royal Court theatre, mysteriously titled *West of Suez*. The celebrated playwright's earlier, 1957 production of *The Entertainer* (with Laurence Olivier's iconic turn in the title role) had delivered a piercing indictment of the Suez crisis, famously depicting the nation-in-microcosm as a crumbling music hall wracked with a bitter nostalgia. But in contrast to the much-vaunted 'anger' and unhinged energy of 1957, *West of Suez* struck an altogether different note. Set on an unnamed Caribbean Island ('neither Africa nor Europe, but some of both, also less than both'), the protagonists are a 'clutch of whites' stranded in the wake of empire. Expatriate author Wyatt Gillman, his four daughters (each born in a different colony), their 'ineffably bored' husbands and a retired brigadier while away their days in dreary, pampered inertia. Whereas once the sun never set, here the set never changes as the characters stroll on and off with a desultory aimlessness. The atmosphere is cloying, claustrophobic – constrained by the truncated purview of a disinherited clique. Taken to task by lukewarm reviewers for mourning a lost colonial vocation, Osborne protested that his real purpose was to explore the 'decaying of tongues ... not just of colonial empires but of emotional empires'. Yet the difficulty surely was distinguishing between the two – the loss of traction in the physical world inducing a debilitating confinement of the spirit. The resulting bewilderment spills over in the final scene, with Wyatt's dying lament: 'Something started without me. Too slow. Never got off the old ground. Never got off the ground. Wasn't sure about the ground at all.'[125]

11

BACKING LITTLE BRITAIN: DISTEMPERS

In the early hours of New Year's Day 1968, some two hundred and forty employees of a South London heating factory clocked into work half an hour early. Braving icy conditions on a day normally associated with absenteeism, the dedicated workers had agreed upon a radical New Year's resolution – to put in an extra thirty minutes each day 'to help put the country back on its feet'.[1] The next morning, a further five hundred of their colleagues at the company's Hampshire plant followed suit, in defiance of their local union's opposition to giving 'buckshee half-hours' to their employer.[2] Within a matter of days, the sudden craze for unpaid overtime had spread to companies all over England, manufacturing everything from carbides to caravans, building materials, fashion accessories, aircraft equipment, headboards, electric pumps, plastics, and meat pies. After years of consistently bad tidings, here was a homespun, all-in push to remedy the nation's ailments. 'This is the Way Ahead', trumpeted the *Daily Mail*: 'Against all the odds and the cynicisms and overwhelming difficulties, Britain can shake off this malady for good and all.'[3] The Confederation of British Industry concurred: 'We think the plan is a hell of a good one.'[4]

The impetus came from an unlikely source – the Orders Department of the Colt Heating and Ventilation Company in the genteel suburb of Surbiton – where five resolute women aged between fifteen and twenty-one asked themselves, 'How Can WE Put This Right?'[5] Responding to an end-of-year exhortation from their sales director to steer away from 'soul-destroying' conversations about Britain's economic woes and 'work just that bit harder in the new year', the soon-to-be-famous five fell upon the idea of sacrificing half an hour each day.[6] A weekend brainstorm produced a battle plan and a serviceable slogan: 'I'm Backing Britain' (the words emblazoned across the horizontal band of a Union Jack). Their modest aim was to 'be the first Company to start the ball rolling' but Valerie White, Joan Southwell, Carol Ann Fry, Christine French and Brenda Mumford could never have anticipated the scale or the swiftness of the response.[7] At a stroke they were thrust into the public glare as the standard bearers of a new spirit of moral

Figure 11.1 The Surbiton Five unveiling their 'I'm Backing Britain' banner, January 1968. From left: Carol Ann Fry, Valerie White, Joan Southwell, Christine French and Brenda Mumford. Source: Shutterstock:1344960a.

uplift. By the end of the week they had contacted more than 40,000 workers throughout the country and secured delivery of 100,000 campaign badges free of charge from a Lincolnshire firm (its workers donating an extra half hour each day to complete the order).[8]

Before long, 'I'm Backing Britain' bumper stickers, mugs, aprons, carry bags and other merchandise were in wide circulation, and a 'Backing Britain' postmark was introduced by the Royal Mail. The Duke of Edinburgh heralded the initiative as the perfect way to 'lick all of our problems', while the Wilson government extolled the 'wholesome, healthy' dedication of its founders.[9] Amid persistent demands for press and television interviews, 'the girls' (as they were invariably dubbed) contended with an avalanche of incoming mail, phone calls and telegrams congratulating them on their selfless dedication, including offers of cash, free holidays, driving lessons and even propositions of marriage – all judiciously declined.

Into the second week of January, the remit widened to include a range of patriotic activities other than working for free. Consumers were enjoined to 'buy British' while companies endeavoured to cut prices for British goods and services (one greengrocer in Kent draping his entire shop in 'Backing Britain' memorabilia). A Surrey hairdresser advertised 'Back Britain Perms on the Cheap' as restaurant owners and hoteliers vied for custom with reduced rates for patrons sporting the 'I'm Backing Britain' badge.[10]

The benefits multiplied when the vicar of Shepherd's Bush pinned one to his cassock and appealed to his congregation, 'Any young couple wearing the same badge as myself can get married at a ten per cent discount.'[11] Housewives were informed that they, too, could earn the right to wear the badge by 'getting their husbands to work half an hour early' and a betting shop in Birmingham presumed to do its bit for productivity by extending opening hours (though without lengthening the odds for badge-bearing punters).[12] Spontaneous contributions suddenly poured into the UK Exchequer from donors of all ages in the form of cheques, postal orders, cash enclosures, even pieces of gold (one donor reminding the chancellor that 'it is for our country and is not a personal present').[13]

Meanwhile the music industry did its bit to amplify the new optimism, with the release of at least two would-be 'Backing Britain' anthems, one recorded within a matter of days by popular entertainer Bruce Forsyth who somewhat artlessly reduced the campaign to its essentials:

> In offices and factories, up and down the country
> an extra half an hour is all we need each day.
> In shops and supermarkets, everybody's started,
> to work a little more without the pay.

His efforts did little to disturb the charts. Nor for that matter did beat rock sensation Herman's Hermits when they announced that all royalties for their new single *I Can Take or Leave Your Loving* would be donated to HM Treasury.[14] Nevertheless, there was an undeniable confluence of popular energy and media fascination. As Bernard Levin recalled: 'Instantly, springing from nowhere like mushrooms after a downpour, the slogan "I'm backing Britain" was ... to be seen and heard everywhere.'[15] Such was the blanket coverage that Cecil Day-Lewis, recently elevated to the royal sinecure of Poet Laureate, dedicated five stanzas to the new civic ardour. Penned with undue haste at the urging of the *Daily Mail*, 'Then and Now' evoked the wartime spirit of grit and resolve:

> Do you remember those mornings after the blitzes
> When the living picked themselves up and went on living –
> Living, not on the past, but with an exhilaration
> Of purpose, a new neighbourliness of danger?

Although the Surbiton typists could have no memory of those dark days, they were nonetheless 'graced with that old selflessness ... Eager to rescue our dear life's buried promise'. As analogies go, it was at the extravagant end of the scale, but by no means uniquely so. The deluge of mail and telegrams only accentuated the moral stakes, including one from the governor of Tasmania stating that the entire island was 'thrilled at the finest action since the Battle of Britain'.[16] Even the ageing A. J. Toynbee – the doyen of 'challenge and response' social theory – recorded how his 'spirits rose' when he heard of the Surbiton scheme: 'Perhaps we were rising to the occasion as we did in 1940 (then, too, at the thirteenth hour).'[17] The Blitz, Dunkirk, 'the Few' – these became the commonplace registers of Backing Britain's emotional resonance, summoning a memory store of past perils to inspire a new generation.

By any yardstick, it was a peculiar episode in post-war Britain, one in which the abstract dilemmas of macro-economic performance collided with popular sentiment in unanticipated ways. Although 'I'm Backing Britain' would soon run into a thicket of adversity, its early capacity to mobilize latent community attitudes and generate a mass following seems extraordinary in retrospect. In most accounts, the recent shock of the November 1967 sterling crisis affords sufficient explanation for the highly receptive public mood.[18] And to be sure, the Wilson government's agonizing decision only six weeks earlier to slash the value of the pound by nearly 15 per cent aroused deep public misgivings at the time. Another factor was the sheer novelty of the fresh-faced instigators themselves, several still in their teens, offering an alluringly simple solution to problems normally associated with the pin-striped doyens of the City and Westminster. As 16-year-old Carol Ann Fry confessed: 'People's impressions of typists ... seems to be of birdbrains doing their nails all day', and it was precisely because 'normally nobody takes much notice of what we say' that their activities seemed so irresistibly newsworthy.[19]

Yet the Backing Britain volunteers were more than mere 'mushrooms after a downpour', spurred to action by the immediate economic travails of 1967. The Surbiton women never seriously entertained ambitions of restoring Britain's ailing current account deficit or propping up the pound. Nor were they responding to any immediate economic downturn in their own company, which had just recorded healthy annual growth figures to the tune of 7 per cent.[20] Theirs was an appeal to the ailing national psyche – a less tangible complex of imagined shortcomings that only dimly registered in the annual balance sheet. As one of them frankly explained: 'We thought if people saw that young people were so worried about Britain they were offering to work more they would realise that something must be wrong.'[21] These were fundamentally vague apprehensions formed over a much longer timescale, harking back more than a decade against a backdrop of tectonic shifts in Britain's global fortunes. It was in the late 1950s that the so-called

'What's Wrong with Britain' genre of political and social commentary spilled over into the laughter and ridicule of the 'satire boom' and the scandalous revelations of the 1963 Profumo affair. Throughout the decade, forecasting Britain's terminal decline became part of everyday political life, vividly encapsulated in the 1967 outburst of Tory grandee Quintin Hogg: 'Can anyone deny that the British people is in the act of destroying itself: and will surely do so if we go on as at present?'[22] Viewed in this broader light, 'I'm Backing Britain' was a makeshift effort to quell the climate of national pessimism anchored in perceptions of Britain's diminished global standing.

What's more, the mood of national introspection was not confined to 1960s Britain but affected a much wider constituency grappling with the manifold disorientations of empire's end. Among the scattered remnants of a British world – especially in Australia, Canada and New Zealand – a proclivity for diagnosing national deficiencies became a recurring feature of the broader political culture. Yet such was the focus on national maladies that these wider commonalities and their shared sources of discontent were almost never remarked upon – even as the practitioners borrowed freely from each other's rhetorical templates. This chapter, then, takes stock of the wider anxieties about the 'state of the nation' that converged around the diminished certainties of Greater Britain. The prognostics of decline, the repudiations of the past and the protracted rummaging around for alternative futures were sustained by a shared predicament. Though rarely acknowledged outwardly, it was the diminished prospects for wider racial endeavour that stoked the appetite for social self-critique, and the attendant scramble for alternative markers of public esteem and collective purpose.

GREAT BRITAIN OR LITTLE ENGLAND?

When *The Guardian*'s international editor Anthony Hartley visited Amsterdam in November 1958, he was immediately struck by the equanimity and quiet confidence of the local citizenry. It seemed such a bold contrast to the social and political temper of Britain that he could not help contemplating the underlying cause: 'They have learned to live in Europe as mere Europeans, and – let us make no mistake – that is the way we ourselves and every ex-colonial Power will have to live in the not-so-distant future.'[23] Hartley marvelled at the extraordinary success of the Dutch in relinquishing an empire state of mind, not only in puncturing the moral imperatives of their civilizing mission overseas but also in their ready embrace of a new, downscaled model of the post-imperial nation. He followed up five years later with a short but illuminating book, *A State of England* (1963), by which time Britain had caught up with the Netherlands in the decolonization stakes. But rather than produce the same beneficial effects, the liquidation of the empire's residual holdings had merely compounded 'a narrowing of horizons and a sense of frustration in English society'.[24] Permeating Hartley's diagnosis were the metaphors of marginalization and retreat, evoking a people 'whose assets of self-respect and conscious international virtue were considerably wasted'.[25]

Hartley was saying nothing intrinsically new. Dean Acheson's 1962 aphorism about a country that had 'lost an Empire, but not yet found a role' seemed to touch a nerve, and remains one of the more quoted one-liners of the decade. 'I have the impression ... that this nation as a whole does not at the moment know where it is going', lamented Liberal peer Gladwyn Jebb to the House of Lords in January 1961, striking much the same pose as the former US secretary of state: 'The process of "de-colonization", as it is called, however desirable and necessary, seems to have left us without any very positive and generally accepted notion of our position in the world.'[26] The ensuing debate elicited an indignant rebuttal from Conservative whip Lord Hastings who managed to flaunt all the tell-tale symptoms of not-yet-finding-a-role in his evocation of Britain as 'a pride of lions roaring their challenge in the face of the adversary'.[27]

Such exchanges were to become emblematic of a time when leading writers, scientists, soothsayers and social commentators conducted a sustained dissection of the nation's shortcomings. From the early 1960s, the first of a steady stream of 'state-of-the-nation' books began to appear, bearing titles that strove to outdo one another in grim foreboding – from Michael Shanks's *The Stagnant Society* in 1961 to Paul Einzig's *Decline and Fall?* at the close of the decade.[28] Arthur Koestler's *Suicide of a Nation?* (1963) pitched its claim at the upper end of the misery scale, while Penguin opted for the more prosaic 'What's Wrong with Britain?' for a series of short books that gnawed persistently at the national fabric.[29] Few of these works were entirely bereft of hope (even Shanks conceded that his title was 'a harsh ... and in some ways unjust one'); indeed, most of them urged that it was 'not too late' for remedial action. But whatever the intent, talking up Britain's downside clearly brought buoyant returns (*The Stagnant Society*, for example, shifted a not-so-stagnant 60,000 copies), which inevitably prompted publishers to commission more of the same. Such was the persistent pall of gloom that Peter Donaldson found it necessary to preface his 1965 *Guide to the British Economy* with the disclaimer that it was 'certainly not intended as another of those "state-of-the-nation" assessments which are currently so much in vogue'.[30]

By no means all of these bleak forecasts were fixated on Britain's diminished global standing. Much of the conversation was remarkably unfocused, striking out in every conceivable direction at all manner of contemporary ills. In what has been described as 'the first full-dress statement' of the new despondency, Labour's Anthony Crosland racked up a bewildering array of grievances in the October 1960 issue of *Encounter*. 'A dogged resistance to change now blankets every segment of our national life', he grimly observed. 'A middle-aged conservatism, parochial and complacent, has settled over the country; and it is hard to find a single sphere in which Britain is pre-eminently in the forefront.'[31] Productivity, export performance, technological innovation, trade unions, parliament, the civil service, the universities, the transport system, attitudes to homosexuality, architecture and town planning were all thrown in to the turbulent mix. Although he also alluded to the embarrassment of playing 'the obsolete role of an imperial power', this was largely obscured by the bewildering 'blanket' of national deficiencies.

Although much of the critique was aimed at the underperformance of the British economy – its halting productivity, poor export returns and chronic underinvestment in manufacturing – even here the lines were blurred by a raft of ill-defined cultural deficiencies. Principal among these was an archaic social hierarchy that protected the inherited wealth, titles and privileges of an out-of-touch ruling elite. C. P. Snow's famous excoriation of a 'traditional culture' that strangled initiative by rewarding literary and cultural pursuits at the expense of science and technology was the most prominent landmark in a wide-ranging critique of the amateurism and stuffiness of Britain's class system.[32] A few years earlier, the notion of a British 'establishment' had gained currency – an invisible clique who wielded authority and influence through a carefully cultivated web of social connections.[33] It was this charmed circle that came under increasing scrutiny as the failures of the post-war era seemed to grow steadily more apparent. In particular, Harold Macmillan's Conservative government came to represent all that seemed to have gone wrong, lambasted as an assortment of 'blimps, permanently stranded in Edwardian England, who had somehow contrived to miss the fast train to the second half of the twentieth century'.[34]

Such was the consensus that virtually no one cared to question the underlying premise. 'Something' was presumed to be endemically defective, and it was only left to debate the underlying causes. Much of the rhetoric tended to distort the overall picture of the country's real material prosperity, due to an overreliance on relative economic disparities (Britain's declining share of world trade, for example) and an almost wilful blindness to the many achievements of the era across a broad spectrum of social and economic indicators. Unprecedented advances in welfare provision, employment levels, consumption, poverty alleviation, housing and education, were habitually overlooked in 'state of the nation' accounting.[35] Viewed over a longer perspective, Britain achieved perfectly respectable rates of economic growth throughout the 1950s and 1960s and to the extent that these lagged behind their major competitors in Europe and the United States, it was largely due to global structural adjustments beyond the capacity of any ruling 'establishment' to rectify. If there were systemic failures, these stemmed as much from political as economic flaws, notably the exaltation of the pound as a global reserve currency and the bipartisan commitment to maintaining overseas defence commitments which placed severe burdens on an otherwise sustainable economic foundation.[36]

The phenomenon of 'declinism', then, needs to be understood in terms of a more fluid set of assumptions shaping popular perceptions of the nation's wellbeing – a point freely conceded by a number of the declinists themselves. Michael Shanks was quite explicit that Britain's underlying malaise was 'not a question of institutions or economics at all. It concerns our national character, the way we behave and feel towards each other as a people.'[37] Arguing about British decline was about cultivating a psychological climate for reform, furnishing powerful rhetorical leverage for those seeking far-reaching political and social change.[38] The Labour Party's 'white heat' election campaign that secured Harold Wilson's historic win in 1964 was the culmination of years of highly effective stigmatization of Macmillan's Tories as the party of archaic values, economic mismanagement and studied neglect. But the spectre of decline could mean a host of other things to rival interest groups: a sense of moral panic in an increasingly permissive society; concern about the corrosive social effects of the faltering 'old industries' (textiles, coal, steel and shipbuilding); or indeed, anxieties about Britain's capacity to compete with the Soviet-style planned economy.

The abiding point of reference, however, was the self-evident setting of the imperial sun – providing a meta-index of national failure that was instantly relatable to all. At a time when the empire had lost all political legitimacy (mourned openly, only by the most diehard traditionalists), it became all the more urgent to root out imperial values still corroding the system from within. Hugh Thomas exemplified the technique in his withering verdict on a public school system geared 'to provide a continuous stream of socially gifted and athletic amateurs to act as proconsuls in ... an empire that no longer exists'.[39] With the requisite dose of irony, a passing reference to fallen empires could invoke the aura of national decline far more efficiently than any quantitative survey or statistical chart. Arthur Koestler's modest attempt at questioning the premise ('what ails Britain is not the loss of empire but the loss of initiative') was promptly negated by the majority of his own contributors to *Suicide of a Nation?*, who continued to wax breezily about 'the hangover of "Empire"', 'an empire now on which the sun never rises', the 'painful predicament ... of an ex-imperial nation' and the 'damage the gentle passing of empire has done to the spirit of our own islands'.[40]

By far the most influential of these works was Anthony Sampson's 1961 bestseller, *Anatomy of Britain* – a comprehensive guide to the myriad individuals in politics, business, industry, education, finance, the media and the military who controlled the sinews of power. More than any other single intervention, Sampson's book cemented the idea that Britain's maladies were the product of an ailing body politic – pioneering the use of medical metaphors to expose a whole physiology of congenital defects. The Duke of Edinburgh himself lent his authority to the idea on the dust-jacket: 'Just at this moment we are suffering a national defeat comparable to any lost military campaign, and, what's more, it is self-inflicted.' Sampson's abiding question, 'Who runs Britain?', flowed from the conviction that, whoever it was, they were failing miserably and needed putting out to pasture. Yet when it came to identifying the root cause, he invariably cast his eye far from Britain's shores. 'It is hardly surprising', he ventured, 'that, in twenty years since the war, Britain should have felt confused about her purpose – with those acres of red on the map dwindling, the mission of the war dissolving, and the whole imperial mythology of battleships, governors and generals gone for ever.'[41] Similar reflexes surfaced in his many interviews with prominent business and political figures such as Colonial Secretary Ian Macleod, where the panorama of imperial retreat again furnished a serviceable backdrop. Responding with remarkable candour to a question about why Britain had 'been in the doldrums for some time', the minister had this to offer:

> You see, I think it's very difficult for people in Britain, and this certainly includes myself, to accept the fact that we aren't now the power we once were. Most of us, even people like myself in their forties, remember the day when at school a third or a quarter of the map was coloured red, and you did get some sort of consolation for being in this bright little, tight little island, and all the old jingo phrases, because of the very vastness of the empire, of which Britain was not only the head but the owner. Now all that is changing.[42]

Macleod was quick to add that change was 'a very exciting thing', performing the customary doublethink of 1960s progressives whose very social conditioning obliged them to welcome the long-awaited liberation of the colonial empire while harbouring unexamined hankerings for the 'consolation of vastness'.

There was something distinctly 'respectable' about 'What's Wrong with Britain' writing, appealing principally (if ironically) to the relatively well-off, tertiary educated middle class reaping the benefits of post-war affluence. As such, they became easy targets of satire, such as Bernard Levin's gentle send up of the 'prophets of doom . . . numerous as weeds in a graveyard and about as cheerful . . . warning and recommending, exhorting and condemning, admonishing and insisting, telling what we must do to be saved and informing us the end was nigh, in some cases that the end was nigh even if we did what we must to be saved'.[43] What passed largely unnoticed, however, was the almost complete lack of engagement with new critical perspectives from African and Caribbean intellectuals probing the sources of racial iniquity in 1960s Britain. Names such as George Lamming, Stuart Hall, and Claudia Jones were absent from the line-up, as though operating in an entirely different sphere – just as wider international critiques of the enduring mentalities of colonialism (Nkrumah, Césaire, Memmi, Fanon) completely failed to resonate. It was a glaring omission in a genre that otherwise dwelt at length on the unextinguished embers of empire. It seems never to have occurred to Michael Shanks, for example, to consider race relations at all in *The Stagnant Society* (despite chapter headings such as 'The Social Barrier', 'Anglo-Saxon Attitudes', '"Them" and "Us"' and 'Equal and Dynamic?'). But a fleeting remark in his closing statement revealed the presumptive whiteness of his readership:

> What sort of an island do we want to be? ... A lotus island of easy, tolerant ways, bathed in the golden glow of an imperial sunset, shielded from discontent by a threadbare welfare state and an acceptance of genteel poverty? Or the tough, dynamic race we have been in the past, striving always to better ourselves, seeking new worlds to conquer in place of those we have lost, ready to accept growing pains as the price for growth?[44]

For all the overt applause for the historic milestone of decolonization, an expectation of British primacy remained. Dynamism, toughness, and self-improvement could still be prized as inherently racial qualities, conferring a unique flair for audacity and conquest. It was a rare confession of the crisis of racial authority that hovered warily between the lines.

This was the fundamental irony of 'What's Wrong with Britain' writing. Unable to resist past greatness as the measure of contemporary ills, these works nevertheless disowned the historical scourge of colonialism. Aspiring to the vision and purpose of old, they could still rail against a debilitating imperial nostalgia. For Anthony Hartley, it was precisely those who had championed the post-Suez retreat from empire who were most severely afflicted, because they 'could hardly admit even to themselves that they regretted the past'.[45] He pinpointed the real source of bewilderment for the contemporary English intellectual: 'How to give his own position its necessary universality from within a society which was no longer the centre of the world picture, how to move on the earth without a fixed point on which to support himself.'[46] It was the original conceit of Greater Britain, where reverence for constitutional liberties always rested uneasily with a presumptive racial pre-eminence. It would produce a special kind of inertia at a time when imperial and racial aspirations could no longer be outwardly indulged.

'THE COMFORT OF CLEAVING TO SOMETHING BIGGER': ANTIPODEAN ECHOES

By 1963, the surge in 'state of the nation' writing had acquired all the attributes of a bandwagon. Critics such as Henry Fairlie lost no time pointing this out, savaging the entire genre as easy editorial fodder – the product 'of a certain kind of noise', vaguely reminiscent of Tigger's battle cry 'worraworraworraworraworra' in *The House at Pooh Corner*.[47] Ever attuned to the eddies of fashion, the satirical magazine *Private Eye* published an 'All-Purpose "What's Wrong With Britain" Graph' – plotting a neat sequence of downward trajectories that could reliably gauge any conceivable index of national decline. One group of eighteen writers led by Arthur Seldon compiled a spirited riposte, *The Rebirth of Britain*, with the aim of refuting 'the moan that "Britain has had it"' (though unwittingly subverting their cause by furnishing countless remedies of their own for the nation's perceived flaws).[48] As *The Economist* wryly remarked, any overseas visitor to London in 1963 could hardly avoid being 'hit between the eyes by this passionate soul searching ... The British have become, suddenly, the most introspective people on earth.'[49]

One such visitor was the forty-one-year-old Australian writer and editor Donald Horne, who arrived in the middle of 1963 having just completed a two-page synopsis for a work of introspection of his own. Horne was one of the leading lights of a new brand of critical journalism in Australia, starting out in Britain before returning to Sydney in the mid-1950s to edit *The Observer* (not to be confused with its UK namesake) and the veteran news magazine *The Bulletin*. Although politically conservative, he was a devotee of a certain liberal humanism and an avowed sceptic, sharing much in common with the new progressive voices in Britain associated with *The Economist*, *Encounter* and *The Spectator*. In late 1962 he was approached by representatives of Penguin's new branch office in South Melbourne with a novel proposition: 'Our English people are very keen to have a fairly useful critical survey of Australia.'[50]

The idea was cast in the mould of Penguin's UK 'Specials' series, anticipating that 'it could be a real winner' in the light of the extraordinary success and 'wide international influence' that the 'English "specials"' had achieved. The timing of Horne's arrival in London could not have afforded a more thorough immersion in the climate of critical self-examination.[51] Little is known of his visit – whom he associated with, what he read or even how long he stayed – but he left a small hint in his memoirs that it was the experience of 'wandering around the world talking about Australia with dozens of people' in 1963 that 'made writing a book about it seem more likely'.[52] It is clear that he absorbed something of the agitated state of UK political and social commentary, noting the jarring contrast between the vastly improved material conditions of ordinary people and the doomsday prophecies of the intellectuals. 'The fact that Average Britons seemed to be mildly pleased with life', he recalled years later, 'was taken as evidence of moral decay, even of the suicide of a nation.'[53] It was during his London sojourn that Horne despatched the prospectus for his book to Penguin Australia, and immediately on his return in October 1963 he signed the contract for what would become his enduring literary achievement: *The Lucky Country: Australia in the Sixties*.[54]

Appearing in December 1964, Horne's searing critique was an instant publishing sensation, selling out its initial print-run in only nine days and kick-starting an extended debate on the dilemmas of contemporary Australia. Best remembered for the author's pithy assessment that 'Australia is a lucky country run mainly by second-rate people who share its luck' (implying throughout that their good fortune was due to expire), the book delivered a broadside against the philistinism and provincialism of an Australia mired in the values and aspirations of a bygone age. Chief among the principal targets was the prime minister of the day, Sir Robert Menzies, whom Horne caricatured as 'more British than the British, always running several years behind London, expressing dreams of Commonwealth that had something of the flavour of progressive discussion in 1908'.[55] Like a growing number of his contemporaries, Horne diagnosed a 'general "national identity" crisis' that hinged on the 'sudden shocks of reorientation' precipitated by the collapse of Europe's vast colonial holdings and, consequently, the rationale behind a British Australia.[56]

Horne's frame of reference was resolutely Australia and its region, tackling pressing issues from the 'White Australia' immigration policy, to Indigenous rights, the American alliance and Australia's place in Asia. On many subjects, he voiced positions that were both challenging and ahead of their time, with a freshness of style and authorial verve that drew applause and indignation in equal measure. When Penguin's co-founder, Allen Lane, remarked in 1961 that Australia was 'about to emerge, speaking from a publishing point-of-view, into a creative phase in place of an absorbent one', he could not have imagined how resoundingly a title such as *The Lucky Country* would prove him right.[57] Building on a recent upsurge in Australia-themed titles such as A. A. Philips's *The Australian Tradition* (1958), Russel Ward's *The Australian Legend* (1958), Peter Coleman's *Australian Civilization* (1962) and the first volume of Manning Clark's *History of Australia* (1962), Horne not only consolidated a rapidly emerging trend, but also harnessed it to a more critical social and political agenda.[58] What none of these earlier works could rival was Horne's unforgiving eye for Australia's multiple shortcomings and his sharply honed prescriptions for overdue change, inspiring a new, more penetrating brand of social commentary that proliferated into the late 1960s and 1970s.[59]

Yet it is equally clear that Horne's achievement was bound up in a much wider publishing phenomenon. The fact that the original idea for the book came from his UK publisher is particularly revealing, not least the manner in which the request was issued 'from our English people' like some latter-day colonial decree.[60] Equally telling is the way the author was hand-picked for his pugnacious style that carried distinct echoes of the more opinionated 'Penguin Specials' flooding the British market at that time.[61] Horne himself would later describe how he 'had done [his] own jeering at the myths of "being Australian"', including a special series of articles for *The Bulletin* dedicated to 'What's Wrong with Australia' – clearly aligning himself with the new 'state of the nation' niche journalism.[62] Not long before he signed up with Penguin, he was recruited to write occasional pieces in the UK for *The Spectator*, then under the deputy editorship of one of the original 'What's Wrong' writers, Anthony Hartley – delivering copy very much in the contrarian mould (his first offering opened with: 'One of the embarrassments of being an Australian . . . ').[63] When the chief luminary of British self-critique, Tony Crosland, paid a visit to Australia in June 1963, Horne was among the first people he encountered in Sydney's Belvedere Hotel.[64] In other words, it would be hard to envisage a more likely conduit for the new spirit of British social commentary into the Australian literary and intellectual scene.

Indeed, the initial brief from his publisher was to write 'somewhat after the style of Anthony Sampson's *Anatomy of Britain*' – so much so that his working title was 'Anatomy of Australia' throughout the drafting phase.[65] Horne's chief advisor and prime mover at Penguin's new Australian outfit, Geoffrey Dutton, was a dedicated Sampson fan, writing effusively in 1963 that Sampson's *Anatomy* 'should be read by all Australians capable of reading a book', not least for its stripping away of the 'moth-eaten robes' that still shrouded Australian perceptions of an idealized England.[66] He was therefore delighted to receive Horne's final manuscript, noting how the book exposed so many 'faults and absurdities in our national set-up', while stopping short of an appeal to 'hoist our moral underpants'.[67] Though Horne shared Sampson's singular aim of pulling the rug from under a complacent system, his was a more compact, penetrating and ultimately more durable work.

There were also subtle differences of emphasis between Horne and his UK counterparts which nevertheless stemmed from a shared point of departure. Both railed against the ignorance and amateurism of their respective governing classes, but whereas British writers stressed the stodgy Edwardian manners of a public-school educated patrician class, Horne excoriated an entrenched clique whose conservative values were 'largely a third-rate imitation of the paternalistic postures of the nineteenth-century *British* upper class'.[68] The British obsession with 'losing an empire' was rendered in Horne's work in terms of an Australian establishment unable to contemplate a world without British hegemony ('What use is your Britishry to you now?' he asked of Menzies and his ilk).[69] Where British writers preached the necessity of relinquishing imperial mentalities and embracing the new Europe, for Horne it was the imperative of decoupling from the British world as the precondition for 'coming to terms' with Asia.[70] And in place of the 'imperial nostalgia' that was routinely cited as an impediment to Britain's search for a new self-understanding, Horne railed against the 'ceremonial clinging to Britain' that was key to the 'delusional structure of the people who now run Australia'.[71] It was a case of alternative vernaculars for invoking the same thing – with Koestler's talk of impending 'suicide' echoed by Horne's high stakes of 'national survival'.[72]

But whereas an Australian writer like Horne could disaggregate his subject from the failures of an obsolete Britishness, the task was considerably more complex for a mother country that continued to carry the imperial can. No English writer, however disaffected, could quite match Horne's categorical certainty that 'to describe [ourselves] as "British" is wrong'. The key to curing 'Australia's malaise' was the kind of hard medicine that 'will divorce it from the largely irrelevant problems of the British'.[73] It is significant that both Horne and Dutton were soon to advocate the severing of ties to the monarchy and the inauguration of an Australian Republic – dismissing the queen variously as a 'novelty item', a 'cheap luxury', an 'official sedative' and decidedly un-Australian.[74] Such a straightforward parting of company was unavailable to English writers, or at least the vast majority who remained wedded to the monarchy and the Union.

There runs an unmistakable seam of irony – some might say hypocrisy – through the remedial exertions of Australia's new breed of 1960s intellectuals. For all their dedication to dismantling provincial habits of mind and combatting 'false orientations to English taste', they themselves were arguably taking their cue (indeed, their editorial instructions) from derivative British templates.[75] The evident admiration for contemporary UK literary fashion ran completely counter to the conviction that Australian writers and intellectuals should strike out on their own. Yet it is important to distinguish between the production context (in which the obvious asymmetries of the British and Australian book trade dictated the terms from London) and the broader ferment of ideas that reproduced the 'What's Wrong' writing boom in multiple hemispheres. Although Horne's work was undoubtedly influenced by English models, other sources of inspiration were also at hand, including the critically engaged 'new journalism' emerging in the pages of American magazines such as *Esquire, Harper's, New York* and *Atlantic Monthly*; as influential among British writers as their antipodean counterparts.[76] The ease of transmission suggests a burgeoning readership for social critique among a new, tertiary-educated post-war generation. But the critical edge varied according to local circumstances – so much so that the underlying similarities were rarely observed by those who presumed to take the national temperature.

This emerges more clearly if the scope is widened to consider the cross-fertilization of ideas in New Zealand where, within a year of the success of *The Lucky Country*, a major publication with similar ambition (although falling short of the same roaring success) was rushed into print. *Colony or Nation?* by the esteemed New Zealand civil servant Bill Sutch was more in the mould of Michael Shanks in focusing on the dysfunctionality of the New Zealand economy (not least its 'unhealthy' reliance on the historic role of shipping foodstuffs to Great Britain) but he nevertheless echoed Horne in deprecating the 'colonial', 'dependant' and 'immature' outlook of the country more generally, claiming that nothing short of New Zealand's 'destiny' was at stake. Just as UK writers seemed convinced of Britain's unique incapacity to adjust to the rapidly changing realities of a post-imperial world, so too, Sutch recorded his conviction that 'nearly all other countries of the world [i.e. except New Zealand] are adjusting their economic systems, even their whole way of life, in order to meet these changes'.[77] He was particularly affronted by the contrast 'between Australia's developing independence and New Zealand's backward-looking mentality of dependence' – a habit that persisted 'because we need the comfort of cleaving to something bigger'.[78] In accounting for New Zealand's unparalleled timidity, he inadvertently evoked a few striking parallels of his own:

> It is ... because of our social heritage, of our patterns of thought and customary ways, and of our amiable inferiority. All of these stem from nineteenth-century colonial society. In universities, the press, and in schools; in public meetings and official pronouncements, the mental activity reflects the thought-patterns of the mother society, the thought-patterns of England nearly a century and more ago.[79]

Here, the 'thought-patterns' of the 'What's Wrong' fraternity begin to take on a more capacious scope. Like Crosland, Shanks, Koestler, Horne and a host of others before him, Sutch was convinced that the nation's economic woes were not the result of structural failings ('it is not', he insisted, 'that the basis of our wealth has suddenly gone') but more an expression of deep-seated moral and cultural flaws. It was the antipodean equivalent of the confounded feelings about the empire among British progressives – at once a source of acute embarrassment, yet also lamented as a fading endorsement of their intellectual and moral authority. Ambivalence about the past pervaded the ardour of future aspiration, inducing what Sutch described as 'a condition of inertia'.[80]

'ALONE IN THE ARCTIC WASTE': FINDING CANADA

It was in Canada, however, that the nagging presence of hard-to-name afflictions assumed endemic proportions. Here, the late 1950s inaugurated a new phase of national hand-wringing, building on the impressive form of earlier disputes over the designation of Canadian citizenship, the use of the term 'dominion', the appointment of a Canadian-born governor-general and

Canada's role in the Suez crisis of 1956.[81] The catalyst was the election of the Conservatives under John G. Diefenbaker in 1957 on a platform of restoring the traditional emphasis on the British connection. This was compounded by the 'Quiet Revolution' of Quebec separatism in the early 1960s, itself largely a localized eddy of the wind of change.[82] The unravelling of an imperially ordered world raised further anxieties about a slow drift into the arms of the United States, setting the stage for an unending seminar on the robustness (or otherwise) of Canadian nationhood that flooded the opinion pages of virtually every major newspaper and news magazine. Whatever might have been wrong with Britain in the early 1960s, it paled in comparison with the persistent prodding and probing of Canada's perceived maladies.

Toronto's *Global and Mail* was a particularly attentive witness, proclaiming in July 1961 that a stark change had come over 'the attitude of the Canadian people'. In place of the audacity, vision and confidence of earlier generations a new 'hesitation, indecision, even timidity seem to be the rule as we face our present difficulties'. Foremost among the challenges facing Canada in the years ahead was 'to be less imitative of other countries, to set our own standards – in short to be a real nation'.[83] The *Halifax Chronicle* chimed in the same day with a soliloquy on the 'loss of healthy, vigorous patriotism' among a people 'too amenable to reason, too dispassionate'.[84] The *Toronto Daily Star* went even further, arguing that 'we have an almost psychotic addition to national soul-searching', without ever arriving at qualified answers to the problem of Canadian nationality, or indeed 'whether it exists at all'.[85]

Just as we have seen in British and Australasian contexts, a bevy of books met the demand for self-contemplation. Arthur R. M. Lower's *Canadians in the Making* in 1958 was a key landmark – a work that lamented English Canada's 'dingy reflection of that ineffably glorious world across the stormy Atlantic', but also held out hope for an alternative future founded on more authentically Canadian experience. Equating 'genuine nationhood' with the point 'when the old past ceases to absorb the new society's own past', Lower approached Canadian history in utilitarian terms – as a means of relinquishing the psychological grip of colonialism and provincialism.[86] He was shortly followed by Frank Underhill's *In Search of Canadian Liberalism* (1960), which singled out Lower as a rare exception to Canada's failure to produce 'prophets, seers and philosophers' who could generate the kind of intellectual ferment necessary to forge a 'separate nationality of our own upon this continent'. Fundamental to this aim was offloading the burden of 'the old attitudes of mind, habits of action, maxims of conduct, traditions, slogans, clichés and myths that we inherited from this happy British century of our experience'.[87] It was a progressive Canadian take on what Donald Horne described as a 'commendable emptiness' – dispensing with the baggage of Britishness to allow room for 'a new rhetoric, a new approach, as if Australia were beginning all over again'.[88]

Progressives did not have it all their own way, however, and conservative elements let it be known that they were perfectly content with the nationality they already had. The *Calgary Herald*, for example, cast aspersions on the whole tenor of the debate:

> Some day in the future an historian studying the Canadian people will surely assume that they were a melancholy lot … torturing their souls and tearing their hearts out in an agonized self-examination … trying to decide 'what is a Canadian'. What a wailing, miserable, tear-soaked, self-pitying, moaning, timid bunch they were, the historian will conclude.[89]

Yet the *Herald* harboured tear-soaked sentiments of its own – mourning the passing of an age when 'Canadianism was a much more solid thing', when British subjecthood was 'accepted without demur', people sang 'God save the King' 'without thinking it strange or inappropriate', and the Union Jack seemed 'as much their flag as anyone else's'.[90] The post-war world had eroded the familiar landscape of old, leaving many of its loyal adherents in a state of subdued disorientation – subdued, because it was attended by no profound material hardship or external threat to physical survival, yet all the more disturbing for the seeming lack of consequence.

These were the kind of pent-up frustrations that compelled the conservative philosopher George Grant to pen his landmark 1965 essay, *Lament for a Nation* – in large part a reaction against the pervasive liberal-progressive exhortations to 'real' nationhood. Taking aim at Frank Underhill's 'obviously ridiculous' credo, 'Stop being British if you want to be a nationalist', Grant looked back despondently at the fading traditions of British conservativism. 'Growing up in Ontario', he recalled, 'the generation of the 1920's took it for granted that they belonged to a nation. The character of the country was self-evident. To say it was British was not to deny it was North American.' For Canadians reared in this environment, the agenda pursued by the Liberal Party since the Second World War had 'led inexorably to the disappearance of Canada' as they conceived it:

> We find ourselves like fish left on the shores of a drying lake. The element necessary to our existence has passed away … [and] we must be allowed to lament the passing of what had claimed our allegiance … The history of the race is strewn with gasping political fish.[91]

Grant would later regret that he wrote with 'too little irony', allowing 'simple people' to mistake the book for 'a lament for the passing of the British dream of Canada'. But his insistence that it was 'rather a lament for the *romanticism* of the original dream', brought little in the way of clarification – or indeed irony.[92] To be sure, Grant acknowledged that John Diefenbaker's cloying attachment to Britain carried an 'air of unreality' at a time when the 'English ruling class had come to think of its Commonwealth relations as a tiresome burden'. But he refused to join 'the clever and the rootless' in condemning the older generation's obsolescent Britishness, preferring instead 'to sympathise with these men of deep loyalty, who found themselves impotent in the face of their disappearing past'.[93] No less than the 'history of the race' seemed to be drawing to a close, much as Michael Shanks had portended four years earlier.

These misgivings were stirred, not by any specific longing for greater intimacy with Britain in any programmatic sense, so much as the feeling that Canadian liberals were eagerly dismantling the foundations of Canada's separate existence without inserting any stable or durable markers in their place. This was the abiding theme of the Ottawa-based political columnist and chief chronicler of Canada's culture wars, Peter C. Newman, who devoted much of the decade to a relentless critique of contemporary Canadian political life directed equally at conservatives and progressives.[94] Although Newman suffered no obvious hankerings for the British connection (which he dismissed as an outdated relic 'entombed forever'), he found little emotional satisfaction in the promise of emergent 'maturity'.[95] Rather he remained fixated on 'that terrible ingrained uncertainty in us, the absence of knowing who we are and why we are here, that is gradually depriving us of our nationhood'.[96] In early 1968 he published his acclaimed portrait of Canada in the 1960s, choosing a title which might equally have served its purpose in Australia, New Zealand or indeed the United Kingdom itself: *The Distemper of Our Times.*

Ostensibly a survey of Canadian politics in the Diefenbaker–Pearson era, Newman's *Distemper* was an attempt to delve deeper into a decade of 'dismay and frustration with our politics that was hardening into cynicism and despair', documenting a collective 'alienation' among Canadians 'they had never known before'. His flair for political theatre was ideally suited to an era when 'the church, our long-praised phlegmatic stability, the old idea of allegiance to Empire, all the comforting touchstones of the familiar past were being displaced by the urgent demands of a disquieting present'. The painful death throes of British Canada and the stalled promise of a new nation 'seeking a political midwife to be born' formed the twin pillars of his perspective, furnishing an unedifying glimpse into the 'Kiplingesque world' of the Canadian political class 'caught up in the vain hopes of a long-gone epoch'. Leaving it to 'some astute historian of the future' to discern a deeper pattern, he could only register 'dim awareness' that 'we were enduring the pains of passage from the safety of the past to we knew not what'.[97]

It is unlikely that Newman was schooled in Antonio Gramsci's concept of *interregnum* – the 'great variety of morbid symptoms' arising 'precisely in the fact that the old is dying and the new cannot be born'.[98] But he had surely familiarized himself with the 'What's Wrong' formula – exasperation, despair and impatience for change, set against the backdrop of an empire-derived political culture urgently in need of renewal. Significantly, he would go on to expose the inner-workings of the nation's elites in *The Canadian Establishment* (three volumes, 1975–88) – a work bearing more than a passing resemblance to Sampson's *Anatomy* (by then in its third edition). For all the blinkered focus on their own national maladies, the 'What's Wrong' writers of the 1960s exhibited a remarkable readiness to draw inspiration indirectly from one another. 'Has our good luck, taken for granted for so long, run out?', asked Newman in the opening salvo of *Distemper*, borrowing freely from the literary blueprint of another *Lucky Country* – apparently secure in the expectation that the two works would never be read side by side. It was not exactly plagiarism, more a veiled acknowledgement that the generation of Newman, Sampson and Horne were ploughing the same out-of-empire furrow, seeking a new purchase on unfamiliar terrain.

Horne, for his part, was more aware than most of these intersecting maladies, embarking on a new work of critical scrutiny at the end of the decade, only this time turning his attention to the mother of all identity crises in Great Britain itself. Here, he took the now cliché-laden landscape of 'state of the nation' writing as his point of departure in his 1969 Penguin offering, *God is an Englishman*:

> Nothing has been added to *la crise anglais* since [1949], except the extension of its existence. It has become institutionalised: it is now part of the British way of life. Come to Britain and see the crisis. Those who were born during the devaluation of 1949 were starting their careers by the devaluation of 1967; they had spent the intervening years growing up in a nation that could never seem officially certain of itself for more than two years on end … It is a crisis of habit, in particular of affronted habits of self-esteem.[99]

It was an attempt to enlarge on his Australian success via the time-honoured ritual of 'trying one's luck' at the imperial hearth, drawing freely on his own successful formula, right down to the opening sentence of the first chapter: 'Britain is one of the fortunate countries.'[100] It was an ironic move, perhaps deliberately so, completing the circle from his early years in Britain, the cultivation of his combative journalism in the *Observer* years, the influence of Sampson, Hartley, Crosland and others in his seminal Australian work, finally to compose his own take on the 'imperial obsessions' that continued to haunt contemporary Britain. What distinguished Horne's perspective was a greater readiness to find parallels among the constituent societies of what he termed 'Anglo-Saxondom' (to which he devoted an entire chapter).[101] He noted, for example how Britain's version of the modern identity crisis was 'not a crisis of the people as it is, say, of Canada, for roughly speaking, the people know who they are. It is a crisis of Britain's elites caused by their over-ambition.'[102] Here was a rare acknowledgement that Britain's predicament (and indeed Canada's) formed part of a broader matrix. No other writer in the 'What's Wrong' stable came as close to recognizing this complex weave of mutual self-understanding. For the most part, national myopia seemed the surest way forward.

God is an Englishman was to be Donald Horne's least successful book by a considerable margin, making virtually no impression in either Australia or Britain and to this day remains almost entirely forgotten in his homeland.[103] The reason seems to have little to do with the inherent value of the book itself, which combines all of Horne's signature qualities of wit, audacity, economy of style and a formidable breadth of field. Part of the difficulty was undoubtedly his outsider status, pitching a book into the closed circle of metropolitan punditry. Moreover, Horne's defining theme of creeping imperial obsolescence hardly augured well for a bumper readership in Australia, Canada or indeed anywhere else in the creepingly obsolete empire.

But the greatest obstacle was the perceived tiredness of the genre itself – certainly among the British reading public for whom a torrent of such works had (in Horne's own words) 'thrown up the misty shapes of an official sense of identity' for more than a decade without bringing much in the way of clarity or resolution.[104] Horne surveyed the succession of phases and phrases that had punctuated the debate since the time of the coronation – the new Elizabethanism, Never Having it so Good, White Heat, Swinging Britain, culminating in the 1967 devaluation and the 'I'm Backing Britain' campaign, replete with the Union Jack serving as both 'an article of apparel' and 'an advertising gimmick'. For Horne, the five Surbiton typists and the short-lived 'show of humility that became fashionable at the beginning of 1968' were merely a novel articulation of an old theme, a new way of 'heightening the crisis'. In this way, he seems fully to have anticipated the perils of breaking into a beleaguered UK publishing market: 'New worlds and slogans, new manufactured images, floated through the air, but none of them landed ... nothing seems to stick.'[105]

'BACK IN OUR OWN ISLAND': EXHORTATION FATIGUE

'Nothing seems to stick' might equally have served as an elegy for the Backing Britain campaign itself – shortly to become another victim of 'What's Wrong' fatigue. After the initial surge of popular support and an overwhelmingly supportive press, there were clear indications that the going would be tough over the longer term. The *Daily Telegraph* raised a note of caution at the outset about 'the Niagara of exhortation we have endured in the last two decades', which had not brought 'the slightest visible effect on our performance'.[106] For all the early momentum and enthusiasm, it was perhaps inevitable that the idea of solving the nation's problems by working half an hour for free would encounter serious difficulties. Most obviously, the trade union movement found little reason to rejoice in the mobilization of patriotism to undermine painstakingly negotiated work-place bargains, and a bitter stand-off quickly emerged between the Colt Heating employees and the Amalgamated Engineering Union who sought to forbid its workers from taking part in the scheme. Colt's shop stewards elected to continue to Back Britain, earning them an official court-martial and a ban on holding office for five years amid howls of indignation from the Fleet Street press. Union leaders were unsparing in their invective, insisting that 'we are as patriotic as anyone banging the drum on this wave of national hysteria' and attacking the 'economic illiteracy' that reduced the complexities of labour, productivity, marketing and efficient management to a simple matter of clocking in early.[107] The president of the Electrical Trades Union predicted that 'as a matter of hard fact this sort of campaign will fail. The regrettable thing is that the spirit which gave rise to the suggestion might be destroyed in the process.'[108]

The objections of the unions proved fatal to the prospects of building a truly nationwide movement. For all its early success in recruiting workers and businesses to the cause, the Backing Britain support base derived from a narrow socio-economic demographic, typically small to medium-scale businesses with non-union staff (as per Colt's Surbiton office) or light industrial manufacturers in and around the urban centres of England. Like the 'What's Wrong' medicine itself, the movement appealed primarily to private enterprise and a white-collar, middle-class constituency.

Conspicuous by its absence was heavy industry of any kind (a thousand workers at the Ford Dagenham plant voted overwhelmingly against the scheme) and public service employees were never tempted to join, despite ample proposals for how they might become involved. Early critics had pointed out that 'white-collar Surbiton is a long way from the steel mills of Lincolnshire or the coal-fields of Scotland' and this dilemma was never resolved.[109]

Even more revealing is the absence of any genuinely 'British' dimension to what was a thoroughly English affair. Scotland remained entirely non-plussed by the self-denying ordinance (one unnamed Scottish trade union-ist reportedly spluttered 'Work for nowt? It's stark raving mad!'), while the lone Scottish nationalist in the House of Commons, Winifred Ewing, was scathing about the cost to taxpayers of the 'Backing Britain' postmark.[110] Greater inroads were made in Wales but the message became garbled when Welsh nationalists produced posters and car stickers rendering the slogan as *Rwy'n Bacio Cymru* ('I'm Backing Wales') – hardly a vote of confidence in the campaign's core message of national unity.[111]

Figure 11.2 'I'm Backing Britain' bunting spills onto Carnaby Street, London, 10 February 1968. By then, the early momentum behind the campaign had already stalled. Source: Bettmann/Getty Images.

Meanwhile the Wilson government adopted an ambiguous pose, on the one hand welcoming the distraction from the relentless negativity about the government's own performance, but at the same time wary of the longer-term prospects with more bad news on the horizon. Just two weeks after the campaign launch, Harold Wilson was obliged to inform the House of Commons that the government would accelerate the withdrawal of Britain's military presence East of Suez – a move widely regarded as yet another humiliating setback which hardly augured well for the fledgling spirit of national self-help that had seen in the New Year. Inevitably, the defeatism of the defence cuts was thrown into sharp relief against the pluck and resolve of the Surbiton typists, though with little consensus about what the contrast might actually mean. Some felt certain (such as Adam Fergusson in *The Times*) that the whole point of Backing Britain was to maintain Britain's position of strength in the world, and that 'the Government would be imperilling the Back Britain mood, to say nothing of itself, if it were to make permanent sacrifices now of necessary bases, valuable assets and deep friendships'.[112] Lord Bathurst passionately advanced this position in the Upper House, proclaiming 'I am ready to "back Britain"; millions of men and women throughout the country will back Britain' but he could not see how that object would be served should Britain 'cease to be reckoned as a great World Power by our friends and foes alike'. Rising to his theme with a fervour only a hereditary peer could muster, he cast his mind to 'the Bathursts scattered throughout the world' – in Gambia, South Africa, Canada and Australia – all 'dangerous places of the world' that might 'need our help tomorrow'.[113] His conception of Britain seemed to encompass one vast landed estate, elevating the defence requirements of the sheep pastures of New South Wales above the solvency of the UK Exchequer. Bathurst's Liberal counterpart, Gladwyn Jebb, took an entirely different view, arguing that the 'so-called "I'm Backing Britain" movement . . . is at least a sign that the British people are beginning to be conscious of the dangers of their present position in the world, and of the fact that nobody owes them a living'. In this view, Backing Britain was a means to 'find another outlet for the energy, the intelligence and the huge capacity of our ex-Imperial people' – in other words, an opportunity to recognize that 'we are back in our own island'.[114]

Meanwhile back in Surbiton, the Colt Heating Company was unable to cope with the surge of public interest in the campaign.[115] Or as the five instigators themselves more plainly put it, 'thanks to all the interviews and things, we just didn't get any typing done'.[116] Attempts to find more secure institutional backing produced an unedifying split between two rival organizations, each claiming to carry the Surbiton torch.[117] By the end of February, the shop floor at Colt had elected to return to normal working hours, prompting a slew of elegiac newspaper reports that praised the much-needed 'psychological stimulus' of the Backing Britain movement while making no bones about the underwhelming results. 'Whereas a mood of quick enthusiasm can be worked up from a sense of national humiliation and frustration', declared *The Times*'s leader on 12 February, it was another matter entirely to work out how 'this enthusiasm can best be utilised more permanently.'[118]

The sense of deflation was conveyed with an affecting modesty by the young Lord Faversham, aged only twenty-three and delivering his inaugural parliamentary speech that same month:

> As a Victorian youth, I should have been 'brainwashed' into the knowledge that I was British, and that Britain was something. Today I am vaguely aware of being a Yorkshireman, but I have not a clue what Britain is or where it is going, if it has not gone already. I know that it must be kept tidy, and it is whispered that I must back it. I presume that I must back it to win—but to win what?[119]

Faversham's bewilderment reflected the uniquely painful predicament of his social class, for whom the coordinates of a British world no longer furnished a reliable political inheritance. Though such overt despondency was not widely shared, its trace elements were abundantly in evidence amid the residue of exhortation fatigue. A more typical response was to laugh the entire matter off as an unfortunate misfire that only amplified the nation's diminished fortunes. The opening scene of *Dad's Army* – a new BBC sitcom piloted in April 1968 – depicted retired Captain George Mainwaring reminiscing with his platoon while launching the Walmington-on-Sea 'I'm Backing Britain' campaign. The joke – which seems obscure in retrospect – would not have been lost on contemporaries.[120]

◆

Viewed against a wider backdrop, the unprecedented boom in 'What's Wrong' social commentary appears less an enquiry into the state of any particular nation and more a diffuse exercise in reconfiguring complex categories of selfhood. This was part and parcel of the decolonization process among the newly created post-colonial states of Asia, Africa and the Caribbean, where the aspirations of nationalism needed to be given constitutional legitimacy and symbolic form. But similar questions were also foisted upon those who had done most of the colonizing, not least the inhabitants of Britain and the one-time 'white dominions' where the end of empire marked the eclipse of a belief system founded on shared racial patrimony. Fundamental to that system was the authority of white liberal progress projected onto a world stage – long-encumbered with glaring contradictions, now all the more bereft of answers as the empire contracted and its legacies grew increasingly suspect.

In Britain itself, the literary boom in 'declinism' doubled as an opportunity for the liberal political establishment to distance themselves from the legacies of empire. For all the searing critique of hidebound imperial values corroding the body politic, there was little genuine interest in exploring the enduring social implications – most were in a hurry to leave the empire behind. But a Britain 'no longer at the centre of the world picture' – its claims to universality punctured by its own disavowal of imperial ambition – left nagging questions for the few who cared to confront the matter head on. It brought added complications by virtue of the fact that there could be no easy disowning of the 'link with Britain', however self-serving that option could be in Australia, Canada and New Zealand. In a more fundamental sense, however – as the remaining chapters will reveal – the 'British connection' proved no less vulnerable to scrutiny in Britain, as influential currents in Scotland, Wales, Northern Ireland and even England began to reconsider their separate designations in a similar light.

The 'I'm Backing Britain' episode shows how the furrowed brows of 'What's Wrong' intellectuals could merge seamlessly with popular perceptions and everyday experience. Despite chronic divisions and endemic confusion over the campaign message, virtually no one had the temerity to suggest that the five heroines of Surbiton had nothing much to worry about. In a conversation overwhelmingly monopolized by highly opinionated white men (not a single female author contributed to the 'What's Wrong' genre), here were clear indications that the other half of the population would not be pushed aside. Indeed, part of the 'refreshing' appeal of the campaign was the veiled rebuke to the nation's demoralized menfolk at a time when 'the smack of firm leadership has yet to be heard'.[121] Gendered metaphors abounded, implying a more fundamental failure of British manhood that resonated all the more powerfully at the nadir of the white man's world. The steady resolve of the 'five pretty typists of Surbiton' could be held up as a shining example for the women of Britain, but it also cast a heavy pall of masculine impotence. The *Daily Mirror*'s Marjorie Proops was 'not a bit surprised' that it took only one day for 'five young dolly girls' to take 'the first genuinely practical step to wake us up from the national torpor into which we have sunk. While men sit around conference tables talking – and doing damn all.'[122]

The Surbiton Five were to make one last encore as the 'Surbiton martyrs' in one of the final instalments of the 'What's Wrong' genre – Paul Einzig's toxic 1969 diatribe, *Decline and Fall? Britain's Crisis in the Sixties*. Where Shanks and Sampson had trained their sights on a stuffy Edwardian establishment, here, unfettered scorn was heaped onto ordinary Britons themselves – or what Einzig termed 'the deterioration of the British character'.[123] 'Only thirty years ago Britain was *the* leading world power', he marvelled, 'the Commonwealth and Empire had a very real meaning.'[124] Just as 'the Empire was built up and maintained by the devotion of the British people', so too, the corrosion of those sterling qualities could now be named as 'the main cause of Britain's decline'.[125] It was a rare acknowledgement of the underlying wellspring of discontent, charged with undisguised contempt for the British people in their feeble response to the 'simple formula' of the five Surbiton typists.[126] What might have been the true 'Dunkirk spirit' reborn, or the latter-day equivalent of the economic sacrifices of the 1930s, had soon degenerated into a cycle of media 'victimization' and trade union 'despotism'.[127] In a book that announced itself as an enquiry into whether the nation was 'really doomed to share the fate of the great empires of the past', it was a revealing juxtaposition.[128] Averting the fate of fallen empires was presumably the last thing weighing on the minds of Valerie, Brenda, Christine, Carol Ann and Joan as they embarked on their fifteen minutes of fame. But as the strange twists of the entire episode attest, their symbolic capital was never really theirs to define.

Though widely laughed off as a comic misfire, the distempers were not easily dissipated. Many would breathe a sigh of relief that a nascent chauvinism had been put back in the bottle. The Wilson government had grown increasingly wary of 'undesirable jingoistic currents in public opinion' that needed close monitoring, and backpedalled furiously on its earlier policy of 'discretely stimulating' the campaign.[129] Meanwhile, the *New Statesman* pointed to the unsettling implications of being 'constantly confronted with the Union Jack', and issued a nervous plea to 'put out less flags'.[130] *The Economist* similarly adopted a wary posture towards a movement that seemed symptomatic of a deeper disaffection and popular alienation from the political process – while drawing comfort from the fact that Britain was 'lucky that there is no demagogue of sufficient ability around to exploit it'.[131]

It was surely a premature assessment. In April 1968, as the last murmurs of 'I'm Backing Britain' quietly petered out, a new populist swell was building around the anti-immigration rhetoric of Enoch Powell, culminating in a march on parliament by angry London dock workers in defence of the renegade Tory MP. Brandishing placards declaring 'Don't Knock Enoch' and 'Back Britain, not Black Britain', it became clear how effortlessly the 'Niagara of exhortation' could be harnessed to the new populist currents of racial exclusion.[132] Coincidentally, it would be in Surbiton the following year that a Conservative Party constituency branch would rebel against its sitting MP, throwing their support behind an independent Powellite candidate. Although Powell himself was no admirer of 'those Surrey typists' (whom he dismissed as 'not only ineffably silly, but positively dangerous'), he would prove highly adept in the months ahead at tapping into the nervous energy that Backing Britain had stirred.[133]

12

THE LAST REFUGE: COMING HOME TO ENGLAND

Ranjanbala Vaid's fantastic voyage began with the death of her mother in Nairobi in 1968. The twenty-two-year-old had spent most of her life among Kenya's thriving Asian merchant class – the descendants of the traders, artisans and railway workers who had oiled the wheels of early colonization. The Vaid family were relative late-comers, having arrived from India in the wake of independence in the late 1940s, swept up in the mass displacements of Britain's imperial retreat. Ranjan herself may never have given a moment's thought to questions of citizenship or nationality, but left suddenly to fend for herself, she was fortunate enough to be in the possession of a 'United Kingdom and Colonies' passport. When the Kenyan Government revoked her right to work in March 1969 she had little choice but to strike out for new horizons, resolving to join her brother Shantilal then working as an accountant in London. An initial approach to the UK High Commission in Nairobi to secure an entry permit resulted in an unexpected rebuff, and so she took matters into her own hands, boarding a Lufthansa 707 in early February 1970 in a bid to blaze her own path to Britain and a better future.

Arriving at Heathrow via Frankfurt on 3 February, she was immediately refused entry. Ever since the passage of the 1968 Commonwealth Immigrants Act, Kenyan Asians who had not taken up Kenyan citizenship found themselves drifting tenuously between two moorings – liable to be denied the means to earn a living in Kenya, but without the automatic right to take up residency in the United Kingdom. Ranjan's onward journey was to dramatize this precarious state of affairs in absurdly vivid terms. Despite her brother's desperate on-the-spot offer to act as financial guarantor, UK immigration officers refused to turn a blind eye to her passport irregularities and deported her straight back to Frankfurt. Meanwhile the German authorities saw no reason why she should be their responsibility and dispatched her promptly to Zurich where BOAC ran a direct service to Kenya – evidently without clearing the decision with BOAC who similarly refused the task and returned her to sender. Back in Frankfurt, airport officials agonized over her situation before reluctantly imploring Lufthansa – at the carrier's expense – to fly her all the way back to Nairobi.

There the matter might have ended but for the extraordinary events upon her arrival the following day. Without so much as an exchange of pleasantries she was handed a curt note by Kenyan immigration authorities stating: 'You are hereby required to leave Kenya forthwith.' As a foreign passport holder with no Kenyan work permit, she was ordered back onto the same Lufthansa jet she had disembarked less than an hour before, now bound for Johannesburg. It was at this point that journalists began to take notice of Ranjan's plight, describing her in tears at Nairobi airport 'clutch-ing the third deportation order' she had received in so many days.[1] 'What a way to see the world' exclaimed Kenya's *Daily Nation*, tracking her forlorn flight path with a quickening fascination.[2]

The inclination to take pity on Ranjanbala Vaid was almost universal, the weight of the world having seemingly descended on her 'diminutive, sari-clad' frame.[3] Measuring barely five feet tall, swaddled in a cardigan and speaking very little English, she seemed the epitome of the innocent abroad. Allowed briefly to speak to journalists at Nairobi airport, she explained that she had been staying with a cousin in Kenya since her mother died without any means of subsistence, forced to choose between whittling away her passage to England or 'trying her luck' with Lufthansa. All fortune having now deserted her, she had been 'told to go to Johannesburg and I will have to go', her parting words registering only the weariest of protests: 'I am fed up with travelling like this for so many days.'[4] At Jan Smuts Airport in Johannesburg she was similarly denied entry and found herself once again winging her way back to Nairobi. Friends and relatives who rallied with food and clothing in the dead of night were turned back by airport officials who, on this occasion, refused her permission even to disembark the refuelling aircraft. Lufthansa's flight crew described Ranjan's emotional state as 'very frightened', allowing their exasperation to show when ordered by Kenyan authorities to deliver her yet again to Frankfurt. 'She can't make a home out of airports', blurted one company representative before complying with the deportation order.[5] Nairobi's *East African Standard* was similarly incredu-lous, enquiring whether 'she [is] to be shuffled to and fro, a captive of the air, and spend the remainder of her life flying?'[6]

The following day she began to appear in newspapers throughout the world as the 'human shuttlecock', while her brother complained loudly in London about the way she had been 'kicked around like a football'.[7] After stopovers in Athens and Vienna she made her fourth touchdown in Frankfurt, where she was subjected to one last attempt by the British

Consul to block her onward progress. But by this stage the whole extraordinary affair was becoming a source of embarrassment to Harold Wilson's Labour government, then gearing up for an election year. Under pressure from his own party and mounting criticism from the press, the UK home secretary James Callaghan made an 'exceptional' exemption, permitting Ranjanbala Vaid finally to enter the UK on 10 February 1970. It was the culmination of a nine-day odyssey spanning 17,069 miles and traversing the equator three times, all the while shuttling between airplanes and flight terminals with precious little sleep and nothing but rolls and coffee for subsistence.[8]

Under interrogation in the House of Commons, Callaghan insisted that it was 'those who encouraged or advised her to try and jump the queue' who bore the responsibility for Ranjan's inhumane treatment; clearly aiming to taint her innocent aura with a touch of premeditated mischief.[9] The home secretary dodged repeated questions (largely from his own party) about the legal anomaly her case had brought to light, insisting that there would have been no anomaly at all had she simply stayed put in Nairobi. The onslaught was taken up in the House of Lords by Liberal and Labour peers, one of whom asked pointedly whether it was 'conducive to British prestige that holders of British passports should be wandering about the world like Flying Dutchmen'.[10] Fenner Brockway pressed the need for clarification, pointing out that Ranjan's situation was by no means unique – indeed, there were 'three stranded in Zurich; three others stranded in Paris, stateless, and seventeen others detained in this country'. Lord Byers summed up the predicament from the Liberal benches: 'The overseas Government refuses permission to work; the British Government refuse permission to enter the United Kingdom; and the Asian is left to live on his or her resources until only the air fare remains. Can anyone blame these people at that stage for wanting to get out while the going is good?'[11]

The anomaly foisted on Kenyan Asians – or 'British Asians' as the Kenyan Government insisted on calling them[12] – is normally ascribed to the 'Africanization' campaign implemented by President Jomo Kenyatta in 1967, designed to enhance the employment and career prospects of Indigenous Africans by dislodging Asian workers from the Kenyan labour market. This prompted a near-doubling of the rate of departures for Britain in the latter part of the year, spurred by the risk of imminent job losses and fears of further discriminatory measures against the Asian community. By January 1968, the much-touted 'exodus' had begun to dominate the news cycle in Britain with televised footage of new arrivals burdened with all their worldly belongings painting a 'strong visual impression . . . of an unending stream of Asians entering the country'.[13] This added fuel to the widely circulating rumours that Britain was about to impose drastic entry restrictions, thus precipitating a 'beat the ban' rush that became self-fulfilling. Responding to the urgent pleas of UK officials to ease the pressures of Africanization, Kenyatta insisted that the British could easily defuse the crisis themselves by the simple expedient of publicly disavowing any intention to impose controls.[14] But the Wilson government chose the opposite tack, hastily enacting legislation in February 1968 that removed the right of entry to all UK passport holders overseas who could not demonstrate a familial connection to the United Kingdom.

There was far more to this episode than the unedifying stand-off between the Kenyan and British governments, however. Fundamentally, it was an accident waiting-to-happen, not dissimilar to the circumstances that had left the *Komagata Maru* stranded on Vancouver's Burrard Inlet more than half a century earlier.[15] Ranjanbala Vaid was an unlikely successor to Gurdit Singh, but her plight brought the same contradictions to the fore – a nominally unbounded Britishness, suddenly forced to reckon with in-built racial exclusions. In contrast to 1914, however, the escalating *perception* of crisis seemed all the more disconcerting at a time when imperial authority had been all but completely discredited. Viewed in these terms, the Kenyan Asian furore counts as a late convulsion of Greater Britain at the very nadir of its political shelf life.

In particular, two contemporaneous developments served to heighten the tension: the November 1967 devaluation of sterling and the January 1968 acceleration of Britain's military withdrawal from East of Suez. The damaging blow to confidence in the pound resonated around the world, not least amongst overseas holders of sterling who promptly revised their belief in Britain's capacity to bear unlimited financial responsibilities. Likewise, the winding up of Britain's defence capability in the Far East sounded the alarm for Commonwealth allies who continued to rely on British defence guarantees. Both episodes compounded the image of a defeated nation pulling up the drawbridge.

This chapter sets out to join this wider context to the presumptive threat posed by inward migration. As the *Evening Standard* trumpeted, the watchword had suddenly changed from 'Backing Britain' to 'Britain Can't Cope', compounding the 'panic of Kenya's Asians instead of dieting it fairly'.[16] Though neither defence cuts nor devaluation materially affected the entitlements of UK passport holders in Kenya, the steady drip of adverse headlines sent out a signal that time was running desperately short to secure a passage to Britain. The rush to board passenger airliners in spring 1968 was but a localized expression of a much wider crisis of confidence in the global currency of Britishness.

These offshore tremors would also register profoundly at the heart of Britain itself. Within weeks of the government's ban on Kenyan Asians, Enoch Powell entered the Midlands Hotel in Birmingham to deliver one of the most controversial political statements of the twentieth century. Although his 'Rivers of Blood' speech contained no references to the Kenyan Asians, his emergence as the political embodiment of stringent immigration controls had its genesis entirely in that context. Throughout the early months of 1968, newspaper columnists and television specials agonized over the apparently sudden scourge of 'racialism' sullying the nation's good name. But for all his racially explosive rhetoric, the real object of Powell's populism was not the 'British' race in the global sense of Dilke or Seeley. His relatively late conversion to immigration restriction unfolded in tandem with his equally belated discovery of 'what it is that binds us together' – the sacred core of Englishness. Powell's England was the final fallback, the last refuge where the wounds of a thousand cuts could heal. Describing his generation as 'one which comes home again after years of distant wandering', he was as much preoccupied with Britain's receding frontiers as the families scrambling to board a plane out of Nairobi. Though his journey was conducted in considerably greater comfort than that of Ranjanbala Vaid, it was no less winding, tortured or vexed by the disorientations of empire's end.

ANATOMY OF A CRISIS: THE KENYAN ASIANS

The conditions that produced the Kenyan Asian crisis arose out of the last days of the Macmillan era, at the intersection of changing attitudes to Commonwealth immigration and the sweeping consequences of African decolonization. As we saw in Chapter 6, controversial immigration restrictions had already been imposed on British subjects throughout the Commonwealth under the terms of the 1962 Commonwealth Immigrants Act.[17] But little more than a year later, with the conclusion of Kenya's independence negotiations, certain categories of British subject were exempted from the 1962 controls, mainly with a view to securing the interests of Kenya's white settler population. Those who chose not to take up Kenyan citizenship (which accounted for the vast majority of whites as well some 90 per cent of the Asian community) were permitted not only to retain their British nationality, but also to exercise the right of free entry into the United Kingdom.[18]

Thus, when these exemptions were suddenly revoked by the Wilson government in February 1968 (targeting specifically the Kenyan Asians while preserving the privileges of white settlers), the burning question was whether Britain had dishonoured a solemn 'pledge'. This was the main charge levelled by angry opponents of the 1968 Bill – that the Conservative government had done the honourable thing in 1963, partly as a reward to Kenyan Asians for decades of loyal imperial service but more crucially to placate widespread fears of ethnic persecution at the hands of the newly sovereign African state. Former colonial secretary Iain Macleod famously aired his disgust in an article in *The Spectator*, insisting that as far as he was concerned, a binding promise had been made in 1963: 'I gave my word, I meant to give it, I wish to keep it.'[19] Meanwhile vocal supporters of the clampdown on Kenyan Asians (which comprised the bulk of Macleod's own Tory Party including the former Commonwealth secretary Duncan Sandys) professed to be totally bewildered by this interpretation, citing the absence of any written accord, or even an informal understanding, to vouchsafe particular segments of the Kenyan community. In this view, assiduously cultivated by Labour's Jim Callaghan at the Home Office, the Kenyan Asian exemption was merely an 'unforeseen loophole' in the 1962 Commonwealth Immigrants Act which needed urgently to be sealed off to forestall an East African floodtide numbering in the hundreds of thousands.[20]

In fact, neither side of the argument could claim much in the way of historical validity. The special dispensation for Kenyan Asians (which also included Asian communities in Uganda and Tanganyika) arose, not out of a sense of moral obligation but from the cumbersome mechanism chosen to exclude Commonwealth immigrants in the 1962 legislation.[21] In order to avoid the dreaded charge of racism, the Macmillan government had elected to discriminate against certain categories of passports (as distinct from the people who carried them) – namely, all travel documents issued by offshore colonial and Commonwealth governments.[22] From the moment the Act came into force in July 1962, only passports issued directly by the United Kingdom Government bestowed the right of unfettered entry, and hence for a brief period Kenyan Asians were indeed restricted during the dying days of the Kenyan colonial government. The exemption came into effect with the convoluted terms of the independence settlement in December 1963, where citizenship of the new Kenyan state was not con-ferred automatically regardless of colour or creed, but only on those born in Kenya who could prove that at least one parent also was born there. This effectively ruled out some 150,000 Kenyan Asians, who were forced to fall back on their prior United Kingdom and Colonies (UKC) citizenship until such time as they applied for naturalization in Kenya. But it also brought the unexpected windfall that their passports henceforth would be issued by the newly established British High Commission in Nairobi – which, as a United Kingdom agency, exempted the bearers from the 1962 controls. Although Kenyan Asians were given a two-year window to apply for Kenyan citizenship, the vast majority chose not to, preferring instead to exchange their old 'colonial' passports for the new, duty-free UKC travel document as insurance against any future persecution at the hands of their new political masters.[23]

In other words, there is no evidence of any conscious design on the part of the UK Government to provide a safe haven for a potentially vulnerable segment of the Kenyan community. Macleod himself never directly cited the solemn obligation he purportedly discharged in 1963, and he had in any case been ousted as colonial secretary long before the Kenyan Independence deal was struck. Randall Hansen has produced evidence of Macleod's successor, Duncan Sandys, publicly acknowledging the reactivation of unrestricted entry rights for all Kenyan holders of British passports in July 1962, but this in no sense took the form of a sacred oath or guarantee.[24] On the contrary, virtually every contemporary Whitehall assessment regarded the entry rights of Kenyan Asians with the most grudging acquiescence, describing their position variously as a 'problem', a 'concern' and an 'anomaly' deriving from 'the gloomy effects of the Kenyan independence settlement which follow the lines we had feared'.[25] The entire matter was deemed exceedingly delicate, laced with dim bureaucratic warnings that 'care needs to be taken', 'there is no alternative', no 'way of curing this one' and even a despairing 'what is to be done?'[26] Such was the veil of conspiratorial silence that one dossier was subtitled: 'this brief to be used only if unavoidable' – in other words, only if controversy should erupt. The responsible minister was advised not to 'attempt to evade' the issue, but nor should he unduly publicize the fact that 'these Asians will acquire a right of entry here'.[27] The innate defensiveness goes a long way to explaining why, when controversy finally flared up in late 1967, the UK High Commission in Nairobi could regard the rights of Kenyan Asians as a mere 'technicality' in the 1962 law rather than an altruistic gesture by a compassionate Tory government.[28]

But it was equally disingenuous to claim that the escalating Kenyan Asian crisis had been entirely unforeseen. As early as 1963, both the Home Office and Commonwealth Relations Office (CRO) had prepared assessments of the likelihood of a major influx of Asians, and in each case the potential for large-scale mobility was acknowledged. Although much was made of the fact that there was 'no tradition of Asian immigration from east Africa to the United Kingdom', and hence 'no intrinsic reason why the Kenyan Asians should come here in large numbers next year', the difficulty of predicting the communal dynamics after independence was obvious. Anticipating Kenyatta's Africanization drive by several years, the Home Office noted the 'clamours for nationalization of Asian-owned businesses', but concluded that there was unlikely to be any large-scale exodus 'unless there are outbreaks of violence or marked signs of oppression' – an eventuality that could 'not, of course, be discounted'.[29] The CRO concurred that it was 'impossible to say' under what circumstances conditions might deteriorate for the Asian community, while pointing to the possibility that a sizeable portion might willingly opt for Kenyan citizenship. 'Apart from hoping that some will do so', officials glumly conceded that 'no practical solution to this problem has been found.'[30] Even as the flow of arrivals rose steadily into the mid-1960s, the Whitehall response was to be 'rather surprised – and relieved' that Kenyan Asians had not been relocating in larger numbers, all the while flagging the possibility that the situation could change at a moment's notice.[31]

Which raises the question of why the issue became so volatile in February 1968 as to require a complete legislative overhaul, rendering hundreds of thousands of British citizens in East Africa effectively stateless. The Home Office under Callaghan was bound by exactly the same constraints that had hamstrung officials in the early 1960s – the legal quagmire of renouncing citizenship rights, the inevitable charge of racial discrimination, the flagrant breach of multiple international treaties and conventions – and yet the government nevertheless went ahead with measures that had seemed, if not unthinkable then certainly unmentionable only four years previously. Callaghan's advisers also anticipated a further difficulty that had escaped the attention of the Macmillan government, namely the legal shambles that would attend any refusal by the Kenyan authorities 'to accept people whom we had refused to admit' – precisely the citizenship limbo that awaited Ranjanbala Vaid and countless others in the years ahead. Indeed, this was one of the key reasons why Commonwealth Secretary George Thomson resolutely opposed the bill, while the UK High Commissioner in Nairobi similarly warned of the embarrassment that could arise from Kenyan expulsions of UK passport holders: 'I can not (repeat not) see which country other than the United Kingdom could be obliged to take them.'[32] Yet Callaghan ploughed on, advising the Cabinet in late February 1968 of his decision to advise all commercial airlines that henceforth, 'only holders of United Kingdom passports who have employment vouchers' would be allowed to enter the United Kingdom.[33] It was thus with eyes wide open that the Wilson government rushed the 1968 Commonwealth Immigrants Act through parliament in record time, deliberately saddling commercial airlines with heavy consular responsibilities. The packed jetliners that touched down too late to meet the midnight deadline of 1 March would be the first to be turned away, their passengers among the original 'shuttlecock' Britons to be stranded between two states.

To what extent, then, can a tipping point be discerned between the relative complacency of 1963 and the fraught scenes at Nairobi Airport in late February 1968, when virtually anyone who could procure an empty seat hastily embarked at a moment's notice?[34] The draconian measures of July 1967 requiring Kenyan Asians to make way for Africans in the labour market are an obvious starting point, precipitating an immediate spike in departures for Britain in September 1967 and drawing attention to what had hitherto been a relatively invisible flow of migration. This was compounded by the increasingly alarmist rhetoric of key opposition parliamentarians in autumn 1967 – notably Duncan Sandys, Cyril Osborne and Enoch Powell – whose calls for government action to stem the 'flood' of Kenyan Asian arrivals generated mounting media interest. The UK High Commission in Nairobi was particularly sensitive to this latter factor, noting how statements by leading UK politicians were 'examined in Kenya with a fine tooth comb!', particularly those of Duncan Sandys, who acquired something of a hypnotic hold over the Kenyan dailies, his every utterance splashed across their front pages 'with the usual effects on the exodus'.[35]

But while these factors undoubtedly lent fuel to an already combustible situation, none of them should be taken at face value. There is a tendency, for example, to exaggerate the immediate hardship of Kenyatta's discriminatory employment voucher scheme, which had barely been implemented at the time of Callaghan's legislation.[36] Virtually none of the many thousands of arrivals prior to Callaghan's cut-off date had been officially refused the right to work in Kenya, and indeed local reporters at Nairobi airport struggled to find any outbound passengers who had even applied for a work voucher, let alone been refused.[37] Asked why he was leaving without seeking the right to stay and work, one man responded: 'What is the use of applying for a work permit? . . . Isn't it better to go now?' Another confessed that his work permit had been approved but that he was leaving in any case 'to try his luck'.[38] The records of the Kenyan Interior Ministry reveal the scant resources available to enforce the permit requirement, giving Asian employers any number of ways to evade detection.[39] To the extent that 'Africanization' was part of the cause of the early exodus, it was more from a sense of trepidation about what might lie ahead.

The same might be said of the 'exodus' itself, where the sheer weight of numbers is often assumed to have placed intolerable constraints on the Wilson government's room for manoeuvre.[40] Although the 13,000 arrivals from Kenya in 1967 represented a doubling of the numbers from the previous year, this was still only a modest proportion of the overall annual intake of registered Commonwealth Immigrants in 1967 (60,000 by the Home Office's estimate) and it was in any case amply offset by the 238,000 white British citizens who left the UK in 1967 for permanent settlement in other countries.[41] British departures to New Zealand alone were a sufficient counterweight to the Kenyan Asian arrivals in 1967. Indeed, over the two-year period of 1968–9, Australia received the equivalent of the entire Kenyan Asian population in (whites only) newcomers from the UK, all comfortably absorbed despite a host population of only 12 million – barely a fifth of that of the United Kingdom.[42] To the extent that Britain was hit by a 'floodtide' in 1967, it was the invisible net outflow of 155,000 souls seeking their fortunes elsewhere in the world. Nor for that matter was there anything particularly remarkable about the pressure of right-wing agitation to turn the immigrant tide. It had been nearly ten years since the 'white riots' of Nottingham had galvanized race as a volatile political issue in Britain, as veteran race-baiters such as Sir Cyril Osborne frequently boasted.[43] And it was more than three years since Labour's Patrick Gordon Walker had been ousted in the 1964 general election by the virulently anti-immigration Conservative campaign in Smethwick.[44] Right-wing reaction had thus been the constant companion of the Wilson government from the moment it took office – not a sudden flare-up demanding an urgent response.

The only discernible novelty in 1967 was the presence of two prominent faces on the opposition frontbench in Sandys and Powell among the advocates of drastic immigration reform.[45] Both were late converts to the cause, and neither built their case – at least initially – around the swelling numbers of Kenyan Asians entering the United Kingdom. Far more politically volatile were the racial disturbances in the United States in 1967, particularly the five days of open rioting in Detroit in late August that drew obsessive media attention.[46] Sandys and Powell were both avid collectors of press clippings of these events, and penned virtually identical cautionary tales in leading UK newspapers that same summer.[47] Powell's *Sunday Express* piece in early July ('Can We Afford to Let Our Race Problem Explode?') marked the beginning of his extended foray into racial polemics – accompanied by an unusually toxic cartoon by Michael Cummings (even by Cummings's unusually toxic standards). Advocating a reduction of the migrant intake to 'nil', the shadow defence secretary stressed the dangers of complacent inaction with the grim warning: 'We dare not look across the Atlantic and say, with folded arms, "It can't happen here.'"[48] Less than two weeks later, Sandys published 'Race Riots: Could They Happen Here?' in the *News of the World*, setting out his stall with the most implausible of anecdotes: '"Detroit today, London tomorrow". That was the threat uttered a few days ago by a British negro agitator.' No details were provided about the identity of the alleged 'British negro' or the cause of his agitation, but it was enough to bring the recent racial strife in the United States into vivid proximity. Less endowed with the rhetorical panache that came so naturally to Powell, Sandys wielded the bluntest of instruments in imploring readers: 'My answer is: Yes, it could [happen here]. But there is still time to prevent it.'[49] Neither article made any reference to Kenyan Asians, indeed there is no indication either Sandys or Powell had the slightest inkling of East Africa as a potential touchstone of white resentment in July 1967.

It was only when Kenyan Asian departures began to attract scrutiny from the press in autumn 1967 that these prophets of racial strife began paying attention. Sandys initially broached the matter in mid-September with Kenya's high commissioner in London, Tom Mboya, the exchange of letters betraying his profound ignorance on the matter at that time.[50] He would leave it to Powell to launch the first major assault against the Kenyan Asian 'influx' in a speech delivered a few weeks later in Kent on 18 October, deliberately timed to upstage the Conservative Party conference then taking place in Brighton. From the moment of Kenyan Independence, Powell intoned, 'hundreds of thousands of people in Kenya who had not belonged to this country before and never dreamt that they did started to belong to it just like you and me'. It was 'quite monstrous', he continued, that such an added burden to Britain's Commonwealth migrant intake could be actuated by an 'unforeseen loophole' in Britain's immigration rules.[51]

Shortly afterwards, Powell set off on his first ever visit to the United States, an experience that would only further inflame 'his increasingly apocalyptic view' (in the words of his principal biographer) of Britain's failure to control immigration.[52] Meanwhile, Sandys would follow suit in a Commons debate on 15 November, insisting that whatever was intended by the terms of Kenyan independence 'it was certainly never intended that this arrangement should provide a privileged back-door entry into the United Kingdom'. Drawing again on the American example, he warned that the government would similarly be 'held accountable by future generations for the misery and bitterness which will result' from a failure to take urgent remedial action.[53] Clearly, then, Kenyan Asians were not the primary impetus behind these dire premonitions. As far as Powell and Sandys were concerned, they were but a timely pretext to tout dystopian racial futures fomented by events unfolding on the other side of the Atlantic.

All of which is to say that it was only relatively late in the day (from November 1967 at the very earliest) that the rights of Kenyan Asians to enter the United Kingdom could in any sense be described as a deepening political 'crisis' – ironically, at the very time when the numbers had briefly subsided. The initial spike of 2,661 arrivals in September had already declined to an October figure of 1,916, dropping again to 1,334 in November – effectively halving the inflow from the first wave of Africanization 'panic'.[54] By the end of October, UK officials in Nairobi could happily report 'a certain calming down of passions in the Asian community on this subject at present'.[55] It was also at this time that Commonwealth Secretary George Thomson arrived for an official call on President Kenyatta, in which Kenyan Asian migration was placed a distant third on the agenda behind the Rhodesian stand-off and the war in Biafra (the migration issue only included belatedly at the behest of the UK high commissioner).[56] The talks themselves produced little in the way of constructive dialogue, with Kenyatta declaring bluntly that 'the fewer "Indians" that remained in Kenya, the better'. Although he would 'do nothing to force them out', he nevertheless insisted that the long-term solution was for the UK simply to 'close [its] doors to them' and divert the migrant flow to India 'where they rightly belonged'.[57] Even in the face of this cavalier attitude, the CRO did not consider the matter an urgent priority in October 1967.[58]

But in surprisingly short order, the Wilson government would be panicked into a radical overhaul of the rights of British citizenship, breaking all records for legislative efficiency from the first Cabinet submission of 12 February to the passage of the ban through parliament just over a fortnight later. From his perspective in the Cabinet Room, Richard Crossman marvelled at how only 'a few years ago everyone there would have regarded the denial of entry to British nationals with British passports as the most appalling violation of our deepest principles'.[59] Yet in truth, it was only a matter of a few short months. Among the voices that fell strangely silent during the crucial Cabinet deliberations were renowned civil libertarians such as Callaghan's predecessor at the Home Office, Roy Jenkins, and the veteran rights campaigner Barbara Castle (who would claim for the rest of her life that she had tragically fallen asleep during the fateful Cabinet meeting).[60] Short of attributing extraordinary powers of persuasion to the speeches of Sandys and Powell, it becomes crucial to consider the deeper fault lines that invested an otherwise distant and marginal dispute with such paradigm-shifting potential.

'YOUR £ DEVALUED! YOUR PASSPORT DEVALUED!':
NOVEMBER 1967

It was on the cusp of the Kenyan Asian crisis in late 1967 that the Wilson government reached an even more critical juncture – the 19 November decision to devalue the pound. Such was the political tumult that all other issues were swept aside, leaving a pall of psychological gloom that lingered well into 1968. The effects of the November devaluation are rarely, if ever, factored into the escalating drama of the Kenyan Asians dispute. The mounting pressures on sterling had beleaguered Britain's economic performance for years, due to an overheated appetite for foreign exchange and a corresponding weakness in international demand for the pound, forcing the government into costly offshore borrowing arrangements to maintain sterling at the sacrosanct rate of $2.80. The countervailing struggle to control the flow of Commonwealth immigration had no bearing whatsoever on these financial woes, nor did the economic implications of devaluation hold any overt sway over the measures subsequently introduced to curtail citizenship rights. Thus, the sterling debacle warrants little more than a passing footnote in virtually all accounts of the Kenyan Asian crisis (and vice versa), to the extent that it is mentioned at all.[61]

Yet the sterling crisis dovetailed with the plight of Kenyan Asians in complex, hard-to-quantify ways, affecting the calculations of virtually all of the main protagonists. The most obvious link is James Callaghan himself, transferred from the Treasury to the Home Office on 29 November as part of the political fallout of the devaluation debacle. Having repeatedly sworn off any intention to deflate the pound, it came as a personal humiliation when the moment finally arrived, causing him to lapse into 'a mood of deep gloom and pessimism' which he carried over to his gruelling tenure as home secretary.[62] He was surely the least equipped of Wilson's ministers to absorb the pressure of an all-new political impasse, and having borne much of the stigma of devaluation he resolved not to be wrong-footed a second time by indecision or loss of nerve. Although any assessment of the fog that followed him from the Treasury is bound to be speculative, there are clear traces of 'over-correction' in his political judgement, with the former crisis seemingly inflating the scale and urgency of the latter. His Cabinet colleagues were certainly struck by his singular refusal to brook dissent, bearing 'the air of a man whose mind was made up' as he steered his immigration reforms with bulldozer-like resolve.[63]

Equally discernible are the broader patterns of community response that drew these otherwise disparate episodes into an overarching narrative of a nation under siege. In the case of the embattled pound, an attitude of

Figure 12.1 Chancellor of the Exchequer James Callaghan leaves Downing Street for the House of Commons to deliver his historic statement on Britain's devaluation of the pound, 19 November 1967. Source: Hulton Archive/Getty Images.

martial defiance became the principal strategy for fending off the dreaded prospect of devaluation.[64] Sterling had long been the bearer of more than mere purchasing power, signifying a whole gamut of reassuring qualities – certainty, reliability, 'first-rateness' – that had survived the buffeting of Britain's eclipse as an imperial power. In its continuing role as a global reserve currency it symbolized one of the final vestiges of Britain's worldly self-projection, lumbered with weighty expectations out of all proportion to its function as a medium of commercial exchange. As David Blaazer has shown, the prolonged effort to maintain sterling at a fixed rate of exchange was consistently couched in the overwrought metaphors of military engagement, in which the pound was a 'citadel' enduring a serial 'bombardment' from the 'foreign enemies' of speculation.[65] Press coverage across the board continually reproduced these spurious analogies, obligingly spelt out by *The Sun* in dramatic upper case: 'BRITAIN UNDER SIEGE TO SAVE POUND'.[66]

Thus, when the prime minister's fateful announcement of a 14 per cent depreciation finally arrived, it could only be comprehended in terms of a historic 'capitulation' and an abject 'surrender' which no amount of government spin could counter. The ensuing clamour for drastic reductions in Britain's foreign exchange requirements – principally by offloading costly military commitments overseas – now became impossible to resist. The accelerated withdrawal from all residual bases 'East of Suez' two months later on 16 January 1968 only reinforced the perception of devaluation as the last sorry sequence in a prolonged national humiliation. Years later, Roy Jenkins would chide his own government 'for having made the defence of the $2.80 rate into a sort of British Dien Bien Phu' – calling to mind the ultimate imperial siege drama of the post-war era.[67]

It is here that the mounting agitation from late 1967 to resist the 'onslaught' of Kenyan Asians seems more than a mere coincidence. Lord Milverton's depiction of 'an unrestricted Asiatic invasion of this country' was constantly recycled in political commentary in an unmistakable echo of the perceived external 'attack' on sterling that persisted into 1968.[68] In January, the Home Office hastily collected data on every conceivable offshore claimant to a right of entry into the UK, not just in East Africa but also India, Malaysia, Singapore, Zambia, Malawi, Trinidad, Jamaica and Cyprus, arriving at the grossly inflated figure of 1.3 million potential passport holders that gained wide circulation, even though the vast majority of these would-be invaders had dual citizenship and thus could never be forced out of their homes.[69] Callaghan himself gestured to these spurious hordes in parliament, stoking fears of an 'invasion of a size which I have indicated' while attempting to have it both ways with a mollifying: 'even though it is not likely'.[70]

The two crises converged around the question of regulating the levers of exchange between Britain and the outside world. In both spheres, the British had long been accustomed to dictating the terms themselves with vastly favourable outward flows of capital and migrants, amply offsetting any inward liabilities. Now, with their capacity to control the balance considerably weakened, the threat of imminent harm at the hands of cynical overseas speculators came sharply to the fore, intensifying political pressure for evasive action. Moreover, both issues were laden with moral baggage about the cost to Britain's international standing should the government place too heavy a hand on the scale. Certainly, *The Times* was persuaded of the general public's 'primitive tribal attachment to the currency as a symbol of national vigour'.[71] The same considerations became entangled in the immigration debate, with Quintin Hogg at pains to assure parliament that 'I have always regarded the tenure of a British passport as something of which people can be proud and can be sure' – indeed, he could 'not conceal from the House the fact that I view the idea of devaluing a British passport with the utmost abhorrence'.[72] Parallels were drawn between the crisis of confidence among Commonwealth holders of sterling balances (who according to Lord Aldington had 'shown confidence in this country . . . and burnt their fingers') and the severe blow to 'the tremendous confidence' in British citizenship throughout the Commonwealth which, according to a petition sent to Buckingham Palace, had been 'seriously undermined'.[73] Conversely, those demanding an immediate ban likened the Kenyan Asian arrivals to 'customers of a bank' who had 'all entered and asked for payment of their outstanding balance at the same time'.[74] In this way, the recent memory of an offshore run on the pound became an efficient means of conveying the moral exigencies of curbing a precipitate run on the passport.

Figure 12.2 Kenyan Asians at Nairobi Airport objecting to the imposition of new entry restrictions for 'non-patrial' British subjects in the 1968 Commonwealth Immigrants Act, 26 February 1968. Source: Mirror/Mirrorpix/Almay Stock Photo.

Before long, 'devaluation' found its way into the everyday vernacular of immigration control, with Liberal Leader Jeremy Thorpe among the first to quip that Callaghan 'having devalued the pound, was moved to the Home Office to devalue the passport'.[75] The message was not lost in Nairobi, where protesters flocked to the airport brandishing placards decrying the 'Great British Betrayal: Your £ Devalued! Your Passport Devalued!' Meanwhile dissenting voices in the House of Lords berated a government that had 'devalued and debased the status of our diplomats and ministers' who henceforth would 'be met with mocking and mourning laughter' at international assemblies around the world in the officially designated 'Year of Human Rights'. Lord Willis lamented the tragic turning of the tables on Britain's moral leadership in the world, adding a tinge of post-colonial irony with the help of Shakespeare's Richard II:

> England, bound in with the triumphant sea,
> . . . is now bound in with shame,
> With inky bolts and rotten parchment bonds:
> That England, that was wont to conquer others,
> Hath made a shameful conquest of itself.[76]

On both sides of the Kenyan Asian dispute, attitudes and emotions were distorted by the perception that Britain's net worth had suffered a severe setback – galvanizing the anti-immigration lobby while stoking liberal indignation at Britain's squandered assets of tolerance and goodwill. The sentiments themselves were by no means without precedent, having accumulated over many years of presumptive national 'decline'. But the potent symbolism of November 1967, with external exigencies seemingly battering the nation on all sides, produced fertile ground for panic-driven measures to hold an increasingly un-British world at bay. The Kenyan Asians were the hapless trigger of these pent-up energies.

'NO ROOM IN THIS SMALL ISLAND': THE CONTRACTION OF ENGLAND

Shutting the entry gate to Kenyan Asians closed off another avenue of the Greater British imaginary. Although rarely (if ever) associated with the original Dilkean conception, the claims of Kenya's Asian community nevertheless rested on an expansive Britishness now seemingly collapsing inwards on itself. Meanwhile in Britain, the pervasive sense of encirclement brought renewed attention to the inner life of the nation. Duncan Sandys spelt out the implications in an urgent plea to the House of Commons: 'We cannot go back into history. We cannot let in all who had any connection with the British Empire, through their parents and grandparents. We just have not got room in this small island.'[77] 'History' had bequeathed the British people a more modest bearing, the flipside of their downgraded travel documents. It was therefore time for the nation's true dimensions to be cautiously surveyed. After more than three hundred years of outward endeavour, the constraints of geography suddenly seemed to matter a great deal when it came to refashioning a sense of the people for a world without empire. But as we shall see, it was not principally a 'British' people that emerged into view.

The mechanism chosen to distinguish 'undesirable' Kenyan Asians from their white settler counterparts was the legal concept of 'patriality', granting exemptions to those whose father or grandfather had been born within the territorial limits of the United Kingdom (later amended to include mothers as well). It was to become the crucial test of another new term invented for the occasion – the criteria of 'belonging', hitherto unheard of in international jurisprudence, now urgently summoned to explain the logic behind the latest exclusions. Identifying citizens 'who do not belong to the United Kingdom' provided moral justification for saying that Kenyan Asians had no real right to come, regardless of what might be written in their passports. In the tortured semantics of the Home Office, they were 'non-belongers', unlike their white settler neighbours whose direct line of descent bound them to British soil.[78]

Critics of these provisions saw straight through the subterfuge, protesting loudly that 'for the first time racism is written into British law'.[79] Callaghan was acutely sensitive to this, going out of his way to stress that 'the test that is adopted is geographical, not racial' – relying on what he termed a 'qualifying connection' to the physical realm of the United Kingdom.[80] But few were convinced, dismissing this 'piece of hypocrisy' as little more than a studied exercise in adding 'insult to injury' (in the words of the Liberal Party's David Steel).[81] Subsequent histories of the period have been equally disdainful, denouncing the 1968 Act as the 'most gratuitous instance of racialized controls', which served to remove the last residual 'inhibitions against defining the nation as a white one'.[82]

Yet Callaghan's insistence on the primacy of geography and a direct physical connection to British soil nevertheless warrants closer scrutiny, for it contained one crucial novelty: it dispensed entirely with the elastic frontiers that had profoundly shaped British civic thought and practice for generations. Even as other Commonwealth countries anchored their citizenship laws within their respective territorial boundaries in the wake of the Second World War, Britain had persisted with its expansive nationality provisions and unwieldy 'United Kingdom and Colonies' citizenship. Callaghan's patriality clause thus forced a dramatic break with tradition – more so, perhaps, than he himself realized. Although he was at pains to emphasize that there was 'no intention to deprive these persons of British nationality' (it was simply a matter of 'forming a queue', he insisted) the introduction of a patriality test represented the very antithesis of Dilkean logic. The upshot was a permanent retraction of the imaginative reach of British nationality, affecting all who fell within its narrowing dispensation.[83]

For the many supporters of the 1968 clampdown, the finer distinctions of patriality were merely common-sense statements of the obvious. Nevertheless, spelling it out as a legal maxim invited closer scrutiny of the territorial unit to which 'belongers' were presumed to be part of. The 1968 Bill consistently named 'the United Kingdom' as the place to which 'patrials' were inherently bound, yet it is striking how rarely 'the UK' figured in vernacular renderings, which were often left remarkably vague and unspecified (as in: 'this country', or simply 'here'). Nor, for that matter, did 'Britain' feature particularly prominently as the physical entity to which Kenyan Asians lacked a 'qualifying connection'. Instead, what came to the fore, evidently with more emotional purchase *as a place* than either Britain or the UK, was the rarefied realm of England.

For the likes of Enoch Powell, the 'undeniable truth' of being English raised the bar to belonging even for the children of immigrant families. With characteristic moral certainty, he declared during the early stages of the crisis: 'The West Indian or Asian does not by being born in England become an Englishman. In law he becomes a United Kingdom citizen by birth; in fact he is a West Indian or Asian still.'[84] Powell could not have made the distinction clearer between the 'United Kingdom' – a clinical term reserved for obfuscating legal niceties – and the true spirit of nationality which only England could evoke. Other prominent voices spoke out in similar terms, such as Lord Elton who excoriated the 'mad, make-believe world of Whitehall' that was incapable of distinguishing between 'Mrs Jones, Mrs Brown and Mrs Robinson', on the one hand, and the 'newcomer to Birmingham who cannot speak English, and three months ago had never heard of Birmingham or even of England' on the other. For the noble lord the matter was 'as simple as that', yet surely not so simple given the conspicuous lack of alignment between the object of his patriotic fervour and its formal legal designation.[85] Even Jim Callaghan – who meticulously observed the protocols of 'United Kingdom' and 'Britain' in his parliamentary oratory – could be described by his cabinet colleague Richard Crossman as 'sensible, constructive, sturdy, *thoroughly English*, doing his job' at the height of the Kenyan Asians crisis.[86]

Further evidence of these English proclivities can be discerned at the level of local politics, particularly those parts of the country where Kenyan Asians established themselves in larger numbers. Together with Coventry and Birmingham, Leicester was one of the major destinations of the earliest arrivals and the *Leicester Mercury* followed the story avidly from November 1967 through to the clampdown in March 1968. Devoting front-page coverage during the entire month of February, the *Mercury* made no secret of its editorial line which it conveyed in simple, forthright terms: 'Action to stem the flood is imperative.'[87] Headlines trumpeting 'Asians Heading for Leicester' left little doubt about the local implications, employing the familiar rhetoric of an uncontrolled surge that urgently needed 'sorting out'.[88] Even the most idle rumour or innuendo was considered newsworthy, including a bogus story that a 'Berlin-style airlift' was underway to spirit the entire Kenyan Asian community to Britain to thwart the ban.[89] Nor were any discernible editorial standards applied to the *Mercury*'s reader page, which unleashed a dirge of agitated and ill-tempered protest letters voicing a mixture of frustration, fear and sheer disbelief at the nation's apparent powerlessness to save itself.

Again, it was not 'Britain' (let alone the United Kingdom) that featured in these diagnostics so much as an embattled Englishness, determined that its voice should be heard. Much was made of the plight of 'the average English person', until recently 'very tolerant of all coloured people' but now 'beginning to feel bitter resentment' and anxiety for the 'future of our children in England'.[90] Of particular concern was the new-fangled 'rights activism' of the more militant newcomers, some of whom needed to be reminded that they were 'talking of England, the Englishman's home and heritage, not an Indian's, Jamaican's or Pakistani's country'.[91] Surveying more than a month of page four letters, one contributor was struck by 'the heart-felt worry and indignation of the English people' at the hands of the government's 'stupid handling' of the crisis.[92] The list of alleged hardships they had to endure was formidable, principal among them 'being taken over by these people and told what we should do and what we should not do' – a core grievance that gave rise to any number of unsubstantiated claims: 'Englishmen like myself cannot express opinions'; immigrants were 'given priority in all things over native-born Englishmen'; the government would soon 'make illegal, any discrimination in favour of the native Englishman'; indeed, the time was fast approaching 'when the native Englishman' would be 'a second-class citizen in an Afro-Asian community'.[93] The frequent resort to the term 'native' was an ironic means of reasserting primacy, pressed into service by a nervous constituency grasping for a form of words to distinguish themselves from presumptive outsiders. To have called themselves 'British' would have fallen short of the mark due to the legal rights of the 'non-belongers' to avail themselves of that very category, robbing it of 'nativist' connotations.

Indeed, to the extent that anyone in Leicester talked about Britishness, it was generally the Asian communities themselves and their various advocacy groups. Protesters who marched through the city on 2 March waved banners condemning discrimination against 'British Nationals', while their spokespeople from the Indian Workers Association appealed directly to the 'moral duty' of the government to respect 'fundamental rights as British citizens' and allow 'free and unrestricted entry to Britain'.[94] Hecklers by the roadside chanted 'out, out, out' while one of the rally organizers, twenty-three-year-old Mohinder Singh, received violent threats in an obscene letter signed by 'A Thoroughbred Englishman'.[95] Again, the adjective (and indeed the noun) served as a deliberate riposte, asserting physical ties that were more authentic and enduring than the Asians' tenuous statutory claims to an abstract idea. In this view, the long tradition of the 'open door' was only ever meant to serve 'those men and women of the British Isles who wished to return to their native land'.[96] No one had imagined that it might operate as a swing door. To correct the historical anomaly, the importance of being English took on a whole new moral significance.

Much as Duncan Sandys himself had foreshadowed, the newly assertive England came with downsized physical dimensions, befitting the diminutive stature of a people once deemed synonymous with capaciousness and reach. 'Just get an atlas out and look at these little islands', one *Mercury* reader implored. 'They cannot have open doors forever. There is no room.'[97] Others associated smallness with the squandered privileges of a disinherited people, predicting that 'soon we shall have no rights in this little island which once we called so proudly "England my country"'.[98] That the newcomers were the root cause of everything seemed beyond question, with one writer combining the themes of decline, diminished scale and the migrant deluge into a single pithy sentence: 'This poor little island of ours is slowly but surely sinking through overloading.'[99] For some, the 'only option' was to look further afield in the pioneering spirit of old: 'We are an English family and were once proud to be English. Now our thoughts are turning to emigration.'[100] Others were drawn to more combative language, such as the 'worried' correspondent who felt 'our only hope lies in forming an English Nationalist party to safeguard the future of our children'.[101]

More sinister still was the author of 'Logical Outlook' who recalled how 'two wars have proved that the English people will be pushed just so far before taking the initiative', warning of the dire consequences 'if this mass invasion is not stopped immediately'.[102]

The *Leicester Mercury* was no provincial penny dreadful but one of Britain's largest regional titles with a daily circulation of more than 180,000, a nominally 'liberal' pedigree and a respectable standing throughout Leicestershire.[103] Yet over a period of several months it saw fit to print an uninterrupted stream of racial invective by correspondents wielding *nomes de plume* such as 'White Johno', 'English Nationalist', the 'New Nationalists', 'Prospective Emigrant' and 'Saxon' – all striking the same rhetorical pose as the 'Thoroughbred Englishman' who vowed that 'bloodshed will be all you get'.[104] Precious few letter writers chose British-derived pennames, and the few who did – such as 'Pro Brittannia [*sic*]' – seemed ill at ease with the idiom of Britishness.[105] Thus, as Kenya's Asian community increasingly turned to Britain as a place of refuge, the destination itself was being busily refashioned as a white English redoubt.

'AMID THE FRAGMENTS OF DEMOLISHED GLORY': POWELL'S ENGLAND

When Leicester University students marched on the *Mercury* office in May 1968 to protest the paper's illiberal stance on Kenyan Asians, the paper's editor E. J. F. Fortune was wholly unapologetic, noting how his anti-immigrant line 'appears to be meeting with wider support among politicians of all parties'.[106] The veiled reference to the rising political fortunes of Enoch Powell is hard to miss, only weeks after his convulsive Birmingham speech in April 1968. The *Mercury* editor drew an implicit correlation between the political showdown over the Kenyan Asians in February and the refreshing (to his mind) new dispensation to voice racially discriminatory views more openly. Powell's sworn adversaries also understood the connection, condemning the Wilson government for unleashing demons that were 'the logical outcome of the betrayal of the Kenyan Asians' (in the words of the Communist Party's John Gollan).[107] Viewed in this light, there can be little doubt that the Kenyan Asian crisis was a crucial precursor to Powell's 'Rivers of Blood', alerting him to the untapped potential of a new brand of ethnic populism.[108] It is equally clear that it marked the self-conscious mobilization of English sentiment as a means of unlocking that potential. In the preamble to the Birmingham speech, Powell meditated on 'the supreme function of statesmanship' to speak out against preventable evils, and the daunting backlash awaiting those who dared rock the boat of political conformity. His idea of England was not only central to subverting the rules of polite conversation about race, but also the key to improvising a safe haven for Englishmen after empire.

Indeed, this latter preoccupation had engaged his intellectual energies for much of the preceding decade. Paul Foot was among the first in 1969 to map out Powell's intricate pathway from arch imperialist to avowed little Englander. The member for Wolverhampton South-West had entered British politics at the tipping point of imperial decline in 1950, and throughout his early career he had thrown himself wholeheartedly into the task of arresting the slide. It was during an earlier, failed attempt to enter parliament in the south Yorkshire coal mining constituency of Normanton in January 1947 that he had described the empire as 'the structure on which we are dependent for our very existence'.[109] Shortly afterwards, the announcement of Mountbatten's appointment to steer India towards independence would leave Powell in a state of stunned disbelief, and for years he would regale listeners with the story of his all-night sojourn through the streets of London, wandering aimlessly in search of solace. 'Occasionally I sat down in a doorway, my head in my hands, one's whole world had been altered.'[110] Whether this was indeed Powell's reaction in August 1947 or merely a parable later contrived to dramatize the effect, it is nevertheless hard to refute Foot's contention that 'resentment against the abandonment of the most glittering jewel of Empire died hard in Enoch Powell'.[111]

For Powell, it was more than a matter of relinquishing an object of deep personal investment. Writing in 1959, Peregrine Worsthorne predicted that Britain's stratified social structure would look very different with the implosion of imperial authority abroad. 'Everything about the British class system', he ventured 'begins to look foolish and tacky when related to a second class power on the decline.'[112] The early 1960s saw the arrival of the much-vaunted 'satire boom' on the British stage and screen, taking aim at the pretensions and inadequacies of the nation's ruling elites. In the words of one of its chief practitioners, Jonathan Miller: 'The smug courtesy of the public school sixth former, neatly adjusted to the demands of loyal service in a growing Empire', was 'at last becoming an object of ridicule.'[113] By the mid-1960s, A. P. Thornton could detect an emerging rift in the *raison d'être* of Britain's governing classes, particularly those of a Conservative persuasion. For all the political expediency of Britain's scramble out of Africa, he reflected, 'decolonization was not carried out without damage to the Tory concept of authority itself, with all its duty and habit'.[114] These misgivings transformed the end of empire from a series of unfortunate setbacks into an existential struggle in

Powell's rendering. Camilla Schofield points to a wider set of anxieties – about the demise of social deference, a new permissiveness, declining patterns of religious worship, and the 'hybridizing effects' of inward migration. In other words, it was not merely the empire but the very 'structures of social difference which had once ordered British imperial rule' that had begun to unravel.[115]

Thus, from the early 1960s Powell began to cut his losses, voicing a readiness to abandon his imperial vocation and seek alternative totems of authority and civic order. It was on St George's eve in 1961 (in an address to the Royal Society of St George) that he began openly to question the imperial logic of an expansive Britishness:

> There was a saying, not heard today so often as formerly, 'What do they know of England who only England know? It is a saying which dates. It has a period aroma . . . which the historian Sir John Seeley, in a now almost forgotten but once immensely popular book, called *The Expansion of England*. In that incredible phase, which came upon the English unawares, as all true greatness comes upon a nation, the power and influence of England expanded with the force and speed of an explosion.[116]

Powell deliberately geared the speech to his audience's patriotic instincts, offering a rousing tribute to the 'invincible seapower' that had brought the 'islands and continents' from the Rockies to the Australian deserts and the lakes of Africa 'under the spell of England'. But no sooner had he invoked these familiar comforts than he revealed his true purpose, turning an unsentimental eye to the present: 'That phase is ended, so plainly ended that even the generation born at its zenith, for whom the realization is the hardest, no longer deceive themselves as to the fact.' It was vintage Powell, describing developments he knew his audience would find difficult and unsettling as though they were inescapably obvious to all but the most hopelessly deluded. 'That power and that glory have vanished', he pressed on, and it was up to the present generation to find out 'what it is that binds us together'.[117]

That Powell should have chosen Seeley as the foil for his first major excursion into post-imperial patriotism was no accident. Of all the nineteenth-century sages of Greater Britain, Seeley remained the most enduring and respected figure. But in Powell's rendering he also symbolized the antiquated mindset that had blinded people to the opportunity that now presented itself:

> So we today at the heart of a vanished empire, amid the fragments of demolished glory, seem to find, like one of her own oak trees, standing and growing, the sap still rising from her ancient roots to meet the spring, England herself. Perhaps after all we know most of England who only England know.[118]

374

All along, Powell maintained, England had lain patiently in wait for her people to return, to reconnect with the innate 'affinities with earlier generations of English, generations before the "expansion of England", who felt no country but this to be their own'.[119] England thus restored need never rely on the empire as the 'structure on which we are dependent for our very existence', for the nation had deeper roots in the pre-imperial soil, 'beyond the grenadiers and the philosophers of the eighteenth century, beyond the pikemen and the preachers of the seventeenth, back through the brash adventurous days of the first Elizabeth and the hard materialism of the Tudors'.[120] The bedrock of Powell's patriotism was thus not only pre-imperial but pre-British. It was emphatically 'England' he saw rising from the ashes.

This would become Powell's credo in the years ahead, as he strove to recover a proportionate sense of political selfhood. By the mid-1960s he would go as far as claiming that the British empire 'never existed' – and that its enduring mental grip was merely 'the psychological tension between our emotions and observable reality'.[121] But for all the passionate renunciations, the constant diatribes against the 'persisting illusion that there is a world elsewhere', the excoriation of empire as a debilitating wound that had sapped the people's energies, Powell was never himself able fully to jettison behaviours and attitudes learned over a lifetime of 'distant wanderings' of his own.[122] As Bill Schwarz contends, decolonization may have afforded Powell 'the opportunity for a more profound, revivified patriotism to emerge', but at the same time he continued to imagine England 'from the vantage of a man for whom the precepts of colonial order remained the natural order of things'.[123] If there were an 'illusion', it was surely Powell's presumption in rewinding the clocks to Tudor England, expunging the effects of three centuries of imaginative engagement with the wider world. He might disavow his former enthusiasms, but he could not erase the deeply internalized habits that precluded him from accepting Asians or West Indians, wherever they were born, as fellow nationals.[124] Englishness provided an emotionally satisfying dodge – and a convenient release from the unwanted connotations of being British.

It might be objected that such intricate manoeuvres were the special preserve of English Tories of a very particular stripe. But it was not only conservatives who made sense of their Englishness through the prism of fallen empires. As Raphael Samuel once noted, 'for the "Progressives" of the 1960s, empire, the British national identity itself, was something to escape from'.[125] Even an apparently inert source such as the 1965 edition of *Fowler's Dictionary of Modern English Usage* could allude to the moral stakes, offering

unsolicited advice to anyone inclined to quibble over the popular prefer-
ence for England over Britain: 'How should an Englishman utter the words
Great Britain with the glow of emotion that for him goes with *England?* ... It is
unreasonable to ask forty millions of people to refrain from the use of the
only names that are in tune with patriotic emotion.'[126] The novelist John
Fowles addressed the issue with unusual candour in a 1964 essay 'On Being
English but not British' – framing the conflict between Englishness and
Britishness as a relatively recent phenomenon:

> For a decade now I have been haunted by the difficulty of defining the
> essence of what I am but did not choose to be: English ... Increasingly, I see
> my Britishness as a superficial conversion of my fundamental Englishness,
> a recent façade clapped on a much older building. 'Britain' is an
> organizational convenience, a political advisability, a passport word.[127]

Though in no sense an enthusiast for Powellism, his inner reflections reveal
an uncannily similar reasoning, not least his depiction of Britishness as
something recently 'clapped on' to a more organic Englishness. To be
British was quite literally to be afforded a 'passport' to a world of entitlement, still prized by those who believed that Britain 'was and should be
stronger than any other country'.[128] But it was increasingly a world of
diminishing returns. Disavowing any 'Little Englander' agenda, Fowles
drew what seemed to him the inevitable conclusion:

> The time has come when there is no other but administrative and
> political necessity to talk about being British; and the agonizing
> reappraisal we English-Britons have had to make of our status as
> a world power since 1945 in fact permits us to be much more English
> again ... In neither of the great political parties do the moderate
> majorities any longer defend this antiquated concept of an Imperial
> Britain on Whom the Sun Never Sets, a concept now at least twenty
> years stranded in the past. But it creates a kind of afterglow, it pervades
> many of our moods with a nostalgia, it hampers our present, and worst of
> all, it still obscures the Green England.[129]

Here, Powell's core sensibilities were faithfully replicated. In dismissing
'Britain' as a mere 'passport word', Fowles foreshadowed the logic that
would strip tens of thousands of offshore passport holders of their claim
to belonging only four years later. Yet there can be no easy categorization of
Fowles as a fellow traveller of Powellite ethnic populism. Rather, his testimony shows how widely and pervasively the resurgence of England resonated. No single political persuasion held a monopoly over the recalibrations
of empire's end. The need to find a secure footing could affect anyone

whose outlook had in some unselfconscious way been anchored in an imperially ordered world – Liberal, Labour or Tory renegade. This helps to explain Powell's extraordinary political traction, riding roughshod over conventional party-political lines with an intensity fired by the knowledge that long-established categories were breaking down.

When Harold Wilson made a television appearance on 19 November 1967 to break the grim news of the devaluation of sterling, he committed the infamously ill-advised gaffe that 'the Pound in your pocket' would remain unaffected – a clumsy attempt to instill calm in an otherwise alarming situation. But arguably more significant were his closing remarks, where he succumbed to the general foreboding: 'We are on our own now. It means Britain first.'[130]

It was a strange thing to say. If the British people were on their own, with whom or what had they parted company? What priorities had previously taken precedence, and why should they now be so relegated? Wilson may have been hinting at a sense of liberation from overseas currency speculators or the crippling terms of Swiss bankers, but such a reading fails to square with his choice of words (and he would soon find in any event that he had freed himself from neither). More likely he was referring to the interests of offshore holders of sterling throughout the Commonwealth whose 'confidence' in the pound had been one of the major psychological barriers to devaluation. In shaking off these encumbrances and placing Britain's own economic survival above the value of Commonwealth sterling balances, Wilson invoked the declaratory procedures of national independence, drawing on language and imagery that would have been immediately intelligible to his listeners. But it was not in the style of a Nehru, Nkrumah or Kenyatta – no 'tryst with destiny', no battles won or freedom extolled. To be 'on our own', to put 'ourselves first' suggested a more grudging disposition, recalling the resent-ments and disenchantment of white settlers with the broken promise of Greater Britain. It was precisely the sort of thing Ian Smith might (and in fact did) say in 1965; or Hendrik Verwoerd in March 1961 upon his eviction from the Commonwealth.[131] It was likewise a direct echo of Australian and New Zealand primary producers in 1962, alarmed at the prospect of British entry into Europe.[132] Just as Greater Britain was founded on shared myths, memories and mutual regard, so too its precipitate demise summoned a common vocabulary of contingent selfhood.

The problems multiplied in the latter months of 1967, when the shock of devaluation and the sudden obsession with Kenyan Asian arrivals signalled the arrival of a world stripped of the former possibilities for outward endeavour. But the political response, whether it be the mannered rhetoric of Enoch Powell or the unalloyed racism of the *Leicester Mercury* readers' page, was to put anything but 'Britain' first. When Harry Goulbourne published his pioneering study of race and post-war nationality in the early 1990s, he framed the introduction of Commonwealth immigration restrictions in terms of an attempt 'to redefine post-imperial *British* national community'.[133] But it also marked a push to substitute 'British' with something else; the moment when the blurred boundaries long inherent in the British-English axis underwent a subtle realignment in England's favour.

Finally, a word on race, the elemental lodestone of the Kenyan Asians crisis and much else besides. Fenner Brockway put it succinctly in the House of Lords on the eve of the clampdown in February 1968: 'This Bill would never have been introduced if the Asians from Kenya pouring into this country had been British and had been white ... we are not being true to the facts if we do not recognise that it arises from circumstances of racist psychology and conditions which encourage it.'[134] None of this would have been lost on Ranjanbala Vaid, whose multiple deportations boiled down to the complexion of her skin, far more than the administrative protocols of her passport or the birthplace of her grandparents. In Bill Schwarz's formidable body of work, memories of an idealized empire are shown to have been dramatically stirred by the sudden arrival of non-white nationals in increasing numbers, infiltrating 'the syntax of Englishness' in remarkably explicit ways. 'From the ruins of colonial empires across the globe', he writes, 'there emerged, among the white populations themselves, a recharged, intensified self-consciousness of their existential presence as white.'[135] This is largely borne out by the evidence presented here – the 're-racialization of England' at empire's end, necessitating substantial borrowings from settler colonial experience to make sense of it all.[136]

But although whiteness was reassigned as the essence of being English (indeed, the very quality that rendered it preferable to a racially compromised Britishness), it should not be assumed that Powellite populism merged effortlessly with the white racial affinities of old. Far from exhibiting continuities, it was a radically truncated version. Memories of empire could stoke the fires of ethnic patrimony, but as decolonization encroached closer to home and England emerged as the last refuge, the physical frontiers of nationhood were drastically curtailed. The renunciations of empire, so often coupled with repudiations of being British, were the necessary corollary of the contraction of England at a time when new distinctions were constantly being drawn. As older transoceanic affinities broke down, whiteness remained essential, but no longer sufficient as the arbiter of who belonged. Relinquishing these last residual investments in the idea of Greater Britain would mark the first unwitting steps towards the disaggregation of Britain itself.

13

'BRITISH WE ARE AND BRITISH WE STAY': TROUBLES

West Briton is the title of a 1962 memoir by Irish journalist and broadcaster Brian Inglis, chronicling the twilight of the 'old Protestant Ascendancy' in his hometown of Malahide to the north of Dublin Bay. An affectionate but by no means uncritical account, Inglis marvels at the durability of a micro-community populated by elderly widows and retired Indian Army officers, seemingly unaffected by the 'great betrayal' of the interwar years. The 1921 Treaty that partitioned Ireland into a nationalist south and loyalist north was but a mere 'passing phase' for these diehard Britishers, their symbols of defiance as innocuous as they were ubiquitous – the Tennis Club, Miss Ahern's junior school, St Andrews Church on the hill, the 'Island' golf course across the estuary and the peeling stucco of the mock-palladian Grand Hotel.[1] Carrying on life as they had always known it, they were not so much in open revolt as collective denial that their world could be rent asunder by the 'signatures of English politicians they despised and local nationalist leaders they detested'.[2] Yet for all their resilience the author's tone is retrospective, documenting an almost imperceptible decline as life slowly 'ceased to be so aggressively English' and a new generation emerged that was 'no longer so cut-off from the Brendans and Kevins, with whom they had achieved a tacit clubbable understanding'.[3] Inglis ascribed this, not to the sudden conflagration that followed the First World War but the more subtle social changes in the wake of the Second, as new economic forces stimulated the growth of a Catholic middle class who were 'not content to be pushed around'.[4] The 'Malahide set' might still be 'West Brits', but by the early 1960s they had been absorbed, as if by osmosis, into the republican world around them.

Eight years later, a radically different portrait of the Ascendancy's demise appeared in *Troubles* – the first of J. G. Farrell's acclaimed empire trilogy, later to be awarded the 'Lost Booker' for 1970. Set in 1919 on a stretch of Ireland's south-east coast, Farrell's fictional village of Kilnalough is the mirror image of Malahide, replete with the time-worn grandeur of the Hotel Majestic that takes centre stage. But it is not the long recessional of Anglo-Ireland that sets the pace. Here, it is the smouldering nationalist insurgency in the aftermath of the Great War that encircles and ultimately engulfs the Protestant redoubt within. Unlike the lingering, genteel shabbiness of Inglis's Malahide, the fate of loyalist Kilnalough is sealed in a matter of days as the insurrection closes in and the 'separate, luxurious species, which had ruled Ireland for almost five hundred years' is forcibly turned out.[5] In the climactic scene the hotel is set ablaze, the assembled townsfolk awestruck by its 'blinding magnificence'. Against this backdrop, 'flaming, shrieking creatures' leap from the burning gutters and windows into the darkness like 'fiery demons pouring out of the mouth and nose of a dying Protestant'.[6] The outcome is as brutal as it is abrupt, coldly compressed in Farrell's matter-of-fact finale: 'And that was the end of the Majestic.'[7]

Composed at opposite ends of the 1960s, these equally absorbing accounts might have been written in alternate centuries for their wildly divergent depictions of the eclipse of Anglo-Ireland – the one piecemeal and quiescent, the other spontaneous and highly combustible. To account for the disparity, we need to look north of the border to the dramatic rekindling of sectarian strife that punctuated the intervening years. Inglis's memoir appeared at a time of relative calm in Northern Ireland, conditioned by some forty years of Protestant and Unionist domination of the Stormont Assembly in Belfast. Despite periodic clashes and bottled resentments, there was little in 1962 to signal the violence that would flare up at the close of the decade. By the time Farrell began scouting locations for his novel, however, the descent into communal turmoil had already begun, its traumatic consequences unfolding as the work neared completion. As he later affirmed: 'I was trying to write about now as well as then.'[8]

No account of the global convulsions of Britishness in the decades after the Second World War can ignore the outbreak of the Northern Ireland Troubles. Of all the myriad setbacks to Britain's worldly dispensation during these years, none were so divisive, disruptive or enduring in their implications. More elusive, however, is the matter of why such a perennial political quarrel erupted into wholesale violence when it did. As Richard Bourke observes, all too often the language and imagery used to describe the chaotic sequence of events have tended to 'distort the object they are seeking to understand'.[9] The frequent resort to 'tribalism', 'atavism' and an indelible sectarian fervour has lent the Troubles an inexorable quality, apportioning blame to 'implacable hatreds' and 'ancient antagonisms'.[10] While fulfilling an understandable need to condemn the bloodshed as irrational and barbaric, such explanations overlook the contemporary dynamism that brought organized violence to the fore. Arguably, the distinguishing feature of the Troubles was their *explosive* character – catching the Ulster Unionist government of Captain Terrence O'Neill largely unawares. O'Neill's ineptitude in handling the escalating unrest soon cost him his job – ironically, for a Stormont premier who had presided over a period of tentative reform and a discernible thaw in communal relations.[11] Although in retrospect his efforts to combat sectarianism seem wholly ineffective, there were any number of contemporaries in the O'Neill years – Protestant and Catholic alike – who voiced guarded optimism for the future, dismissing loyalism and republicanism as outdated encumbrances.[12]

The question that goes to the heart of the Troubles outbreak is: what changed? What were the combustible materials, the key flashpoints that punctured the mood of cautious confidence, tipping the scale towards internecine strife? Any number of possible socio-economic causes have been canvassed – the decline in shipbuilding and textile manufacturing, rising unemployment, the radicalization of nationalist resistance and a widening rift in living standards between Northern Ireland and the rest of the UK. While none of these factors can be ignored, there is a wider perspective that tends to be overlooked – namely the end of empire, and specifically the creeping obsolescence of Britishness abroad. Ulster was by no means insulated from the larger story that concerns us here. On the contrary, by the late 1960s it was arguably the standout variable that distinguishes this period from so many earlier phases of sectarian discord.

Prior to the pivotal events of this decade, the matrix of Ulster's competing identity claims had been woven into a broader Britannic fabric, in a world of imperial provinces, dominions, dependencies and domains where the persistence of a British enclave in an otherwise republican Ireland had a plausible logic anchored in a wider legitimacy. Despite the ordeal of partition and the uneasy truce of the 1921 Treaty, the empire afforded Northern Ireland's loyal inhabitants a certain continuity and wider connectivity, acting as a psychological bulwark against the threat of absorption by the South. Conversely, if Ulster unionism was 'primarily an imperial, not a metropolitan variety of Britishness', the stripping away of the imperial backdrop in the decades after 1945 increasingly cast the province in a very different light, aligning it with other late imperial flashpoints around the world.[13] To be sure, most of the empire had been effectively liquidated by the time the first barricades were raised in the streets of Derry and Belfast. But it was precisely the advanced stage of imperial decline that posed highly charged questions about the long-term viability of a virulently loyal British outpost in the face of a newly energized nationalist challenge.

For decades, an often-fierce debate has raged over whether Ireland ought properly to be considered a 'colony' of the British empire. This chapter sidesteps that conceptual logjam to advance two core claims. First, that regardless of how Northern Ireland is categorized, the eclipse of Greater Britain provided ample encouragement and legitimacy to the 'anti-colonialist' credentials of militant nationalism. Precisely how this filtered down to the level of street battles and civil disorder, however, requires careful qualification. Second, and more significantly, the reaction of the Unionist majority cannot be viewed in isolation from the wider repercussions of Britain's imperial endgame. Although Northern Irish Protestants rarely mobilized any concerted opposition to the dismantling of the British empire, it was the cumulative weight of Westminster's perceived duplicity and 'betrayal' of embattled Britons around the world that aggravated long-harboured suspicions of an impending sell-out of Ulster.

Misgivings about Britain's mettle in the face of the nationalist challenge were as old as Carson and the Covenant, but with the empire reduced to a few scattered overseas territories, a devalued pound and a protracted withdrawal from 'East of Suez' on the cards, these doubts acquired a new, combative edge. When the Heath government reached the fateful decision to close Stormont and impose direct rule in March 1972 'the bile of bitterness against Britain rose high', consolidating a division of the loyalist community into rival moderate and extremist elements that placed the future viability of the United Kingdom in jeopardy.[14] 'The Great Britain concept is within a measurable distance of ending in Northern Ireland', declared the ultra-loyalist Ulster Vanguard in early 1972. 'Paradoxically, it may yet prove to be that mainland Britain cannot survive without Ulster.'[15]

ANTI-COLONIALISM AND THE TROUBLES OUTBREAK

Pinpointing precisely when the Troubles began is an inexact science. Popular memory calls to mind the open street clashes and barricades of the 'Battle of the Bogside' in Derry in August 1969, but there were earlier tremors around the fiftieth anniversary of the Easter Rising in 1966.[16] Virtually all accounts emphasize the formation of the Northern Ireland Civil Rights Association (NICRA) in February 1967 – a loosely integrated network of activists and social justice groups that targeted specific grievances in the allocation of housing, discrimination in employment, and above all the gerrymandered local electoral system that entrenched Unionist political dominance. 'One man one vote' was the abiding slogan of an avowedly peaceful movement that identified with much of the progressive social agenda of the late 1960s.

It was NICRA's impatience with the glacial pace of reform under Terrence O'Neill (himself increasingly under fire within his own ranks for moving too fast) that led to the adoption of 'direct action' in the form of non-violent street protest and civil disobedience. The initial flame was lit by a sectarian tenancy dispute in Country Tyrone in June 1968, when a council house in the village of Caledon was allocated to the nineteen-year-old private secretary of a local Unionist politician, bypassing two Catholic families squatting in homes on either side. The episode snowballed into a major political controversy when nationalist MP Austin Currie staged a sit-in on the premises amid a welter of publicity. Televised images of the squatters' forcible removal garnered a rapid surge of sympathy and support, directly inspiring a series of large-scale civil rights marches throughout the summer and autumn of that year.[17]

The new spirit of public protest and civic activism ran headlong into the indignation and ire of Protestant reaction. Organizations such as the Rev. Ian Paisley's Ulster Protestant Volunteers lost no time mobilizing in defence of the status quo, setting the scene for a protracted sectarian clash. The flashpoint came in October 1968, when the Stormont government imposed a series of restrictions on a planned civil rights march in Derry. The protest went ahead in defiance of the decree, only to be confronted by the truncheons and water canon of the Royal Ulster Constabulary. Reports of seventy-seven civilians treated for bruises and lacerations were corroborated by television footage of unrestrained beatings of unarmed protesters.

Three months later the scene was repeated when protesters marching from Belfast to Derry were ambushed at Burntollet Bridge by loyalists armed with cudgels and makeshift missiles. In a satellite age, such disturbing images circulated rapidly around the world, and 'at a stroke rewrote the basic grammar of Northern Ireland politics'.[18] Accusations of police harassment and destruction of property in Derry's Bogside in the days after the Burntollet incident only stiffened Catholic resolve, and the first 'Free Derry' barricades were raised on 5 January 1969. By the summer of that year, Terrence O'Neill had been hounded out of office by his own party and the civil rights agenda had given way to open rioting, pitched street battles between police and protesters and newly resurgent paramilitary forces on both sides taking matters into their own hands. On 14 August, the British Army was deployed to restore order, a move that in the long run only served to compound sectarian polarization and entrench mutual enmities.[19]

Figure 13.1 British troops arrive at Derry's Bogside, 1 August 1969. Source: Express/ Stringer/Getty Images.

Conventional accounts of the Troubles outbreak have tended to emphasize patterns of causation explicable largely in terms of Ireland's internal religious and social structures. While national and sectarian divisions are obviously axiomatic, they are insufficient to capture the wider international setting that helped to produce such an incendiary outcome – as several historians have argued in recent years. Some have drawn parallels with the larger pattern of civil disturbances and student protests that erupted throughout Europe in spring 1968, going so far as to claim that Northern Ireland 'should be considered in the same breath as Paris, Rome and Berlin'.[20] Others have depicted the Troubles more broadly as an Irish affiliate of the Civil Rights movement in the American South – a connection frequently made at the time by the NICRA protestors themselves, bearing placards heralding 'Alabama hits Dungannon' and demanding justice for 'White Negroes'.[21] Some of the leading activists themselves have recalled how they absorbed 'the tactics of Martin Luther King in America' – particularly the emphasis on non-violent street marches as a means of raising public awareness and mobilizing popular sympathy.[22] Conversely, transatlantic connections have been drawn between Protestant militancy and the support network of right-wing

American fundamentalist groups, apprehending a shared struggle against a wider conspiracy of Catholicism, ecumenism and the insidious heresy of the social gospel.[23]

It seems remarkable, therefore, that virtually no attempt has been made to explain the Troubles in terms of the wider dynamics of a declining British empire, despite ample historical parallels and an abundance of speculation by contemporaries to that very effect. One possible source of hesitation lies in the unresolved dispute over whether Ireland ought properly to be regarded as a 'colony' of Britain. The intricacies of the debate need not delay us here, suffice it to say that more is at stake than the finer details of historical classification.[24] As Stephen Howe cautions, 'invocations of the idea of Northern Ireland as "Britain's last colony"' have a strong tendency to posit 'a teleology by which the province must itself be destined for imminent decolonisation, the final unfinished business of the global collapse of empires'.[25] In other words, the incendiary nature of the conceptual debate is part and parcel of the broader sectarian conflict itself, making it a particularly precarious exercise to distinguish the late imperial *context* from its polemical battlefield.[26]

Nevertheless, it is at least plausible that Britain's truncated imperial purview might have wielded a decisive influence over the Troubles outbreak, irrespective of whether Ireland be deemed a colony or otherwise. The polemical evidence itself is an obvious place to start, notably the quickening conviction among nationalists that they were engaged in the final act of a global anti-colonial struggle. Leading Sinn Féin activists such as Gerry Adams wasted no opportunity in characterizing the Troubles in these terms, insisting that 'Violence in Ireland is the result of British Imperialism, of the British connection and the British presence' – often drawing direct comparisons with other imperial flashpoints from which the British had duly extricated themselves.[27] At issue here is not the veracity or verifiability of these convictions, but whether they were in some way actuated or emboldened by the wider circumstances of Britain's imperial retreat.

How novel this situation was is not always fully recognized. To be sure, anti-imperialism had a long history in nationalist advocacy, reaching back at least as far as the withering critiques of the mid-nineteenth-century nationalist press.[28] But it was not until a century later, with the eclipse of the British world-system, that it emerged fully formed as *anti-colonialism*. For all the rhetorical disdain for 'imperialism' among earlier generations of Irish radicals, it was rare for them to make genuine common cause with colonial iniquities elsewhere in the world, and even when they did it was invariably 'an ironic exercise in racialized self-deprecation' – in other words, the analogy was frequently and indeed intentionally superficial.[29]

Leading nineteenth-century nationalist icons from Daniel O'Connell to William Smith O'Brien drew clear distinctions between Ireland's cause and the colonization schemes of Asia, Australasia, Africa and North America, which they rarely opposed and often wholeheartedly supported.[30] The more conservative streak of nationalism continued to insist that the colonies 'belonged to Ireland as much as England – we paid dearly enough for them';[31] and while radical Fenians and home rulers could occasionally voice sympathy for Zulus, Afghans and other fellow antagonists of Britain, there remained a strong undercurrent of moral ambiguity – with the clear implication that the white folk of Ireland were more obvious candidates for self-determination.[32] When Eamon de Valera embarked on an extended fundraising tour of the United States in June 1919, he showed little interest in the injustice of racial segregation, campaigning instead on the grievance that Ireland 'was the only white nation on earth still in the bonds of political slavery'.[33] Significantly, the Proclamation of the Irish Republic in Easter 1916 said nothing about any wider struggle to eradicate colonialism worldwide.[34]

It would not be until the 1960s that Irish nationalism articulated an unreservedly anti-colonial worldview, buoyed by a surge in anti-colonial activism worldwide. The emphasis on colonial questions in the United Nations and other international fora furnished ample precedent for construing the problems of contemporary Ireland in this wider setting. The nationalist *Irish News*, for example, condemned the October 1968 Derry riots in terms of unalloyed solidarity: 'The white men of Derry have the same rights as the black men of Rhodesia, and they will take what your government will not give.'[35] Liam de Paor pressed the analogy in the opening lines of his highly influential *Divided Ulster* in 1970: 'In Northern Ireland Catholics are blacks who happen to have white skins ... The Northern Ireland problem is a colonial problem, and the "racial" distinction (and it is actually imagined as racial) between the colonists and the natives is expressed in terms of religion.'[36] Such a conceptualization – widely reflected in press commentary of the day – contained echoes of much older patterns of Irish identification with oppressed non-European peoples.[37] With the empire's rapid disintegration, the use of colonial analogies to ensure that Irish grievances did not pass unnoticed became far more commonplace, acquiring fresh conviction and greatly enhanced rhetorical purchase. Richard Bourke describes a 'recrudescence in anti-imperialist rumination' on the back of Asian and African decolonization in the late 1960s, but the apparent continuities mask a qualitative shift in the principles and potency of anti-colonial sentiment.[38]

Consequently, there was no shortage of equally impassioned scepticism about Irish Nationalism's anti-colonial credentials. Conor Cruise O'Brien dissected the colonial analogy at length in his seminal *States of Ireland* (1972), drawing on his background as a UN diplomat in the Congo crisis to rule out 'the stark, dramatic Manichean contrasts between *le colon* and *le colonisé*', which, although superficially tempting, were 'too simple for the [Irish] situation'.[39] He went on to suggest that it was the Republic of Ireland's demand for a united Ireland, irrespective of the wishes of Northern Protestants, that was 'essentially a colonial claim' – unable to resist a colonial counter-analogy of his own.[40] Both sides of the debate, in other words, were susceptible to the newfound polemical force of an anti-colonialism which was cutting deep inroads into Northern Irish politics.[41]

That this was no mere academic feud can also be gleaned from the rhetoric of militant nationalist groups seeking to exploit the more favourable international climate for anti-colonial mobilization. In one 1970 strategic appraisal, Sinn Féin surveyed Britain's diminished standing in the world and concluded that there had never been a better time to be an Irish nationalist, with the sudden convergence of 'factors which disturb the ability of the imperialists to govern in the manner to which they had previously been accustomed, and which create a political crisis for imperialism'. Specifically, the advanced stage of decolonization worldwide had 'given tremendous impetus to national liberation movements everywhere'. Britain being 'increasingly unable to stand on her own as an imperial power' presented Republican Ireland with a unique 'opportunity to take advantage of Britain's weakness and isolation and to strike out on an independent political and economic course'. Indeed, the outlook seemed 'more favourable than ... 50 years ago. An Irish Republic in the seventies would have many friends in the world which did not exist then.'[42] Here we see a latter-day iteration of the 1916 maxim 'England's difficulty is Ireland's opportunity'[43] – only here the difficulty pertained to a British world-system in tatters. It rendered explicit what was already implicit in much of the resurgent militancy of the era: that the rules of engagement had profoundly altered. To this extent, the timing and trajectory of the Troubles can be linked to a new belligerence emboldened by a transformed international setting.

But some caution is also warranted, not least when we consider more broadly the range of radical activist groups in Northern Ireland that adopted an anti-colonial platform in these early years of civil strife. By no means all civil rights protesters were nationalists, particularly elements within NICRA and its more radical offshoot, People's Democracy (PD; founded by Queen's University students in the aftermath of the 1968 Derry street march). For some of the most articulate critics of 'imperialism', the object was not *national* liberation but a romantic neo-Marxist programme of working-class resistance, embracing the exploited proletariat on both sides of the sectarian divide.[44] Thus, when the charismatic co-founder of PD, Bernadette Devlin, invoked Ireland's long history of continual struggle 'to end British occupation, British imperialism, and British capitalism', the key to her thinking was the juxtaposition of the latter two ingredients, the perennial bedfellows of Marxist–Leninist theory.[45] Indeed, she was often at pains to distinguish the twin evils of imperialism and capitalism from the British people themselves. 'We are not fighting the British', she revealed to a perplexed audience at Berkeley in 1971, 'most of our allies are in the British working class. We are not fighting any narrow national struggle.'[46] In this scheme of things, the Protestant working class were also hapless victims of the imperial system, duped by a 'few paltry privileges' into believing their 'chains were a little less heavy' than their Catholic counterparts.[47] Similarly, the pages of PD's *Free Citizen* frequently and emphatically proclaimed that 'the root cause of the trouble in Ireland is British Imperialism', but with strikingly little in the way of exemplification, which was more readily drawn from the Vietnam War, Cuba or the rural guerrilla struggle in Latin America than anything relating directly to British colonial experience.[48] Although PD was emphatic that 'the border must go because it is a relic of imperialism', the critique was applied indiscriminately to the governing structures on both sides, insisting that 'in order to root out imperialism, we [also] have to root out the neo-imperialist set-up in the South'.[49]

In other words, 'imperialism' could encompass a great many things, often wrenched from any identifiably 'British' coercive context. Leading PD activist Eamonn McCann offered some revealing reflections on the raucous public meetings and rousing rhetoric in Derry's Bogside in the heat of the street battles of August 1969. Although 'British imperialism took a lot of stick', he recalled, 'we never got down to defining with any precision what British imperialism was. We implied that it was the thing the Bogside had been fighting against for the past year and that we, the left-wingers, were more against it than anybody else.'[50] This suggests only scant engagement with the particulars of Britain's residual imperial holdings – a point further illustrated by McCann's recollections of the arrival of the British Army after three days of bitter street fighting:

> There was confusion as to what the proper attitude to the soldiers might be. It was not in our history to make British soldiers welcome ... Bernadette Devlin, her voice croaking, urged 'Don't make them welcome. They have not come here to help us', and went on a bit about British imperialism,

Cyprus and Aden. It did not go down very well. The fight had been against the [Royal Ulster Constabulary], to 'defend the area'. The RUC was beaten ... It was victory enough for the time being.[51]

Amid the petrol fumes and tear gas there was evidently little motivational force in a call to arms against a more generalized *imperial* tyranny. Though nationalists welcomed the transformed international setting that hampered 'the ability of the imperialists to govern', they remained overwhelmingly focused on their own liberation struggle. Indeed, to the extent that 'British imperialism' resonated in the Bogside at all, it functioned largely as a theoretical abstraction via Marx, Hobson and Lenin. Bourke puts the case succinctly: 'As imperialism rose in the minds of its various critics to the heights of omnicompetence, it disappeared from the field of reality as a definite plan of action associated with a specific set of agents.'[52] It may even be that the empire's precipitate demise somehow facilitated this conceptual looseness, obscuring any present-day field of vision against which such claims might be verified. 'Militant Republicanism was reborn', Bourke avers, 'so British imperialism had to be reinvented.'[53]

Figure 13.2 Independent Unity MP for Mid-Ulster Bernadette Devlin in Derry during the Battle of the Bogside. Source: Hulton Archive/Getty Images.

But this should not imply that the imperial or anti-colonial dimensions of the Troubles were wholly illusory. What Ronald Robinson once termed the 'moral disarmament of empire' was absolutely cardinal in Northern Ireland, furnishing a powerful new aspirational plank to nationalist ambitions.[54] Anti-imperialism was not simply the 'reinvention' of militant republicanism but its accompanying baggage, each drawing critical purchase from the wider collapse of the European colonial order over the preceding decades. Whether it be the abstract speculations of neo-Marxist theory or the more prosaic assessments of militant nationalist groups, the perceived dawning of a new era furnished an abundance of polemical weaponry and spiritual uplift. In ways that were simply unavailable to earlier generations of republican radicals, the passing of the British empire as an incontrovertible fact lent a palpable sense that history was on their side. Whether colonial analogies afforded an accurate or logically sustainable characterization of the Northern Ireland situation is beside the point. The cauldron of contested claims that spilled over into the streets of Northern Ireland were part and parcel of a new and uncertain dispensation in a post-imperial world.

'ABANDONED COLONY'? THE UNIONIST RESPONSE

If these undercurrents helped to mobilize civil libertarian and nationalist protest, they had an equally galvanizing effect on loyalist resentment and reaction. For decades, the empire had comprised one of the pillars of Unionist certainties, alongside Protestantism, the monarchy, the Orange Order and the Union itself. Unsurprisingly therefore, the adverse tidings for imperialism were met with a jittery response, particularly when it came to acknowledging the implications for Ulster. Protestant opinion was generally loath to countenance any colonial dimension to the Troubles, or indeed any correlation between the end of empire and the future of Northern Ireland. 'If there is anything likely to raise the hackles of any Ulster Protestant', opined the *Portadown News* at the outset of the Troubles in 1969, 'it is the suggestion that he is not an Irishman. He may describe himself as British but certainly not as "planter."'[55] The Belfast *News Letter* similarly went out of its way to debunk analogies that posited Catholics 'as the "native" population of Ulster, with Protestants as colonial intruders' – a view echoed by the Unionist government at the highest level.[56] The prickly defensiveness stemmed from the surge of unwelcome speculation about the implications of the end of empire for Northern Ireland. Hugh Trevor-Roper's take was typical of the genre:

> [Ireland] was the first English colony—and the first also to be voluntarily decolonized. But even now that decolonization is not complete, a residue of Britain remains, more intensely British, more nationalist, than any other part of Britain, because it is an isolated, insecure, but tenacious outpost in an abandoned colony. That residue, that outpost, is Ulster.[57]

The characterization of the Protestant majority as the beleaguered and excitable occupants of an 'abandoned colony' had a variety of wellsprings, none more conspicuous than the behaviour of its own extreme factions. The first major civil rights clash in Derry in October 1968, for example, 'provoked a Pavlovian defensiveness among most Unionists'.[58] The excessive nature of the response – the restrictions imposed on the marchers' route, the doggedness of loyalist counter-demonstrations obstructing their every progress, the exuberance of the Royal Ulster Constabulary (RUC) in bringing proceedings to a halt – all served to escalate an ostensibly non-violent protest into three days of rioting. The unrestrained thuggery of the police is a matter of (televised) historical record, widely corroborated by contemporary witness accounts of RUC batons and water canon wielded 'vigorously and indiscriminately'.[59] Leading civil rights activists such as John Hume described a 'line of policemen ... with looks on their faces I have never seen before in my life', while the chief organizer of the march, Dermie McClenaghan recalled how the police crackdown 'seemed to be all out of proportion' to the modest demands of the non-violent protesters.[60] Even Prime Minister Harold Wilson compared the RUC's actions unfavourably with the restraint shown by the Metropolitan police during the anti-Vietnam demonstrations in Grosvenor Square earlier in the year.[61] But if the police response seemed disproportionate to the provocation, the question arises as to why loyalist threat perceptions were on such high alert in 1968.

A variety of explanations have been put forward, drawing chiefly on the internal dynamics of the conflict. For some, it was largely a matter of a Unionist movement habituated to stubborn defiance and unaccustomed to compromise. 'The fact that Unionists had never tried to implement serious reforms', argues Niall Ó Dochartaigh, 'meant that they could only respond ... with resistance and repression, thus beginning a cycle of conflict'.[62] Alternatively, Marc Mulholland points to the pronounced thaw in sectarian tensions in the early 1960s that unleashed the demons of loyalist extremism.[63] The few studies to seriously consider the late imperial dimensions of resurgent loyalist militancy have done so with the broadest of brush strokes, alluding to generalized patterns of causation detached from the immediate course of events.[64] Ian McBride is the exception, diagnosing a 'particularly virulent form of disorientation' among Ulster loyalists at empire's end, due to the loss of the wider 'sense of common purpose' that deprived Protestant Ulster 'of its traditional role in the wider British world' – hinting at a more immediate causal relationship. But the connection has never been properly elaborated.[65]

In one crucial respect, the cross-currents of British imperial decline furnished a combustible element in its own right – namely, the widening rift between loyalist Ulster and the United Kingdom Government, where patterns of mutual incomprehension and mounting impatience contributed enormously to the deteriorating situation. It is generally overlooked that in the very week of the fateful Derry march of October 1968, Harold Wilson found himself anchored off Gibraltar on board HMS *Fearless*, locked in futile negotiations with rebel Rhodesia's Ian Smith.[66] Thus, when the prime minister issued a personal summons to O'Neill and his senior ministers only weeks later, he was in no mood for a second serving of loyalist stonewalling.[67] The ensuing meeting at 10 Downing Street on 4 November has been described variously as a 'mauling', a 'roasting' and a 'harangue' – it was certainly devoid of diplomacy or tact, with Wilson threatening 'the complete liquidation of all financial agreements with Northern Ireland' unless the Stormont Government were prepared to make substantial concessions to the Catholic minority.[68] He did not need to spell out Northern Ireland's dependence on an array of Westminster subsidies, all of which essentially became hostage to British Government demands for reform. Wilson warned O'Neill that parliamentary agitation was 'about to grow on a massive scale' and would become considerably worse unless signs of 'unmistakable movement' on civil rights reforms rapidly emerged. He singled out the restrictions on the local government franchise as particularly 'indefensible in the 20th century'.[69]

Although ostensibly held in secret, the combative nature of the encounter was duly leaked to the press, prompting a sea of speculation about Northern Ireland's future in a changing political climate, nationally as well as internationally. As the loyalist Belfast *News Letter* reflected, 'circumstances had changed to our disadvantage with post-war loyalty and sentiment counting for much less than they did'.[70] Or as one disgruntled reader more pithily concluded: 'It is "thanks to the British" that the Unionist party leaders have been . . . brought to London and in effect told that being in the United Kingdom is one thing and being of it another.'[71] Asked by reporters after the meeting whether he had given any promise of worthwhile reforms, O'Neill replied gingerly, 'I never give a promise I cannot keep.'[72]

This was the crux of O'Neill's dilemma. The surge in direct action and other forms of popular protest in Northern Ireland was amply countered by Ian Paisley's politics of righteous indignation. The disturbances of autumn 1968 seemed to vindicate persistent Paisleyite attacks on O'Neill's lack of resolve in the face of 'Ulster's enemies' – a message that resonated particularly powerfully among less affluent Protestants who felt that years of unstinting 'loyalty' had gone unrewarded.[73] Crucially, loyalist extremism was not a wholly new departure in 1968 but reflected tensions that had been simmering since the mid-1960s when Paisley first emerged from relative obscurity at the helm of the Free Presbyterian Church to become a major thorn in O'Neill's side. Spurred initially by the controversial January 1965 visit to Belfast of Irish taoiseach Sean Lemass (the first Irish premier to cross the northern border), Paisley had rapidly built up a following under the auspices of 'Ulster Protestant Action', a multi-pronged movement that managed to infiltrate both the Orange Order as well as local Unionist Party associations by appealing directly to rural and urban working-class Protestants.

The fiftieth anniversary of the Easter Rising in 1966 provided the occasion for Paisley's transformation 'from an irritant in the wings to a centre-stage scene stealer'.[74] His preferred technique was the 'counterdemonstration', often going to extraordinary lengths to ensure a hostile loyalist presence at each and every manifestation of civil rights advocacy or nationalist dissent.[75] Already by 1966, the Northern Ireland Government apprehended the existence of an extremist 'Paisleyite Movement' comprising a range of organizations including the paramilitary 'Ulster Volunteer Force' that posed a potentially greater threat to public order than republican dissident groups.[76] Paisley always vehemently denied the paramilitary connection, but his repeated refusals to keep the peace earned him his first jail stint in July 1966 – an inconvenience that did no harm to his surging popularity among disaffected Protestants.

Paisley's pre-Troubles career serves as a useful reminder that Protestant extremism was not simply an overwrought response to the civil rights campaigns of 1968 but largely preceded them. Or as one major study concludes, 'the threats to public order and paramilitary support did not spring from outside the Unionist party but were nurtured in [its] branches'.[77] Specifically, the policy of 'hindering and harrying' civil rights marchers at every turn was not a makeshift response but a carefully refined tactic, prefigured by several years of unease at the pace of liberal reform agendas emanating from

Figure 13.3 Founder of the Protestant Unionist Party (and later Democratic Unionist Party), Ian Paisley, leads a demonstration from Trafalgar Square to Downing Street, London, 1967. Source: Hulton Archive/Getty Images.

mainland Britain.[78] Such proactive measures sowed the seeds of later sectarian violence – as evidenced by the nail-studded cudgels wielded at a counter-protest in Armagh in November 1968 (earning Paisley a second prison term) or the bottles and stones that rained on the civil rights march at Burntollet in January 1969.[79] Moreover, Paisley's activities helped to cloak an avowedly ecumenical civil rights campaign in sectarian garb, creating an opening for republican dissidents to infiltrate and ultimately redirect civil libertarian protest towards nationalist ends. No one was more aware of this than the RUC, who viewed Paisley's activities as a key contributory factor in sustaining the climate of civil rights discord. 'If the Reverend gentleman could only be persuaded to leave it to the Government and police', concluded one influential assessment of July 1969, 'the C[ivil] R[ights] attendances would probably continue to fall away. CR only feeds and thrives on such opposition.'[80]

For the ruling Ulster Unionists at Stormont, wedged between Wilson's intransigence and the reactionary fervour of their own extremists, there seemed little room for manoeuvre. The result was a debilitating party split between pro- and anti-O'Neill factions, with the former inclined to move forward with social justice reforms and the latter regarding any concession to the Wilson government as a species of base treason. Home minister and inveterate hardliner Bill Craig rapidly emerged as the extremists' figure-head, laying down the gauntlet in a December 1968 speech in which he defiantly opposed 'any effort by any government in Great Britain, whatever its complexion might be, to exercise that power to in any way interfere with the proper power and jurisdiction of the parliament and government of Northern Ireland'.[81] His words were widely interpreted as a direct challenge for the party leadership, leading to his swift dismissal from the Cabinet and enhancing his leadership credentials among fellow dissenters. It was to address mounting opposition within his own party that O'Neill delivered his crunch-time 'Crossroads' television address on 9 December 1968:

> There are, I know, today some so-called loyalists who talk of independence from Britain ... These people are not merely extremists. They are lunatics ... They are not loyalists but *dis*loyalists: disloyal to Britain, disloyal to the Constitution, disloyal to the Crown, disloyal – if they are in public life – to the solemn oath they have sworn to Her Majesty the Queen.[82]

Thus, already by the end of 1968, well before the civil rights agenda had been overwhelmed by sectarian violence, the widening rift between the O'Neill and Wilson governments had punctured the inner unity of the ruling Unionist Party – an organization for whom solidarity was an existential creed. At issue was not the threat posed by Irish nationalists so much as the fealty and fortitude of the British Government in London. For O'Neill and his sup-porters, there was simply no alternative to working in concert with Harold Wilson, as any fundamental breach of British solidarity would threaten the foundations of Northern Ireland's economic and political viability. For the likes of Craig, Paisley and their considerable following, however, it was their fellow Britons across the Irish Sea who posed the most immediate threat. It was in some respects a re-run of the Irish crisis of 1912–14, when a populist Unionist groundswell faced down the prospect of Home Rule, threatening to tear down H. H. Asquith's minority government. Here, however, it was the Ulstermen themselves who grappled with internal schism and disarray.

It was at this juncture, as Graham Walker contends, that 'Protestant Ulster once more perceived the fact of siege for which mythically they were ever ready'.[83] But despite the familiar historical resonances, this was a wholly new state of affairs – one in which Unionism began to turn inwards upon itself. When O'Neill called a snap election at the end of February 1969 in a bid to shore up his mandate, many Protestant seats were contested for the very first time by pro- and anti-O'Neill candidates (including O'Neill's own Bannside seat, which he narrowly held against a full-scale onslaught from Paisley himself). The O'Neill faction appealed to the electorate to reject the anti-British attitudes of the extremists, campaigning on a slogan of 'Greater Britishness' versus 'Little Ulsterism'.[84] In reality, however, the prospects for greater Britonism had rarely seemed bleaker. Although O'Neill was able to scrape home at the polls, he was to suffer a fatal setback within a matter of weeks when a series of arson attacks targeted the Belfast water supply – another spectacular act of self-harm by dissident Unionists who sought to pin the blame on the IRA. Although Paisley was incarcerated at the time, his *Protestant Telegraph* freely indulged the falsehood, rousing sectarian ire with ominous visions of 'the struggle that lies ahead and the supreme sacrifice that will have to be made in order that Ulster will remain Protestant'.[85]

As the situation grew more volatile, evidence abounded of a widening gulf between 'mainland' British sympathies and the loyalist cause, casting the latter in the role of estranged relatives. High on the list of Unionist grievances was the alleged pro-Catholic bias of the British media. Whatever the merits of the charge, it is generally agreed that loyalists lost the 'propaganda war' from very early on, never managing to regain the initiative in combatting English media stereotypes of Unionist bigotry, intransigence and religious fanaticism.[86] Viewed from the vantage point of progressive, cosmopolitan, 'swinging' London of the late 1960s, it is not hard to see how Protestant militancy seemed like an atavistic throwback to the seventeenth century. Even traditionally sympathetic outlets such as the *Daily Express*, while dismissing civil rights as the work of 'either hooligans looking for a punch-up or anarchists with a grudge against society', tended to condemn all forms of extremism and support O'Neill's faltering programme of moderation and reform.[87]

Equally lamentable in Unionist eyes were the extraordinary levels of mainland British ignorance of Northern Irish affairs. In April 1969, *The Observer* commented on 'the surprising apathy towards Ulster in the rest of the United Kingdom', noting that 'most people would bitterly resent being caught up in what would be seen as an almost meaningless, faction-ridden, religious war'.[88] It was an extraordinary juxtaposition – indifference in the face of imminent domestic civil disorder – suggesting that whatever species of 'Britishness' lay at the heart of the conflict, it was a foreign commodity in the eyes of a substantial portion of the British public. Surveying the scene for *The Spectator* in September 1969, Tory MP David Walder confessed that his sole emotional investment in the Ulster crisis was 'a sneaking sympathy with the average British incomprehension of things Irish'. It was not for the want of reliable information. For all the saturation of media coverage throughout the turbulent 1969 summer, the physical barrier of the Irish Sea 'seemed to provide sufficient insulation from any real sense of involvement', bracketing Ulster with a vanishing British world, out of sight and increasingly out of mind:

> Since 1921 the British have experienced a surfeit of contests with the forces of nationalism in various forms, in India, Africa and Palestine, in Malaya, Cyprus and Arabia. Rightly or wrongly they are tired and bored. The sacred cause of 'law and order' *outside this island* has no appeal.[89]

Similarly, the debate about the wisdom of deploying British troops to keep the peace was conducted as though Ulster were a remote offshore condominium, replete with warnings about the folly of despatching 'our young men to be shot at by both sides, as they once were in Palestine and in Cyprus'.[90] These apprehensions dogged the UK Government's early handling of the problem, with Defence Minister Dennis Healey urging his Cabinet colleagues in May 1969 to remember that 'Northern Ireland has completely different conditions from Britain and we shall be as blind men leading the blind if we have to go in there knowing nothing about the place.'[91] Such blithe ignorance of his own sovereign jurisdiction was not unique to Healey, but entirely consistent with a broader tendency to discern Ulster's difficulties through the dim twilight of empire. Home Secretary James Callaghan maintained that the army was no longer 'emotionally involved' in saving Ulster, while Richard Crossman's Cabinet diary reveals how the deteriorating situation was bracketed instinctively with other costly overseas entanglements – dismissing the crisis as yet 'another adventure' for Harold Wilson's reckless interventionist streak. Between bouts of anguish about 'being dragged closer and closer to the precipice of protecting the Orangemen in Ireland', Crossman needed to remind himself that 'Northern Ireland is of course far more important than Rhodesia, infinitely more important than Anguilla, here we are on the edge of civil war'.[92]

Thus, even before the violent surge of the 1969 summer, the British establishment gave every indication of seeking to extricate themselves – psychologically if not physically – from a dangerous imbroglio in a remote corner of their own kingdom. 'With the end of empire', argues Pamela Clayton, 'the underlying notion of Northern Ireland as an "imperial garrison" was no longer as credible as it had been', placing clear limits on mainland British ownership of the problem.[93] Such aloofness was not a neutral position but a volatile factor in its own right, not least because it became so infuriatingly apparent to militant loyalists who registered their resentment and disgust accordingly. Even time-honoured myths such as the 1689 siege of Derry were refitted to capture the new mood of disillusionment with mainland Britain (replete with 'London Lundies' symbolizing a whole new brand of treachery). As the fear of imminent betrayal escalated, the 1689 rallying cry of 'No Surrender' took on a new set of meanings, no longer serving 'as a reminder of Britain's debt to Ulster, but as a historical justification for Protestant rebellion'.[94] In the dying days of his doomed premiership, Terrence O'Neill was obliged to devote the vast bulk of his energies to the incipient militancy and separatism within his own loyalist constituency, far more than the actual grievances of the civil rights movement. As Mulholland contends, 'the unionist attitude to Britain, not to the catholic minority, was the burning issue of the day'.[95]

'END OF THE ROAD FOR ULSTER?' THE SHADOW OF OFFSHORE BRITONS

If Protestant extremism was stoked by the belief that British benevolence could no longer be guaranteed, it drew added conviction from the example of other ostensibly 'loyal' communities facing a similar predicament in the late 1960s. Six months prior to the ill-fated Derry march that sparked the initial riots, a day of civil unrest erupted in the western Mediterranean enclave of Gibraltar where the civilian population – descended from Maltese, Genoese, Moroccan, Portuguese, Spanish and other sojourners through the ages – spontaneously asserted their civil rights in none-too-civil terms. The local denizens had only recently achieved a degree of responsible government after centuries of Garrison rule, but this in no way dimmed their attachment to the British connection, voting by a margin of 95.8 per cent to retain the link with Britain in a sovereignty referendum of September 1967. The claims of Francoist Spain persisted, however, prompting a group of Gibraltarian businessmen to advocate compromise in spring 1968 rather than risk the economic turmoil of a unilateral border closure. Styling themselves 'the Doves', these leaders of business and commerce engaged in secret activities (including clandestine negotiations with Madrid) to reach an economically viable settlement, the details of which soon leaked to an astonished and enraged public who promptly took matters into their own hands.

On the morning of 6 April 1968, a handful of disaffected locals descended on the governor's residence demanding that the Doves and their families be expelled from the colony for high treason. When their cries went unheeded, their attention turned to the homes and businesses of the alleged traitors and their numbers quickly swelled. By lunchtime, a swarm of protesters estimated between 600 and 1,000 had joined in an unbridled rampage, ransacking shops and commercial premises, overturning buses and cars and setting fire to a yacht in the marina. The police were wholly ill-equipped to deal with the situation, and suspicions lingered that their hands-off approach to riot management stemmed from an underlying sympathy with the troublemakers' cause. 'British we are and British we stay' the dissidents chanted as they paraded through the narrow streets and alleyways, interspersed with periodic outbursts of the Ulster loyalist credo 'No Surrender'.

Caught in the middle of the maelstrom was the local police commissioner, an Irishman from Sligo named Luke Hannon whose prior policing experience in Palestine, Nyasaland, Cyprus and the Bahamas had left him evidently ill-prepared for the peculiar wrath of Gibraltar's besieged Britons. Upon hearing of the disturbances, Hannon set off to survey the scene personally with two senior officers, arming himself with a couple of tear gas canisters as he left the station. Within minutes he found himself beating a retreat down Gibraltar's Main Street pursued by the mob, imploring them to halt their trail of wanton destruction. As the rioters closed in on the panic-stricken commissioner, he hurriedly unleashed one of the gas canisters, engulfing the entire cavalcade of men, women and children and incapacitating the few able-bodied officers at his disposal.[96]

According to multiple witnesses and police testimony, this marked the point when the locals put aside their enmity towards Spain and refocused their ire on 'the Englishman'.[97] From the chorus of 'British we are, British we stay', the tune quickly changed to an enraged chant – in Spanish – of 'kill the commissioner'.[98] Hannon fled the scene and found refuge in a nearby apartment, reportedly 'very badly shaken' by the incident and forced to relinquish command.[99] Throughout the afternoon other incidents were reported of identifiably 'English' officers being targeted by the mob with cries of 'ese es otro Ingles otro hijo de puta mas' ('that one is also an Englishman another son of a whore') and 'tu eres un hijo de puta ingles me cago en tus muertos' ('you are an English son of a whore, I shit on your dead').[100] By the end of the day some fifteen officers had been treated for injuries ranging from sprained limbs, blows to the head, bites on the arm and one officer hospitalized for a 'kick in the testicles'. It was not until late in the afternoon that the British garrison was called in (much against the wishes of the civilian government) and order was restored by sunset.

Here, in the space of a single afternoon, were many of the volatile elements that would later blight the streets of Derry and Belfast, albeit on a much reduced scale: the pervasive threat of absorption by a hostile neighbour; a restive community suspicious of Britain's intentions; the conviction that disorderly measures were justified to uphold British standards; allegations of complicity among the local police; the impassioned slogans of loyalist defiance; and the eventual deployment of British troops to enforce an uneasy truce. The presence of a lone Irish lawman conspicuously failing to restore order only compounded the irony, not least the fact that he was mistaken for an Englishman. While in no way condoning the rioters, the *Gibraltar Post* was unable to resist a sardonic note:

> Hoist up the Union Jack in your garden. Rejoice and put on your red, white and blue panties, for last weekend we made history. We have been the only territory in the whole world-wide British Empire, or what is left of it, to have had policemen and soldiers having to quell a very riotous pro-British demonstration. If Queen Victoria had been alive she would have declared it a 'national holiday'.[101]

Although an unusual, and in many ways unique chapter in Britain's drawn-out imperial endgame, the underlying impulse was hardly without parallel. On the contrary, there were other straws in the wind in spring 1968 that pointed to a wider arc of offshore British disquiet. As we saw in the previous chapter, it was in March of that year that Kenyan Asian passport holders were denied the right of entry into the UK, unleashing a political tempest and condemning tens of thousands of British subjects to a citizenship limbo. Belfast's *News Letter* was quick to decry the betrayal of these stranded Britons abroad, less out of genuine sympathy for their British bona fides and more with an eye on Ulster's fate at the hands of a government 'which has shown once again how maladroit its methods are'.[102] The same month saw the establishment of a new and increasingly vocal source of Greater British reaction – the Falkland Islands Lobby – established, not to counter resurgent Argentinian designs on the Islands per se, so much as to mount sustained resistance against the perceived irresolution of the British Government. And the following year in March 1969, British forces were despatched to the Caribbean island of Anguilla to quell a popular revolt claiming the right to remain British rather than be shackled to the sovereignty of nearby St Kitts.[103] Although it is hard to imagine a series of episodes less obviously connected in terms of scale, causation or community dynamics, all were fundamentally about thwarted identity claims mediated through the same ambivalent end-of-empire nexus. Even in far-off New Zealand, the announcement of Britain's weary retreat from East of Suez in January 1968 could elicit wounded misgivings from a leading daily newspaper:

> The Pax Britannica has long since gone ... the enthusiasm for Kipling, the nostalgia for the 'sun-shine an' the palm trees an' the tinkly temple bells' has dwindled. Oddly enough, the Kipling spirit seems to be kept alive more by non-Britons than the British themselves. Who was most shocked by Mr Wilson's announcement this week? ... If anyone received a traumatic shock it was in this part of the world, not in Britain.[104]

In a world where the fortunes of offshore Britons had taken a distinct turn for the worse, this broader confluence of remonstration and regret provided the deeper emotional backdrop to the Northern Ireland Troubles. Virtually everywhere loyalists looked, Britain seemed to prevaricate in its support for its most ardent supporters, pointing inexorably to Ulster's imminent betrayal. More than at any other time in the long history of sectarian enmity, the external setting fostered a climate of militant vigilance.

Above all, it was the example of white Rhodesia that compounded Unionist distrust of a British Labour government more concerned with currying international favour (as they saw it) than supporting its own kinsfolk. In many respects, the similarities were entirely superficial – Rhodesian settlers were a one-in-ten minority in a continent rapidly making the transition to majority rule, whereas Ulster Protestants were themselves majority stakeholders with only the dimmest self-perception as a settler population. Nor were there discernible sectarian dimensions to the Rhodesian crisis, which was entirely racial rather than religious in character. But the pathos of an isolated and avowedly loyal community openly defying the British Government so as to safeguard their Britishness was enough to invite frequent comparison. Harold Wilson instantly saw the resemblance, remarking bluntly to Terrence O'Neill at their very first encounter in August 1966: 'I suppose Northern Ireland is rather like Rhodesia.'[105] The parallels were even more apparent to ardent loyalist elements in Northern Ireland who saw events unfolding in Rhodesia as marking 'The End of the Road for Ulster.'[106] Extremist publications such as the *Protestant Telegraph* and the *Ulster Protestant* assiduously cultivated a sense of common cause with Ian Smith's Rhodesian Front, depicting white Rhodesian compatriots as victims of the Devil's own work personified by the Pope and the Labour

Party (with Irish Catholic missionaries routinely accused of stoking the passions of African avarice). Meanwhile Smith himself was roundly applauded as the embodiment of Protestant self-discipline and resolve, despite the inconvenient presence of several Rhodesian Catholics in his Cabinet.[107]

Rhodesia's defiance of the British Government in November 1965 was routinely likened to Ulster in 1912 where 'necessary steps' had similarly been taken against metropolitan tyranny. 'There is no treason in such an action', readers of the *Protestant Telegraph* were assured, 'but Harold Wilson should be indicted for treason.'[108] Donal Lowry has teased out the intriguing commonalities, noting how for the Paisleyites it was Wilson himself who had 'put Britishness into temporary abeyance', placing the onus on 'the two loyalist communities to uphold the imperial cause'.[109] The *Ulster Protestant* consistently portrayed the Rhodesian crisis as an object lesson for Ulster, railing frequently against the government's 'sordid' attempts to engineer Smith's downfall.[110] As the political and social chaos of spring 1969 unfolded, there could be no doubt about where to apportion blame:

> In one decade Britain has lost her commanding position in the moral leadership and enlightenment of the nations and has been rendered despicable by her supine policies at home and abroad ... We are ruled by men to whom our greatness does not mean a thing, and who by their deeds profess they are ashamed of the history of the land which gave them birth and liberty. We have dissolved the Empire and created in its place a monstrous affair misnamed the Commonwealth in which the alleged 'mother' country is treated with contempt and insult. We have, under the rule of successive administrations of guilty men, abdicated our responsibilities.[111]

This wider vista of an empire cravenly squandered was fundamental to the extremist worldview, infusing the cause with enhanced moral purpose and a renewed sense of urgency. One striking feature was the sheer bewilderment, bordering on disbelief at the extent of the ground that had given way. As one baffled *Ulster Protestant* correspondent from Australia lamented: 'Who would think that this British family, the most stable bloc of nations in the world could ever show signs of disintegrating. Yet this is happening. Why?'[112] A sense of being deeply misunderstood by their own kind was replicated across the Ulster–Rhodesia divide, with one letter-writer to the Belfast *News Letter* remonstrating: 'Ian Smith has said that only about 1 per cent of the people of England know the facts or want to know the facts about Rhodesia. This is also true of the average Englishman's attitude to Ulster.'[113]

Meanwhile the disgraced Unionist minister Bill Craig toyed openly with the idea of a Rhodesian-style 'Unilateral Declaration of Independence' – indeed, he came out in support of Smith's rebel cause as early as March 1966.[114] Throughout the early phase of sectarian unrest, the initials 'UDI' became ubiquitous in Ulster press and political commentary in a cycle of will-they-or-won't-they speculation.[115] It exposed Unionists to a degree of ridicule at the hands of their opponents, such as Bernadette Devlin's caustic assessment of 1969:

> The Paisleyites are sort of caricatures of Ulster Protestants, out-Britishing the British by a long shot. They are mad keen on the Union Jack, but ... don't really want to have anything to do with England, because England has forgotten it's British. At one point they were talking about UDI—a Unilateral Declaration of Independence, on the model of Ian Smith and Rhodesia—which would leave Ulster the only unsullied little corner of the British Isles.[116]

More moderate Unionists were so alarmed by the comparison that they felt bound to speak out against the potentially catastrophic economic consequences of following the Rhodesian example.[117] Others stressed the grave tactical error of keeping such dubious company: 'It does not help our image to say that we are modelling ourselves on a regime which is universally condemned by democrats.'[118] Terrence O'Neill was particularly alarmed by the swirling UDI rumours, devoting a few carefully chosen words of disparagement in his December 1968 'Crossroads' broadcast. 'Rhodesia in defying Britain from thousands of miles away at least has an Air Force and an Army of her own', he countered. 'Where are the Ulster Armoured Divisions and the Ulster Jet Planes?'[119]

Indeed, such were O'Neill's apprehensions that he worked actively behind the scenes to bring about Ian Smith's downfall. During the early years of UDI he forged a very personal alliance with the embattled Rhodesian governor, Sir Humphrey Gibbs, providing moral and material support to the entire Gibbs family during their four years of isolation at Government House in Salisbury. In autumn 1966, Gibbs's wife, Molly, made an extended visit to Ulster as a personal guest of the O'Neills, during which time the two families hatched an intricate plot to bring the Rhodesian crisis to a rapid resolution. The gist of the plan was to 'smuggle' the queen mother into Rhodesia to quell the rebellion – conveyed secretly to Harold Wilson in a handwritten missive on 1 October 1966:

> A plane could leave England after dark carrying officials. It would be known that Lady Gibbs was on board – perhaps even a female Gibbs relative could

be said to be in the party. At Salisbury airport the secret would emerge, but the QM's fantastic natural charm would win the day. Vast crowds would gather outside Government House to express their loyalty. Smith would be 'on the spot'. If he tried to expel the Queen Mother the Regime would risk offending the string of latent pro-British sentiment ... All those in the regime of British stock would fall over themselves to meet her at Government House. She might just bring it off![120]

The scheme was fanciful to say the least, and Whitehall's advice to Wilson was to give it no encouragement. When O'Neill failed to take the hint and submitted a revised version a few months later, the prime minister weighed in personally and 'killed it' (in his own words). But tellingly, Wilson was also cautioned against raising the matter in the presence of O'Neill's ministerial colleagues who were said to be 'very suspicious' of their leader over Rhodesia.[121] Evidently, it was not prudent for a Unionist premier to be seen assisting the British Government in bringing rebellious loyalists abroad to heel.

Other contemporary parallels such as Gibraltar and the Falklands were less constantly in focus, but when they did arise there were loud proclamations of Ulster's filial loyalty to their cause. As with Rhodesia, what gave these examples a special resonance were the subtle indications that the British Government might be prepared to renege on earlier assurances and negotiate with Spain and Argentina, respectively. When Lord Shephard was despatched by Wilson to Gibraltar in February 1968 to smooth ruffled feathers, he was astonished at the level of scepticism about the government's true intentions. 'We are wedded to Gibraltar as Gibraltar wishes to be wedded to the United Kingdom', he pleaded with more than a hint of exasperation.[122] Later that same year it was Lord Chalfont's turn to reassure the Falkland Islanders during a visit to Port Stanley, where he was pursued for days by protesters bearing placards calling on Britain to keep its word and keep the Falklands British.[123] The Falkland Islands lobby had launched an energetic campaign under the banner 'As British As You Are' – virtually ignoring Argentina in a PR strategy myopically focused on Britain (the 'you' implicit in the slogan). The contemporary resonances with Protestant Ulster were unmistakable, and the Unionist press was quick to make the connection:

> There is similarity at all points in the demands by the inhabitants of the Falkland Islands and those of Gibraltar that there should be no transfer of sovereignty without their consent. The assertion of this fundamental right should find full sympathy in Northern Ireland ... If Argentine friendship is to be conditional upon the imposition of alien administration on a group of British citizens, however small it may be, the price is too great.[124]

Figure 13.4 Residents of the Falkland Islands voice their support for remaining British outside the Anglican Cathedral, Port Stanley, 1 January 1968. Source: Express/Stringer/ Getty Images.

Paisley's *Protestant Telegraph* was even more explicit, hammering home the message that if British diplomats were prepared to accept UN mediation in places such as the Falklands and Gibraltar, 'why not Ulster?'.[125] Meanwhile a visiting Australian professor at Queen's University questioned the supposed uniqueness of Ulster's plight, venturing that 'Ulster is not like the rest of Britain or the rest of Europe but has much more in common with areas outside Europe' – a situation he broadly likened to that of Gibraltar.[126] Indeed, the threat of a Spanish takeover presented itself as a microcosm of the wider loyalist predicament, exemplifying the tipping point between filial devotion and militant defiance that became so characteristic of vulnerable British enclaves cut adrift at empire's end.

This is not to suggest any moral equivalence or even ideological coherence across a diffuse chain of self-styled 'Britishers' located variously offshore – all of whom were stirred by complex motivations and conflicting emotions rooted in their respective local settings. But there was more than mere coincidence to the simultaneous spawning of loyalist misgivings at the twilight of empire. The alarming portents of a mother country relinquishing its wider vocation fuelled an unusually strong appetite among loyalists for taking matters into their own hands. Although Unionist militancy was a fringe movement, never representative of the broad base of Protestant opinion, its influence in igniting the Troubles was always disproportionate to its numerical strength. The susceptibility of these various groups to the receding tide of imperial Britishness therefore needs to be factored squarely into the pattern of causation that sparked the sudden outbreak of sectarian violence in 1968–9. For the Paisleyites and the loyalist paramilitaries, it was the looming uncertainty of a post-British world that brought fresh exigency to age-old enmities, serving as justification for any and every resort to proactive measures to entrench their position.

'BEFORE AN EMPIRE'S EYES': VANGUARD'S EMPTY PROMISE

On the afternoon of Tuesday 28 March 1972, more than 100,000 loyalist protesters braved wind and rain to assemble in the grounds of the Stormont Parliament in Belfast. Some wore the uniform of the newly formed 'Ulster Defence Association', others belted out renditions of 'The Sash My Father Wore' to the rhythm of Lambeg drums. Many defiantly waved the 'Red Hand of Ulster' flag or the Ulster Banner of the Northern Ireland parliament. Unusually for such a gathering, virtually no one paraded the Union Jack.[127] It was the largest loyalist demonstration in Ulster's history, the culmination of a two-day work stoppage to oppose the actions of the Conservative government of Edward Heath who only days earlier had suspended the Stormont assembly.[128] Three years of escalating violence and civic disorder, including the Bloody Sunday massacre in Derry only two months previously, had finally forced the government's hand in imposing the direct rule of Westminster. As a show of Ulster's resolve, the heaving crowd outside Stormont had been summoned by the 'Ulster Vanguard' movement, launched only weeks earlier by Bill Craig in anticipation of Britain's impending 'sell-out'. What distinguished Vanguard from Paisleyism and other strands of loyalist extremism was its determination to pursue – 'if there is no alternative' – complete separation from Britain.[129] Just prior to Craig's appearance on the Stormont balcony alongside deposed Unionist premier Brian Faulkner, the central stanza of Rudyard Kipling's 1912 poem 'Ulster' had been read aloud in the closing session of the Northern Irish Assembly:

> Before an Empire's eyes
> The traitor claims his price.
> What need of further lies?
> We are the sacrifice.[130]

Even in Kipling's day it was something of a stretch to invoke the 'empire's eyes' as a singular line of sight. By 1972 it was naive at best to imagine anyone watching at all. The persistence of the anachronism bears out Steve Bruce's assessment of the 'datedness' of loyalism's image of Britain and the world, endeavouring to be 'British in the way in which Kipling was British . . . British in the way in which Anglo-indians and other marginal groups are British.'[131]

Although Ulster loyalism could still rely on occasional words of encouragement and sympathy from around the world, not least in Britain, by the 1970s their belief in a deeper, organic, transoceanic Britishness could hardly be sustained. With the closure of Stormont, even a staunch metropolitan defender of the status quo such as the *Daily Express* could broach the possibility that 'the British people have had enough of this mediaeval nonsense and they are certainly not prepared to tolerate the British Army being sacrificed to perpetuate a barbaric struggle'.[132] Such attitudes were themselves subtly conditioned by imperial precedent. When in February 1972 the *Daily Mirror* proposed to 'end the killing' by substituting UN peacekeepers for the British Army, it drew explicitly on the reassuring (albeit selective) memory of Britain's orderly imperial retreat. 'Britain set

Figure 13.5 Leader of the Ulster Vanguard, William Craig, addresses a rally from the steps of Belfast City Hall, 20 May 1972. Source: Images Press/Contributor/Getty Images.

an example to the world in relinquishing an Empire with the minimum of violence and the maximum of financial aid. Let Britain now set another example to the world.'[133]

The Ulster Vanguard was fashioned out of the anger that poured into the widening rift. Its early pamphlets and propaganda were adamant that 'the greatest threat to the loyalist cause is not the assault of Irish nationalism in the form of IRA physical violence' – that was a known quantity and had been safely seen off countless times before. The real existential threat lay across the Irish Sea in the 'changing mood of the people of Great Britain' – a mood that now fluctuated along a scale of 'indifference to outright hostility'. The persistent 'taunts of the British press' were only too apparent – 'they have called us backwoodsmen, barbarians and they have meant it . . . In this sense the British are the Ulster problem.' The collapse of UK-wide solidarity in the face of the nationalist threat was only the most visible sign of a deeper divergence, one that touched upon every aspect of public decency and private morality. Whether in terms of the rise of sexual 'permissiveness', the decline in religious observance or changing attitudes to civic duty, the Vanguard leadership faced the unhappy prospect that 'urbanised society in Great Britain is far out of step with Ulster . . . by virtue of different historical experience [and] different scales of reference by which to measure, weigh and judge'.[134] It was a remarkably astute assessment. Age-old defects in the chain of mutual empathy had become strained to breaking point by divergent historical time scales – a disparity made manifest by the demarcation line of global decolonization. But what Vanguard decried as a species of 'British parochialism' applied equally, if not more so to their own self-isolation, as indeed to other offshore loyalists whose stake in the inviolate bonds of Britishness turned out to be a lonely investment.

Despite auspicious beginnings, Vanguard's momentum soon expired for the want of a coherent programme of action. Though logic and reason pointed inexorably to a fully independent Ulster, the movement faltered when it came to relinquishing once and for all the bedrock claim to being British. In seeking to have it both ways – described variously as 'the establishment of an independent British Ulster', a 'British entity within or without the Union' or a new nation 'on the northern approaches to Europe . . . democratic, flexible, imaginative and deeply British' – Vanguard never managed to cut through the contradictions.[135] Failing to distinguish itself from mainstream Unionism, the constant threat of secession turned out to be merely another means of leveraging metropolitan sympathy. As with so many prior examples of unrequited Britishness, they tended to misconstrue the problem as a matter of getting their message across. On the eve of

Stormont's closure, a series of double-spread newspaper advertisements implored readers to 'Tell Everyone Why You Want to Stay British' – precisely the flawed tactic deployed by beleaguered British settlers in Kenya two decades earlier.[136] Drawing further inspiration from offshore counterparts, the campaign also belatedly embraced the Gibraltarian rallying cry: 'British we are. And British We'll stay'.[137]

———————◆———————

Ultimately, imploring each and every Protestant to shout out their Britishness was symptomatic of the problem. It was the amplified zeal that betrayed the fragility of the cause – a weakness only too readily exploited by their opponents. Frequently lampooned was the forlorn figure of the Ulster Protestant who 'feels he must continually prove he's British' – as though he were saying: 'We *are* British ... aren't we?'[138] The brittle terms of endearment placed Ulster loyalists at one remove, a predicament highlighted by the radical Protestant reformer (and founding member of the Civil Rights movement) Jack Bennett in a penetrating essay of December 1972. Whenever loyalists trumpeted their determination to 'remain British', he observed, they subtly flagged 'the possibility that they may either remain British – or they may not'. This was to expose the debilitating fudge at the core of their belief system:

> It is a sub-conscious recognition that even if they claim to be British by name, they are not, in fact, British by nature. For ultimately, whether they remain British or not is entirely up to Britain to decide. And should Britain decide otherwise, it is difficult to imagine what degree of determination would enable them to remain British in any realistic sense unless that determination included the ability to row a boat.[139]

The asymmetry of feeling had long been apparent – consciously or otherwise – to successive generations, influencing calculations on all sides. For decades, British governments had worked from the premise that the political stability of Northern Ireland required Westminster's ready compliance with the wishes of the Protestant majority. Only twenty years earlier, the Attlee government had established the firm principle of majority-consent to constitutional change in the crucial Ireland Bill of 1949 – a decision wholly based on the need to placate loyalist anxieties. The logic was fully spelt out in the Cabinet minutes of the day: 'Unless the people of Northern Ireland felt reasonably assured of the support of the people of this country, there might be a revival of the Ulster Volunteers and of other bodies intending to meet any threat of force by force; and this would bring nearer the danger of an outbreak of violence in Northern Ireland.'[140] By the late 1960s, however, this consensus had completely broken down.

To return, then, to the question broached at the outset: what changed? Why did the Labour government of the late 1960s cease to abide by the maxims of its predecessor two decades earlier? The pronounced shift in metropolitan priorities had multiple wellsprings, but by far the most significant was the overhaul of expectations wrought by post-war decolonization. An empire–commonwealth that seemed worth fighting for in the 1950s – in Kenya, Malaya, Suez, Aden and Cyprus – became an increasing liability as more and more colonies achieved independence in a transformed international landscape. By the late 1960s, the guiding precepts of British political culture had long since caved to the logic of relinquishing colonial rule, while public opinion had slowly (if unevenly) turned against the use of naked force to suppress demands for self-determination. In short, the Wilson government was confronted with an entirely new set of international ground rules compared to the Attlee ministry of 1949. 'The signs and portents were in the skies of Northern Ireland', affirmed veteran Unionist MP Edmund Warnock at the start of the Troubles in December 1968. 'But none of us, although we may have seen signs of the gathering storm, had the least conception that instead of a wind of change [we] were going to be met with a hurricane.'[141] It was a shrewd choice of metaphor, fashioned from the embers of empire.

Added to this were heightened local enmities that became all the more polarized as the tide turned against imperialism worldwide. Northern Ireland's civil rights movement drew fresh impetus and inspiration from the wider challenges to British authority, while militant nationalism was greatly emboldened by the 'tremendous impetus to national liberation movements everywhere' in the 1960s.[142] The sense of wider connectivity may have been more rhetorical than real (few, if any links were forged with Africa's proliferating liberation movements) but it was a rhetorical purchase that brought its own grim realities (and ample moral justification) as the violence of the Troubles escalated. Conversely, the 'evangelical vaudeville' of Paisleyism was essentially a traumatized response to Britain's impaired capacity (and diminished will) to meet global challenges to its authority with its customary 'resolve'.[143] Here, the predicament of other offshore Britishers grappling with similarly lukewarm metropolitan backing was an unmistakable omen, stoking expectations of a catastrophic downgrading of Ulster in mainland British sympathies. The resort to a siege mentality was by no means a new feature of Protestant identity, but it acquired a fatalistic (and ultimately fatal) edge with the unravelling of the British world-system.

The 'apparent paradox' of loyalist rebellion – as Ian McBride suggests – can be better understood 'if Britishness is viewed, not as a single, homogenous entity, but as a plurality of identities brought together by common historical experience yet retaining distinctive characteristics'.[144] The argument advanced here is that the 'plurality' of Britishness traversed a much broader geographical sweep than the diverse regions of the United Kingdom. Far from presenting a paradox, loyalist defiance was paradigmatic at a time when 'independent systems of expectation' that had long negotiated a shaky co-existence were pitted directly against each another.[145] The languages of loyalism and the charge of betrayal were constant bedfellows across a range of historical experience, albeit with widely varying inflections and outcomes. Ultimately, this wider fracturing of the Greater British firmament rendered offshore British identities untenable, raising an implicit challenge to the integrity of the Union itself. Northern Ireland occupied the precarious crossroads between the two.

It should not be overlooked that the Northern Ireland Troubles were by no means Britain's only 'harrowing aftermath of empire' (as one newspaper termed it at the height of the 1969 summer).[146] Only two weeks prior to Terrence O'Neill's fateful resignation in April 1969, the Wilson government announced a wholesale inquiry into the inner workings of the British constitution following a surge in support for separatist political parties at the ballot box in Scotland and Wales. Although by no means identical to the volatile situation in Ulster, electoral pressure from Scottish and Welsh nationalists lingered at the margins of the early Troubles, much as Rhodesia and Gibraltar furnished a compelling offshore counterpoint. Amid the first street clashes in Derry of August 1969, the *Daily Mirror* managed to combine these highly charged ingredients into a single cautionary tale:

> The ineptitude of Asquith and Lloyd George in dealing with Ireland between 1912 and 1922 led directly to the dissolution of the British Empire. The Indians and Africans were watching. Similar ineptitude by Harold Wilson and his successor might lead, with equal speed, to the dissolution of the United Kingdom; Welshmen and Scots are watching.[147]

Evocatively titled 'Lifting the Lion's Paw', the piece exhorted the government to tread warily in the sight of history. Not for the first time, a show of resolve in Ireland was deemed crucial to subduing a new restiveness in Scotland and Wales.

14

'STOP THE WORLD': CELTIC DEPARTURES

The route that winds through the Tywi Valley in south-west Wales seems an unlikely road to revolution. The scene is serenity itself, verging on parody: the gentle arc of the River Tywi shrouded in mist; scattered flocks grazing in the shadows of castle ruins; and hedgerows buttressed by sloping hills in every shade of green. At the western reach lies the ancient market town of Carmarthen, its tangled lanes inscribed with visual markers of the Union with England. The remains of Carmarthen Castle, stronghold of the first Norman intruders of the early twelfth century, dominate the townscape on the edge of Nott Square. At centre stage stands Sir William Nott himself, an obscure Afghan war hero whose bronze effigy (personally financed by Queen Victoria) was fashioned from canon captured at the Battle of Maharajpur. Nearby, St Peter's Church boasts the sixteenth-century tomb of Rhys ap Thomas, slayer of Richard III at Bosworth Field and loyal lieutenant of the Tudors. He is thought to be the first Welshman successfully to petition parliament to be turned into an Englishman.[1]

It was here on the evening of 14 July 1966 that Welsh National Party leader Gwynfor Evans journeyed from his home in the Upper Tywi Valley to claim a majority as the first Plaid Cymru member of the House of Commons. After more than twenty years at the helm of his party, the mild-mannered market gardener from Llangadog had finally secured a breakthrough. The Carmarthen by-election had followed immediately on the heels of the general election in March of that year, with the death of popular Labour MP Megan Lloyd George. Although Evans had made substantial gains at the earlier poll, increasing his vote from 11 to 16 per cent, he was widely expected to run a respectable second – itself an impressive result for a party with radical ideas for a self-governing Wales. In the event, the Plaid Cymru leader more than trebled his vote to 39 per cent, trouncing both the Liberals and Conservatives and securing a comfortable 6 per cent majority over his nearest rival, Labour.[2] It was the most significant single-constituency result in Welsh history, catapulting to

413

prominence a movement that had long been accustomed to failure, mockery and political marginalization. As the pubs closed and expectant crowds poured into Carmarthen's Guildhall Square to strains of the Welsh anthem *Hen Wlad fy Nhadau*, a hush descended as the four candidates appeared on the balcony. When the results were read out, the scale of Evans's win was drowned in a jubilant roar.[3]

Sixteen months later, in the south Lanarkshire town of Hamilton on the River Clyde, an even more startling by-election was won by the Scottish National Party's Winifred Ewing. Unlike her veteran Welsh counterpart, Ewing was a political novice; an aspiring lawyer with a young family standing for office for the first time. She was able to turn this to her advantage on the hustings, however, striking a vivid contrast to the main parties with a highly mobile and energetic campaign heralding a 'real fighter' for Scotland versus 'the grey nonentity that represents Westminster'. Tactical innovations such as thirty-car convoys and celebrity endorsements (including 007 himself, Sean Connery) only added to the raw energy of her candidacy. When polling day arrived on 2 November 1967, she proceeded to decimate the Labour and Conservative vote by 30 and 17 per cent, respectively, winning by a margin of nearly two thousand in Labour's second safest Scottish seat. Ewing later described 'the strongest feeling of euphoria I have ever felt' as she emerged from Hamilton Town Hall to address a rain-drenched crowd huddled beneath umbrellas. 'Stop the World, Scotland wants to get on', she shouted to delirious applause – a virtual rerun of the ecstatic scenes at Carmarthen the previous year.[4]

Contemporaries were quick to conflate the two events, the *Glasgow Herald* detecting a 'nationwide problem' in the tumult of Hamilton and Carmarthen, and a 'widespread feeling of remoteness from government [that] is not confined to Scotland and Wales'.[5] If Carmarthen had seemed an aberration, the combined effect of Evans and Ewing could not be written off as a mere protest vote. *The Times* pointedly called on Britain's political elite to 'think in a fundamentally new way about Celtic nationalisms before it is too late'.[6] Then, as now, the twin-victories were viewed as a major portent, marking the dawn of devolutionary politics in a more fragmentary political scene. From electoral obscurity, both the SNP and Plaid Cymru had become credible political alternatives virtually overnight, generating a momentum that would carry over into the 1970s. Suddenly, the future of the Union – the fate of Britishness itself – was a question worth posing. In the words of the *New Statesman*, Carmarthen and Hamilton marked the beginning of 'a forest fire certain to consume more'.[7]

Figure 14.1 Newly elected Scottish National Party MP, Winnie Ewing, arrives at the House of Commons accompanied by Plaid Cymru Leader and MP for Carmarthen, Gwynfor Evans, 16 November 1967. Source: Mirrorpix/Getty Images.

That these electoral ruptures occurred at the very nadir of Britain's global fortunes did not escape notice, fuelling speculation about a possible connection between the collapse of imperial authority abroad and the fracturing of civic loyalties at home. For *The Guardian*, it was 'the shock of discovering Britain's reduced status in the world' that had put 'large groups of voters ... in a highly emotional mood'.[8] Tom Nairn was more explicit, linking the separatist surge in Scotland and Wales to the 'slow, festering decay of British State and society' – twin forces of disintegration that 'prefigure the dismemberment of the united British society which built up the imperial system itself'.[9] The candidates provided ample corroboration, with Ewing's 'Stop the World' rhetoric echoing Plaid Cymru's slogan for 1964: 'Wales must join the World'.[10] A sense of lost latitude pervaded the language of both parties, suggesting more was at stake than the isolated whims of the electors of Carmarthen and Hamilton. For all the undoubted significance of local grievances, a larger story was unfolding – of Celtic departures, abandoning England to its ailments and engaging with a new global dynamism.

Surprisingly, historians have shown a remarkable wariness about making too much of the connection between the end of empire and the separatist agenda of the 1960s, to the extent that the connection has been taken seriously at all. Keith Webb was among the first to debunk the 'decline of empire thesis', arguing in 1977 that there was precious little evidence to support the idea, or indeed to interpret SNP electoral gains as a belated 'awakening' of Scottish identity at the expense of prior attachments to being British. The two had comprised a delicate balance for generations.[11] 'The fault of this type of theory', he continued, 'is that the mere overlap of two historical sequences is taken as evidence that the one is causing the other.'[12] Keith Robbins similarly cautioned that it was 'most unwise' to assume any broader structure or pattern in the early momentum of Scottish nationalists, as though it were 'part of some grand, uniform historical phenomenon with an inevitable success'.[13] When T. M. Devine revisited the question decades later, he too was inclined to dismiss the end of empire as a moment that 'failed to produce much political concern in Scotland' – and hence of little consequence for the sudden political momentum that spurred the SNP's early electoral success. The real breakthrough came much later under Mrs Thatcher, who had 'an infinitely greater claim to be the midwife of Scottish devolution than the factor of imperial decline'.[14]

Only Tom Nairn's seminal *The Break-Up of Britain* (1977) gave the matter serious scholarly treatment, albeit in terms that made no pretence of scholarly detachment. His scathing critique of Britain's 'backward' state configuration – geared for centuries to running an overseas empire – applied equally to Scottish elites who had readily sacrificed their nationality 'during the prolonged era of Anglo-Scots imperialist expansion', effectively relinquishing the prize of separate statehood 'for a hugely profitable junior partnership in the New Rome'. With the passing of empire, however, this was all set to change. For Nairn, it was not merely the Scots but also the English who needed 'to rediscover who and what they are, to reinvent an identity of some sort better than the battered cliché-ridden hulk which the retreating tide of imperialism has left them'.[15] But Nairn aside, the issue has been left largely to conjecture, with little attempt to consider the upswing in the fortunes of separatist politics in any wider context.[16] The oversight is particularly conspicuous in the case of Wales, where not even the vague outlines of a historical debate have ever emerged.

To what extent, then, can the imprint of imperial decline be detected in these early Celtic departures? How pervasive or prominent were global perspectives in the local politics of Carmarthen or Hamilton, and the more general consolidation of separatist support in the 1960s? In what ways did the logic or example of decolonization shape the devolution agenda, if at all? Above all, how did the success of Gwynfor Evans and

Winifred Ewing converge with the receding frontiers of Britishness else-where in the world? The answers are by no means straightforward; but it will be shown that these early tremors can only be fully comprehended in terms of global cross-currents and empire-wide antecedents.

'FROM THE WRECKAGE OF EMPIRE': THE SEPARATIST SURGE

The most striking feature of the separatist electoral surge in the 1960s was its remarkable spontaneity. Founded in 1925 and 1934, respectively, Plaid Cymru and the SNP were amalgamations of various organizations and interest groups devoted to fostering a national agenda, vaguely and vari-ously defined. The disappointing upshot of 'Home Rule all round' in the pre-1914 era had shown the futility of relying on the major parties to devolve sovereignty to Scotland and Wales, hence the need for distinct and dedi-cated political movements to advance the cause. Their founding members were drawn from a wide spectrum of personalities and political persuasions, and thus their precise aims were subject to divergent interpretations, with calls for outright independence tempered by more moderate demands for greater autonomy 'within a loose association of British peoples'. Among the core principles of the SNP in 1934, for example, was the expectation that 'Scotland shall share with England the rights and responsibilities they, as mother nations, have jointly created and incurred within the British Empire' – hardly a principled objection to imperialism per se.[17]

For much of this early period, political emancipation took second place to the more immediate question of cultural advancement, whether in terms of language, literature, the arts or community awareness more generally. Many of the early party protagonists were themselves artists, writers and intellectuals rather than seasoned political operators, and thus both parties were marked by weak organization and consistently disappointing electoral results throughout their formative decades.[18] As late as 1960, the SNP and Plaid Cymru continued to dwell at the extreme fringes of the political landscape, with no parliamentary presence in Westminster and few obvious prospects to expand their electoral base. The SNP polled no more than 1.3 per cent of the overall Scottish vote between 1945 and 1959, while Plaid Cymru never secured more than 10 per cent in the constituencies it con-tested – well short of posing a threat to the major parties.[19]

But in the early 1960s the fortunes of both parties started to turn, coinciding with a shift to an overtly separatist platform calling for a more fundamental break with Britain.[20] The early portents appeared in a series of by-elections beginning in November 1961, when Ayrshire farmer Ian

Macdonald polled an impressive 18 per cent for the SNP at Glasgow-Bridgeton, seemingly out of nowhere. The following year Billy Wolfe emerged in West Lothian as one of the new leading lights of the SNP, securing a surprise second place with nearly a quarter of the vote. In neither case was the swing sufficient to win the seat, but the shock to the political system was substantial – inspiring John Strachey's gloomy forebodings about the 'Balkanization of Britain' discussed in the opening pages of Part I.[21]

Meanwhile in Wales a new generation of nationalists brought greater urgency and dynamism to the movement with the establishment of *Cymdeithas yr Iaith Gymraeg* (the Welsh Language Society), founded in 1962 for the purpose of preserving and promoting the Welsh tongue, if necessary by way of mildly subversive measures (not least its trademark vandalism of English signposts). Another galvanizing issue was the controversial flooding of the Tryweryn Valley in 1965 to provide a massive new reservoir for Liverpool, submerging the entire Welsh-speaking village of Capel Celyn in the process. The decade-long struggle to stop the dam not only furnished a potent symbol of Welsh subservience to England, but also gave birth to the so-called 'Free Wales Army' – a paramilitary organization modelled loosely on the IRA, albeit with a far more modest membership and limited means.[22] These developments initially brought considerable strain to Plaid Cymru's unstable coalition of supporters, with a pronounced rift between a politically moderate old guard led by the teetotalling, deeply Christian and socially conservative Gwynfor Evans, and a younger, restless and altogether less patient cohort demanding 'direct action' to address urgent Welsh grievances. Signs of a deepening rift along generational and ideological lines caused a temporary dip in support at the 1964 general election, but over the longer term the party's electoral appeal seems to have benefitted from widening the tent, influencing popular perceptions of the iniquities of the Union.

The combined success of Evans and Ewing was thus no mere flash in the pan but the culmination of a series of milestones in their internal political organization and electoral momentum. By 1968, SNP membership had increased sixtyfold in the space of only six years (from 2,000 members in 1962 to 120,000 in 1968) while branch organizations proliferated from 21 to 472 over the same period.[23] The party was reorganized along more professional lines, acquiring a full-time party organizer, propaganda unit, research department, communications office and a more efficient fundraising machine. Similarly in Wales, victory in Carmarthen was shortly followed by the near-defeat of Labour in its Welsh mining heartland at the Rhonda West by-election of March 1968, with the Plaid Cymru candidate recording a fivefold increase in support. Three months later, again in the Welsh valleys at Caerphilly, another by-election saw Plaid Cymru quadrupling its vote to come within a thousand votes of taking the seat.[24] Both results suggested that the nationalist message could resonate beyond the *Cymru Cymraeg* (the Welsh-speaking Welsh) in the north, west and south-west of the country.

Surveying these remarkable developments, it is hard to ignore the broader confluence of anti-colonial independence movements the world over. From the time of Harold Macmillan's 'Wind of Change' moment in February 1960 to the Wilson government's retreat from 'East of Suez' in January 1968, the electoral fortunes of the SNP and Plaid Cymru seemed to improve in inverse proportion to the empire's diminished holdings. By the time Winnie Ewing took up her seat in parliament in November 1967, the crippling external pressures on the British economy had reached their denouement with the devaluation of sterling that very month, widely regarded as the last, humiliating pinprick to Britain's global standing.[25] Long before Gwynfor Evans's breakthrough in Carmarthen, operatives of both parties had begun to exploit the perceived correlation between imperial and national trends. The SNP-aligned *Scots Independent* surveyed the dwindling assets of the 'Empire states' of Europe in 1965, noting the inwardly corrosive effects on the Union and the attendant opportunity for Celtic nationalism: 'This is now happening to the Scottish people ... The wind of change just doesn't blow suddenly as some English politicians would have us believe and then subside.'[26]

Similar sentiments were voiced by the SNP's London secretary Kenneth Tucker the following year, excoriating a 'redundant' British state apparatus that was now being 'discarded' by the Irish, Scots and Welsh due to one overriding factor: 'The fundamental reason for the creation of the British state, world empire is a thing of the past and one cannot see circumstances in which it is ever likely to rise again.'[27] The unexpected windfall of surging membership subscriptions permitted a complete makeover of the *Scots Independent* in 1968, with a revamped design and professionalized management. The inaugural issue of the new-look magazine (sporting the SNP political logo) trumpeted its editorial line on the front page: 'From the start England has been determined that Great Britain should be merely a normal pseudonym to cloak her desperate ambitions. The same is even more true today with the empire gone and world influence rapidly declining.'[28]

Meanwhile Plaid Cymru's two official newspapers (in English and Welsh, respectively) furnished elaborate assessments of the factors that underpinned the party's triumph in Carmarthen. 'Post-imperialist'

Britain, ventured the *Welsh Nation* in August 1966, had reached a turning point: 'England bereft of the "empire on which the sun never set" and of her worldwide maritime power, has, so to speak, awoke disillusioned in the cold grey light of unromantic dawn.'[29] Here, the SNP win in Hamilton was not merely an extension of the Carmarthen breakthrough but the latest in a much longer sequence of English setbacks the world over. 'Where did the old empire go?' inquired *Y Ddraig Goch* in the aftermath of Ewing's victory:

> India and Africa have long since gone. The Island of Cyprus has gone. The islands of Malta have gone. And the situation is not healthy in Hong Kong. All that remain are the countries that were first conquered by England, and the situation is not healthy there either. To tell the truth the will for parliaments in Scotland, Wales and Cornwall is growing so quickly that it is not inappropriate to ask 'for how much longer must we wait'? Is it not time for us to give one more big push so that a Welsh parliament meets in 1970?[30]

More significantly, nationalist party leaders themselves drew freely on these analogies to advance their cause. At the 1960 Plaid Cymru Party Conference, founding member J. E. Jones declared that 'African freedom movements have greatly influenced and strengthened the Welsh demand for complete self-government', in what he termed a 'wind of change over Wales'.[31] From the same conference podium, Gwynfor Evans surveyed the international scene and drew conclusions for Wales that are worth quoting at length:

> Empires are bursting at their seams, unable to contain the tremendous power of nationalism. Throughout the world this has been a liberating force to which hundreds of millions are grateful. In 1960 alone a tremendous surge is carrying seven African countries to statehood and full national freedom. Our politicians are resolved that Wales shall not take part in the great movement of the age, although its fruit could be welcomed here with greater confidence than in many countries ... Their choice is to play safe, to keep Wales a backwater where no contribution of great value is ever likely to be made again, well away from the world's vital stream ... Conditioned by their parties' imperialist past our professional politicians are bewildered by this new world and are petrified by the thought of Wales taking her place alongside Eire and a score of other equally small countries in the U.N. Their sterile ambition is to prevent Wales becoming a nation which can act in international affairs. This is the meaning of their common determination, Tory and Labour alike, 'to maintain the union with England'.[32]

The entire framing of the speech underscores the influence of global trends on nationalist political messaging in two key respects. First, it marked the beginning of a shift away from 'dominion' or 'Commonwealth status' as the standard bearer of Welsh national aspirations and towards a demand for a fully independent Welsh seat at the UN. Second, and more significantly, it signalled an opportunity to depict Plaid Cymru's opponents as timid reactionaries, stranded on the wrong side of history. In likening the Union to a species of latter-day imperial servitude, Evans aligned his own emancipatory project with the irreversible tide of human progress that had ushered Europe's empires into oblivion. 'From the wreckage of empire', he implored his audience, 'a truly inter-national order is emerging, based soundly on the co-operation of free nations.'[33] The changing colonial and international landscape thus not only refashioned Plaid Cymru's core demands, but also profoundly altered their approach to packaging nationalist politics for the 1960s.

The SNP's leading lights were less florid in their pronouncements, but here too the deteriorating climate for colonialism brought a distinct change of emphasis. The career of the party's star performer prior to Hamilton, Billy Wolfe, is particularly instructive. Far from exhibiting a lifelong commitment to the nationalist cause, the middle-class accountant and shovel manufacturer from Bathgate was only belatedly moved to join the SNP in 1959, 'convinced by the facts of Scotland's decline in the 1950s and by the logic of the double contention that if there is a nation of Scots it is entitled to self-government'.[34] By mid-1962 he had become 'moved to indignation and frustration' because he 'realized anew that the essence of Scotland was being so diluted and destroyed ... It was a kindly English imperialism that was destroying them.'[35] At the October 1964 general election, Wolfe's first political advertisement proclaimed: 'Nyasaland now has independence – what about Scotland – but of course Scotland is a profitable colony. So long as we are a nation of labourers in our own land we will remain England's last satellite.'[36] His arch-nemesis – Labour's Tam Dalyell, who would hold out against Wolfe's designs on West Lothian at a further six elections – complained wearily of the latter's 'laser-like fixation on Scottish Statehood', as though it were some idle distraction from what politics ought to be about.[37]

Time and again during the 1960s, the two nationalist parties would pin their hopes on Britain's diminished place in the world. Amid the pronounced anger at the flooding of the Tryweryn Valley in 1965, Evans resorted to Dean Acheson's famous dictum 'England has lost an Empire ... without finding a role', adding pointedly: 'Do the Welsh people feel that their submerged country has a role in the world?'[38] On other occasions, not least following his Carmarthen triumph, he turned the hackneyed metaphor of an imperial sunset to more positive ends: 'I can see something different from the light of the setting sun. It looks more like the rising of a new dawn. "Westward look the land is bright."'[39] By the end of the decade, the SNP research department had devised a similar ploy, tapping into feelings of British enfeeblement to rally a sense of nationalist optimism. Candidates were encouraged to stress the stark choice faced by Scottish voters – either 'rejoin the international community as a self-governing nation in her own right', or 'remain a province of England, a poor relation to the sick man of Europe'.[40] SNP chairman Arthur Donaldson put the matter plainly in his response to the 1967 devaluation of sterling: 'We are on a sinking ship. We have left it rather late to take the necessary steps. But Scotland must get a boat of her own.'[41]

It is not that events unfolding elsewhere in the world somehow dictated the course of Scottish and Welsh politics. It was more a matter of separatist agendas aligning with a new global politics of national aspiration. What gave the cause an electoral boost was not any widespread sympathy for (still less identification with) the Kenyattas and Kaundas, so much as an altogether less tangible sense of the diminished scope for being British in the world. Though only dimly perceived, these wider impulses would force a subtle recalibration of the old British–Scottish duality in favour of the latter.

'EXPLOIT LOCAL GRIEVANCES': CARMARTHEN AND HAMILTON

But this only gets us so far. The fact that leading nationalist figures such as Evans and Wolfe could draw direct parallels between Celtic and colonial contexts certainly attests to the importance of the empire's demise in shaping their 1960s agenda. But it need not necessarily follow that this was the crucial ingredient in their sudden run of success. Closer attention to local patterns of causation reveals a more complex picture, especially at the level of grass-roots party organization, political activism and the specific strategies adopted at Carmarthen and Hamilton to swing voters behind Evans and Ewing. The official records of both the SNP and Plaid Cymru bear witness to a very different – and avowedly provincial – set of preoccupations, with sustained attention to the minutiae of party organization, canvassing tactics, internal political jostling, branch management, finance, publicity and the meticulously recorded minutes of endless sub-committees. References to wider issues affecting Britain's place in the world in general, or the empire in particular, are conspicuous by their absence, suggesting that these issues operated at a level of political awareness at one remove from the business of day-to-day door knocking. Nor did the end of empire feature prominently in the campaign material of either party during the two crucial by-elections, where the sustained focus was Westminster's indifference to the material hardships affecting Scottish and Welsh voters.

Gwynfor Evans's written instructions to branch offices was quite explicit in this regard: 'Use local press, appointing press officers, constantly and intelligently; and exploit local grievances.'[42] The energetic horde of student canvassers bussed in for the 1966 campaign was instructed to play down talk of a seat for Wales at the UN and emphasize instead the candidate's qualities as an able and honest local resident dedicated to his constituents. 'On no account' were they to be caught wearing the Free Wales Army uniform.[43] Issues such as roads, railways, infrastructure, health care, schools and pit closures furnished the dominant register in a highly localized operation that seemed, on the face of it, impervious to the wider international scene. As Carmarthen's *Western Mail* commented, 'the campaign has been conducted in terms of local problems and their relation to national policy rather than in the reverse order'.[44] This was also reflected in the party's own post-election assessment of 'why Carmarthen was won', which boiled down to Evans's personal popularity in the electorate, his extensive support network, and the fact that he was able to concentrate on his own seat rather than simultaneously canvass the entire country as party president. 'Bad roads, closure of railways, depopulation, the closure of small schools; these were definite reasons why voters were willing to support a man who fought for the betterment of the rural districts and an improvement in infrastructure.'[45] Such was the local emphasis that one English press correspondent lamented that the entire campaign 'thwarted outside attempts at assessment. For one thing it was conducted largely in Welsh.'[46]

In Hamilton there was the added ingredient of the 'well-earned unpopularity' of the Wilson Labour government, widely derided for its alleged 'masterly inactivity' in Scotland.[47] This was relentlessly hammered home by the *Hamilton Herald*, an SNP news sheet dedicated to cataloguing Labour's failings in housing, education, unemployment and faltering productivity.[48] The local *Hamilton Advertiser*, although by no means enamoured of the SNP, described Winnie Ewing as a 'kiss of life to a public that was suffocating from lack of interest', ascribing her victory almost exclusively to her 'bubbling whirl of vigour, charm and plain talking' that provided welcome respite from the 'political rut' exemplified by the main parties. Viewed from a grass-roots perspective, Hamilton was won by the fortuitous combination of a refreshingly optimistic candidate at a time of widespread voter fatigue.

Figure 14.2 Winnie Ewing's Hamilton by-election campaign in 1967 drew a stark contrast between the 'grey non-entity that represents Westminster' and the promise of national renewal with the SNP, emphasizing youth, vigour and an abrupt break with the past. SNP supporters, left to right, Sheila Ferguson, Myra Thornton, Julie Hutchison and Sylvia McGrady, Sunday 8 October 1967. Source: Mirrorpix/Getty Images.

'She did nothing short of bowl them over', the *Advertiser* concluded, 'running an exemplary campaign and giving a welcome spark of life to what, without her, could only have been another political foregone conclusion.'[49]

The weight of local evidence therefore calls for a degree of caution. In certain contexts, for certain purposes, the panoramic sweep of a decolonizing world could convey a plausible broad-brush portrait of the nation-in-waiting. But for the more immediate purpose of canvassing votes, it could be less helpful, perhaps even a liability – a deft balancing act that required careful political judgement. No sooner had Gwynfor Evans secured victory in Carmarthen, for example, than his rhetoric reverted almost immediately to the bigger picture, releasing a commemorative LP

('Wales Resurgent') replete with references to the 'oppressive yoke of England ... being thrown off'.[50] His maiden speech in the House of Commons was equally panoramic in scope. Denied the right to take the oath in Welsh, he launched a broadside against a British government and a British state that 'never will invest in our country ... never will take the necessary steps to build up a healthy balanced economy in Wales. What, therefore, should they do? They should get out of Wales, and leave the government of that country to the Welsh people themselves.' Here, he unfurled his core objection to a parliament and a political system that placed 'England's prestige above all else':

> Sterling, the pound, the hydrogen bomb, Aden and Singapore – your costly efforts to keep these relics of an imperial past place a devastating burden upon the Welsh economy ... If you were prepared humbly to accept the reality of your present position in the world, there would be no talk of financial or economic crisis today and no panic Tory measures. This is an English crisis, but, as usual, the Welsh people have to pay more than their share of the price.[51]

Not a word about the closure of the Carmarthen–Aberystwyth rail line or other local irritants. Context was crucial; a historic, set-piece speech in the House of Commons furnished a more promising forum to excoriate centuries of imperial misrule than a community hall in the Tywi Valley.

The two registers of political signification cannot be considered in isolation, however. As Evans astutely judged, charges of chronic under-investment in regional infrastructure could be attributed to the misguided priorities of a British government bent on salvaging the last vestiges of a world role. The key was to connect the burden of costly overseas commitments to the immediate concerns that resonated with the local community – even where the connection was far from convincing. For all the talk of Westminster's indifference to Scottish and Welsh prosperity, it is often overlooked that the 1960s were a time of significantly enhanced income redistribution, when the Wilson government in particular campaigned heavily on regional issues and established a Welsh Office with its own secretary of state to deal with key policy areas such as health, agriculture and education. Wilson announced in 1964 that the new minister would 'express the voice of Wales', ensuring that the Welsh people were given 'a fair crack of the whip'. The first secretary of state, Cledwyn Hughes, went out of his way to draw a line under the perceived neglect of the past, offering the wry assurance: 'I do not propose to consent to the drowning of any villages in Mid Wales.'[52] It could not have been a lack of political awareness in Westminster that fuelled the perception of studied metropolitan neglect.

But the redoubled efforts of the Welsh Office seem in no way to have satisfied nationalist grievances or diminished Welsh demands for a greater say in governing themselves – indeed the opposite seems to be the case.[53] Likewise in Scotland, the familiar charge of Westminster's alienation from Scottish problems escalated at a time of unprecedented government investment in the North. T. M. Devine notes the spectacular 900 per cent increase in public expenditure in Scotland between 1964 and 1973, pushing per capita spending over the national average by one-fifth. New infrastructure projects, bridges, pits, smelters, schools and administrative bodies proliferated, while the number of universities doubled from four to eight. These initiatives were also dispersed widely throughout the country, leaving 'no part of Scotland ... untouched'.[54] Yet despite this frenetic activity, the entrenched perception was one of political aloofness and remote control.

The point is not that Welsh and Scottish discontents were groundless. But it does highlight a more complex weave of causation that fed into perceptions of government neglect and forged an unusually receptive climate for separatist political messaging in the latter half of the 1960s. At a time when endemic 'declinism' emanated from London, when 'what's wrong' journalism multiplied throughout Britain, Australasia, Canada and elsewhere, concerns about the present and future prosperity of Scotland and Wales could similarly be viewed in the light of Britain's serial shortcomings.[55] SNP stalwart and future party leader Gordon Wilson stressed the confluence of real material hardship and waning political morale wrought by external factors; the collapse of empire had not only undermined the 'prestige and power of the British state', but also removed a major source of Scottish economic prosperity and opportunity.[56] Whether this was understood in terms of the decline of old 'imperial' industries such as shipping, steel, coal and jute (much of which had already begun decades earlier) or merely the half-remembered fragments of former industrial pre-eminence, it nevertheless filtered directly into public perceptions of Scotland's social and economic woes. Similarly for Wales, the burden of redundant ambitions abroad was spelt out by *Y Ddraig Goch* in 1967:

> The cost of the upkeep of the English Empire signalled the last gasp of death for us in Wales. It is like a rope around our necks. If England wants to sink into disorder and hopelessness through continuing to play with its imperialism let her be. But it is a matter of life and death for our nation to take our heads out of the noose.[57]

Kenneth Morgan rightly points out that Plaid Cymru's victory in Carmarthen 'was too sweeping to be explained solely by reference to purely local or fortuitous factors'.[58] As important as local grievances undoubtedly were, it was the way they were melded to perceptions of wider British adversity that secured the breakthrough – and the attendant promise of a separate future unencumbered by the stigma of national failure. Likewise in Hamilton, unknown, untried candidates do not secure swings in excess of 40 per cent purely on the strength of local discontent. Talk of Britain's standing in the world may not have been at the forefront of voter intentions when they entered the ballot box, but it was crucial to investing local grievances with a heightened immediacy and urgency – a point vividly captured by the *Hamilton Advertiser* on the eve of the poll:

> Britain has lost its vocation, its sense of destiny as a nation. Having handed over an empire, we are left without a role – our occupation is gone. America has nearly disowned us; de Gaulle's France has rejected us; we cannot make our national will felt over a quarter of a million white Rhodesians; and we have forfeited the respect of peoples whom once we proudly ruled.[59]

It was this spiritual vacuum that Winnie Ewing skilfully exploited to overwhelm a Labour candidate with a 16,000-vote majority. Her 'Stop the World' victory cry outside Hamilton Town Hall was no random rhetorical flourish but the subtext of the entire campaign. Vowing to 'put Scotland on the map', SNP campaign posters featured the candidate sitting confidently astride an imposing bronze globe. The inspired image was captured – of all places – in the commemorative forecourt of David Livingstone's birthplace in nearby Blantyre. Once a symbol of Britain's (and indeed Scotland's) imperial reach, the Livingstone orb now furnished powerful visual testimony for Scotland's separate, sovereign destiny in a world after empire.

'GO BACK TO CAMBRIDGE, CHARLIE BOY': THE ESTABLISHMENT RESPONDS

As with the outbreak of the Troubles in Northern Ireland, one of the immediate effects of separatist electoral success in Scotland and Wales was to galvanize the major parties into devising an urgent response. Greater heed was suddenly paid to the nationalist agenda and its discontents, now regarded as a distinct political movement that needed somehow to be checked, co-opted or absorbed. One BBC *Checkpoint* programme in January 1968 surveyed seventy-one Scottish MPs and found that more than half – forty-three in total – were in favour of some sort of devolved assembly for Scotland. Only sixteen were opposed. The *Glasgow Herald* raised eyebrows at the belated conversion of so many honourable members, but the fact remained: 'For so many Scottish MPs to make an admission which would have been unthinkable for all except the Liberals a short time ago is something of a landmark.'[60] Within a matter of months, Opposition Leader Edward Heath had publicly aired the possibility of devolved regional assemblies while the Wilson Labour government – not to be outdone – announced a Royal Commission on the Constitution in April 1969, charged with considering 'whether any changes are desirable ... in the present constitutional and economic relationships between the various parts of the United Kingdom'. Despite the dry-as-dust terms of reference, there could be no mistaking the recrudescence of an issue that had lain dormant since the Anglo-Irish Treaty of 1921.

Reactions were not confined to the promise of constitutional reform, however, particularly when it came to Wales. Far more imaginative was the decision to stage a full-scale royal pageant in Caernarfon in July 1969 for the formal investiture of the twenty-one-year-old Charles, Prince of Wales. The decision itself had been taken a decade earlier in Cardiff at the closing ceremony of the 1958 Empire and Commonwealth Games, stipulating only that the investiture should take place when the young prince was 'grown up'. But the delicate matter of timing became enmeshed in the new challenge posed by political separatism in the mid-1960s. When the newly established Welsh Office first approached the palace in 1965, the queen made it clear that the ceremony should wait until Charles had completed his Cambridge education in the early 1970s, but it was soon brought forward to summer 1969. As John S. Ellis has shown, 'it was only at the insistent cajoling' of the secretary of state for Wales that the queen agreed, 'with some misgivings' to the change of plan.[61] This was in February 1967, barely six months after Plaid Cymru's shock win in Carmarthen, and although it was never referred to explicitly in palace correspondence it is clear that the Welsh Office had ulterior motives for bringing the investiture forward.[62] To ensure that the prince should 'not be a complete stranger to Wales', it was also decided that he should spend a two-month period of study at the University College of Wales in Aberystwyth prior to his investiture, so that he might become conversant in the Welsh language.[63]

The announcement was met with widespread ambivalence, bordering on cynicism. Labour had long benefitted from strong electoral support in the coal-mining valleys of South Wales – now particularly vulnerable to nationalist incursions – and questions were inevitably raised about the propriety of co-opting the royal family for such brazen political ends. A. J. P. Taylor prominently denounced 'the sordid plot to exploit Prince Charles', though not out of sympathy for Welsh nationalism which he dismissed completely out of hand – adding insult to injury with the gratuitous putdown: 'I can think of many universities where a year's residence might benefit the history student ... Aberystwyth is not among them.'[64] Even *The Times* judged the entire event a 'public relations and political sop to pacify the nationalist stirring in Wales', while *The Observer* likened the situation to the 1920s when Charles's predecessor, the Duke of Windsor, was kept preoccupied touring the empire during the long prelude to his short-lived career as Edward VIII:

> But now there is no Empire to tour ... So how is Charles to become a useful member of society? ... The Government's long-term idea is to turn him into a Welsh-speaking Welshman, get him to take a serious and continued interest in the life and future of the nation. Then bingo: the restless Welsh are pacified, Charles has a useful role, the Monarchy is saved and the Labour Party holds a few key marginal seats in the valleys.[65]

Few dared to suggest openly that the royal family had been willingly co-opted to stall Plaid Cymru's electoral momentum, but such considerations were never far from view – not least among the Plaid Cymru leadership, for whom the whole problem of Prince Charles posed an intractable dilemma. In theory, the monarchy itself was a non-issue. The party's constitutional position on self-government had always recognized the Crown as an integral component of 'Commonwealth status' and thus a Prince of Wales need not have raised any graver difficulties than it did for Canada or New Zealand. But it was equally clear that many of the party's younger recruits took a dimmer view of the monarchy as self-evidently English and hence a potent symbol of Welsh subjugation, all the more so in the dramatized setting of an occupying power anointing its own successor. The scene was thus set for damaging internal divisions which were never fully resolved.

Gwynfor Evans prevaricated from the outset, describing the event as a 'tremendous honour' for Charles while claiming to be 'unenthusiastic' about it personally. Privately he believed that the Wilson government had set a 'trap' for Plaid Cymru which needed to be handled with the utmost care at a time when the party was seeking to broaden its electoral appeal without alienating its more ardently nationalist support base.[66] Internal party research was also equivocal, noting that while the entire affair 'must be categorized as fundamentally obnoxious', the overriding electoral imperatives dictated a 'calculated coolness'. Evans personally adopted the tactic of remaining as 'quiet as possible' in the futile hope that ignoring the investiture might make it go away, electing to absentee himself from the Caernarfon ceremony itself, but making a point of meeting the prince when he visited Carmarthen a few days later.[67] This only invited criticism from all sides, with the *Carmarthen Times* demanding to know 'why nationalists have shut up?' in the presence of the prince's ineluctable charm.[68]

It was left to the younger generation of Plaid activists, largely under the auspices of *Cymdeithas yr Iaith Gymraeg*, to denounce the investiture as a 'continuation of the historic insult to our Nation' and the 'greatest farce of modern Welsh history'. Dafydd Elis Thomas, then leader of Plaid Cymru's youth wing, issued a memorable appeal in the Party magazine, *I'r Gad*: 'Don't come to Caernarfon in 1969 – but go back to Cambridge, Charlie boy, Wales has her own leaders and her own destiny now.'[69] Slogans, satire and a slew of placards and bumper stickers became the order of the day, ranging from 'Senned Nid Tywysog' ('parliament not Prince') to 'Cymru nid Prydain' ('Wales not Britain') and 'Dim Sais yn Dywysog Cymru' ('no Englishman for Prince of Wales').[70] In January 1969, popular Welsh folk artist Dafydd Iwan released the satirical single 'Carlo' (a Welsh variation on 'Charles' but also a common name for a pet dog), dominating the Welsh language pop charts for several weeks.[71] When the moment finally arrived on 31 May for Prince Charles to deliver his first public address in Welsh at the Urdd Eisteddfod in Aberystwyth, the first two rows silently filed out in protest, amid physical scuffles, booing and general rancour.[72]

More ominous were the threats of sabotage and paramilitary violence from the Free Wales Army and the *Mudiad Amddiffyn Cymru* (Movement for the Defence of Wales) in the days and months leading up to the ceremony, with several bombs exploding in public locations throughout Wales, including the Welsh Office in Cardiff in May 1968. Although the numerical strength and capacity of these groups were greatly overestimated, at the time they seemed a genuine public menace, prompting a massive security operation throughout the country with more than a hundred prominent nationalists placed under constant surveillance (with the most conspicuous paramilitaries rounded up in advance and subjected to legal proceedings that were slow-tracked to keep them behind bars until the festivities were over). By spring 1969, a swarm of Special Branch, MI5 and Army bomb disposal personnel had poured into Wales, particularly the potential hot spots of Aberystwyth and Caernarfon. The Aberystwyth Student Union complained of the sudden influx of 'mature students who look amazingly like agents from the Special Branch' while the townsfolk of Caernarfon complained of living 'in a goldfish bowl in a Scotland yard office'. As *The Sun* reported on the eve of the investiture: 'In Caernarvon yesterday there were an awful lot of people watching other people.'[73]

Yet even this failed to neutralize the threat completely. On the day before the ceremony on 30 June, a mail bomb exploded in a Cardiff post office while later that evening, two men were killed in Abergele by the untimely detonation of their own bomb, intended for the railway line carrying the Queen and Prince Philip to Wales.[74] The following night, a military police van at the castle gate in Caernarvon was targeted by an explosion that incinerated the driver. And most infamously, a bomb that failed to detonate along the route of the prince's procession was discovered by eleven-year old Ian Cox four days later, resulting tragically in an amputated leg. Only one bomb managed to go off on the day itself, in a nearby field as the prince's entourage made its way to the castle in an open carriage. Secretary of State for Wales George Thomas records the following surreal exchange with the prince at the time of the blast:

> He turned to me: 'What is it Mr Thomas?' I improvised 'It's a royal salute, Prince Charles'. When he said it was a peculiar royal salute, I could only reply, 'There are peculiar people up here, Prince Charles'.[75]

The ceremony itself went ahead as planned, with the ghostly ruins of Caernarfon Castle given an ultra-modern makeover with a circular slate dais raised under a giant perspex canopy, designed by the smartly clad Lord Snowdon. The simplest of lightweight, rectilinear stools sufficed as thrones for the main protagonists – a deft merger of the venerable and the new-vogue. Much was made of the impending Apollo 11 mission, amid talk of a 'medieval pageant staged in the month of the moon walk'.[76] The exhaustive six-hour television coverage, broadcast live to half a dozen countries, attracted a record audience – conveying all the reverence of timeless tradition tweaked for the satellite age. As Charles dedicated himself to his new principality 'as much as possible', he was flanked by thirty-four 'representatives of Welsh youth' enlisted to portray the prince as 'the young leader of a young Wales'.[77] In the words of Cledwyn Hughes, it was not merely 'the dedicating of a Prince but also the rededication of a nation'. For those who missed the point, George Thomas rammed it home: 'In my view, our Prince has given us another chance to become one Wales, not two.'[78]

Figure 14.3 The investiture of Prince Charles, Caernarvon Castle, 1 July 1969. Source: Hulton Royals Collection/Getty Images.

But although the investiture succeeded in squeezing the nationalist support base and temporarily wrong-footing Plaid Cymru, it proved a failure as a touchstone of unity. Opinion polls may have pointed to solid majorities rallying behind the prince and the pageantry of Caernarfon, but the very proliferation of pollsters asking probing questions – like the influx of Special Branch spooks – was indicative of a more fractious affair. As the Welsh language weekly *Y Cymro* ventured, the entire episode would prove 'of great interest to future historians' because of the obvious questions it raised. Above all: 'was Welsh nationalism considered so much of a threat that . . . it was necessary to throw the whole weight of the Crown into the political battlefield to try and extinguish it?'[79] The controversies that seemed to erupt at every turn only amplified the underlying problem. As Ellis affirms, over the longer term, rather than 'burying nationalist protest culture' the investiture ultimately helped to define and consolidate Plaid Cymru's presence in a transformed political arena.[80]

'BACK IN OUR OWN COUNTRY FOR KEEPS':
THE PATH TO 1979

In the short term, the 1970 general election took some of the wind out of the nationalist sails, with both Evans and Ewing losing their seats with only a single compensatory gain for the SNP in the Western Isles. The frustration was compounded by the electoral system's notorious bias against smaller parties, with Plaid Cymru enjoying a threefold increase in vote share right across Wales yet still losing their only seat in the Commons.[81] No sooner were Ewing and Evans removed than the major parties lost interest in vying for the hearts and minds of nationalist voters, and the appetite for constitutional reform rapidly abated. When Lord Kilbrandon's Royal Commission finally brought down its findings in October 1973, the recommendation for devolved assemblies in Scotland and Wales, coupled with further regional devolution throughout England, was quietly brushed to one side.[82]

The expectation that separatist politics would quickly be snuffed out proved to be premature, however. Margo MacDonald's successful SNP by-election campaign for the seat of Glasgow Govan in 1973 signalled an upswing in nationalist fortunes, with the much-publicized discovery of North Sea oil providing fresh impetus (coinciding with the quadrupling of the oil price during the 1973 OPEC crisis). The SNP's 'It's Scotland's Oil' campaign brought immediate dividends in 1974 when two successive general elections delivered handsome gains, culminating in nearly a third of the Scottish vote and eleven seats in the Commons (Winifred Ewing returning in her new constituency of Moray and Nairn).[83] Gwynfor Evans, too, regained Carmarthen in 1974 together with two new Plaid Cymru members: Dafydd Elis Thomas in Merioneth and Dafydd Wigley winning the symbolically charged seat of Caernarfon. Together with the eleven SNP members they comprised a substantial rump of nationalist MPs, the likes of which would have been unimaginable ten years earlier. With a new Wilson Labour government returned with the slimmest of majorities, the receptive climate for nationalist demands was renewed, just as the demands themselves gained a new self-assurance. At the launch of the SNP's independence blueprint in September 1974, Britain was confidently deemed to be stranded 'at the end of an imperial era and ... there was no reason why the four nations within Britain should not live in an independent state'.[84]

By this stage, the fallen empires analogy was not merely a matter of separatist propaganda; it now provided a ready backdrop for making sense of the see-sawing political landscape, with a steady supply of books and essays unequivocally aligning recent trends in Scotland and Wales with the broader sweep of imperial decline. Michael Hechter's *Internal Colonialism* made a timely appearance in 1975, the most significant work to date likening 'English rule' of 'Celtic lands' to the age-old practice of 'colonialism overseas'.[85] That same year, the Scottish theologian, Daniel Jenkins, rolled out the largely forgotten figure of J. R. Seeley to posit an inversion of his famous aphorism: 'If the British Empire was built in a fit of absent-mindedness, the United Kingdom could easily, and quite unnecessarily, become the disunited Kingdom in the same way.'[86] Shortly afterwards came the most sophisticated elaboration of the theme in Tom Nairn's *The Break-Up of Britain*, attributing the separatist impulse to the wider failures of a sclerotic, hierarchical and inherently imperial British state. The one-time tormenter of nationalist 'sporranry' had become the leading figure in 'defining modern Scottish nationalism as a language of anti-imperialism'.[87]

Even more significant was the way the imperial parallel became commonplace in mainstream political commentary, with the leader writer for *The Times*, Owen Hickey, buying in to its evolving logic:

> While Great Britain was, or was still regarded by many of its citizens as being, an imperial power and a major economic, political and military force in the world, there were compensations to make up for Scotland's submerged nationhood. The scale of British operations abroad opened up an almost endless range of opportunities; and dominating Scotsmen were afforded the opportunity of ruling an empire in exchange for ruling themselves in the north of the British Isles. Those compensations have faded . . . It would not be surprising if the hold of British patriotism over the Scots had weakened as Britain's status has declined.[88]

Here, Scotland's emergence from empire was no longer a simple case of casting off the shackles of dominion. It was an exercise in cutting losses, electing to rule themselves once more now that ruling the world was no longer an option. The premise was crude but sufficiently tempting to draw all the major parties once more into the devolution debate, amid tortuous parliamentary negotiations to find viable constitutional solutions for Scotland and Wales. The Labour Party had fought the 1974 elections on a promise to move forward with devolutionary measures but these quickly became bogged down in bureaucratic red tape and internal party discord. The first, ill-fated attempt was the Scotland and Wales Bill, introduced by the Callaghan government in 1976 'to give the Scottish and Welsh people a surer guarantee and a more relevant instrument of national identity than a protest vote thrown to an extreme theory' – in other words, a thinly veiled attempt to thwart the advance of the SNP and Plaid Cymru. The prime minister sought to play down the magnitude of his own measures, presenting them as 'the outcome of steady development' through a series of milestones harking back to the establishment of the Scottish Office in 1885.[89]

But in the ensuing debate, speaker after speaker from all sides of the House depicted a country at an unprecedented constitutional crossroads, with the long shadow of empire's end furnishing the (by now) predictable backdrop. Labour's Jim Sillars (Ayrshire South, who would later defect to the SNP) described the demand for self-government in Scotland as 'a natural process of imperial decline', with the 'minority nations' in the United Kingdom merely 'seeking a new post-imperial partnership with England' that members would disregard at their peril.[90] Even Conservative voices north of the border could not resist the implications. 'How important to England is the United Kingdom?' asked Alexander Fletcher, Conservative member for Edinburgh North (and future under-secretary for Scotland under Thatcher). 'Having lost the Empire and while retaining a rather tenuous link with the Commonwealth would it really matter very much if Scotland and Wales were to do their own thing and go their own separate ways?'[91]

English Tories could not allow themselves to be so sanguine. At the pessimistic end of the spectrum was John Biffen's Powellite pamphlet *A Nation in Doubt* (1976), citing the separatist threat in the north among the major social challenges facing the party and the nation in the years ahead. He contrasted the extraordinary electoral success of the SNP in 1974 with the situation only twenty years earlier when the Conservatives held a majority of seats in Scotland, urging: 'We are stumbling towards a cataclysm' – the causes of which were far more complex than the discovery of oil or a late flowering of 'regionalism'. Here too, the 'dissolution of the British Empire' made an appearance as the great precursor event that was 'bound to have consequences upon the kingdom that had been its heart'. But in Biffen's rendering it was not the shared material dividends of overseas adventure that mattered, so much as the incalculable cost 'to imagination and pride'. It was a moral and emotional deficit that was eroding the core of a common Britishness.[92]

Needless to say, the SNP had every reason to exploit the crisis of confidence, but even here the anti-colonial fervour of old was giving way to a different emphasis. The newly elected member for Clackmannan and East Stirlingshire, George Reid, offered some sober reflections on the deeper historical forces at work, neither excoriating nor apologizing for the shared enthusiasms of the imperial past:

> English MPs fail to understand that the United Kingdom is not a nation. Do they recite 'O to be in the United Kingdom now that April's here' or sing

'There'll always be a United Kingdom'? The United Kingdom is a multinational State comprising the separate nations of the British Isles ... What is taking place ... is that we have come to the end of the Empire and the United Kingdom is currently in a state of economic decline. No one here would deny that. I may be making a point against myself, but we Scots had a privileged position in the days of Imperial grandeur. We were both Scots and British. We ran the docks in Hong Kong, the judicial system in the Punjab and held Burns suppers in temperatures of 102 degrees in India. Those days are gone and those options are no longer open to us. We stay at home. The young Scots in Scotland today, looking at the obvious degradation and neglect, are not prepared to tolerate these conditions. They are back in our own country for keeps and wish to do something about the situation—usually by joining the SNP.[93]

Rarely was the issue framed so matter-of-factly in terms of a cold repudiation of a historic partnership that no longer paid a serviceable dividend. Nothing in Reid's perspective implied a state of 'internal colonialism' or a restless chafing at the last vestiges of imperial rule. It was about sloughing off the burden of empire-building and relinquishing privileges 'no longer open to us' as the necessary prelude to building a viable future on a greatly reduced scale. It meant being 'back in our own country for keeps'; a compelling metaphor for the diminished prospects for overseas reward.

But as David McCrone points out, the metaphor was frequently mistaken for a deeper explanatory paradigm – as though the mere fact of the empire's passing signalled a foregone conclusion from which there could be no escape.[94] This partly accounts for the misplaced optimism of the nationalist parties in the lead-up to the first devolution referendums in 1979. Party operatives would soon discover the world of difference between exploiting disenchantment with the status quo and delivering on political solutions to advance the nationalist cause. The original Scotland and Wales Bill had been defeated by a rebellion of Labour and Liberal MPs in February 1977 and was subsequently divided into two separate bills for Scotland and Wales, respectively. These were to have an equally difficult passage through the legislature and only succeeded following a Labour backbench amendment requiring that the two referendums be passed not only by an absolute majority of voters but also by 40 per cent of the electorate as a whole – effectively dooming the process from the outset. No post-war British government had ever come close to meeting such a daunting threshold.

The results nevertheless came as a shock to nationalists. Although the 1 March 1979 referendum delivered a slim 51.6 per cent majority of Scottish voters in favour, the turnout was poor, falling well short of the stiff requirements of the 40 per cent rule. Meanwhile, Welsh electors – on St David's Day no less – voted against their own regional assembly by an overwhelming majority of nearly 80 per cent, including a majority in every county. As one of the chief advocates of the new Assembly, Secretary of State for Wales John Morris glumly concluded: 'When you see an elephant on your doorstep, you know that it's there.'[95] For the SNP, to be denied victory on a technicality seemed intolerably unfair, prompting a last-ditch attempt by the party leadership to lodge a United Nations protest under Resolution 1514 (better known as the 'Resolution on Decolonisation'). Fired with indignation, Billy Wolfe could 'not rule out the possibility of catalytic action, such as the Easter Rising of 1916 in Ireland, resulting in at last galvanising the Scottish electorate into active support for the struggle'.[96] It was a profound misreading of the situation. The UN protest proved a spectacular misfire, bringing little satisfaction and considerable ridicule from the SNP's Unionist adversaries.

The Labour government immediately abandoned the devolution project, sparking a revolt among SNP members who promptly withdrew their parliamentary support – convinced that the electorate would rally around them in protest over the dubious voting procedures. The results of the 1979 general election suggested otherwise, not only delivering a Tory victory to Margaret Thatcher, but also completely decimating the parliamentary ranks of the nationalists (famously scorned as 'turkeys voting for an early Christmas' by outgoing Prime Minister James Callaghan).[97] The two standard bearers of Welsh and Scottish separatism, Gwynfor Evans and Winnie Ewing, both lost their seats once more – the latter falling to a Conservative rival by a mere 420 votes – with neither destined ever to return to the House of Commons. For Welsh nationalists, it felt like the end of the road, as though Wales had written '*finis* to nearly 200 years of Welsh history'.[98] Likewise for an SNP reduced from eleven to only two seats, it was a dispiriting moment that seemed to have 'effectively removed Scotland, for the time at least, from the map'.[99]

'THE LEAST THAT ANCIENT SCOTLAND CAN EXPECT': IMPERIAL PARALLELS

What to make, then, of the remarkable ebb and flow of separatist politics in the two decades from 1960 to 1979, and the pronounced readiness to attribute causation to the inner workings of empire's end? It was at the peak of the nationalist surge in the mid-1970s that the post-imperial metaphor seemed most apposite, widely reiterated in contemporary political and social commentary. But it was by no means a static proposition, containing any number of inconsistencies and glaring contradictions that were hardly ever acknowledged, let alone reconciled. The eleventh-hour bid for Scotland to be 'decolonized' by the UN chimed awkwardly with George Reid's frank admission that it was only because the 'privileged position' of empire had fallen by the wayside that the iniquities of the Union now needed to be urgently addressed. For all the readiness to draw imperial parallels, there remained a conspicuous gap between invocations of the empire as a generalized form of rhetorical persuasion and the specific material and moral consequences of imperial decline.

It also needs to be borne in mind that Scottish nationalists did not always endorse the notion that their sudden run of success was imperially ordained. At her first Bannockburn Day rally following the euphoria of Hamilton, Winifred Ewing set out to refute the 'propagandists' and 'political myth-makers' who denied the SNP any real credit for their spectacular political gains, taking aim specifically at 'the legend of our rise is due to the British Empire's fall'.[100] Her emphatic rejection of the galvanizing properties of imperial decline flew directly in the face of much contemporary commentary, but there were obvious political reasons for preferring a deeper legitimacy aligned with the fourteenth-century legacies of William Wallace and Robert the Bruce. Clearly, it did not always suit the SNP's emotional temper to depict Scottish separatism as a belated response to an obsolescent Britishness. But as with the Livingstone globe that adorned her campaign posters, the fact that imperial parallels were largely implicit – and frequently unselfconscious – in no way diminished their powers of signification.

All of which suggests a certain evasiveness in nationalist perceptions of the end of empire as a factor in their improved electoral prospects – and a more complex interplay with events unfolding elsewhere in the world. In the early 1960s, it was the example of independence movements in the wind of change era that were normally cited as inspiration, such as Billy Wolfe's parallel with Nyasaland or Gwynfor Evans's pivot to the 'tremendous surge' throughout Africa to 'full national freedom'.[101] From an early stage, the SNP's *Scots Independent* voiced unalloyed sympathy for African peoples seeking to 'end a system which condemns them to inferiority', drawing direct comparisons with Scotland's plight: 'It has surprisingly little to do with colour, for our own working classes experienced the same emotions when they set about claiming a voice in politics. The racial question merely complicates the problem; it is not in itself the crux of the matter.'[102]

Invoking a spirit of solidarity with subjugated peoples in other parts of the world was a largely perfunctory move, however – aligning the separatist cause with the latter's political momentum without going to the trouble of engaging seriously with the alleged similarities (or indeed the obvious differences). As with Irish nationalist affiliations with the US civil rights movement, Welsh and Scottish nationalist appeals to Asian and African precursors were often tainted with unacknowledged resentment at their own relegation to the ranks of second-class whites. An SNP pamphlet circulated for the 1964 general election conveyed something of the general gist:

> Proud imperial powers no longer steer their own course regardless of the rest of humanity ... Does it not seem odd to you that, despite these tremendous changes in the outside world, no thought is given in London to the need for an equally thorough-going reorganization within the British Isles? ... Surely, you think, when the British Government can confer full nationhood so freely on former colonial peoples in Africa and Asia, the least that ancient Scotland can expect is federal self-government within a customs union.[103]

If equal treatment with Asians and Africans was *the least* Scotland could expect, the implication was that they deserved considerably more, presumably by virtue of their prior standing as co-sponsors of the empire project. 'How much longer must we wait?', asked *Y Ddraig Goch* with more than a hint of outworn patience.[104] These were the objections of self-consciously white protagonists, unwittingly aligning themselves, for example, with the frequent Southern Rhodesian refrain that if Nyasaland and Zambia were allowed to secede from the Central African Federation as independent nations, it was the height of impertinence to deny fellow whites the same entitlement. Not that the Rhodesian situation in any sense directly influenced separatist aspirations in Scottish and Welsh political culture. The SNP hierarchy roundly condemned Ian Smith's Unilateral Declaration of Independence in November 1965 (damning Smith's Tory sympathizers in England into the bargain).[105] Rather, it was a case of a broader crisis of Greater British authority producing similar patterns of critical reflection among disparate communities grappling with the diminished scope to imagine their political lives. The option of severing emotional ties to Britain and going it alone was one obvious pathway available, with all manner of local variations and moral implications.

Lest the Rhodesian connection seem far-fetched, consider the enthusiastic letters that Evans and Ewing both received from well-wishers in Southern Africa who (mistakenly or otherwise) saw a broad moral equivalence with their own struggle against the Wilson government. Often, these messages were couched in terms of common *Celtic* grievances, while some of the incoming mail to Evans was demonstratively written in Welsh – such as the disgruntled settler from Bulawayo who ventured, 'Wales and Rhodesia are united in their wish to escape the clutches of the Englishman's Government – a government that does not understand the local environment and judges every nation as being lower than themselves.'[106] One especially prominent letter-writer was the Scottish peer and Rhodesian stud farmer Angus Graham (and leading member of Ian Smith's Rebel Rhodesian Cabinet) whose father had been a founding member of the SNP in the 1930s and who naturally expected to find a kindred spirit in Winnie Ewing. In an elaborate three-page letter, he commended her warmly on the Hamilton triumph, assuring her that 'the battle for Scottish independence is against the same enemy as we are battling' – while discoursing at length on the remarkable achievements of white minority rule in Rhodesia. Despite the best efforts of 'Mr Wilson and his henchmen', he boasted, 'you can walk with greater safety by day or night from one end of Rhodesia to the other than you can walk across Glasgow!'[107]

Graham might conceivably have struck a chord with Ewing's spirited critique of a Labour government that 'cares more about dead birds on English beaches than about living men in Glasgow'.[108] But the new MP for Hamilton responded evasively, declining an invitation to visit Rhodesia (on the grounds that she needed to go in 'boots and all' for Scottish independence) and posing uncomfortable questions about African welfare, education and especially the prospects for universal suffrage.[109] Had Graham followed the Hamilton by-election more closely he would have received ample warning of Ewing's more progressive take on Scottish nationalism, not least her unimpeachable anti-colonial credentials. But his presumption was not entirely fanciful either. Ultimately, if ironically, Ewing's cause shared more fundamental similarities with white Rhodesia than neighbouring Nyasaland in terms of the broader historical trajectories that pitted both movements against the unwelcome intrusions of British sovereignty.

Contemporaries were also known to make the Rhodesian comparison, and both the SNP and Plaid Cymru therefore took every opportunity to distance themselves from the taint of white reaction. Evans made sure he was seen prominently at anti-Smith rallies outside Rhodesia House on the Strand, while Ewing consistently denounced the serial travesties of racial justice in Southern Africa. This occasionally wrong-footed their own supporters, with one letter-writer from Pretoria reporting 'the dismay caused in the Scottish Community by the already appalling voting record of Mrs

Ewing' – notably on Apartheid and arms sales to South Africa – which could only alienate 'a nation which has nothing but well being [*sic*] towards a Free Scotland'.[110] In reply to a query from a New Zealand journalist in November 1967, party chairman Arthur Donaldson clarified that the SNP 'would like to remain in the Commonwealth. There are times when we wonder whether it will remain with us!' – vaguely alluding to popular disenchantment with Commonwealth racial disharmony, so prevalent at the time in England.[111]

Donaldson's remark also points to a stark generational divide that opened up in these years – unsurprisingly given the spectacular growth in recruitment of younger members attracted by the SNP's anti-establishment credentials. The party chairman was himself a scion of the SNP old guard; a founding member who was briefly interned in 1941 on suspicion of wartime subversion. Donaldson embodied a culturally conservative streak that bordered on provincial chauvinism, ill at ease with some of Winnie Ewing's more progressive pronouncements on racial inclusion. Devising a consensual SNP immigration policy was therefore a delicate balancing act between an overtly liberal opposition to 'discrimination against a person because of class, creed or colour', and a more conservative hankering for 'strict immigration control even after ensuring that the Scots in Scotland and the Scots overseas, had been looked after'.[112] When Ewing voted against the Wilson government's February 1968 measures to exclude Kenyan Asian holders of British passports, she was subjected to a public grilling at a party meeting in Dundee with questions ranging from 'Why let the coloured people into Scotland when our people are leaving?' to 'Why do we allow foreigners in to our country if we have not enough employment for our own people?' Some even asked whether Scotland would 'declare UDI after an SNP victory?'

Though Ewing held her ground, she had to grapple with the likes of old India hand James W. Moncur, who pledged his loyalty to the SNP (as the only party likely to secure Scotland's freedom) while making plain that 'I wish Scotland to be kept white and Christian and I shall fight you every inch of the way if your policy does not guarantee that this will be so.'[113] Both the party chairman and the SNP's political weekly stressed that Ewing was 'entitled to follow her own conscience' on Kenyan Asian immigration, creating a subtle distance from her fundamental principles and suggesting that she was moved mainly by the belief 'that people who were given British passports' and 'actively encouraged to think of themselves as "British"' should not have their rights suddenly withdrawn.[114] Clearly a door was being held ajar for SNP supporters drawn to nationalism as a means of jettisoning the multi-racial implications of Britishness and regrouping around an undisturbed white core. One correspondent living in Cheltenham put the position plainly:

> the time has come for Scotland to make a complete break. This would secure for her a place in world affairs. All our money would be kept in our sporrans and wouldn't be going over to independent/republic countries who have already told us that they are quite capable of handling their own affairs, thus when Scotland obtains her independence, she will be able to give them the great honour of doing just that . . . It is the poor Englishman's lot down here that he hasn't got fair representation for himself. Scotland, on the other hand, is lucky. She has the alternative of complete separate Scottish nationalism. She doesn't require to bother herself with the other fellow, she can think for Scotland and the Scots.[115]

Here, obvious parallels emerge with Enoch Powell's rediscovery of a racially untarnished England 'amid the fragments of demolished glory', or the Ulster Vanguard's flirtation with secession in the early 1970s as a means of preserving their besieged polity and entrenched privileges.[116] Though the SNP consistently condemned Powell and applauded his dismissal from the Conservative Shadow Cabinet following the 'Rivers of Blood' speech, the party chairman allowed ample room for equivocation. Scots should not 'be too sure that we are fundamentally different on this colour question', he conceded; indeed, Powell was 'merely saying from a public platform what masses of the people are saying among themselves'. Fortunately, he assured members, Commonwealth immigration was 'overwhelmingly an English problem' thanks to relatively low rates of new arrivals north of the border. But there could be no masking his underlying message: 'Where we have advantages in less or lessening friction let us hold on to them' – by maintaining 'constant vigilance'.[117]

It would miss the point of the comparison to align Winifred Ewing with the racial bigotry of Powellite reaction. Just as Powell's rediscovery of England appealed to a much wider constituency than xenophobic nationalism, so too there was scope for progressive alternatives in other parts of the United Kingdom. Powell himself never secured much in the way of a Scottish following and fell largely out of favour after some ill-judged comments likening government subsidies to Upper Clyde shipbuilding to the hand-feeding of prairie dogs on US nature reserves.[118] But again, the timing and framing of the convulsions – if not their precise moral or ideological bent – suggests an underlying confluence. Mrs Ewing's political priorities were much closer to Labour's Barbara Castle than the member for

Wolverhampton South West – no more a 'Tartan Tory' than a 'Paisley Paisley' – but the circumstances that thrust her into the political limelight arose out of the same lapsed coordinates of a Greater British world.

A final – and more fundamental – parallel can be found in the nationalist conviction that Britain was a spent force internationally, which also broadly echoed cross-currents in other parts of the world. Virtually every episode recounted in these pages, from the venting of white rage in the grounds of Government House Nairobi to the indignation of Queensland cane growers denied their customary access to the British market, to the stalled momentum of the Ulster Vanguard vowing to break with Britain once and for all, combined an element of disenchantment with Britain's staying power in the world with the need urgently to reassess local political allegiances. In Chapter 11 we saw how Australian and Canadian writers drew on a wider reckoning with imperial decline to disabuse themselves of their British outlook, spurred by the 'sudden shocks of reorientation' of the post-war world.[119] Donald Horne's crusade against the 'ceremonial clinging to Britain' not only reverberated among white liberals throughout the Commonwealth, but also appeared in modified form in the rhetoric of prominent Caribbean figures seeking a new purchase on post-imperial belonging.[120] When Trinidad and Tobago achieved independence in 1962, Prime Minister Eric Williams called for a wholesale recalibration of popular loyalties: 'There can be no Mother England and no dual loyalties; no person can be allowed to get the best of both worlds.' Barbados followed suit in November 1966 (only months after Gwynfor Evans's more modest breakthrough in Carmarthen), with Premier Errol Barrow similarly calling on his fellow citizens to disavow the 'historical accident' of their residual British identity.[121]

It is not that the specifics of any of these episodes became internalized in Scottish and Welsh politics. But a hazy conception of a disappearing world 'offshore' frequently made its presence felt. One satirical item from *The Scotsman* in January 1968, amid the rupture of the Wilson government's 'East of Suez' reversal, depicted the hapless 'Bill and Mabel' paddling furiously in a chaotic nautical scene: 'Mabel, Mabel; snap out of your torpor, old girl and pull yourself together. Be calm – and if it's not too big a laugh these days – be British.' The 'old ship of state' was sinking fast, but where could the lifeboat be steered to safety? Australia? Not ideal, with 'everyone calling you a drongo or a pongo or whatever they label new arrivals'. New Zealand seemed all too tedious 'where the pubs close at six' and 'the people are more British than the British'. Nor would South Africa do, where 'the colour scheme wouldn't suit us' ('they tends to see everything in terms of black and white ... and not in the subtle tones of grey like we do'). Which left only Canada, where everyone seemed absorbed in the crass 'pursuit of the mighty dollar', hardly an edifying prospect. Ultimately, there was 'no place left for us, we'll have to stay on the old ship' – manning the pumps was 'the only thing left to do'.[122] The joke – for all its comic simplicity – relied on a complex weave of intrinsic knowledge; at once a wry salute to the jaded mindset of Greater Britain, and a frank acknowledgement of its fading resonance.

When the Scottish broadcaster Ludowic Kennedy told a BBC audience in June 1968 that 'it was the empire above all, that made and kept us British', he was rehearsing the rhetorical procedures of a much wider conversation.[123] No two variants produced a perfect likeness, such was the strength of regional influences and local imperatives. But nor was it a historical accident that the end of Britain figured so prominently as a galvanizing force across so many distinct political cultures. While supporters and operatives of the SNP and Plaid Cymru were rarely, if ever, tuned directly into this wider civic landscape, nor were they entirely insulated from the extended chain of consequence arising from the serial ruptures of empire's end.

———————◆———————

Writing a year before the electoral shakeout at Carmarthen in 1966, prominent Welsh nationalist A. D. Rees reflected on the inner turmoil of being simultaneously Welsh and British, concluding: 'If Britishness is an illusion, it is a very powerful illusion.'[124] It was a frank concession from an otherwise committed nationalist, flagging a problem that would dog separatist ambitions for decades: the extraordinary durability of the Union in the face of the nationalist challenge. That a solid majority of Scottish and Welsh voters held firm to the British connection throughout the three decades of post-war imperial retrenchment requires no elaboration. Indeed, it was in order to gauge the resilience of Unionist convictions that pollsters developed an appetite for prying into every conceivable aspect of popular loyalties, from the standard 'do you feel more British or Welsh/Scottish?' to more subtle inquiries into the depth and dimensions of separatist feeling. Although largely inconclusive, the statistics nevertheless paint a picture of a nationalist support base as fragile as it was fitful. Nationalist voters were not always separatists, and indeed many of their concerns and aspirations were shared by those who continued voting for the major parties.

But the longer-term significance lies in the fact that such questions were being posed at all. While there was no spontaneous mass conversion to the cause of Welsh or Scottish independence, the normalization of the separatist parties in the 1960s and 1970s marks a critical watershed – turning the spotlight on rival shades of patriotic feeling and drawing nationwide attention to the inherent fragility of the Union. Nationalists persistently worked these fault lines, their passionate disavowals of British sentiment carrying as much – and sometimes more – conviction than their claims to separate, sovereign selfhood. In the words of Welsh philosopher J. R. Jones in his 1966 treatise, *Prydeindod* (*Britishness*): 'There already exists such a thing as a British nationality: it is the English one.'[125] When Gwynfor Evans visited Glasgow shortly after his Carmarthen triumph, he similarly appealed to his fellow nationalists:

> It is high time that the people of Scotland insisted on doing their duty as a nation and taking their due place in the life of the world. Their due place is in the van of nations – not in the dim, grey provincial existence of the British state. There is no such thing as a British nation. A British state – yes – but a British nation is a creature of a state.[126]

Evans was in the habit of calling Britishness a 'sickness', and it was ultimately not his love of Wales so much as his flat repudiation of any wider allegiance that distinguished his personal brand of Welshness from equally passionate Unionist variants. Significantly, even his staunchest Welsh opponents could convey an underlying ambivalence about being British. During the investiture furore in 1969, former Cardiff Lord Mayor Sir James Lyon described his affinities in terms that would have seemed unremarkable to contemporaries: 'I love Cardiff and I love Wales, but I want it to be part of Great Britain and the world.'[127] The declining affective register laid bare the priorities: Britain was the name that dared not speak its love. Being a 'part of Great Britain' was evidently not something that stirred the heart, in marked contrast to the emotions freely bestowed on Cardiff and Wales. Britishness was an altogether more prosaic affair, providing ready access to 'the world' with which it could still be so habitually bracketed.

As Keith Webb argued in the 1970s, the challenge in accounting for the sudden emergence of separatist politics lies not in explaining the existence of intense national feeling, which had long been an intrinsic feature of the Union compact. 'What is needed', he said, 'is an explanation for why nationalist feelings already held … became politicized when they did.'[128] For the nationalists themselves the answer seemed clear enough: Britishness had outlived its material and indeed moral usefulness, calling for an urgent reappraisal of sub-national priorities. But what gave the claim persuasive force was the wider arc of global British sentiment that so spectacularly faltered in the decades after the Second World War. The inhabitants of the

United Kingdom were not alone in sensing the diminished latitude of their Britishness. Yet virtually nowhere was the eclipse of Greater Britain experienced as a clean break, without hesitations, complications or recidivist tendencies. Inconclusive outcomes were part and parcel of the empire's enduring legacies, entirely in keeping with the residual hold of Britishness elsewhere in a world where devising credible, consensual alternatives would prove anything but straightforward.

15

'COSMOLOGIES OF OUR OWN': AFTER BRITAIN

Charles Dilke and J. R. Seeley can be credited with popularizing the idea of Greater Britain, but their late Victorian audience was well-primed by the earlier exertions of Thomas Babington Macaulay, whose five-volume *History of England* (1848–61) became something of a mid-century publishing sensation. More than perhaps any other figure, Macaulay instilled the twin legacies of liberty and progress in the British historical imagination – both as the supreme achievement of the Williamite Revolution that cemented constitutional checks on arbitrary power and as a beguiling justification for Britain's subsequent rise to naval and commercial pre-eminence in the world. His life's work was an exercise in mass civic enchantment, 'civilizing subjects', in Catherine Hall's memorable phrase, 'through its history, rather than the legislative practices of the state'.[1]

Though 'England' was Macaulay's main rubric, he ranged effortlessly across all of Britain and Ireland, his portraits of the Siege of Derry and the Glencoe Massacre counting among his most famous passages. Employing the conventional English–British lexical switch through all five volumes, he nevertheless hinted at a careful distinction in his opening teaser to Volume One. 'Nothing in the early existence of Britain indicated the greatness which she was destined to attain', he declaimed. But all that was to change dramatically with the conversion of the 'Saxon colonists' to Christianity. 'At length the darkness begins to break; and the country which had been lost to view as Britain reappears as England' – the first of 'a long series of salutary revolutions'.[2] In Macaulay's biblical scheme, Britain stood for the original 'darkness', abandoned by classical civilization to the 'squalid cabins and uncleared woods' of the 'aboriginal Britons'. But it also doubled as the ultimate achievement of a uniquely English liberty that emerged from the gloom, radiating outwards to share the benefits of constitutional freedom, moral progress and material prosperity in a wider, composite and inherently imperial Britishness.[3]

For all Macaulay's reverence for 'remote ancestors', however, his vision was tempered by periodic bouts of despair at the possibility of achieving 'anything worthy to be remembered with pride by remote descendants'.[4] His famous evocation of a time far-distant 'when some traveller from New Zealand shall, in the midst of a vast solitude, take his stand on a broken arch of London Bridge to sketch the ruins of St Paul's' signalled a momentary but revealing lapse in his otherwise unstinting confidence in continuous progress. Macaulay's forlorn New Zealander was copiously reproduced in Victorian literary and artistic representations; the rhetorical crutch of every small-town orator, such that already by the 1860s it was targeted by *Punch* as woefully 'hackneyed' and urgently in need of 'retirement'.[5] More often than not, the scene was invoked to ward off its disconcerting portents. Anthony Trollope was one of many to assure his readers that it would never come to pass; that through a process of enlightened reform it would be

Figure 15.1 Inspired by Thomas Babington Macaulay's 1840 prophecy, 'The New Zealander' on London Bridge became a popular motif in mid-century Britain. This engraving by Gustave Doré is from *London: A Pilgrimage*, by Gustave Doré and Blanchard Jerrold, 1872. Source: Hulton Archive/Getty Images.

possible to 'postpone the coming of the New Zealander'.[6] But crucially, the scene in all its variations was depicted as profoundly moving to the New Zealander himself; as much his own loss as that of the vanquished English. Though often assumed to be a returning settler, Macaulay's London Bridge pilgrim was indisputably Maori – personifying the noble savagery from whence Britain had come, just as the scene itself presaged its inevitable return.[7]

It would be a New Zealander of a very different stripe who journeyed forth more than a hundred years later to depict the scene that played so heavily on Macaulay's mind. John Greville Agard Pocock, one of New Zealand's most renowned intellectual exports of the last half-century, arrived in his hometown of Christchurch in 1973 to deliver the keynote for the centenary celebrations of the University of Canterbury. Just as Macaulay in his darker moods contemplated the implosion of his grand design, so too, Pocock reflected ruefully on the ruins of the British world-system.[8] Central to his purpose were the timing and the setting – only four months after Britain's formal accession to the European Economic Community (EEC) in January 1973, from the perspective of a country especially hard-hit by the economic fallout. Pocock discoursed at length on the disruptions this had caused, not in the familiar strains of lost export opportunities for New Zealand butter and lamb, but the altogether more pressing issue of the lost history to which 'we knew ourselves as belonging'.[9] He addressed his audience in a spirit of shared grievance, impugning the English as fair-weather friends, eager to erase the memory of wider British endeavour so as to cement their newfound European credentials. 'If it has been psychologically possible for them to annihilate the idea of the Commonwealth', he speculated, 'it is not altogether beyond the bounds of possibility that "United Kingdom" and even "Britain" may someday become similarly inconvenient and be annihilated, or annihilate themselves, in their turn.'[10]

This was the view from London Bridge, surveying a belief system in figurative ruins – all centred on the derelict dome where Leslie Howard had once expounded on Britishness with a small 'b'. If the myth of Greater Britain was destined for annihilation, how were New Zealanders and other 'tangential cultures' to avoid being marginalized in its wake? Pocock's solution was to reconfigure history itself, in a radical departure from the Anglo-centric conventions of 'English History' to encompass a worldwide 'diversity of interacting and varyingly autonomous cultures'.[11] According to these lights, the expansion of England was no unidirectional movement emanating from the imperial centre but the product of multiple kingdoms and peoples interacting variously 'so as to modify the conditions of one another's existence'.[12] It was thus incumbent on 'the rest of us' to refashion the past, each according to their own needs, out of the sum of which an entirely new subject would emerge that Pocock called 'British history' – ironically predicated on the diminishing possibilities of actually being British:

> The British cultural star-cluster is at present in a highly dispersed condition, various parts of it feeling the attraction of adjacent galaxies; the central giant has cooled, shrunk and moved away, and the inhabitants of its crust seem more than ever disposed to deny that the rest of us ever existed. Since it no longer emits those radiations we felt bound to convert into paradigms, we are free and indeed necessitated to construct *cosmologies of our own*.[13]

As the son of a classics professor who himself studied classics 'because that was the way to become educated and had been for a thousand years', Pocock was instinctively drawn to the Aristotelian notion of *cosmos* – not pertaining to the stars per se, but to the contemplation of the universe and universals.[14] His quest for 'cosmologies of our own' was a profoundly personal response to what he saw as a collective crisis of 'historical self-awareness'.[15] If imperial expansion for Macaulay had been 'the recipe for the universalization of English liberty', it was the converse for Pocock, for whom imperial decline signalled the eclipse of a universal Britishness and the need for remedial action.[16] Whereas Macaulay's *English* history was a monumental edifice, Pocock's *British* history was essentially a salvage operation geared to restoring 'some sort of harmony and vitality' in a fragmenting world.[17]

But it was a flawed mission, for reasons to be considered in this closing chapter that explores the scramble for 'cosmologies of our own' that accompanied the end of Britain-in-the-world. Throughout the former empire, few were inclined to pursue Pocock's abstract design, preferring the more straightforward path of remaking history as a national enterprise – producing any number of new departures, but also a pervasive uncertainty as to who or what comprised a viable post-imperial story. New national symbols also acquired a special potency in these years, as the need to remove the stigma of imperial patrimony seemed ever more urgent. In the former dominions in particular, devising simple, serviceable and consensual alternatives to British-derived flags, anthems and other totems of collective selfhood proved to be a protracted affair, not least due to the tenacity of older British affinities that persisted much longer than Pocock had envisaged. Meanwhile, residual pockets of Greater British sentiment continued to thrive in places such as Gibraltar, Hong Kong and the Falkland Islands where unresolved legacies endured. It will be argued here that many of these same tensions were reproduced with local inflections in the United Kingdom, particularly in Scotland where the continuities and entanglements are especially striking. As in Macaulay's day, the practice of history remained closely aligned to the imagined contours and character of the people, and thus the peoples of the 'Atlantic Archipelago' (Pocock's preferred term for the anachronistic 'British Isles') would not be spared the search for new configurations compelled by the eclipse of Greater Britain.[18]

AN UNDERSTUDY OR AN UNDERTAKER: HISTORIANS

Pocock was not alone in exploring the restorative potential of a radically reordered conception of the past. But his entire approach was out of sync and indeed sympathy with the generation of New Zealand historians that emerged in the 1960s, who tended to see 'British history' as the problem rather than the solution. It was 'New Zealand history' that was needed; a category that had rarely featured in high school or university curricula, but which began to make headway from the late 1950s. In *The Story of New Zealand* (1960), W. H. Oliver described New Zealanders as engaged in a new 'step in the process of self-knowledge' in which 'the heritage of England and Europe has ceased to be an overpowering substitute for independent thought'.[19] The watchword was 'independence', an ambiguous term in a traditionally loyal white British outpost, heavily reliant on the cultural circuitry of Greater Britain.

More than any other historian of his generation, Keith Sinclair made it his life's mission to liberate New Zealand from an inhibiting colonial mindset, signalled by the publication of his landmark *History of New Zealand* in 1959. Sinclair's wartime experiences in Britain had left a lasting impression of the iniquities of class in British society (not least the habitual condescension towards the more lowly ranked 'dominion' servicemen) and he elected to return to New Zealand in 1946 to complete his studies rather than follow the well-worn path to Oxford or Cambridge. National self-respect was his guiding principle in establishing 'New Zealand history' as a stand-alone subject (later founding the *New Zealand Journal of History* in the late 1960s) – such that Pocock himself would later concede the mantle of 'founding father' of New Zealand history to his Auckland rival.[20] Asking pointedly whether 'we [can] conceive for our country a future more important or meaningful than success at exporting lambs and butter?', Sinclair was convinced that the colonial economic model was not only a demeaning way of earning a living, but also a humiliating reflection of a more general cultural subservience. In early 1963, he delivered a scathing verdict on the nation's tired and timid British instincts, wondering how these would fare in the eyes of posterity:

> Since Britishness lies at the source of many of the silliest of our excesses, one can feel sure that [any] future historian will have a good deal of fun with it ... The future historian won't fail to see that the effort to be British was a source of strength as well as weakness, providing a code to live up to ... But I feel sure that New Zealand will be much less British when the future historian writes. Moreover, I am satisfied with that prospect, not as a critic of British life (indeed, I would rather be in London than anywhere else in the world outside of Auckland), but because we never can have a high civilization that is British. For us to want to be British is a poor objective, like wanting to be an understudy or a caretaker – or an undertaker.[21]

Not that Sinclair was immune to the instincts he so resolutely shunned. The idea of London – its cultural sophistication and intellectual allure – continued to exert an irresistible pull, even as the idea of New Zealand Britishness invited abundant scorn. Years later, Bill Oliver also acknowledged the mesmerizing attractions that pervaded these early attempts to break the habit. 'When one says "Not British"', he reflected, 'one is still paying a tribute, even if an ambiguous one, to Britishness.'[22]

Similar developments can be traced in Canada and Australia, where unprecedented levels of interest in the national past underwrote the careers of a new generation of post-war historians writing predominantly for a home readership. It was largely an exercise in elaborating a sense of national 'identity', accounting for the emergence of a distinctive national ethos out of a presumptively unique set of social, economic and environmental conditions.[23] For early exponents of the genre, the white settler experience remained the overwhelming source of intellectual curiosity, constrained by the same racialized moral order inherited from imperial templates. Australia's Manning Clark made no secret of his ambition to produce an authoritative statement of Australian historical experience worthy of the greats of British, European and American History. His six-volume *History of Australia* (1962–87) adopted the romantic procedures of monumental history, modelled loosely on Macaulay's *History of England*, albeit geared to relinquishing 'the comforters of the past, the myth of British civilisation and so forth'.[24] It proved an extraordinary commercial success (much in the way of Macaulay's achievement a century earlier), propelling Clark into the public sphere as one of the country's leading public intellectuals, frequently consulted by politicians and the press on all manner of pressing subjects – an ironic instance of a historian inhabiting 'the role created by the very same historical moment he observed'.[25] Indigenous perspectives figured only at the outer margins (as Clark would lament in later years) – much like other early works of nationalist history that sought to graft a story of white deliverance out of the illusory promise of empire and Britishness.

This was the white settler equivalent of the contemporary surge of new national histories throughout Asia, Africa and the Caribbean where the transfer of power to newly independent states was invariably accompanied by the legitimizing power of a self-validating national story. Often these works were composed by nationalist leaders themselves, such as Jomo Kenyatta's *Facing Mount Kenya* (composed prior to the independence struggle in 1938) and Jawaharlal Nehru's *The Discovery of India* (written in the heat of battle during the last of his prison stints in 1946); each in their own way conjuring the nation in waiting. Eric Williams's *History of the People of Trinidad and Tobago* was a monument in its own right, published as a gift to his newly liberated people on Independence Day in August 1962.[26] Though these emancipatory accounts would later be challenged by the emergence of 'subaltern' histories that unsettled the received myths of revolutionary elites, they nevertheless performed a crucial role in the transition to new forms of post-imperial political legitimacy.[27]

If attempts to refashion the white histories of the former dominions fundamentally mirrored these developments, they were also hamstrung by the absence of any coherent liberation struggle from which to structure a self-sufficient narrative.[28] For Bill Oliver in New Zealand, a semblance of historical continuity could be gleaned from a long overdue reckoning with British loyalty itself – by revisiting the countless disappointments in the nation's history when 'Britain was not British enough', when the 'priorities of imperialism were the source of acute New Zealand disquiet', when the cumulative force of repeated betrayals 'enforced the conclusion that Great Britain was not entirely trustworthy'. Britain's determination to join the European Common Market had incited so much resentment in New Zealand, he argued, not because it came as any great surprise but because it seemed so true to historical form. For the best part of a century, 'running alongside the blind holistic assumption that Great Britain could do no wrong', there had prevailed 'a strong awareness that she both could and did do wrong, that she was a flawed model'. It had always been 'a reformed, not an actual, Great Britain', that furnished the true object of New Zealand loyalties – universalized as the font of unique privileges and freedoms. Preempting Pocock by several years he viewed the prospect of British entry into Europe in seismic terms: 'Our experience suggests, if it does not prove, that Britain, simply because she is part of Europe, is likely to prove faithless; that the old world is all too likely to destroy the new.'[29]

Pocock himself abhorred the rhetorical procedures of the 'search for identity', with its endless striving and questing for some ineffable quality that always lay tantalizingly out of reach. Far from furnishing the antidote to the historical marginalization of places such as New Zealand, it served only as temptation 'to take part in this marginalization by constructing autochthonous narratives which know nothing of any history but that they have made for themselves'.[30] As Ian McBride suggests, his new British history was 'an act of imaginative repossession', allowing New Zealanders to assert control over a British culture from which they could never entirely be emancipated.[31] But Pocock was virtually alone among antipodean historians in seeking solutions along these lines; his prescriptions conspicuously failed to catch on in the very historical setting that originally inspired them.

Nor did it initially take root in those parts of the United Kingdom that might otherwise have been energized. Already a decade earlier, the Edinburgh philosopher George Davie had produced his landmark statement of Scottish popular sovereignty, *The Democratic Intellect* (1961) – a work far more in tune with Keith Sinclair's critique of the slavishly loyal undertaker. Davie railed against an endemic 'defeatism' that was 'unable to see anything in Scottish history but an uninterrupted, irreversible trend towards conformity with England', mounting a compelling case for the ongoing relevance of a uniquely Scottish civic ethos that had survived the loss of formal political institutions in 1707.[32] It was because the Union was primarily political in nature, he argued, permitting separate secular institutions such as the law, the Church and particularly the universities to thrive, that a 'distinctive code regulating Scottish life' was fundamentally preserved.[33] As Ben Jackson has shown, *The Democratic Intellect* was 'saturated by the language of independence', steeped in the mythology of an enduring Scottish tradition 'repeatedly threatened and eroded by English cultural influences and heavy-handed, unsympathetic union-state management'. Davie's book would prove foundational for a generation of Scottish historians as the political climate for separatism came into its own and the matter of 'Scottish national identity' was increasingly asserted, argued about and acted upon from the 1960s onwards.[34]

One of Davie's most avid disciples was a young New Zealander, H. J. Hanham, only thirty-five years of age when appointed founding professor of politics at Edinburgh in 1963, who delivered his inaugural lecture on the theme of 'the Scottish Political Tradition'. He would only stay five years before moving on to prestigious posts at Harvard and MIT, but his brief tenure afforded him the vantage point of the New Zealander on London Bridge, surveying the early portents of the break-up of Britain. Hanham was among the first to view the rekindling of Scottish separatism in the 1960s as part of a global historical trend, likely to continue to the point where 'Home Rule in one form or another is surely inevitable'.[35] In *Scottish Nationalism*, a major study completed just prior to his departure for the United States in 1969, he hinted at a New Zealander's sympathy for the 'higher national purpose' of the emerging separatist movement, compared with the 'purely provincial Scotland' that had long contented itself with 'second-class status within the United Kingdom'.[36] Hanham was particularly attuned to the links between surging support for Scottish autonomy and the wider dissolution of the British empire – a connection that must have seemed all the more tempting for an itinerant Aucklander:

> At the height of its popularity the Union was inspired by a sense of purpose. Scots felt that they were sharing in a great imperial venture and took pride in the achievements of Scots all over the world. Now that the Empire is dead, many Scots feel cramped and restricted at home … To give themselves an opening to a wider world the Scots need some sort of outlet, and the choice appears at the moment to be between emigration and re-creating the Scottish nation at home.[37]

It was a rare example of 'de-dominionizing' sentiment in the former settler empire filtering directly into separatist political agendas in the United Kingdom. But Hanham was not simply unpacking his own antipodean 'cosmologies' and applying them to Scottish experience. His own world view was equally affected by the new currents emerging in his adopted home in the early 1960s.

Nor was Scotland the only example of the push for self-sufficient historical narratives in Britain. It was in the most provincial of English settings in June 1963 – the South-West Norfolk Conservative Fete – that Enoch Powell called on his rural audience to 'seek to re-establish our confidence and our faith in ourselves upon a new basis'. This, he said, could only be achieved by devising 'a new patriotism befitting this changed world, to replace the old, imperial patriotism of the past'. As a system of logic, it was not unlike Pocock's prescription in Christchurch ten years later, but whereas the latter sought to channel the shared patrimony of British descent into a 'diversity of interacting and varyingly autonomous cultures', Powell sought to exorcize the empire completely. As he elaborated two years later in a speech in Manchester: 'I am not quite saying that the new history will be "Britain without Empire," but it will be very nearly "Britain with the imperial episode in parenthesis."'[38] As we saw in Chapter 12, Powell found it much easier to wrest 'England' from the stigma of empire than 'Britain', as such – a theme he pursued with relish in his speeches and writings throughout the decade.[39]

The appearance of the final volume of the *Oxford History of England* that same year seemed to answer Powell's call for a history re-centred around its core subject. The author, A. J. P. Taylor, made much of the profound changes since the first volumes in the series had appeared in the 1930s – a time when '"England" was still an all-embracing word. It meant indiscriminately England and Wales; Great Britain; the United Kingdom; and even the British Empire.'[40] But in 1965 this would no longer do. Taylor not only voiced his intention to keep the empire at arm's length, but also caused a minor furore by removing Scotland entirely from his scholarly remit (insisting, for good measure, on referring to them as 'the Scotch', the more correct 'English' term). These and other outlying appendages, he declared, would only impinge on his story where necessary to illuminate issues and themes of relevance to the 'geographic area' of England. To compound matters, he claimed that he merely wished to avoid offending Scottish sensibilities (i.e. by appropriating their history under an English rubric). But he clearly derived some sort of personal satisfaction from adopting exclusively English blinkers. At no stage did he consider framing his subject as a history of 'Britain', stating emphatically: 'I never use this incorrect term, though it is sometimes slipped past me by sub-editors.' On one occasion when the broader collective noun could not be avoided, he made a point of noting: '"British" here means, perhaps for the last time, the peoples of the Dominions and the Empire as well as the United Kingdom.'[41]

Taylor's provocation provided the original spark for Pocock's 'new British history', which he expressly formulated as an antidote to the Englishman's 'flat and express denial that the term "Britain" has any meaning'.[42] Upbraiding English presumption was emotionally satisfying, but it also produced the fundamental flaw in Pocock's own lopsided design. The urge to escape the impress of Taylor's arrogance ultimately trapped his thinking within those very strictures, leaving unresolved the fundamental asymmetry of a history saddled with England-heavy ballast.[43] If British history was to incorporate 'the historiography of no single nation but of a problematic and uncompleted experiment in the creation and interaction of several nations', by what means could (or even should) the subject be bound within a single rubric at all?[44]

Significantly, it would take the best part of twenty years for Pocock's prescription to bear intellectual fruit, but not in the transoceanic dimensions he had originally intended. From the late-1980s, his ideas started to reappear in the more limited guise of 'Four Nations' history, confined largely to the study of 'conflict and cross-breeding' in early modern England, Scotland, Wales and Ireland.[45] Thus stripped of the global optics of the original Christchurch prospectus (and screening out the all-important view from London Bridge), the 'new British history' was more a rear-guard attempt to make the composite British state cohere at a time when its unity of purpose was beginning to falter. To be sure, the new framing brought valuable intellectual scrutiny to the standard-bearers of early modern historiography – the Civil War, the Restoration, the 'Glorious Revolution' – all of which appeared in a revelatory new light. Nevertheless, there is a wider sense in which a project primarily conceived as 'an exercise in mapping the historical consciousness' became reduced to a mere fragment thereof, at a time when Britain's global projections were conspicuously fading from view.[46] Raphael Samuel was not wide of the mark in 1995 when he ascribed the emergence of Four Nations history 'to a vertiginous sense of impending loss', arising out of the very portents of the end of Britain that had been so integral to Pocock's original blueprint of 1973. The 'break-up of Britain in the present', he surmised, and the collapse of any number of 'taken-for-granted certainties' in the wake of imperial decline, had suddenly made 'us more aware of its contingent character in the past'.[47]

SYMBOLS IN SEARCH OF A PEOPLE

On the very day of Pocock's May 1973 Christchurch lecture, the New Zealand Labour Party's annual conference in Wellington debated proposals for a new national flag, a New Zealand republic, the adoption of a New Zealand honours system in place of royal honours and the substitution of 'God Save the Queen' with 'God Defend New Zealand' as the national anthem. Though none of the resolutions were passed, they generated heated debate and no shortage of support arising from the perceived irrelevance of Britain in the light of the barriers recently raised to the free passage of New Zealand goods (and the people who produced them).[48]

This was the symbolic face of the 'search for identity', enlisting the energies of government, political parties and civil society in devising new national totems befitting a more self-sufficient people, navigating a path between British sentiments that could no longer be sustained and more local allegiances that were yet to take symbolic form. Finding workable solutions was to prove extraordinarily complex and divisive, however, not least due to enduring attachments to older loyalist emblems and rituals among a sizeable number of white English-speakers (whose self-designation also became part of the conundrum – 'English Canadians', 'Anglo-Celts' in Australia, while the Maori term 'Pakeha' began to acquire traction among white New Zealanders). But more fundamentally, the hesitations arose from a general lack of ready-made alternatives to the symbolism and syntax of Britishness. Much as Pocock called on New Zealanders 'to decide in what sense if any we continue to be British or have a British history', similar dilemmas arose whenever governments began tinkering with new national symbols – whether to emphasize continuity or rupture; to refashion the familiar emblems of old or devise freshly minted alternatives.[49]

Such matters were by no means purely symbolic. From the early 1920s, when the Irish Free State embarked on a new nation-building project out of the brittle compromise with the British government (adopting 'as many of the symbols of independent nationhood as it could get away with'), the question of refitting the national fabric assumed paramount importance.[50] As Ewan Morris has shown, devising unifying emblems for a partitioned Ireland occurred at a time when the public were at their most divided. Anthems, coins, flags, stamps, coats of arms, badges, pillar-boxes and other public ornaments were variously charged with meaning, open to rival interpretations and conflicting aspirations with the potential to rekindle violent clashes.[51] Similarly in South Africa, the introduction of a new national flag in the 1920s proved bitterly divisive, not least over the issue of whether a Union Jack should be incorporated in the new design. Amid the threat of secession from ever 'loyal' English-speaking Natal, a compromise was reached which entirely failed to satisfy British community sentiment by incorporating a Union flag visible 'only with a microscope and at close range' (in the damning verdict of the *Sunday Times*). The *Natal Mercury* similarly stoked the indignation of its readers, who would henceforth regard the new South African flag as little more than an 'In Memoriam Notice' – 'a visible sign to South Africa that the Union Jack has been laid to rest'.[52]

Indian independence in 1947 marked the beginning of two decades of extraordinary patriotic invention as Union Jacks were hauled down all over the world and home-grown replacements installed. Though the vast majority of Britain's former colonies opted for membership of the 'new' Commonwealth, it nevertheless went without saying that they should dispense with imperial adornments and acquire the outward trappings of full independence. Though it cannot be assumed that these new national symbols were inherently unifying or instantly embraced by diverse and often divided constituencies, their adoption was rarely attended by controversy or open dispute. When Lord Mountbatten, for example, sought to foist colonial ensigns on both India and Pakistan (featuring the Union Jack in the upper quadrant as per the self-governing dominions), the proposal was politely brushed aside by the Congress and Muslim League leadership alike.[53] Such unwanted encumbrances helped to forge a momentary consensus around the flag of independent India, despite a prior history of sharp disagreements between rival factions and 'the inherent contradictions of the nationalist project of unity in diversity'.[54] Nor was the new flag of Pakistan adopted by way of community consultation of any kind, but hurriedly put together only days before independence by adding a white stripe to the Muslim League's green flag. But this in no way seems to have impaired its popular reception.

This pattern was to be reproduced in dozens of Independence Day celebrations around the world, which over time developed a liturgical quality of their own through sheer force of repetition, reinforcing a sense that British symbols projected overseas were now fundamentally out of place. The funeral rites were well established by the time Jamaica and Trinidad achieved independence in August 1962, where both the colonial ensign and 'God Save the Queen' were retired with few regrets. Trinidad followed the precedent set by India in 1947, with the flag selected by an official committee with very little popular input, while the anthem was hurriedly composed from the remnants of the hymn originally commissioned for the (now defunct) West Indies Federation. Independent Jamaica chose a different route, improvising the practice of holding an open competition to solicit ideas from the public for a new national flag and anthem, selecting the winning entries from a pool of 360 flags and more than a hundred anthems (while convening a special committee to arrive at official designations of the national flower, tree, fruit and bird). In no sense was there any popular resistance to the legitimacy of these emblems or wider questioning of their fundamental purpose, though doubts would continue to be raised in press commentary about the capacity of Jamaica's political class to 'create a cultural identity for ourselves'.[55] Popular endorsement for going it alone had already been firmly secured in the September 1961 referendum, and the symbolic trappings of new nationhood were therefore widely embraced as a natural and welcome change.

The sense of inevitability surrounding the switch from imperial to national symbols in so many former British colonies soon forced similar questions on the one-time 'dominions' (the term 'dominion' itself counting among the adornments to be discarded), but what distinguished the process in these countries was the absence of any clear-cut moment of separation from which new national emblems might be fashioned. In the absence of the outward ceremony of a formal transfer of power, the need for a national symbolic makeover never carried the same conviction or urgency – even as perceptions multiplied that something was vaguely amiss with the continued reliance on old-world emblems. In contrast to the 'new' Commonwealth, the task of overhauling the symbolism of empire and Britishness occurred in a constitutional vacuum, wrenched clean from any legal or political significance.

Canada was at the forefront of attempts to simulate the ceremonial passage to full nationhood, most notably with the adoption of the Maple Leaf flag on 15 February 1965. The influence of Independence Day celebrations throughout the empire was unmistakable, with the solemn rites of an official changeover ceremony observed across the country (and televised nationwide from the main event at Ottawa's Parliament Hill). But the outward display of unity could not conceal the deep social and political schisms that attended the entire selection process. Opposition Leader John Diefenbaker publicly shed tears as the old colonial 'Red Ensign' was lowered and replaced with a more recognizably Canadian emblem – as though mourning the loss of nationhood itself.

Ever since the end of the Second World War, the Canadian Tories had accused successive Liberal governments of actively seeking to obliterate the sentimental ties to Britain and the Commonwealth, and the charge was renewed with the Liberal victory under Lester Pearson at the 1963 election. Pearson's determination to replace the flag was partly a means of placating separatist sentiment in Quebec, but the necessary downgrading of Canada's ties to Britain struck deep reservoirs of resentment among influential community organizations still very much invested in the idea of Canadian Britishness – from the Royal Canadian Legion to the Orange Lodge, Provincial Premiers and the influential Imperial Order Daughters of the Empire (IODE) – all of whom strenuously asserted their attachment to the Union Jack in the Red Ensign's upper canton.[56] A group of distinguished Canadian historians in mid-1964 urged Pearson to retract the maple leaf design, arguing that 'its only advantage is that it is innocuous, that it produces tepid approval, mild disapproval, or indifference, that it can therefore be adopted without any display of strong feeling whatever'.[57] Others were more impassioned, such as the Manitoban senator claiming to speak for millions of Canadians who felt 'mortally wounded at the tearing away of the Union Jack', while the writer and novelist Scott Symons was even more forthright: 'Every time I look at that frigging Maple Leaf I dissolve. I simply cease to exist ... It's a non-flag.'[58] Such sentiments are often dismissed by Canadian historians as the reactionary instincts of alienated, diehard Tories 'bewailing their loss' from the political margins, but contemporary opinion polls suggest that a slender majority of English-speaking Canadians in 1964 were not only unimpressed by the change, but uneasy about its implications.[59] Diefenbaker's tears were not merely personal, but targeted at a substantial political constituency.

Figure 15.2 The Canadian prime minister, Lester B. Pearson, defends his original preferred design for a new Canadian flag in the face of bitter 'loyalist' opposition of every stripe in this 1964 cartoon 'The Rockslide' by Al Beaton in the *Toronto Telegram*, 4 May 1964. Source: Library and Archives Canada, Peter Dobush fonds/2874301.

The intensity of the political furore over the Canadian flag is one reason why the governments of Australia and New Zealand steered clear of the issue, focusing instead on revamping the national commemorative calendar to make up for the lack of a unifying national holiday. But it was far from obvious what national milestone or achievement should be marked by such an occasion – in the absence of a clear date or event denoting separate nationhood. When the New Zealand government decided in 1973 to inaugurate 'New Zealand Day', the date of 6 February was chosen for the new nationwide holiday, marking the anniversary of the 1840 Treaty of Waitangi between the British government and a coalition of Maori peoples in the Bay of Islands. But controversy immediately erupted over the date, the name and the appropriate form of observance. Criticism flew from all sides over the decision to drop the former name 'Waitangi Day' in order to foster a conception of 'New Zealand as one country of many people' – clearly and indeed expressly intended to deflect attention from 'Maori discontents'.[60] Maori community leaders objected vehemently to the bestowal of 'a Pakeha name' on an occasion of such overwhelming Indigenous significance, while at the conservative end of the political spectrum, the custodians of the Auckland Historical Society lamented the diminished focus on the historical moment 'by which New Zealand *became British*'.[61]

Meanwhile, similar attempts in Australia to endow the anniversary of colonization (26 January) with enhanced national significance were met with vehement Aboriginal protest and a resigned shrug on the part of the white population – the Melbourne *Age* dismissing Australia Day as 'a festival in search of a meaning' that only served 'to demonstrate our uncertainty as to what we stand for and where we are going'. In a remarkable concession, the Lord Mayor of Sydney addressed a Martin Place crowd on Australia Day 1971 with the feeble entreaty: 'If the present function does not suit the needs of our times, would you please let us know what you suggest?'[62] When a new Labor government two years later sought to bring greater clarity by launching a nationwide national anthem competition (echoing the Jamaican example a decade earlier), the results were underwhelming. Not one of the 2,400 entrants were deemed sufficiently worthy to be put to the popular vote, and it was eventually decided to exhume a much older hymn composed in the 1870s – Peter McCormack's 'Advance Australia Fair'. The song was duly crowned by popular plebiscite; though not before expurgating three stanzas of awkward references to 'true British courage', 'from England soil' and 'Britannia rules the waves'.[63]

Claude Ryan, editor of the Montreal daily *Le Devoir*, dubbed this the 'new nationalism' – a phenomenon he thought peculiar to *les Canadiens anglaise*.

As he astutely pointed out, it was fundamentally a reaction against older forms of imperially derived patriotism in order to give voice, 'perhaps awkwardly' to something 'that seeks to be more completely Canadian', without ever quite securing agreement on what that might entail. Had Ryan cast a wider net he could have equally applied his term to the other former dominions where the spur to civic renewal was largely driven by the climate of adversity for older British affinities – more so than any compelling vision of what the nation-in-waiting should become. The persistence of stubborn pockets of loyalist resistance at virtually every turn suggests that achieving consensus about a coherent national 'identity', cut clean from the lineaments of Greater Britain, was bound to be a prolonged and combative process.

The key components of the 'new nationalism' can also be discerned in contemporary Scotland, where the political breakthrough of the SNP similarly spawned a quest for self-validating myths that could be rendered as viable national symbols. The availability of a home grown 'ancient' iconography gave Scottish nationalists a clear edge over their dominion counterparts, furnishing a ready-made archive of thistles, saltires, unicorns and patron saints. But the SNP also engaged actively in symbolic refurbishment and renewal – again, with inconclusive results. At the very moment when Australia and Canada were casting around for a new national anthem, for example, the SNP leadership was considering a range of new musical compositions for similar purposes – running into much the same adversity in securing broad consensus around a single tune. The genre itself tended to bring nineteenth-century romantic clichés to the fore, with dated references to ethnic purity and 'Scottish blood' that could offend contemporary sensibilities. Responding to one of many such compositions, Billy Wolfe wrote to the party chairman in 1968 requesting that the words 'let's revive the old racial fire' be substituted with 'Scottish fire'.[64]

In much the same vein, when SNP activists set about refurbishing Bannockburn Day as a unifying annual event in 1968, they imagined themselves tapping into deep temporal continuities harking back to the spirit of Robert the Bruce's 1314 victory over Edward II. But the present-day affinities with the reboot of Australia Day and Waitangi Day were far more tangible, even if contemporaries were largely oblivious to each other's exertions.[65] The SNP's case for refitting the 24 June anniversary would have been familiar to frustrated nation-builders elsewhere – lamenting the low levels of public participation (barely resonating at all outside of Stirling), an unimpressive ceremonial element and 'a general lack of joie de vivre'. Only by revamping the entire occasion would the Scottish people 'be brought to realize . . . their abiding national aspirations' and acquire the stuff of 'real' nationhood.[66] As with so many parallels played out in other parts of the world, these exhortations largely failed to elicit much in the way of spontaneous fervour – and to this day Scots do not typically indulge in mass memorialization of the 1314 victory over England.[67]

Indeed, the symbolic dimensions of Scottish separatism in the 1960s and 1970s never fully cohered – for reasons that largely echoed the dominion experience. The case for independence was acutely vulnerable to the charge of national chauvinism, even bigotry – one reason why Tom Nairn initially abhorred Winifred Ewing's SNP breakthrough at Hamilton in 1967. Years before he emerged as the leading theorist of the 'break-up of Britain', Nairn relentlessly caricatured the 'great Tartan Monster' comprising 'lumpen-provincials whose parochialism finds its adequate expression in the asinine idea that a bourgeois parliament and an army will rescue the country from provincialism'. Left-wing critics took much the same view of the SNP's narrower conception of the people as staunchly conservative and Unionist opponents, assuming it to be uniform, hegemonic and inherently regressive. It would be years before Nairn would change his mind, drawn to the potential of Scottish separatism as a path to a more radical programme of social reform. But he stopped short of embracing the cause of symbolic renovation, romantic nationalism or indeed anything else that might stir the 'monster'.[68]

These same hesitations ensured a bumpy ride in the transition from imperial to national symbols throughout virtually all of the successor states of Greater Britain. The post-war era witnessed a growing scepticism about patterns of public conformity more generally, questioning the ideological demands of the Cold War and the tarnished legacy of patriotic fervour in the wake of two destructive world wars. A spirit of cultural rebellion, alienated youth, and what subsequently became known as the 'counterculture' made for anything but an opportune moment to rally people unquestioningly around the flag.[69] The wide-ranging critique of the status quo – from social inequality to civil rights, gender roles, immigration reform, peace advocacy and anti-war activism – could help generate momentum behind the push to dismantle overtly imperial symbols and civic structures, but it could not easily be harnessed to consensual alternatives. Australia's Donald Horne captured the predicament: 'How could people in a modern, industrialised 1960s affluent society be expected to fabricate something so alarmingly old-fashioned as new national symbols?'[70] It is largely for this reason that so many of the overt symbolic trappings of Greater Britain survive to this day, captive to the ambivalence of Pocock's elusive cosmologies.

AFTERLIVES: THE FALKLANDS, GIBRALTAR
AND HONG KONG

There can thus be no neat, clear-cut, across-the-board demarcation between the end of Britain and the new nationalisms that emerged fitfully in its wake. The evident failure of Britain to come to an end raises obvious complications, notwithstanding the almost constant weight of decades of expectation. As we saw in the previous chapter, the 1979 devolution referendums in Scotland and Wales brought the momentum of impending 'break-up' to an abrupt halt, dousing the fires of nationalist aspiration and engendering renewed complacency among advocates of the status quo. Though the Thatcher era would ultimately rekindle separatist ambition through a combination of arrogance and spectacular ineptitude, it also exhibited powerful continuities with the Greater British mindset of old.

The unexpected flare-up of the 1982 Falkland Islands dispute was the most visible sign that the habit of projecting Britain's frontiers far from its own shores would be a long time dying. The despatch of a naval task force to retake a distant territory of dubious strategic value witnessed a remarkable recrudescence of instincts and assumptions reminiscent of former times. The irrepressible urge to domesticate the Falkland Islanders as 'quintessentially English', from their red pillar boxes to their rural seaside setting and – especially – their iconic depiction as an 'island race', echoed the pattern of previous offshore deployments of British forces in striking ways. Receiving the accolades of the Conservative Party at Cheltenham racecourse at the end of the conflict, Mrs Thatcher lauded the 'newfound confidence' of a nation that had 'found herself again in the South Atlantic', chiding the 'waverers' who felt that 'Britain was no longer the nation that had built an empire and ruled a quarter of the world'.[71]

The ease with which Mrs Thatcher could rally the country to such an out-of-the-way conflict has led many to question whether three full decades of relentless downsizing had left any kind of lasting impression at all. The Dilkean myth seemed to hold firm as ever, with the popular imagery of battleships, bunting and wild injunctions to 'rejoice' in a far-flung victory seemingly at odds with Britain's obviously diminished standing as a world power. Left-wing critics were quick to denounce signs of a debilitating recidivism. 'At the very moment when Britain patently no longer rules the waves or an empire', Eric Hobsbawm objected, 'that song has resurfaced and has undoubtedly hit a certain nerve.'[72] Anthony Bartlett diagnosed a people in the grip of a 'moral imperialism' that not only insisted that 'a British voice must speak out' but also 'that the Anglo-Saxon accent can and should arbitrate across all frontiers'.[73] Talk of an 'imperial atavism' that had 'settled like a sentiment in the consciousness of the British people' became a commonplace register for voicing opposition to the war and its absurdly marginal southern latitude.[74]

Though dissenters were in the minority at the time, they were by no means peripheral, and it is perhaps this more than anything else that complicates any simple reading of the Falklands conflict as a case of imperial ardour undimmed.[75] For all the outpouring of sympathy for the Falkland Islanders, even mainstream media outlets could lend a wry touch to depictions of a people leading 'strange, lonely lives many thousands of miles away from the Mother Country'. The physical remoteness of the islands doubled as a distant temporal latitude, evoking an isolated community still 'quintessentially British in a way that Britain had not been for a very long time, or perhaps never had been'.[76] Though intended to be endearing, the accent on quaintness introduced an element of the absurd, accentuating the gap between rhetoric and reality. The Foreign Office ministers who eventually resigned for having failed to prevent the outbreak of hostilities declared solemnly that 'it matters not whether the invasion took place 80 or 8,000 miles away'. But they only drew attention to the ironic distance, which evidently did matter and needed somehow to be explained away.[77] As Andrew Thompson suggests, the veneer of jubilation at the successful defence of the Falklands was tempered by an implicit sense that the Islanders themselves were something of an anachronism.[78]

Moreover, the outward display of national unity did not capture the whole story. Throughout the conflict and especially its immediate aftermath, any number of political and social divisions revealed themselves across the United Kingdom. Nationalist parties in Scotland, Northern Ireland and Wales took a more sceptical view, with Tom Nairn leading the indictment of a British government that had 'refused self-rule to the Scots, who voted for it' while justifying the liberation of the Falkland Islands in the name of 'self-determination'.[79] Perspectives from Wales were additionally complicated by enduring cultural ties to the old nineteenth-century Welsh settlement in Patagonia (still numbering around 20,000 in the early 1980s with a strong contingent of Welsh speakers). The Plaid Cymru leadership directly lobbied the prime minister, urging that 'those who are prepared to use arguments about "kith and kin" in their own contexts' should show greater 'understanding for the validity of this feeling'.[80] Meanwhile in Buenos Aires, the even larger 'Anglo-Argentine' community was thrown into disarray by the prospect of war with Britain, causing bitter internal divisions and the severance of many of their traditional ties. In Ezequiel

Mercau's fine-grained account, a battle fought to defend one small fragment of Greater Britain proved remarkably effective in extinguishing the embers of another. Taking a wider view than the euphoric dockside reception for the returning troops, the Falklands War clearly 'magnified latent tensions over the meaning of Britishness' in a United Kingdom slowly fraying at the seams.[81]

Much the same can be said of the British Nationality Act of 1981, which sparked a fresh round of recriminations right across the residual empire of overseas bases, crown colonies and 'dependent territories', in some cases at a critical juncture in relations with covetous neighbours. The Act itself was largely concerned with nomenclature (the right of abode in the UK having already been removed by the 1962 Commonwealth Immigrants Act) to address the anomaly whereby residency rights and nationality had 'over the years parted company with each other' (in the words of Thatcher's home secretary, Willie Whitelaw). It spelt the end of the antiquated 'Citizenship of the United Kingdom and Colonies', introducing harder distinctions between British Citizens and British 'Overseas' Citizens so as to distance 'certain categories of people from the United Kingdom'.[82] But some stood to lose real privileges, like the citizens of Gibraltar who objected vehemently to the prospective denial of entry entitlements. The Gibraltar lobby in Westminster managed to secure an amendment restoring full citizenship rights, deploying the familiar argument that they were somehow 'more British than the British'. It was another instalment of the well-rehearsed sequence of rumoured 'betrayal' followed by political and moral outrage and a hurriedly cobbled-together compromise. On the face of it, the UK government had yielded to Greater British instincts once more, exempting from immigration controls a tiny Mediterranean enclave of less than 20,000 people who could still leverage remarkable sentimental capital. But contemporaries also seemed tacitly aware that such attachments were becoming increasingly marginal as Britain's overseas holdings grew progressively thinner, judging by one account from 1978:

> No one will really begrudge this symbol, this last corner-stone . . . a nation once top dog needs a sheet anchor sometimes to fall back on in a storm, the very thought of which makes it feel secure again . . . Take the Rock away from us and there will be a deep vacuum, a great sadness, a void in the community of things British.

This was a far cry from earlier invocations of Gibraltar as the 'keystone' in a far-flung chain of British possessions. The collapse of the outward form drained confidence in the symbol itself, relegating Gibraltar to a 'last corner-stone' at the end of the line. The effect was complete with the announcement of the closure of the Naval Dockyard in 1983, sparking murmurs of protest in the House of Lords that for the first time 'since the Tudors reigned over this country' there would be no permanent British naval presence in the Mediterranean. But in the absence of valid strategic arguments in a nuclear age, appeals to the livelihood of 'happily British subjects' at a distant remove no longer carried sufficient weight.[83] Among Gibraltarians too, the appeal to Greater British sentiment now had to be balanced against the need to articulate and uphold local attachments to 'the Rock'. At a time of mounting concern over a possible transfer deal with Spain, vigilance was required lest over-identification with Britain could result in a mass 'repatriation' to the UK. Though the customary cry of loyalty remained the dominant register, political leaders were now eager to emphasize that British nationality was in no way inconsistent with local Gibraltarian feeling, any more than it eroded 'the identity of the Welsh, the Scots or the people of the Channel Isles'.[84]

These shifting mental coordinates during Thatcher's tenure were even more apparent in Hong Kong, not least with the opening of negotiations for the anticipated handover to China. When talks commenced in September 1982, they were occasioned by a 10 per cent drop in the Hong Kong stock market and a momentary plunge for the Hong Kong dollar.[85] The diplomatic complexities of the expiry of the ninety-nine-year lease invested the new British Nationality Act with enormous significance, raising suspicion that it signalled a deliberate downgrading of Hong Kong in British priorities (an impression reinforced by the favourable concessions devised for Gibraltar). The feeling that 'we are losing our Britishness' was confined largely to the privileged classes of Hong Kong's business elite, but was nevertheless fervently articulated.[86] The *South China Morning Post* ran a sustained campaign to restore residency rights throughout the 1980s, resorting to rhetoric borrowed from earlier crunch-moments in other offshore settings. 'The tragedy of the current debate', opined the 16 October 1981 edition, 'is that no one in the UK Government is prepared to recognize that people can be British in sentiment, life style, thinking or attitudes, without once having trodden on home ground. And to cast these people into the nether world ... is a total rejection which is deeply humiliating and disappointing.'[87] It was the old Dilkean formula stripped of its racially exclusive baggage, now pressed belatedly into service to defend the last bastion of Britain's extended frontiers. But as with other such aftershocks, beneath the veneer of moral indignation a weary resignation can be discerned. Though a cosmetic change was agreed to create a new category of 'British National

(Overseas)' – exclusively for Hong Kong subjects so as to preserve the reassuring cadence of British *nationality* – no British government was likely to offer entry entitlements for the roughly half of Hong Kong's five million residents who held British passports. The upshot may have been 'humiliating and disappointing', but by the 1980s it was hardly surprising.

The official handover sixteen years later in July 1997, staged in driving rain mixed with the tears of departing British dignitaries, doubled as a farewell pageant to a near-extinct way of life. UK media outlets strove to outdo each other in elegiac tributes, amid widespread scepticism as to how Hong Kong would fare under Chinese administration. Much of the coverage rehearsed Britain's record of achievement in the Far East, with headlines borrowed almost verbatim from the independence rites in India half a century earlier – 'Flag Comes Down but We Can Hold our Heads High' (*Daily Mail*), 'Last Hurrah for a Symbol of Empire' (*Guardian*) and 'Look Back with Pride' (*Daily Mirror*). But on this occasion, there was the added sense of a final curtain call – a 'Tearful Salute to the Last Jewel in the Crown', and the moment when 'An Empire Closes Down'. The outward display of emotion proved to be short-lived, however, and largely retrospective – a momentary burst of dignified self-pity at reaching the endpoint of 'an extraordinary era in British history' (*The Times*).[88] Indeed, the entire occasion carried a distinctly belated feel, such that an element of irreverence and even flippancy crept in. 'So Long Hong Kong', declaimed *The Sun* cheerily, replete with a British-Chinese page three girl presented as 'a little Hong Kong phewy to mark today's transfer'.[89] Within a matter of days, Hong Kong vanished almost completely from the contemporary UK news cycle. Though misgivings about China's designs remained, there was virtually no lingering sense of having forsaken the legitimate moral claims of fellow Britons.[90]

THE PEOPLE'S CHOICE: NEVERENDUM

The Falkland Islanders, by contrast, never let up in applying moral pressure on the British government, all too aware of the conditional nature of Britain's long-distance affections. Only four years after their liberation by British forces in 1982, they took steps to bolster their position by holding a popular referendum that resulted in a 96 per cent endorsement of their irreducible Britishness. The exercise was repeated in 2013 (the margin widening to 99.8 per cent), as much to remind the British government of its familial obligations as to gauge the temper of public opinion. Gibraltar adopted a similar tactic in 2002 to combat the principle of 'shared sovereignty' between Britain and Spain, with 98.97 per cent falling in with a predictably solid pro-British majority. The resort to direct democracy in both instances was driven by the perceived flimsiness of British government guarantees, and the need constantly to cattle-prod an increasingly apathetic British public.

Remarkably, to the extent that referendums have been held to address the residual anomalies of Greater Britain over the last half-century or so, they have tended to follow the Falklands and Gibraltar in favouring the persistence of British constitutional arrangements. In almost every instance, the opportunity to dispense with the civic remnants of Britishness has been refused, as witnessed by the outcomes of the Quebec 'sovereignty-association' referendum (1980), the Tuvalu republican referendum (1986), the Bermuda independence referendum (1995), the Quebec independence referendum (1995), the Australian republican referendum (1999), the Tuvalu republican referendum (again, in 2008), the St Vincent and the Grenadines republican referendum (2009) and the elaborate consultative process to choose a distinctively New Zealand flag in place of the old colonial ensign (2016) – not to mention the Scottish independence referendum of 2014.[91] With the notable exception of the Scottish and Welsh devolution referendums of September 1997 (where voters supported the introduction of national assemblies in Cardiff and Edinburgh), in every other instance the less 'British' alternative failed to muster a majority, despite the exertions of passionate advocates for change. When Barbados finally made the switch to a republican constitution in 2021 (a move repeatedly deferred since 2008), it was the first former British colony to loosen its constitutional ties to Britain in more than forty years. On this occasion, the formalities of a constitutional referendum were dispensed with, perhaps with the poor recent showing in other jurisdictions in mind.

But it would be wrong to view this pattern as indicative of the tenacious resilience, let alone a spirited revival of global British sensibilities. With each episode, the mere fact of holding a referendum accentuated the anomaly of persisting with British-derived constitutional arrangements, while the results in Quebec, Australia, New Zealand, St Vincent and latterly Scotland were notable for the stark divisions they exposed and the undimmed aspirations of the losing side. Only in Bermuda could the matter be considered to have been finally settled (with three-quarters of the electorate voting to remain under the British Crown), while elsewhere, speculation about the prospect of revisiting the question at some later date has persisted (presumably until such time as the people produce the desired answer). Viewed in a broader context, the proliferation of referendums addressing such foundational issues suggests an ongoing and incomplete reckoning with the identity politics of empire's end. The eminent constitutional authority Ivor Jennings once hinted at a fundamental flaw in the Wilsonian conception of self-determination: 'The people cannot decide', he averred, 'until someone decides who are the people.'[92] It is this latter question – who are 'the people' and what are their defining characteristics – that has persisted even as the matter of self-determination has been satisfactorily resolved. Rather than simply gauge the popular will, the proliferation of plebiscitary politics throughout the Commonwealth in recent decades has itself underlined the difficulty of substituting imperial categories of selfhood with 'cosmologies of our own'.

This is no more evident than in Britain itself, where referendums were traditionally held to be antithetical to the sacred British principle of parliamentary sovereignty. That these convictions have eroded over time reflects the cumulative weight of precedent elsewhere in the Greater British world. The Northern Ireland Border Poll of March 1973 was the first of its kind in UK constitutional history. Nearly four years into the Troubles, with the closure of Stormont and the stalemate of sectarian discord conspicuously unresolved, electors in Northern Ireland were asked to decide whether they wished 'to remain part of the United Kingdom' or to 'be joined with the Republic of Ireland'. The precise implications were left extraordinarily vague, with the Conservative prime minister Edward Heath naively hoping that an elaborate exercise in consulting the people 'might remove the emotive subject of the border from the centre of Northern Ireland politics'.[93] Government ministers were unable to agree even on a consistent nomenclature ('referendum', 'plebiscite' and 'poll' were used interchangeably throughout proceedings), underscoring the jarring cadence of direct democracy in UK constitutional language. The decision of Catholic and nationalist leaders to stage a wholesale boycott ultimately robbed the episode of any real political significance. But it remains important for the simple fact that it happened at all, conceding the principle that one part of the United Kingdom might conceivably vote itself out of the Union (a powerful precedent for Scotland and Wales in the years ahead). David Owen pointed to the wider implications from the opposition benches in the House of Commons:

> the more complex the decision, the more difficult the decision, the worse an instrument for decision making a referendum is. If we want vision, judgment, timing, and flexibility, I put my support firmly and squarely behind representative democracy, not behind periodic plebiscites and

a plebiscitary democracy ... We are introducing into one part of the United Kingdom a constitutional practice which we have resisted introducing in any other part of the British constitution ... I hope that this little Bill will not be the first chink in the armour of the overall strength of our present system of government.

Owen's question was no idle debating point: why, indeed, introduce 'into one part of the United Kingdom' a practice widely deemed antithetical to the spirit and logic of British constitutionalism? Why, when 'we have resisted it when it has been pressed on all parties by the Scottish Nationalists and by the Welsh Nationalists', should the same consultative mechanism now be deemed appropriate for Northern Ireland?[94]

Here, the peculiar geographic location of Northern Ireland assumes enormous significance, straddling the crossroads of empire and nation. Consulting the people directly may have been alien to UK constitutional practice, but it had become increasingly familiar as a means of determining the wishes of subject peoples offshore. The North-West Frontier Provence referendum of July 1947 was to be the first of many decolonizing measures where a simple plebiscite was used to determine who belonged where (the exercise repeated the same day in the eastern Bengal district of Sylhet). The same procedures were devised the following year when two referendums were held in Newfoundland to canvass the people's preference between three options: revert to dominion status; continue to be controlled by Britain; or become a province of Canada (with the latter proposition narrowly winning out). British colonial authorities also administered plebiscites in British Togoland in 1956 (where a majority opted for a merger with soon-to-be-independent Ghana) and British Cameroons in 1961 (where the Southern majority went with independent Cameroon while Northern Cameroon chose integration with Nigeria), again with little sense that the practice was alien to British experience or even mildly suspect.

Two referendums in particular can be seen as important precursors that helped open the door to plebiscitary politics as a means of 'determining selfhood' in the United Kingdom. In Malta in February 1956, a proposal for full 'integration with Britain', with three seats to be reserved for Maltese MPs in the House of Commons, received the endorsement of a remarkable 77 per cent of voters. The initiative came from the Maltese Labour government of Dom Mintoff, primarily for the purpose of weaving British wage and welfare standards into the Maltese social fabric and locking-in Britain's commitment to Malta's physical and economic security. Why the idea was ever entertained by the Eden government in Britain can be gleaned from the advice of Foreign Secretary Harold Macmillan in July 1955: 'At this moment in our history the voluntary and patriotic desire of Malta to join us is something we ought not to repel. Centrifugal forces are very strong at the moment. Let us cherish any centripetal movement that we can find.'[95] Throughout the campaign, the example of Northern Ireland was cited both by staunch advocates of integration (arguing that Malta having its own local legislature while returning MPs to Westminster would be no different from the situation pertaining to Stormont) as well as those vehemently against (on the grounds that Northern Ireland would expect more from the UK Exchequer if Malta received too generous a deal). Opponents also warned that Scotland and Wales might revive their nineteenth-century demands for local assemblies if Malta were conspicuously allowed the same privilege.[96] Though the decision was never implemented (with voters opting for independence at a later poll in 1964), it remains a significant moment in terms of bringing the assumptions and practice of direct democracy into closer dialogue with the politics of Unionism in Britain.

Even more direct parallels can be drawn with the first Gibraltar Referendum in September 1967 where electors were asked to choose whether they wished 'to pass under Spanish Sovereignty' or 'voluntarily to retain their link with the United Kingdom'.[97] The overwhelming majority for remaining British (95.8 per cent) was widely regarded as running counter to the prevailing currents of decolonization, so much so that UK press coverage was roundly criticized for making Gibraltarians 'look like a primitive tribe eager to crawl under Queen Victoria's blanket'.[98] And to be sure, there is good reason to be sceptical of the notion that Gibraltarians were somehow woefully out of step with the times. The referendum campaign was not some stolid defence of the old order but a dynamic event in its own right that permanently altered Gibraltar's civic landscape (literally so, judging from the ongoing custom of painting the town red, white and blue). British officials judged that the mere fact of staging such an all-in community exercise had the effect of consolidating support behind the link with Britain.[99] Rather than simply furnish an inert mechanism for ascertaining the popular will, the referendum was a unique occasion for bringing inherently vague notions of Gibraltarian selfhood into sharper relief.[100]

While there can be no clear line of causation from Gibraltar 1967 to Northern Ireland 1973, the similarities are more than merely coincidental. Aside from the almost identical framing of the question, in neither instance was the fundamental intention to bring about change but rather the very opposite – to mount a case for the status quo that could be anchored in new forms of legitimacy drawn from post-imperial precedent elsewhere. As in

Malta, both polls arose out of the need to refute the logic of 'centrifugal forces' pulling the British people inexorably apart. Arguably, without the wider impress of plebiscitary politics it is unlikely that either referendum would ever have been deemed desirable or even particularly necessary. In this sense, the border polls in Gibraltar and Northern Ireland were not merely interrelated, but also interlaced with the broader bureaucratic procedures of determining selfhood at empire's end. Moreover, it is significant that Northern Ireland seemed a more obvious or opportune place to experiment with direct democracy in the United Kingdom. Though not itself formally a colony, it was nevertheless parked precariously 'offshore', marking it out as the detached portion of the Union where imported principles could more readily be applied.

Harold Wilson's EEC referendum came only two years later in 1975 – the first ever nationwide consultative poll of its kind in UK history. It, too, can be seen in retrospect as a species of grappling with a shared sense of belonging in the light of radical reconfigurations of Britain's place in the world. As Robert Saunders has shown, the rhetoric of both sides of the campaign was saturated with assumptions inherited from the imperial past – the 'no' case pleading the cause of Commonwealth solidarity and Britain's natural inclination to push 'out, and into the world'; the 'yes' campaign steeped in talk of Europe as a 'new frontier' where the country's unique qualities of global leadership would not go to waste.[101] Those who opposed putting the matter to a popular vote railed passionately against the intrusion of 'continental' procedures into the sacrosanct domain of parliamentary sovereignty. *The Sun, The Mirror* and the *Daily Mail* were united in denouncing Wilson's referendum as a 'constitutional monstrosity', a 'thoroughly bad innovation' and an act of civic vandalism that left the British Constitution bleeding 'beneath the still-moving rubble of Her Majesty's Government'.[102] They were met with what ought to have been the obvious retort – the ubiquitous use of referendums throughout the Commonwealth, 'all of whose parliamentary traditions have grown out of this country'.[103] Not for the first time, Greater Britain could confer a sense of continuity and political legitimacy on the governing assumptions of Britain itself.

One of the great myths of referendums is that they resolve divisive issues, rallying the people behind a clear manifestation of the collective will. That may be the case for settling relatively mundane political matters amenable to simple yes/no propositions. But in the realm of identity politics, the evidence of 'British' experience suggests that referendums rarely produce clear-cut solutions – and are almost never the end of the story.

More often than not a residue of emotionally charged frustration on the part of the losing cause has tended to keep the issue alive, sustained by the conviction that time, and an underlying political momentum, must surely be on the side of change. The Scottish independence referendum of 2014 is only the most prominent example of a 'once in a generation' defeat refusing to lie down, buoyed by the everyday indications that Britishness is losing ground.

Equally buoyant in defeat was the campaign leadership of 'Change the NZ Flag' in March 2016, despite two years of painstaking selection of a new design to replace the old colonial ensign, and a devastating referendum defeat by a margin of 57 per cent. What ought to have been a deeply humbling moment, the equivalent of an unmitigated landslide in general election terms, was blithely brushed aside by the campaign chair, Lewis Holden. The majority may have spoken, he conceded, but 'for everyone else, this debate is far from over'. Citing any number of spurious reasons to draw encouragement, he predicted confidently that 'a growing yearning for independent symbols that unite all New Zealanders will not go away … If anything the call will grow louder.' Without a shred of irony, he summoned the ghost of Winston Churchill to clinch the argument: 'This is not the end, it is not even the beginning of the end. But it is perhaps the end of the beginning.'[104]

Exactly three months later, a UK-wide majority of just under 52 per cent elected to leave the European Union, producing the decisive political fault line of twenty-first-century British politics. The Brexit referendum was about many things, too complex to consider in detail here. But for at least a sizeable portion of its supporters, there was an underlying unease about Britain's diminished global standing that had persisted for decades, of which membership of the EU was only the most persistent reminder. As with so many precursor events elsewhere, it was yet another exercise in 'determining selfhood' with immediate repercussions for the future of both Scotland and Northern Ireland in the Union. It is by no means fanciful to see oblique parallels between the Brexit vote and the contemporaneous tussle over New Zealand's flag unfolding on the other side of the world in real time. Despite vast differences in the magnitude and complexity of what people were being asked to consider, both campaigns addressed a popular, but by no means universal, desire to regroup the nation around a narrower set of coordinates. Some commentators remarked on the irony that while Britain chose 'leave', New Zealand opted – figuratively at least – for 'remain' in its retention of the Union Jack. But this overlooked the shared set of dilemmas that brought two otherwise wholly disconnected episodes into the same frame.

To be sure, Brexit cannot simply be caricatured as yet another item of unfinished imperial business, or its significance submerged in the crush of plebiscitary politics since the onset of decolonization. But nor can the irony of restoring sovereignty by re-engaging with 'global Britain' be detached from its worldwide antecedents – particularly when the deliberative instrument itself was borrowed from wider Commonwealth experience.

———————————◆———————————

J. G. A. Pocock could not have foreseen this latter-day confluence of British and New Zealand destinies in 1973, but it is unlikely he would have disapproved. He never sought to hide his contempt for the European Union (and specifically Britain's decision to join), and he must surely have regarded the idea of removing the Union Jack from New Zealand's flag as a prime example of 'the negation of our historic existence as neo-Britains' – the kind of 'harm to our understanding of ourselves' that shaped his entire approach to Britishness as a historical subject.[105] His prescription for preserving some wider connectivity in an otherwise fractured polity – under the rubric of a 'new British history' – spectacularly failed to garner a following among the very 'neo-Britains' for whom it seemed to him so urgent. When it finally did catch on, it was for the far more limited purpose of reconfiguring the 'Four Nations' of the United Kingdom in ways that only enhanced the perception of deeper centrifugal forces at work.

But nor did the 'new nationalism' that emerged as the main rival to Pocock's design achieve any lasting paradigmatic status. If British markers of identity had acquired distinctly moribund connotations, it did not necessarily follow that self-evident, self-sufficient national myths were ready to hand to forge an alternative popular consensus. Rival interest groups invariably squared off in pursuit of competing agendas, all vaguely geared towards realizing the elusive goal of 'real' nationhood. Unsurprisingly, it would not be long before 'identity fatigue' set in. In 1967, the centennial year of Canadian Confederation, Ramsay Cook caused a minor sensation by wondering out loud whether 'the search is worth the effort'. In a wide-ranging essay questioning the incessant clamour for an overly self-conscious nationalism, he asked himself whether 'the frame of reference is wrong':

> Perhaps instead of constantly deploring our lack of identity, we should attempt to understand and explain the regional, ethnic and class identities that we do have. It might just be that it is in these limited identities that 'Canadianism' is found, and that except for our over-heated intellectuals, Canadians find this situation quite satisfactory.[106]

476

'Limited Identities' would soon be taken up under different labels at different times in all parts of the disaggregated British world, exploring the 'heterogenous pluralism' advocated by Cook and others.[107] It was a pluralism widely at variance from Pocock's 'diversity' of British cultures and allegiances, dispensing not only with Greater British grand narratives but also the expectation of a uniform national story to take their place.[108] It enabled perspectives hitherto obscured or indeed completely ignored – Indigenous, migrant, subaltern – to come to the fore, as well as wider scope for gender, class and sub-regional variations. Fitfully at first, but with gathering momentum, these new departures would jostle for attention in the years ahead alongside more conventional national histories in 'identity' mode, producing periodic bouts of 'history wars' over the moral implications of the past.[109] Though frequently centred on the legacies of colonialism and the injustices of Indigenous dispossession, the outwardly 'British' dimension itself nevertheless tended to fade from view. As Miranda Johnson's work has shown, Indigenous experience would ultimately provide 'something of use to the settler state' – a timeless connection to an autochthonous past rooted in their 'own geographies'. For all the unresolved discord over Indigenous entitlements, this too, she argues, could form 'part of the project of dissolving ties with Britain'.[110]

The proliferation of limited identities has also enabled multiple variants of British identity to persist on a smaller scale in the United Kingdom, often wildly at odds with one other. A casual stroll along Belfast's Shankill Road presents a visual feast of British-themed mural art that only local initiates can fully appreciate. The 12 September celebration of Gibraltar Day (marking the anniversary of the 1967 referendum) triggers an annual outpouring of distinctly Mediterranean British euphoria that goes largely unnoticed in Britain itself. Britishness has also continued to resonate as a marker of Black and minority ethnic identification throughout the UK, sometimes as a foil for the more 'nativist' undertones of 'Four Nations' affiliations. In 2007, the Institute of Public Policy Research revealed polling data suggesting that Asian and Black Britons were 'more likely to see themselves as British first', compared with an increasingly fragmented white constituency drawn towards English, Scottish, Welsh and Northern Irish affinities. Five years later, the same institute announced the exact same 'finding', buttressed by a regular stream of anecdotal evidence of the more inclusive properties of Britishness.[111]

Paul Gilroy famously exploded these assumptions in *There Ain't No Black in the Union Jack* (1987), laying bare the 'ethnic absolutism' that was equally embedded in British discourses of race and nation.[112] Years later, recalling his decision to identify as English rather than British, he explained how he was 'worried with the idea of Britishness that it would only end up being the Black and minority ethnic populations who took it seriously'.[113] The idea that ethnic minorities more easily qualify as British persists, however, partly on account of the inherently composite nature of British identities but also due to the memory of a more capacious territorial remit that retains a residual hold. That such memories are brutally selective was demonstrated by the 2018 'Windrush scandal', involving the wrongful deportations of especially Caribbean British subjects born before the tightening of nationality laws in the 1970s and 1980s. It was a prime example of the past colliding with the present in unanticipated ways, giving rise to the renewed currency of the once familiar charge of British 'betrayal' – warped by the displacements of time and historical context.[114]

Meanwhile, the exclusively white cadence of Greater Britain still makes its presence felt at regular intervals and continuities are not hard to find, whether it be the periodic enthusiasms for a global English-speaking fraternity – latterly redubbed the 'Anglosphere', with the emphasis on a shared linguistic and cultural inheritance to avoid the discredited racial slant of the Dilkean original – or the more recent push for 'Global Britain' as the abstract ideal of successive Conservative governments seeking cover from the fallout of exiting the European Union.[115] These enthusiasms speak to the residue of older, racialized mentalities rooted in former times, but they can still arouse tacit (and sometimes even explicit) support among influential vested interests in all the former 'dominions'. Over time, however, they have become increasingly difficult to sustain, surviving as a source of comfort for a diverse and disaffected constituency unreconciled to the sweeping changes of the last half-century or more that have progressively undermined their privileged status.

Taking the longer view from the onset of global decolonization in the late 1940s to the early twenty-first century, the idea of Britishness as a credible marker of globally resonant values, beliefs, history, culture, ethnicity and civic identity has been in almost constant retreat – unevenly so, and with recidivist tendencies at every turn, but with ever fading resonances over time. This book has sought the widest possible vantage point, teasing out the worldwide antecedents of the disparity of fellow feeling that has accrued in recent decades among the constituent nations of the United Kingdom. In no single instance or episode has the eclipse of British sentiment been seamless or smooth, but that is entirely in keeping with the haphazard procedures that invested Britishness with such unprecedented civic latitude to begin with. Those at the forefront of defending it into the twenty-first century (whether they be Unionist, 'loyalist' or 'global' Britishers) cannot ignore the historical weight of imperial parallels and precedent. The entanglements run deep and persist to this day.

But equally, those at the forefront of championing the break-up of Britain could benefit from the wider optics advocated here. In a June 2020 interview, the elder statesman of Scottish nationalism, Tom Nairn, remained upbeat about the approaching dawn of independence despite having waited more than forty years for his predictions finally to come to fruition. 'We're making it up as we go along' he enthused. 'What was once Great Britain, the British Empire, we're struggling along to replace that with something else, with something new.' Surveying the extraordinary changes that have occurred since the 1977 publication of *The Break-Up of Britain*, there can be no denying that the gap between aspiration and fulfilment has narrowed considerably. But Nairn was surely wide of the mark in proclaiming: 'No one has ever done this before.'[116]

CONCLUSION

Being British was always something of a stretch. From its earliest iterations it had a speculative quality; the product of an expansive mindset grasping for new categories that could traverse immense distances. For all the popular mythology of an insular people, closing ranks and 'standing alone' against outside adversity, the first Britons were as likely to be found offshore, in scattered clusters of uprooted, itinerant, indentured, enlisted, and enslaved peoples all engaged – unequally – in new patterns of social organization. Britishness was only one vernacular improvised for the occasion, and it would take centuries for it to evolve into a loose-fitting identity for an imperial age. Simultaneously, and by dint of similar processes of migration, military conquest, commercial exchange and industrial innovation, it also emerged as an umbrella term for the peoples of the United Kingdom. Three scales of signification – empire, Union and a plethora of distinct localities – joined in a running dialogue to produce a global civic idea, called upon to do unprecedented work all over the world.

Even at peak efficiency, to be British was heavily modulated by local inflections and a tangle of conflicting priorities. At no time during its roughly three hundred years of popular currency did it provide watertight categories of inclusion or resonate uniformly from one constituency to the next. Any number of ethnic, religious, regional, socio-economic and ideological factors could alter the terms of endearment, furnishing enormous scope for misunderstanding and periodic shocks of mutual 'misrecognition'. Yet it nevertheless managed to circulate freely as a unifying category under a variety of labels. This, arguably, was the key to its wide dissemination at a time of incipient globalization – its extraordinary elasticity, and an almost limitless capacity to generate shared resonances. In time, these same shape-shifting qualities would precipitate its protracted unmaking in the second half of the twentieth century. Finding a fresh purchase on this critical closing phase has been the principal aim of this book.

Part of the puzzle lies in the extraordinary variations themselves, and the lack of an agreed terminology – or even agreement on what *kind* of group consciousness Britishness signified. Though the criteria for membership overlapped conspicuously with the trappings of nationalism – language, race, religion, culture, history, and shared civic ideals – these were never matched by any serious conviction that the British people should be joined in popular sovereignty on a planetary scale.[1] But nor was the sense of mutual expectation and reciprocal obligation merely perfunctory. Contemporaries often resorted to allegory to describe an 'organic' unity, 'instinctive' ties and vague allusions to 'a spirit, an attitude of mind, an unconquerable hope' (as John Buchan would have it in 1906) that seemed somehow more dependable and enduring than formal treaties or alliances.[2] This was the fundamental paradox of colonial over-reach, producing expectations of a binding transoceanic compact among a vast interconnected network of peoples whose core convictions (and the uncertain contingencies of long-distance relationships) bred a stubborn attachment to local autonomy. Britishness was the imperfect solution to the conundrum.

Imperfection was also the leitmotif of Charles Wentworth Dilke in his 1868 account of his travels throughout the British world. Dilke fell upon the idea of 'Greater Britain'; a term that soon found a prominent place in the political lexicon, reaching peak circulation around the turn of the twentieth century.[3] It has been revisited here as a much-needed conceptual handle – not because it ever gained universal acceptance or even a stable set of meanings, but because it was conceived out of the very fault lines that would later produce the endemic fracturing of the post-war years. Dilke's journey occurred at a time of rich possibilities to rethink mental maps, when 'the scale of socialization and aspiration became vastly wider'.[4] That he even contemplated such an elongated voyage was testimony to the technological revolution that made it possible, inspiring him not only to describe the various destinations along the way but also to imagine them as parts of a globally integrated whole. It was a prime example of a historical space constituted 'by virtue of the time by which it can be traversed' – and hence be given a name.[5] But Dilke not only furnished a serviceable name, he also exemplified the logical discrepancies that were Greater Britain's chief asset, and ultimately its cardinal flaw. Like his contemporary J. R. Seeley, he was deeply ambivalent about the status of the non-white colonial empire in his grand design. Unable to detour around British India (spending months, in fact, traversing the length and breadth of the Indian empire from Ceylon to Sindh), he was equally ill-disposed to embrace it as his own.

This was the core conceit of Britain-in-the-world that both Dilke and Seeley epitomized – evoking an expansive sense of the people with avowedly liberal overtones, shot through with racial, religious and ideological barriers to inclusion. The disparities soon worked their way into the everyday imagining of a British world, not least the persistent 'slippage of terms' that became so characteristic of the British condition.[6] If Greater Britain is taken at face value as a vast white man's estate where 'in essentials, the race was always one', its analytical value will inevitably be limited.[7] But as a flawed system of logic predicated on the export of English constitutional liberties for the presumptive benefit of all who resided under the British flag, it becomes a more intricate matter entirely – traceable through recurring patterns of conflict, crisis and compromise that came to a head in the crucial three decades after the Second World War. The fundamental paradox of 'a liberal, commercial society incubating in a world of illiberal, colonial empires' allows us to see Greater Britain in all its moral and ideological complexity, furnishing the key to its disorderly undoing.[8]

That the system was always inherently defective was in no way difficult for contemporaries to discern – indeed, it was obvious to anyone who cared to examine it more closely. As we saw in Part I, Winston Churchill, Joseph Chamberlain, Lord Milner, even Dilke himself could be counted among those who quietly acknowledged the inconsistencies. Yet the effort to wrap these in a veneer of high principle seemed not only worthwhile but also crucial to insulating the whole enterprise from prying eyes. Gurdit Singh was by no means the first to expose the incompatibility of British liberty with the veneration of the 'British race' (Paul Bogle, J. J. Thomas, M. K. Gandhi and a host of others had visited it long before). But the arrival of SS *Komagata Maru* on Vancouver's Burrard Inlet in spring 1914 lifted the veil in dramatic fashion – at a time when a Canadian leader of the UK Conservatives was poised to ride roughshod over the British liberties of Irish Catholics.

It would be decades before the implications fully emerged, however. Some, like William Cooper, Solomon Plaatje, Learie Constantine and Ranjanbala Vaid continued to press the anomalies in a bid to secure admission, convinced that the theory could be made to work in practice. But the onset of decolonization from the late 1940s marked the beginning of an irresistible fragmentation. It was during these years that the tension between boundless constitutional liberty and the 'global colour line' reached a dramatic tipping point, placing renewed pressure on successive British governments to make good on the universal promise of British freedoms. Meanwhile the descendants of white settlers deployed all manner of strategies to arrest the slide in their privileged status, determined that the shaky edifice of racial unity should hold firm. Others, however, arrived at a rejection of their British affinities entirely, out of despondency at the failure of the system to underwrite their interests in a changing world order. There can be no easy generalizations in this regard – the emotional register accommodated wide discrepancies of feeling – but in straining to be all things to all people, in the end Britishness could satisfy none.

What distinguished the post-war period was as much a matter of degree as kind. The great precursor event was the mid-century collapse of the British world-system, symbolized by the fall of Singapore in February 1942.[9] The transformed international setting would amplify three debilitating factors that had always nagged at the edges of Greater British convictions. The capacity of the United Kingdom to meet the enormous cost of global commitments and fiscal liabilities – a logistical problem that had long hampered imperial strategy – now assumed endemic proportions for a nation morally and materially depleted by two world wars. This was compounded by the dwindling returns of an economic model structured around the exchange of colonial raw materials for metropolitan manufactures – again, a development foreshadowed by pre-war trends. And third, the ideological demands of a bipolar world fostered a new climate of adversity for racial injustice in general and colonial empires in particular. Here, too, it was a case of ramping up the momentum of the interwar period, spawning liberation movements of every stripe – local, national, religious and ideological. In particular, the proliferation of new conceptions of universal rights and civic entitlements posed unique challenges for a system premised on mutual assistance and reciprocal regard among a globally dispersed cohort of English-speaking whites.

Any or all of these factors could have punctured confidence in the idea of Greater Britain, but they were compounded by one last crucial factor – an explosive new potential for direct contact between self-styled British communities hitherto consigned to separate geographic spheres. The virtual proximity furnished by new audio and visual broadcasting technologies, coupled with a greatly expanded scope for human mobility, would cast Charles Dilke's celebrated 'imperfections' in a new and searching light. The Trinidadian clergyman M. E. Farquhar remarked perceptively in 1948 on the changes that had brought 'the opportunity of acquaintance with England to a comparatively large number of West Indians', anticipating acute difficulties arising from what he termed the 'altered conception of remoteness'.[10] The effects would multiply across any number of trajectories, of which the metropole–colony axis was only the most prominent. The 'independent systems of expectation' that had long co-existed among widely dispersed communities of Britishness could not easily withstand tighter patterns of proximity, producing serial ruptures as rival British sensibilities squared off against each other in the decades after 1945.[11]

Above all, the expectation that a community of race, language and constitutional liberties automatically conferred a community of interest was put to the test in these years, and persistently found wanting – fitfully at first, but with accelerating momentum into the 1960s. The creeping obsolescence of the empire project itself, and the taint of inevitability that attended each stage in its drawn-out demise, ultimately drained confidence in the verities of an unbounded Britain. A moral world of universal entitlements that (in practice) favoured people of a certain caste, complexion or locality could not escape critical scrutiny, exposing divisions even among the presumptive core of English-speaking whites when called upon to choose between liberal principles and racial patrimony. It was a recipe for misrecognition and mutual disenchantment on a scale arguably never seen before, pushing the question of separate 'identities' increasingly to the fore. This book has presented a way of explaining how those dynamics played out in the broadest terms, with profound implications for the long-term political viability of the British of Britain.

THE SENSE OF AN ENDING

Communities, like individuals, have a way of locating themselves in time, making sense of shared experience as part of a wider temporal order. 'We all share certain fictions about time', wrote the literary critic Frank Kermode in 1967, arising out of a fundamental need 'in the moment of existence to belong, to be related to a beginning and to an end.'[12] In Australia in the 1970s, the myth of a young country whose time had finally come enjoyed a remarkable resurgence, despite the notion itself being more than a century old. One of the finalists in the 1973 national anthem competition couched his verse in the future tense, heralding a nation-in-waiting that 'approaches every minute / and bids us speak the right / Oh, come let us begin it / Before the fall of night' – evidently untroubled by how such sentiments would fare with the passing of the years. It was eventually decided to dispense with novelty and turn to the more familiar strains of Peter McCormack's 'Advance Australia Fair'. Originally composed in 1878, it needed to be thoroughly worked over to expunge the imprint of imperial loyalty (with more than half the song ultimately consigned to the dustbin). But somehow the opening salvo, 'for we are young and free', survived the refurbishment, and still passes muster fifty years on. As Barry Humphries quipped at the time, it was a country 'endlessly coming of age'.[13]

Australia's aura of eternal youth would have seemed tired and jaded were it not for the passing of a much older order. For a country and a people conspicuously steeped in the legacies of transoceanic Britishness, the new tidings were shaped by what Kermode famously termed 'the sense of an ending' – in this case, the end of Britain-in-the-world as the symbol of a wider ethnic and cultural unity. There was no neat temporal dividing line between the two states of mind – more a matter of inextricable entanglement, the fading verities of being British serving as vivid testimony to a nation reborn. Nor was the condition confined to the white majority for whom talk of new beginnings generated such enthusiasm. The 1960s also witnessed a distinct change of tactic among Indigenous activists, asserting Aboriginal entitlements as fundamentally self-validating while casting aside petitioning practices subordinated to British constitutional liberties. In this, and countless other ways, older circuits of self-knowledge were giving way to new possibilities.

The sense that Britain's world was coming to an end resonated across a remarkably broad spectrum of political, social and cultural life – of which only an indicative sample has been presented in the six chapters that comprise Part II. Already from the late 1940s, stark disagreements over the meaning and applicability of the adjective 'British' among the political class of the 'new Commonwealth' signalled early tidings of what lay ahead. The colonial administration of Kenya seemed clearly to sense what was afoot, taking remedial action in the form of a permanent royal residence to ensure that 'home' retained a sense of long-range reciprocity. Meanwhile, West Indian sojourners in London were now reminded on a daily basis that the mutual recognition of British subjecthood could in no sense be taken for granted, their mere presence in a metropolitan setting sparking debate about the universal properties of Greater Britain. Further afield, English South Africans grappled with the twin prongs of an Afrikaner majority determined to override their paramount status, and a burgeoning Black resistance calling time on the bogus liberties invested in the British Crown. Even humble trade commodities were not immune to the contingencies, unable to rely on older consumer loyalties in the face of tectonic shifts in the terms of trade and the attractions of new markets outside of the British orbit. Likewise, the long arm of British justice was caught embarrassingly short when the Wilson government failed to suppress a rebellion of a few hundred thousand unrepentant white Rhodesians, whose agitation stemmed from the realization that they could no longer 'be British as they understood the term'.[14] Taken together, these six episodes document the sheer range and complexity of the break-up of Greater Britain as it unfolded across multiple registers and diverse historical geographies.

Crucially, the sense of an ending could not be quarantined offshore – the overriding theme of Part III. For metropolitan pundits, politicians and the people they represented, the lost latitude of the post-war era could assume existential dimensions wholly out of proportion with the material stakes – culminating in the dogged defence of 'global reach' that was the Suez crisis of 1956. Such trepidations not only influenced the outlook of Suez 'hawks', but also spilled over into the grim projections of 'state of the nation' writers in the 1960s whose relentless forecasts of national decline inspired the moral defiance of the 'I'm Backing Britain' campaign at the end of the decade – albeit fleetingly and with only marginal returns. Reflecting on the publication of *The Sense of an Ending* thirty years later, Kermode recalled an era when 'it seemed more than merely possible that there was a bad time coming, possibly a terminally bad time', which clearly influenced the temper of his 1967 classic. He counted Cuban missiles, race riots, anti-Vietnam War marches and US political assassinations among 'the imminence of events that could without too much exaggeration be characterized as apocalyptic' – ensuring that his work immediately struck a chord. Remarkably, Kermode made no mention of the winding up of the British empire and the serial ruptures of collective selfhood that proceeded in its wake.[15] But for a writer working at the high noon of sterling's humiliation and the retrenchment of Britain's long-range defence posture, the sense of a people fallen on hard times could not have been far from his mind.

As the closing chapters of this volume variously attest, Britain's narrowing horizons carried all manner of implications for the constituent 'Four Nations' – none more crucial than a heightened awareness of their separate existence. The Kenyan Asians crisis of 1967–8 was a particularly resonant moment, at once highlighting the no-man's land occupied by holders of British passports issued overseas, while subtly magnifying the finer distinctions between England and Britain on the home front. The sudden urge to close the perceived 'loophole' of a liberal, capacious, expansive Britishness prompted a resignification of the category of Englishness in a newly circumscribed nation. It was an ingenious, if largely unselfconscious means of discounting the bona fides of those Asian families who rushed to 'beat the ban' in March 1968, while avoiding the overt stigma of 'racialism'. In this way, the looser, empire-derived affinities of Britishness could be downgraded without relinquishing the badge of ethnicity available only to the 'true-born'. But repatriating the frontiers of nationhood raised implicit questions about what ultimately bound the constituent parts of the Union together – questions that would become increasingly explicit as the shared global projections of Greater Britain receded into the past.

Few Kenyan Asians made their presence felt in Northern Ireland, but the spectacle of a British government turning its back on long-standing moral commitments abroad (from East of Suez to Rhodesia, Gibraltar and the Falkland Islands) only heightened suspicion that Protestant Ulster would be next in line. Such apprehensions could seem paranoid, but they were reinforced by rational observation – of Britain's rapid global retreat and a Westminster establishment ever-prone to unburden itself of overseas encumbrances. Ultimately, it was as much to combat English incomprehension of their plight that Protestant loyalists resorted to a beleaguered militancy as the touchstone of their Britishness; a strategy that only served to distance them further from their 'mainland' counterparts. Meanwhile, the same sense of Britain's diminished capacity to deliver on the promise of global reach was viewed as a rare opportunity by Scottish and Welsh separatist parties, whose stunning rise to electability between 1961 and 1974 cannot be viewed in isolation from the broader indications of a nation retracting inwards on itself. Here, the end of Britain was the avowed political prize, persistently and effectively packaged in the aspirational politics of 'stopping the world' so that older nationalities might be retooled for a post-British age.

Making sense of the interconnections between the course of events unfolding overseas and the decades-long push for the dissolution of the United Kingdom cannot be a straightforward matter of cause and effect. In 2009, the veteran Scottish writer and editor Ian Jack laid out the conventional view in his collection of essays and reminiscences, *The Country Formerly Known as Great Britain*:

> First the empire went and then most of the manufacturing industry. Protestantism survives in ill-attended churches only as one faith among many, and all of them no more than little islands of religion in a sea of unbelieving materialism. There is hardly a British institution – the monarchy, the BBC, the Royal navy – that doesn't fear for its future.[16]

First the empire went. As with so many invocations of this familiar sequence, the end of empire furnishes the crucial tipping point, beyond which so much else falls effortlessly away. But it is misleading as a guide to the shifting patterns of relationships that have produced such bleak prospects for the Union. The eclipse of British identities elsewhere in the world were as much occasioned by changing priorities in Britain itself – hence the frequent charge of 'betrayal' that remained so integral to the language of loyalty. British scales of belonging had always rested historically on a wider sense of connectivity – imperial, Unionist and sub-national alike – and hence relied on multiple staging posts for mutual affirmation. Long-distance affinities and the opportunities these beckoned were the fundamental rationale for accentuating British identities vis-à-vis more localized attachments, whether they be in Bermuda, Brisbane, Bulawayo or Birmingham. The implosion of the British world-system and the attendant waves of mutual misrecognition affected disparate communities equally, if unevenly, across a wide spectrum of everyday experience – in ways that cannot simply be reduced to the empire's fatal 'impact' on metropolitan Britain.

If Australia qualifies as a nation 'endlessly coming of age', there is a sense in which Britain since the 1970s has become a country endlessly coming to an end – apparently with no end in sight. But that in no way punctures the certainty of those eagerly awaiting the final mortal blow; or for that matter, the anxieties of those at pains to preserve the familiar coordinates of old. Superficially, the persistence of the Union in the face of decades of gloomy prophesy might be viewed as a sign that the UK is somehow uniquely resilient – still standing more than half a century after the first tell-tale cracks appeared. But shared categories of belonging rarely permit clear-cut patterns of 'closure'. That the end itself is incomplete and indistinct is entirely in keeping with the many offshore encounters examined here, where enduring dilemmas and loose ends abound. The pervasive *sense* of an ending, however, can be all too readily discerned and extensively documented, albeit according to divergent rhythms and disparate timescales. Like Britishness itself, it has traversed an extraordinarily vast terrain, the loss of confidence in each separate sphere lending weight to a cumulative, collective disenchantment. Viewed in this light, the end of Britain is indisputably a matter of historical record.

In one crucial respect, however, the constituent four nations of the United Kingdom present a special case; namely their immediate geographic proximity, which brings its own unique entanglements. Whatever the future trajectory of devolutionary politics, the inhabitants of these islands will need to find a way of living together that respects their fundamental interdependence. So long as there is a British state, the possibility of future accommodations or compromise that might perpetuate something going by that name obviously cannot be ruled out, even if only as a matter of political expediency. But framing the issue in global terms suggests the unlikelihood that it can be anything more, or that the underlying centrifugal pressures over the longer term will somehow subside. Taking a global perspective allows us to see the contemporary travails of the Union as just one dimension of a much wider depletion of emotional investments in being British harking back to the Second World War – a composite tale, encompassing peoples in all parts of a precariously aligned British world. How that sense of an ending has endured, merging into an endemic cycle of 'neverendum', presents not so much a puzzle as a paradigm – with a worldwide profusion of subplots and scattered legacies.

Acknowledgements

Books incur debts, far beyond what can adequately be accounted for in a brief afterword. When I first presented my initial, admittedly vague ideas for this book many years ago to the eminent historian of Britishness, Linda Colley, her immediate response was two short but memorable words: 'Good luck!' And it so happens that I've been extremely fortunate in terms of the resources put at my disposal and the reservoir of experience, expertise and collegial goodwill that I have been able to draw upon. Richard Drayton offered sage advice in the very early stages, which he may have long since forgotten, but which nevertheless influenced my approach to the subject in significant ways. I have also benefitted from the example of two of Britain's leading global historians of empire, John Darwin and the late C. A. Bayly, each of whose major works provided something of a springboard. A running conversation with Bill Schwarz spanned most of the duration of this work, pushing me to revisit one or two assumptions and rethink aspects of the broader project design. Elizabeth Buettner, Sarah Stockwell and Wendy Webster have also been welcome fellow travellers, their own outstanding books on related themes having appeared long before this one.

I would never have made a serious start without a further stroke of good fortune: the award of a major research grant from the Velux Foundation for the 'Embers of Empire' project at the University of Copenhagen. Velux not only provided the financial resources for the extensive travel and fieldwork requirements, but also presented the opportunity to supervise a cohort of talented doctoral research students all working with Britain's tangled imperial afterlives. Tóra Djurhuus, Ezekiel Mercau, Kalathmika Natarajan, Jimmi Østergaard Nielsen, Christian D. Pedersen and Astrid Rasch have now all moved on with their own promising careers, but the work they produced in the Embers project and the international camaraderie and team spirit they generated remained a source of genuine inspiration throughout. Ezekiel and Astrid also contributed research assistance at key junctures, and I was additionally well served in that regard by Harriet Mercer for Chapters 6 and 12, and Gareth Owen for Chapter 14 (who worked alongside me in

Aberystwyth at the National Library of Wales, translating Welsh language sources *in situ*).

The project could never have been completed without the generous support of a Carlsberg Foundation Monograph Fellowship. A scheme designed to allow researchers a period of respite to finish their (often overdue) manuscripts could not have come at a better time. Sincere thanks are also due to the (then) dean of the Faculty of Humanities at the University of Copenhagen, Jesper Kallestrup, for agreeing to a period of leave for this purpose, and to his successor Kirsten Busch Nielsen for her support and understanding in permitting so much time away from my post. One of my closest collaborators in recent years, David Bloch, very generously took over as head of the Saxo Institute during my absence, making it abundantly clear that I was not to contemplate returning without a complete draft. To all of my colleagues at Saxo – historians, ethnologists, archaeologists, classicists and our dedicated secretariat – I offer my thanks for the indulgence of not turning up to work for so much of 2021.

I have additionally benefitted from two visiting research fellowships along the way that helped maintain writing momentum and bring fresh perspective. In spring 2017, Richard Toye, Martin Thomas and Andrew Thompson invited me to the Imperial and Global History Centre at Exeter University under their 'Visiting International Academic Fellow' scheme, where I had the opportunity to present the broad outlines of the project. And in 2018 I spent a very rewarding summer (or winter, as these things turn out) as a visiting research fellow at the Australian National University, kindly sponsored by Frank Bongiorno and Angela Woollacott. In addition to the vibrant programme of seminars and abundance of source material that Canberra has to offer, I also had the pleasure of working alongside my co-visitor at the ANU School of History, Phillipa Levine. The occasional weekend retreat at the bush hideout of Mark and Fiona McKenna capped off an extremely worthwhile stay.

Old friends and colleagues from Australia and New Zealand have continued to provide a ready source of advice and encouragement. Mark McKenna was extremely generous in responding to chapter drafts that popped up periodically on his screen. Likewise, my one-time co-author, James Curran, might well have wondered at times whether he was co-writing this one as well. Harshan Kumarasingham and Christina Twomey have also helped to keep the project on the rails in various ways, while Andrew May came up with a title suggestion for one of the chapters that chimed in perfectly. Deryck Schreuder has always been on hand with a supportive email, and it would be remiss of me not to mention the influence of Neville Meaney, who originally set me on this path nearly three decades ago, but who sadly did not live to see where it has led.

The series of workshops I convened during the six years of the Embers of Empire project also presented the opportunity to engage with an extraordinary community of scholars. For taking the time to join us at one time (and venue) or another I must thank: Jocelyn Alexander, Casper Andersen, Clare Anderson, Sarah Ansari, Neal Ascherson, Jordanna Bailkin, Jennifer Ballantine-Perera, James Belich, Robert Bickers, Luke Blaxill, Elleke Boehmer, Elizabeth Buettner, Jodi Burkett, Antoinette Burton, Sebastian Conrad, John Darwin, Andrew Dilley, Katie Donnington, Richard Drayton, Saul Dubow, Andreas Eckert, Caroline Elkins, Mark Hampton, Peter Harder, Morten Heiberg, Philip Holden, Tony Hopkins, Stephen Howe, Ian Jack, Maya Jasanoff, Steven Jensen, Ravinder Kaur, Dane Kennedy, Michael Kenny, Yasmin Khan, Harshan Kumarasingham, Miles Larmer, Joanna Lewis, Charles Lock, Donal Lowry, John M. MacKenzie, Mark McKenna, Javed Majeed, Dirk Moses, Radhika Natarajan, Olivette Otele, Fintan O'Toole, Kennetta Hammond Perry, Simon Potter, Hilary Sapire, Camilla Schofield, Bill Schwarz, Jean Smith, Sarah Stockwell, Casper Sylvest, Nils Arne Sørensen, David Thackeray, Andrew Thompson, Richard Toye, Kim Wagner and Wendy Webster. For the abundance of good advice (including copious critical feedback on chapter drafts) as the project has evolved, I owe this group an enormous collective debt of gratitude. They cannot, of course, in any way be held responsible for whatever shortcomings remain.

Virtually all of the chapters have been presented as papers at seminars and conferences too numerous to list here, but three stand out as particularly consequential. An invitation from Zoë Laidlaw and Catherine Hall to present Chapter 14 at the 'Reconfiguring the British' seminar at London's Institute of Historical Research in October 2016 brought 'tough but fair' critique at just the right time, as well as the chance to meet Susan Pennybacker with whom I've kept up a valuable correspondence ever since. In May 2019, Dan Geary invited me to present Chapter 13 at a specially convened workshop at Trinity College Dublin. The written responses of Dan himself, as well as Eunan O'Halpin and Niall Ó Dochartaigh, were extremely useful and encouraging. Finally, the opportunity to be part of Erik Linstrum and Krishan Kumar's 'Decolonizing Britain' seminar series at the University of Virginia in autumn 2021 provided the perfect forum to test the foundations of the argument as a whole – just in time to pre-empt the final submission.

While I have resisted the temptation to pre-publish these chapters in article form, certain parts of the manuscript (and portions of some of the source material) have inevitably appeared elsewhere. The middle section of Chapter 6 was published in modified form as '"How Come England did not Know Me": The "Rude Awakenings" of the Windrush Era', in Christian D. Pedersen and Stuart Ward (eds.), *The Break-Up of Greater Britain* (Manchester University Press, 2021). Some of the Scottish material in Chapter 14 formed part of an early collaboration with Jimmi Østergaard Nielsen, published as '"Cramped and Restricted at Home": Scottish Separatism at Empire's End', *Transactions of the Royal Historical Society*, 25 (2015), pp. 159–85. Trace elements of Chapter 15 can also be found in my contribution ('The Redundant Dominion') to Matthew Hayday and Raymond Blake's first volume of *Celebrating Canada* (Toronto University Press, 2016), while a greatly condensed version of the argument in Chapter 11 appeared in the October 2017 edition of *Prospect Magazine*. Antoinette Burton's timely suggestion that I contribute an essay about J. G. A. Pocock to her 2021 'Intimations of Brexit' project (which appears as 'Machiavellian Moments and the Exigencies of Leaving', *Historical Reflections*, 47:2, Summer 2021, pp. 49–64) involved some cross-referencing with the opening salvo of Chapter 15. Sincere thanks are due to the editors and publishers of all five pieces for their invaluable cooperation.

Nearly a decade has passed since Michael Watson from Cambridge University Press walked up and introduced himself on an Edinburgh street, having heard that I was 'up to something' that might make for an interesting book. It was the beginning of an extremely fruitful working partnership that has endured through countless emails and meetings in the UK, the US and Denmark, from the initial proposal right down to the submission of the final manuscript. His capacity to see the overarching shape of a book before it emerges, respond swiftly to drafts, lend encouragement and criticism in equal measure – while somehow managing the bulging in-tray of a commissioning editor – has never ceased to impress, and I can only hope the end product is worthy of his patience and dedication to the process.

In the final stages of production, I found myself in the very capable and efficient hands of Ruth Boyes, Stephanie Taylor and Emily Plater at CUP who skilfully saw the book through to completion. I was particularly well-served by the copy-editing of Jan Baiton, whose attentive eye picked out any number of infelicities. It was also at this closing stage that I benefitted enormously from the response of two readers of the entire manuscript. Richard Toye generously took time out from his summer break to offer penetrating advice about the overarching design and structure of the book, particularly the opening sequence. And Andrew Thompson was an especially assiduous critic, providing extensive written feedback on each chapter, as well as invaluable assistance in distilling the main contours of the argument for the conclusion. I have made use of their insights to the best of my ability, and they can rest assured that the hours and effort they invested have been hugely appreciated.

Finally, on a personal note, this project has taken unreasonable amounts of time away from my family, for too many years. Now that 'the book' (as it became known, not always affectionately) is finally out of the way, it only remains to record my love and thanks to Lill, Oscar and Amelia for their understanding and forbearance, and to promise that the next one won't be quite so all-consuming.

Notes

INTRODUCTION

1. Mike Bartlett, *King Charles III*, Act II, Wyndham Theatre, 2014.
2. Tom Nairn, *The Break-Up of Britain: Crisis and Neo-Nationalism* (London: Verso, 1977).
3. Gwyn A. Williams, 'When was Wales?', BBC Wales Annual Radio Lecture, 12 November 1979, pp. 6–23 (repr. in G. A. Williams, *The Welsh in Their History* (London: Croom Helm, 1982), p. 190).
4. Linda Colley, *Britons: Forging the Nation, 1707–1837* (London: Vintage, 1996, 1st ed. 1992), pp. 395–6. See also her thoughts on why 'Britain is bound now to be under immense pressure', pp. 6–7.
5. See Ailsa Henderson and Richard Wyn Jones, *Englishness: The Political Force Transforming Britain* (Oxford: Oxford University Press, 2021). For just one recent example of 'Britishness' polling see *The Times*, 'Union in crisis as polls reveal voters want referendum on Scottish independence and united Ireland', 23 January 2021.
6. With titles ranging from the ominous to the cautiously optimistic. For a representative sample, see Peter Hitchens, *The Abolition of Britain* (London: Quartet Books, 1999); John Redwood, *The Death of Britain?* (London: Macmillan, 1999); Andrew Marr, *The Day Britain Died* (London: Profile Books, 2000); Tom Nairn, *After Britain: New Labour and the Return of Scotland* (London: Granta, 2000); Simon Heffer, *Nor Shall My Sword: The Reinvention of England* (London: Weidenfeld and Nicolson, 1999). The 'end of Britain tome' is borrowed from Stephen Moss's review of Marr and Nairn in *The Guardian*, 24 February 2000.
7. As exemplified by Nairn's *After Britain* and, in a different vein, Christopher Harvie's, *No Gods and Precious Few Heroes: Twentieth-Century Scotland* (Edinburgh: Edinburgh University Press, 2016, 1st ed. 1981).
8. Or, indeed, the recent surge of English nationalism as the driver of devolutionary pressures, as in Gavin Esler's invaluable *How Britain Ends: English Nationalism and the Rebirth of Four Nations* (London: Head of Zeus, 2021).
9. Alvin Jackson, *The Two Unions: Ireland, Scotland, and the Survival of the United Kingdom, 1707–2007* (Oxford: Oxford University Press, 2012), p. 342.
10. Janan Ganesh, 'A Bad Campaign is Not the Real Unionist Problem for Scotland', *Financial Times*, 8 September 2014.

11. Andrew Marr, 'Andrew Marr on the Imperilled State of the Union', *Prospect Magazine*, 26 February 2021.

12. Colley, *Britons*; J. G. A. Pocock, *The Discovery of Islands: Essays in British History* (Cambridge: Cambridge University Press, 2005); Raphael Samuel, 'Unravelling Britain' in *Island Stories*, vol. 2 (London: Verso, 1998); Krishan Kumar, *The Making of English National Identity* (Cambridge: Cambridge University Press, 2003); Norman Davies, *The Isles: A History* (London: Macmillan, 1999), especially p. 1053.

13. See, for example, Fintan O' Toole, *Heroic Failure: Brexit and the Politics of Pain* (London: Head of Zeus, 2018). On the persistent intrusions of the imperial past in the Brexit debate, see Stuart Ward and Astrid Rasch (eds.), *Embers of Empire in Brexit Britain* (London: Bloomsbury, 2019).

14. Andrew Gamble, 'A Union of Historic Compromise', in Mark Perryman (ed.), *Imagined Nation: England after Britain* (London: Lawrence and Wishart, 2008), p. 38. On the empire's 'disappearing act' in the historiography, see Stuart Ward, 'The Anatomy of Break-Up', in Christian Damm Pedersen and Stuart Ward (eds.), *The Break-Up of Greater Britain* (Manchester: Manchester University Press, 2021).

15. David Marquand, 'How United is the Modern United Kingdom?', in Alexander Grant and Keith J. Stringer (eds.), *Uniting the Kingdom? The Making of British History* (London: Routledge, 1995), pp. 287–8.

16. Charles W. Dilke, *Greater Britain: A Record of Travel in English-Speaking Countries during 1866 and 1867* (New York: Harper and Brothers, 1869, 1st ed. 1868).

17. The 'too soon' argument is well made by Keith Robbins, '"This Grubby Wreck of Old Glories": The United Kingdom and the End of the British Empire', *Journal of Contemporary History*, 15:1 (1980), pp. 81–95. The 'too late' side of the equation appears in T. M. Devine, 'The Break-up of Britain? Scotland and the End of Empire', *Transactions of the Royal Historical Society*, 16 (2006), pp. 163–80. For a critique of the latter, see Jimmi Østergaard Nielsen and Stuart Ward, 'Three Referenda and a By-Election: The Shadow of Empire in Devolutionary Politics', in John M. MacKenzie and Bryan Glass (eds.), *Scotland, Empire and Decolonisation in the Twentieth Century* (Manchester: Manchester University Press, 2015), pp. 204–9, 217–19.

18. Michael Hechter, *Internal Colonialism: The Celtic Fringe in British National Development, 1536–1966* (London: Routledge & Kegan Paul, 1975).

19. Marquand, 'How United is the Modern United Kingdom?', pp. 287–8. Tom Nairn was the first to develop a theory of the inherently imperial underpinnings of the British state in *The Break-Up of Britain* (and assorted essays in the *New Left Review*), though it is less clear whether he thought the idea of a British *people* could also be conceptualized in imperial terms.

20. John Darwin, *The Empire Project: The Rise and Fall of the British World-System, 1830–1970* (Cambridge: Cambridge University Press, 2009).

21. A. G. Hopkins, *American Empire: A Global History* (Princeton: Princeton University Press, 2018), p. 691 and see generally pp. 696–707.

22. Or Rosenboim, *The Emergence of Globalism: Visions of World Order in Britain and the United States, 1939–1950* (Princeton: Princeton University Press, 2017), pp. 1, 6–7 and ch. 4. See also Glenda Sluga, *Internationalism in the Age of Nationalism* (Philadelphia: University of Pennsylvania Press, 2013); Mark Mazower, *No Enchanted Palace: The End of Empire and the Ideological Origins of the United Nations* (Princeton: Princeton University Press, 2009).

23. Adom Getachew, *Worldmaking after Empire: The Rise and Fall of Self-Determination* (Princeton: Princeton University Press, 2019), p. 4; on the contingency of post-empire nation-building, see also Frederick Cooper, *Citizenship between Empire and Nation: Remaking France and French Africa, 1945–1960* (Princeton: Princeton University Press, 2014).

24. Timothy J. Hatton, 'Emigration from the UK, 1870–1913 and 1950–1998', *European Review of Economic History*, 8:2 (August 2004), pp. 149–71.

25. Simon Potter, *Broadcasting Empire: The BBC and the British World, 1922–1970* (Oxford: Oxford University Press, 2012), p. 146; A. James Hammerton and Alistair Thomson, *Ten Pound Poms: Australia's Invisible Migrants* (Manchester: Manchester University Press, 2005).

26. Charles Taylor, *Multiculturalism: The Politics of Recognition* (Princeton: Princeton University Press, 1995), pp. 36, 25, 32–3.

27. Stuart Hall with Bill Schwarz, *Familiar Stranger: A Life between Two Islands* (Durham, NC: Duke University Press, 2017), pp. 184–7. The term also appears in ch. 6 to refer to the way white Britons lumped all West Indians together as Jamaicans: 'just one instance of the misrecognitions in play', p. 165.

28. On this, see especially Susan Pennybacker, *From Scottsboro to Munich: Race and Political Culture in 1930s Britain* (Princeton: Princeton University Press, 2009); Marc Matera, *Black London: The Imperial Metropolis and Decolonization in the Twentieth Century* (Berkeley: University of California Press, 2015).

29. Erik Linstrum, *Age of Emergency: Living with Violence at the End of the British Empire* (Oxford: Oxford University Press, 2023), Introduction. See also Caroline Elkins' acclaimed *Legacy of Violence: A History of the British Empire* (New York: Knopf, 2022).

30. De-dominionization is Jim Davidson's term, see 'The De-Dominionisation of Australia', *Meanjin*, 38 (1979), pp. 139–53; Jim Davidson, 'De-Dominionisation Revisited', *Australian Journal of Politics and History*, 51 (2005), pp. 108–13.

31. Richard Bourke, 'Pocock and the Presuppositions of the New British History', *Historical Journal*, 53:3 (2010), pp. 747–70, 750, 754–5, 758, 762. Bourke labels this 'Ulsterization' – co-opting the British Government's declared policy after the closing of the Stormont Parliament at the height of the Northern Ireland 'Troubles' in the early 1970s but encompassing a much wider phenomenon – indeed, a 'generic feature of British imperial history' that could be traced across any number of historical settings. Though the high-stakes, hyper-loyalist example of Protestant Ulster seems ill-fitting as a general characterization, the recurring pattern of mutual misrecognition is crucial to understanding the broader dynamics at work. Trevor Burnard, for example, has borrowed Bourke's terminology to describe

how, as early as the 1750s, the white West Indian planter-oligarchy 'became the first in a long line of settler peoples of British descent to have their claims to Britishness denied by metropolitan opinion' (noting in passing that 'Ulsterization' might just as pertinently have been named after white Jamaicans). Trevor Burnard, 'Harvest Years? Reconfigurations of Empire in Jamaica, 1756–1807', *Journal of Imperial and Commonwealth History*, 40:4 (2012), pp. 533–55, 533, 550.

32. J. G. A. Pocock, 'British History: A Plea for a New Subject', *New Zealand Journal of History*, 8 (1974), pp. 3–21, 5.
33. Pocock, *Discovery of Islands*, p. ix; 'tangential identity' is from the 1973 lecture, 'Plea for a New Subject', p. 21.
34. Pocock, *Discovery of Islands*, p. 182.
35. Pocock, 'Plea for a New Subject', pp. 4–5.
36. Bourke, 'Presuppositions of the New British History', pp. 754, 758.
37. Eliga H. Gould, 'A Virtual Nation: Greater Britain and the Imperial Legacy of the American Revolution', *American Historical Review*, 104:2 (April 1999), pp. 476–89, 478, 482.
38. Bartlett, *King Charles III*.
39. See Sebastian Conrad's useful discussion of 'shifting scales' in *What is Global History?* (Princeton: Princeton University Press, 2016), pp. 132, 137.
40. 'Social self-worship' is borrowed from Ernest Gellner, *Nations and Nationalism* (Ithaca: Cornell University Press, 1983), p. 56.

1 OFFSHORE FORMATIONS: THE UNBEARABLE BANDWIDTH OF BEING BRITISH

1. Gordon T. Stewart, 'The Strange Case of Jute', in John M. MacKenzie and Bryan Glass (eds.), *Scotland, Empire and Decolonisation in the Twentieth Century* (Manchester: Manchester University Press, 2015), pp. 80–1. 'Cinderella of the Textile Industries' was the message delivered to the president of the Board of Trade, Stafford Cripps, when he visited in 1945, see p. 77. See also Gordon T. Stewart, *Jute and Empire* (Manchester: Manchester University Press, 1998); Jim Tomlinson, *Dundee and the Empire: Juteopolis 1850–1939* (Edinburgh: Edinburgh University Press, 2014).
2. Quoted in Tam Dalyell, *Devolution: The End of Britain?* (London: Jonathan Cape, 1977), p. 83.
3. Prior to 1970, the SNP had only fielded candidates in Dundee on three occasions (in 1945, 1952 and 1963), never polling more than 7.5 per cent in either of the town's two constituencies (subdivided into Dundee East and West in 1950). By the October 1974 general election, support had surged to 35 per cent in Dundee West and an extraordinary 47.7 per cent in Dundee East, more than enough to secure the seat for Party Leader Gordon Wilson who would hold it for the next thirteen years.

4. John Strachey, *The End of Empire* (London: Victor Gollancz, 1959), dustjacket and p. 7. It was also the first title in English ever to use that simple but evocative phrase to refer to the British empire.

5. Strachey, *End of Empire*, pp. 63, 66, 90, 96, 140, 154, 190, 215. On Strachey's conversion to Marxism, see Noel Thompson, *John Strachey: An Intellectual Biography* (Basingstoke: Macmillan, 1993).

6. Strachey, *End of Empire*, p. 154.

7. Strachey, *End of Empire*, p. 216.

8. Strachey, *End of Empire*, p. 204.

9. Strachey, *End of Empire*, pp. 214–15.

10. Max Beloff, *Imperial Sunset*, vol. 1: *Britain's Liberal Empire, 1897–1921* (London: Methuen, 1969), p. 19; Richard Price, *An Imperial War and the English Working Class* (London: Routledge and Kegan Paul, 1972), p. 241; James Morris, 'The Popularisation of Imperial History: The Empire on Television', *Journal of Imperial and Commonwealth History*, 1 (1973), pp. 113–18, 113.

11. A. J. P. Taylor, *English History, 1914–1945: The Oxford History of England*, vol. XV (Oxford: Oxford University Press, 1965), p. 600.

12. Peter Calvocoressi, *The British Experience, 1945–75* (London: Bodley Head, 1978), pp. 224–5.

13. At the risk of lumping quite different traditions and perspectives into the one basket, some representative examples include Bernard Porter, *The Absent-Minded Imperialists: What the British Really Thought about Their Empire* (Oxford: Oxford University Press, 2004); Ronald Hyam, *Britain's Declining Empire: The Road to Decolonisation, 1918–1968* (Cambridge: Cambridge University Press, 2006); P. J. Marshall, 'No Fatal Impact? The Elusive History of Imperial Britain', *Times Literary Supplement*, 12 March 1993; For my critique specifically of Porter, see Stuart Ward, 'Echoes of Empire', *History Workshop Journal*, 62 (2006), pp. 264–78.

14. David Edgerton, *The Rise and Fall of the British Nation: A Twentieth Century History* (London: Allen Lane, 2018). Edgerton is mainly concerned to minimize the significance of empire in the period after 1945 (allowing his national optics to emerge more clearly into view), leaving to one side as 'an open and debated question' the matter of whether this applied equally to earlier periods, p. 19.

15. Edgerton, *Rise and Fall*, pp. 26, 255, 286, 269.

16. Edgerton, *Rise and Fall*, pp. 316, 388, 9.

17. Edgerton, *Rise and Fall*, p. xxi.

18. Not that any neat counter-consensus has emerged, but for a representational sample, see Wendy Webster, *Englishness and Empire, 1939–65* (Oxford: Oxford University Press, 2005); Andrew S. Thompson, *The Empire Strikes Back?: The Impact of Imperialism on Britain from the Mid-Nineteenth Century* (Harlow: Longman, 2005); Bill Schwarz, *The White Man's World: Memories of Empire*, vol. 1 (Oxford: Oxford University Press, 2011); Jordanna Bailkin, *The Afterlife of Empire* (Berkeley: University of California Press, 2012); Camilla Schofield, *Enoch Powell*

and the Making of Postcolonial Britain (Cambridge: Cambridge University Press, 2013); Elizabeth Buettner, *Europe after Empire: Decolonization, Society and Culture* (Cambridge: Cambridge University Press, 2016); Sarah Stockwell, *The British End of the British Empire* (Cambridge: Cambridge University Press, 2018); Stephen Howe, 'Internal Decolonization? British Politics since Thatcher as Post-colonial Trauma', *Twentieth Century British History*, 14:3 (2003), pp. 286–304; Ezequiel Mercau, *The Falklands War: An Imperial History* (Cambridge: Cambridge University Press, 2019); Christian Damm Pedersen and Stuart Ward (eds.), *The Break-up of Greater Britain* (Manchester: Manchester University Press, 2021). For an early critique see Stuart Ward (ed.), *British Culture and the End of Empire* (Manchester: Manchester University Press, 2001), and for a more recent and more personal reflection, see Sathnam Sanghera, *Empireland: How Imperialism Has Shaped Modern Britain* (London: Viking, 2021). Much of this work arises out of the 'empire and metropolitan culture' paradigm pioneered in the 1980s by John M. MacKenzie's *Propaganda and Empire: The Manipulation of British Public Opinion, 1880–1960* (Manchester: Manchester University Press, 1984). Other key titles include John M. MacKenzie (ed.), *Imperialism and Popular Culture* (Manchester: Manchester University Press, 1986); Catherine Hall and Sonya O. Rose (eds.), *At Home with the Empire: Metropolitan Culture and the Imperial World* (Cambridge: Cambridge University Press, 2006); Andrew Thompson (ed.), *Britain's Experience of Empire in the Twentieth Century* (Oxford: Oxford University Press, 2012); Antoinette Burton, *Empire in Question: Reading, Writing and Teaching British Imperialism* (Durham, NC: Duke University Press, 2011).

19. See Krishan Kumar, *Visions of Empire: How Five Imperial Regimes Shaped the World* (Princeton: Princeton University Press, 2017), p. 321.

20. Strachey was unable to get the work published at the time, though his letters and pamphlets circulated widely (including one account of being shipwrecked in Bermuda that is generally credited as the inspiration for Shakespeare's *The Tempest*). The book finally appeared in print in the mid-nineteenth century: *The Historie of Travaile into Virginia Britannia* (London: Hakluyt Society, 1849), p. 4. The direct line of descent from John Strachey's great grandfather, Henry Strachey, to the author of *Virginia Travaile* is traced in *The Baronetage of England: Or the History of the English Baronets and such Baronets of Scotland as are of English Families*, vol. V. See Entry 469. 'Strachey of Sutton-Court Somersetshire' (London: E. Lloyd, 1805), pp. 431–3.

21. Malcolm Gaskill, *Between Two Worlds: How the English Became Americans* (Oxford: Oxford University Press, 2014), pp. 20–1.

22. Purchas, cited in David Armitage, *The Ideological Origins of the British Empire* (Cambridge: Cambridge University Press, 2000), p. 85.

23. Michael Drayton, 'To the Virginian Voyage', in *Poems of Michael Drayton: Edited with an Introduction by John Buxton*, vol. 1 (Cambridge MA: Harvard University Press, 1953), p. 123.

24. 'James I on the Union with Scotland, 1607', printed in J. R. Tanner, *Constitutional Documents on the Reign of James I, 1603–1625* (Cambridge: Cambridge University Press, 1960, 1st. ed. 1930), p. 35.

25. Jenny Wormald, 'The Creation of Britain: Multiple Kingdoms or Core and Colonies?', *Transactions of the Royal Historical Society*, 2 (1992), pp. 175–94, 184.

26. David Armitage, 'Literature and Empire', in Nicholas Canny (ed.), *The Oxford History of the British Empire*, vol. 1: *The Origins of Empire* (Oxford: Oxford University Press, 1998), pp. 111–12. Andrew Hadfield also underlines the classical resonance of Johnson's *Nova Britannia*: 'Britain's past can be repeated in the "New World" and a new Britain established there', see *Shakespeare, Spenser and the Matter of Britain* (London: Palgrave, 2004), p. 73.

27. Andrew Fitzmaurice notes how the English 'produced more literature promoting colonization in this period than any other European country', precisely because of the heavy demands of persuasion for a project with relatively little material backing from the state. Success 'rested upon bringing something unfamiliar together with something familiar' – in this instance the promise of building a 'new commonwealth' drawing on humanist ideals in which the intended audience would have been well versed. Fitzmaurice, *Humanism and America* (Cambridge: Cambridge University Press, 2003), pp. 8–9, 15.

28. Strachey, *Historie of Travaile*, pp. 24–5.

29. Armitage also shows how its entanglement in the dynastic struggles of the sixteenth century lent it a decidedly polemical edge, ill-suited to the aspirational language of civic idealism. See *Ideological Origins*, pp. 7–8 and especially ch. 2.

30. Armitage, *Ideological Origins*, pp. 57, 59, quoting the revised articles of the plantation of 1610 (among other early records). Emphasis in original. On the broader context, see especially Nicholas Canny, *Making Ireland British, 1580–1650* (Oxford: Oxford University Press, 2001).

31. Anthony Pagden, *Lords of All the World: Ideologies of Empire in Spain, Britain and France c.1500–c.1800* (New Haven: Yale University Press, 1995), p. 161.

32. Gaskill, *Between Two Worlds*, p. xi.

33. In contrast to French or Spanish counterparts in the Americas who had always been more tightly controlled, the thirteen colonies (and the slave plantations of the West Indies) were founded as private ventures by Royal Charter, fostering intense fealty to the monarch as distinct from the metropolitan legislature. See Pagden, *Lords of All the World*, especially ch. 5.

34. The indispensable authority remains John Brewer's *The Sinews of Power: War, Money and the English State 1688–1783* (London: Unwin Hyman, 1989).

35. The literature is vast but James Vernon, for example, stresses the enduring influence of the veneration of sacred constitutional principles in *Politics and the People: A Study in English Political Culture, c.1815–1867* (Cambridge: Cambridge University Press, 1993), p. 298.

36. Evan Gottlieb, *Feeling British: Sympathy and National Identity in Scottish and English Writing, 1707–1832* (Lewisburg: Bucknell University Press, 2007), p. 11.

37. Karin Bowie, *Public Opinion in Early Modern Scotland c. 1560–1707* (Cambridge: Cambridge University Press, 2020), pp. 228–36 (the Duke of Hamilton quoted on p. 187).

38. 'The Queen's Speech on Passing the Act of Union', 6 March 1707, in *Cobbett's Parliamentary History of England* (London: Bagshaw, 1810), p. 576.

39. Linda Colley, *Britons: Forging the Nation, 1707–1837* (London: Vintage, 1996).

40. Colley, *Britons*, pp. 4, 18. On Colley's reasons for having 'deliberately not written about Ireland', see p. 8.

41. Colley, *Britons*, pp. 10, 69–75, 94–105.

42. Colley, *Britons*, p. 130. The intensification of transatlantic British feeling in the light of the Seven Years War is persuasively developed in Eliga H. Gould's, *The Persistence of Empire: British Political Culture in the Age of the American Revolution* (Chapel Hill: University of North Carolina Press, 2000). Colley, too, addressed this theme more directly in her subsequent study, *Captives*, documenting how, from the mid-eighteenth century, the quickening flows of human and material exchange with the American colonies produced a clear affective response: 'this vast territory and all its complex dangers came to seem to Britons at home infinitely more real and absorbing'. See Linda Colley, *Captives: Britain, Empire and the World, 1600–1850* (London: Jonathan Cape, 2002), p. 161, ch. 7.

43. Colley, *Britons*, p. 137. John Robertson, 'Empire and Union: Two Concepts of the Early Modern European Political Order', in John Robertson (ed.), *A Union for Empire: Political Thought and the Union of 1707* (Cambridge: Cambridge University Press, 1995), p. 3.

44. Colin Kidd, *Subverting Scotland's Past: Scottish Whig Historians and the Creation of an Anglo-British Identity, 1689–c. 1830* (Cambridge: Cambridge University Press, 1993), pp. 1, 6–7, 206–7. Kidd qualifies this in the conclusion in terms of a 'dismal failure to construct a wholeheartedly "national" British identity *different in form from loyalty to crown or to Empire*' – seemingly acknowledging the existence of genuinely 'British' affinities but ascribing the 'failure' to their inability to attach squarely to a 'Four Nations' polity. See p. 272.

45. Ernest Gellner, *Nations and Nationalism* (Ithaca: Cornell University Press, 1983), p. 1. See also Chapter 1.

46. Jack P. Greene, 'Empire and Identity', in P. J. Marshall (ed.), *The Oxford History of the British Empire*, vol. III: *The Eighteenth Century* (Oxford: Oxford University Press, 1998), p. 215.

47. Josiah Tucker, Dean of Gloucester cathedral (1757), quoted in T. H. Breen, 'Ideology and Nationalism on the Eve of the American Revolution: Revisions Once More in Need of Revising', *Journal of American History*, 84: 1 (June 1997), pp. 13–39, 18.

48. Jack P. Greene, *Evaluating Empire and Confronting Colonialism in Eighteenth-Century Britain* (Cambridge: Cambridge University Press, 2013), p. xii.

49. Quoted in Gordon S. Wood, *The Americanization of Benjamin Franklin* (New York: Penguin, 2004), p. 150. On the similar indignities perceived by Jamaican

oligarchs, see Trevor Burnard, 'Harvest Years? Reconfigurations of Empire in Jamaica, 1756–1807', *Journal of Imperial and Commonwealth History*, 40:4 (2012), pp. 533–55, 543.

50. Granville Sharp, *A Declaration of the People's Natural Right to a Share in the Legislature, which is the Fundamental Principle of the British Constitution of State* (London: 1774), pp. 13–14.

51. Kathleen Wilson, *The Sense of the People: Politics, Culture and Imperialism in England, 1715–1785* (Cambridge: Cambridge University Press, 1998), p. 25.

52. Maya Jasanoff, *Edge of Empire: Lives, Culture, and Conquest in the East, 1750–1850* (New York: Alfred A. Knopf, 2005), p. 10.

53. Michael Zuckerman, 'Identity in British America: Unease in Eden', in Nicholas Canny and Anthony Pagden (eds.), *Colonial Identity in the Atlantic World* (Princeton: Princeton University Press, 1987), pp, 115–57, 115. Eliga Gould takes this a step further when he suggests that 'George III lost the greater part of his North American empire' because his colonial subjects 'had become so thoroughly "British" that they refused to sacrifice any of the rights of self-government enjoyed by their cousins on the European side of the Atlantic'. Eliga H. Gould, 'A Virtual Nation: Greater Britain and the Imperial Legacy of the American Revolution', *American Historical Review*, 104:2 (April 1999), pp. 476–89, 481.

54. Breen, 'Ideology and Nationalism', p. 39. See also Jack P. Greene, 'The American Revolution', *American Historical Review*, 105:1 (2000), pp. 93–102.

55. P. J. Marshall, 'A Nation Defined by Empire, 1755–1776', in Alexander Grant and Keith J. Stringer (eds.), *Uniting the Kingdom? The Making of British History* (London: Routledge, 1995), pp. 208–22, 220, 221.

56. Colley, *Britons*, p. 121.

57. Maya Jasanoff, *Liberty's Exiles: The Loss of America and the Remaking of the British Empire* (London: Harper Press, 2011).

58. Itself a 'jagged, broken and faltering move' rather than a clear demarcation line effective immediately upon the cessation of hostilities. See Stephen Conway, 'From Fellow-Nationals to Foreigners: British Perceptions of the Americans, circa 1739–1783', *The William and Mary Quarterly*, 59:1 (January 2002), pp. 65–100, 67.

59. J. G. A. Pocock, 'Empire, State and Confederation: The War of American Independence as a Crisis in Multiple Monarchy', in Robertson (ed.), *Union for Empire*, pp. 346–8.

60. See generally C. A. Bayly, *Imperial Meridian: The British Empire and the World, 1780–1830* (London: Longman, 1989).

61. C. A. Bayly, *The Birth of the Modern World, 1780–1914* (Oxford: Blackwell, 2004), pp. 6, 12. On the transformative impact of steam power in particular, see John Darwin, *Unlocking the World: Port Cities and Globalization in the Age of Steam, 1830–1930* (London: Allen Lane, 2020).

62. James Belich, *Replenishing the Earth: The Settler Revolution and the Rise of the Anglo-World, 1783–1939* (Oxford: Oxford University Press, 2009), pp. 4–5. The figure

of eight million migrants is from Eric Richards, *Britannia's Children: Emigration from England, Scotland, Wales and Ireland Since 1600* (London: Hambledon & London, 2004), p. 180. See also Kent Fedorowich and Andrew S. Thompson (eds.), *Empire, Migration and Identity in the British World* (Manchester: Manchester University Press, 2013).

63. James Belich, 'How Much Did Institutions Matter? Cloning Britain in New Zealand', in Jack P. Greene (ed.), *Exclusionary Empire: English Liberties Overseas, 1600–1900* (Cambridge: Cambridge University Press, 2010), pp. 248–68.

64. Peter Cochrane, *Colonial Ambition: Foundations of Australian Democracy* (Melbourne: Melbourne University Press, 2006), p. 221; Phillip A. Buckner, *The Transition to Responsible Government: British Policy in British North America, 1815–1850* (Westport: Greenwood Press, 1985), p. 8.

65. Overseas migration was, in effect, 'an extension of long distance internal migration' – a matter of degree rather than kind – and was frequently foreshadowed by one or more relocations elsewhere in Britain. Colin Pooley and Jean Turnbull, *Migration and Mobility in Britain since the Eighteenth Century* (London: Routledge, 1998), pp. 257, 276.

66. John Darwin, *The Empire Project: The Rise and Fall of the British World-System, 1830–1970* (Cambridge: Cambridge University Press, 2009), pp. 58–9, 47.

67. Jennifer Ridden, 'Britishness as an Imperial and Diasporic Identity: Irish Elite Perspectives, c. 1820–70s', in Peter Gray (ed.), *Victoria's Ireland?: Irishnesss and Britishness, 1837–1901* (Dublin: Four Courts Press, 2004), p. 89.

68. Belich, *Replenishing the Earth*, pp. 208, 460, 557. Many of these 'vectors' have been the subject of specialized studies, such as Simon Potter's work on the imperial circuitry of information and news. See Simon Potter, *News and the British World: The Emergence of an Imperial Press System, 1876–1922* (Oxford: Oxford University Press, 2003).

69. Joel Mokyr, *The Enlightened Economy: An Economic History of Britain, 1700–1850* (New Haven: Yale University Press, 2009), pp. 368–81.

70. Gary B. Magee and Andrew S. Thompson, *Empire and Globalisation: Networks of People, Goods and Capital in the British World, c. 1850–1914* (Cambridge: Cambridge University Press, 2010), pp. 166–7, 134.

71. Indigenous interactions with settler colonialism had multiple dimensions, with patterns of resistance overlapping with strategies of accommodation. See Zoë Laidlaw and Alan Lester (eds.), *Indigenous Communities and Settler Colonialism: Land Holding, Loss and Survival in an Interconnected World* (London: Palgrave Macmillan, 2015); Martin Daunton and Rick Halpern (eds.), *Empire and Others: British Encounters with Indigenous Peoples, 1600–1850* (Philadelphia: University of Pennsylvania Press, 1999).

72. Alan Lester, 'British Settler Discourse and the Circuits of Empire', *History Workshop Journal*, 54 (2002), pp. 25–48, 39.

73. Alan Lester, *Imperial Networks: Creating Identities in Nineteenth Century South Africa and Britain* (London: Routledge, 2001), p. 63.

74. *Sydney Morning Herald*, cited in Lester, 'British Settler Discourse', p. 33; and 31 January 1848, cited in C. D. Rowley, *The Destruction of Aboriginal Society*, vol. 1: *Aboriginal Policy and Practice* (Canberra: Australian National University Press, 1970), pp. 111, 113.

75. Lester, 'British Settler Discourse', p. 25; Alan Lester, 'Humanism, Race and the Colonial Frontier', *Transactions of the Institute of British Geographers*, 37:1 (2012), pp. 132–48, 140.

76. Catherine Hall, *Civilising Subjects: Metropole and Colony in the English Imagination, 1830–1867* (London: Polity, 2002), pp. 12, 20, 338, 440; See also Thomas Holt, *The Problem of Freedom: Race, Labor, and Politics in Jamaica and Britain, 1832–1938* (Baltimore: Johns Hopkins University Press, 1992). Kay Anderson views this as part of a deeper crisis of the human–nature distinction in classical humanism, which was sacrificed in order to 'dignify dispossession and all manner of subordinating practices' on settler–colonial frontiers – a signal moment she evocatively describes as 'a rattle in the cage of the anthropological machine that had tried to fix the ground and class of human "being"'. *Race and the Crisis of Humanism* (London: Routledge, 2007), pp. 200, 32.

77. Hall, *Civilising Subjects*, pp. 365, 368.

78. Quoted in Duncan Bell, *Reordering the World: Essays on Liberalism and Empire* (Princeton: Princeton University Press, 2016), p. 50; See also Rande W. Kostal, *A Jurisprudence of Power: Victorian Empire and the Rule of Law* (Oxford: Oxford University Press, 2005), p. 466.

79. Onur Ulas Ince, *Colonial Capitalism and the Dilemmas of Liberalism* (Oxford: Oxford University Press, 2018), p. 2. See also Uday Mehta, *Liberalism and Empire: A Study in Nineteenth-Century British Liberal Thought* (Chicago: University of Chicago Press, 1999).

80. *Pall Mall Gazette*, 1865, quoted in Kostal, *Jurispridence of Power*, p. 462.

81. Kostal, *Jurispridence of Power*, pp. 468, 20.

82. Quoted in Theodore Koditschek, *Liberalism, Imperialism, and the Historical Imagination: Nineteenth-Century Visions of a Greater Britain* (Cambridge: Cambridge University Press, 2011), p. 99.

83. Thomas R. Metcalf, *Ideologies of the Raj* (Cambridge: Cambridge University Press, 1995), pp. 199–200.

84. Jennifer Pitts, *A Turn to Empire: The Rise of Imperial Liberalism in Britain and France* (Princeton: Princeton University Press, 2005), pp. 250–1, 59–61.

85. Priyamvada Gopal, *Insurgent Empire: Anticolonial Resistance and British Dissent* (London: Verso, 2019), pp. 85–8. On Indigenous petitioning in the Victorian era, see, for example, Sarah Carter and Maria Nugent (eds.), *Mistress of Everything: Queen Victoria in Indigenous Worlds* (Manchester: Manchester University Press, 2016).

86. The theoretical literature is vast but for the former proposition, see, for example, Anthony D. Smith, *The Ethnic Origins of Nations* (Oxford: Blackwell, 1986); Adrian Hastings, *The Construction of Nationhood: Ethnicity, Religion and*

Nationalism (Cambridge: Cambridge University Press, 1997); the most complete statement of the 'modernist' conception of nationalism is Ernest Gellner's, *Nations and Nationalism* (Ithaca: Cornell University Press, 1983), but even more influential is Benedict Anderson's, *Imagined Communities: Reflections on the Origins and Spread of Nationalism* (London: Verso, 2006, 1st ed. 1983).

87. Neville Meaney, 'Britishness and Australia: Some Reflections', in Carl Bridge and Kent Fedorowich (eds.), *The British World: Diaspora, Culture and Identity* (London: Cass, 2003), pp. 121–35. The phrase, 'more British than the British' became commonplace from the late nineteenth century, ventured both as a measure of loyalty and, occasionally, by way of critique of colonial subservience. See, for example, 'Why Canada Is At War' by 'A Canadian', *The Quarterly Review*, 1916, p. 13.

88. John Kendle, *Federal Britain: A History* (London: Routledge, 1997), p. 37 and see the discussion of the staunch metropolitan foe of imperial federation, E. A. Freeman, on p. 50. See also Duncan Bell, *The Idea of Greater Britain: Empire and the Future of World Order, 1860–1900* (Princeton: Princeton University Press, 2007), pp. 15, 6.

89. Henry Parkes, 'Our Growing Australian Empire', *Choice Literature: A Monthly Magazine* (September–December 1883), pp. 281–6, 285. My emphasis.

90. *Brisbane Courier*, 17 May 1888.

91. The authority in question was none other than the prominent Liberal parliamentarian Charles Dilke, of whom more shortly. Quoted in Bell, *Greater Britain*, p. 15.

92. Quoted in Dermot Meleady, *Redmond: The Parnellite* (Cork: Cork University Press, 2008), p. 77.

93. Anderson, *Imagined Communities*, p. 7. Lorenzo Veracini proposes that Greater Britain be conceptualized as an 'isopolity', referring to 'a single political community joining separate jurisdictions' that enables 'the seamless transfer of people *and their rights* between separate polities'. His solution offers a means of reconciling nationalism's 'exclusive and demanding' precepts that do 'not easily accommodate double allegiances', because 'an isopolitical union allows one to be faithful to a *relationship*; one does not have to choose'. It also permits the equality of status that was so central to the myth of Greater Britain, challenging the imperial hierarchies of core and periphery. See Lorenzo Veracini, 'Isopolitics, Deep Colonizing, Settler Colonialism', *Interventions*, 13:2 (2011), pp. 171–89. Though theoretically ingenious, the label tends to impose an unhelpful degree of precision and exactitude that was never achieved by contemporaries, overlooking the perennial imperfections of Greater Britain and the persistence of imperial hierarchies, peripheries and inequalities that persisted within a theoretically liberal multi-polity.

94. Reginald Horsman, *Race and Manifest Destiny: The Origins of American Racial Anglo-Saxonism* (Cambridge, MA: Harvard University Press, 1981), ch. 4; Hall, *Civilising Subjects*, pp. 367–8; See also Duncan Bell, *Dreamworlds of Race: Empire and the Utopian Destiny of Anglo-America* (Princeton: Princeton University Press, 2021); Marilyn Lake, *Progressive New World: How Settler Colonialism and Transpacific Change Shaped American Reform* (Cambridge, MA: Harvard University Press, 2019).

95. Quoted in Schwarz, *White Man's World*, p. 79.

96. Quoted in S. R. Mehrotra, 'On the Use of the Term "Commonwealth"', *Journal of Commonwealth Political Studies*, 2:1 (1963), pp. 1–16, 4. Nicholas Mansergh, *The Commonwealth Experience*, vol. 1: *The Durham Report to the Anglo-Irish Treaty* (London: Macmillan, 1982), p. 21.

97. Dilke, *Greater Britain*, p. ix.

98. Dilke, *Greater Britain*, p. 67. On Dilke's surprising views about the United States and Canada, given his subsequent elevation as the oracle of a Greater Britain centred squarely on the British empire, see Dane Kennedy, 'The Dream of Greater Britain', in *Historical Reflections*, 47:2 (Summer 2021), pp. 105–17, 106–8.

99. Dilke, *Greater Britain*, p. 525.

100. J. R. Seeley, *The Expansion of England: Two Courses of Lectures* (London: Macmillan, 1891, 1st ed. 1883), pp. 11, 50, 72, 158–9. Seeley was equally enamoured of Dilke's 'Greater Britain' and was largely responsible for the rapid dissemination of the term in the 1880s and 1890s.

101. Seeley, *Expansion of England*, pp. 11, 301–2.

102. The 'British World' has jostled for prominence in recent decades alongside 'Britain and the World', 'Britannic Nationalism', 'Britishness Abroad', 'Imperial Citizenship' and 'British Race Patriotism' to name only a few contenders, all of which have been subjected to varying lines of critique. Prominent titles include works cited earlier by Darwin, Belich, MacGee and Thompson, as well as Carl Bridge and Kent Fedorowich (eds.), *The British World: Diaspora, Culture and Identity* (London: Cass, 2003); Phillip Buckner and R. Douglas Francis (eds.), *Rediscovering the British World* (Calgary: University of Calgary Press, 2005); Daniel Gorman, *Imperial Citizenship: Empire and the Question of Belonging* (Manchester: Manchester University Press, 2006); Kate Darian-Smith, Stuart Macintyre and Patricia Grimshaw (eds.), *Britishness Abroad: Transnational Movements and Imperial Cultures* (Melbourne: Melbourne University Press, 2007); Barry Crosbie and Mark Hampton (eds.), *The Cultural Construction of the British World* (Manchester: Manchester University Press, 2015). For a critique, see Tehila Sasson, James Vernon, Miles Ogborn, Priya Satia and Catherine Hall, 'Britain and the World: A New Field?', *Journal of British Studies*, 57 (October 2018), pp. 677–708; Rachel K. Bright and Andrew R. Dilley, 'After the British World', *The Historical Journal*, 60:2 (2017) pp. 547–68.

103. As Catherine Hall terms it in *Civilising Subjects*, p. 437.

104. Dilke, *Greater Britain*, p. ix.

105. Andrew S. Thompson, 'The Languages of Loyalism in Southern Africa, c. 1870–1939', *English Historical Review*, cxviii (2003), pp. 617–50, 635.

106. Donal Lowry, 'The Crown, Empire Loyalism and the Assimilation of non-British White Subjects in the British World: An Argument Against "Ethnic Determinism"', in Bridge and Fedorowich, *The British World*, pp. 96–120.

107. See the renowned Canadian historian's reflections on his childhood quoted in Phillip Buckner, 'The Long Goodbye: English Canadians and the British World', in Buckner and Francis (eds.), *Rediscovering the British World*, pp. 181–208, 191.

108. On the settler colonies as sites where 'Four Nations' affinities were consolidated, see John M. MacKenzie, 'Irish, Scottish, Welsh and English Worlds? The Historiography of a Four-Nations Approach to the History of the British Empire', in Catherine Hall and Keith McClelland (eds.), *Race, Nation and Empire: Making Histories, 1750 to the Present* (Manchester: Manchester University Press, 2010), pp. 133–53; John M. MacKenzie with Nigel Dalziel, *The Scots in South Africa: Ethnicity, Identity, Gender and Race, 1772–1914* (Manchester: Manchester University Press, 2012).

109. Harrison's 1898 essay 'A Word for England' is quoted in Georgios Varouxakis, '"Great" Versus "Small" Nations: Size and National Greatness in Victorian Political Thought', in Duncan Bell (ed.), *Victorian Visions of Global Order: Empire and International Relations in Nineteenth-Century Political Thought* (Cambridge: Cambridge University Press, 2007), pp. 136–58, 149.

110. Bell, *Greater Britain*, p. 24. He cited Edward Said as the main foil for his argument, but he might also have included Linda Colley's 'Britishness and Otherness: An Argument', *Journal of British Studies*, 31:4 (October 1992), pp. 309–29.

111. Seeley, *Expansion of England*, p. 109.

112. Dilke, *Greater Britain*, p. 384.

113. Darwin, *Empire Project*, p. 178.

114. Seeley, *Expansion of England*, pp. 11, 50–1. Dilke also ventured the possibility that at some point in the future 'when the connection rests mainly upon sentiment, it may still last indefinitely'. Charles Dilke, *Problems of Greater Britain*, vol. I (London: Macmillan, 1890), p. 274.

115. Lytton Strachey, *Eminent Victorians* (London: Continuum edition, 2002, 1st ed. 1918), p. 3.

116. Strachey, *Eminent Victorians*, p. 3.

117. See Vernon's contribution to Sasson et al., 'Britain and the World', p. 691.

2 THE LIMITS OF LOCATION: GREATER BRITAIN

1. Local historians have also noted the rapid surge of industry along the waterfront on both the Coal Harbour and False Creek sides of the city, 'alienating Vancouverites from their connections with the water and even the precious view of the mountains'.

See Vancouver Historical Society, 'The Story of Vancouver', www.vancouver-historical-society.ca/blog/introduction/iii-vancouver's-economic-and-commercial-development/.

2. Norbert MacDonald, 'A Critical Growth Cycle for Vancouver, 1900–1914', *BC Studies*, 17 (Spring 1973), pp. 26–42, 28–9. Europeans other than British accounted for some 10 per cent, while a smaller contingent from China and Japan amounted to around 3 per cent of the emigrant intake.

3. R. E. Gosnell, 'A Greater Britain on the Pacific', *Westward Ho! Magazine*, 2:1 (January 1908), pp. 7–12. Available at https://issuu.com/showbc/docs/westward_ho_-_british_columbia_magazine_1908_jan_v. See also W. Peter Ward, *White Canada Forever: Popular Attitudes and Public Policy Toward Orientals in British Columbia* (Montreal and Kingston: McGill-Queen's University Press, 2002, 1st ed. 1978), p. 93.

4. Norbert MacDonald, 'Population Growth and Change in Seattle and Vancouver, 1880–1960', *Pacific Historical Review*, 39:3 (August 1970), pp. 297–321. MacDonald noted the high proportion of British-born mayors, lawyers and company executives, their influence 'so pervasive, long standing, and taken for granted that there has been very little scholarly investigation of it', p. 312.

5. MacDonald, 'Growth Cycle for Vancouver', p. 42.

6. Quoted in Hugh J. M. Johnston, *The Voyage of the Komagata Maru: The Sikh Challenge to Canada's Colour Bar* (Vancouver: UBC Press, 2014, 1st ed. 1989), p. 72.

7. Then, as later, 'the line on the map . . . presented no real containment'. See Grechen Poiner and Sybil Jack (eds.), *Limits of Location: Creating a Colony* (Sydney: Sydney University Press, 2007), pp. 9–10.

8. Alan Atkinson, 'Conquest', in Deryck M. Schreuder and Stuart Ward (eds.), *Australia's Empire* (Oxford: Oxford University Press, 2008), pp. 37–9.

9. Catherine Hall, *Civilising Subjects: Metropole and Colony in the English Imagination, 1830–1867* (London: Polity, 2002), p. 20.

10. Anjali Gera Roy underlines the distinction: as far as 'movements triggered by imperial policies and agendas' were concerned, Sikhs and other South Asian peoples were frequently relied upon as beneficial recruits to the imperial cause. But when it came to 'movements initiated by himself, the Sikh was resignified as hostile stranger', in need of meticulous regulation. Anjali Gera Roy, 'Making and Unmaking of Strangers: The *Komagata Maru* Episode and the Alienation of Sikhs as Undesirable Aliens', *Sikh Formations: Religion, Culture, Theory*, 12:1 (2016), pp. 67–86, 68.

11. Antoinette Burton, *At the Heart of the Empire: Indians and the Colonial Encounter in Late-Victorian Britain* (Berkeley: University of California Press, 1999).

12. Canadian Labour Minister, Rodolphe Lemieux, quoted in Ward, *White Canada Forever*, p. 75.

13. Quoted in Johnston, *Voyage of the Komagata Maru*, p. 5.

14. T. R. E. McInnes, son of a former lieutenant governor who had been commissioned by the Federal Interior Ministry to conduct a secret investigation into the Vancouver riots, quoted in Marilyn Lake and Henry Reynolds, *Drawing the Global Colour Line: White Men's Countries and the Question of Racial Equality* (Melbourne: Melbourne University Press, 2008), p. 185. The specific concern was that British Columbians might seek to throw in their lot with their equally Asia-averse neighbours on the US Pacific Coast. See also John Price, *Orienting Canada: Race, Empire, and the Transpacific* (Vancouver: UBC Press, 2011).

15. Kirt Niergarth, '"This Continent Must Belong to the White Races": William Lyon Mackenzie King, Canadian Diplomacy and Immigration Law, 1908', *International History Review*, 32:4 (December 2010), pp. 599–617, 611.

16. Johnston, *Voyage of the Komagata Maru*, pp. 44–52.

17. Quoted in Johnston, *Voyage of the Komagata Maru*, pp. 66, 72.

18. See, for example, local parliamentarian H. H. Stevens to Borden, 6 July 1914, Borden Papers, MG 26, H1(a), Vol. 40, 17286–17949, Library and Archives Canada (hereafter LAC).

19. *Vancouver Sun*, 'Government Asked to Send an Armed Force to Vancouver', 23 June 1914.

20. Henri-Marc Ami to British Columbian Premier Sir William McBride, 29 March 1914, McBride Papers, MS-0347, British Columbia Archives, Victoria. Emphasis in original. Ami had for thirty years been a prominent member of the Geological Survey of Canada, itself an instrument of colonization in documenting the vast extent of the terrain under white Canadian sovereignty.

21. Telegram from Passengers of the *Komagata Maru* to the Canadian Governor-General, the Duke of Connaught, 13 July 1914, Borden Papers, MG 26, H1(a), Vol. 40, 17286–17949, LAC.

22. Quoted in Johnston, *Voyage of the Komagata Maru*, p. 135. The UK secretary of state for the colonies, Lewis Harcourt, also gently raised the 'possibility of compassionate grant to British Indian subjects who have been misled by promoters of voyage' in correspondence with the Canadian Governor-General, 16 July 1914, Sir Robert Borden Papers, MG 26, H1(a), Vol. 40, 17286–17949, LAC.

23. The order regarding guns seems not to have come from Ottawa, with Borden urgently cabling: 'Do not understand ... reference to use of ship's guns, and cannot conceive how use could possibly become necessary ... absolutely opposed to so extreme a measure.' Borden to Martin Burrell, 21 July 1914, Borden Papers, MG 26, H1(a), Vol. 40, 17286–17949, LAC.

24. Martin Burrell to Borden, 21 July 1914, Borden Papers, MG 26, H1(a), Vol. 40, 17286–17949, LAC.

25. Baba Gurdit Singh, *Voyage of Komagatamaru or India's Slavery Abroad* (Calcutta: The Compiler, 1928), p. 107.

26. Twenty passengers were given permission to land upon submitting evidence of prior residence in British Columbia.
27. Renisa Mawani, *Across Oceans of Law: The* Komagata Maru *and Jurisdiction in the Time of Empire* (Durham, NC: Duke University Press, 2018), pp. 132–5.
28. Mawani, *Oceans of Law*, p. 137.
29. It did, however, lead to tragic consequences for the *Komagata Maru* – now a 'marked ship' that received a hostile reception at every port, culminating in a violent showdown on its return to Bengal in late September that resulted in the death of twenty passengers at the so-called 'Budge Budge Riot'. See Johnston, *Voyage of the Komagata Maru*, ch. 10 ('marked ship' on p. 148; casualty figures p. 161).
30. Lake and Reynolds, *Global Colour Line*, Introduction, p. 4. The term is an adaptation from the contemporary critique of the Black American intellectual W. E. B. Dubois.
31. Mawani, *Oceans of Law*, p. 30.
32. Ali Kazimi, *Undesirables: White Canada and the Komagata Maru – An Illustrated History* (Vancouver: Douglas and McIntyre, 2012), p. 6.
33. It goes unmentioned in Andrew Thompson and Martin Thomas (eds.), *The Oxford Handbook of the End of Empire* (Oxford: Oxford University Press, 2018), to name but one example; the same applies to studies more specifically focused on the period such as Pankaj Mishra's *From the Ruins of Empire: The Revolt against the West and the Remaking of Asia* (London: Allen Lane, 2012) as well as Lake and Reynolds's *Global Colour Line*. On the inadequacy of Canadian national paradigms see Rita Kaur Dhamoon, Davina Bhandar, Renisa Mawani and Satwinder Kaur Bains (eds.), *Unmooring the* Komagata Maru*: Charting Colonial Trajectories* (Vancouver: UBC Press, 2019).
34. This fascinating piece was unearthed by Mawani in *Oceans of Law*, pp. 116–17.
35. On the elaborate stage-managing and 'street theatre' of these events, see Daniel Jackson, *Popular Opposition to Irish Home Rule in Edwardian Britain* (Liverpool: Liverpool University Press, 2009).
36. Quoted in Ronald McNeill, *Ulster's Stand for the Union* (London: John Murray, 1922), p. 80.
37. See Ronan Fanning, *Fatal Path: British Government and Irish Revolution, 1910–22* (London: Faber & Faber, 2013), pp. 109–14. Jackson mounts a convincing argument that these sympathies were not confined to the British Army but were anchored in wider reservoirs of public sympathy. Jackson, *Popular Opposition*.
38. Robert Blake, *The Unknown Prime Minister: The Life and Times of Andrew Bonar Law, 1858–1923* (London: Eyre & Spottiswoode, 1955), p. 97.
39. On Bonar Law's 'unrelenting Ulsterization of the Home Rule struggle', see Thomas C. Kennedy, 'Troubled Tories: Dissent and Confusion Concerning the Party's Ulster Policy, 1910–1914', *Journal of British Studies*, 46:3 (July 2007), pp. 570–93, 571.

40. Quoted in Ian S. Lustick, *Unsettled States, Disputed Lands: Britain and Ireland, France and Algeria, Israel and the West Bank-Gaza* (Ithaca: Cornell University Press, 1993), p. 202.
41. Quoted in Kennedy, 'Troubled Tories', p. 579.
42. Thomas Bartlett, *Ireland: A History* (Cambridge: Cambridge University Press, 2010), p. 368.
43. See Alvin Jackson, *Home Rule: An Irish History, 1800–2000* (Oxford: Oxford University Press, 2003), pp. 32–5.
44. A. T. Q. Stewart, *The Ulster Crisis: Resistance to Home Rule, 1912–14* (Belfast: Blackstaff Press, 1997), p. 55.
45. Bill Schwarz, 'Forgetfulness: England's Discontinuous Histories', in Stuart Ward and Astrid Rasch (eds.), *Embers of Empire in Brexit Britain* (London: Bloomsbury, 2019), p. 53.
46. Richard Bourke, 'Pocock and the Presuppositions of the New British History', *Historical Journal*, 53:3 (2010), pp. 747–70, 750.
47. Quoted in McNeill, *Ulster's Stand*, p. 91.
48. Historians have tended to stress Bonar Law's Coleraine origins rather than the equally crucial Canadian connection. See, for example, Nicholas Mansergh, *The Unresolved Question: The Anglo-Irish Settlement and Its Undoing, 1912–72* (New Haven: Yale University Press, 1991), pp. 77–8; Jackson, *Home Rule*, pp. 116–18.
49. Recollections of veteran Canadian journalist Beverley Baxter, who later followed Bonar Law into the UK House of Commons as a Conservative MP: 'The Passing of Bonar Law', *McLean's Magazine*, July 1921, p. 50. Baxter depicted a devout 'son of the Manse' who 'never renounced his loyalty to the land of his birth'. On Bonar Law's intimate friendship with Beaverbrook, see Anne Chisholm and Michael Davie, *Beaverbrook: A Life* (London: Pimlico, 1993), pp. 71–6.
50. Chisholm and Davie, *Beaverbrook*, pp. 71–6.
51. Bonar Law, speech at Leeds, December 1911: www.britishpoliticalspeech.org/speech-archive.htm?speech=79.
52. An item in the *Montreal Gazette* in 2008 took exception to this, mounting a case for Bonar Law's 'Canadian' credentials with mock indignation. See 'The Forgotten PM from Canada', 16 September 2008, https://montrealgazette.com/news/the-forgotten-pm-from-canada.
53. W. L. Dence, County Secretary, Vancouver LOL to H. H. Stevens, MP, undated, 1914, Borden Papers, MG 26, H1(a), Vol. 40, 17286–17949, LAC.
54. J. R. Seeley, *The Expansion of England: Two Courses of Lectures* (London: Macmillan, 1891, 1st ed. 1883), pp. 158–9; Charles W. Dilke, *Greater Britain: A Record of Travel in English-Speaking Countries during 1866 and 1867* (New York: Harper and Brothers, 1869, 1st ed. 1868), p. ix.
55. Exceptions apply due to the inevitable imprecision of imperial language generally, where Greater Britain was occasionally tossed out as a synonym for the entire empire. But as Duncan Bell affirms, though alternative 'modulations

circulated widely, the most frequent usage was in reference to the settler colonies'. Duncan Bell, *The Idea of Greater Britain: Empire and the Future of World Order, 1860–1900* (Princeton: Princeton University Press, 2007), p. 7.

56. Bell, *Idea of Greater Britain*, p. 24.

57. Bell, *Idea of Greater Britain*, pp. 25, 63, 65.

58. Bell, *Idea of Greater Britain*, p. 119.

59. On the latter see John C. Mitcham, *Race and Imperial Defence in the British World* (Cambridge: Cambridge University Press, 2016), especially ch. 7.

60. Bell, *Idea of Greater Britain*, p. 30. Seeley quoted p. 111.

61. Quoted in Douglas Cole, '"The Crimson Thread of Kinship": Ethnic Ideas in Australia, 1870–1914', *Historical Studies*, 14:56 (April 1971), pp. 511–25, 515–16.

62. Lake and Reynolds, *Global Colour Line*, pp. 118–19.

63. Diary entry, 28 June 1883, quoted in Graeme Powell, 'A Diarist in the Cabinet: Lord Derby and the Australian Colonies, 1882–85', *Australian Journal of Politics and History*, 51:4 (2005), pp. 489–90.

64. Roger C. Thompson, *Australian Imperialism in the Pacific: The Expansionist Era, 1820–1920* (Melbourne: Melbourne University Press, 1980), p. 92.

65. Bill Schwarz, *The White Man's World: Memories of Empire*, vol. 1 (Oxford: Oxford University Press, 2011), pp. 65–6.

66. Schwarz, *White Man's World*, p. 66.

67. Seeley, *Expansion of England*, pp. 296, 302. On the problem of reconciling British India with liberal convictions, see Thomas R. Metcalf, *Ideologies of the Raj* (Cambridge: Cambridge University Press, 1995), pp. 199–200, 231.

68. Quoted in J. Lee Thompson, *A Wider Patriotism: Alfred Milner and the British Empire* (London: Pickering and Chatto, 2007), p. 4.

69. Quoted in Schwarz, *White Man's World*, p. 95.

70. P. J. Marshall, *'A Free though Conquering People': Eighteenth-Century Britain and Its Empire* (Aldershot: Ashgate, 2003).

71. On the conviction that Greater Britain could defy historical gravity and 'attain permanence, a kind of historical grace', see Duncan Bell, 'Escape Velocity: Ancient History and the Empire of Time', in Duncan Bell, *Reordering the World: Essays on Liberalism and Empire* (Princeton: Princeton University Press, 2016), p. 121.

72. Bell, *Idea of Greater Britain*, p. 115. Schwarz points out how Dilke himself was an exception in this regard, expounding at length on colonial violence against Indigenous peoples as 'the inevitable function of the expansion of "Saxondom"'. But he attributes this to the fact that Dilke was writing 'at an earlier moment when the violent conquest of native peoples was still in progress'. By the end of the century, Indigenous peoples had become relegated to an amnesia-inducing invisibility. Schwarz, *White Man's World*, p. 76.

73. Seeley, *Expansion of England*, p. 50. Seeley did, however, make a point of excluding India from his frame of reference by virtue of racial difference.

74. Quoted in Lake and Reynolds, *Global Colour Line*, pp. 122, 119–20.

75. R. A. Huttenback, 'The British Empire as a "White Man's Country": Racial Attitudes and Immigration Legislation in the Colonies of White Settlement', *Journal of British Studies*, 13:1 (November 1973), pp. 108–37, 109.
76. Lake and Reynolds, *Global Colour Line*, pp. 119–20, 122, 124. *Natal Mercury* quoted p. 120.
77. H. Kumarasingham, 'The Historical Constitution', in Peter Cain and H. Kumarasingham (eds.), *The Cambridge Constitutional History of the United Kingdom*, vol. 1 (Cambridge: Cambridge University Press, 2023).
78. Cited in Robert A. Huttenback, 'Racism and Imperialism in the Antipodes', *Southeast Asia Series*, 19:2 (January 1971), pp. 1–15, 3.
79. Kumarasingham, 'Historical Constitution'.
80. Cited in Huttenback, 'Racism and Imperialism', p. 8.
81. Lake and Reynolds, *Global Colour Line*, p. 128.
82. McBride to Digby Denham, Premier of Queensland, 19 September 1914, McBride Papers, MS-0347, British Columbia Archives, Victoria.
83. Keith Thomas, quoted in Kumarasingham, 'Historical Constitution'; see generally James Vernon, *Politics and the People: A Study in English Political Culture, c.1815–1867* (Cambridge: Cambridge University Press, 1993).
84. Kumarasingham, 'Historical Constitution'. See also H. Kumarasingham, 'Constitution and Empire', in Peter Cain and H. Kumarasingham (eds.), *The Cambridge Constitutional History of the United Kingdom*, vol. 2 (Cambridge: Cambridge University Press, 2023).
85. To paraphrase Seeley, *Expansion of England*, pp. 296, 302.
86. Quoted in Lake and Reynolds, *Global Colour Line*, p. 232.
87. The quote is from the Australian-born advocate of imperial federation Francis Labilliere in the early 1880s, who insisted that 'if the British Empire is to be one nation, we must not talk of Canadian nationality, or Australian nationality, or South African nationality'. Quoted in Margaret A. Banks, *Sir John George Bourinot: Victorian Canadian* (Montreal and Kingston: McGill-Queen's University Press, 2001), p. 84.
88. Quoted in Deryck Schreuder, 'The Making of the Idea of Colonial Nationalism', in John Eddy and Deryck Schreuder (eds.), *The Rise of Colonial Nationalism* (Oxford: Oxford University Press, 1988), p. 84.
89. Jebb's 'Britannic Alliance' never caught on; nor did he achieve a following for his valiant attempt to impose semantic consistency by confining 'British' to 'things appertaining to Britain, or the United Kingdom', as distinct from 'Imperial' for the entire empire, with the suitably grand adjective 'Britannic' reserved for 'the autonomous States of the Empire, viz. Britain, Canada, Australia, New Zealand, South Africa and Newfoundland'. See Richard Jebb, *The Britannic Question: A Survey of Alternatives* (London: Longmans, Green & Co., 1913), pp. 15–16.
90. Daniel Gorman, *Imperial Citizenship: Empire and the Question of Belonging* (Manchester: Manchester University Press, 2006), quoting Buchan's *A Lodge in the Wilderness* (1906), p. 78.

91. See especially Caspar Hirschi, *The Origins of Nationalism: An Alternative History from Ancient Rome to Early Modern Germany* (Cambridge: Cambridge University Press, 2012), p. 28.

92. See Neville K. Meaney, *A History of Australian Defence and Foreign Policy,* vol. I: *The Search for Security in the Pacific* (Sydney: Sydney University Press, 1976), pp. vii–viii, 6; Douglas Cole made a similar case for Canada in 'The Problem of "Nationalism" and "Imperialism" in British Settlement Colonies', *Journal of British Studies,* 10:2 (May 1971), pp. 160–82.

93. Schwarz, *White Man's World,* ch. 1, pp. 397–99, 61.

94. Schwarz notes that despite Dilke's perspective as 'a self-professed radical', his conception of Greater Britain 'depended more on his concept of race than it did on his regard for the traditional practices of English constitutionalism'. Schwarz, *White Man's World,* p. 72.

95. Schwarz, *White Man's World,* pp. 83, 102.

96. Gurdit Singh, *Voyage of Komagatamaru,* p. 103. Emphasis added.

97. Gurdit Singh, *Voyage of Komagatamaru,* pp. 1, 2, 5, 108, 125.

98. Schwarz, *White Man's World,* p. 105.

3 'BRITISH WITH A SMALL "B"': THE IMPRESS OF INTERNATIONALISM

1. *From the Four Corners* (1941); 35mm b&w, Australian War Memorial, Acc. F01475, www.awm.gov.au/collection/F01475. Sincere thanks to Richard Toye for drawing my attention to this source.

2. On the remarkably deliberate and frequently disingenuous 'inclusiveness' of official imperial messaging during the Second World War in order to 'create a good impression' in the colonial empire, see Wendy Webster, *Mixing It: Diversity in World War Two Britain* (Oxford: Oxford University Press, 2018), ch. 3, pp. 110–11.

3. Glenda Sluga, quoting C. A. Bayly in 'The Transnational History of International Institutions', *Journal of Global History,* 6 (2011), pp. 219–22, 219. See especially Glenda Sluga, *Internationalism in the Age of Nationalism* (Philadelphia: University of Pennsylvania Press, 2013); Akira Iriye, *Cultural Internationalism and World Order* (Baltimore: Johns Hopkins Press, 2000).

4. Or Rosenboim, *The Emergence of Globalism: Visions of World Order in Britain and the United States, 1939–1950* (Princeton: Princeton University Press, 2017), pp. 3–4.

5. James Belich, *Replenishing the Earth: The Settler Revolution and the Rise of the Anglo-World, 1783–1939* (Oxford: Oxford University Press, 2009), p. 460.

6. Mosley was not principally concerned with the Dilkean inflections of the term, but see Evan Smith, 'The Pivot of Empire: Australia and the Imperial Fascism of the British Union of Fascists', *History Australia,* 14:3 (2017), pp. 378–94.

7. Duncan Bell, *The Idea of Greater Britain: Empire and the Future of World Order, 1860–1900* (Princeton: Princeton University Press, 2007), pp. 19, 264.

8. W. K. Hancock, *The Modern Map* (Oxford: Oxford University Press, 1941), pp. 44–8. Hancock's conceptualization derived from University of London Professor of Education, Sir Fred Clarke's, '"British" with a Small "b"', *The Nineteenth Century and After*, 119:710 (April 1936), pp. 428–39. Clarke's small 'b' Britishness was later warmly endorsed by the Canadian historian Frank Underhill (discussed later in Chapter 11) in the mid-1950s, distinguishing between 'large B' manifestations such as the Monarchy, the peerage and the BBC, and *Britannia Rules the Waves*, while reserving small 'b' Britishness for 'the long tradition of the freedom and dignity of the individual, the habit of reaching decisions by discussion, the spirit of toleration, the flair for compromise, a sense of limits, social solidarity, the independence of the judiciary, a free press, free political parties, free churches, free trade unions'. See R. Douglas Francis, 'Historical Perspectives on Britain: The Ideas of Canadian Historians Frank H. Underhill and Arthur R. M. Lower', in Philip P. Buckner and R. Douglas Francis (eds.), *Canada and the British World: Culture, Migration and Identity* (Vancouver: UBC Press, 2006), pp. 309–21, 319–20. See also Jim Davidson, *A Three-Cornered Life: The Historian, W. K. Hancock* (Sydney: UNSW Press, 2010), pp. 271, 277.
9. Bell, *The Idea of Greater Britain*, p. 92.
10. H. Duncan Hall, *Commonwealth: A History of the British Commonwealth of Nations* (London: Van Nostrand Rheinhold, 1971), p. 26.
11. See W. David McIntyre, 'The Strange Death of Dominion Status', *Journal of Imperial and Commonwealth History*, 27:2 (May 1999), pp. 193–212, 194.
12. Hall, *Commonwealth*, p. 4. The name itself is generally attributed to Lord Rosebery, who as early as 1884 had declared in the Adelaide Town Hall: 'There is no need for any nation, however great, leaving the Empire, because the Empire is a commonwealth of Nations.' But it would take several decades for the term to catch on. Quoted in S. R. Mehrotra, 'On the Use of the Term "Commonwealth"', *Journal of Commonwealth Political Studies*, 2:1 (1963), p. 4.
13. See Mark Mazower, *No Enchanted Palace: The End of Empire and the Ideological Origins of the United Nations* (Princeton: Princeton University Press, 2013), ch. 2.
14. Curtis to J. S. Ewart, 7 May 1941, quoted in 'Official Title of the Commonwealth', 23 October 1948, CAB21/1815, The National Archives, Kew (hereafter NA).
15. Smuts was even congratulated in some quarters for putting 'the lid on Messers Lionel Curtis & Co.', see Saul Dubow, 'The Commonwealth and South Africa: From Smuts to Mandela', *Journal of Imperial and Commonwealth History*, 45:2 (2017), pp. 284–314, 290.
16. Quoted in 'Official Title of the Commonwealth', 23 October 1948, CAB21/1815, NA.
17. Quoted in Thomas R. Metcalf, *Ideologies of the Raj* (Cambridge: Cambridge University Press, 1995), p. 223.
18. William Redmond, quoted in John Darwin, *The Empire Project: The Rise and Fall of the British World-System, 1830–1970* (Cambridge: Cambridge University Press, 2009), p. 255.

19. Hall, *Commonwealth*, pp. 196–7.
20. Both Zimmern and Curtis, for example, lent their insights to the formation of the League of Nations, see Dubow, 'Commonwealth and South Africa', p. 286. On Curtis's conception of the Commonwealth as the 'Sermon on the Mount' inscribing the 'moral and political building block for a new federal and democratic world order', see Rosenboim, *Emergence of Globalism*, pp. 107–14.
21. The Rt. Hon J. C. Smuts, 20 June 1921, in Arthur Berriedale Keith (ed.), *Speeches and Documents of the British Dominions, 1918–1931: From Self-Government to National Sovereignty* (Oxford: Oxford University Press, 1961, 1st ed. 1932), p. 58.
22. Susan Pedersen, *The Guardians: The League of Nations and the Crisis of Empire* (Oxford: Oxford University Press, 2015), pp. 4–5. See also Daniel Gorman, *The Emergence of International Society in the 1920s* (Cambridge: Cambridge University Press, 2012).
23. The Rt. Hon W. C. Massey, 20 June 1921 (Prime Minister of New Zealand) in Keith, *Speeches and Documents*, p. 60. See also Australia's W. M. Hughes, p. 55. It was not just the assembly itself but also the precise circumstances of their gathering that lacked a serviceable name. Neither Massey nor Hughes were inclined to experiment with names or constitutional form, however (the latter seeking to present the ambiguity as a source of strength, resting on an inherent trust and confidence that defied constitutional formula).
24. Mackenzie King to McDonald, 7 August 1921 in Keith, *Speeches and Documents*, p. 345.
25. The Irish Free State was represented by three senior ministers led by Justice Minister Kevin O'Higgins.
26. Imperial Conference 1926, Committee on Imperial Relations, Minutes of the First Meeting Held on Wednesday 27 October 1926, p. 5.
27. Darwin, *Empire Project*, p. 407.
28. Imperial Conference 1926, Inter-Imperial Relations Committee Report, 18 November 1926, p. 2.
29. H. Duncan Hall, 'The Genesis of the Balfour Declaration of 1926', *Journal of Commonwealth Political Studies*, 1:3 (1962), pp. 169–93, 169.
30. Hall, *Commonwealth*, pp. 681, 645. This created the revealing anomaly that the Commonwealth was 'within the British Empire' for the purposes of the Balfour formula, but placed explicitly 'without' for the purposes of the League.
31. R. F. Holland, *Britain and the Commonwealth Alliance, 1918–1939* (London: Palgrave, 1981), p. 53.
32. Australia ratified the Statute in 1942 while New Zealand waited until 1947. See W. J. Hudson and M. P. Sharp, *Australian Independence: Colony to Reluctant Kingdom* (Melbourne: Melbourne University Press, 1988).
33. Linda Colley, *Acts of Union and Disunion: What Has Held the UK Together – and What is Dividing It?* (London: Profile Books, 2014), p. 140.
34. See Menzies' foreword to Hall, *Commonwealth*, p. xxii.
35. R. P. Singh, 'The Irwin Declaration of 1929: Its Background and Implications', *Proceedings of the Indian History Congress*, 38 (1977), pp. 460–8, 461.

36. Carl Bridge, *Holding India to the Empire: The British Conservative Party and the 1935 Constitution* (New York: Envoy Press, 1986), p. 5.
37. Metcalf, *Ideologies of the Raj*, p. 160.
38. Kim A. Wagner explores the long shadow of 'white vulnerability' beneath displays of 'exemplary violence' such as Amritsar in *Amritsar 1919: An Empire of Fear & The Making of a Massacre* (New Haven: Yale University Press, 1919), pp. xxi–xxiii, 258.
39. Andrew S. Thompson, *Imperial Britain: The Empire in British Politics. c. 1880–1932* (Harlow: Pearson Education, 2000), p. 184.
40. Archibald R. Colquhoun, 'The Proposed British Zollverein', *North American Review*, 177:561 (August 1903), pp. 172–82, 173.
41. Gary B. Magee and Andrew S. Thompson, *Empire and Globalisation: Networks of People, Goods and Capital in the British World, c. 1850–1914* (Cambridge: Cambridge University Press, 2010), pp. 166, 108.
42. Gary B. Magee, 'The Importance of Being British? Imperial Factors and the Growth of British Imports, 1870–1960', *Journal of Interdisciplinary History*, xxxvii:3 (Winter, 2007), pp. 341–69, 351–3.
43. Magee and Thompson, *Empire and Globalisation*, pp. 117–18, 154, 167. Adele Wessell similarly argues that 'food consumed in the Australian colonies ... was not simply the residue of old food habits, or traces of colonial history, but a device to reaffirm cultural and historical bonds and sustain a shared sense of British identity'. Adele Wessell, 'There's No Taste Like Home: The Food of Empire', in Kate Darian-Smith, Patricia Grimshaw, Kiera Lindsey and Stuart Macintyre (eds.), *Exploring the British World: Identity, Cultural Production, Institutions* (Melbourne: RMIT Publishing, 2004), pp. 811–21, 811.
44. On the eve of the Second World War the UK share of Australian, Canadian and New Zealand export income was 49.5, 41.6 and 76.7 per cent, respectively. W. K. Hancock, *Survey of British Commonwealth Affairs*, vol. II: *Problems of Economic Policy, 1918–1939* (London: Oxford University Press, 1940), pp. 306–10.
45. Belich, *Replenishing the Earth*, pp. 179, 208.
46. Belich, *Replenishing the Earth*, p. 447.
47. Such was the impact of refrigerated shipping that James Belich regards the year 1882 – marking the first ever passage of a refrigerated cargo from New Zealand to Britain – as the '1066' of New Zealand history. See *Paradise Reforged: A History of the New Zealanders from the 1880s to the Year 2000* (Auckland: Penguin, 2001), ch. 2.
48. Felicity Barnes, *New Zealand's London: A Colony and Its Metropolis* (Auckland: Auckland University Press, 2012), p. 163; David Thackeray, 'Buying for Britain, China, or India? Patriotic Trade, Ethnicity, and Market in the 1930s British Empire/Commonwealth', *Journal of Global History*, 12 (2017), pp. 386–409, 406.
49. Magee and Thompson, *Empire and Globalisation*, p. 167. Barnes, *New Zealand's London*, p. 124.

50. Frank Trentmann, *Free Trade Nation: Commerce, Culture and Civil Society in Modern Britain* (Oxford: Oxford University Press, 2008), p. 2.

51. Andrew Thompson details the various preferential tariff measures implemented by Rhodesia (1896), Canada (1897), the South African colonies (1903), New Zealand (1903, 1906) and Australia (1907) in *Imperial Britain*, pp. 90–6. See also Trentmann, *Free Trade Nation*, pp. 162–4.

52. David Edgerton, *The Rise and Fall of the British Nation: A Twentieth Century History* (London: Allen Lane, 2018), pp. 19–20, 88.

53. Magee and Thompson, *Empire and Globalisation*, p. 133. Moreover, Trentmann notes that free trade policies surprisingly do not seem to have affected trade patterns to any measurable degree over the longer term, which suggests that 'non-market' discriminating factors could still operate freely within a non-discriminatory trading regime. *Free Trade Nation*, p. 10.

54. Hancock, *Survey of British Commonwealth Affairs*, p. 94.

55. Hancock, *Survey of British Commonwealth Affairs*, pp. 95, 99, 100.

56. Trentmann, *Free Trade Nation*, p. 285. Andrew Thompson also demonstrates how the 'organisational base of the tariff reform movement was significantly broadened' at this time, see *Imperial Britain*, pp. 178–80.

57. Hancock, *Survey of British Commonwealth Affairs*, p. 140.

58. The scope of their activities widened to include Australia in 1925 and Canada and South Africa in 1928. See Thackeray, 'Buying for Britain', p. 388.

59. Trentmann, *Free Trade Nation*, pp. 230–1.

60. Sir Henry Cowan, quoted in Kaori O'Connor, 'The King's Christmas Pudding: Globalization, Recipes, and the Commodities of Empire', *Journal of Global History*, 4:1 (2009), pp. 127–55, 140.

61. Frank Trentmann, 'Before "Fair Trade": Empire, Free Trade, and the Moral Economies of Food in the Modern World', *Environment and Planning D: Society and Space*, 25 (2007), pp. 1079–102, 1085. On the female consumer generally, see Matthew Hilton, *Consumerism in Twentieth Century Britain: The Search for a Historical Movement* (Cambridge: Cambridge University Press, 2003), pp. 41–6.

62. O'Connor discusses the difficulty in apportioning the ingredients equitably among the many countries for potential inclusion, some of whom reacted bitterly to being left out of the original recipe of 1926. See 'The King's Christmas Pudding', pp. 141–50. *The Times* quote is at p. 146.

63. Anne Clendinning, 'Exhibiting a Nation: Canada at the British Empire Exhibition, 1924–1925', *Social History*, 39:77 (2006), pp. 79–107, 93–4.

64. Barnes, *New Zealand's London*, p. 141.

65. Mackenzie King in *The Times*, 26 February 1924, quoted in Christopher Tait, 'Brushes, Budgets and Butter: Canadian Culture and Identity at the British Empire Exhibition, 1924–25', in Buckner and Francis (eds.), *Canada and the British World*, pp. 234–49, 236–7.

66. David Thackeray and Richard Toye, 'What Was a British Buy? Empire, Europe and the Politics of Patriotic Trade in Britain, c.1945–1963', in

David Thackeray, Andrew Thompson and Richard Toye (eds.), *Imagining Britain's Economic Future, c.1800–1975: Trade, Consumerism, and Global Markets* (London: Palgrave, 2018), p. 135.

67. Stephen Constantine, '"Bringing the Empire Alive": The Empire Marketing Board and Imperial Propaganda', in John M. MacKenzie (ed.), *Imperialism and Popular Culture* (Manchester: Manchester University Press, 1986), p. 217.

68. Felicity Barnes, 'Bringing Another Empire Alive? The Empire Marketing Board and the Construction of Dominion Identity, 1926–33', *Journal of Imperial and Commonwealth History*, 42:1 (2014), pp. 61–85, 64. David Thackeray has shown how this 'exclusion of marginal groups from full participation' acted as encouragement to diasporic peoples in India and Singapore to devise 'competing patriotic trade networks, which sought to develop connections between them and their ancestral homelands'. 'Buying for Britain', p. 408.

69. Thus, Canadian honey and apples were ranged alongside British-built ships; New Zealand sheep stations were juxtaposed with British woollen mills; and Australian dairy production was visually paired with British steelworks. Barnes, 'Another Empire', pp. 72, 75.

70. Barnes, 'Another Empire', p. 67.

71. Quoted in Francine Mackenzie, 'Trade, Dominance, Dependence and the End of the Settlement Era in Canada, Australia, New Zealand and South Africa, 1920–73', in Christopher Lloyd, Jacob Metzer and Richard Sutch (eds.), *Settler Economies in World History* (Leiden: Brill, 2013), p. 479.

72. Nixon and Yeabsley, cited in Mackenzie, 'Trade, Dominance, Dependence', p. 479.

73. Trentmann, *Free Trade Nation*, p. 234.

74. Far from imagining the bucolic farmlands of the southern oceans, Willoughby was bound for China (via the fabled north-east passage through the Russian arctic) and perished in the attempt. The quotation (unattributed in the EMB poster) is from the letters patent of Edward VI to Sir Hugh just prior to his departure in 1553. The poster is reproduced in Stephen Constantine, *Buy and Build: The Advertising Posters of the Empire Marketing Board* (London: Public Record Office, 1986).

75. Andrew Markus, 'William Cooper and the 1937 Petition to the King', *Aboriginal History*, 7:1 (1983), pp. 46–60, 47.

76. Markus, 'William Cooper', p. 53.

77. Markus, 'William Cooper', p. 51. See also Bain Attwood and Andrew Markus, *Thinking Black: William Cooper and the Australian Aborigines League* (Canberra: Aboriginal Studies Press, 2004), pp. 1–11.

78. Clive Turnbull interview in the *Melbourne Herald*, 7 August 1937, quoted in Attwood and Markus, *Thinking Black*, p. 79.

79. Quotations sampled from the extensive collection of Cooper's letters reprinted in Attwood and Markus, *Thinking Black*, see variously documents 8, 13, 25, 31, 32,

37, 44, 45, 50, 51, 62, 63, 72 and 84. See also Tim Rowse, *Indigenous and Other Australians since 1901* (Sydney: UNSW Press, 2017), pp. 190–2.

80. Elsewhere he decried 'all thought of breeding the half-caste white' as 'a creature of the white mind'. Quoted in Attwood and Markus, *Thinking Black*, document 38. For further evidence that Cooper's 'deployment of Britishness was something other than assimilationist', see Alison Holland, '"Does the British Flag Mean Nothing to Us?" British Democratic Traditions and Aboriginal Rights Claims in Interwar Australia', *Australian Historical Studies*, 50:3 (2019), pp. 321–38, 324, 336. Russell McGregor also warns against regarding Indigenous activists as 'mere dupes of a dominant ideology, rather than as political actors who made conscious and deliberate choices from the range of options which had some currency in the 1930s'. See Russell McGregor, 'Protest and Progress: Aboriginal Activism in the 1930s', *Australian Historical Studies*, 25:101 (October 1993), pp. 555–68, 556, 568.

81. Tim Rowse, 'The Identity of Indigenous Political Thought', in Lisa Ford and Tim Rowse (eds.), *Between Indigenous and Settler Governance* (Abingdon: Routledge, 2013), pp. 95–107, 105.

82. Fred Clarke (Hancock's colleague who originally proposed small 'b' usage) once described his turn of phrase as marking 'precisely the features of British civilization that have a universal appeal' – according to the recollections of Canadian historian Frank Underhill in the 1950s. See Francis, 'Historical Perspectives on Britain', p. 320.

83. The coupling was not Cooper's invention but had its origins in enlightenment political philosophy. The constitutional reformer Granville Sharp, for example, declared in 1774 that 'as all British subjects, whether in Great-Britain, Ireland, or the Colonies, are equally free by the law of Nature, they certainly are equally entitled to the same Natural Rights that are essential for their own preservation, because this privilege of "having a share in the legislation" is not merely a British Right, peculiar to this island, but it is also a Natural Right, which cannot, without the most flagrant and stimulating injustice, be withdrawn from any part of the British Empire by any worldly authority whatsoever'. Granville Sharp, *A Declaration of the People's Natural Right to a Share in the Legislature, which is the Fundamental Principle of the British Constitution of State* (London, 1774), p. 4.

84. Not that redress was forthcoming in Cooper's lifetime, however. His lifelong campaign for Indigenous recognition is now the subject of a major biography, see Bain Attwood, *William Cooper: An Aboriginal Life Story* (Melbourne: Melbourne University Press, 2021).

85. Alison Holland shows that his 'appeal to British democratic traditions was more widespread' at the time, both in Australia and elsewhere. Holland, 'Does the British Flag Mean Nothing to Us?', p. 322.

86. Attwood and Markus, *Thinking Black*, p. 7. Heather Goodall also sees in the activities of Cooper and his many predecessors, not a 'remnant of misplaced loyalties to a colonising Queen' but the 'conviction that Aboriginal rights to

land had been recognised at the highest levels of the British state' – thus investing the Crown with the potential 'to assert the equivalent dignity of their own authorities and power structures'. See Heather Goodall, *Invasion to Embassy: Land in Aboriginal Politics in New South Wales, 1770–1922* (Sydney: Sydney University Press, 2008, 1st ed. 1996), p. 122.

87. Sarah Carter and Maria Nugent, 'Introduction', in Sarah Carter and Maria Nugent (eds.), *Mistress of Everything: Queen Victoria in Indigenous Worlds* (Manchester: Manchester University Press, 2016), p. 1.

88. See Chapter 6, p. 167.

89. Michael Belgrave, '"We Rejoice to Honour the Queen, for She is a Good Woman, who Cares for the Maori Race": Loyalty and Protest in Maori Politics in Nineteenth-Century New Zealand', in Carter and Nugent (eds.), *Mistress of Everything*, pp. 54–77, 56, 73.

90. Deskaheh, 'I am Going to Geneva' (1923), in Daniel M. Cobb (ed.), *Say We Are Nations: Documents of Politics and Protest in Indigenous America since 1887* (Chapel Hill: University of North Carolina Press, 2015), pp. 45–9.

91. Deskaheh, 'I am Going to Geneva', p. 48.

92. Quoted in Keith Newman, *Ratana the Prophet* (Rosedale: Raupo, 2009), p. 87.

93. Newman, *Ratana the Prophet*, p. 93.

94. Newman, *Ratana the Prophet*, p. 97.

95. Pedersen, *The Guardians*, p. 5.

96. Ravi de Costa, 'Identity, Authority, and the Moral Worlds of Indigenous Petitions', *Comparative Studies in Society and History*, 48:3 (July 2006), pp. 669–98, 685; see also (in the context of the League of Nations mandate in South-West Africa) Tilman Dedering, 'Petitioning Geneva: Transnational Aspects of Protest and Resistance in South West Africa/Namibia after the First World War', *Journal of Southern African Studies*, 35:4 (December 2009), pp. 785–801.

97. De Costa, 'Moral Worlds of Indigenous Petitions', pp. 670, 673, 680.

98. See Hancock, *Modern Map*, cited pp. 44–8.

99. Mackenzie King Diaries, April 4, 1946, MG26-J13, Library and Archives Canada.

100. A useful overview is provided by José Igartua, *The Other Quiet Revolution: National Identities in English Canada, 1945–71* (Vancouver: UBC Press, 2006), pp. 30–3. For a different emphasis, see Raymond B. Blake, 'From Dominion Day to Canada Day, 1946–82: History, Heritage and National Identity', *Asian Journal of Canadian Studies*, 17:2 (2001), pp. 1–32. See also Matthew Hayday and Raymond B. Blake, *Celebrating Canada*, vol. 1: *Holidays, National Days, and the Crafting of Identities* (Toronto: University of Toronto Press, 2016).

101. *Ottawa Journal*, quoted in Igartua, *Other Quiet Revolution*, p. 31.

102. Both quotations from Igartua, *Other Quiet Revolution*, pp. 30–2.

103. Quoted in Blake, 'From Dominion Day', p. 11.

104. Elmore Philpott in the *Vancouver Sun*, quoted in Igartua, *Other Quiet Revolution*, p. 32.

105. Darwin, *Empire Project*, pp. 476–8, 512–13. Darwin's 'Eurasian revolution' of the 1930s is not to be confused with his earlier revolution of the same name between the 1750s and 1830s that fostered the preconditions that gave the European states 'a commanding lead over the rest of Eurasia . . . to project their power into the heartlands of the great Asian empires', as elaborated in John Darwin, *After Tamerlane: The Global History of Empire* (London: Allen Lane, 2007), ch. 4, p. 160.
106. Darwin, *Empire Project*, p. 513.
107. Darwin, *Empire Project*, pp. 655, 649.
108. Personal testimony of G. Morgan of the Malayan Public Works Service, July 1942, quoted in Christopher Bayly and Tim Harper, *Forgotten Armies: Britain's Asian Empire & the War with Japan* (London: Penguin, 2005), p. 130.
109. See Lynn Hollen Lees, *Planting Empire, Cultivating Subjects: British Malaya, 1786–1941* (Cambridge: Cambridge University Press, 2017), pp. 285, 309.
110. Robert Bickers, 'Cut Loose: The British in China and the Aftermath of Empire', in Christian Damm Pedersen and Stuart Ward (eds.), *The Break-Up of Greater Britain* (Manchester: Manchester University Press, 2021), ch. 2.
111. *The Times*, 24 February 1942.
112. Max Beloff, 'Empire Reconsidered', *Journal of Imperial and Commonwealth History*, 27:2 (May 1999), pp. 13–26, 14.
113. Richard Toye, 'An Imperial Defeat? The Presentation and Reception of the Fall of Singapore', in Brian F. Farrell (ed.), *Churchill and the Lion City: Shaping Modern Singapore* (Singapore: NUS Press, 2011), pp. 108–22, 121–2. The term 'heroic failure' is from Stephanie Barczewski, *Heroic Failure and the British* (New Haven: Yale University Press, 2016).
114. Quoted in Toye, 'An Imperial Defeat?', p. 115.
115. See James Curran, *Curtin's Empire* (Cambridge: Cambridge University Press, 2011), p. 3. Curran makes the point that Curtin (and his successor Ben Chifley) used the phrase on more than one occasion, and it therefore cannot be put down to a 'slip of the tongue'.
116. 'Thwarted Britishness' is Neville Meaney's term; see 'Britishness and Australian Identity: The Problem of Nationalism in Australian History and Historiography', *Australian Historical Studies*, 32:116 (2001), pp. 76–90, 89.

4 'WE MUSTN'T USE THE WORD "EMPIRE"': THE BRITISH NAME

1. Undated newsreel from the 1950 general election featured in the television documentary *The Churchills*, Thames Television 1991, episode 1.
2. A simple Hansard word search bears this out. Before the war, the term 'empire' was used in parliament roughly a thousand times each year during the 1930s. By the time of Indian independence in 1947, it was down to 908 utterances, before dwindling to 542 times in 1950, the year of Churchill's lament. He had quite

rightly intuited a steep decline which would continue throughout the decade, striking a low of 159 mentions in Hansard in 1959 (by then, typically couched in the past tense).

3. John Darwin, 'Fear of Falling: British Politics and Imperial Decline since 1900', *Transactions of the Royal Historical Society*, 36 (1986), pp. 27–43, 41–2.

4. Nicholas J. White, 'Reconstructing Europe through Rejuvenating Empire: The British, French and Dutch Experiences Compared', *Past and Present*, 210 (2011) supplement 6, pp. 211–36; Frederick Cooper, 'Reconstructing Empire in British and French Africa', *Past and Present*, 210 (2011) supplement 6, pp. 196–210, 200; Andrew S. Thompson, 'Unravelling the Relationships between Humanitarianism, Human Rights, and Decolonization: Time for a Radical Rethink?', in Martin Thomas and Andrew S. Thompson (eds.), *The Oxford Handbook of the Ends of Empire* (Oxford: Oxford University Press, 2018), pp. 453–76.

5. Martin Thomas and Richard Toye, 'Introduction: Rhetorics of Empire', in Martin Thomas and Richard Toye (eds.), *Rhetorics of Empire: Languages of Colonial Conflict after 1900* (Manchester: Manchester University Press, 2017), p. 5. Andrew Thompson also notes how 'the meaning of words like "empire" and "imperialism" did not change accidentally' but were subject to complex societal processes that could not simply be administered from on high. See Andrew Thompson, *Imperial Britain* (London: Longman, 2000), p. 15.

6. Richard Toye, 'Words of Change: The Rhetoric of Commonwealth, Common Market and Cold War, 1961–3', in L. J. Butler and Sarah Stockwell (eds.), *The Wind of Change: Harold Macmillan and British Decolonization* (Basingstoke: Palgrave, 2013), p. 141. On the pitfalls of 'empty rhetoric' see James Curran, *The Power of Speech* (Melbourne: Melbourne University Press, 2004).

7. R. Palme Dutt, *Britain's Crisis of Empire* (London: Lawrence and Wishart, 1950), p. 7.

8. See Quentin Skinner, 'Some Problems in the Analysis of Political Thought and Action', *Political Theory*, 2 (1974), pp. 277–303.

9. What sociolinguists term 'intersubjectivity' is the first casualty when words are no longer able to contain the communities they are devised to serve. Peter Harder refers to a 'loss of onomasociological salience' when the semantic range of a given term fails to keep pace with the changing social realities it is presumed to encompass. See Peter Harder, 'Cognitive Sociolinguistics, Language Systems and the Fall of Empires', in Jocelyne Daems, Eline Zenner, Kris Heylen, Dirk Speelman and Hubert Cuyckens (eds.), *Change of Paradigms – New Paradoxes* (Berlin: Mouton de Gruyter, 2015), pp. 237–51.

10. Cabinet Minute, 108th Conclusions, Confidential Annex, 31 December 1946, in Nicholas Mansergh (ed.), *Constitutional Relations Between Britain and India: The Transfer of Power* (hereafter TOP), Vol. IX, pp. 427–31.

11. See Stuart Ward, 'The European Provenance of Decolonization', *Past and Present*, 230 (2016), pp. 227–60.

12. Significantly, he was the first viceroy to appoint a full-time press attaché. See Chandrika Kaul, '"At the Stroke of the Midnight Hour": Lord Mountbatten and the British Media at Indian Independence', *The Round Table*, 97:398 (October 2008), pp. 677–93.

13. See Chapter 3, p. 81. Mountbatten regarded India's future in the Commonwealth as 'the most important single problem' he faced, a point he repeatedly impressed on his viceregal staff. Viceroy's Staff Meeting, 19 April 1947 and 9 May 1947, TOP, Vol. X, pp. 329, 703. The primacy of the Commonwealth link in Mountbatten's priorities is reiterated by his biographer, Philip Ziegler, *Mountbatten: The Official Biography* (London: Collins, 1985), p. 469.

14. John Darwin, 'Decolonization and the End of Empire', in Robin Winks (ed.), *The Oxford History of the British Empire*, vol. V: *Historiography* (Oxford: Oxford University Press, 1999), p. 547.

15. Nehru's trial statement, 17 May 1922, quoted in Ram Gopal, *The Trials of Jawaharlal Nehru* (Bombay: The Book Centre, 1962), p. 14.

16. Nehru's address in the school's 'Speech Room' quoted in *The Harrovian*, LXXIII:22 (12 May 1960).

17. Quoted in Sarvepalli Gopal, *Jawaharlal Nehru: A Biography*, vol. 1: *1989–1947* (London: Jonathan Cape, 1975), p. 111.

18. Jawaharlal Nehru, *The Discovery of India* (New York: John Day, 1946), p. 41.

19. H. Kumarasingham, 'The "Tropical Dominions": The Appeal of Dominion Status in the Decolonisation of India, Pakistan and Ceylon', *Transactions of the Royal Historical Society*, 23 (2013), pp. 223–45, 233.

20. Kumarasingham, '"Tropical Dominions"', pp. 234–5.

21. Hugh Tinker, 'Jawaharlal Nehru at Simla, May 1949. A Moment of Truth?', *Modern Asian Studies*, 4:4 (1970), pp. 349–58, 356.

22. Kumarasingham, '"Tropical Dominions"', p. 239.

23. V. P. Menon's Note on a Talk with Nehru, Simla, 8 May 1947, in Sarvepalli Gopal (ed.), *Selected Works of Jawaharlal Nehru*, 2nd ser, vol. 2 (New Delhi: Orient Longman, 1973), pp. 114–16 (hereafter SWJN).

24. Minutes of Viceroy's 11th Miscellaneous Meeting, Simla, 10 May 1947, TOP, Vol. X, p. 735.

25. Record of a Meeting between Rear-Admiral Mountbatten and Mr Krishna Menon, 17 April 1947, TOP, Vol. X, pp. 310–12; Minutes of Viceroy's 13th Staff Meeting, Simla, 10 May 1947, TOP, Vol. X, p. 729.

26. Minutes of Viceroy's 27th Staff Meeting, Simla, 7 May 1947, TOP, Vol. X, p. 659.

27. Gopal, *Nehru*, p. 356.

28. Mountbatten to Lord Ismay (India Office), 8 May 1947, TOP, Vol. X, p. 699; Viceroy's Staff Meeting, 18 April 1947, TOP, Vol. X. pp. 313–14; Viceroy's Conference Paper 40, 'A Method of Transferring Power to Successor Authorities in India Which Could Result in a Form of Transitional Constitution Analogous to Dominion Status', 1 May 1947, p. 527.

29. Brook to Attlee, 12 May 1947, TOP, Vol. X, p. 794. The phrase 'bring in new members without losing the old' is Ismay's.
30. Prime Minister's Personal Minute, 14 May 1947, TOP, Vol. X, p. 819.
31. Smuts to Attlee, 12 May 1947, TOP, Vol. X, pp. 796–7.
32. Neville Meaney, 'Britishness and Australia: Some Reflections', in Carl Bridge and Kent Fedorowich (eds.), *The British World: Disapora, Culture, Identity* (London: Cass, 2003), p. 131. On the 'British-speaking race', see Chapter 3, p. 99.
33. Draft Cabinet Paper, 'Future Relations of India and the British Commonwealth', 3 February 1947, TOP, Vol. IX, pp. 603–9. On British motivations for retaining India in the Commonwealth, see Anita Inder Singh, 'Imperial Defence and the Transfer of Power in India', *International History Review*, 4:4 (November 1982), pp. 568–88; 'Keeping India in the Commonwealth: British Political and Military Aims, 1947–49', *Journal of Contemporary History*, 20:3 (July 1985), pp. 469–81.
34. See, for example, 'The Last Viceroy', the ninth episode of his personal documentary series *The Life and Times of Lord Mountbatten* (Thames Television, 1969). Needless to say, Mountbatten's view of the matter is highly contested. For a particularly scathing verdict on his role, see Stanley Wolpert, *Shameful Flight: The Last Years of the British Empire in India* (Oxford: Oxford University Press, 2009); Shahid Hamid, *Disastrous Twilight: A Personal Record of the Partition of India* (Barnsley: Leo Cooper, 1986).
35. Chandrika Kaul notes the remarkable media consensus that seemed to dissolve the normally deep partisan and political divisions among rival British newspaper outlets. Kaul, 'Midnight Hour', p. 689.
36. Quoted in Kaul, 'Midnight Hour', p. 681.
37. Quoted in Nicholas Owen, '"More Than a Transfer of Power': Independence Day Ceremonies in India, 15 August 1947', *Contemporary Record*, 6:3 (1992), pp. 415–51, 443.
38. Bevin Circular 0138, 25 July 1947, DO35/2255, The National Archives, Kew (hereafter NA).
39. Cabinet Committee Gen 186, 2nd Meeting, 'Commonwealth Relations', 9 June 1947, TOP, Vol. XI, p. 222.
40. See R. J. Moore, *Making the New Commonwealth* (Oxford: Clarendon Press, 1987), pp. 111–14.
41. Attlee to Nehru, 11 March 1948, PREM8/820, NA.
42. Nehru Memorial Library, New Delhi (hereafter NML), Nehru to Krishna Menon, 16 April 1948. Despite Attlee's explicit request 'to have your views on these high matters', Nehru deliberately evaded the issue ('it is not easy for me to answer adequately ... I am, therefore, not attempting answer at this stage'). Nehru to Attlee 18 April 1948, PREM8/820, NA.
43. Menon to Nehru, undated but mid-1948, JN (SG) File no. 15 (I), NML.

44. Australia and South Africa were represented by senior government ministers, with Eric Louw attending on behalf of the newly elected Nationalist Party Government in South Africa, and Australia's Foreign Minister H. V. Evatt deputising for Prime Minister Ben Chifley. Illness prevented W. L. Mackenzie King from attending, and he was substituted by his successor as prime minister, Louis St Laurent, towards the end of proceedings.

45. See Mary Kenny, *Crown and Shamrock: Love and Hate between Ireland and the British Monarchy* (Dublin: New Island, 2009).

46. Mackenzie King Diary entry, 15 October 1948, item 32666, MG26-J13, Library and Archives Canada (hereafter LAC).

47. Mackenzie King diaries, private and personal memorandum by Mackenzie King, 'Problem of Crown and Commonwealth', 10 October 1948; 13 October 1948, MG26-J13, LAC.

48. Royal Archives Windsor (hereafter RA), Lascelles to George VI, 10 October 1948, PS/PSO/GVI/PS/MAIN/09196.

49. Beasley to Chifley, 18 November 1948, A1838, 899/1/5, National Archives of Australia (hereafter NAA). Beasley also concluded that it had been a 'great mistake' that the matter had not been dealt with in open session at the 1948 Conference.

50. External Affairs Memorandum, 'Official Title of the Commonwealth', 25 January 1949, RG25-A-3-b, Vol. 4234 File Part 1, LAC.

51. Quoted in Moore, *Making the New Commonwealth*, p. 154.

52. 'Prime Ministers' Conference London: October 1948, Note by Sir Girija Shankar Bajpai', undated, JN (SG) File no. 14, NML.

53. Reported in Snelling (Wellington) to Syers, 24 February 1949, DO35/2255, NA.

54. Snelling to Syers, 24 February 1949, DO35/2255, NA.

55. *Melbourne Sun*, 26 October 1948.

56. Extract from cable HC Canberra to CRO, 14 January 1949, DO35/2255, NA.

57. *The Telegraph* (Sydney), 14 January 1949.

58. 'Guest of Honour', by Dr H. V. Evatt, broadcast on ABC Radio, Sunday 16 January 1949.

59. Rough translation of Malan's address to the Nationalist Party Cape Congress, 26 October 1948, reported in Australian High Commission Pretoria to Canberra, 27 October 1948, A1838, 899/1/5, NAA.

60. *Rand Daily Mail*, 23 October 1948; *Rand Daily Mail*, 25 October 1948.

61. Hansard, 28 October 1948, cc. 242–72.

62. Cabinet Minute 48 (67th Conclusion), 28 October 1948, CAB21/1815, NA.

63. Memorandum by the Prime Minister 'Commonwealth Nomenclature', December 1948, CAB21/1815, NA.

64. Syers to Laithwaite, 13 January 1949, DO35/2255, NA.

65. *Daily Express*, 22 January 1949.

66. Noel-Baker to Attlee, 1 February 1949, DO35/2255, NA.
67. See H. Kumarasingham, *A Political Legacy of the British Empire: Power and the Parliamentary System in Post-Colonial India and Sri Lanka* (London: I. B. Tauris, 2013), pp. 39–40.
68. As he described them to Sardar Patel on 26 March 1949, see transcript in Durga Das (ed.), *Sardar Patel's Correspondence, 1945–50*, vol. VIII (Ahmedabad: Navajivan Press, 1973), p. 5.
69. CRO paper 'The Commonwealth Relationship: Constitutional Questions', February 1949, CAB21/1824, NA.
70. Nehru to all Provincial Premiers, 16 April 1949, JN (SG) File no. 22 (II), NML. In a separate minute to Krishna Menon he reiterated: 'I should like to make it clear that we cannot possibly accept the description "British Commonwealth of Nations"', Nehru to Menon, 14 April 1949, JN (SG) File no. 22 (II), NML.
71. Noel-Baker to Attlee, 'India's Foreign Policy and Her Relation to the Commonwealth', 20 April 1949. Annex B 'References by Other Commonwealth Prime Ministers to the Implications of India's Membership of the Commonwealth on Foreign Policy', CAB21/1824, NA.
72. H. Kumarasingham, 'The "New Commonwealth" 1947–49: A New Zealand Perspective on India Joining the Commonwealth', *The Round Table*, 95:385 (2006), pp. 441–54. See also H. Kumarasingham, *Onward with Executive Power: Lessons from New Zealand, 1947–57* (Wellington: Institute of Policy Studies, 2010).
73. Frederick Doidge, future external affairs minister and later high commissioner to the UK in the Sidney Holland Government of the 1950s, quoted in *The Dominion* (Wellington), 20 April 1949.
74. Fraser to St Laurent, 24 March 1949, EA1 153/27/1 Part 1, Archives New Zealand (hereafter ANZ).
75. Noel-Baker to Attlee, 'India's Foreign Policy and Her Relation to the Commonwealth', 20 April 1949. Annex B 'References by Other Commonwealth Prime Ministers to the Implications of India's Membership of the Commonwealth on Foreign Policy', CAB21/1824, NA.
76. *The Times*, 12 March 1949.
77. Frank Bongiorno, '"British to the Bootstraps? H. V. Evatt, J. B. Chifley and the Australian Policy on Indian Membership of the Commonwealth, 1947–49', *Australian Historical Studies*, 36:125 (2005), pp. 18–39, 28–9.
78. Hector Mackenzie, 'An Old Dominion and the New Commonwealth: Canadian Policy on the Question of India's Membership', *Journal of Imperial and Commonwealth History*, 27:3 (September 1999), pp. 82–112, 99. The document itself appears in JN (SG) File no. 22 (II), NML. See also Das, *Sardar Patel's Correspondence*, pp. 10–11.
79. See Philip Murphy, *Monarchy and the End of Empire* (Oxford: Oxford University Press, 2013), ch. 3; Nicholas Mansergh, *The Commonwealth Experience*, vol. 2: *From British to Multiracial Commonwealth* (London: Macmillan, 1982).

80. Minutes of Commonwealth Prime Ministers' Conference (third and fourth meetings), 25–26 April 1949, CAB133/89, NA.

81. Commonwealth Prime Ministers' Meeting, 1949, Final Communiqué 27 April 1949 in Nicholas Mansergh, *Documents and Speeches on British Commonwealth Affairs, 1931–52*, vol. 2 (Oxford: Oxford University Press, 1953), p. 846. My emphasis.

82. Nehru to Patel, 23 April 1949, in Das, *Sardar Patel's Correspondence*, p. 17. Nehru would later draw attention to the significance of the disappearance of 'British' in an address to the Indian Constituent Assembly on 16 May, strongly implying that the old designation would officially be superseded by the new nomenclature upon the ratification of India's Republican Constitution. Mansergh, *Documents*, p. 847.

83. Ivor Jennings, 'Commonwealth Terminology: A Suggested Usage', *The Times*, 14 May 1949.

84. The King's Speech to the Prime Ministers of the Commonwealth, 27 April 1949; Leo Amery to Lascelles, 28 April 1949, Royal Archives Windsor, PS/PSO/GVI/C/310/22.

85. Lascelles to Amory, 29 April 1949, Royal Archives Windsor, PS/PSO/GVI/C/310/22.

86. *Daily Mail*, 28 April 1949.

87. *The Guardian*, 28 April 1949.

88. Cablegram, Beasley to Chifley, 2 May 1949 with Evatt's annotation, A1838, TS899/6/1 Part 1, NAA.

89. Evatt to Beasley, 23 April 1949 in Pamela Andre (ed.), *Australia and the Postwar World: The Commonwealth and Asia, Documents 1948–49* (Canberra: Department of Foreign Affairs and Trade, 1998), pp. 121–2.

90. *The Argus*, 29 April 1949; *Sydney Morning Herald*, 29 April 1949.

91. *Sydney Morning Herald*, 29 April 1949. Chifley's statement is in A1838, TS899/6/1 Part 1, 3 May 1949, NAA.

92. Quoted in *Sydney Morning Herald*, 29 April 1949; *Goulbourne Evening Post*, 29 April 1949.

93. *Ottawa Journal*, 29 April 1949.

94. 2 May 1949, extract in Mansergh, *Documents and Speeches*, p. 1210.

95. Syers to Brook, 3 August 1949, DO35/2255, NA.

96. Minutes of Proceedings and Evidence of the Standing Committee on External Affairs of the House of Commons, 18 November 1949, RG25-A-3-b Vol. 4234, File Part 1, LAC.

97. Quoted in Information Division memorandum, 8 February 1950, RG25-A-3-b Vol. 4234, File Part 1, LAC.

98. Shannon (HC Ottawa) to Syers, 16 March 1949, DO35/2255, NA.

99. Surprisingly in the light of subsequent events, Northern Ireland was not considered an obstacle to the change, nor was the Stormont Parliament consulted.

100. Maud (Pretoria) to Sandys, 27 December 1960, DO161/148, NA.

101. Maud (Pretoria) to Sandys, 27 December 1960, DO161/148, NA.

102. Oliver (Canberra) to Sandys, 13 January 1960, DO161/148, NA.
103. Cumming-Bruce (Wellington) to Sandys, 23 December 1960, DO161/148, NA.
104. Garner (Ottawa) to Sandys, 19 December 1960, DO161/148, NA.
105. Cabinet Submission, 'Nomenclature: Britain or UK' (Duncan Sandys), 27 March 1961, CAB 21/5492, NA.
106. This latter point was made in an annex to the Cabinet submission, 27 March 1961.
107. Brook to Butler, '"Britain" or "U.K."', 27 March 1961, PREM 11/3652, NA.
108. Briefing paper, '"Britain" and "British": Summary of three main difficulties put to Commonwealth Secretary by Sir Norman Brook', undated, June 1961, PREM11/3652, NA.
109. Norman Brook to Clutterbuck, 2 May 1961, DO161/148, NA.
110. Norman Brook to Clutterbuck, 2 May 1961, DO161/148, NA.
111. Macmillan to Sandys, 1 May 1961, DO161/148, NA.
112. Macmillan to Sandys, 20 June 1961, PREM11/3652, NA.
113. Memorandum for the Prime Minister, 'Proposal that the terms "Britain" and "British" should be used instead of "United Kingdom"', 10 July 1961, RG25 Vol. 5200 Part 2, LAC; For the Australian reaction, see External Affairs memorandum, 'Use of "Britain" and "British" for "United Kingdom"', 17 November 1961, A1838, 67/1/3, Part 3, NAA.
114. Clutterbuck to Governors-General, Governors and Administrators of the Colonies, 6 September 1961, DO161/148, Gen. 203/182/01, NA.
115. *The Times*, 21 October 1961.
116. *The Economist*, 6 January 1962.
117. Gore-Booth (Delhi) to Clutterbuck (Permanent Undersecretary, CRO), 15 September 1961, DO161/148, NA.
118. This had become a familiar theme of Gore-Booth's, see Gore-Booth to Sandys, 18 December 1960, DO161/148, NA.
119. According to Gore-Booth's successor in a despatch a year later. See R. H. Belcher (Delhi) to Garner, 27 August 1962, DO161/149, NA.
120. *Vancouver Sun*, 'The British name', 3 November 1961.
121. The lack of 'warmth or affection' was the case against 'the UK' made by Whitehall to the BBC and the British Council (in the context of the official changes of 1961). See DO161/148, 9 August 1961, Con. 91/63/2, NA.
122. 4 June 1947, quoted in Alex Von Tunzelmann, *Indian Summer: The Secret History of the End of an Empire* (London: Pocket Books, 2007), p. 194.
123. George VI, cited in Murphy, *Monarchy and Empire*, p. 34. My emphasis.
124. Attlee to Churchill, 22 July 1942, quoted in Peter Caterall, '"Efficiency with Freedom"? Debates about the British Constitution in the Twentieth Century', in Peter Caterall, Wolfram Kaiser and Ulrike Walton-Jordan (eds.), *Reforming the Constitution: Debates in Twentieth-Century Britain* (London: Cass, 2000), p. 27.
125. Mackenzie King diary entry, 30 October 1948, MG26-J13, LAC. King was explicitly referring to the nomenclature question.

5 HOMES AWAY FROM HOME: THE HOUSES OF WINDSOR

1. Simon Potter notes how the late 1940s marked a reassertion of the BBC's 'Britannic and imperial roles'; a time when radio still reigned supreme, extending its reach further than ever before with little awareness that it would prove to be a false dawn – both for global Radio and for the pan-British sentiments it propagated. See Simon Potter, *Broadcasting Empire: The BBC and the British World, 1922–1970* (Oxford: Oxford University Press, 2012), pp. 144–7.

2. Quoted in Graham Viney, *The Last Hurrah: The 1947 Royal Tour of South Africa and the End of Empire* (London: Robinson, 2019), p. 2.

3. Letters of Margaret and Elizabeth to Queen Mary quoted in Viney, *The Last Hurrah*, pp. 358, 265.

4. Telegram Circular 110, 'Wedding of HRH Princess Elizabeth', 30 September 1947, CER 22/3, Kenyan National Archives (hereafter KNA).

5. Anthony Trollope, 'Returning Home', in *Tales of All Countries* (London: Chapman and Hall, 1867), p. 300.

6. Thomas Pownall, quoted in Anthony Pagden, *Lords of All the World: Ideologies of Empire in Spain, Britain and France c.1500–c.1800* (New Haven: Yale University Press, 1995), p. 155.

7. Ranajit Guha, 'Not at Home in Empire', *Critical Inquiry*, 23:3 (Spring, 1997), pp. 482–493, 482. See also Catherine Hall and Sonya O. Rose, 'Introduction: Being at Home with the Empire', in Catherine Hall and Sonya O. Rose (eds.), *At Home with the Empire: Metropolitan Culture and the Imperial World* (Cambridge: Cambridge University Press, 2006).

8. 'X', 'The Mingling of Nations', *St John's Review* (1934) quoted in Vivian Kong, 'Multiracial Britons: Britishness, Diasporas, and Cosmopolitanism in Interwar Hong Kong', PhD Dissertation, University of Bristol (March 2019), p. 61.

9. Alison Blunt, *Domicile and Diaspora: Anglo-Indian Women and the Spatial Politics of Home* (Oxford: Blackwell, 2005); see also Alison Blunt and Robyn M. Dowling, *Home* (New York: Routledge, 2006). 'Miniaturizes and occasionally intensifies' is from Bridget Bennett and Hamilton Carroll, 'Imagining the Place of Home: Research Review', Arts and Humanities Research Council Report, 2014, p. 4, www.leeds.ac.uk/arts/info/125130/imagining_the_place_of_home.

10. Alison Blunt, 'Imperial Geographies of Home: British Domesticity in India', *Transactions of the Institute of British Geographers*, New Series, 24:4 (1999), pp. 421–40, 421.

11. Maya Jasanoff describes the estrangement among loyalist refugees in London in the wake of the American Revolution: 'For all that many Americans had been raised to consider Britain as "home", this was emphatically a foreign country.' *Liberty's Exiles: The Loss of America and the Remaking of the British Empire* (London: Harper Press, 2011), pp. 113–14. Cf. Felicity Barnes, '"Familiar London": New Zealand Travel Writing and the Imagined Metropolis, 1890–1940', *Studies in Travel Writing*, 14:4 (2010), pp. 397–409; Astrid Rasch, 'Autobiography after

Empire: Individual and Collective Memory in Dialogue', PhD Thesis, University of Copenhagen (August 2016).

12. Menzies, diary entry 21 March 1935, quoted in A. W. Martin and Patsy Hardy (eds.), *Dark and Hurrying Days: Menzies' 1941 Diary* (Canberra: National Library of Australia, 1993), p. 1.

13. Blunt, *Domicile and Diaspora*, p. 4.

14. See Keith Sinclair, *A Destiny Apart: New Zealand's Search for National Identity* (Wellington: Allen & Unwin, 1986), pp. 104–8.

15. Bennett and Carroll, 'Imagining the Place of Home', p. 7.

16. Malcolm Macdonald (Governor of Kenya) to Sir Michael Adeane (Private Secretary to the Queen), 1 August 1963, CO822/3254, The National Archives, Kew (hereafter NA).

17. The Colonial Office records are remarkably silent on the matter, as are the Royal Archives at Windsor who were unable to locate a single document on the subject. The only reliable sources are available in the Kenyan Archives in Nairobi, but here, too, one of the key files on the transfer of the house appears to have gone missing.

18. Executive Council Minute 560/47, 'Wedding Present Princess Elizabeth', undated, 1947, CER 22/3, KNA.

19. Although no record of these discussions is available, the general outlines of Mitchell's understanding with the palace can be gleaned from the UK National Archives. See Mitchell to Sir Thomas Lloyd (Permanent Undersecretary, Colonial Office), 7 November 1950, CO967/63, NA. In his public announcement, Mitchell also hinted at a tacit agreement with the princess that she should not feel pressured to make an appearance, as reported in the *East African Standard*, 28 November 1947.

20. Mitchell to Creech-Jones, 30 May 1947, CO847/35/6, NA.

21. Governor Mitchell's speech at Nakuru, November 1948, cited in George Bennett and Alison Smith, 'Kenya from White Man's Country to Kenyatta's State, 1945–63', in D. A. Low and Alison Smith (eds.), *History of East Africa*, vol. 3 (Oxford: Clarendon Press, 1976), p. 110.

22. Mitchell to Creech-Jones, 30 May 1947, CO847/35/6, NA.

23. An official brochure from Queen Elizabeth's 1983 visit to Kenya where she was the official guest of President Daniel Arap Moi at Sagana Lodge (her first and only return visit) put the cost at £250,000. If accurate, this places the cost between £7 and 8 million in present-day values. See *The Queen's Visit to Kenya, 10–14 November 1983*, Official guide. The UK National Archives in Kew are surprisingly silent on the issue of financing.

24. Lascelles to Lloyd, 31 October 1950; Charteris to Lloyd, 22 November 1950, CO967/63, NA.

25. Lloyd to Mitchell, 24 November 1950; Mitchell to Lloyd, 29 November 1950; Mitchell to Lloyd, 7 November 1950, CO967/63, NA. In the same

correspondence, Mitchell also conveyed his irritation that his requests to include Kenya in the abortive tour of King George VI to Australia were also given short shrift.

26. The original *Essai sur le don* appeared in *L'année sociologique* in 1925 but did not appear in book form until 1950. The lines quoted are from the 1990 translation by W. D. Halls (with a foreword by Mary Douglas) *The Gift* (London: Routledge, 1990), pp. 3, 5 and 'Foreword: No Free Gifts', p. x. For a good overview see Alan D. Schrift (ed.), *The Logic of the Gift: Toward an Ethic of Generosity* (New York: Routledge, 1997).

27. *East African Standard*, 'Royal Wedding', 20 November 1947.

28. *East African Standard*, 'A Royal Welcome', 1 February 1952.

29. Also reported in *The Times*, 19 January 1952.

30. *News of the World*, 3 February 1952.

31. *East African Standard*, 'Her One Speech: They hope to come back often', 4 February 1952. Cf. the editorial in the same issue: 'Kenya has captivated them and they have promised to come back often'.

32. *The Times*, 'Royal Lodge in Kenya', 19 January 1952.

33. *Evening News*, 'Royal Cottage', 31 January 1952.

34. *Daily Graphic*, 'The House in the Trees', 22 January 1952.

35. *East African Standard*, 'Forest Lodge', 4 February 1952.

36. *Daily Express*, 9 January 1952; 5 February 1952.

37. *Home Chat*, 'Royal Retreat', 19 January 1952.

38. *Daily Mail*, '"It's a Lovely Home" Says Princess', 4 February 1952.

39. *The Lady*, 'Princess Elizabeth's House in the African Bush', 31 January 1952.

40. *Press and Journal*, 'Princess's Highland Home in Kenya', 1 February 1952.

41. *East African Standard*, 'Do You Care If We Lose the Empire?', 1 February 1952.

42. *East African Standard*, 'A Royal Welcome', 1 February 1952.

43. *Daily Graphic*, 'Princess at Her Kenya Home', 4 February 1952; *Daily Express*, 9 January 1952; *Home Chat*, 'Royal Retreat', 19 January 1952.

44. Blunt and Dowling, *Home*, p. 150.

45. *Nottingham Guardian*, 'Into the Blue', 30 January 1952.

46. *East African Standard*, 'Bleak Britons Check up on East Africa', 5 February 1952.

47. See, for example, *The News of the World*, 3 February 1952; *Nottingham Guardian*, 5 February 1952.

48. *News Chronicle*, 5 and 6 February 1952.

49. *Evening Standard*, 'So Near to Home', 11 February 1952.

50. *Daily Express*, 7 February 1952; *Daily Mail*, 7 February 1952.

51. *Daily Express*, 7 February 1952.

52. *Daily Mirror*, 'A Whisper Turned Laughter into Tears', 7 February 1952.

53. Mrs H. Jones to Mrs B. Palmer, published in *Western Gazette*, 'A Missing Light', 22 February 1962. Some reports suggested that the locals had the presence of mind to remove the flags or lower them to half-mast, although this seems

unlikely and was probably an attempt to depict the scene with due solemnity. See, for example, conflicting reports in *The Times* and the *Daily Telegraph* on 7 February 1952.

54. *Evening Standard*, 'So Near to Home', 11 February 1952.
55. David Edgerton, *The Rise and Fall of the British Nation: A Twentieth Century History* (London: Allen Lane, 2018), p. 256.
56. *Sunday Express*, 'Let's Now Have Youth!', 10 February 1952.
57. *Daily Mail*, 'We Shall Return Says the Queen', 8 February 1952.
58. *The Times*, 'Royal Message to Kenya: We Greatly Hope to Return', 12 February 1952.
59. See particularly John Lonsdale, 'Mau Maus of the Mind: Making Mau Mau and Remaking Kenya', *Journal of African History*, 31:3 (1990), pp. 393–421; Dane Kennedy, 'Constructing the Colonial Myth of Mau Mau', *International Journal of African Colonial Studies*, 25:2 (1992), pp. 241–60.
60. The two most prominent and widely debated works are David Anderson's *Histories of the Hanged: Britain's Dirty War in Kenya and the End of Empire* (New York: W. W. Norton, 2005), based primarily on the trial records of the thousands of Kikuyu sent to the gallows, and Caroline Elkins's *Britain's Gulag: The Brutal End of Empire in Kenya* (London: Pimlico, 2005), which focuses on the government's exceedingly harsh 'rehabilitation' system for suspected insurgents, known as 'the pipeline'. Although differences of emphasis and interpretation remain, both authors ascribe the uprising to deeper iniquities in the pattern of land distribution with their roots in the interwar years.
61. See Daniel Branch, *Defeating Mau Mau, Creating Kenya: Counterinsurgency, Civil War and Decolonization* (Cambridge: Cambridge University Press, 2009), pp. 36–8.
62. Anderson, *Histories of the Hanged*, p. 44.
63. Anderson, *Histories of the Hanged*, p. 45.
64. The terms 'moderate' and 'militant', 'rebel' and 'loyalist' are hardly adequate to capture the complexity of the divisions within Kikuyu society in these years. Daniel Branch notes how these ever-shifting divisions were as much 'a product of the conflict rather than a cause or catalyst of the violence' and that any naming convention can only function as convenient shorthand. He advises that to gain any understanding of the distinctions and divisions between loyalists and militants, 'it is necessary to place ambiguity at the centre of our analysis'. Branch, *Defeating Mau Mau*, pp. 2, 9, 52, 209.
65. Branch, *Defeating Mau Mau*, p. 45.
66. *Daily Record and Mail*, 'The Princess, the Duke and the Witchdoctors', 14 January 1952.
67. Anderson, *Histories of the Hanged*, p. 47.
68. Anderson, *Histories of the Hanged*, p. 53.
69. *The Argus*, 24 October 1952. Less than two years later, the Treetops Hotel where Elizabeth succeeded to the throne met the same fate.

70. Stephen Chappell, 'Air Power in the Mau Mau Conflict: The Government's Chief Weapon', *Rusi Journal*, 156:1 (2011), pp. 64–70, 67.

71. See, for example, the *Daily Express* report on the Fergusson and Bingley murder, quoted in Wendy Webster, *Englishness and Empire, 1939–65* (Oxford: Oxford University Press, 2005), p. 131.

72. Graham Greene, *Ways of Escape* (London: Vintage, 1999, 1st ed. 1980), p. 188.

73. *East African Standard*, 'The Front-line Settler Says What He Thinks of It All', 26 January 1953.

74. Blunt and Dowling, *Home*, p. 142; Penelope Tuson, 'Mutiny Narratives and the Imperial Feminine', *Women's Studies International Forum*, 21:3 (1998), pp. 291–303.

75. Mihaly Csikszentmihalyi and Eugene Rochberg-Halton, *The Meaning of Things: Domestic Symbols and the Self* (Cambridge: Cambridge University Press, 1981), p. 104.

76. Webster, *Englishness and Empire*, pp. 130, 133.

77. *Daily Express*, 7 January 1953 quoted in Webster, *Englishness and Empire*, p. 134; the front page of the *Daily Mail*'s 21 October 1952 edition announcing the state of emergency featured the headline 'Women Put Guns in their Handbags', see Joanna Lewis, '"Daddy Wouldn't Buy Me a Mau Mau": The British Popular Press and the demoralization of Empire', in E. S. Atieno Odhiambo and John Lonsdale (eds.), *Mau Mau and Nationhood: Arms, Authority and Narration* (Oxford: James Currey, 2003). See also the *Daily Mail*'s feature extolling 'The Courage of the Women of Kenya' on 26 January 1953, depicting one 'charming hostess' clad in 'a black silk dress' which, on closer inspection, 'revealed an automatic pistol hanging at her hip'.

78. Webster, *Englishness and Empire*, p. 130.

79. Webster, *Englishness and Empire*, p. 121.

80. Fred Majdalany, *State of Emergency: The Full Story of Mau Mau* (London: Longmans, 1962), p. 147. On Majdalany's pro-settler perspective and influence, see Anderson, *Histories of the Hanged*, p. 308.

81. Cited in Anderson, *Histories of the Hanged*, p. 309.

82. Branch, *Defeating Mau Mau*, pp. 5–6.

83. See, for example, the report in the *Sunday Dispatch* of an impending 'night of the long knives' on 24 August 1952, cited in Susan Carruthers, *Winning Hearts and Minds: British Governments, the Media and Colonial Counter-Insurgency, 1944–60* (London: Leicester University Press, 1995), p. 133. The colonial authorities also anticipated widespread attacks on settlers on a scale that never eventuated. See Carruthers, *Winning Hearts and Minds*, p. 136.

84. Elsbeth Huxley, *A Thing to Love* (London: Chatto and Windus, 1954).

85. Memorandum for Parliamentary Delegation, 13 January 1954, cited in Carruthers, *Winning Hearts and Minds*, p. 159.

86. Margery Perham, quoted in Carruthers, *Winning Hearts and Minds*, p. 134. The 'pathologization' of Mau Mau was central to its depiction as a peculiarly chilling species of psycho-horror. One early example of this was a report for the colonial

authorities compiled by the psychiatrist J. C. Carothers, *The Psychology of Mau Mau* (Nairobi: Government Printer, 1954). Sloan Mahone has shown how earlier violent outbreaks in the colonization of Kenya were prone to similar diagnoses, representing East Africans as unusually predisposed to 'episodic mass hysteria'. See Sloan Mahone, 'The Psychology of Rebellion: Colonial Medical Responses to Dissent in British East Africa', *Journal of African History*, 47 (2006), pp. 241–58.

87. Carruthers notes that although standards of good taste militated against publishing such images, Colonial Office officials made sure that they were circulated among a narrow circle of newspaper editors and politicians (including a sample deposited in the parliamentary library at Westminster) so that their impact might be felt indirectly. *Winning Hearts and Minds*, pp. 168–9.

88. *East African Standard*, 'Armed to the Teeth, even by Day', 30 January 1953.

89. Anderson, *Histories of the Hanged*, p. 94.

90. Majdalany, *State of Emergency*, p. 124.

91. British pathé, 16 February 1953, www.britishpathe.com/video/mau-mau-victims-funeral/query/murder.

92. Anderson, *Histories of the Hanged*, p. 93.

93. *Daily Mail*, 26 January 1953. On the Hankey angle see, for example, 'Peer's Niece is Found Slashed to Death', *Daily Mirror*, 26 January 1953.

94. *Daily Mail*, 'Paradox in Africa', 27 January 1953.

95. Erik Linstrum, *Ruling Minds: Psychology in the British Empire* (Cambridge, MA: Harvard University Press, 2016), pp. 182–3.

96. Erik Linstrum, 'Facts about Atrocity: Reporting Colonial Violence in Postwar Britain', *History Workshop Journal*, 84 (Autumn 2017), pp. 108–27.

97. Linstrum, 'Facts about Atrocity', p. 112.

98. Quoted in Lewis, 'Daddy Wouldn't Buy Me a Mau Mau', p. 236.

99. *Daily Mirror*, 'Open Letter to Sir Evelyn', 12 December 1952.

100. Rande W. Kostal, *A Jurisprudence of Power: Victorian Empire and the Rule of Law* (Oxford: Oxford University Press, 2005), p. 20.

101. Linstrum, 'Facts about Atrocity', p. 115.

102. As Lewis shows in the case of the *Daily Mail*, for example. Carruthers argues that even the mainstream liberal press such as the *Manchester Guardian* and the *New Statesman and Nation*, despite some initial scepticism, adopted a line remarkably similar to the settler interpretation of Mau Mau. See Carruthers, *Winning Hearts and Minds*, p. 180.

103. Lewis notes that it was conventionally regarded as 'British' to avoid excess. Lewis, 'Daddy Wouldn't Buy Me a Mau Mau', p. 239. Linstrum also notes the 'epistemological conservatism' that governed the profession at the time, tending to focus on 'events rather than causes, consequences or meaning' out of an aversion for crossing the line between observation and 'advocacy'. 'Facts about Atrocity', pp. 115, 118–19.

104. Quoted in Carruthers, *Winning Hearts and Minds*, p. 175.

NOTES TO PAGES 151–5

105. Carruthers, *Winning Hearts and Minds*, p. 173.
106. Quoted in Anderson, *Histories of the Hanged*, pp. 180, 260.
107. Ronald Hyam, *Britain's Declining Empire: The Road to Decolonisation, 1918–1968* (Cambridge: Cambridge University Press, 2006), p. 171.
108. See Richard Toye, *Churchill's Empire* (London: Macmillan, 2010), p. x.
109. *East African Standard*, 28 January 1953. As early as October 1952 the Kenyan Government despatched a journalist, Granville Roberts, to London as Public Relations Officer for the purpose of counteracting bad press in Britain. See Carruthers, *Winning Hearts and Minds*, p. 144.
110. Esme Ruck's personal correspondence printed in *East African Standard*, 'Armed to the Teeth, Even by Day', 30 January 1953.
111. *East African Standard*, 'The Front-Line Settler Says What He Thinks of It All', 26 January 1953.
112. Michael Blundell's personal recollections in *So Rough a Wind* (London: Weidenfeld and Nicolson, 1964), p. 126. Expurgation of 'f—' is from the original source (where 'n—s' is spelt out).
113. Blundell, *So Rough a Wind*, p. 124. See also *East African Standard*, 'Europeans Demonstrate at Government House', 27 January 1963.
114. *East African Standard*, 'The Front-Line Settler Says What He Thinks of It All', 26 January 1953.
115. Elkins, *Britain's Gulag*.
116. See Chapter 3. Nor, for that matter, with the Black British subjectivities of the West Indies to be examined later in Chapter 6.
117. See, generally, Branch, *Defeating Mau Mau*.
118. *East African Standard*, 27 January 1953.
119. *East African Standard*, 'The Front-Line Settler Says What He Thinks of It All', 26 January 1953.
120. Letter to the Editor, *East African Standard*, 2 February 1953. A palpably angry debate unfolded in the letters pages over several days about the appropriateness of the crowd's behaviour.
121. David Anderson, 'Mau Mau at the Movies: Contemporary Representations of an Anti-colonial War', *South African Historical Journal*, 48:1 (2003), pp. 71–89, 75.
122. Anderson, 'Mau Mau at the Movies', p. 76.
123. Michael Paris, 'Africa in Post-1945 British Cinema', *South African Historical Journal*, 48:1 (2003), pp. 61–70, 67.
124. Lewis, 'Daddy Wouldn't Buy Me a Mau Mau', p. 242. Similar conclusions were reached by Howard Smith in his study of BBC coverage of racial issues in South Africa in the 1950s: 'Apartheid, Sharpeville and "Impartiality": The Reporting of South Africa on BBC Television, 1948–61', *Historical Journal of Film, Radio and Television*, 13:3 (1993), pp. 251–8.
125. Quoted in James Gibbs, 'Uhuru na Kenyatta: White Settlers and the Symbolism of Kenya's Independence Day Events', *Journal of Imperial and Commonwealth History*, 42:3 (2014), pp. 503–29, 524.

126. Although Kenya was initially slated to become a republic, it remained a constitutional monarchy in its first year due to complications in defining the president's powers. See Philip Murphy, *Monarchy and the End of Empire* (Oxford: Oxford University Press, 2013), pp. 92–3.

127. The palace advised the outgoing Kenyan Colonial Government in 1963 that the lodge had 'been somewhat on [the Queen's] mind and particularly the question of upkeep after Independence'. Adeane to N. B. J. Huijsman (Government House Nairobi), 7 August 1963, CO822/3254, NA.

128. Adeane to N. B. J. Huijsman (Government House Nairobi), 7 August 1963, CO822/3254, NA.

129. MacDonald to Adeane, 1 August 1963, CO822/3254, NA.

130. Huijsman to Adeane, 14 August 1963, CO822/3254, NA; on the reasons for the Queen's non-attendance at independence ceremonies, see Murphy, *Monarchy and the End of Empire*, p. 81.

131. A plotline not dissimilar to Shute's own flight from Labour-governed Britain to Australia in 1950. See Neville Shute, *In the Wet* (London: William Heinemann, 1953).

132. Murphy, *Monarchy and the End of Empire*, pp. 96–100.

133. See Stuart Ward, 'Sir Alexander Downer and the Embers of British Australia', in Carl Bridge, Frank Bongiorno and David Lee (eds.), *The High Commissioners* (Canberra: Department of Foreign Affairs and Trade, 2010), pp. 145–63, 156.

134. Notably, it was Treetops that was chosen for the site of a 60th jubilee memorial in 2012.

135. Juliet Barnes, *The Ghosts of Happy Valley: Searching for the Lost World of Africa's Infamous Aristocrats* (London: Aurum Press, 2013), p. 5.

136. Elspeth Huxley, *A Man from Nowhere* (London: Chatto & Windus, 1964), p. 52.

137. Huxley, *A Man from Nowhere*, pp. 278–9.

6 IMPERIAL WELCOME: THE BRITISH SUBJECT

1. Quoted in Gavin Stamp, *Lost Victorian Britain: How the Twentieth Century Destroyed the Nineteenth Century's Architectural Masterpieces* (London: Aurum Press, 2010), p. 61.

2. Legal proceedings reported in *The Times*, 20 June 1944; 29 June 1944 (my expurgation of the original). Constantine published his own brief account ten years later in *Colour Bar* (London: Stanley Paul, 1954), pp. 137–8.

3. See Bill Schwarz (ed.), *West Indian Intellectuals in Britain* (Manchester: Manchester University Press, 2003), especially chs., 2, 3 and 6.

4. *Evening Standard*, 4 September 1943.

5. *Daily Mirror*, 4 September 1943.

6. *Evening Standard*, 3 September 1943; *Daily Telegraph*, 3 September 1943.

7. Quoted in the *Daily Mirror*, 3 September 1943.

8. Mr Justice Birkett, quoted in Peter Fryer, *Staying Power: The History of Black People in Britain* (London: Pluto, 1984), p. 366.

9. Hansard, 23 September 1943, Vol. 392, cc. 443–4.

10. *Evening Standard*, 3 September 1943; see also *Daily Herald*, 3 September 1943; *Daily Mirror*, 3 September 1943; *Spectator*, 9 September 1943.

11. *Evening Standard*, 7 September 1943.

12. See Wendy Webster, *Mixing It: Diversity in World War Two Britain* (Oxford: Oxford University Press, 2018), pp. 123–4.

13. This point is elaborated in Anne Spry Rush, 'Imperial Identity in Colonial Minds: Harold Moody and the League of Coloured Peoples', *Twentieth Century British History*, 13:4 (2002), pp. 356–83.

14. Minute by J. L. Keith, 13 September 1943, CO859/80/8, The National Archives, Kew (hereafter NA). The Colonial Office ultimately decided against legislative action, partly on the grounds that Constantine's contractual suit against the hotel rendered the matter *sub judice*, and partly to avoid stirring further adverse publicity about the racial prejudices of American servicemen in Britain.

15. Quoted in Webster, *Mixing It*, pp. 116–17.

16. Quoted in Kathleen Paul, *Whitewashing Britain: Race and Citizenship in the Postwar Era* (Ithaca: Cornell University Press, 1997), p. 21.

17. Anne Spry Rush, *Bonds of Empire: West Indians and Britishness from Victoria to Decolonization* (Oxford: Oxford University Press, 2001).

18. Kennetta Hammond Perry, for example, frames it as a moment when the 'ideological possibilities of imperial belonging collided with the practical realities of British citizenship'. See Kennetta Hammond Perry, *London Is the Place for Me: Black Britons, Citizenship and the Politics of Race* (Oxford: Oxford University Press, 2016), p. 50. Later she invokes a 'penetrating schism between the possibilities of British citizenship and the realities of exclusion and non-belonging', p. 88.

19. Perry, *London Is the Place for Me*, p. 12. See also Jordanna Bailkin's *The Afterlife of Empire* (Berkeley: University of California Press, 2012) and Daniel Gorman's conceptualization of the nationality issue as a mode of 'domestic decolonisation' in *Imperial Citizenship: Empire and the Question of Belonging* (Manchester: Manchester University Press, 2007), p. 214.

20. See, for example, Z. Nia Reynolds (ed.), *When I Came to England: An Oral History of Life in 1950s and 1960s Britain* (London: Black Stock, 2001); the shock of arrival theme is also ubiquitous in scholarly accounts that emphasize the 'myth of the mother country … shattered' by the experience of migration, see, for example, Elizabeth Thomas-Hope, 'Hopes and Reality in the West Indian Migration to Britain', *Oral History*, 8:1 (Spring 1980), pp. 35–42, 40.

21. Andrea Levy, *Small Island* (London: Headline, 2004), p. 141.

22. Perry, *London Is the Place for Me*, p. 14; Barnor Hesse, 'Diasporicity', in Barnor Hesse (ed.), *Un/settled Multiculturalisms* (London: Zed Books, 2000), pp. 97–99. See especially Tony Kushner's extended critique of the reductive

and distorting Windrush mythology, which he argues was 'rediscovered' some forty years after the event for largely contemporary purposes. See Tony Kushner, *The Battle of Britishness: Migrant Journeys, 1685 to the Present* (Manchester: Manchester University Press, 2012), ch. 7.

23. Matthew Mead, 'Empire Windrush: The Cultural Memory of an Imaginary Arrival', *Journal of Postcolonial Writing*, 45:2 (June 2009), pp. 137–8.

24. Mike Phillips and Trevor Phillips, *Windrush: The Irresistible Rise of Multiracial Britain* (London: Harper Collins, 1998), p. 79.

25. The Home Office was aware of reports that *Empire Windrush* might be the harbinger of things to come, but remarked that the 'grounds for this fear are not clear'. A. W. Peterson (assistant private secretary to the prime minister) to F. L. T. Graham-Harrison (Home Office), 5 July 1948 in S. R. Ashton and David Killingray (eds.), *The West Indies: British Documents on the End of Empire*, Series B, vol. 6 (London: The Stationary Office, 1999), p. 6. Labour's Colonial Secretary Arthur Creech Jones assured parliament that it was 'very unlikely that a similar event to this will occur again in the West Indies', Hansard (Commons) 16 June 1948, vol. 452, c. 422; Fryer, *Staying Power*, p. 372.

26. Winston James, 'The Black Experience in Twentieth-Century Britain', in Philip D. Morgan and Sean Hawkins (eds.), *Black Experience and the Empire* (Oxford: Oxford University Press, 2004), p. 378.

27. Stephen Howe, 'C. L. R. James: Visions of History, Visions of Britain', in Schwarz, *West Indian Intellectuals*, p. 161.

28. David Killingray, '"A Good West Indian, a Good African, and, in Short, a Good Britisher": Black and British in a Colour-Conscious Empire, 1760–1950', *Journal of Imperial and Commonwealth History*, 36:3 (2008), pp. 363–81, 364. Bill Schwarz concurs that 'Britishness was indeed a capacious category, and it could offer a resource to the dispossessed' in '"Shivering in the Noonday Sun": The British World and the Dynamics of "Nativisation"', in Kate Darian-Smith, Stuart Macintyre and Patricia Grimshaw (eds.), *Britishness Abroad: Transnational Movements and Imperial Cultures* (Melbourne: Melbourne University Press, 2007), p. 23.

29. Schwarz, '"Shivering in the Noonday Sun"'. See also Rush, *Bonds of Empire*, ch. 2.

30. Perry, *London Is the Place for Me*, pp. 26, 37.

31. Lara Putnam, 'Citizenship from the Margins: Vernacular Theories of Rights and the State from the Interwar Caribbean', *Journal of British Studies*, 53:1 (January 2014), p. 172.

32. Rush, *Bonds of Empire*, pp. 9–10.

33. Rush, *Bonds of Empire*, pp. 6, 10.

34. Perry, *London Is the Place for Me*, p. 61.

35. Howe, 'C. L. R. James', p. 158; Perry, *London Is the Place for Me*, pp. 35, 39; Rush, *Bonds of Empire*, p. 10. There remains, however, a certain equivocation between imperial manipulation and Caribbean agency that is never fully squared in most accounts.

36. Quote from 1916 in Howard Johnson, 'The Black Experience in the British Caribbean in the Twentieth Century', in Morgan and Hawkins, *Black Experience*, p. 320.
37. C. L. R. James, *Beyond a Boundary* (Durham, NC: Duke University Press, 2013, 1st ed. 1963), pp. 7–8.
38. Marilyn Lake and Henry Reynolds, *Drawing the Global Colour Line: White Men's Countries and the International Challenge of Racial Equality* (Cambridge: Cambridge University Press, 2008); R. A. Huttenbuck, 'The British Empire as a "White Man's Country": Racial Attitudes and Immigration Legislation in the Colonies of White Settlement', *Journal of British Studies*, 13:1 (1973), pp. 108–37.
39. Charles W. Dilke, *Greater Britain: A Record of Travel in English-Speaking Countries during 1866 and 1867* (New York: Harper and Brothers, 1869, 1st ed. 1868), p. ix.
40. J. R. Seeley, *The Expansion of England: Two Courses of Lectures* (London: Macmillan, 1891, 1st ed. 1883), p. 10.
41. Seeley, *Expansion of England*, pp. 11, 301–2.
42. Seeley, *Expansion of England*, p. 12.
43. This now largely forgotten passage is in the conclusion to Churchill's celebrated 'Iron Curtain' speech at Fulton Missouri in March 1946.
44. James Anthony Froude, *The English in the West Indies* (London: Longmans, Green, and Co., 1888), p. 287.
45. Froude, *The English in the West Indies*, pp. 364–5.
46. Catherine Hall, 'What is a West Indian?', in Schwarz (ed.), *West Indian Intellectuals*, p. 46.
47. J. J. Thomas, *Froudacity: West Indian Fables by James Anthony Froude* (Philadelphia: Gebbie and Co, 1890, 1st ed. 1889), pp. 9, 125; See Bill Schwarz, 'Introduction', in Schwarz (ed.), *West Indian Intellectuals*, p. 4.
48. Thomas, *Froudacity*, pp. 128–9.
49. N. Darnell Davis, 'Mr. Froude's Negrophobia: or Don Quixote as Cook's Tourist', *Timehri: Journal of the Royal Agricultural and Commercial Society of British Guiana*, 2, new series (1888), pp. 85–129.
50. Quoted in Putnam, 'Citizenship from the Margins', p. 180.
51. See Thomas Koditschek, *Liberalism, Imperialism, and the Historical Imagination: Nineteenth-Century Visions of a Greater Britain* (Cambridge: Cambridge University Press, 2011), pp. 200–2.
52. Quoted in Anthony Bateman, *Cricket, Literature and Culture: Symbolising the Nation, Destabilising Empire* (London: Routledge, 2009), pp. 162, 164.
53. Which is not to dismiss the myriad other, more subtle ways that the colonial Caribbean interacted with imperial subjectivities in the metropole. See, generally, Catherine Hall, *Civilising Subjects: Metropole and Colony in the English Imagination, 1830–67* (London: Polity, 2002).
54. Putnam, 'Citizenship from the Margins', pp. 188–9.
55. *Evening Standard*, 22 June 1948.

56. Stuart Hall (with Bill Schwarz), *Familiar Stranger: A Life between Two Islands* (London: Allen Lane, 2017), p. 12.
57. *Barbados Advocate*, 25 June 1948.
58. W. A. S. Hardy, quoted in the *Daily Gleaner*, 'West Indian "Inrush" Regretted', 27 June 1948. Hardy, a Black Jamaican journalist resident in London since the 1930s, went on to record the experiences of ordinary West Indians in England in the Colonial Service radio series, *Biography of an Exile*. See Rush, *Bonds of Empire*, p. 188.
59. *Trinidad Guardian*, 20 June 1948.
60. M. E. Farquhar, 'Candid Comments', *Trinidad Guardian Weekly*, 27 June 1948.
61. Vince Reid, testimony in Phillips and Phillips, *Windrush*, p. 64.
62. *Evening Standard*, 22 June 1948.
63. Putnam, 'Citizenship from the Margins', p. 164. I have enlarged on the theme of individual recollections of sudden disenchantment in Stuart Ward, '"How Come England Did Not Know Me": The "Rude Awakenings" of the Windrush Era', in Christian D. Pedersen and Stuart Ward (eds.), *The Break-Up of Greater Britain* (Manchester: Manchester University Press, 2021), pp. 84–102.
64. Putnam, 'Citizenship from the Margins', p. 164.
65. *The Times*, 22 June 1948. The following day, a mere ten lines were devoted to 'Jamaicans arrive to seek work', clearly treating the matter as a mere passing curiosity.
66. Hansard (Lords), 21 June 1948, Vol. 156, cc. 998–9.
67. Quoted in Randall Hansen, *Citizenship and Immigration in Post-War Britain* (Oxford: Oxford University Press, 2000), p. 50.
68. Home Office officials did notice the 'unfortunate' coincidence that the 'Jamaica party' should have arrived in the middle of the debate on the Nationality Bill and voiced concern that 'it may introduce an extraneous element into the discussion in the Commons'. But these concerns never materialized. See A. W. Peterson to F. L. T. Graham-Harrison, 5 July 1948 in Ashton and Killingray (eds.), *The West Indies*, p. 5.
69. As Kathleen Paul notes, the Common Code was formally codified in the 1914 *British Nationality and Status of Aliens Act*, but the informal practice had existed since at least the seventeenth century. See Kathleen Paul, '"British Subjects" and "British Stock": Labour's Postwar Imperialism', *Journal of British Studies*, 34:2 (1995), pp. 233–76, 236–7.
70. Ann Dummett and Andrew Nicol, *Subjects, Citizens, Aliens and Others. Nationality and Immigration Law* (London: Weidenfeld and Nicolson, 1990), p. 134.
71. On nationalist interpretations, see Jatinder Mann, 'The Evolution of Commonwealth Citizenship, 1945–48 in Canada, Britain and Australia', *Comparative Politics*, 50:3 (2012), pp. 293–313, 294–5; see also, for example, Valerie Knowles, *Forging Our Legacy: Canadian Citizenship and Immigration, 1900–1977* (Ottawa: Citizenship and Immigration Canada, 2000).
72. Mann, 'The Evolution of Commonwealth Citizenship', p. 296.

73. Conservative MP Donald Fleming, cited in José E. Igartua, *The Other Quiet Revolution: National Identities in English Canada, 1945–71* (Vancouver: University of British Columbia Press, 2006), p. 21. Sections of the English-speaking press shared these suspicions, including the *Ottawa Journal* that criticized the 'unseemly haste of certain people in this country ... to rid Canada of anything suggesting the British connection'. Igartua, *The Other Quiet Revolution*, p. 26.
74. Quoted in Mann, 'The Evolution of Commonwealth Citizenship', p. 296.
75. Quoted in Paul, *Whitewashing Britain*, p. 14.
76. Paul, '"British Subjects" and "British Stock"', p. 250.
77. Paul, '"British Subjects" and "British Stock"', p. 246.
78. The idea was originally proposed by the Bermudan governor Sir Ralph Leatham, see Leatham to Creech Jones, 30 October 1946, CO323/1869/11 Part 1, NA. See also the Colonial Office internal minute that ultimately decided in favour of CUKC in CO323/1869/11, Part 2, November 1946.
79. Quoted in Hansen, *Citizenship and Immigration*, p. 53.
80. 'Starkly myopic' in Putnam, 'Citizenship from the Margins', p. 186; 'misguided idealism' in Bevan (1986) and excessive generosity in Freeman (1979), both quoted in Hansen, *Citizenship and Immigration*, p. 56. The charge of disingenuousness is implicit throughout Paul's account, describing the Act as a 'last stand against encroaching colonial independence and imperial disintegration'. See Kathleen Paul, 'Communities of Britishness: Migration in the Last Gasp of Empire', in Stuart Ward (ed.), *British Culture and the End of Empire* (Manchester: Manchester University Press, 2001), pp. 180–99, 183. Perry also presents the Act as a cynical exercise in keeping up imperial appearances in *London Is the Place for Me*, p. 59.
81. Hansen, *Citizenship and Immigration*, pp. 55–6.
82. See Chapter 4.
83. Neville Meaney, 'The End of "White Australia" and Australia's Changing Perceptions of Asia, 1945–1990', *Australian Journal of International Affairs*, 49:2 (1995), pp. 171–89; Ann-Mari Jordens, *Redefining Australians: Immigration, Citizenship and National Identity* (Sydney: Hale & Iremonger, 1995), p. 6.
84. Minister of Internal Affairs William Parry, introducing the legislation to the New Zealand Parliament on 17 August 1948 in W. David McIntrye and W. J. Gardner (eds.), *Speeches and Documents on New Zealand History* (Oxford: Oxford University Press, 1971), p. 295. In Australia it was Immigration Minister Arthur Calwell who presided over Citizenship and who also saw fit to underline how 'nationality has been placed in the forefront ... it is a bill relating first, to British nationality, and, secondly, to Australian citizenship'. Quoted in Mann, 'The Evolution of Commonwealth Citizenship', p. 306. See also J. C. Beaglehole, 'The Development of New Zealand Nationality', *Journal of World History*, 2 (1954), pp. 106–23.
85. Quoted in Jatinder Mann, *The Search for a New Identity: The Rise of Multiculturalism in Canada and Australia, 1890s–1970s* (New York: Peter Lang, 2016), p. 122.

86. Quoted in Mann, 'The Evolution of Commonwealth Citizenship', p. 307.

87. Nicholas Mansergh, *Survey of Commonwealth Affairs: Problems of Wartime Cooperation and Post-war Change* (London: Frank Cass, 1968), pp. 386–7. See Chapter 2.

88. Saul Dubow notes that the 1949 Citizenship Bill did not in itself deprive Black South Africans of citizenship, but the kind of legislation it enabled 'marked a step in the process of making citizenship exclusive and race dependent'. Saul Dubow, 'South Africa and South Africans: Nationality, Belonging, Citizenship', in Robert Ross, Anne Kelk Mager and Bill Nasson (eds.), *The Cambridge History of South Africa*, vol. 2: *1885–1994* (Cambridge: Cambridge University Press, 2012), p. 55.

89. Dr Arthur Keppel-Jones of the University of Witwatersrand in the *Sunday Times* (Johannesburg), 17 July 1949. 'It is too clear', he averred, 'that what the South African Government want to withhold from British immigrants is not the citizen's status but the vote.'

90. Quoted in Ronald Hyam and Peter Henshaw, *The Lion and the Springbok: Britain and South Africa since the Boer War* (Cambridge: Cambridge University Press, 2003), p. 310; on the electoral implications see p. 284.

91. *Cork Examiner*, 29 January 1946.

92. British Nationality Act 1948, Part 1, s. 2(1).

93. Rieko Karatani, *Defining British Citizenship: Empire, Commonwealth and Modern Britain* (London: Frank Cass, 2003), pp. 117–18; J. Mervyn Jones, 'British Nationality Act, 1948', *British Yearbook of International Law*, 25 (1948), pp. 158–79, 161–2.

94. As Canadian officials concluded: 'It would seem inevitable that we should find ourselves in an embarrassing position regarding our immigration policy if we agreed to a scheme under which the essential feature of the Commonwealth connection would be the common status of Commonwealth citizenship'. Memorandum by Canadian Department of External Affairs, 'India and the Commonwealth: A Preliminary Survey', 3 March 1949 in Hector Mackenzie (ed.), *Documents on Canadian External Relations*, vol. 15, 1949 (Ottawa: DFAIT, 1995), pp. 1315–16. The same reservations were expressed in Australia, see Cabinet Submission 'India and the British Commonwealth' 7 April 1949 in Pamela Andre (ed.), *Australia and the Postwar World: The Commonwealth, Asia and the Pacific, Documents 1948–49* (Canberra: DFAT, 1998), pp. 116–17.

95. British Nationality Act 1948, Part 1, s. 1(2).

96. See commentary by the CRO's constitutional adviser, Sir Charles Dixon in DO35/10303, NA; see also 'Commonwealth Nomenclature: Draft of a Note by the First Parliamentary Counsel', December 1949, CAB21/8185, NA.

97. H. E. Davies (Delhi) to Harrison (CRO), 23 April 1955; D. W. H. Wickson (CRO) to D. M. R. Skinner (Delhi), 7 November 1956, DO35/1030, NA. The terms appears in the Act solely to refer to citizens of other Commonwealth countries, not Indians.

98. Extract of Indian parliamentary debates, 27 August 1958, in DO35/10303, NA. Smedley (Delhi) to Chadwick (CRO), 30 August 1958 in DO35/10303, NA. Other examples of dissent and confusion over the designation of Indians as British subjects are documented in Kalathmika Natarajan, 'Entangled Citizens: The Afterlives of Empire in the Indian Citizenship Act, 1947–55', in Pedersen and Ward (eds.), *The Break-Up of Greater Britain*, pp. 63–83.

99. Quoted in Paul, *Whitewashing Britain*, p. 142.

100. The BBC programme is discussed in Wendy Webster, *Englishness and Empire, 1939–65* (Oxford: Oxford University Press, 2005), pp. 159–62; Learie Constantine, *Colour Bar* (London: Stanley Paul, 1954).

101. Edward Pilkington, *Beyond the Mother Country: West Indians and the Notting Hill White Riots* (London: I. B. Tauris, 1988). See also Paul, *Whitewashing Britain*, pp. 155–6; Webster, *Englishness and Empire*, pp. 164–5; Perry, *London Is the Place for Me*, pp. 89–91.

102. As extensively documented in Perry's *London Is the Place for Me*, ch. 3.

103. Foreign Office telegram to overseas posts, 3 September 1958, quoted in Perry, *London Is the Place for Me*, p. 106.

104. *Barbados Advocate*, 'The Heart of the Matter', 9 September 1958; 'Take it Easy', *Daily Gleaner*, 9 September 1958; 'The Truth about Notting Hill', *Sunday Gleaner*, 7 September 1958.

105. *Daily Gleaner*, 4 September 1958; 6 September 1958.

106. Perry, *London Is the Place for Me*, p. 109.

107. *Economist*, 5 September 1958. The now-famous cartoon in the *Daily Mirror* on 2 September depicting the ghost of Adolf Hitler looming over a rioting 'Teddy Boy' had much the same effect.

108. See article in *The Times* referring to the 'sadly misnamed "race riots"', cited in Perry, *London Is the Place for Me*, p. 112 and Merrick Winn's bald assertion in the *Daily Express* that the riots had 'nothing to do with race or colour', 2 September 1958.

109. 'How to Live as Neighbours' and 'Why? What Fans the Hatred', *Daily Express*, 2 September 1958.

110. *Daily Mirror*, 3 September 1958; 8 September 1958. Emphasis in original.

111. *The Times*, 'A Family of Nations', 4 September 1958.

112. Macmillan conceded in his memoirs that the riots provided an added spur to government action, see *At the End of the Day* (London: Macmillan, 1973), p. 74.

113. Ian R. G. Spencer, *British Immigration Policy since 1939: The Making of Multi-Racial Britain* (London: Routledge, 1997), p. 109.

114. These rival standpoints are argued respectively by Hansen's *Citizenship and Immigration* (who emphasizes the court of public opinion) and Paul's *Whitewashing Britain* (which stresses the 'succession of officials and politicians' who over a period of thirteen years 'had taken an extremely proactive role in developing enough momentum to make control acceptable', p. 166).

115. Norman Manley, 'A National Jamaica' (1938), reprinted in Rex M. Nettleford (ed.), *Norman Washington Manley and the New Jamaica: Selected Speeches and Writings, 1938–68* (Kingston: Longman Caribbean, 1971), p. 101.
116. 'taking our place' is Trinidad's Albert Gomes, 'Federation in the British West Indies' in A. Curtis Wilgus (ed.), *The Caribbean: Its Political Problems* (Gainesville: University of Florida, 1956), p. 277; 'liquidating vestiges' is W. A. Crawford of Barbados, quoted in Elizabeth Wallace, *The British Caribbean: From the Decline of Colonialism to the End of Federation* (Toronto: University of Toronto Press, 1977), p. 100.
117. Harold N. McDermott, 'Towards "That Republic in Which Complexions Do Not Matter": Derek Walcott's Drums and Colours Fifty Years On', *Anthurium: A Caribbean Studies Journal*, 11:2 (2014).
118. See Samuel J. Hurwitz, 'The Federation of the West Indies: A Study in Nationalisms', *Journal of British Studies*, 6:1 (November 1966), pp. 158–9; see also Wallace, *The British Caribbean*, pp. 116–17.
119. Hurwitz, 'Federation of the West Indies', p. 144.
120. 'The idea of Federation', Mary Chamberlain avers, 'was born in the trans-national belongings and dreams of West Indians overseas and soon acquired status as a kind of mythical homeland'. Mary Chamberlain, *Empire and Nation-Building in the Caribbean: Barbados, 1937–66* (Manchester: Manchester University Press, 2010), pp. 184–5. Wallace also noted 'the saying' in the 1970s that 'the Federation and West Indian nationhood were conceived in London and Toronto rather than in the Caribbean', see *The British Caribbean*, p. 225; George Lamming, *The Pleasures of Exile* (London: Michael Joseph, 1960), p. 214.
121. 'Passage to the Promised Land?' (1996) BBC Radio 2. 'No Opportunities in Grenada' – Alex Pascall, broadcaster and oral historian.
122. Schwarz, 'Introduction', p. 8.
123. Donald Hinds, *Journey to an Illusion: The West Indian in Britain* (London: Bogle-L'Ouverture, 2001, 1st ed. 1966). 'Struck dumb' is Hinds's term in *Mother Country: In the Wake of a Dream* (London: Hansib, 2014).
124. Interview in Ian Thomson, 'Scotland Yard: The Jamaican-British Encounter', *Nation*, 11 March 2011. Hinds was not unique in this regard. The racial justice campaigner Baron Baker recalled how, before the Notting Hill riots 'I was British – I was born under the Union Jack. But the race riots made me realize who I am and what I am. They turned me into a staunch Jamaican.' Quoted in Paul Ward, *Britishness Since 1870* (London: Routledge, 2004), p. 137.
125. Bill Schwarz, 'Claudia Jones and The West Indian Gazette: Reflections on the Emergence of Post-colonial Britain', *Twentieth Century British History*, 14:3 (2003), pp. 264–85, 270.
126. Donald Hinds, 'The West Indian Gazette: Claudia Jones and the Black Press in Britain', *Race and Class*, 50:1 (2008), pp. 88–97, 92.
127. Quoted in Schwarz, 'Claudia Jones', pp. 273–4.

128. The description is from a 1992 letter to his grandson, Liam James Marcelle, published in the 2001 edition. See Hinds, *Journey to an Illusion*, p. xvii.
129. The title of the last chapter in Lamming's *Pleasures of Exile*.
130. Hinds, *Journey to an Illusion*, p. 5.
131. Hinds, *Journey to an Illusion*, pp. 157, 159.
132. Sam Selvon, *The Lonely Londoners* (London: Penguin, 2006, 1st ed. 1956), p. 124.
133. Paul, *Whitewashing Britain*, p. 167.
134. That is to say, without applying for an entry permit. There were exceptions, to be taken up in Chapter 12.
135. Thornberry would later play a formative role in the civil rights movement in Northern Ireland: 'British Nationality Act', *The Modern Law Review*, 28 (March 1965), pp. 197–200, 197.
136. Quoted in Paul, *Whitewashing Britain*, p. 166.
137. J. V. Scott (NZ High Commission, London) to Secretary of External Affairs, 'Immigration into the United Kingdom', 3 August 1961, ABHS 7148 W4628 65/10/9, Archives New Zealand, Wellington.
138. Alexander Downer (snr) quoted in Stuart Ward, *Australia and the British Embrace: The Demise of the Imperial Ideal* (Melbourne: Melbourne University Press, 2001), p. 137.
139. *Sydney Morning Herald*, 'Loosening the Ties of the Commonwealth', 23 April 1962; see similar sentiments in the *Canberra Times*, 23 April 1962.
140. *Barbados Advocate*, 'British Migration Bill is Anti-Colour', 18 November 1961.
141. *Barbados Advocate*, 'Britain has Fallen on Evil Days', 13 October 1961.
142. *Barbados Advocate*, 'Sir Grantley Speaks Strong Words on Curb Bill', 5 November 1961.
143. Agency tape report of Sir Grantley Adams's comments at Heathrow Airport, 4 December 1961; 'Note for the Record', 4 December 1961, PREM11/3623, NA.
144. 'Note for the Record', 4 December 1961, PREM11/3623, NA.
145. See, for example, the more benign treatment by Robert Best in the *Barbados Advocate*, 19 April 1962 and the editorial of the *Trinidad Guardian*, 25 April 1962.
146. *Barbados Advocate*, 20 October 1961; 18 November 1961.
147. A line of argument honed and perfected by Trinidadian premier Eric Williams. See, for example, his remarks likening the migration to Britain of unemployed West Indians as 'Britain's chicken coming home to roost' in PREM13/2433, NA.
148. Wallace, The British Caribbean, pp. 93, 109.
149. A point also made in Chamberlain, *Empire and Nation Building*, p. 187.
150. 'could not be wholly separated', Chris Waters, '"Dark Strangers" in Our Midst: Discourses of Race and Nation in Britain, 1947–63', *Journal of British Studies*, 36:2 (April 1997), pp. 207–38, 208; 'collided head-on', Elizabeth Buettner, *Europe*

after Empire (Cambridge: Cambridge University Press, 2016), p. 259; 'made race central', Webster, *Englishness and Empire*, p. 171.

151. Waters, '"Dark Strangers"', p. 217; Schwarz, 'Claudia Jones', p. 266. See also Webster, *Englishness and Empire*, p. 181.

152. Perry, *London Is the Place for Me*, p. 48; Amanda M. Bidnall, 'West Indian Interventions at the Heart of the Cultural Establishment: Edric Connor, Pearl Connor, and the BBC', *Twentieth Century British History*, 24:1 (2013), pp. 58–83, 59.

153. Perry, *London Is the Place for Me*, p. 12.

154. Schwarz, 'Claudia Jones', p. 267.

155. Quoted in Perry, *London Is the Place for Me*, p. 54.

156. Perry, *London Is the Place for Me*, pp. 6, 49.

157. This 'inward-turn' is discussed in Schwarz, 'Claudia Jones', p. 284. An earlier study by Paul B. Rich also notes how as late as 1962, 'black political thinking was still governed more by the idea of asserting rights as citizens of the Commonwealth than as permanent members of British society' – a situation that was shortly to change. *Race and Empire in British Politics* (2nd ed., Cambridge: Cambridge University Press, 1990), p. 199.

158. The 'whimper' is stressed by Erik Bleich, *Race Politics in Britain and France: Ideas and Policymaking since the 1960s* (Cambridge: Cambridge University Press, 2003), pp. 61, 69; Gavin Schaffer is more upbeat in his assessment in 'Legislating against Hatred: Meaning and Motive in Section Six of the Race Relations Act of 1965', *Twentieth Century British History*, 25:2 (2014), pp. 251–75, 251.

159. Sheila Patterson, *Immigration and Race Relations in Britain, 1960–67* (New York: Oxford University Press, 1969), p. 87.

160. The other two members were Mark Bonham Carter (Chairman and former Liberal MP) and Bernard Langton (Lord Mayor of Manchester).

161. Greater London Council quoted in Hermione Hobhouse, *Lost London: A Century of Demolition and Decay* (London: Macmillan, 1971), p. 207. All that remains of the original Imperial Hotel are the five tower bells and some original statues, situated in the forecourt of its aesthetically unambitious substitute erected on the same Russell Square site.

7 THE WIND CHANGES: HUMAN RIGHTS AFTER SMUTS

1. Alan H. Jeeves, 'Arthur Keppel-Jones: Scholar, Teacher, Liberal Intellectual', *South African Historical Journal*, 32:1 (1995), pp. 24–33 ('historical extrapolation' was the assessment of Keppel-Jones's compatriot, Cornelis W. de Kiewiet of Cornell University, quoted on p. 24). Keppel-Jones himself described it as an attempt at 'working out the next half-century of South African history as it is likely to be shaped by the political forces which at present dominate the scene';

Arthur Keppel-Jones, *When Smuts Goes: A History of South Africa from 1952–2010, First Published in 2015* (London: Victor Gollancz, 1947), pp. 7–8.

2. Keppel-Jones, *When Smuts Goes*, pp. 96, 97.

3. Keppel-Jones, *When Smuts Goes*, p. 88 and generally ch. 5. The premonition was never meant to be taken literally. As Keppel-Jones explained to an audience at Chatham House in March 1947, the book was intended as both 'a prophecy and a warning' to shake his countrymen from their complacency and 'contempt for purely South African threats against their nationality'. Quoted in John Lambert, '"Welcome Home": White English-speaking South Africans and the Royal Visit of 1947', *South African Historical Journal*, 69:1 (2017), pp. 101–12. Or as he re-framed it years later, he hoped that 'the warning would prevent the prophecy from coming to pass'. Alan H. Jeeves, 'Interview with Arthur Keppel-Jones', *South African Historical Journal*, 32:1 (1995), pp. 11–23, 15.

4. Jeeves, 'Interview with Keppel-Jones', pp. 15, 17, 19.

5. Keppel-Jones, *When Smuts Goes*, p. 95.

6. The term is from James Belich, *Replenishing the Earth: The Settler Revolution and the Rise of the Anglo-World, 1783–1939* (Oxford: Oxford University Press, 2009), p. 472. See also Chapter 1 in this volume.

7. Saul Dubow, 'South Africa and South Africans: Nationality, Belonging, Citizenship', in Robert Ross, Anne Kel Mager and Bill Nasson (eds.), *The Cambridge History of South Africa,* vol. 2: *1885–1994* (Cambridge: Cambridge University Press, 2012), pp. 17–65, 51.

8. Bill Schwarz, *The White Man's World: Memories of Empire*, vol. 1 (Oxford: Oxford University Press, 2011), p. 278.

9. These assessments from Smuts's contemporaries are cited in Schwarz, *White Man's World*, pp. 283, 285, 287.

10. Saul Dubow, 'How British Was the British World? The Case of South Africa', *Journal of Imperial and Commonwealth History*, 37:1 (2009), pp. 1–27, 15.

11. Schwarz, *White Man's World*, pp. 288–9.

12. See L. J. Butler and Sarah Stockwell (eds.), *The Wind of Change: Harold Macmillan and British Decolonization* (Basingstoke: Palgrave, 2013).

13. See, for example, Adom Getachew's argument that 'anti-colonial nationalists were not solely or even primarily nation-builders', in *Worldmaking after Empire: The Rise and Fall of Self-Determination* (Princeton: Princeton University Press, 2019); see also Frederick Cooper, *Citizenship between Empire and Nation: Remaking France and French Africa, 1945–1960* (Princeton: Princeton University Press, 2014).

14. More than thirty years ago, John Darwin identified the 'emergence' of 'Afro-Asian nationalism' as the most 'widely favoured' explanation for the 'defeat of colonial rule'. Although himself sceptical of such reductive accounting, the effects of an undifferentiated 'nationalism' nevertheless continue to assume prominence across a wide spectrum of historical writing. See John Darwin, *Britain and Decolonisation: The Retreat from Empire in the Post-War World* (London: Macmillan, 1988), p. 17. See

also John Darwin, *The End of the British Empire: The Historical Debate* (Oxford: Basil Blackwell, 1991).

15. Dubow, 'How British Was the British World?', p. 4.
16. See Dubow, 'How British Was the British World?', especially, pp. 13–15 and his observations about Dilke on p. 5.
17. See, particularly, Andrew S. Thompson, 'The Languages of Loyalism in Southern Africa, c. 1879–1939', *English Historical Review*, 118:477 (June 2003), pp. 617–50.
18. Dubow, 'How British Was the British World?', p. 14.
19. Hilary Sapire, '"We Have Seen the Son of Heaven/We Have seen the Son of our Queen": African Encounters with Prince Alfred on his Royal Tour, 1860', in Sarah Carter and Maria Nugent (eds.), *Mistress of Everything: Queen Victoria in Indigenous Worlds* (Manchester: Manchester University Press, 2016), pp. 25–53, 26. See also Chapters 3 and 6.
20. Shula Marks, *The Ambiguities of Dependence in South Africa: Class, Nationalism, and the State in Twentieth-Century Natal* (Baltimore: Johns Hopkins University Press, 1986), p. 48.
21. Andrew Thompson cites several examples of this reductive approach in 'The Languages of Loyalism', p. 619; see also Marks, *Ambiguities of Dependence*, p. 48; Hilary Sapire also treats the loyalism of African elites and traditionalist chiefs as more complex and layered than 'the naïve internalisation of the imperial creed by craven "Black Englishmen"'. See Sapire, 'We Have Seen the Son of Heaven', p. 26.
22. Hilary Sapire, 'Ambiguities of Loyalism: The Prince of Wales in India and Africa, 1921–2 and 25', *History Workshop Journal*, 73 (Spring 2012), pp. 37–65, 39.
23. Sapire, 'Ambiguities of Loyalism', pp. 39, 42, 58, 59.
24. Peter Limb, 'Early ANC Leaders and the British World: Ambiguities and Identities', *Historia*, 47:1 (May 2002), pp. 56–82, 58.
25. Marks, *Ambiguities of Dependence*, pp. 55–6.
26. Limb, 'Early ANC Leaders', p. 73.
27. Limb, 'Early ANC Leaders', pp. 62, 76. Dubow also notes the 'conspicuous evidence of British forms of address and dress' among the early ANC leadership, in terms of both 'its verbal pronouncements and visual self-representation'. Dubow, 'How British Was the British World?', p. 12.
28. Schwarz, *White Man's World*, ch. 5, note 51.
29. Quoted in Peter Walshe, *The Rise of African Nationalism in South Africa: The African National Congress, 1912–52* (Berkeley: University of California Press, 1971), p. 64.
30. Limb, 'Early ANC Leaders', p. 71.
31. Peter Limb, 'The Empire Writes Back: African Challenges to the Brutish (South African) Empire in the Early 20th Century', *Journal of Southern African Studies*, 41:3 (2015), pp. 599–616, 604.
32. Limb, 'Empire Writes Back', p. 610.
33. Limb, 'Early ANC Leaders', p. 70.

34. Quoted in Andrew Markus, 'William Cooper and the 1937 Petition to the King', *Aboriginal History*, 7:1 (1983), pp. 46–60, 51. See Chapter 3, pp. 90–2.
35. Saul Dubow, *South Africa's Struggle for Human Rights* (Athens: Ohio University Press, 2012), p. 47.
36. Limb, 'Early ANC Leaders', p. 69.
37. Adom Getachew, 'A Great Wall to Batter Down', *London Review of Books*, 22:10 (21 May 2020).
38. Quoted in Limb, 'Empire Writes Back', p. 615.
39. Walshe, *Rise of African Nationalism*, p. 328.
40. Which is not to say that the Crown henceforth became irrelevant to Indigenous claims, but the emphasis shifted markedly. See Mark McKenna, '"An Audience with the Queen": Indigenous Australians and the Crown, 1954–2017', *Royal Studies Journal*, 5:1 (2018), pp. 157–67. See also Joel Hebert, '"Sacred Trust": Rethinking Late British Decolonization in Indigenous Canada', *Journal of British Studies*, 58:3 (2019), pp. 565–97.
41. See Hilary Sapire's critique of the 'resistance paradigm' in South African historical writing, in which various modes of 'black loyalism', implicitly and explicitly, 'are portrayed as "regressive", "naïve", and "backward" and hence inauthentic, awaiting their inevitable substitution by more intrinsic modes of Indigenous selfhood'. Hilary Sapire, 'African Loyalism and Its Discontents: The Royal Tour of South Africa, 1947', *Historical Journal*, 54:1 (March 2011), pp. 215–40, 220. Dubow also notes the 'cautious ambivalence' of much South African historiography in dealing with modes of Black loyalism 'because of the assumption that resistance necessitated overt and consistent rejection of imperial hegemony'. 'How British Was the British World?', p. 12.
42. Elizabeth Borgwardt, *A New Deal for the World: America's Vision for Human Rights* (Cambridge, MA: Harvard University Press, 2005), p. 4.
43. Sapire, 'Ambiguities of Loyalism', p. 70; 'African Loyalism and Its Discontents', p. 231.
44. Quoted in Sapire, 'We Have Seen the Son of Heaven', p. 25.
45. Sapire, 'African Loyalism and Its Discontents', p. 232.
46. Sapire, 'African Loyalism and Its Discontents', p. 226.
47. Quoted in Sapire, 'African Loyalism and Its Discontents', p. 234; on the thwarted ANC boycott more generally see pp. 234–7.
48. The literature is vast but the 'cascading' metaphor is from Lynn Hunt's *Inventing Human Rights: A History* (New York: Norton, 2007).
49. Samuel Moyn, *The Last Utopia: Human Rights in History* (Cambridge, MA: Harvard University Press, 2010), p. 7.
50. Samuel Moyn is even more explicit in *Human Rights and the Use of History* (London: Verso, 2017), taking aim at the 'most troubling shortcoming' of conventional human rights history: 'It distorts the past to suit the present' (p. 1). He urges that 'human rights history should turn away from ransacking the past as if it provided good support for the astonishingly specific

international movement of the last few decades' (p. xiii). Moyn principally had in mind Hunt's *Inventing Human Rights.*

51. Moyn, *Human Rights and the Use of History,* pp. 12–13.

52. A. W. Brian Simpson, *Human Rights and the End of Empire: Britain and the Genesis of the European Convention* (Oxford: Oxford University Press, 2001), p. 5. The characterization of anti-colonialism as a 'single issue struggle' is implicit in Simpson but the quotations are from Reza Afshari's influential 2007 essay, arguing that anti-colonial movements had 'no significant impact … on the evolution of human rights' and that 'no human rights consciousness blossomed as the darkness of colonialism was lifted'. See Reza Afshari, 'On Historiography of Human Rights: Reflections on Paul Gordon Lauren's *The Evolution of International Human Rights: Vision Seen*', *Human Rights Quarterly,* 29:1 (2007), pp. 1–67, 44, 65. See also Christian Reus-Smit's insistence that 'if decolonization was about rights, it was about collective rights not individual rights'. Christian Reus-Smit, *Individual Rights and the Making of the International System* (Cambridge: Cambridge University Press, 2013), p. 152.

53. Afshari, 'On Historiography', p. 44.

54. Moyn, *Last Utopia,* p. 86.

55. Moyn, *Last Utopia,* p. 7.

56. The injudicious formulation is Moyn's own, see *Last Utopia,* p. 3. For the 'Big Bang' critique, see Steven L. B. Jensen, *The Making of International Human Rights: The 1960s, Decolonization and the Reconstruction of Global Values* (Cambridge: Cambridge University Press, 2016), p. 10.

57. Jensen, *The Making of International Human Rights,* p. 3.

58. Jensen, *The Making of International Human Rights,* p. 21.

59. See also Roland Burke, *Decolonization and the Evolution of International Human Rights* (Philadelphia: University of Pennsylvania Press, 2010).

60. 'Breakthrough' is also the organizing principle for Jan Eckel and Samuel Moyn (eds.), *The Breakthrough: Human Rights in the 1970s* (Philadelphia: University of Pennsylvania Press, 2015).

61. This becomes increasingly apparent in Moyn's *Last Utopia* as the author exhausts his vocabulary to diminish the significance of human rights prior to the 1970s, discounting them variously as 'irrelevant', 'peripheral', 'marginal' and 'an empty vessel'; they were 'minor products' of the wartime settlement, 'not main features', 'already on the edge of the stage' before being 'pushed off'. Human rights were 'a story of death in birth', entering history 'as a throwaway line, not a well-considered idea', their arrival heralded 'not with a bang but in passing', achieving only a 'vanishingly slight prominence'. They 'never did percolate in public and around the world'; they 'could and did not take off', 'masked other agendas', 'solved no problems' and ultimately 'failed quite spectacularly', leaving little evidence that they ever 'captured the imagination of contemporaries'. 'Above all', human rights were 'not even an especially prominent idea', and thus it 'would be hard to identify an issue in which an

appeal to rights, as such, could or did matter.' The onset of the Cold War, 'far from being their death-knell, only extended the original mortification of their birth'. In short, the stark dichotomy signalled in Moyn's opening gambit – that the dawn of human rights in the 1940s was 'less the annunciation of a new age than a funeral wreath laid on the grave of wartime hopes' – is tenaciously sustained throughout.

62. Moyn, *Last Utopia*, p. 42.
63. Frederick Cooper, 'Afterword: Social Rights and Human Rights in the Time of Decolonization', *Humanity: An International Journal of Human Rights, Humanitarianism, and Development*, 3:3 (Winter 2012), pp. 473–92, 477.
64. Dubow notes how early ANC proposals to 'opt out' of a unitary South Africa and 'stress a common African or black identity . . . were not always easily contained in the civic and political boundaries of South Africa'. As the prominent ANC intellectual Z. K. Matthews recalled of these early years, 'the makers of the world did not count us as a nation or as part of any nation'. Dubow, 'South Africa and South Africans', pp. 45–6.
65. Cooper, 'Afterword', p. 478.
66. The term is Steven Jensen's, who uses it in a more formal diplomatic context in 'Introduction', *The Making of International Human Rights*.
67. Robin Blackburn, 'Reclaiming Human Rights', *New Left Review*, 69 (May–June 2011), pp. 126–38, 135. Blackburn's remarks are aimed specifically at Moyn's emphasis on a 1970s human rights 'breakthrough', arguing that Moyn's 'insistent denial of any and all antecedents is exaggerated and wrong' (p. 130).
68. Moyn, *Last Utopia*, p. 109.
69. *Africans' Claims in South Africa*, including 'The Atlantic Charter from the Standpoint of Africans within the Union of South Africa' and 'Bill of Rights', adopted by the ANC Annual Conference, December 1943. South African History Online: www.sahistory.org.za/archive/africans-claims-south-africa-adopted-anc-1943-annual-conference.
70. *Africans' Claims in South Africa*.
71. *Africans' Claims in South Africa*.
72. Dubow, *South Africa's Struggle for Human Rights*, p. 57. Rob Skinner reminds us that the ANC was not the only protest organization to internalize the spirit of the Atlantic Charter, noting the activities of the 'Campaign for Right and Justice', a multi-racial alliance of left-liberal groupings whose founding Charter of Rights in 1943 'shared many similarities' with the ANC's *Africans' Claims in South Africa*. See Rob Skinner, *The Foundations of Anti-Apartheid: Liberal Humanitarians and Transnational Activists in Britain and the United States, c.1919–64* (London: Palgrave, 2010), p. 69.
73. This was the so-called 'Three Doctors' Pact' of 9 March 1947, entered into with the leaders of the Natal Indian Congress and the Transvaal Indian Congress (all of whom, like Xuma, happened to be medical doctors). The text of the pact appears at www.sahistory.org.za/archive/three-doctors-pact-march-9–1947.

74. Dubow, *South Africa's Struggle for Human Rights*, p. 55.
75. Quoted in Saul Dubow, 'Smuts, the United Nations and the Rhetoric of Race and Rights', *Journal of Contemporary History*, 43:1 (2008), pp. 45–74, 70.
76. Quoted in Luli Callinicos, *Oliver Tambo: Beyond the Engeli Mountains* (Claremont: David Philip, 2004), p. 145.
77. Quoted in Walshe, *Rise of African Nationalism*, p. 330.
78. Mark Mazower, *No Enchanted Palace: The End of Empire and the Ideological Origins of the United Nations* (Princeton: Princeton University Press, 2009), p. 61.
79. Quoted in Dubow, 'Smuts, the United Nations', p. 62. Dubow's account sheds considerable light on how Smuts was able to reconcile the evident contradictions in his approach.
80. The June 1946 Act was only the latest instalment in a dispute between Indian communal leaders and the South African Government that had simmered for decades. See Lorna Lloyd, '"A Family Quarrel". The Development of the Dispute over Indians in South Africa', *The Historical Journal*, 34:3 (September 1991), pp. 703–25.
81. The argument rested on the fact that the migration of Indians to South Africa had been 'encouraged' by nineteenth-century indenture agreements between the two countries which bore the resemblance of international treaties; hence the Indian government was 'morally bound' to pursue the matter. See Lorna Lloyd, '"A Most Auspicious Beginning": The 1946 United Nations General Assembly and the Question of the Treatment of Indians in South Africa', *Review of International Studies*, 16:2 (April 1990), pp. 131–53, 133.
82. Nehru, quoted in Mazower, *No Enchanted Palace*, p. 179.
83. Mazower, *No Enchanted Palace*, p. 178.
84. Smuts to J. H. Hofmeyr, 6 May 1945, quoted in Dubow, 'Smuts, the United Nations', p. 54; Smuts to M. C. Gillett, 14 January 1947 in Jean van der Poel (ed.), *Selections from the Smuts Papers*, vol. VII: *August 1945–October 1950*, doc. 738 (Cambridge: Cambridge University Press, 1973), p. 117.
85. Smuts to M. C. Gillett, 17 November 1946 in Poel, *Selections*, doc. 733, p. 110; Smuts to Florence Lamont, 8 December 1946 in Poel, *Selections*, doc. 734, p. 111.
86. Smuts to M. C. Gillett, 17 November 1946 in Poel, *Selections*, doc. 733, p. 110.
87. Smuts to M. C. Gillett, 14 January 1947 in Poel, *Selections*, doc. 738, p. 117; Smuts to M. C. Gillet, 1 February 1947, in Poel, *Selections*, doc. 740, p. 121.
88. Dubow, 'Smuts, the United Nations', p. 72.
89. Smuts to M. C. Gillet, 1 February 1947, in Poel, *Selections*, doc. 740, p. 121.
90. According to Pandit's memoir, quoted in Lloyd, '"A Most Auspicious Beginning"', p. 148.
91. Quoted in Jensen, *The Making of International Human Rights*, p. 35; Dubow, *South Africa's Struggle for Human Rights*, p. 13.
92. Bain Attwood, *Possession: Batman's Treaty and the Matter of History* (Melbourne: Miegunyah, 2009), p. 262. Attwood also emphasizes the stark discontinuities in

Indigenous rights claim-making in the post-war era in *Rights for Aborigines* (Sydney: Allen & Unwin, 2003), p. xiv.

93. Ravi de Costa, 'Identity, Authority, and the Moral Worlds of Indigenous Petitions', *Comparative Studies in Society and History*, 48:3 (July 2006), pp. 669–98, 685. Which is not to say that human rights gained a stable or permanent foothold in the political landscape; see Dubow, *South Africa's Struggle for Human Rights*, pp. 68, 72. Rob Skinner also stresses how the 'moment passed' into the 1960s. See Rob Skinner, 'Humanitarianism and Human Rights in Global Anti-Apartheid', in Anna Konieczna and Rob Skinner (eds.), *A Global History of Anti-Apartheid: 'Forward to Freedom' in South Africa* (London: Palgrave, 2019), p. 46.

94. Mazower, *No Enchanted Palace*, p. 179.

95. Smuts to M. C. Gillet, 1 February 1947, in Poel, *Selections*, doc. 740, p. 121.

96. Quoted in Dubow, 'South Africa and South Africans', p. 57.

97. Keppel-Jones very occasionally referred to 'the English-speaking population' or 'English-speaking section' in *When Smuts Goes*; but never once did he describe them as 'English-speaking South Africans'.

98. Dubow, 'South Africa and South Africans', p. 57.

99. Dubow, 'South Africa and South Africans', pp. 56–7.

100. Quoted in Jeeves, 'Arthur Keppel-Jones', p. 28.

101. See, generally, Chapters 10 and 11.

102. John Lambert, 'An Unknown People: Reconstructing British South African Identity', *Journal of Imperial and Commonwealth History*, 37:4 (2009), pp. 599–617, 609. Lambert overlooks the exception of Northern Irish Catholics or, depending on one's perspective, Scottish and Welsh nationalists.

103. See Christian Damm Pedersen, 'African Decolonisation and the Fate of Britishness, 1959–1965', PhD Thesis, University of Copenhagen (2016), p. 127.

104. Heaton-Nichols to Lord Swinton (Secretary of State for Commonwealth Relations), 9 June 1953, DO35/5095, The National Archives, Kew (hereafter NA).

105. Salisbury to Swinton, 27 May 1953; Swinton to Heaton-Nichols, 16 June 1953, DO35/5095, NA. See, generally, P. S. Thompson, *Natalians First: Separatism in South Africa, 1909–1961* (Johannesburg: Southern Book Publishers, 1990).

106. Quoted in Lambert, 'An Unknown People', pp. 609–10.

107. John Bond, *They Were South Africans* (Cape Town: Oxford University Press, 1956), pp. 1, 4.

108. See Keppel-Jones's column in the *Sunday Times* (Johannesburg), 17 July 1949. See also Chapter 6, p. 178.

109. See, generally, Ronald Hyam and Peter Henshaw, *The Lion and the Springbok: Britain and South Africa since the Boer War* (Cambridge: Cambridge University Press, 2003), ch. 12, quoting *Die Transvaler*, 16 April 1957, on p. 292.

110. Hyam and Henshaw, *Lion and Springbok*, p. 291.

111. Quoted in Cherry Michelman, *The Black Sash of South Africa: A Case Study in Liberalism* (London: Oxford University Press, 1975), p. 32.

112. 'Letter to Prime Minister D. F. Malan on Behalf of the African National Congress', 21 January 1952, www.sahistory.org.za/sites/default/files/ARTIC LES%2C%20SPEECHES%20AND%20LETTERS%20BY%20W.A.%20SISUL U.pdf.

113. Walshe puts the figure at 8,577 arrests of passive resistance volunteers. See *Rise of African Nationalism*, p. 402.

114. Dubow views the Freedom Charter as marking the beginning of a move away from universalist towards collectivist claims which would become more pronounced into the 1960s. He points to the fact that every major signatory had the word 'South African' in its title, suggesting that individual rights would be subordinate to 'the achievement of a common or supra-South African nationality'. *South Africa's Struggle for Human Rights*, pp. 68, 72–3.

115. Quoted in Saul Dubow, *Apartheid, 1948–1994* (Oxford: Oxford University Press, 2014), pp. 70–1.

116. Rob Skinner, 'The Moral Foundations of British Anti-Apartheid Activism, 1946–1960', *Journal of Southern African Studies*, 35:2 (2009), pp. 399–416, 405.

117. Trevor Huddleston, *Nought for Your Comfort* (New York: Doubleday, 1956), pp. 17–18, 75–6.

118. Paul B. Rich, *White Power and the Liberal Conscience: Racial Segregation and South African Liberalism, 1921–60* (Manchester: Manchester University Press, 1984), p. 120. On the change in British media representations of South Africa and apartheid in the 1950s, see Howard Smith, 'Apartheid, Sharpeville and "Impartiality": The Reporting of South Africa on BBC Television 1948–61', *Historical Journal of Film, Radio and Television*, 13:3 (1993), pp. 251–98. See also Hyam and Henshaw, *Lion and Springbok*, ch. 13.

119. See Neil Roos, *Ordinary Springboks: White Servicemen and Social Justice in South Africa, 1939–1961* (Aldershot: Ashgate, 2005).

120. Michelman, *Black Sash*, p. 24.

121. Michelman, *Black Sash*, pp. 39, 41.

122. Dubow, 'How British Was the British World?', p. 14.

123. Quoted in Michelman, *Black Sash*, p. 8.

124. Jeeves, 'Arthur Keppel-Jones', p. 28.

125. Sir John Maud (UK High Commissioner, Pretoria) to Macmillan, 6 February 1960, PREM11/3073, NA.

126. 'Note of a conversation in Dr Verwoerd's Room in the Assembly Building, Cape Town, 3 February 1960' (Macmillan and Graaff), PREM11/3071, NA.

127. See, for example, Oliver Lyttleton to Macmillan; Hunt to Clutterbuck, 8 February 1960, DO35/9187, NA.

128. Maud to Home (Secretary of State for Commonwealth Relations), 18 February 1960, DO/35/10572, NA. See also Hunt to Clutterbuck, 8 February 1960, DO35/9187, NA.

129. See Philip Frankel, *An Ordinary Atrocity: Sharpeville and Its Massacre* (New Haven: Yale University Press, 2001). See also Saul Dubow, 'Were There Political

Alternatives in the Wake of Sharpeville-Langa Violence in South Africa, 1960?', *Journal of African History*, 56:1 (2015), pp. 119–42.

130. Burke, *Decolonization and the Evolution of International Human Rights*, p. 56.

131. www.nobelprize.org/prizes/peace/1960/lutuli/lecture/.

132. Pedersen, 'African Decolonisation ', p. 118.

133. *Natal Mercury*, 7 March 1960, quoted in Pedersen, 'African Decolonisation', p. 158.

134. Undated referendum campaign memorandum, 133/1, United Party Archives, UNISA, Pretoria (hereafter UPA).

135. UPA, Graaff Papers, 111.3 Referendum Speeches. The East London speech was on 1 September 1960.

136. A presumption that Verwoerd's Nationalists were at pains to dispel.

137. Pedersen, 'African Decolonisation', p. 164. My emphasis.

138. Australia's often tortured path from uncritical partnership to a position of ambivalent repudiation is skilfully mapped out in Roger Bell, *In Apartheid's Shadow: Australian Race Politics and South Africa, 1945–75* (Melbourne: Australian Scholarly Publishing, 2019).

139. *Sunday Times* (Johannesburg), 2 October 1959.

140. *Natal Mercury*, 'I Oppose a Republic' by C. B. Downes, 1 October 1960.

141. Front-page editorial, 'Republic Must Be Rejected', *Natal Witness*, 5 October 1960.

142. Sir John Maud to Sir Alexander Clutterbuck, CRO, 14 October 1960, DO161/107, NA.

143. Quoted in Terry Wilks, *The Biography of Douglas Mitchell* (Durban: King and Wilks, 1980), p. 137.

144. Wilks, *The Biography of Douglas Mitchell*, p. 138.

145. Sheila Henderson, 'Douglas Mitchell (1896–1988): A Personal Memoir', p. 67, https://natalia.org.za/Files/19/Natalia%20v19%20obituaries%20Mitchell.pdf.

146. *Manchester Guardian*, 'The Boer Millennium', 31 May 1961.

147. The controversy was covered by the Black Sash members' magazine in a piece entitled 'The English-Speaking Whites: Are They the Lowest Form of South African Political Life?', *The Black Sash*, September 1961.

148. The Natal Coast branch, for instance, was reduced to 150 members from a 1957 cohort of 950, giving rise to intense discussion about their future viability. See Black Sash National Conference, Natal Coastal Region Report, 31 October 1960, p. 3. Black Sash Papers, File 317, Killie Campbell Africana Library, University of Kwa-Zulu Natal, Durban.

149. 'Chairman's Report to the National Conference, November 1960'. Black Sash Papers, File 317, Killie Campbell Africana Library, University of Kwa-Zulu Natal, Durban. The divisions over the position to adopt in the event of a Nationalist Republic are documented in files 317 and especially 321.

150. 'Have They a Future', *Black Sash*, September 1961.

151. 'This Is the Start of the Head-On Clash', *The Star* (Johannesburg), 12 May 1961.
152. Television interview with ITV reporter Brian Widlake on 31 May 1961, quoted in Thula Simpson, *Umkhonto we Sizwe: The ANC's Armed Struggle* (London: Penguin, 2019).
153. Mandela to Graaff, undated but the context points clearly to on or around 21 May 1961, Graaff Papers 246, UPA.
154. Graaff to Mandela, 26 May 1961, Graaff Papers 246, UPA.
155. Mandela to Graaff, undated (21 May 1961), Graaff Papers 246, UPA; 'closing a chapter' is from the interview with Mandela in Simpson, *Umkhonto we Sizwe*.

8 PRIDE IN THE GOODS: THE MORAL ECONOMY OF THE COMMON MARKET

1. Barry O. Jones, 'Pollard, Reginald Thomas (1894–1981)', *Australian Dictionary of Biography*, vol. 18: *1981–1990, L-Z* (Melbourne: Melbourne University Publishing, 2012), pp. 299–300. Of the other sixty-odd federal Labor MPs returned at the 1958 election, only Victoria's Frank Courtnay, Tasmanian Gil Duthie and the Northern Territory's Jock Nelson had any hands-on experience on the land.
2. Reg Pollard, *Commonwealth Parliamentary Debates* (Representatives), Vol. 32, 17 August 1961, p. 255.
3. *The Guardian*, 'Britain Will Ask to Join EEC', 1 August 1961.
4. Hansard (Commons), 3 August 1961, Vol. 645, c. 1665.
5. As pointed out by David Thackeray, Andrew Thompson and Richard Toye (eds.), in their introduction to *Imagining Britain's Economic Future, c.1800–1975: Trade, Consumerism, and Global Markets* (London: Palgrave, 2018), p. 8. The theme is taken up in the latter chapters of David Thackeray, *Forging a British World of Trade: Culture, Ethnicity and Market in the Empire-Commonwealth, 1880–1975* (Oxford: Oxford University Press, 2019).
6. For 'emotional communities' see Barbara Rosenwein, 'Worrying about Emotions in History', *American Historical Review*, 107 (2002), pp. 821–45; 'emotional regimes' derives from William Reddy's, *The Navigation of Feeling: A Framework for the History of Emotions* (Cambridge: Cambridge University Press, 2001); the older term 'emotionology' was coined by Peter and Carol Stearns, 'Emotionology: Clarifying the History of Emotions and Emotional Standards', *American Historical Review*, 90 (1985), pp. 813–36. Each of these terms has been applied variously – and not always consistently – across a wide body of scholarship.
7. Rob Boddice, *The History of Emotions* (Manchester: Manchester University Press, 2018), p. 196.
8. Martin Frances, 'Tears, Tantrums and Bared Teeth: The Emotional Economy of Three Conservative Prime Ministers, 1951–63', *Journal of British Studies*, 41 (July 2002), pp. 354–87, 355, 357. Frances regarded the study of these outward signs of 'performativity' as somehow distinct from 'a genuine emotional economy'

comprising 'inner psychic processes' – a distinction he left unexplored. Other early proponents were equally imprecise in formulating the term. Ann Laura Stoler and Karen Strassler rendered it virtually synonymous with Raymond Williams's much older notion of 'structures of feeling', again, an implicitly discursive analytical practice with few evident 'economic' implications. See 'Casting for the Colonial: Memory Work in "New Order" Java', *Comparative Studies in Society and History*, 42:1 (2000), pp. 4–48, 6.

9. Claire McLisky, 'The Emotional Economies of Protestant Missions to Aboriginal People in Nineteenth-Century Australia', in David Lemmings and Ann Brooks (eds.), *Emotions and Social Change: Historical and Sociological Perspectives* (New York: Routledge, 2014), pp. 82–98, 85–6, 95.

10. Sara Ahmed makes the most rigorous case for affective economies, arguing that emotions are not psychological dispositions residing in the individual, but mobile forms of capital that 'circulate and are distributed across a social as well as psychic field'. Drawing on the Marxian critique of the logic of capital, she likens the accumulation of affect as it circulates between objects and signs to the movement of commodities and money, generating surplus value. Ahmed concedes, however, that the comparison is based on a narrow reading of Marx's concept of value 'and hence relies on a limited analogy'. See Sara Ahmed, 'Affective Economies', *Social Text* 79, 22:2 (Summer 2004), pp. 117–39, 119–21.

11. Quoted in Robert Frank Dewey, *British National Identity and Opposition to Membership of Europe, 1961–63: The Anti-Marketeers* (Manchester: Manchester University Press, 2009), p. 1.

12. *Daily Express*, 16 January 1962, quoted in Dewey, *British National Identity*, p. 2.

13. On 'declinism' see Chapter 11.

14. Quoted in Miriam Camps, *Britain and the European Community* (Princeton: Princeton University Press, 1964), p. 288.

15. See Mathias Haeussler, 'The Popular Press and Ideas of Europe: The Daily Mirror, the Daily Express, and Britain's First Application to Join the EEC, 1961–63', *Twentieth Century British History*, 25:1 (2014), pp. 108–31, 124.

16. Quoted in Benjamin Grob-Fitzgibbon, *Continental Drift: Britain and Europe from the End of Empire to the Rise of Euroscepticism* (Cambridge: Cambridge University Press, 2016), p. 279.

17. Neil Rollings, *British Business in the Formative Years of European Integration, 1945–73* (Cambridge: Cambridge University Press, 2007), pp. 129–37. Business generally came on board, however, once negotiations got underway.

18. In a personal letter to the prime minister of 8 August 1962, quoted in Dewey, *British National Identity*, p. 106.

19. Quoted in Dewey, *British National Identity*, pp. 40–1.

20. Quoted in Dewey, *British National Identity*, p. 89.

21. On the lack of Commonwealth consensus over the adjectival 'British', see Chapter 4.

22. Quoted in Dewey, *British National Identity*, p. 100.

23. See Gaitskell's speech of 3 October 1962 at www.cvce.eu.

24. See Chapter 3.

25. See James Ellison, *Threatening Europe: Britain and the Creation of the European Community, 1955–1958* (Basingstoke: Macmillan, 2000).

26. Quoted in Glen St J. Barclay, *Commonwealth or Europe* (St Lucia: University of Queensland Press, 1970) p. 84. Macmillan's reference to 'our first purpose' appears in a letter to Australian Federal Treasurer, Arthur Fadden, 15 September 1956, Crawford Papers, MS4514, Box 14, National Library of Australia (hereafter NLA).

27. Quoted in Alex May, 'Commonwealth or Europe?: Macmillan's Dilemma, 1961–63', in Alex May (ed.), *Britain, the Commonwealth and Europe: The Commonwealth and Britain's Applications to Join the European Communities* (Basingstoke: Palgrave, 2001), pp. 90–1.

28. Macmillan to Fadden, 15 September 1956, Crawford Papers, MS4514, Box 14, NLA.

29. Broadly speaking, the debate about Britain's motivations in turning to Europe can be divided into three camps: the exclusively economic; the exclusively political; and those who concede a complex admixture of both. For representative titles, see, respectively, Alan S. Milward, *The Rise and Fall of a National Strategy, 1945–1963: The UK and the European Community*, vol. 1 (London: Frank Cass, 2002); Wolfram Kaiser, *Using Europe, Abusing the Europeans: Britain and European Integration, 1945–63* (London: Macmillan, 1996); N. Piers Ludlow *Dealing with Britain: The Six and the First UK Application to the EEC* (Cambridge: Cambridge University Press, 1997).

30. See European Economic Association Committee, 'The Implications of Signing the Treaty of Rome: Commonwealth Free Entry', 12 June 1961, CAB134/1821, EQ(61)18, The National Archives, Kew (hereafter NA).

31. Memorandum by the Prime Minister, 29 December 1960–3 January 1961, PREM11/3325, NA, original emphasis.

32. James Belich, *Paradise Reforged: A History of the New Zealanders from the 1880s to the Year 2000* (Auckland: Penguin, 2001), p. 432.

33. John Perkins, *Geopolitics and Green Revolution: Wheat, Genes and the Cold War* (New York: Oxford University Press, 1997); see also Alison Bashford, *Global Population: History, Geopolitics and Life on Earth* (New York: Columbia University Press, 2014), ch. 10.

34. Andrew Dilley, 'Un-Imagining Markets: Chambers of Commerce, Globalisation and the Political Economy of the Commonwealth of Nations, 1945–1975', in Thackeray, Thompson and Toye (eds.), *Imagining Britain's Economic Future*, p. 73. See also Andrew Dilley, 'A Tale of Two Commonwealths? The (British) Commonwealth of Nations, Decolonisation and the Break-Up of Greater Britain', in Christian Damm Pedersen and Stuart Ward (eds.), *The Break-Up of Greater Britain* (Manchester: Manchester University Press, 2021).

35. UK Permanent Secretary to the Board of Trade, Sir Frank Lee, 1956, quoted in May, 'Commonwealth or Europe?', p. 89. Francine McKenzie identifies a tipping point circa 1950 beyond which a distinctly imperial political economy went into rapid decline. See Francine McKenzie, 'Trade, Dominance, Dependence and the End of the Settlement Era in Canada, Australia, New Zealand, and South Africa, 1920–1973', in Christopher Lloyd, Jacob Metzer and Richard Sutch (eds.), *Settler Economies in World History* (Leiden: Brill, 2013), pp. 463–89.

36. See, for example, polls cited in Dewey, *British National Identity*, p. 31; David Thackeray and Richard Toye, 'What Was a British Buy? Empire, Europe and the Politics of Patriotic Trade in Britain, c.1945–1963', in Thackeray, Thompson and Toye (eds.), *Imagining Britain's Economic Future*, p. 147; and May, 'Commonwealth or Europe?', p. 90.

37. The change was implemented at the 1960 Congress in Canberra. See Dilley, 'Un-Imagining Markets', pp. 261–2.

38. Dilley, 'Un-Imagining Markets', p. 253.

39. Glen O'Hara, 'Imagining New Zealand's Economy in the Mid-Twentieth Century', in Thackeray, Thompson and Toye (eds.), *Imagining Britain's Economic Future*, p. 80.

40. Belich, *Paradise Reforged*, p. 433; see Stuart Ward, 'A Matter of Preference: The EEC and the Erosion of the Old Commonwealth Relationship', in May (ed.), *Britain, the Commonwealth and Europe*, pp. 163–4.

41. Quoted in David Hall, *Emerging from an Entrenched Colonial Economy: New Zealand Primary Production, Britain and the EEC, 1945–1975* (London: Palgrave, 2017), pp. 82, 158. See also Paul Robertson and John Singleton, 'The Old Commonwealth and Britain's First Application to join the EEC: 1961–3', *Australian Economic History Review*, 40:2 (2000) pp. 159–77.

42. 'Statement by the Prime Minister to the Commonwealth Prime Ministers' Conference', 11 September 1962, A5819/2 vol. 10, National Archives of Australia (hereafter NAA).

43. See Stuart Ward, *Australia and the British Embrace: The Demise of the Imperial Ideal* (Melbourne: Melbourne University Press, 2001), ch. 5.

44. Jack McEwen, 'Address to the Australia Club', London, 17 April 1962, A1838/275 727/4/2, Part 2, NAA.

45. See Stuart Ward, 'Worlds Apart: Three "British" Prime Ministers at Empire's End', in Phillip Buckner and Doug Francis (eds.), *Rediscovering the British World* (Calgary: University of Calgary Press, 2005).

46. Letter to Diefenbaker from Canadian High Commissioner in London (and Diefenbaker's predecessor as Party Leader) George Drew, April 1962, quoted in J. L. Granatstein, *Canada, 1957–67: The Years of Uncertainty and Innovation* (Toronto: McClelland and Stuart, 1986), p. 52. Milward notes how Drew made no secret of his opposition to Britain's membership bid and made a point of

boycotting Heath's periodic Commonwealth briefings. Milward, *Rise and Fall*, p. 365.

47. *Vancouver Sun*, 16 September 1961; *Calgary Herald*, 2 March 1961; 8 September 1962.

48. Canadian Cabinet Conclusions no. 104/61, 26 September 1961, RG2, vol. 6177, Library and Archives Canada (LAC).

49. *Ottawa Journal*, 15 September 1962. On this, see Andrea Benvenuti and Stuart Ward, 'Britain, Europe and the "Other Quiet Revolution" in Canada', in Phillip Buckner (ed.), *Canada and the End of Empire* (Vancouver: University of British Columbia Press, 2005), pp. 165–82.

50. Nehru in *Times of India*, 26 July 1961; Desai in *Times of India*, 14 September 1961, both quoted in Rajendra K. Jain, 'Jawaharlal Nehru and the European Economic Community', *India Quarterly*, 71:1 (2015), pp. 1–15, 5–6.

51. Quoted in Jain, 'Jawaharlal Nehru', p. 7.

52. The phrase 'hewer of wood' was used by Ghana's first high commissioner to the UK, Sir Edward Asafo Adjaye, to describe EEC 'Associate' membership in February 1962. Quoted in Ali A. Mazrui, 'African Attitudes to the European Economic Community', *International Affairs*, 39:1 (January 1963), pp. 24–36, 28.

53. See also Lindsay Aqui, 'Macmillan, Nkrumah and the 1961 Application for European Economic Community Membership', *International History Review*, 39:4 (2017), pp. 575–91.

54. See Mazrui, 'African Attitudes', pp. 33, 34–5.

55. See, for example, S. R. Ashton and David Killingray, *British Documents on the End of Empire, Series B*, vol. 6: *The West Indies* (London: Institute of Commonwealth Studies, 1999): Document 140, Record of a Meeting with West Indian Ministers at Lancaster House on 8 November 1960, p. 379; Document 169, Williams to Reginald Maudling, 11 November 1961, p. 466.

56. *Barbados Advocate*, 30 July 1961; Sir Archibald Cuke, quoted in the *Sunday Advocate* (Barbados), 9 September 1962.

57. Quoted in May, 'Commonwealth or Europe?', pp. 102–3.

58. See Chapter 6.

59. Grantley Adams to Macmillan, 17 November 1961, Document 170 in Ashton and Killingray (eds.), *British Documents*, p. 467.

60. Quoted in Dewey, *British National Identity*, p. 40.

61. Montgomery, 'I Say We Must Not Join Europe', *The Times*, 4 June 1962. To broaden the appeal, Beaverbrook commissioned a series of anti-Marketeer articles two months later by former Labour PM Clement Attlee under the heading 'I say halt!'. See Dewey, *British National Identity*, p. 163.

62. Ludlow, *Dealing with Britain*, p. 85. Macmillan explicitly informed Cabinet that public feeling was 'really centred upon the old Commonwealth countries' and that the task of persuading the British people needed to take account of this. See

Memorandum by the Prime Minister, 'Commonwealth Conference', 4 September 1962, CAB133/262 PMM(UK)(62)4, NA.

63. Tehila Sasson, *The Solidarity Economy: Nonprofits and the Postimperial Origins of Neoliberalism*, forthcoming, Princeton University Press, ch. 3. With thanks to the author for the opportunity to read a pre-published version.

64. Quoted in Richard Toye, 'Words of Change: The Rhetoric of Commonwealth, Common Market and Cold War, 1961–63', in L. J. Butler and Sarah Stockwell (eds.), *The Wind of Change: Harold Macmillan and British Decolonization* (Basingstoke: Palgrave, 2013), p. 147.

65. Quoted in Toye, 'Words of Change', p. 146.

66. 'Rapport fait au nom de la Commission du commerce extérieur sur les aspects commerciaux et économiques de la demande d'adhesion du Royaume-Uni à la CEE', 16 January 1962, BAC24/1967 E13, Historical Archives of the European Union, Florence (hereafter HAEU). The phasing-out period generally agreed on was seven years which, if implemented, would have extinguished the imperial preference system by 1970.

67. Jean Chauvel (French Ambassador, London) to Maurice Couve de Murville (French Foreign Minister), 'La Grande Bretagne et le Commonwealth', 26 February 1962, Ministère des affaires étrangères, MAEF48/OW, Microform 321, HAEU.

68. Macmillan, diary entry, 12 September 1962, in Peter Catterall (ed.), *The Macmillan Diaries,* vol. II: *Prime Minister and after* (London: Macmillan, 2011), p. 496.

69. Heath's private comments quoted in C. D. Wiggin (FO) to Bottomley (CRO), 11 July 1962, DO159/60, NA.

70. Cumming-Bruce to Lintott (Commonwealth Relations Office), 16 March 1962, DO159/64, NA.

71. The speech is reproduced in the appendix to Harold Macmillan, *At the End of the Day: 1961–63* (London: Macmillan, 1973).

72. Quoted in Dewey, *British National Identity,* p. 335.

73. Macmillan, diary entry, 12 September 1962, in Peter Catterall (ed.), *The Macmillan Diaries,* p. 496.

74. Arjun Appadurai, 'Introduction: Commodities and the Politics of Value', in Arjun Appadurai (ed.), *The Social Life of Things: Commodities in Cultural Perspective* (Cambridge: Cambridge University Press, 1986), pp. 3, 15.

75. T. H. Breen, 'An Empire of Goods: The Anglicization of Colonial America, 1690–1776', *Journal of British Studies,* 25:4 (October 1986), pp. 467–99.

76. T. H. Breen, 'Ideology and Nationalism on the Eve of the American Revolution: Revisions Once More in Need of Revising', *Journal of American History,* 84:1 (June 1997), pp. 13–39, 17.

77. T. H. Breen, '"Baubles of Britain": The American and Consumer Revolutions of the Eighteenth Century', *Past and Present,* 119 (May 1988), pp. 73–104, 76, 98.

78. E. P. Thompson, 'The Moral Economy of the English Crowd in the Eighteenth Century', *Past and Present*, 50 (February 1971), pp. 76–136, 78–9, 89–90. Thompson's celebrated study of eighteenth-century English food riots critiqued the 'crass economic reductionism' that overlooked that way communities bring their own social configuration to bear on their economic relationships – regardless of the putative 'morality' of their self-understanding or indeed whether such processes actually secured their material welfare.

79. Joel Mokyr, *The Enlightened Economy: An Economic History of Britain, 1700–1850* (New Haven: Yale University Press, 2009), pp. 379, 381.

80. See also Chapter 3, pp. 83–90; Frank Trentmann, 'Before "Fair Trade": Empire, Free Trade, and the Moral Economies of Food in the Modern World', *Environment and Planning D: Society and Space*, 25 (2007), pp. 1079–102, 1079, 1085–6, 1097.

81. Matthew Hilton, *Consumerism in Twentieth Century Britain: The Search for a Historical Movement* (Cambridge: Cambridge University Press, 2003), pp. 137–8.

82. Lawrence Black, *Redefining British Politics: Culture, Consumerism and Participation, 1954–70* (London: Palgrave, 2010), p. 14, citing the example of the 'Consumers' Association' founded in the late 1950s, ch. 2. The notion of the consumer as the 'sovereign ruler of the capitalist economy' was first articulated by the British economist William H. Hutt in the late 1930s; see Niklas Olsen, *The Sovereign Consumer: A New Intellectual History of Neoliberalism* (London: Palgrave Macmillan, 2019), p. 20.

83. Erika Rappaport, *A Thirst for Empire: How Tea Shaped the Modern World* (Princeton: Princeton University Press, 2017), pp. 235, 377, 403. Rappaport shows how 'the empire shopping ideal lost much of its vigor' already by the late 1930s and was never fully revived after the Second World War, p. 264.

84. Rappaport, *A Thirst for Empire*, p. 394.

85. Thackeray and Toye, 'What Was a British Buy?', pp. 135, 142, 150.

86. Thackeray, *Forging a British World of Trade*, pp. 130, 167.

87. Thackeray, *Forging a British World of Trade*, pp. 160–2; Rappaport, *Thirst for Empire*, p. 361. The rebranding of tea was achieved in spite (or perhaps because) of the fact that British commercial interests in post-war international tea production and marketing remained largely unaffected by the end of empire.

88. Thackeray, *Forging a British World of Trade*, pp. 162–4; see also Håkon Thörn, *Anti-Apartheid and the Emergence of a Global Civil Society* (London: Palgrave, 2006).

89. Quoted in Dewey, *British National Identity*, pp. 76–7. Dewey notes the ironic twist whereby imperial protectionists such as Beaverbrook were able to deploy the 'cheap food' rhetoric of their former arch-rival Free Trade, 'expropriating the label and inverting its meaning for anti-Market purposes'.

90. Quoted in Dewey, *British National Identity*, p. 136.

91. Haeussler, 'The Popular Press', pp. 120, 126; See also Thackeray, *Forging a British World of Trade*, pp. 174–5.

92. Quoted in Simon Potter, *Broadcasting Empire: The BBC and the British World, 1922–1970* (Oxford: Oxford University Press, 2012), pp. 201–2.

93. See Chapter 3.

94. See Ludlow, *Dealing with Britain*, p. 85.

95. Piers Ludlow, 'Commercial Preferences: Economics and Britain's European Choices, 1945–2016', in Thackeray, Thompson and Toye, *Imagining Britain's Economic Future*, p. 290.

96. Sasson, *Solidarity Economy*, ch. 3.

97. Frank Trentmann, *Empire of Things: How We Became a World of Consumers, from the Fifteenth Century to the Twenty-first* (London: Allen Lane, 2016), p. 573, and Chapter 13 generally.

98. *Australian Financial Review, Sydney Morning Herald*, 19 April 1962.

99. The classic account is Sidney Mintz, *Sweetness and Power: The Place of Sugar in Modern History* (New York: Viking-Penguin, 1985).

100. Eric Williams, *Capitalism and Slavery* (Chapel Hill: University of North Carolina Press, 1944), p. 149.

101. See Warwick Anderson, *The Cultivation of Whiteness: Science, Health and Racial Destiny in Australia* (New York: Basic Books, 2003), especially ch. 5.

102. *The Story of Queensland Sugar*, Compiled by the Queensland Cane Growers' Council, 10 November 1927, pp. 3, 19. State Library of Queensland, Brisbane.

103. Stefanie Affeldt, *Consuming Whiteness: Australian Racism and the 'White Sugar' Campaign* (Berlin: Lit Verlag, 2014), p. 512.

104. Jack P. Greene, 'Changing Identity in the British Caribbean: Barbados as a Case Study', in Nicholas Canny and Anthony Pagden (eds.), *Colonial Identity in the Atlantic World, 1500–1800* (Princeton: Princeton University Press, 1987), pp. 239, 241.

105. Quoted in Anderson, *Cultivation of Whiteness*, pp. 73–4.

106. *Barbados Advocate*, 4 November 1961. Ten years earlier, Patrick Leigh Fermor had depicted the capital Bridgetown as a 'completely English town, a town on the edge of London … all the familiar landmarks were there'. Quoted in Robert B. Potter and Mark Wilson, 'Barbados', in Robert B. Potter (ed.), *Urbanization, Planning and Development in the Caribbean* (London: Mansell, 1989), p. 123.

107. If their local newspapers are to be believed, 'the greatest day in Mackay's history' was the Monday morning in March 1954 when Queen Elizabeth and Prince Philip graced the town with their presence for an hour and 55 minutes; while the *Barbados Advocate* could hail the 'great esteem' extended to the 'extremely popular' Princess Margaret on her visit the following year in 1955, even though she never actually left the boat. *Daily Mercury*, 6 April 1962; *Barbados Advocate*, 4 November 1961.

108. Thackeray, *Forging a British World of Trade*, p. 182.

109. 'The United Kingdom and the European Communities', Cmnd. 4715, July 1971, p. 17.

110. 'Common Market': Mr Rippon's Speech to Conservative Summer School, 5 July 1971, text in SRS1043/1/3204 640 Part 1, Queensland State Archives (QSA).

111. Rippon in the Commons, quoted in John Southgate, *The Commonwealth Sugar Agreement, 1951–74* (London: Czarnikow, 1984), p. 46. Southgate explains how 'Commonwealth sugar had been turned into an issue on which opponents of the Common Market, defenders of the Commonwealth and champions of the third world could unite'. He adds that this 'was the real reason' for Rippon's willingness to negotiate concessions for Commonwealth sugar, p. 47.

112. *Advocate-News*, 15 May 1971, echoing sentiments the day before in the *Trinidad Guardian*, 14 May 1971: 'either Britain protects us or we perish'.

113. S. Norman Girwar, 'The Future of Commonwealth Sugar in an Enlarged EEC', presented to the Eleventh AGM of the Caribbean Cane Farmers' Association, Kingston, Jamaica, 28 August 1972, p. 11. Emphasis in original.

114. *Advocate-News*, 'Last Chance for Our Sugar Case', 2 June 1971.

115. *Advocate-News*, 14 May 1971.

116. 'Notes for a Talk by Lord Campbell to the Committee on Development and Cooperation of the European Parliament', 23 October 1973, pp. 4, 11: SRS1043/1/3205 640 Part 2, QSA.

117. *Advocate-News*, 2 June 1971. Similar objections were raised during Britain's first EEC membership bid in 1961 by independent federal MP Albert Gomes from Trinidad, who urged the West Indian people 'to forget about riding into the Common Market on Britain's coat tail, or of cringing like beggars on the Common Market's doorstep, by becoming an associate member of what was nothing but an exchange of British colonialism for a neo-European colonialism'. *Barbados Advocate*, 22 July 1961.

118. Guyanese delegate Sonny Ramphal, quoted in *Advocate-News*, 4 June 1971.

119. A logic that was vehemently contested by Australian sugar interests; see, for example, the official statement by the Chairman of the Colonial Sugar Refining Company Sir John Dunlop on 13 June 1971 in SRS1043/1/3205 640 Part 2, QSA.

120. *Sydney Morning Herald*, 27 October 1967; *Australian*, 26 October 1967; *Mercury*, 30 October 1967; *The Age*, 16 October 1967; *Canberra Times*, 16 October 1967. See also James Curran and Stuart Ward, *The Unknown Nation: Australia after Empire* (Melbourne: Melbourne University Publishing, 2010), ch. 2.

121. *Telegraph*, 2 June 1971.

122. Statement by Sir John Dunlop, Chairman of the Colonial Sugar Refining Co. Ltd, 13 July 1971, SRS1043/1/3205 640 Part 2, QSA.

123. *Townsville Daily Bulletin*, 25 June 1971; *Daily Mercury*, 4 July 1971.

124. *Daily Mercury*, 11 June 1971. Prompting one local MP to call on 'British officials visiting north Queensland' to stop 'taking our people for hicks'. *Daily Mercury*, 12 June 1971.

125. News Release, Premier's Department Brisbane, 'Premier Questions Terms for British Entry into the Common Market', 2 June 1971, and see also Bjelke-Petersen

to UK Minister for Agriculture Jim Prior, 27 May 1971, SRS1043/1/3204 640 Part 1, QSA.

126. Queensland's Agent-General in London reported that 'the overall publicity given by newspapers ... was disappointing' and 'several papers did not even mention it'. N. C. Seeney to Bjelke-Petersen, 15 June 1971; Telegram from Queensland House, London, 2 June 1971; SRS1043/1/3204 640 Part 1, QSA. The premier's efforts did, however, register with Mackay's *Daily Mercury*, which loudly sang his praise for ensuring that 'Australia's voice is now being heard loud and clear' (4 July 1971). The gratitude of local producer organizations is also apparent from the correspondence in SRS4344/2/8 Vol. 18, QSA.

127. *The Townsville Daily Bulletin*, 25 June1971.

128. *North Queensland Register*, 19 June 1971.

129. *Daily Mercury*, 'The Fading Glory', 12 June 1971.

130. See especially Dilley, 'Un-Imagining Markets', p. 266. Curiously, much of this gradualist emphasis comes from recent work on New Zealand, where the economic and cultural reverberations converged more potently than virtually anywhere else. See, for example, Jim McAloon, *Judgements of All Kinds: Economic Policy-Making in New Zealand 1945–1984* (Wellington: Victoria University Press, 2013); Hamish McDougall, 'Buttering up: Britain, New Zealand and Negotiations for European Community Enlargement, 1970–71', *International History Review*, 43:2 (2021), pp. 333–47. Brian Easton concedes the symbolic dimension, suggesting that EEC entry was a 'political, cultural and even emotional event for New Zealand', more so than an 'economic event' – though how he draws such distinctions is unclear given the economic triggers of the crisis of sentiment. See Brian Easton, *In Stormy Seas: The Post-War New Zealand Economy* (Dunedin: University of Otago Press, 1997), p. 80. David Hall's study of New Zealand primary producer organizations provides ample evidence of the sharp wake-up call delivered by the Common Market crisis (a phenomenon, he says, which 'should be celebrated, not mourned'), yet nevertheless comes down firmly in favour of the gradualist view. See Hall, *Emerging from an Entrenched Colonial Economy*, pp. 52, 309.

131. Milward makes a similar point in *Rise and Fall*, p. 370.

132. *Courier Mail*, 'Australia – the Land "Forgotten"', 26 June 1971.

133. Thompson, 'The Moral Economy', p. 79.

134. *Morning Telegraph* (Business Extra), 9 June 1971.

9 UNCOMMON LAW: THE REACH OF BRITISH JUSTICE

1. Many Zimbabwean place names were changed after independence to expunge the traces of white Rhodesian authority, but in the following account the older terminology of the colonial era is used to avoid confusion with naming practices in the quoted source material from the time. Thus, Harare appears as 'Salisbury',

Mutare is rendered as 'Umtali', while the mountainous south-eastern area of Manicaland is called by its colonial designation 'Melsetter' (present-day Chimanimani).

2. Interview with one of the demonstrators, Dr Linda Kirk (then a lecturer at the University College of Rhodesia) August 2015.

3. *Daily Telegraph*, 8 March 1968; *Bulawayo Chronicle*, 8 March 1968.

4. *Rhodesia Herald*, 9 March 1968. The editor was also critical of the protestors for their 'ill-conceived' gesture that was 'bound to arouse resentment'.

5. *The Times*, 'Envoys Pelted by Africans', 13 March 1968.

6. *The Guardian*, 13 March 1968.

7. C. A. Bayly, *The Birth of the Modern World, 1780–1914* (Oxford: Blackwell, 2004), p. 145.

8. Eva Mackey, 'Unsettling Expectations: (Un)certainty, Settler States of Feeling, Law, and Decolonization', *Canadian Journal of Law and Society/Revue Canadienne Droit et Société*, 29:2 (2014), pp. 235–52, 237. See also Lauren Benton, *Law and Colonial Cultures: Legal Regimes in World History, 1400–1900* (Cambridge: Cambridge University Press, 2002).

9. Rande W. Kostal, *A Jurisprudence of Power: Victorian Empire and the Rule of Law* (Oxford: Oxford University Press, 2005), p. 7.

10. Martin Wiener, *An Empire on Trial: Race, Murder, and Justice under British Rule, 1870–1935* (Cambridge: Cambridge University Press, 2009), pp. 10, 19. Wiener sees the colonial courtroom as an extension of the early nineteenth-century clashes between settlers and metropolitan humanists over the rights of Indigenous peoples under the law. See also Alan Lester, 'British Settler Discourse and the Circuits of Empire', *History Workshop Journal*, 54 (Autumn 2002), pp. 25–48.

11. Kostal, *Jurisprudence of Power*, p. 20.

12. *Umtali Post*, 26 August 1964; 9 December 1964.

13. National Archives of Zimbabwe, Harare (hereafter NAZ), 'The Murder of Petrus Johannes Andries Oberholtzer, 4 July 1964', s. 3061 1071/64.

14. The term 'hokoyo' literally means 'lookout' in Shona but its meaning in this context is ambiguous. The *Rhodesian Herald* transcribed the note as '*Boss of Crocodile Group will soon kill all whites*', but this reading does not stand up to scrutiny of the original document where the word 'bossop' is clearly used. *Rhodesia Herald*, 12 December 1964.

15. The 'Battle of Sinoia' of 18 April 1966 is conventionally understood (and commemorated) as the beginning of the armed struggle, but some accounts include the Crocodile group as a noteworthy precursor. See, for example, Michael Raeburn, *Black Fire: Accounts of the Guerilla War in Zimbabwe* (London: Julian Friedmann, 1978), p. 53; H. Ellert, *The Rhodesian Front War: Counter-Insurgency and Guerrilla War in Rhodesia, 1962–80* (Gweru: Mambo Press, 1993), p. 7; Baxter Tavuyanago, 'Ndangana and the Crocodile Group Operation', History Honours Dissertation, University of Zimbabwe (1985; available in the university library).

16. Police file memo, 7 July 1964, s. 3061 1071/64, NAZ.
17. 'Statement by Amos Kademaunga', 9 July 1964, s. 3061 1071/64, NAZ. His testimony at the trial was heard *in camera* to protect the witness from political reprisals. *Umtali Post*, 11 December 1964.
18. Tavuyanago, 'Ndangana and the Crocodile Group', p. 8; 'Statement by Amos Kademaunga', 9 July 1964, p. 2, s. 3061 1071/64, NAZ; CID Report, undated, p. 3, s. 3061 1071/64, NAZ.
19. This claim appears in Terrence Ranger's account but is not mentioned in the CID file. See 'Violence Variously Remembered: The Killing of Pieter Oberholtzer in July 1964', *History in Africa*, 24 (1997), pp. 273–86, 282.
20. Police file memo, 7 July 1964, s. 3061 1071/64, NAZ. According to Kademaunga's testimony, he and Ndangana even sat in the gallery for some of the court proceedings, see 'Statement by Amos Kademaunga', 9 July 1964 in s. 3061 1071/64, NAZ.
21. Dhlamini and Mlambo would plead that this latter task was not revealed to them until they had arrived in the Nyanyadzi district. The prosecution witness Kademaunga corroborated this, claiming that 'everyone was afraid' of Ndangana. *Umtali Post*, 14 December 1964.
22. 'Statement by Amos Kademaunga', 9 July 1964, p. 4, s. 3061 1071/64, NAZ.
23. The notes appear in photostat in s. 3061 1071/64, NAZ. It was at this point that the fifth member of the group, Amos Kademaunga, lost his nerve and fled. See Tavuyanago, 'Ndangana and the Crocodile Group', p. 14.
24. Ndangana would later make a name for himself in the bush war in the 1970s, becoming deputy minister for defence in Mugabe's first cabinet. He would subsequently die in a collision with an army vehicle in 1989 under suspicious circumstances. Master Tresha was later apprehended in another attack on white farmers in May 1966 and identified and charged as one of the Oberholtzer killers. He escaped the gallows on account of being under eighteen but served a long prison sentence, see J. R. T. Wood, *So Far and No Further! Rhodesia's Bid for Independence during the Retreat from Empire, 1959–65* (Bloomington: Trafford Publishing, 2005), p. 220.
25. Interview, Paul Naish, August 2015.
26. *Umtali Post*, 9 December 1964.
27. *Umtali Post*, 11 December 1964.
28. *Rhodesia Herald*, 15 December 1964; *Umtali Post*, 11 December 1964.
29. Specifically, James arrived in Chipinga with a bleeding lip wound that he claimed to be the result of a punch in the face. *Umtali Post*, 14 December 1964; *Rhodesia Herald*, 10 and 15 December 1964. The accusation was vehemently denied by police during the trial (who testified that the two were 'completely cooperative' at the time of their arrest) and reiterated decades later by arresting officer Constable Paul Naish in 2015. Dhlamini's bleeding wound from his lip, they insisted, was sustained during a fall on the long trek to Chipinga. *Umtali Post*, 9 December 1964; interview Paul Naish, August 2015.

30. *Rhodesia Herald*, 12 December 1964.

31. In contravention of s. 31(1)(a) of the Law and Order (Maintenance) Act 1960. In order to secure a conviction, the court needed to be satisfied that each of the accused had used petrol to set fire to the family or the vehicle. Although Mrs Oberholtzer could not identify precisely which of the four men had done so, Mlambo's own statement confessed to lighting one of the petrol bombs. Dhlamini's statement contained no such admission, but the court held that the two were involved in a 'combined operation' as witnessed by the notes left at the scene. Dhlamini's fingerprints were also reportedly found on a petrol bomb left behind after the attack on Nyanyadzi police station. *Rhodesia Herald*, 11 December 1964; *Umtali Post*, 9 December 1964, 16 December 1964.

32. This was the description of the Rhodesian Chief Justice at their appeal trial, who might have understood the legal niceties a little better. See 'Dhlamini and Others v. Carter, N.O. and Another.' (1), Appellate Division Salisbury, Beadle CJ, Quenet, JP, Macdonald JA, 26–29 February 1968, *Rhodesian Law Reports*, 1968, Part I, Ministry of Justice, Rhodesia, 1968, p. 148. Mrs Oberholtzer testified that she 'definitely saw four people but saw only one person using a knife'. *Rhodesia Herald*, 9 December 1964.

33. Several published accounts of the Oberholtzer murder have appeared over the years; by Ndabaningi Sithole himself, written in prison in the 1960s; by the author and filmmaker Michael Raeburn in the late 1970s, fired with optimism for the Mugabe era; by the young Zimbabwean student Baxter Tavuyanago in a fascinating honours thesis of 1985; and a fourth by the Zimbabwean writer Peter Godwin who chose the Oberholtzer murder as the opening template of his 1990s memoir, *Mukiwa* (imaginatively reconstructing his six-year-old self at the scene of the crime). Yet none of these works provide any real glimpse into the two lives that would ultimately be extinguished by the tide of events. Terrence Ranger considered the conflicting accounts in 'Violence Variously Remembered'. Sithole's version was smuggled out of prison and published in 1970: Ndabaningi Sithole, *Obed Mutezo: The Mudzimu Christian Nationalist* (Nairobi: Oxford University Press, 1970); Raeburn, *Black Fire*, pp. 65–8. Tavuyanago's thesis was published more than twenty-five years later in article form as 'The "Crocodile Gang" Operation: A Critical Reflection on the Genesis of the Second Chimurenga in Zimbabwe', *Global Journal of Human Social Science*, 13:4 (2013), pp. 1–10; Peter Godwin, *Mukiwa: A White Boy in Africa* (London: Picador, 1996).

34. Tavuyanago's account is the most informative, based largely on interviews in the 1980s with Ndangana and other ZANU local members involved in assisting the group. Tavuyanago, 'Ndangana and the Crocodile Group', p. 6.

35. Crime Salisbury to all stations, 20 July 1964, s. 3061 1071/64, NAZ.

36. *Umtali Post*, 16 December 1964.

37. The notes were signed 'David' (the suspect's middle name) and according to police records, Dhlamini admitted to having written the notes which he

discarded when he realized he had no way of posting them. CID Umtali to CID headquarters, Salisbury, 'Oberholtzer Murder', 30 July 1964, s. 3061 1071/64, NAZ.

38. See, for example, Benjamin Grob-Fitzgibbon, *Imperial Endgame: Britain's Dirty Wars and the End of Empire* (London: Palgrave Macmillan, 2011); Stacy Hynd, 'Killing the Condemned: The Practice and Process of Capital Punishment in British Africa, 1900–1950s', *Journal of African History*, 49 (2008), pp. 403–18.

39. Walima T. Kalusa, 'The Killing of Lilian Margaret Burton and Black and White Nationalisms in Northern Rhodesia (Zambia) in the 1960s', *Journal of Southern African Studies*, 37:1 (March 2011), pp. 63–77, 65.

40. Kalusa, 'The Killing of Lilian Margaret Burton', p. 64.

41. *Umtali Post*, 6 July 1964. The *Rhodesia Herald* raised 'the question of public measures to counter the evil of attacks on vehicles', demanding that 'the authorities' consider relaxing restrictions on the right of ordinary citizens to own and bear firearms. *Rhodesia Herald*, 6 July 1964.

42. The Rhodesian Air Force provided helicopter assistance to enhance police mobility, but a unit of the Rhodesian Light Infantry stationed nearby at Chipinga was not called in. *Umtali Post*, 8 July 1964. Bhebe and Ranger note how the Rhodesian authorities were generally slow to perceive nationalist violence in terms of a military threat in the early years of the struggle. See Ngwabi Bhebe and Terrence Ranger (eds.), *Soldiers in Zimbabwe's Liberation War* (London: James Currey, 1995).

43. Dated 7 July 1964. The report is cited in Donal Lowry, 'Rhodesia, 1890–1980', in Robert Bickers (ed.), *Settlers and Expatriates* (Oxford: Oxford University Press, 2010), p. 142.

44. Tavuyanago, 'The Crocodile Gang Operation', p. 34; Ellert, *The Rhodesian Front War*, p. 3.

45. Desmond Lardner-Burke, *Rhodesia: The Story of the Crisis* (London: Olbourne, 1966), pp. 57–8.

46. Quoted in Robert C. Good, *UDI: The International Politics of the Rhodesian Rebellion* (London: Faber, 1973), p. 80.

47. Quoted in *Rhodesia Herald*, 16 November 1965; see also Chengetai J. Zvogbo, 'Church and State in Rhodesia: From the Unilateral Declaration of Independence to the Pearce Commission, 1965–72', *Journal of Southern African Studies*, 31:2 (June 2005), pp. 381–402.

48. On the politics of sanctions and Wilson's dealings with Rhodesia more generally, see Elaine Windrich, *Britain and the Politics of Rhodesian Independence* (London: Groom Helm, 1978); Richard Coggins, 'Wilson and British Policy Towards Rhodesia', *Contemporary British History*, 20:3 (2006), pp. 363–81.

49. Quoted in Good, *UDI*, pp. 18–19. The complex negotiations that ensued between the two governments on HMS *Tiger* (1966) and *Fearless* (1968) will not be rehearsed here but see J. R. T. Wood, *A Matter of Weeks rather than Months: The Impasse between Harold Wilson and Ian Smith, 1965–1969* (Bloomington:

Trafford Publishing, 2008); Windrich, *Britain and the Politics of Rhodesian Independence*.

50. Smith denied that the governor moved to dismiss him at their first meeting immediately after UDI, a point which Gibbs's biographer persuasively rebuts. See Alan Megahey, *Humphrey Gibbs: Beleaguered Governor* (Basingstoke: Macmillan, 1998), p. 109.

51. Good, quoting 'a leading Conservative' in *UDI*, p. 60. Two important studies have emphasized the technical feasibility of a British invasion and occupation and downplay contemporary rumours that British servicemen might have mutinied at the prospect of military engagement with fellow British troops in Rhodesia, although they differ on the tactical wisdom of Wilson's public disavowal of military force. See Carl Watts, 'Killing Kith and Kin: The Viability of British Military Intervention in Rhodesia, 1964–65', *Twentieth Century British History*, 16:4 (2005), pp. 382–415; Philip Murphy, '"An Intricate and Distasteful Subject": British Planning for the Use of Force against the European Settlers of Central Africa, 1952–65', *English Historical Review*, cxxi:492 (June 2006), pp. 746–77.

52. Barfoot informed Gibbs point blank that he had to obey Smith or he would 'lose his job'. Transcript of oral testimony of Gibbs's secretary comptroller in the UDI years, John Pestell, 'Rhodesia and UDI', 1993. Sir John Pestell Papers, Bodleian Library, Oxford, Mss. Afr. 2208 (hereafter JPP) Box 4, 4/2; see also Megahey, *Humphrey Gibbs*, p. 108.

53. Quoted in Megahey, *Humphrey Gibbs*, p. 110.

54. Lowry, 'Rhodesia', p. 114.

55. Quoted in Richard Bourke, *Peace in Ireland: The War of Ideas* (London: Pimlico, 2012, 1st ed. 2003), p. 39.

56. Josiah Brownell, '"A Sordid Tussle on the Strand": Rhodesia House during the UDI Rebellion, 1965–80', *Journal of Imperial and Commonwealth History*, 38:3 (2010), pp. 471–99, 477.

57. Lowry, 'Rhodesia', p. 114.

58. *Rhodesia Herald*, 13 November 1965.

59. For an astute analysis of Beadle's torn instincts see Manuele Facchini, 'The "Evil Genius": Sir Hugh Beadle and the Rhodesian Crisis, 1965–1972', *Journal of Southern African Studies*, 33:3 (September 2007), pp. 673–89.

60. Quoted in Good, *UDI*, p. 81.

61. *Rhodesia Herald*, 13 November 1965.

62. Gibbs's £7,500 a year salary was terminated by the Smith government after UDI, and he refused the offers of the British Government to compensate his loss. The £1,000 per month upkeep of Government House was maintained out of a fund set up by (mainly Rhodesian) well-wishers, supplemented by Sir Humphrey's own private means. See the Sir Humphrey Gibbs Archive, Peterhouse College, Marondela, Zimbabwe (hereafter HGA), Box PC18.

63. Ian Smith's own account provides a reliable guide to the emotional stakes of the break-up of the federation in *The Great Betrayal: The Memoirs of Ian Douglas Smith*

(London: Blake, 1997), ch. 4; See also Philip Murphy, *Party Politics and Decolonisation: The Conservative Party and British Colonial Policy in Tropical Africa, 1951–1964* (Oxford: Oxford University Press, 1995).

64. *Rhodesia Herald*, 12 November 1965.

65. Quoted in Wendy Webster, '"There'll Always be an England": Representations of Colonial Wars and Immigration, 1948–68', *Journal of British Studies*, 40 (October 2001), pp. 557–84, 581.

66. See Smith's full UDI broadcast in *Rhodesia Herald*, 12 November 1965 where he also underlined that 'we in this country have no quarrel whatsoever with the people of Great Britain; the differences of opinion which we have are entirely with successive British Governments'.

67. Smith to Her Majesty the Queen, 23 November 1965, DO207/295, The National Archives, Kew (hereafter NA).

68. Clifford Dupont, *The Reluctant President* (Bulawayo: Books of Rhodesia, 1978), p. 174. The 'wind of change' remark is quoted in the transcript of the BBC programme 'From our Own Correspondent', 15 May 1965 (episode on 'Who Leads Rhodesia'), 5th Marquess of Salisbury Papers, Hatfield House, Box WW.

69. *Daily Mail*, 'The Voices of Rhodesia', 9 September 1968. Gibbs's biographer also notes the intricacies of avoiding Dupont at the Club, not always successfully. See Megahey, *Humphrey Gibbs*, p. 120.

70. Dupont, *Reluctant President*, p. 180.

71. Pestell diary entry, 8 June 1968, Box 1, 1/4, JPP.

72. Pestell diary entry, 4 November 1967, Box 1, 1/4, JPP.

73. Peter Godwin and Ian Hancock, *Rhodesians Never Die: The Impact of War and Political Change on White Rhodesia, 1970–1980* (Oxford: Oxford University Press, 1993), p. 11.

74. Megahey, *Humphrey Gibbs*, p. 99.

75. See Chapter 7.

76. *Natal Witness*, 12 November 1965.

77. Good, *UDI*, p. 22. The vice-chancellor at the time was Smith's brother-in-law, Owen Horwood, who harboured pro-apartheid sympathies and who later became leader of the National Party in Natal. On the South African government's refusal to impose sanctions, see A. S. Mlambo, '"We Have Blood Relations over the Border": South Africa and Rhodesian Sanctions, 1965–1975', *African Historical Review*, 40:1 (2008), pp. 1–29.

78. Undated handwritten memorandum by Menzies, 'Rhodesia – my story of what turned out to be my problem', Menzies Papers, MS4936, 421/4, National Library of Australia.

79. National Archives of Australia (hereafter NAA), A5827/1, Vol. 35, Cabinet Minute, Decision no 1373, 'Unilateral Declaration of Independence by Rhodesia', 12 November 1965.

80. Diary entry of Federal Minister for Air, Peter Howson, 12 November 1965, quoted in Carl Watts, '"The Men Who Smell Fear": The Menzies Government

and Rhodesia's Unilateral Declaration of Independence', *Australian Journal of Politics and History*, 62:3 (2016), pp. 404–18, 412.

81. The left-wing *Daily Sketch* concluded on 8 January 1966: 'We know exactly why the Australian Prime Minister is fuming over the Commonwealth Prime Ministers' Conference. Australia is as much a race-baiter as Ian Smith of Rhodesia'.

82. Foreign Affairs and Defence Committee Minutes, decision nos 1445 (7 December 1965) and 1446 (10 January 1966), A5828/1 Vol. 5, NAA. These instincts had to contend with considerable misgivings in official circles that over-identification with Rhodesia would be greatly to the detriment of Australia's international standing. See, for example, Matthew Jordan, '"Australia in this Matter is under Some Scrutiny": Early Australian Initiatives to the Rhodesian Problem, 1961–64', *International History Review*, 42:1 (2020), pp. 77–98.

83. Alan J. Campbell (Australian Country Party of Queensland Trustees) to McEwen, 7 December 1966; J. W. D. Lee (Delegate to 1966 NSW Conference) to McEwen 15 December 1966, M58/113, NAA.

84. Press release by Deputy Prime Minister John McEwen, 'Rhodesia', January 1967, M58/113, NAA.

85. *The Advertiser*, 15 November 1965; *The Australian*, 15 November 1965; *Courier Mail*, 15 November 1965; *Daily Telegraph*, 17 November 1965; the *New Zealand Herald* ran a similar line on 19 November 1965.

86. The governments who at various times called on Wilson to deploy troops included Sierra Leone, Uganda, Trinidad and Tobago, Zambia, Ceylon, Ghana and Tanzania. See *Courier Mail*, 13 January 1965; *The Mercury* (Hobart), 13 January 1965; *Daily Telegraph*, 17 January 1965; *Canberra Times*, *West Australian*, *Sydney Morning Herald*, all 14 January 1965.

87. *Melbourne Herald*, 12 November 1965; the only robust criticism of Rhodesian whites was in Sydney's left-leaning *Daily Mirror*, which condemned a lifestyle founded on 'ebony house slaves who ... pick up endlessly behind outrageously spoiled children'. *Daily Mirror*, 12 November 1965.

88. *Auckland Star*, 12 November 1965.

89. Quoted in Malcolm Mackinnon (ed.), *New Zealand in World Affairs,* vol. II: *1957–72* (Wellington: New Zealand Institute of International Affairs, 1991), p. 103.

90. Archives New Zealand, Wellington (hereafter ANZ), ABHS 950 W4627 Box 4171 245/8/3 Part 17, 'Guidance survey 33/65, Rhodesia', 6 December 1965.

91. *Sunday Times* (Wellington), 28 November 1965. See also the *Sunday News*, 'Give Smith a Chance', 28 November 1965.

92. *Christchurch Star*, 4 December 1965.

93. *New Zealand Truth*, 19 January 1966.

94. Quoted in Camilla Schofield, *Enoch Powell and the Making of Post-Colonial Britain* (Cambridge: Cambridge University Press, 2013), p. 196. Emphasis in original.

95. Quoted in Alice Ritscherle, 'Disturbing the People's Peace: Patriotism and "Respectable" Racism in British Responses to Rhodesian Independence', in Philippa Levine and Susan Grayzel (eds.), *Gender, Labour, War and Empire* (London: Palgrave Macmillan, 2008), pp. 201–2.
96. Hansard, 8 December 1966, Vol. 737, c. 1621.
97. Ritscherle, 'Disturbing the People's Peace', pp. 208–9.
98. Dingle Foot Papers, Churchill Archives Centre, Cambridge (hereafter DFP) DGFT 5/30, Timeline of key events, 'Rhodesia'.
99. The 5th Marquess of Salisbury Papers in Hatfield House (Boxes VV, WW, XX, YY and ZZ) are stuffed full with letters of gratitude from Rhodesians and Rhodesian sympathizers around the world, particularly Britain. See also Christian Damm Pedersen, 'African Decolonization and the Fate of Britishness, 1959–1965', PhD thesis, University of Copenhagen (2016).
100. Bill Schwarz, *The White Man's World* (Oxford: Oxford University Press, 2011), p. 37.
101. H. M. Bailey to Salisbury, 10 December 1965, Salisbury Papers, Box XX.
102. A. Smith (Tambours Kloof, Cape Town) to Salisbury, 2 December 1965, Salisbury papers, Box XX.
103. Mrs Beringer to Salisbury, 12 November 1964, Salisbury Papers, Box VV.
104. Geoffrey Boys (Huntingdon, Cambridgeshire) to Salisbury, 16 November 1965; F. Violet Agnew to Salisbury, 16 November 1965. The latter purged her inner self in elaborate terms: 'I am only a rotten Englishwoman and deeply ashamed of my nationality'. Salisbury Papers, Box XX.
105. Grace Boddington to Salisbury, 26 August 1965. She and her husband, too, were 'ashamed of being English, and are ready to fight for what we believe in over Rhodesia'. Salisbury Papers, Box XX.
106. His comments were made on the BBC *World at One* programme on 28 August 1967 and quoted in *The Times* as follows: 'After all, they and we are on the same side . . . Like resistance fighters in the last war, these fighters are fighting for a very similar cause – against alien rule and against the doctrine of the master race'.
107. All of these letters are contained in the Foot papers, DGFT 8/17. The Tunbridge Wells letter was from a Mrs Kathleen Williams, dated 6 September 1967.
108. Quoted in Donal Lowry, 'Ulster Resistance and Loyalist Rebellion in the Empire', in Keith Jeffrey (ed.), *'An Irish Empire'? Aspects of Ireland and the British Empire* (Manchester: Manchester University Press, 1996), p. 204.
109. Quoted in Ritscherle, 'Disturbing the People's Peace', p. 214. On the Kenyan Asians episode see Chapter 12.
110. Quoted in Timeline of Key Events, 'Rhodesia', DGFT 5/30, Foot papers.
111. The details of the scene are assembled here from various reports in the Bulawayo *Chronicle, Daily Mail* and *The Sun*, all 7 March 1968, and the *Sunday*

Times, 10 March 1968. The interview with Mlambo's father was with *The Sun*'s correspondent Malcolm Stewart.

112. File Note, 'Numbers and Details of Persons under Sentence of Death in Rhodesia', 8 March 1968, PREM13/2333, NA.

113. *Daily Telegraph*, 8 March 1968; *Bulawayo Citizen*, 8 March 1968; *Rand Daily Mail*, 11 March 1968.

114. *Daily Mail*, 7 March 1968; *Daily Telegraph*, 7 and 8 March 1968.

115. See Chapter 14.

116. See *Daily Mail*, 7 March 1968; *Daily Express*, 7 March 1968. See also Brownell, 'A Sordid Tussle', p. 483.

117. Needless to say, the Murder (Aboliton of Death Penalty) Act was entirely unrelated to UDI. The Act only suspended the death penalty for a period of five years, but as this was reaffirmed in 1969 it marked the end of capital punishment in the UK.

118. *The Times*, 7 March 1968.

119. The two depictions of Beadle referred to here are taken from undated and unattributed press cuttings in Humphrey Gibbs's personal scrapbook. Box PC 18, HGA.

120. Note, however, that two of the five judges in *Madzimbamuto v. Lardner-Burke* (otherwise known as the 'Constitutional Case') of 29 January 1968, Macdonald and Quenet, held that the government now had to be regarded as both de facto and *de jure*. Both of these judges would sit in judgement on Mlambo, Dhlamini and Shadreck.

121. 'Dhlamini and Others v. Carter, N.O. and Another' (2), Appellate Division Salisbury, Beadle CJ, Quenet, JP, Macdonald JA, 1 March 1968, *Rhodesian Law Reports*, 1968, Part I, Ministry of Justice, Rhodesia, 1968, pp. 157–60. My emphasis.

122. The other took the unusual step of issuing his own statement from the bench, dissecting the judgement as an effective bestowal of *de jure* recognition on the illegal 1965 Constitution. See Justice Dendy Young's statement dated 4 March 1968 in Box 3, 3/2, JPP; Justice Fieldsend's resignation is described at length in his unpublished 'Judicial History of Rhodesia's Unilateral Declaration of Independence', Box 3, 3/3, JPP.

123. *The Times*, 11 March 1968; Hailsham's remarks are recorded in Pestell's diary, 2 March 1968, Box 1, 1/3, JPP.

124. Palliser to Williams, 1 March 1968, PREM13/2333, NA.

125. 'Dhlamini and Another v. Carter, N.O. and Another', Appellate Division Salisbury, Beadle CJ, Quenet, JP, Macdonald JA, 4 March 1968, pp. 160–4, *Rhodesian Law Reports*, 1968, Part I, Ministry of Justice, Rhodesia, 1968.

126. Salisbury to Whitehall, 2 March 1968, PREM13/2333, NA. The source (Gibbs's comptroller, John Pestell, who was present at the meeting) observed that Beadle seemed 'very wrought up as though he knew he had gone, or been pushed, too far'.

127. This would also explain the absence of signatures on the execution notices nailed to the prison gates, the fact that no minister made any personal public statement, and that the official 'Statement by the Rhodesian Government' broadcast immediately after the hangings was read out by an anonymous government newsreader.

128. Gibbs to Pestell, 29 November 1981, Box 4, 4/2, JPP.

129. *Cape Times*, 12 March 1968.

130. *Daily Express*, 7 March 1968; *Sunday Telegraph*, 10 March 1968. Similar sentiments were voiced in the *Daily Mail* editorial 'Smith's Lonely Path', 7 March 1968. By no means all newspapers were scathing of Smith, with several apportioning at least part of the blame to the Wilson government for driving Smith 'into the arms of his extremists by the obtuse and pedantic handling from London', see *Daily Telegraph*, 7 March 1968; see also *News of the World*, 10 March 1968, which criticized Wilson's 'personal vendetta' against Smith. However blame was apportioned, it was universally recognized that a rubicon had been crossed.

131. See Foot and MP for Croydon Mr Winnick reported in the *Daily Telegraph*, 7 March 1968.

132. Quoted in Phillip Ziegler, *The Authorised Life of Lord Wilson of Rievaulx* (London: Weidenfeld and Nicolson, 1993), p. 319.

133. Quoted in Daniel McNeil, '"The Rivers of Zimbabwe Will Run Red with Blood": Enoch Powell and the Post-Imperial Nostalgia of the Monday Club', *Journal of Southern African Studies*, 37:4 (December 2011), pp. 731–45, 737.

134. *Daily Express*, 7 March 1968.

135. *Umtali Post*, 4 March 1968.

136. *Umtali Post*, 8 March 1968.

137. As reported in *The Times*, 25 March 1968.

138. Pestell diary entry, 24 March 1968, Box 1, 1/3, JPP.

139. *Daily Mail*, 9 March 1968.

140. Rhodesian Cabinet memorandum, 'Speech from the Throne', RC(s) (68)94, 8 May 1968, Ian Smith Papers, Cory Library, Rhodes University, Grahamstown, 2/007(A) (hereafter SP).

141. Rhodesian Cabinet Memorandum, 'Queen's Birthday' RC(s) (68) 75, 8 April 1968, 2/007(A), SP.

142. *Rhodesia Herald*, 10 August 1968.

143. *Rhodesia Herald*, 12 August 1968. See also the harmless objections raised in the letters pages of the *Herald* on 13 and 15 November 1968.

144. The lack of a fitting anthem in place of 'God Save the Queen' was widely commented on; see *Rhodesia Herald* and *Bulawayo Chronicle*, 12 November 1968.

145. *Rhodesia Herald*, 11 November 1968.

146. See campaign material in Box 2, 2/2, JPP.

147. *Rhodesia Herald*, 21 June 1969; 3 March 1970.

148. Megahey, *Humphrey Gibbs*, pp. 168–9. The flag returned briefly at the end of the 1970s when Christopher Soames was appointed caretaker governor during the Lancaster House process to create an independent Zimbabwe, but by then it had lost all of its earlier connotations of loyalty and affinity with Britain. It also continued to be raised over Cecil Square each year on 'Pioneer Day', although as much in mourning as celebration. See Schwarz, *White Man's World*, pp. 394–5.

10 EAST AND WEST OF SUEZ: RECEDING FRONTIERS

1. Peter Fleming, 'The Man from Rangoon', *The Spectator*, 5 October 1951, p. 13.
2. Ian Fleming, *Casino Royale* (London: Jonathan Cape, 1953). Fleming commenced work on his first Bond novel in January 1952. See John Pearson, *The Life of Ian Fleming* (London: Bloomsbury, 2013, 1st ed. 1966), p. 266.
3. Jonathan Cape, quoted in Andrew Lycett, *Ian Fleming* (Phoenix: Turner Publishing, 1996), p. 226.
4. See, for example, Tony Bennett and Janet Woollacott, *Bond and Beyond: The Political Career of a Popular Hero* (London: Routledge, 1987); Sam Goodman, *British Spy Fiction and the End of Empire* (London: Routledge, 2016); Simon Winder, *The Man Who Saved Britain* (London: Picador, 2006).
5. See, for example, Bernard Porter, *The Absent-Minded Imperialists: How the British Really Saw Their Empire* (Oxford: Oxford University Press, 2004).
6. Eyre Crowe, 'Memorandum on the Present State of British Relations with France and Germany,' 1 January 1907 reproduced in multiple versions since its original 1934 edition (with a foreword by Hilaire Belloc), most recently in J. S. Dunn, *The Crowe Memorandum* (Newcastle upon Tyne: Cambridge Scholars, 2013).
7. The literature is now substantial, but the foundational works are Paul Kennedy, *The Rise and Fall of British Naval Mastery* (New York: Scribner, 1976); Phillip Darby, *British Defence Policy East of Suez* (London: Oxford University Press, 1973); Jeffrey Pickering, *Britain's Withdrawal from East of Suez: The Politics of Retrenchment* (London: Macmillan, 1997); Saki Dockrill, *Britain's Retreat from East of Suez: The Choice between Europe and the World?* (London: Palgrave Macmillan, 2002); P. L. Pham, *Ending East of Suez: The British Decision to Withdraw from Malaysia and Singapore 1964–1968* (Oxford: Oxford University Press, 2010).
8. Cited in Peter Hennessy, *Having It So Good: Britain in the Fifties* (London: Allen Lane, 2006), p. 2.
9. Sir Olaf Caroe, 'From 1947 On', British Library India Office Collection, Mss Eur. F203 Papers of Sir Olaf Kirkpatrick Caroe. Elizabeth Buettner's study of returnees from India suggests that this might have been a long-standing habit, in which the individual disappointments of diminished status in the metropole were projected onto a nation presumed to be in decline. The period after 1947 would have amplified this tendency given the sheer number of returnees. See especially ch. 5

of Buettner's *Empire Families: Britons and Late Imperial India* (Oxford: Oxford University Press, 2004).

10. A. J. M. Craig, 'Impressions of a Dubai Post', 27 September 1964, Document 116 in S. R. Ashton and Wm Roger Louis (eds.), *East of Suez and the Commonwealth, 1964–71*, British Documents on the End of Empire, Part 1 (London: HMSO, 2004), p. 395.

11. Cyril Radcliffe, 'The Page is Turned', BBC broadcast 2 October 1947, quoted in Hennessy, *Having It So Good*, p. 273. See also Lucy P. Chester, *Borders and Conflict in South Asia: The Radcliffe Boundary Commission and the Partition of the Punjab* (Manchester: Manchester University Press, 2009), ch. 9.

12. On the lingering capacity of colonial graves to stir the imperial imagination long after decolonization, see Elizabeth Buettner, 'Cemeteries, Public Memory and Raj Nostalgia in Postcolonial Britain and India', *History and Memory*, 18:1 (Spring/Summer 2006), pp. 5–42.

13. Cited in Peter H. Hansen, 'Coronation Everest: The Empire and Commonwealth in the "Second Elizabethan Age"', in Stuart Ward (ed.), *British Culture and the End of Empire* (Manchester: Manchester University Press, 2001), p. 57. David Carlton describes the 'media obsession' with a Second Elizabethan Age as a species of 'collective self-delusion which, if anything, added to the country's problems' in the lead-up to the Suez crisis. See *Britain and the Suez Crisis* (Oxford: Blackwell, 1988), pp. 1–2.

14. Quoted in Hennessy, *Having It So Good*, p. 241. See also Peter H. Hansen, 'Confetti of Empire: The Conquest of Everest in Nepal, India, Britain and New Zealand', *Comparative Studies in Society and History*, 42:2 (2000), pp. 307–32; Gordon T. Stewart, 'Tenzing's Two Wrist Watches: The Conquest of Everest and Late Imperial Culture, 1921–1953', *Past and Present*, 149 (November 1995), pp. 170–97.

15. Colonial Office minute, 22 July 1952, Quoted in Ronald Hyam, *Britain's Declining Empire: The Road to Decolonisation, 1918–68* (Cambridge: Cambridge University Press, 2006), p. 179.

16. Address to the Imperial Defence College in 1953, quoted in Hyam, *Britain's Declining Empire*, p. 173.

17. Oliver Lyttleton, *The Memoirs of Lord Chandos* (New York: New American Library, 1963), p. 380. See also Chapter 5 in this volume.

18. Quoted in Saravelli Gopal, 'Churchill and India', in Robert Blake and Wm Roger Louis (eds.), *Churchill* (Oxford: Oxford University Press, 1993), p. 471.

19. Evelyn Shuckburgh (Eden's principal Foreign Office adviser) quoted in Michael Charlton, *The Price of Victory* (London: BBC, 1983), p. 157; See also senior FO mandarin Sir Frank Roberts quoted in Hennessy, *Having It So Good*, p. 278.

20. The memorandum, dated 18 June 1952, is reproduced in full in David Goldsworthy (ed.), *The Conservative Government and the End of Empire, 1951–57* (London: HMSO, 1994), Doc. 3., p. 6; Eden's 'unalterable marrow' is

a reference to the related context of European integration, during an address to Columbia University in January 1952, extracted in Eden, *Full Circle* (London: Cassell, 1960), p. 36.

21. David Goldsworthy, 'Keeping Change within the Bounds: Aspects of Colonial Policy during the Churchill and Eden Governments, 1951–57', *Journal of Imperial and Commonwealth History*, 18:1 (1990), pp. 81–108. The Sudan became independent in January 1956, but this fell outside of the domain of the Colonial Office.
22. Cited in Ronald Hyam and Peter Henshaw, *The Lion and the Springbok: Britain and South Africa since the Boer War* (Cambridge: Cambridge University Press, 2003), p. 243.
23. John Williams, 'ANZUS: A Blow to Britain's Self-Esteem', *Review of International Studies*, 13:4 (October 1987), pp. 423–63; Stuart Ward, *Australia and the British Embrace: The Demise of the Imperial Ideal* (Melbourne: Melbourne University Press, 2001), pp. 23–4.
24. 10 March 1952, quoted in John Darwin, *The Empire Project: The Rise and Fall of the British World-System* (Cambridge: Cambridge University Press, 2009), p. 563.
25. See Michael T. Thornhill, 'Britain, the United States and the Rise of an Egyptian Leader: The Politics and Diplomacy of Nasser's Consolidation of Power', *English Historical Review*, 119 (September 2004), pp. 892–921; Wm Roger Louis, 'Prelude to Suez: Churchill and Egypt', in *Ends of British Imperialism: The Scramble for Empire, Suez and Decolonization* (London: I. B. Tauris, 2006).
26. Elleke Boehmer, *Indian Arrivals: 1870–1915* (Oxford: Oxford University Press, 2015), p. 40.
27. Quoted in Boehmer, *Indian Arrivals*, p. 50.
28. Quoted in Gordon T. Stewart, 'The Strange Case of Jute', in Bryan S. Glass and John M. MacKenzie (eds.), *Scotland, Empire and Decolonisation in the Twentieth Century* (Manchester: Manchester University Press, 2015), p. 69.
29. Somerset Maugham, *East of Suez: A Play in Seven Scenes* (New York: George H. Doran, 1922). The play was also made into a silent movie in 1925, directed by Raoul Walsh.
30. Boehmer, *Indian Arrivals*, p. 48. Boehmer places particular emphasis on the two-way narrated journey, with British perspectives on a waterway opening out to an opulent east 'at once contested and shared' by Indian elites journeying in the opposite direction. See p. 41.
31. Quoted in Keith Kyle, *Suez: Britain's End of Empire in the Middle East* (London: I. B. Tauris, 2011, 1st ed. 1991), p. 7.
32. Leaving aside the French position in North Africa, which was in any case a specifically French interest. See Maurice Vaisse, 'France and the Suez Crisis', in Wm Roger Louis and Roger Owen (eds.), *Suez 1956: The Crisis and Its Consequences* (Oxford: Oxford University Press, 1989), pp. 134–8; see also Martin Thomas, *Fight or Flight: Britain, France and Their Roads from Empire* (Oxford: Oxford University Press, 2014), ch. 6.

33. Quoted in Simon C. Smith, 'Prelude to the Suez Crisis', in Simon C. Smith, *Reassessing Suez 1956: New Perspectives on the Crisis and its Aftermath* (Aldershot: Ashgate, 2008), pp. 29, 31.

34. Quoted in Darwin, *Empire Project*, pp. 593, 600.

35. Salisbury to Churchill, 10 July 1951, cited in Sue Onslow, '"Battlelines for Suez": The Abadan Crisis of 1951 and the Formation of the Suez Group', *Contemporary British History*, 17:2 (2003), pp. 1–28, 11.

36. Albert Hourani, 'Conclusion', in Louis and Owen (eds.), *Suez 1956*, p. 394.

37. On Churchill's agonized and grudging acceptance of this outcome see Louis, 'Prelude to Suez'.

38. Hansard (Lords) 28 July 1954, Vol. 189, cc. 253–4.

39. Quoted in Louis, 'Prelude to Suez', p. 625.

40. David Goldsworthy, *Colonial Issues in British Politics, 1945–61: From 'Colonial Development' to 'Wind of Change'* (Oxford: Oxford University Press, 1971), p. 288.

41. Quoted in Sue Onslow, *Backbench Debate within the Conservative Party and Its Influence on British Foreign Policy, 1948–57* (Basingstoke: Palgrave Macmillan, 1997), p. 116.

42. Onslow notes, however, that by no means all members conformed to the 'old war horse' stereotype, and that in terms of its composition, attitudes and influence, the Group was closer to the centre of the Conservative Party than posterity has generally allowed. See Onslow, *Backbench Debate*, pp. 117–18.

43. Hennessy, *Having It So Good*, pp. 280–1.

44. Hansard (Commons), 21 June 1951, Vol. 489, c. 786.

45. *We the British, Are We in Decline?*, BBC Television Script, Episode 1, broadcast 24 April 1956, BBC Written Archives Centre, Reading, pp. 1–2. The first episode was entitled 'Our position in the world'. Subsequent programmes in the series looked at 'Our economic life', 'Our attitude to work', 'Our moral standards' and 'Our religious faith', followed by a 'Summing up' at the end of the series.

46. Cited in Webster, *Englishness and Empire*, p. 119.

47. *We the British*, pp. 4, 7.

48. Kyle, *Suez*, p. 137.

49. Quoted in Geoffrey Marston, 'Armed Intervention in the 1956 Suez Canal Crisis: The Legal Advice Tendered to the British Government', *The International and Comparative Law Quarterly*, 37:4 (October 1988), pp. 773–817, 776. The company was nominally French, with headquarters in Paris, but the principal shareholder was the British Government. In legal terms the company was Egyptian, subject to Egyptian law and hence a legitimate object of state acquisition.

50. The Eisenhower–Eden correspondence, which left absolutely no doubt as to the president's attitude, is reprinted in Peter G. Boyle (ed.), *The Eden-Eisenhower Correspondence* (Chapel Hill: University of North Carolina Press, 2005). See also Wm Roger Louis, 'American Anti-Colonialism, Suez, and the Special Relationship', *International Affairs*, 61:3 (1985), pp. 409–16.

51. The veracity of the moustache story is, however, dubious. The only credible source was the French defence minister Maurice Bourgès-Maunoury who played a key role at Sèvres and who made the claim during an interview in November 1986 for the BBC2 documentary series *Secrets of Suez*. But the rumour was dismissed as 'absurd' by another eye-witness, Donald Logan (Lloyd's private secretary), who countered that the foreign secretary at no time wore 'any disguise of any kind nor did he contemplate doing so'. Sir Donald Logan to R. M. Cooper, 6 January 1987, FCO 12/181, The National Archives, Kew (hereafter NA).

52. Quoted in Hennessy, *Having It So Good*, p. 439.

53. The roll of honour is at www.palacebarracksmemorialgarden.co.uk/archive/Suez.htm.

54. Hugh Thomas, commenting on the 'macabre humour' of the assault, noted that even the grand old Duke of York 'at least got to the top of the hill'. Hugh Thomas, *The Suez Affair* (London: Weidenfeld and Nicolson, 1966), p. 164.

55. This view was originally popularized by the tell-all memoir by Anthony Nutting, the Foreign Office 'Minister of State' who resigned in disgust over the collusion with France and Israel, and who finally broke his silence in 1967. See *No End of a Lesson: The Story of Suez* (London: Constable, 1967). Subsequent historical accounts have also claimed that drugs and debilitating illness were decisive, such as Richard Lamb, *The Failure of the Eden Government* (London: Sidwick and Jackson, 1987); Bert E. Park, *Ailing, Aging, Addicted: Studies of Compromised Leadership* (Lexington: University of Kentucky Press, 1993), ch. 7; Lord Owen, 'The Effect of Prime Minister Anthony Eden's Illness on his Decision-Making During the Suez Crisis', *QJM: An International Journal of Medicine*, 98:6 (2005), pp. 387–402. Robert Rhodes James, by contrast, refutes the depiction of Eden as a physically enervated figure, dependent on drugs and stimulants in his 1986 biography *Anthony Eden* (London: Weidenfeld and Nicolson, 1986); David Carlton's *Britain and the Suez Crisis* is also sceptical, pp. 16–21, 63–4.

56. Hyam, *Britain's Declining Empire*, pp. 231–2. David Edgerton, *The Rise and Fall of the British Nation: A Twentieth Century History* (London: Allen Lane, 2018), p. 276.

57. Quoted in Hennessy, *Having It So Good*, p. 416.

58. Sue Onslow, 'Julian Amery and the Suez Operation', in Smith (ed.), *Reassessing Suez*, pp. 69–72.

59. Roger Louis has made a similar argument in respect of the 1951 Abadan oil crisis, which he claims was 'one of the root causes of the Suez crisis five years later'. See Wm Roger Louis, *The British Empire in the Middle East, 1945–51: Arab Nationalism, the United States and Postwar Imperialism* (Oxford: Oxford University Press, 1994), p. 668; See also Onslow, *Backbench Debate*, pp. 141–50.

60. Indeed, several conservative newspapers were harshly critical of the government for not having used force earlier in the crisis. Tony Shaw, *Eden, Suez and the Mass Media: Propaganda and Persuasion during the Suez Crisis* (London: I. B. Tauris, 1995), chs. 2–7.

61. All quotations in Dominic Sandbrook, *Never Had It So Good: A History of Britain from Suez to the Beatles* (London: Abacus, 2006), p. 18. See also Ralph Negrine, 'The Press and the Suez Crisis: A Myth Re-examined', *The Historical Journal*, 25:4 (1982), pp. 975–83.

62. *Daily Mail*, 7 November 1956.

63. Lord Butler, *The Art of the Possible* (London: Gambit, 1971), pp. 188–9.

64. Louis, *Ends of British Imperialism*, p. 17. Lord Beloff reached a similar conclusion in 'The Crisis and its Consequences for the British Conservative Party', in Louis and Owen, *Suez 1956*, pp. 329, 332.

65. Epstein's verdict that Suez was 'the moment for the resurgence of an unadulterated imperial spirit' is one early example of a tendency to overdraw the imperial analogy. The spirit was surely 'adulterated' by the advanced stage of imperial retreat. See Leon D. Epstein, *British Politics in the Suez Crisis* (London: Pall Mall Press, 1964), p. 42.

66. Eden to Eisenhower, 30 October 1956 in Boyle, *Eden-Eisenhower*, p. 181.

67. This view was vigorously advanced by the lord chancellor, Lord Kilmuir, and was the basis of the government's repeated claim that armed intervention in no way breached the UN charter. In fact, legal opinion in Whitehall was bitterly divided and Eden went to great lengths to keep his contrarian Foreign Office legal advisers 'completely in the dark'. See Marston, 'Armed Intervention', p. 808.

68. Home in Hennessy, *Having It So Good*, p. 421; Amery in Goldsworthy, *Colonial Issues*, p. 298; Macmillan diary entry 15 September 1956 in Peter Catterall (ed.), *The Macmillan Diaries: The Cabinet Years, 1950–57* (London: Pan, 2004), p. 600; Eden to Eisenhower, 6 September 1956, in Boyle, *Eden-Eisenhower*, p. 167.

69. Eisenhower to Eden, 8 September 1956, in Boyle, *Eden-Eisenhower*, p. 167.

70. Eden, public broadcast, 8 August 1956, available for listening at AP Archive, 'Eden's Suez Speech': www.aparchive.com/.

71. Peter Lyon, 'The Commonwealth and the Suez Crisis', in Wm Roger Louis and Roger Owen (eds.), *Suez 1956: The Crisis and its Consequences* (Oxford: Oxford University Press, 1989), p. 272.

72. *The Age*, 15 August 1956. Eden had reportedly intervened personally with the BBC to get Menzies on the air.

73. W. J. Hudson, *Blind Loyalty: Australia and the Suez Crisis, 1956* (Melbourne: Melbourne University Press, 1989), p. 27. When Labor Opposition Leader H. V. Evatt encountered criticism for his 'anti-British' advocacy of UN mediation he responded: 'The people of Great Britain are our kinsmen and I believe that in this matter they take the same view as that expressed by the Labor Party here.' Quoted in James Eayrs, *The Commonwealth and Suez: A Documentary Survey* (London: Oxford University Press, 1964), p. 185.

74. *Daily Telegraph*, 1 November 1956; *Sydney Morning Herald*, 2 November 1956.

75. Menzies to Eden, 1 November 1956, quoted in Hudson, *Blind Loyalty*, p. xii.

76. 7 August 1956, extract in Eayrs, *Commonwealth and Suez*, p. 60.

77. Malcolm Templeton, *Ties of Blood and Empire: New Zealand's Involvement in Middle East Defence and the Suez Crisis, 1947–57* (Auckland: Auckland University Press, 1994), pp. 67, 128.

78. See, for example, Holland's 'Dear Team' memo of 5 November 1956, reprinted in Templeton, *Ties of Blood*, pp. 222–5. The prime minister had first presented the matter to the New Zealand parliament in the starkest terms on 7 August: 'The Suez Canal is vital to Britain and Britain is vital to New Zealand. Where she is in difficulty we are in difficulty.' Extract in Eayrs, *Commonwealth and Suez*, pp. 60–1.

79. Templeton, *Ties of Blood*, pp. 129, 131.

80. McIntosh to Macdonald, 20 August 1956, Alister McIntosh Papers, MS6759/307, Alexander Turnbull Library, Wellington.

81. Holland to Eden, 1 November 1956, EA W2619, 217/1/12 Part 1, Archives New Zealand.

82. Templeton, *Ties of Blood*, p. 106.

83. Templeton, *Ties of Blood*, p. 136.

84. 'Intervention in Egypt – Protests and Demonstrations in Pakistan', despatch by the Canadian High Commissioner, November 1956, RG25-A-3-b Vol. 6109, Library and Archives Canada (hereafter LAC).

85. *Dawn*, 1 November 1956, quoted in Eayrs, *Commonwealth and Suez*, p. 197.

86. Speech in Hyderabad, 1 November 1956, reproduced in Eayrs, *Commonwealth and Suez*, pp. 251–2; see also Sarvepalli Gopal, 'India, the Crisis and the Non-Aligned Nations', in Louis and Owen, *Suez 1956*, p. 185.

87. Nehru to Eden, 31 October 1956, copy available in MG31-E46 Vol. 8, LAC.

88. Nehru to Vijaya Lakshmi, 11 February 1957, V. L. Pandit papers, 207 – PMH/57, Nehru Memorial Library, New Delhi.

89. Mordechai Bar-On makes a similar point about the Israeli government, which was widely understood to be acting on the basis of a rational, if misguided, calculation of its own vital interests. Indeed he notes that while London 'echoed with outrage right away . . . such indignation and accusations were not heard in Paris, and certainly not in Tel Aviv'. See 'David Ben Gurion and the Sèvres Collusion', in Louis and Owen (eds.), *Suez 1956*, p. 159.

90. St Laurent to Eden, 31 October 1956; 5 November 1956, MG31 E-46 Vol. 8, LAC.

91. Canada House New Delhi, Memorandum on Nehru's forthcoming visit to Canada, 26 November 1956, MG31-E46 Vol. 9, File 2, LAC. Reid later claimed in his memoirs, with some justification, that had Canada 'joined Australia and New Zealand in voting against the first UN Resolution on Suez, the newly established Commonwealth would have been shattered'. Escott Reid, *Hungary and Suez 1956: A View from New Delhi* (Oakville, Ont.: Mosaic Press, 1986), p. 136.

92. John Strachey, *The End of Empire* (London: Victor Golancz, 1959), p. 253. See also Lyon, 'Commonwealth and the Suez Crisis', p. 272 and Beloff, 'Consequences for the Conservative Party', p. 334; Louis concurs that 'the

Commonwealth was never again the same after Suez', *Ends of British Imperialism*, p. 9. On the change of Commonwealth nomenclature, see Chapter 4.

93. José E. Igartua, *The Other Quiet Revolution: National Identities in English Canada, 1945–71* (Vancouver: UBC Press, 2006), p. 115.

94. Igartua, *Other Quiet Revolution*, p. 116.

95. 28 and 5 November 1956, respectively, quoted in Igartua, *Other Quiet Revolution*, pp. 120, 122.

96. Igartua, *Other Quiet Revolution*, pp. 128–9.

97. Pearson to St Laurent, 'The United Kingdom and the Suez Intervention', 18 December 1956, MG26-L, Vol. 219, LAC.

98. Quoted in Reid, *Hungary and Suez*, p. 135.

99. 3 November 1956, quoted in 'Anglo-French Military Intervention in Egypt: An Assessment of its Purposes and Results', Department of External Affairs, Wellington, 10 June 1957, ABHS/950 W4627 Box 4974 217/1/12 part 3, Archives New Zealand, Wellington.

100. Prominent British satirist John Wells quoted in Humphrey Carpenter, *That Was Satire That Was* (London: Victor Gollancz, 2001), p. 32.

101. See Hennessy, *Having It So Good*, pp. 457–9. For an alternative view, see G. C. Peden who goes so far as to suggest that Suez was no more than 'an eddy in the fast-flowing stream of history', and that very few policy reversals can be traced directly to Suez. G. C. Peden, 'Suez and Britain's Decline as a World Power', *The Historical Journal*, 55:4 (December 2012), pp. 1073–96, 1074, 1095. See also M. E. Yapp, 'Suez Was Not the Turning Point', *Times Literary Supplement*, 16 July 1999.

102. Negrine, 'The Press and the Suez Crisis'.

103. Tom Maschler (ed.), *Declaration* (London: MacGibbon & Kee, 1957).

104. Benn diary, 23 June 1958, quoted in Nicholas Owen, 'Four Straws in the Wind: Metropolitan Anti-Imperialism, January-February 1960', in L. J. Butler and Sarah Stockwell (eds.), *The Wind of Change: Harold Macmillan and British Decolonization* (Basingtoke: Palgrave, 2013), pp. 123–4.

105. Jordanna Bailkin, *The Afterlife of Empire* (Berkeley: University of California Press, 2021), p. 55. Bailkin compares VSO with the American Peace Corps, noting how it was formed out of 'a very different impulse: one that was shaped by the loss of global supremacy rather than its acquisition', p. 58.

106. Jean P. Smith, 'Persistence and Privilege: Mass Migration from Britain to the Commonwealth, 1945–2000', in Christian Damm Pedersen and Stuart Ward (eds.), *The Break-Up of Greater Britain* (Manchester: Manchester University Press, 2021).

107. See Lycett, *Ian Fleming*, pp. 302–7, 274–5. Noël Coward recorded his 'core of sadness about England' in his diary in the aftermath of Suez, see Graham Payn and Sheridan Morley (eds.), *The Noel Coward Diaries* (London: Weidenfeld and Nicolson, 1982), p. 342.

108. In the otherwise exhaustive historical literature on Suez, Eden's Jamaican jaunt receives conspicuously short shrift, serving as little more than a dramatic exit for a defeated premier. But see, for example, Simon Winder's take on the near-perfect 'cross-over' between the political world and the world of 'mad fantasy' in *The Man Who Saved Britain*, pp. 136–7.

109. Onslow, '"Battlelines for Suez"', p. 10. To complicate the picture, Ann Fleming's passionate affair with Labour leader Hugh Gaitskell also began around this time. See Brian Brivati, *Hugh Gaitskell* (London: Methuen, 2006).

110. See the *Daily Mail's* 'Eden's Other Island' series, 22, 23, 24 and 26 November 1956.

111. Matthew Parker, *Goldeneye: Where Bond Was Born* (London: Hutchinson, 2014), p. 123.

112. *Evening Standard*, 'The Return of Sir Anthony', 14 December 1956. This piece was particularly wounding, having been penned by Randolph Churchill, the former prime minister's son and Clarissa Eden's cousin.

113. Evelyn Shuckburgh, *Descent to Suez* (London: Weidenfeld and Nicolson, 1986). Butler also noted wryly that 'it did sound the most extraordinarily remote suggestion in the middle of such unprecedented troubles'. Butler, *Art of the Possible*, p. 194.

114. Quoted in Kevin Jeffreys, *Retreat from the New Jerusalem: British Politics, 1951–64* (London: St Martin's Press, 1997), p. 56.

115. Thomas, *Suez Affair*, p. 161.

116. David Marquand, *Britain since 1918: The Strange Career of British Democracy* (London: Phoenix, 2009), p. 166.

117. Darwin, *Empire Project*, pp. 606, 610.

118. Quoted in Philip Murphy, 'Britain as a Global Power in the Twentieth Century', in Andrew Thompson (ed.), *Britain's Experience of Empire in the Twentieth Century* (Oxford: Oxford University Press, 2012), p. 64.

119. The phrase is from the penultimate verse of Kipling's 1892 ballad 'Mandalay' ('Ship me somewheres east of Suez / where the best is like the worst / Where there aren't no Ten Commandments / an' a man can raise a thirst'). Although used in the title of the 1922 Somerset Maugham play referred to earlier on p. 301, and despite some scattered references to 'East of Suez' in interwar political discourse, the phrase did not become commonplace until after the Suez crisis of 1956 and more particularly during the Wilson years.

120. Darwin, *Empire Project*, p. 642.

121. David M. McCourt, 'What was Britain's "East of Suez Role"? Reassessing the Withdrawal, 1964–68', *Diplomacy and Statecraft*, 20:3 (2009), pp. 453–72, 460.

122. Quoted in Edward Hampshire, *From East of Suez to the Eastern Atlantic: British Naval Policy 1964–70* (London: Routledge, 2016), p. 126.

123. Philip Murphy notes how the persistent urge of the British defence establishment to 'punch above its weight' in the world 'is rarely matched by a cogent explanation of why such a global reach is necessary or even desirable' – and

must therefore count as 'a psychological legacy of empire'. See Murphy, 'Britain as a Global Power', p. 33.

124. 'Homage to a Government', *High Windows* (London: Faber & Faber, 1974).
125. John Osborne, *West of Suez* (London: Faber, 1971), p. 84. See also pp. 11, 58–60. The reference to a 'clutch of whites' is taken from J. W. Lambert's review in the *Sunday Times*, 22 August 1971. Osborne is quoted in John Heilpern, 'A Sense of Failure', *The Guardian*, 29 April 2006.

11 BACKING LITTLE BRITAIN: DISTEMPERS

1. *Daily Telegraph*, 30 December 1967. This was in the days before New Year's Day was gazetted as an annual bank holiday.
2. Amalgamated Engineering Union's Portsmouth District official, reported in the *Daily Telegraph*, 4 January 1968.
3. *Daily Mail*, 1 January 1968.
4. *Daily Mirror*, 3 January 1968.
5. 'Your Memo Dated 27 December 1967', signed by Valerie White, Joan Southwell, Carol Ann Fry, Christine French and Brenda Mumford, 28 December 1967, EW4/103, The National Archives, Kew (hereafter NA).
6. 'General Progress Report – December 1967', Memorandum by F. W. Price, Sales Director, Colt Heating and Ventilation Ltd, 27 December 1967, EW4/103, NA. See also *Daily Telegraph*, 30 December 1967.
7. 'Your Memo Dated 27 December 1967', EW4/103, NA.
8. *Daily Telegraph*, 3 January 1968.
9. *Daily Mail*, 6 January 1968.
10. *Surrey Comet*, undated press clipping in EW4/103, NA.
11. The Rev. David Platt of St Katherines, quoted in the *Daily Telegraph*, 8 January 1968.
12. *Daily Mail*, 3 January 1968; *New Statesman*, 'From Surbiton to Whitehall', 12 January 1968.
13. See, generally, T276/88, NA. The 'reminder' was from Veronica Ware to Chancellor Roy Jenkins, 14 February 1968.
14. *Daily Mail*, 5 January 1968.
15. Bernard Levin, *The Pendulum Years: Britain and the Sixties* (London: Jonathan Cape, 1970), p. 427.
16. Dated 8 January, quoted in the *Sunday Times*, 3 March 1968.
17. Toynbee, Letter to *The Times*, 'Backing Britain', 10 February 1968.
18. No major study of the episode has ever been undertaken, and it normally appears (if at all) parenthetically in general histories of post-war Britain as a fleeting fad. See, for example, Dominic Sandbrook, *White Heat: A History of Britain in the Swinging Sixties* (London: Abacus, 2006), pp. 608–11.
19. *Australian Women's Weekly*, 31 January 1968; *Daily Mail*, 1 January 1968.

20. 'General Progress Report – December 1967', EW4/103, NW.
21. *Australian Women's Weekly*, 31 January 1968.
22. Sandbrook, *White Heat*, p. 608.
23. *Manchester Guardian*, Anthony Hartley, 'An Impression of Holland: Freed from Colonial Cares', 1 November 1958.
24. Anthony Hartley, *A State of England* (London: Hutchinson, 1963), p. 15.
25. Hartley, *A State of England*, pp. 20, 74, 77.
26. Hansard (Lords), 25 January 1961, Vol. 227, c. 1245.
27. Hansard (Lords), 25 January 1961, Vol. 227, c. 1245.
28. Michael Shanks, *The Stagnant Society: A Warning* (Harmondsworth: Penguin, 1961); Paul Einzig, *Decline and Fall? Britain's Crisis in the Sixties* (London: Macmillan, 1969).
29. Arthur Koestler (ed.), *Suicide of a Nation?* (London: Hutchinson, 1963) which doubled as the summer 1963 edition of *Encounter*, 21:1 (July 1963). The 'What's Wrong with Britain' series included volumes devoted to 'What's Wrong' with the Unions, the Church, British Industry, Parliament and Hospitals.
30. Quoted in Matthew Grant, 'Historians, the Penguin Specials and the "State-of-the-Nation" Literature, 1958–64', *Contemporary British History*, 17:3 (2003), pp. 29–54, 31.
31. Christopher Booker, *The Neophiliacs: The Revolution in English Life in the Fifties and Sixties* (London: Pimlico, 1969), p. 153. Crosland's original essay appeared as 'Radical Reform and the Left', *Encounter*, October 1960.
32. C. P. Snow, *The Two Cultures and the Scientific Revolution* (Cambridge: Cambridge University Press, 1959); see Guy Ortolano, *The Two Cultures Controversy: Science, Literature and Cultural Politics in Postwar Britain* (Cambridge: Cambridge University Press, 2009).
33. There is some dispute as to whether the term should be attributed to historian A. J. P. Taylor's, 'Review of M. L. Pearle's *William Cobbett*', *The New Statesman*, 29 August 1953, or whether it was the journalist Henry Fairlie who first gave it prominence in 'Political Commentary', *Spectator*, 23 September 1955, p. 380.
34. Dilwyn Porter, quoted in Grant, 'Historians, ... and the "State-of-the-Nation"', p. 43.
35. David Edgerton's work has been pioneering among the 'post-declinist' histories of the period, see particularly, *Warfare State: Britain, 1920–70* (Cambridge: Cambridge University Press, 2006); *Science, Technology and British Industrial 'Decline', 1870–1970* (Cambridge: Cambridge University Press, 1996). He delivers a pungent critique of the flawed logic of declinism in ch. 15 of *The Rise and Fall of the British Nation: A Twentieth Century History* (London: Allen Lane, 2018). See also Jim Tomlinson, *The Politics of Decline: Understanding Post-War Britain* (Harlow: Longman, 2001). Kevin Jeffreys also underlines the paradox that the issue of decline emerged at a time when Britain achieved levels of prosperity that would outstrip both the preceding and the subsequent decades, see *Retreat from New Jerusalem: British Politics, 1951–64* (London: Palgrave, 1997),

p. 110. A similar point is made by Ortolano, who adds that the 1950s was the first decade of the century 'to have ended in better economic shape than it had begun'. *Two Cultures*, p. 164.

36. P. J. Cain and A. G. Hopkins, *British Imperialism: Crisis and Deconstruction* (London: Longman, 1993), p. 289.

37. Shanks, *Stagnant Society*, p. 232. Similarly, Arthur Koestler ventured that 'there seems to be general agreement that we are faced with a "functional" rather than a "structural" disorder. Structural diseases have objective, material causes, functional diseases have subjective, psychological causes'. Koestler, 'Lion and the Ostrich', Introduction to *Suicide of a Nation?*, p. 12.

38. Ortolano, *Two Cultures*, p. 163, See also pp. 170, 258.

39. Hugh Thomas (ed.), *The Establishment: A Symposium* (London: Anthony Blond, 1959), p. 15.

40. Koestler, *Suicide of a Nation?*, pp. 13, 230. See chapters by Muggeridge (p. 36), Seton-Watson (pp. 137, 146), Mander (p. 160), Rees (p. 50), Shanks (p. 54), Connolly (pp. 187–8) and Cunliffe (p. 200).

41. Anthony Sampson, *Anatomy of Britain* (London: Hodder & Stoughton, 1962), p. 620.

42. Quoted in Sampson, *Anatomy of Britain*, p. 91. Macleod was quoting Thomas Dibdin's patriotic song from the time of the Napoleonic wars ('Oh what a snug little island / a right little, tight little island'). In subsequent popular renditions, 'right' was altered to 'bright'.

43. Levin, *Pendulum Years*, pp. 242–4. Christopher Booker was similarly dismissive in *The Neophiliacs*, pp. 158–9, 230.

44. Shanks, *Stagnant Society*, p. 232.

45. Hartley, *State of England*, p. 71.

46. Hartley, *State of England*, p. 76.

47. Henry Fairlie, 'On the Comforts of Anger', in Koestler (ed.), *Suicide of a Nation?*, p. 19.

48. Arthur Seldon (ed.), *Rebirth of a Nation: A Symposium of Essays by Eighteen Writers* (London: Pan, 1964).

49. *The Economist*, 'Britain 1963: Neurosis or New Look?', 14 September 1963.

50. Brian Stonier (Penguin Australia) to Horne, 30 August 1963. Donald Horne Papers, Mitchell Library Sydney, MSS 3525 (hereafter DHP), MLK 02135, L-18, 1963–64.

51. Max Harris to Horne, 29 January 1963. MLK 02135, L-18, 1963–64, DHP.

52. Donald Horne, *Into the Open: Memoirs, 1955–99* (Sydney: Harper Collins, 2000), p. 127.

53. Donald Horne, *God is an Englishman* (Ringwood: Penguin, 1969), p. 88.

54. Horne, *Into the Open*, p. 127.

55. Donald Horne, *The Lucky Country: Australia in the Sixties* (Ringwood: Penguin, 1964), p. 101.

56. Horne, *The Lucky Country*, pp. 24, 111.

57. Quoted in Carl Reinecke, 'The Vanishing Point: The Story of the Publication of *The Lucky Country*', *Meanjin* (Winter 2016); Brigid Magner, 'Case Study: Anglo-Australian Relations and the Book Trade', in Craig Munro and Robyn Sheahan-Bright (eds.), *Paper Empires: A History of the Book in Australia, 1946–2005* (St Lucia: University of Queensland Press, 2006), p. 8.

58. Reinecke notes that between 1961 and 1965, the total value of the domestic publishing industry in Australia doubled. Reinecke, 'The Vanishing Point'.

59. See James Curran and Stuart Ward, *The Unknown Nation: Australia after Empire* (Melbourne: Melbourne University Press, 2010).

60. Brian Stonier (Penguin Australia) to Horne, 30 August 1963, MLK 02135, L-18, 1963–64, DHP.

61. Carl Reinecke offers the most detailed account of the genesis of the book, exploring the tension between the fundamentally collaborative nature of the book's origins and Horne's individual claim to authorship. According to Reinecke, Horne's version of events tends to place the author 'centre stage, dissecting his country, while his fellow citizens lazed about the beach' – an interpretation that is vigorously disputed by Horne's son Nick in a robust rejoinder. See Reinecke, 'Vanishing Point'; Nick Horne, 'Donald Horne and the Story of the Publication of *The Lucky Country*', *Meanjin* (14 August 2017).

62. Horne, *Into the Open*, p. 57.

63. *The Spectator*, 'Australia Obsolescent', 28 December 1962.

64. Frank Bongiorno discovered Horne's first *Spectator* piece among Tony Crosland's papers, suggesting a mutual admiration and indeed influence. See Frank Bongiorno, 'The New Progressivism: Anthony Crosland and the Coming of the Australian Sixties', in Shirleene Robinson and Julie Ustinoff (eds.), *The 1960s in Australia: People, Power and Politics* (Newcastle upon Tyne: Cambridge Scholars Publishing, 2012), pp. 181, 187.

65. Dutton to Horne, 25 March 1963, MLK 02135, L-18, 1963–64, DHP. The title also appears on the original typescript in Horne's papers, and it was only at the eleventh hour that it was altered to *The Lucky Country* after a futile ransacking of the medical lexicon for a serviceable synonym for 'anatomy'. Stonier (Penguin Australia) to Horne, 14 December 1963, MLK 02135, L-18, 1963–64, DHP.

66. Dutton, 'British Subject', *Nation*, 6 April 1963, p. 15.

67. Dutton to Horne, 17 April 1964, MLK 02135, L-18, 1963–64, DHP.

68. Horne, *Lucky Country*, p. 183. Here, Horne was quoting a recent item in the autumn 1964 edition of *Dissent* by political scientist Hugo Wolfsohn. My emphasis.

69. Quoted in James Curran, *Curtin's Empire* (Melbourne: Cambridge University Press, 2011), p. 122.

70. See Mads Clausen, 'Donald Horne Finds Asia', in Agnieszka Sobocinska and David Walker (eds.), *Australia's Asia: From Yellow Peril to Asian Century* (Perth: UWA Publishing, 2012). David Walker, *Stranded Nation: White Australia in an Asian Region* (Perth: University of Western Australia Press, 2019).

71. Horne, *Lucky Country*, p. 84.

72. Horne, *Lucky Country*, p. 88.

73. Horne, *Lucky Country*, pp. 83, 89, 90–1.

74. Horne, *Lucky Country*, p. 89; Geoffrey Dutton, 'British Subject', *Nation*, 6 April 1963, p. 15. See also Geoffrey Dutton (ed.), *Australia and the Monarchy: A Symposium* (Melbourne: Sun Books, 1966).

75. Dutton, 'British Subject', p. 16. Dutton was remarkably frank about the early difficulties in establishing the Australian branch of Penguin, with senior UK executives behaving 'as if Australia were still coloured pink, as on those maps which used to hang on the wall when I was at school, where the British Empire seemed to rule half the world'. Geoffrey Dutton, *A Rare Bird: Penguin Books in Australia, 1946–96* (Ringwood: Penguin, 1996), pp. 36, 41.

76. Horne had in any case already begun to develop some of his major themes as early as 1958 – well before the 'What's Wrong with Britain' fad had taken hold. Under his stewardship in the late 1950s, *The Observer* ran any number of pieces that pre-empted Horne's later themes, such as 'Has Australia Got a Chance?', 'How Equal Are Australians?', 'What Happened to Education?' and 'Living with Asia'. See Horne, *Into the Open*, pp. 17–35.

77. W. B. Sutch, *Colony or Nation? Economic Crises in New Zealand from the 1860s to the 1960s* (Sydney: Sydney University Press, 1966), p. 182.

78. Sutch, *Colony or Nation?*, p. 178.

79. Sutch, *Colony or Nation?*, p. 183.

80. Sutch, *Colony or Nation?*, p. 182.

81. See, generally, José Igartua, *The Other Quiet Revolution: National Identities in English Canada, 1945–71* (Vancouver: UBC Press, 2006). See also Chapters 4 and 10.

82. Michael D. Behiels, *Prelude to Quebec's Quiet Revolution: Liberalism Versus Neo-Nationalism, 1945–1960* (Kingston, Ont.: McGill-Queen's University Press, 1985).

83. *Globe and Mail*, 'Now We Are 94', 1 July 1961.

84. Quoted in Igartua, *Other Quiet Revolution*, p. 165.

85. Quoted in Igartua, *Other Quiet Revolution*, p. 166.

86. Arthur R. M. Lower, *Canadians in the Making: A Social History of Canada* (Toronto: Longmans Green and Co., 1958), pp. 135, xxi.

87. Frank Underhill, *In Search of Canadian Liberalism* (Toronto: Macmillan, 1960), p. 268, 257, 75, 99.

88. Horne, January 1968 quoted in Curran and Ward, *Unknown Nation*, p. 19.

89. *Calgary Herald*, 2 March 1961, 'Oh Canada' by Mathew Seddon.

90. *Calgary Herald* quoted in Igartua, *Other Quiet Revolution*, p. 170.

91. George Grant, *Lament for a Nation: The Defeat of Canadian Nationalism* (Ottawa: Carleton University Press, 1991, 1st ed. 1965), pp. 3–4. It was presumably passages such as this that Underhill had in mind when he dismissed parts of Grant's thesis as

'emotional drivel'. See Kenneth C. Dewar, *Frank Underhill and the Politics of Ideas* (Montreal and Kingston: McGill-Queen's University Press, 2015), p. 169.

92. Grant, *Lament for a Nation*, preface to 1970 edition, p. xi. My italics.

93. Grant, *Lament for a Nation*, pp. 32–3, 34.

94. Robert Wright persuasively argues that it was the provocation of Newman's writing that, above all, spurred George Grant to mount his defence of the old spiritual order, see Robert Wright, 'From Liberalism to Nationalism: *Peter C. Newman's* Discovery of Canada', in Magda Fahrni and Robert Rutherdale (eds.), *Creating Postwar Canada: Community, Diversity and Dissent, 1945–75* (Vancouver: UBC Press, 2008), p. 119.

95. Peter C. Newman, *The Distemper of Our Times: Canadian Politics in Transition, 1963–68* (Toronto/Montreal: McClelland and Stuart, 1968), p. 255.

96. Quoted in Wright, 'Liberalism to Nationalism', p. 130.

97. Newman, *Distemper of our Times*, pp. xi–xiii.

98. Even if Newman had been inclined to consult Gramsci, the relevant passage of his *Prison Notebooks* was not translated into English until the 1970s. See Quintin Hoare and Geoffrey Nowell-Smith (eds.), *Selections from the Prison Notebooks of Antonio Gramsci* (London: Lawrence and Wishart, 1971), p. 276.

99. Horne, *God is an Englishman*, pp. 7–8.

100. Horne, *God is an Englishman*, p. 13. Horne later described the book in terms of a journey back to 'what used to be my obsession with England ... imagining it as a best seller in Australia, in Britain, even in the United States'. He confessed to vaguely attempting 'a kind of *Lucky Country* treatment' of Britain, or 'not exactly a *Lucky Country* treatment but, well what?', equipping himself for the task with 'several armfuls of every known "state of Britain" book'. Horne, *Into the Open*, pp. 136–7.

101. Horne, *God is an Englishman*, ch. 7.

102. Horne, *God is an Englishman*, p. 146.

103. A 2017 celebration of Horne's work edited by his son contains a rich array of extracts and essays spanning his long career, while barely mentioning the 1969 monograph. Nick Horne (ed.), *Donald Horne: Selected Essays* (Melbourne: La Trobe University Press, 2017).

104. Horne, *God is an Englishman*, p. 15.

105. Horne, *God is an Englishman*, pp. 8, 28.

106. *Daily Telegraph*, 2 January 1968.

107. Amalgamated Engineering Union's Portsmouth District Secretary Rory McCarthy, reported in the *Daily Mirror*, 4 January 1968; *Daily Telegraph*, 5 January 1968; 6 January 1968.

108. Leslie Cannon, 'The Five Girls of Surbiton Are Wrong, but They Have Acted as a Catalyst for the Nation', *Sunday Times*, 7 January 1968.

109. *Daily Telegraph*, 2 January 1968.

110. Hansard (Commons), 12 March 1968, Vol. 760, c. 280.

111. 'Car Stickers Now Proclaim "Backing Wales"', *The Guardian*, 22 January 1968.

112. Adam Fergusson, 'Cuts Could Frustrate Back Britain Mood', *The Times*, 12 January 1968.

113. Hansard (Lords) 24 January 1968, Vol. 288, cc. 391–2.

114. Hansard (Lords) 23 January 1968, Vol. 288, cc. 154–61. Jebb's reference to 'back in our own island' is quoted in *The Times*, 12 January 1967. The phrase appears in his January 1968 Lords speech as 'we are indeed back in an island'.

115. Alan O' Hea (Colts) to J. W. Hoaen (DEA), 5 January 1968, EW 4/103, NA.

116. Quoted in the *Sunday Times*, 3 March 1968.

117. One of which was disastrously managed by the maverick publishing magnate Robert Maxwell, who took out a series of full-page advertisements on 7 February exhorting readers to select 'six practical things to help Britain get out of the red' – which was met with widespread ridicule. See, for example, *The Times*, 7 February 1968.

118. *The Times*, 'How to Back Britain', 12 February 1968.

119. Hansard (Lords) 21 February 1968, Vol. 289, cc. 455–6.

120. David Thackeray, *Forging a British World of Trade: Culture, Ethnicity and Market in the Empire-Commonwealth, 1880–1975* (Oxford: Oxford University Press, 2019), p. 142.

121. *Daily Mail*, 1 January 1968; 2 January 1968.

122. *Daily Mirror*, 3 January 1968.

123. Einzig, *Decline and Fall?*, p. ix.

124. Einzig, *Decline and Fall?*, pp. 12–13.

125. Einzig, *Decline and Fall?*, pp. 16, 28–9.

126. Einzig, *Decline and Fall?*, p. 8.

127. Einzig, *Decline and Fall?*, pp. 138–40, 224–7.

128. Einzig, *Decline and Fall?*, p. 1.

129. 'Think British/I'm Backing Britain', memorandum by P. Cowling, 23 January 1968; John Groves (Chief Information Officer, DEA) to Derk, 'The Maxwell Campaign and I'm Backing Britain', 9 February 1968; Currall to Cowling, 'I'm Backing Britain and Mr Robert Maxwell's Campaign', 7 February 1968, EW 4/103, NA.

130. Philip French described this as 'one of the more painful aspects' of the campaign which brought back memories of 'the Tory political meetings of my youth and the odious *Land of Hope and Glory*'. *New Statesman*, 'Put Out Less Flags', 19 January 1968.

131. *The Economist*, 'Who's Really Backing Britain?', 13 January 1968.

132. Simon Heffer, *Like the Roman: The Life of Enoch Powell* (London: Phoenix, 1999), p. 462.

133. Heffer, *Like the Roman*, pp. 555, 442; *The Times*, 11 January 1968.

12 THE LAST REFUGE: COMING HOME TO ENGLAND

1. *East African Standard*, 10 February 1970.
2. *Daily Nation*, 10 February 1970.
3. As depicted in *Daily Nation*, 10 February 1970.
4. *East African Standard*, 10 February 1970.
5. *Daily Nation*, 10 February 1970.
6. *East African Standard*, 10 February 1970.
7. *Chicago Tribune*, 9 February 1970.
8. *Time*, 'The Girl without a Country', 23 February 1970.
9. Hansard (Commons), 10 February 1970, Vol. 795, cc. 1076–80.
10. Quoted in 'The Girl without a Country'.
11. Hansard (Lords), 10 February 1970, Vol. 307, cc. 830–4.
12. *East African Standard*, 17 February 1970.
13. Ann Dummet and Andrew Nicol, *Subjects, Citizens, Aliens and Others: Nationality and Immigration Law* (London: Weidenfeld and Nicolson, 1990), p. 200.
14. Malcolm MacDonald telegram, 19 February 1968, cited in Randall Hansen, *Citizenship and Immigration in Postwar Britain* (Oxford: Oxford University Press, 2000), p. 162.
15. See Chapter 2.
16. 27 February 1968, quoted in Nicole Longpré, '"An Issue That Could Tear Us Apart": Race, Empire and Economy in the British (Welfare) State, 1968', *Canadian Journal of History*, XLVI (2011), pp. 63–95, 92.
17. On the 1962 Act, see Chapter 6, pp. 188–90.
18. Randall Hansen, *Citizenship and Immigration in Postwar Britain* (Oxford: Oxford University Press, 2000), p. 158.
19. Quoted in Hansen, *Citizenship and Immigration*, p. 166.
20. Callaghan reiterated the 'loophole' argument in his memoir *Time and Chance* (London: Collins, 1987), p. 264.
21. Randall Hansen, 'The Kenyan Asians, British Politics, and the Commonwealth Immigrants Act, 1968', *The Historical Journal*, 42:3 (1999), pp. 809–34.
22. Hansen, 'Kenyan Asians', pp. 827–8.
23. See Hansen, *Citizenship and Immigration*, p. 170.
24. Hansen, 'Kenyan Asians', p. 830.
25. See, respectively, the following documents in The National Archives, Kew (hereafter NA): 'Asians in Kenya', Brief no 32, 58/1251, undated but seemingly from autumn 1963, DO175/92; W. N. Hyde (HO) to W. F. G. Le Bailly (CRO) 31 October 1962, HO344/49; K. B. Paice (HO) to G. W. St J. Chadwick (CRO) 5 December 1961, HO344/49; Memorandum by W. N. Hyde, 9 October 1962, HO344/49.
26. HO344/49, Home Office Minute, 21 May 1962, NA; K. B. Paice (HO) to G. W. St J. Chadwick (CRO) 5 December 1961, HO344/49, NA.
27. 'Asians in Kenya', Brief no. 32, 58/1251, DO175/92, NA.

28. Peck (UK High Commissioner, Nairobi) to Commonwealth Office, 10 October 1967, FCO31/250, NA.
29. Assessment by Bennett, 'Commonwealth Immigrants Act: Persons of Asian Origin in Kenya', 16 October 1963, HO344/49, NA.
30. 'Asians in Kenya', Brief no. 32, 58/1251, DO175/92, NA.
31. Memorandum by Younger (Home Office), 12 January 1965, HO344/49, NA.
32. Cabinet Submission by the Secretary of State for Commonwealth Affairs, 'Immigration Legislation', C(68)35, 12 February 1968, CAB129/35, NA; Peck to Commonwealth Office, 10 October 1967, FCO31/250, NA.
33. Memorandum by Home Secretary, 'Asian Immigration from East Africa', C(68) 39, 21 February 1968, CAB129/136, NA.
34. David Steel recounts the sudden departures of those who had merely intended to farewell loved-ones, including one Asian magistrate who left in the middle of hearing a case. See David Steel, *No Entry: The Background and Implications of the Commonwealth Immigrants Act 1968* (London: C. Hurst, 1969), p. 144.
35. Arthur (Nairobi) to Reid (Commonwealth Office) 6 November 1967, FCO31/250, NA; Arthur to Reid, 27 October 1967, FCO31/250, NA; Edward Peck to Commonwealth Office, 9 January 1968, FCO31/251, NA.
36. For an example of this, see Hansen, 'Kenyan Asians', pp. 809–10.
37. 'Statement by the Ministry of Commerce and Industry', 12 February 1968, FCO31/251, NA.
38. See report in the *Daily Nation*, 'The Exodus', 10 February 1968. Some respondents did complain, however, about rumours circulating that work permits were being issued for only limited time periods of three to six months.
39. 'A Report of a Visit to the Coast Province by the Investigating Team, July 1969', 7 August 1969, SF/ADM/12, CA/27/3, Kenyan National Archives, Nairobi.
40. Judith Brown, *Global South Asians: Introducing the Modern Diaspora* (Cambridge: Cambridge University Press, 2006), p. 47. Sana Aiyar refers to a 'full-blown exodus' in *Indians in Kenya: The Politics of Diaspora* (Cambridge: Cambridge University Press, 2015), p. 277.
41. Cabinet memorandum by the Home Secretary, 'Immigration Legislation', C(68)34, 12 February 1968, CAB129/35, NA. The UK emigration figures are sourced from the Office of National Statistics, which records a net outflow for 1967 of 155,000. See https://visual.ons.gov.uk/explore-50-years-of-international-migration/.
42. See figures in A. James Hammerton and Alistair Thompson, *Ten Pound Poms: Australia's Invisible Migrants* (Manchester: Manchester University Press, 2005).
43. Hansard, 15 November 1967, Vol. 754, c. 507.
44. See Elizabeth Buettner, '"This Is Staffordshire Not Alabama": Racial Geographies of Commonwealth Immigration in Early 1960s Britain', *Journal of Imperial and Commonwealth History*, 42:2 (2014), pp. 710–40.
45. Sandys was an ex-frontbencher on account of his sacking from the shadow cabinet the previous year by Edward Heath.

46. See, for example, Malcolm McLaughlin, *The Long, Hot Summer of 1967: Urban Rebellion in America* (New York: Palgrave, 2014).

47. Sandys's US press cuttings are revealingly stored in a file marked 'Immigration 1967' (Sandys Papers, Churchill College Cambridge, DSND 13/20) while Camilla Schofield remarks upon Powell's collection of news clippings about Detroit and Black Power in *Enoch Powell and the Making of Post-Colonial Britain* (Cambridge: Cambridge University Press, 2013), p. 199.

48. *Sunday Times*, 9 July 1967. Although this was pre-Detroit, Powell nevertheless structured his entire argument around a comparison with the racial demographics of the United States, claiming that Britain had inflicted upon itself 'a race problem of near-American dimensions'.

49. *News of the World*, 30 July 1967. Sandys's logic, structure, conclusion and even the demographic statistics he draws upon are so similar to Powell's *Sunday Times* piece (which is included among the press clippings in the Sandys archive) that he seems surely to have drawn directly on it for inspiration.

50. See Sandys's exchange of letters with Mboya (whom he first approached at a September wedding party) in the Sandys Papers DSND14/14; Mboya to Sandys, 8 September 1967; Sandys to Mboya, 26 September 1967. See also Peter Brooke, *Duncan Sandys and the Informal Politics of Britain's Late Decolonisation* (London: Palgrave, 2018).

51. Quoted in Paul Foot, *The Rise of Enoch Powell* (Harmondsworth: Penguin, 1969), p. 106.

52. Simon Heffer, *Like the Roman: The Life of Enoch Powell* (London: Phoenix, 1998), p. 437.

53. Hansard (Commons), 15 November 1967, Vol. 754, c. 507.

54. See Cabinet Submission by the Home Secretary, 'Immigration Legislation', C (68)34, 12 February 1968, CAB 129/135, NA.

55. Arthur to Reid, 27 October 1967, FCO31/250, NA.

56. Peck to Commonwealth Office, 25 October 1967, FCO31/250, NA.

57. Peck to Commonwealth Office, 30 October 1967, FCO31/250, NA.

58. A point also noted at the time by David Steel in *No Entry*, p. 132.

59. Quoted in Hansen, *Citizenship and Immigration*, p. 161.

60. Barbara Castle, *The Castle Diaries: 1964–70* (London: Weidenfeld and Nicolson, 1984), pp. 377–8. Castle failed to account for how she remained equally slumbrous throughout the Bill's passage through parliament the following week.

61. Randall Hansen mentions the sterling crisis in passing on p. 160 of *Citizenship and Immigration*, but it is otherwise left out of accounts of immigration reform. The converse is equally true of leading accounts of the sterling crisis such as Alec Cairncross and Barry Eichengreen, *Sterling in Decline: The Devaluations of 1931, 1949 and 1967* (Oxford: Basil Blackwell, 1983) and Catherine R. Schenk, *The Decline of Sterling* (Cambridge: Cambridge University Press, 2010).

62. Kenneth O. Morgan, *Callaghan: A Life* (Oxford: Oxford University Press, 1999), p. 292. Callaghan described the day of decision to the Cabinet as the

'unhappiest day of my life' and the decision itself as 'the most agonizing reappraisal I have ever had to do'. Quoted in Ben Pimlott, *Harold Wilson* (London: Harper Collins, 1992), p. 482. He reiterated the 'welter of emotions' he felt in his memoirs, recalling how he 'was not at all surprised that it took some time for the emotional effects to wear off in the press and elsewhere'. *Time and Chance*, pp. 219–23.

63. Anthony Howard (ed.), *The Crossman Diaries: A Selection from the Diaries of a Cabinet Minister, 1964–1970* (London: Mandarin, 1991), p. 400. Crossman added that 'he would do it come what may and anybody who opposed him was a sentimental jackass'.

64. David Blaazer, '"Devalued and Dejected Britons": The Pound in Public Discourse in the Mid 1960s', *History Workshop Journal*, 47 (Spring, 1999), pp. 121–40, 121.

65. Blaazer, 'Devalued and Dejected', p. 126.

66. Blaazer, 'Devalued and Dejected', p. 126. The item referred to earlier pressures on sterling the year before.

67. Blaazer, 'Devalued and Dejected', p. 131.

68. Lord Milverton in Hansard (Lords), 29 February 1968, Vol. 289, c. 1012. He also urged that it was not good to 'sit idly by while an indigestible number of people of alien birth descend upon' Britain.

69. Cabinet Submission by the Home Secretary, 'Immigration Legislation', C(68) 34, 12 February 1968, CAB129/135, NA.

70. Hansard, 27 February 1968, Vol. 759, c. 1247.

71. Blaazer, 'Devalued and Dejected', p. 131.

72. Even as he voted for the government's exclusion of the Kenyan Asians. Hansard, 27 February 1968, Vol. 759, c. 1260.

73. Blaazer, 'Devalued and Dejected', p. 137; David Steel, quoting from his own petition to the queen against the 1968 Commonwealth Immigrants Bill in *No Entry*, p. 169.

74. Quintin Hogg in Hansard, 27 February 1968, Vol. 759, c. 1260.

75. Quoted in Steel, *No Entry*. Steel was himself a prominent opponent of the Bill and frequently applied the 'devaluation' tag (along with the related term 'depreciation'), pp. 154, 221, 225. Other contemporaries such as Dilip Hiro reflected on how 'it became necessary even to devalue British passports'. Dilip Hiro, *Black British, White British* (London: Eyre and Spottiswoode, 1971), p. 228.

76. Lord Willis, Hansard, 29 February 1968, Vol. 289, cc. 999, 1002.

77. Hansard, 15 November 1967, Vol. 754, c. 507.

78. Cabinet Submission by the Home Secretary, 'Immigration Legislation', C(68) 34, 12 February 1968, CAB 129/135, NA. See also Appendix III: 'The Form of the Legislation' in the same file. The Attorney-General's Office was confident that any legal challenges could be met by 'the general argument that the persons to be dealt with, although technically our nationals, are not so closely

connected with this country that they can be said to "belong" to it'. Cabinet Submission by the Attorney General, 'Immigration Legislation', C(68)36, 14 February 1968, CAB129/413, NA.

79. Letter to *The Times* by a prominent group of professors, quoted in Steel, *No Entry*, p. 165.

80. Hansard, 27 February 1968, Vol. 759, c. 1251.

81. Steel, *No Entry*, p. 175.

82. 'most gratuitous' in James Hampshire, *Citizenship and Belonging: Immigration and the Politics of Demographic Governance in Postwar Britain* (Basingstoke: Palgrave, 2005), p. 75; 'inhibitions against' in Dummet and Nicol, *Subjects, Citizens*, p. 205; Elizabeth Buettner affirms that 'the right to British citizenship and identity became ever more closely aligned with whiteness' while Kathleen Paul emphasizes the way 'the communities were separated above all by skin colour'. Dilip Hiro's chapter on the episode was simply titled 'White Passports Only'. Hiro, *Black British, White British*, p. 145; Kathleen Paul, *Whitewashing Britain: Race and Citizenship in the Postwar Era* (Ithaca: Cornell University Press, 1997), p. 181; Elizabeth Buettner, *Europe after Empire: Decolonization, Society and Culture* (Cambridge: Cambridge University Press, 2016), p. 270.

83. See Callaghan's first reading speech in Hansard, 22 February 1968, Vol. 759, c. 663.

84. Quoted in Foot, *Rise of Enoch Powell*, p. 66. The reference to the 'undeniable truth' of the difference between immigrants and belongers was asserted a month earlier in Gloucester (p. 104).

85. Quoted in Schofield, *Enoch Powell*, p. 204.

86. Howard, *Crossman Diaries*, p. 508 (my emphasis).

87. *Leicester Mercury*, 12 February 1968. That this was a deliberate and consistent editorial line is affirmed in the newspaper's official history; Steve England, *Magnificent Mercury: The First 125 Years of the Leicester Mercury* (Leicester: Kairos Press, 1999), p. 79.

88. *Leicester Mercury*, 12 February 1968.

89. *Leicester Mercury*, 12 February 1968.

90. *Leicester Mercury*, 'Logical Outlook', 1 March 1968; 'Worried', 5 March 1968.

91. *Leicester Mercury*, 'White Johno', 18 November 1967.

92. *Leicester Mercury*, 'MBK', 19 February 1968; 'Frank Drinkwater', 18 November 1967; 'Had Enough', 28 February 1968; 'Soft-Headed', 15 February 1968; 'M.M.', 18 November 1967.

93. *Leicester Mercury*, 'Logical Outlook', 1 March 1968.

94. *Leicester Mercury*, 'Hecklers Hurl Abuse at Marching Indians', 4 March 1968.

95. *Leicester Mercury*, 'Threats Letter to Organiser of March', 1 March 1968.

96. *Leicester Mercury*, 'MM', 18 November 1968.

97. *Leicester Mercury*, 'Mrs J. Dutton', 15 February 1968.

98. *Leicester Mercury*, 'Fed Up Reader', 15 February 1968.

99. *Leicester Mercury*, 'Lonely Mother', 15 February 1968.

100. *Leicester Mercury*, 'Only Option', 15 February 1968.

101. *Leicester Mercury*, 'Worried', 5 March 1968.

102. *Leicester Mercury*, 'Logical Outlook', 1 March 1968.

103. Circulation figures cited in England, *Magnificent Mercury*, p. 78.

104. *Leicester Mercury*, 'Threats Letter to Organiser of March', 1 March 1968.

105. *Leicester Mercury*, 19 February 1968.

106. England, *Magnificent Mercury*, p. 79.

107. Quoted in Schofield, *Enoch Powell*, p. 246.

108. This argument was first advanced by Paul Foot in 1969, in which he documented Powell's surprising lack of interest in Commonwealth immigration until only months before the 'Rivers of Blood' speech. See Foot, *Rise of Enoch Powell*, p. 101.

109. Foot, *Rise of Enoch Powell*, p. 14.

110. Quotations sourced variously from several versions of the tale, including Foot, *Rise of Enoch Powell*, p. 19; Heffer, *Like the Roman*, p. 115 and Peter Hennessy, *Never Again: Britain, 1945–51* (London: Jonathan Cape, 1992), p. 235.

111. Foot, *Rise of Enoch Powell*, p. 19. For a more recent account of Powell's transformation, see ch. 3 of Schofield's *Enoch Powell*.

112. Quoted in David Cannadine, *Class in Britain* (London: Penguin, 2000), p. 159.

113. Jonathan Miller, 'Can English Satire Draw Blood?', *The Observer*, 1 October 1961. See Stuart Ward, '"No Nation Could Be Broker": The Satire Boom and the Demise of Britain's World Role', in Stuart Ward (ed.), *British Culture and the End of Empire* (Manchester: Manchester University Press, 2001).

114. A. P. Thornton, 'Decolonisation', *International Journal*, 19:1 (Winter, 1963/ 1964), pp. 7–29, 22.

115. Schofield, *Enoch Powell*, pp. 11–12.

116. Quoted in Heffer, *Like the Roman*, p. 335.

117. Quoted in Heffer, *Like the Roman*, pp. 335, 336, 338.

118. Quoted in Heffer, *Like the Roman*, p. 336.

119. Quoted in Heffer, *Like the Roman*, p. 337.

120. Quoted in Heffer, *Like the Roman*, p. 338.

121. Quoted in Schofield, *Enoch Powell*, pp. 148–9.

122. See, for example, Powell's essay in *The Times*, 'Patriotism Based on Reality not on Dreams', 2 April 1964. The article appeared anonymously, but Powell is now widely acknowledged as the author, see Schofield, *Enoch Powell*, pp. 171–2.

123. Bill Schwarz, *The White Man's World: Memories of Empire*, vol. 1 (Oxford: Oxford University Press, 2011), p. 6.

124. See also Wendy Webster, *Englishness and Empire 1939–65* (Oxford: Oxford University Press, 2005), pp. 178–81.

125. Raphael Samuel, *Island Stories: Unravelling Britain* (London: Verso, 1998), p. 83.

126. *Fowlers Dictionary of Modern English Usage* (2nd ed., Oxford: Oxford University Press, 1965), p. 157.

127. John Fowles, 'On Being English but Not British', *The Texas Quarterly*, 2:3 (Autumn, 1964), pp. 154–70, 154.

128. Fowles, 'On Being English', p. 154.

129. Fowles, 'On Being English', p. 156. Matthew Hurwitz argues that Fowles's emotional leanings 'toward a larger project of articulating a new Englishness in light of imperial decline' also found its way into his fiction. See 'Relocating Englishness: The 1960s Postimperial Turn and National Identity in John Fowles's *The Magnus*', *Modern Fiction Studies*, 61:3 (Fall 2015), pp. 446–68, 447.

130. Quoted in Dominic Sandbrook, *White Heat: A History of Britain in the Swinging Sixties* (London: Abacus, 2007), p. 431.

131. Verwoerd's precise words were 'we go now forward, alone. We are standing on our own feet', quoted in Jon Gemmell, *The Politics of South African Cricket* (London: Routledge, 2004), p. 141.

132. See, generally, Chapter 8. Surveying Britain's EEC aspirations in 1962, the *Australian Financial Review* looked 'inexorably to a time when Australia will be increasingly on her own ... We may have to stop thinking about Britain as "Home"'. 25 September 1962.

133. Harry Goulbourne, *Ethnicity and Nationalism in Post-War Britain* (Cambridge: Cambridge University Press, 1991), p. 1. My emphasis. Much of the early work carried out in the 1990s tended to stress the 'equation of whiteness and Britishness' that seemed to define the identity politics of an end-of-empire era 'when Britishness and whiteness became increasingly synonymous'. See Chris Waters, '"Dark Strangers" in Our Midst: Discourse of Race and Nation in Britain, 1947–63', *Journal of British Studies*, 36:2 (April 1997), pp. 207–38, 212, 237. Kathleen Paul's influential work also examined immigration in terms of the existence of 'hierarchies of Britishness' and 'competing communities of Britishness', with the United Kingdom serving as a relatively stable core. See *Whitewashing Britain*, p. xii.

134. Hansard, 29 February 1968, Vol. 289, cc. 955–6.

135. Bill Schwarz, '"The Only White Man in There": The Re-racialization of England, 1956–58', *Race and Class*, 38:1 (1996), pp. 65–78, 65. The argument was later developed and refined in *The White Man's World*.

136. Ibid., pp. 73–4.

13 'BRITISH WE ARE AND BRITISH WE STAY': TROUBLES

1. Brian Inglis, *West Briton* (London: Faber & Faber, 1962), p. 30.
2. Inglis, *West Briton*, p. 12.
3. Inglis, *West Briton*, p. 214.
4. Inglis, *West Briton*, p. 214.
5. J. G. Farrell, *Troubles* (London: Phoenix, 1993), p. 336.
6. Farrell, *Troubles*, p. 443.

7. Farrell, *Troubles*, p. 444.
8. Lavinia Greacen (ed.), *J.G. Farrell, in His Own Words: Selected Letters and Diaries* (Cork: Cork University Press, 2009), p. 217. In a letter dated early November 1968, Farrell indicated that he had begun canvassing the setting for the new novel, which he had originally conceived in early 1967. As the deteriorating Northern Ireland situation dominated headlines into 1969, the author 'superstitiously ... wondered if he had somehow evoked the current troubles'. Lavinia Greacen, *J. G. Farrell: The Making of a Writer* (London: Bloomsbury, 1999), p. 255. He submitted the final manuscript a month after British troops were deployed in Ulster in summer 1969.
9. Richard Bourke, 'Languages of Conflict and the Northern Ireland Troubles', *Journal of Modern History*, 83 (September 2011), pp. 544–78, 544.
10. Bourke traces these rhetorical tropes across a wide spectrum of Irish historiography, including such luminaries as Conor Cruise O'Brien ('atavistic national-religious forces'), J. J. Lee ('tribal religious war') and Roy Foster ('ancient antagonism'), Bourke, 'Languages of Conflict', pp. 559–60.
11. See Marc Mulholland, *Northern Ireland at the Crossroads: Ulster Unionism in the O'Neill Years* (London: Palgrave, 2000).
12. Bob Purdie cites several examples in his mandatory *Politics in the Streets: The Origins of the Civil Rights Movement in Northern Ireland* (Belfast: Blackstaff, 1990), pp. 15–17; Richard English also suggests that 'the striking thing about 1960s Northern Ireland is how much hope and optimism there actually was', in *Irish Freedom: The History of Nationalism in Ireland* (London: Macmillan, 2006), pp. 365–6.
13. Donal Lowry, 'Ulster Resistance and Loyalist Rebellion in the Empire', in Keith Jeffrey (ed.), *'An Irish Empire'? Aspects of Ireland and the British Empire* (Manchester: Manchester University Press, 1996), pp. 208–9.
14. John Biggs-Davidson, 'Torment and Troubles', *The Spectator*, 16 November 1985, p. 34.
15. 'Betrayal in Ulster: The Technique of Conservative Surrender', Ulster Vanguard booklet, 1972, P1244, Linen Hall Library, Belfast (hereafter LHL).
16. A view popularized by Conor Cruise O'Brien's 1972 dictum that 'ghosts were bound to walk, North and South' in the 'great commemoration year' of 1966, see *States of Ireland* (New York: Pantheon, 1972), p. 143. For a more cautious assessment, see Mary E. Daly and Margaret O'Callaghan (eds.), *1916 in 1966: Commemorating the Easter Rising* (Dublin: Royal Irish Academy, 2007).
17. Austin Currie, *All Hell Will Break Loose* (Dublin: O'Brien, 2004), pp. 97–106.
18. David McKittrick and David McVea, *Making Sense of the Troubles* (London: Penguin, 2001), p. 42.
19. Several specialized studies of the start of the Troubles have appeared over the years but see particularly Mulholland, *Northern Ireland at the Crossroads*; Peter Rose, *How the Troubles Came to Northern Ireland* (Basingstoke: Palgrave, 2000); Niall Ó Dochartaigh, *From Civil Rights to Armalites: Derry and the Birth of*

the Troubles (New York: Palgrave Macmillan, 2005); Christine Kinealy, *War and Peace: Ireland since the 1960s* (London: Reaktion Books, 2010); Simon Prince and Geoffrey Warner, *Belfast and Derry in Revolt: A New History of the Start of the Troubles* (Dublin: Irish Academic Press, 2012).

20. Chris Reynolds, *Sous les pavés ... The Troubles: Northern Ireland, France and the European Collective Memory of 1968* (Bern: Peter Lang, 2014), p. 185. Simon Prince concurs that 'Northern Ireland was not under quarantine while the revolutionary contagion raged throughout the West' in 'The Global Revolt of 1968 and Northern Ireland', *The Historical Journal*, 49:3 (September 2006), pp. 851–75, 867. See also Simon Prince, *Northern Ireland's 1968: Civil Rights, Global Revolt and the Origins of the Troubles* (Dublin: Irish Academic Press, 2007), p. 6. For a more cautious view of the 'uneasy and ideologically fractured alliance' with other radical movements, see Niall Ó Dochartaigh, 'Northern Ireland', in Martin Klimke and Joachim Scharloth (eds.), *1968 in Europe: A History of Protest and Activism, 1956–1977* (New York: Palgrave Macmillan, 2008), p. 141.

21. Quoted in Purdie, *Politics in the Streets*, pp. 92–3.

22. Cited in Prince, 'The Global Revolt', p. 861. The Belfast-Derry march of January 1969 is frequently said to have been modelled on King's Selma-Montgomery March four years earlier. See, generally, Brian Dooley, *Black and Green: The Fight for Civil Rights in Northern Ireland and Black America* (London: Pluto, 1998). At times the American parallel is overdrawn, overlooking the racial disparities. On the 'marked reluctance among Irish Americans' to make common cause with African Americans, see Ó Dochartaigh, *From Civil Rights to Armalites*, p. 51. See also Purdie, *Politics in the Streets*, p. 157.

23. Daniel Geary, 'From Belfast to Bob Jones: Ian Paisley, Protestant Fundamentalism, and the Transatlantic Right', in Daniel Geary, Camilla Schofield and Jennifer Sutton (eds.), *Global White Nationalism: From Apartheid to Trump* (Manchester: Manchester University Press, 2020), pp. 131–56.

24. For a sophisticated debunking of the salience of 'imperialism' in diagnosing sectarian discord in Ireland, see Richard Bourke, *Peace in Ireland: The War of Ideas* (London: Pimlico, 2012, 1st ed. 2003). Bourke characterizes the conflict, not as a centuries-old imperial struggle but as a 'recognisably modern dispute about the nature of democracy' in circumstances where the rule of the majority becomes 'a means of prescribing the terms of democratic inclusion in the state' (and where the feeling of perpetual exclusion is mislabelled 'imperialism'). See pp. xvii–xx, 10–11, 40.

25. Stephen Howe, *Ireland and Empire: Colonial Legacies in Irish History and Culture* (Oxford: Oxford University Press, 2000), p. 170. See also Terry Eagleton, 'Afterword: Ireland and Colonialism', in Terrence McDonough (ed.), *Was Ireland a Colony: Economics, Politics and Culture in Nineteenth-Century Ireland* (Dublin: Irish Academic Press, 2005), p. 329.

26. The general wariness among historians on this question persists. In a recent roundtable on 'Decolonising Irish History' convened in the pages of *Irish Historical Studies*, the Troubles are referred to only in passing as a mere 'backdrop' to the polemical furore over whether Ireland counted as a 'Kingdom' or a 'colony'. None of the eight contributors seemed inclined to consider whether decolonization constitutes a discrete period of Irish history with discernible temporal markers and material repercussions. See 'Round Table: Decolonising Irish History? Possibilities, Challenges, Practices', *Irish Historical Studies*, 45:168 (2021), pp. 303–32. Jane Ohlmeyer quoted on p. 318.

27. Quoted in Bourke, *Peace in Ireland*, p. 23. On the alleged continuum between operations in Northern Ireland and other post-war counter-insurgencies, see Edward Burke, 'Counter-Insurgency against "Kith and Kin"? The British Army in Northern Ireland, 1970–76', *The Journal of Imperial and Commonwealth History*, 43:4 (2015), pp. 658–77, 659.

28. See Matthew Kelly, 'Irish Nationalist Opinion and the British Empire in the 1850s and 1860s', *Past and Present*, 204 (August 2009), pp. 127–54.

29. Paul A. Townend, 'Between Two Worlds: Irish Nationalists and Imperial Crisis, 1878–1880', *Past and Present*, 194 (February 2007), p. 146. See also M. C. Rast, '"Ireland's Sister Nations": Internationalism and Sectarianism in the Irish Struggle for Independence, 1916–22', *Journal of Global History*, 10:3 (2015), pp. 479–501.

30. Sean Ryder, 'Defining Colony and Empire in Early Nineteenth-Century Irish Nationalism', in McDonough (ed.), *Was Ireland a Colony*, p. 165. Note, however, that Ryder saw this as no reason to conclude that Ireland 'was not a "colony" in some important sense of the word' in the nineteenth century. See also Joseph Ruane, 'Colonialism and the Interpretation of Irish Historical Development', in Marilyn Silverman and P. H. Gulliver (eds.), *Approaching the Past: Historical Anthropology through Irish Case Studies* (New York: Columbia University Press, 1992).

31. In the memorable words of Home Rule League founder Isaac Butt, quoted in Townend, 'Between Two Worlds', p. 165. Townend makes the case that 'anti-imperialism emerged as an integral, powerful part of Irish national mobilizing rhetoric' from the late 1870s, but much of his formidable body of evidence suggests a more superficial, even opportunistic pattern of identification.

32. Matthew Kelly makes the crucial point that although opposition to the British empire cannot be overlooked as a key rhetorical plank of Irish nationalism's historical evolution, this 'does not necessarily refute the claim that Irish nationalists did not readily identify with non-European colonized people'. Kelly, 'Irish Nationalist Opinion', p. 130.

33. Maurice Walsh, *Bitter Freedom: Ireland in a Revolutionary World 1918–1923* (London: Faber & Faber, 2021).

34. Even the more explicit parallels drawn in the interwar years between the freedom struggles in Ireland and India chimed discordantly with the

philosophical tenets of Gandhian passive resistance. See Kate O'Malley, *Ireland, India and Empire: Indo-Irish Radical Connections, 1919–64* (Manchester: Manchester University Press, 2008), p. 3; Shereen Ilahi, *Imperial Violence and the Path to Independence: India, Ireland and the Crisis of Empire* (London: I. B. Tauris, 2016).

35. *Irish News*, 'Disorders in Derry Debase Britain', 14 October 1968.
36. Liam de Paor, *Divided Ulster* (Harmondsworth: Penguin, 1970), p. xiii.
37. Matthew Kelly has shown how mid-nineteenth-century pamphleteers deployed similar references to 'the White N——s of Ireland' and 'the Celtic Hottentots of Skibereen' in order to 'demonstrate that the Irish were deserving of sympathy too'. See Kelly, 'Irish Nationalist Opinion', pp. 137, 141, 148, 149. My expurgation.
38. Bourke, *Peace in Ireland*, pp. 135–6.
39. O'Brien was referring specifically to Frantz Fanon's use of the binary 'colonized' and 'colonizer', see *States of Ireland* (New York: Pantheon, 1972), pp. 72, 307.
40. He originally made this point in a speech in the Irish Dáil in 1971 (where he served as a Labour Party member from 1969 to 1977), which he reprinted in *States of Ireland*, p. 296.
41. Stephen Howe also notes that anti-colonial discourses only became 'truly widespread in, and in relation to, Ireland' with the Troubles outbreak in 1968. *Ireland and Empire*, p. 172.
42. Sinn Féin (Official), 'The Lessons of History', February 1970, P1374, LHL. 'Official' Sinn Féin distinguished the organization from the breakaway 'Provisionals'.
43. Originally coined by Daniel O'Connell but achieving prominence during the Great War. Patrick M. Geoghegan, *Liberator Daniel O'Connell: The Life and Death of Daniel O'Connell, 1830–1847* (Dublin: Gill and Macmillan, 2010), ch. 3.
44. When asked about the role of the Protestant workers in their revolutionary programme in a 1969 interview, the PD leadership replied, 'Everything depends on winning them over.' 'Explosion in Ulster: PD Militants Discuss Strategy' (Baxter/Devlin/Farrell/McCann/Toman), 20 April 1969, p. 42, PD1969, Public Record Office of Northern Ireland (hereafter PRONI). On the 'intellectual linkage between nationalism and civil rights', see Christopher Hewitt, 'The Roots of Violence: Catholic Grievances and Irish Nationalism during the Civil Rights Period', in Patrick J. Roche and Brian Barton (eds.), *The Northern Ireland Question: Myth and Reality* (2nd ed., Tonbridge: Wordzworth, 2013), pp. 52–4.
45. Bernadette Devlin, *The Price of My Soul* (London: Pan Books, 1969), p. 54.
46. Bernadette Devlin, 'The Irish Fight for Socialism', address to San Francisco Bay Area International Socialists Forum, Berkeley, 20 February 1971, P12801, LHL.
47. 'On this basis', concluded PD activist Eamonn O'Kane, 'British imperialism proceeded to recarve Ireland to its own liking.' Eamonn O'Kane, 'British Imperialism', PD Pamphlet circa 1971, P1496, LHL.
48. *Free Citizen*, no. 4 [n.d. but late 1969], D3219/1/2, PRONI.

49. 'Explosion in Ulster', p. 42.
50. Eamonn McCann, *War and an Irish Town* (London: Pluto, 1993, 1st ed. 1974), p. 123. McCann's frankness about the inherent vagueness of anti-imperialism did not deter him from concluding later in the book, 'The fact was, and is, that the Republican tradition, for all the distortions of history contained within it, stemmed from a genuine, if episodic, anti-imperialist struggle; the Orange tradition was, objectively, pro-imperialist' (p. 177).
51. McCann, *War and an Irish Town*, p. 118.
52. Bourke, *Peace in Ireland*, p. 33.
53. Bourke, *Peace in Ireland*, p. 40.
54. Ronald Robinson, 'The Moral Disarmament of African Empire, 1919–1947', *Journal of Imperial and Commonwealth History*, viii (1979), pp. 86–104.
55. 10 October 1969, quoted in Pamela Clayton, *Enemies and Passing Friends: Settler Ideologies in Twentieth Century Ulster* (London: Pluto Press, 1996), p. 38.
56. 'More Home Truths', *News Letter*, 14 February 1972; see also 'Extracts from the Speech of the Prime Minister', in *News Letter*, 3 March 1972.
57. Hugh Trevor-Roper, 'Why Ulster Fights', *Réalités*, December 1969, p. 48.
58. Graham Walker, *A History of the Ulster Unionist Party: Protest, Pragmatism and Pessimism* (Manchester: Manchester University Press, 2004), p. 165.
59. John Ryan, Anne Kerr, Russell Kerr (MPs), 'Three Eyewitnesses Report on Londonderry', 8 October 1968, HA/32/2/30, PRONI.
60. Hume quoted in Simon Prince, '5 October 1968 and the Beginning of the Troubles: Flashpoints, Riots and Memory', *Irish Political Studies*, 27:3 (2012), pp. 394–410, 403; McClenaghan quoted in Ó Dochartaigh, *From Civil Rights to Armalites*, p. 19.
61. Minutes of Meeting at Ten Downing Street on 4th November 1968, CAB 4/1413, PRONI.
62. Ó Dochartaigh, *From Civil Rights to Armalites*, p. 10.
63. Mulholland, *Northern Ireland at the Crossroads*. Unionism, Mulholland argues, had always been 'defined by negatives, principally its opposition to Roman Catholicism and Irish nationalism' and thus the 'apparent weakening of its enemy threw its own self-identity into crisis', p. 8.
64. See, for example, Christine Kinealy, 'At Home with the Empire: The Example of Ireland', in Catherine Hall and Sonya O. Rose (eds.), *At Home with the Empire: Metropolitan Culture and the Imperial World* (Cambridge: Cambridge University Press, 2006), p. 99; Clayton, *Enemies and Passing Friends*, p. 122; Kevin Kenny, 'Introduction', in Kevin Kenny (ed.), *Ireland and the British Empire* (Oxford: Oxford University Press, 2004), p. 24.
65. Ian McBride, 'Ulster and the British Problem', in Richard English and Graham Walker (eds.), *Unionism in Modern Ireland* (Basingstoke: Macmillan, 1996), pp. 13–14.
66. The Derry incident and its aftermath ran from 5 to 8 October, while the Fearless talks were conducted immediately afterwards on 9–13 October.

67. Cabinet Minute: 'Meeting at 10 Downing St on 4th November 1968', CAB 4/1413, PRONI.
68. See, respectively, McKittrick and McVea, *Making Sense,* p. 44; Mulholland, *Northern Ireland at the Crossroads,* p. 64; Walker, *Ulster Unionist Party,* p. 166.
69. Cabinet Minute: 'Meeting at 10 Downing St on 4th November 1968', CAB 4/1413, PRONI.
70. *News Letter,* 'Ulster Must Be Right', 29 October 1968.
71. *News Letter,* 'Unionist Dilemma', letter from 'Really Amazed', 9 December 1968.
72. Radio interview with O'Neill, 4 November 1968: http://euscreen.eu/item.html ?id=EUS_B3E35AFDA0A24FA1B6609DC3A1A3FB3B.
73. Walker, *Ulster Unionist Party,* pp. 164, 168.
74. Walker, *Ulster Unionist Party,* p. 159.
75. His activities in this regard were constantly monitored by police, see, for example, 'List of Principle Meetings and Other Events Connected with the Paisleyite Movement in October' (1968), CAB 9/B/300/3, PRONI.
76. Margaret O'Callaghan and Catherine O'Donnell, 'The Northern Ireland Government, the "Paisleyite Movement" and Ulster Unionism in 1966', *Irish Political Studies,* 21:2 (2006), pp. 203–22, 210.
77. O'Callaghan and O'Donnell, 'The Northern Ireland Government', p. 219. Mulholland's account fully bears out the theme that 'Loyalist reaction pre-dated catholic mobilization in the civil rights movement', while Steve Bruce concurs that the mounting political crisis was fundamentally driven by a clash 'between O'Neill's reformist Unionism and Paisley's traditionalist stand'. Mulholland, *Northern Ireland at the Crossroads,* p. 113; Steve Bruce, *God Save Ulster! The Religion and Politics of Paisleyism* (Oxford: Oxford University Press, 1986), p. 89.
78. 'Hindering and Harrying' was the proud boast of Paisley supporters in the aftermath of Burntollet, see Bowes Egan and Vincent McCormack, *Burntollet* (London: LRS Publishers, 1969).
79. De Paor, *Divided Ulster,* p. 183.
80. David Johnston (County Inspector, RUC) to John G. Hill (Permanent Secretary, Ministry of Home Affairs), 7 July 1969, HA/32/2/28, PRONI.
81. Quoted in McKittrick and McVea, *Making Sense,* p. 47.
82. 'Ulster at Cross Roads', Monday 9 December 1968, reprinted in Terrence O'Neill, *Ulster at the Crossroads* (London: Faber & Faber, 1969), p. 143.
83. Walker, *Ulster Unionist Party,* p. 172.
84. Walker, *Ulster Unionist Party,* pp. 181–2.
85. *Protestant Telegraph,* 5 April 1969.
86. Alan F. Parkinson, *Ulster Loyalism and the British Media* (Dublin: Four Courts, 1998).
87. *Daily Express,* 'Curbing Violence', 7 January 1969; see also *Daily Express,* 'We Must Back this Man! [O'Neill]', 13 January 1969.
88. *The Observer,* 'How to Avoid a Civil War', 29 April 1969.

89. David Walder, 'Lucky Old Pope', *Spectator* (Political Commentary), 6 September 1969, p. 4. My emphasis.
90. *The Observer*, 'How to Avoid a Civil War', 29 April 1969.
91. Cited in Peter Rose, 'Labour, Northern Ireland and the Decision to Send in the Troops', in Peter Caterall and Sean McDougall (eds.), *The Northern Ireland Question in British Politics* (London: Macmillan, 1996), p. 99.
92. Crossman, unpublished diary entry 27 April 1969 quoted in Rose, *How the Troubles Came to Northern Ireland*, p. 146. Callahan, quoted in Richard Bourke, 'Pocock and the Presuppositions of the New British History', *Historical Journal*, 53:3 (2010), pp. 747–70, 757.
93. Clayton, *Enemies and Passing Friends*, p. 123.
94. Ian McBride, *The Siege of Derry in Ulster Protestant Mythology* (Dublin: Four Courts, 1997), pp. 77, 72–3.
95. Mulholland, *Northern Ireland at the Crossroads*, p. 169.
96. Gibraltar Archives (hereafter GA), 'The Doves: April 1968', Eyewitness Statement by Police Sergeant David Smith, 15 April 1968.
97. Deputy Commissioner Payas testified at the enquiry that it was at this point that 'the attitude of the crowd had changed from the Doves to the Commissioner'. See 'The Doves, April 1968, Enquiry proceedings', Testimony of Deputy Commissioner L. J. Payas, 20 August 1968, p. 111, GA.
98. 'The Doves, April 1968', Witness Statement by Police Inspector Edward Wood, 6 April 1968, GA; 'The Doves: Police Statements', Witness Statement by Police Inspector Joseph Louis Yome, 9 April 1968, GA.
99. 'The Doves, April 1968, Enquiry Proceedings', Testimony of Deputy Commissioner L. J. Payas, 20 August 1968, GA.
100. 'The Doves: Police Statements', Witness Statement by Police Inspector Joseph Louis Yome, 9 April 1968, GA.
101. *Gibraltar Post*, 13 April 1968.
102. *News Letter*, 'A Case of Mishandling', 29 February 1968.
103. See Spencer Mawby, 'Overwhelmed in a Very Small Place: The Wilson Government and the Crisis over Anguilla', *Twentieth Century British History*, 23:2 (2012), pp. 246–74.
104. *Auckland Star*, 'Not Quite Cricket', 20 January 1968.
105. Terrence O'Neill, *The Autobiography of Terrence O'Neill* (London: Rupert Hart-Davis, 1983) p. 83.
106. *Protestant Telegraph*, 'The End of the Road for Ulster', 28 December 1968.
107. See Lowry, 'Ulster Resistance and Loyalist Rebellion', on the loyalist tendency to Protestantize the Smith regime.
108. *Protestant Telegraph*, 'Rhodesia's UDI 1965' (by 'Redhand'), 25 November 1967.
109. Lowry, 'Ulster Resistance and Loyalist Rebellion', pp. 206–7.
110. *Ulster Protestant*, April 1968.
111. *Ulster Protestant*, 'The Plight of Britain Today', April 1969.
112. *Ulster Protestant*, 'British Commonwealth Alliance', April 1970.

113. *News Letter*, 'Invaders Welcomed' (William Brown, letters), 28 October 1968.

114. Mulholland, *Northern Ireland at the Crossroads*, p. 117.

115. The *Belfast Telegraph* first began to report on a 'UDI' tendency in the Unionist Party on 18 October 1968, and it became a frequent reference point thereafter. See Mulholland, *Northern Ireland at the Crossroads*, p. 169.

116. Devlin, *Price of My Soul*, p. 105.

117. See, for example, Robin Briggs, 'Independent Ulster "Not a Good Buy"', *News Letter*, 17 March 1972.

118. *News Letter*, 'Time for Sanity' ('Janus', letters), 13 March 1972.

119. O'Neill, *Ulster at the Crossroads*, p. 143.

120. Handwritten personal note by O'Neill to Wilson, 1 October 1966, PREM13/1762, NA.

121. File note to Wilson, 11 January 1967, PREM13/1762, NA.

122. *Gibraltar Chronicle*, 'Lord Shepherd Surprised at Gibraltar Concern for Future', 9 February 1968.

123. Ezequiel Mercau, *The Falklands War: An Imperial History* (Cambridge: Cambridge University Press, 2019), pp. 38–9.

124. *News Letter*, 'The Right to Decide', 7 December 1968.

125. Quoted in Lowry, 'Ulster Resistance and Loyalist Rebellion', p. 207.

126. Roger D. Scott, 'Ulster in Perspective: The Relevance of Non-European Experience', *Australian Outlook*, 23:3 (1969), pp. 246–57, 246.

127. Simon Winchester, *In Holy Terror: Reporting the Ulster Troubles* (London: Faber, 1974), p. 232.

128. *News Letter*, 29 March 1972.

129. As enunciated in a solemn 'Declaration of Intent and Covenant to Act' of 9 February 1972. Ulster Vanguard Action Rallies, 9 February 1972, HA/32/5/10, PRONI.

130. As reported in the *Daily Express*, 29 March 1972. The stanza (and only that stanza) was read out by Ulster Unionist politician and former government chief whip John Brooke, son of former Unionist prime minister of Northern Ireland Basil Brooke.

131. Bruce, *God Save Ulster!*, p. 252.

132. *Daily Express*, 25 March 1972, Political Commentary by Derek Marks, 'Only One Card Left if this Gamble Fails'.

133. *Daily Mirror*, 3 February 1972, Mirror Comment: 'How to End the Killing in Northern Ireland'.

134. 'Ulster – a Nation', Ulster Vanguard Publication, April 1972, P1240a, LHL.

135. See variously Ulster Vanguard Action Rallies, 'Declaration of Intent and Covenant to Act', 9 February 1972, HA/32/5/10, PRONI; 'Betrayal in Ulster: The Technique of Conservative Surrender', Ulster Vanguard booklet, 1972, P1244, LHL; 'Dominion of Ulster' by Kennedy Lindsay, 1972, D1327/20/4/162, PRONI.

136. See Chapter 5, pp. 151–2.

137. *News Letter*, 10 March 1972. The Gibraltarian catchcry first appeared in autumn 1964 when Chief Minister Joshua Hassan returned from a hearing of the UN Decolonization Committee in New York to packed crowds lining the airport bearing the 'British we are . . . ' banner. See *Pathé* news report 'British We Are British We Stay', www.youtube.com/watch?v=U8XK9ZAu7_M. See also *The Guardian*, 'Gibraltar Crowds Say: "We Stay British"', 12 October 1964.
138. As caricatured by Bernadette Devlin in *The Price of My Soul*, p. 156.
139. Jack Bennett, 'The Northern Conflict and British Power', Irish Sovereignty Movement, Pamphlet no. 1, December 1972, P1755a, LHL.
140. Quoted in McKittrick and McVea, *Making Sense*, pp. 23–4.
141. Quoted in Mulholland, *Northern Ireland at the Crossroads*, p. ix.
142. Sinn Féin (Official) 'The Lessons of History', February 1970, P1374, LHL.
143. 'Evangelical vaudeville' is from Walker, *Ulster Unionist Party*, p. 159.
144. McBride, 'Ulster and the British Problem', p. 14.
145. Richard Bourke, 'Pocock and the Presuppositions of the New British History', *Historical Journal*, 53:3 (2010), p. 762. See discussion of Bourke in the Introduction, pp. 11–12.
146. *The Guardian*, 'Ulster: Survival or Civil War?', 12 September 1969.
147. Constantine Fitzgibbon, 'Lifting the Lion's Paw', *Daily Mirror*, 27 August 1969. Later that year Fitzgibbon would publish a history of the 1916 Easter Rising similarly titled *Out of the Lion's Paw: Ireland Wins Her Freedom* (London: Macdonald, 1969).

14 'STOP THE WORLD': CELTIC DEPARTURES

1. John Davies, *A History of Wales* (London: Penguin, 2007), p. 199.
2. Figures cited in Alan Butt Philip, *The Welsh Question: Nationalism in Welsh Politics, 1945–70* (Cardiff: University of Wales Press, 1975), p. 105.
3. Rhys Evans, *Gwynfor Evans: Portrait of a Patriot* (Talybont: Y Lolfa Cyf, 2008), p. 264; *Daily Telegraph*, 15 July 1966.
4. Winifred Ewing, *Stop the World: The Autobiography of Winnie Ewing* (Edinburgh: Birlinn, 2004), p. 11. See also James Mitchell, *Hamilton 1967: The By-Election that Transformed Scotland* (Edinburgh: Luath Press, 2017).
5. *Glasgow Herald*, 'Back Home', 6 November 1967.
6. *The Times*, 'A Scottish Victory', 4 November 1967.
7. Quoted in Evans, *Gwynfor Evans*, p. 286.
8. *The Guardian*, 'Don't Laugh at the Threat, It Has Promise', 17 November 1967.
9. Tom Nairn, 'The Three Dreams of Scottish Nationalism', *New Left Review*, 49 (May–June 1968), pp. 3–18, 4.
10. Plaid Cymru Papers, National Library of Wales, Aberystwyth (hereafter PCP) C, C90, election leaflet 1964.

11. Keith Webb, *The Growth of Nationalism in Scotland* (Glasgow: Molendinar Press, 1977), p. 87.
12. Webb, *The Growth of Nationalism in Scotland*, p. 87.
13. Keith Robbins, '"This Grubby Wreck of Old Glories": The United Kingdom and the End of the British Empire', *Journal of Contemporary History*, 15:1 (1980), pp. 81–95, 82.
14. T. M. Devine, 'The Break-Up of Britain? Scotland and the End of Empire', *Transactions of the Royal Historical Society*, 16 (2006), pp. 163–80, 163, 166.
15. Tom Nairn, *The Break-up of Britain: Crisis and Neo-Nationalism* (London: New Left Books, 1977), pp. 129, 259.
16. See Jimmi Østergaard Nielsen and Stuart Ward, '"Cramped and Restricted at Home": Scottish Separatism at Empire's End', *Transactions of the Royal Historical Society*, 25 (2015), pp. 159–85.
17. Colin Kidd, *Union and Unionisms: Political Thought in Scotland, 1500–2000* (Cambridge: Cambridge University Press, 2008), pp. 261, 292. Kidd notes that it would only be much later that the 'the aim of negotiating a looser association with England metamorphosed into the goal of ending the English connection altogether' (p. 298). On the early SNP disputes over Scotland's future relationship to the wider empire, see Richard Finlay, 'For or against? Scottish Nationalists and the British Empire, 1919–1939', *Scottish Historical Review*, 71 (1992), pp. 184–206.
18. Robert McIntyre's twelve-week stint as SNP member for Motherwell in 1945 is the one notable exception, secured in abnormal circumstances during the final days of the wartime national government when the major parties had agreed tacitly not to stand against each other. The SNP was not a party to the agreement and hence McIntyre was Labour's only opponent in a historically low turnout. Labour easily regained the seat twelve weeks later at the 1945 general election.
19. Robbins, '"This Grubby Wreck of Old Glories"', p. 92; Butt Philip, *Welsh Question*, pp. 78, 84.
20. Ben Jackson, *The Case for Scottish Independence: A History of Nationalist Political Thought in Modern Scotland* (Cambridge: Cambridge University Press, 2020), p. 2.
21. See Chapter 1, pp. 21–3.
22. For a romanticized account, see Roy Clews, *To Dream of Freedom: The Story of the MAC and the Free Wales Army* (Talybont: Y Lolfa Cyf, 2001).
23. Webb, *The Growth of Nationalism in Scotland*, p. 204.
24. Butt Philip, *Welsh Question*, pp. 109–10.
25. See Chapter 12.
26. *Scots Independent*, 'Where are the Empire States?', 20 February 1965.
27. *Scots Independent*, 'State or Nation?', 29 October 1966; see also *Scots Independent*, 'The British Crisis: Scotland Must Act Herself', 3 September 1966: 'Where can Britain really go? Time is long past when Britain sat smugly on her islands and the world came to her door.'
28. *Scots Independent*, 'History's Next Big Date', 13 January 1968.

29. *Welsh Nation*, August 1966.
30. *Y Ddraig Goch*, 'Yn Rhydd Erbyn 1970?: Ble'r Aeth Yr Hen Ymerodraeth?', December 1967–January 1968, Vol. 36, Nos 12–13. All translations from Welsh sources are by Gareth Owen.
31. Reported in the *Daily Nation*, 31 July 1960.
32. Gwynfor Evans, 'Look Forward Wales', *Welsh Nation*, June 1960, M3/1 (137), Datganiadau i'r wasg, taflenni a phamffledi/Press releases, leaflets and pamphlets 1960–1978, in Gwynfor Evans Papers (hereafter GEP), National Library of Wales, Aberystwyth.
33. Evans, 'Look Forward Wales'.
34. Billy Wolfe, *Scotland Lives: The Quest for Independence* (Edinburgh: Reprographia, 1973), p. 27.
35. Wolfe, *Scotland Lives*, p. 10.
36. Quoted in Wolfe, *Scotland Lives*, p. 53.
37. Tam Dalyell, *The Question of Scotland: Devolution and After* (Edinburgh: Birlinn, 2016).
38. Gwynfor Evans, Plaid Cymru, *Commonwealth Status for Wales* (1965), p. 12.
39. Hansard, 26 July 1966, Vol. 732, cc. 1496–1504.
40. SNP Research Department interim report, 14 March 1969, ACC 11987/110, SNP Archives, National Library of Scotland (hereafter SNPA).
41. *Scots Independent*, Arthur Donaldson's Diary 'The True Significance of Devaluation', 25 November 1967.
42. Evans to Ammanford Cell (Dr Davies), 28 January 1966, C73, PCP.
43. Evans, *Gwynfor Evans*, p. 261.
44. *Western Mail*, 12 July 1966, p. 4.
45. 'Rhai Rhesymau Paham yr Enillwyd Caerfyrddin' ('Some reasons why Carmarthen was won'), by D. Cyril Jones (undated but post-July 1966), I38, PCP.
46. *The Guardian*, 'The Challenge of Plaid Cymru', 16 July 1966.
47. *Hamilton Advertiser*, 'After the Ball', 10 November 1967.
48. These are available in the National Library of Scotland, P.1a.7030, *Hamilton Herald*.
49. *Hamilton Advertiser*, '"Scots wha hinnae" won for Winnie', 10 November 1967. See also Nielsen and Ward, 'Cramped and Restricted at Home', pp. 170–6.
50. See www.youtube.com/watch?v=_ms6JFJqpU0.
51. Hansard, 26 July 1966, Vol. 732, cc. 1496–1504.
52. E. Rowlands, 'The Politics of Regional Administration: The Establishment of the Welsh Office', *Public Administration*, 50 (Autumn 1972), pp. 339, 340–1.
53. Rowlands, 'The Politics of Regional Administration', p. 351.
54. T. M. Devine, 'The Challenge of Nationalism', in T. M. Devine (ed.), *Scotland and the Union, 1707–2007* (Edinburgh: Edinburgh University Press, 2008), pp. 148–9.
55. On this, see Chapter 11.

56. Gordon Wilson, *SNP: The Turbulent Years, 1960–1990* (Stirling: Scots Independent, 2009), p. 247.
57. *Y Ddraig Goch*, 'Yn Rhydd Erbyn 1970?'.
58. Kenneth O. Morgan, *Rebirth of a Nation: Wales 1880–1980* (Oxford: Oxford University Press, 1981), p. 386.
59. *Hamilton Advertiser*, 'Which?', 27 October 1967.
60. *Glasgow Herald*, 'Scottish Surprise', 13 January 1968. From 1885 down to 2005, Scotland had over seventy seats in the House of Commons.
61. John S. Ellis, *Investiture: Royal Ceremony and National Identity in Wales, 1911–69* (Cardiff: University of Wales Press, 2008), p. 147. The following account is largely drawn from this detailed and insightful study, unless otherwise indicated.
62. See the missive by Welsh Office's Goronwy Daniel to Sir Michael Adeane, 'Investiture of Prince Charles', 14 December 1966, and the latter's unforthcoming reply on 16 December 1966, PREM13/2359, The National Archives, Kew (hereafter NA). Two days later Adeane complained to Downing Street about the Welsh Office's pushiness on the matter, 'Royal Family', 18 December 1966, PREM13/2359, NA.
63. *Western Mail*, 2 November 1967, quoted in Ellis, *Investiture*, p. 247.
64. Quoted in Ellis, *Investiture*, pp. 192–3.
65. 'Wither Charles?', *The Observer*, 29 October 1967; *The Times*, 2 July 1969.
66. Evans, *Gwynfor Evans*, p. 285.
67. Ellis, *Investiture*, p. 195.
68. *Carmarthen Times*, 20 June 1969.
69. Quoted in Evans, *Gwynfor Evans*, p. 289.
70. Craig Owen Jones, '"Songs of Malice and Spite"? Wales, Prince Charles, and an anti-Investiture Ballad of Dafydd Iwan', *Music and Politics*, 7:2 (Summer 2013), p. 2.
71. Jones, 'Songs of Malice', pp. 3–4. As *The Times* correspondent in Aberystwyth observed, 'fun poking at the investiture has generated a miniature industry', quoted in Ellis, *Investiture*, p. 200.
72. Ellis, *Investiture*, pp. 15–16.
73. Ellis, *Investiture*, p. 232.
74. Clews, *To Dream of Freedom*, p. 250.
75. George Thomas, *George Thomas, Mr Speaker: The Memoirs of Viscount Tonypandy* (London: Century, 1985), p. 120.
76. *Daily Mail*, 1 July 1969, quoted in Ellis, *Investiture*, p. 257.
77. Ellis, *Investiture*, p. 265.
78. Quoted in Ellis, *Investiture*, pp. 266, 271.
79. *Y Cymro*, 'Cwestiynau o bwys' ('Weighty Questions'), 2 July 1969.
80. Ellis, *Investiture*, p. 306.
81. Compared with their overall result in the 1966 general election, see Butt Philip, *Welsh Question*, p. 123.

82. The members of the commission were unable to reach agreement, resulting in a second minority 'Memorandum of Dissent' which did little to rally political support behind the commission's findings.

83. Robbins, '"This Grubby Wreck of Old Glories"', p. 92.

84. *The Times*, 24 September 1974.

85. Michael Hechter, *Internal Colonialism: The Celtic Fringe in British National Development, 1536–1966* (London: Routledge & Kegan Paul, 1975), p. 342.

86. Daniel Thomas Jenkins, *The British, Their Identity, and Their Religion* (London: SCM Press, 1975), p. 135.

87. Nairn, *Break-Up of Britain*. On Nairn's 'epic' journey in this regard, see Jackson, *The Case for Scottish Independence*, pp. 62, 68–72. For Nairn's critique of SNP 'sporranry' see Chapter 15, p. 464.

88. *The Times*, 18 April 1974.

89. Hansard, 13 December 1976, Vol. 922, cc. 975–6.

90. Hansard, 14 December 1976, Vol. 922, cc. 1320–2.

91. *The Times*, 25 February 1975.

92. John Biffen, *A Nation in Doubt* (London: Conservative Political Centre, 1976), p. 8.

93. Hansard, 14 December 1976, Vol. 922, cc. 1320–2, c. 1359.

94. David McCrone, *Understanding Scotland: The Sociology of a Stateless Nation* (London: Routledge, 1992), p. 62.

95. Quoted in Davies, *History of Wales*, p. 652.

96. Wolfe to Gordon Wilson, 24 August 1979, Acc 13099/2, Political Correspondence, SNPA. Wilson would shortly succeed Wolfe as party leader less than a month later.

97. Quoted in Christopher Harvie, *Scotland and Nationalism: Scottish Society and Politics, 1707 to the Present* (3rd ed., London: Routledge, 1998), p. 201.

98. Quoted in Davies, *History of Wales*, p. 652.

99. *The Guardian*, 30 August 1979.

100. Untitled document in Acc. 6038/6, Folder 4, SNPA.

101. Gwynfor Evans, 'Look Forward Wales', *Welsh Nation*, June 1960, in M3/1 (137), GEP.

102. James Halliday, 'The African Situation', *Scots Independent*, 13 February 1960.

103. Neil Douglas, *How London Spends Your Money* (Edinburgh). Undated, but most likely 1964 judging from its general context and file placement in the Arthur Donaldson Papers, Acc. 6038/2, 'Correspondence of and to Arthur Donaldson', Folder 2, SNPA.

104. *Y Ddraig Goch*, 'Yn Rhydd Erbyn 1970?'.

105. The SNP's Robert McIntyre condemned the entire Rhodesian situation as the work of a people 'living in a state of mental illness so far from world reality . . . that their actions are akin to madness'. See 'English Tory Loyalty', *Scots Independent*, 27 November 1965.

106. Desmond Johnson (Bulawayo) to Evans, 25 July 1966, M2/4 Box 134, GEP. Evans's papers at the National Library of Wales contain numerous such examples from Welsh groups and individuals living in Rhodesia.
107. Angus Graham to Ewing, 8 December 1967, Acc. 10090/113, SNPA.
108. Quoted in *The Observer*, 'Celtic Threat', 18 February 1968.
109. This can only be inferred from Graham's 8 December letter, which is drafted in the form of a reply to Ewing's polite refusal to visit.
110. R. I. Webster (Pretoria) to Arthur Donaldson (Party Chairman), 16 December 1967, Arthur Donaldson Papers, Acc. 6038/6, Folder 3, SNPA.
111. Donaldson to Frank E. B. Molesworth (of the *Northern Advocate*, NZ) 15 November 1967, Arthur Donaldson Papers, Acc. 6038/6, Folder 2, SNPA.
112. *Scots Independent*, 27 April 1968.
113. Notes on a Public Meeting in Dundee, 1 April 1968, Arthur Donaldson Papers, Acc. 6038/6, Folder 7, SNPA; Moncur to Donaldson, 10 April 1968 reporting on the Dundee meeting in ibid.
114. *Scots Independent*, 27 April 1968; Donaldson to Moncur, 19 May 1968, Arthur Donaldson Papers, Acc. 6038/6, Folder 7, SNPA.
115. C. Buchanan (Cheltenham) to Donaldson, 20 December 1967, Arthur Donaldson Papers, Acc. 6038/6, Folder 3, SNPA.
116. See Chapters 10 and 11, respectively.
117. Arthur Donaldson, 'Scots Diary', *Scots Independent*, 4 May 1968. See also *Scots Independent*, 27 April 1968.
118. *Glasgow Herald*, 31 July 1969. Future SNP leader Gordon Wilson pursued the matter publicly, demanding that the Conservative Party leadership distance itself from Powell's 'offensive likening of Scottish shipyard workers to "prairie dogs"'. Wilson to Edward Heath, 30 June 1969 and 30 July 1969 in Gordon Wilson papers, Acc 13099/2, Political Correspondence, SNPA.
119. Donald Horne, *The Lucky Country: Australia in the Sixties* (Ringwood: Penguin, 1964), pp. 24, 111.
120. Horne, *Lucky Country*, p. 84.
121. Eric Williams, *History of the People of Trinidad and Tobago* (London: Andre Deutsch, 1982, 1st ed. 1962), p 279. Barrow quoted in Anne Spry Rush, *Bonds of Empire: West Indians and Britishness from Victoria to Decolonization* (Oxford: Oxford University Press, 2001), p. 235. See Williams's Independence Day remarks extracted in a memorandum by E. L. Sykes, 19 September 1962, DO200/95, NA.
122. Albert Morris, 'Scotsman's Log', *Scotsman*, 18 January 1968.
123. Ludovic Kennedy, 'The Disunited Kingdom', transcript of BBC broadcast, 12 June 1968, Acc. 10090/113, SNPA.
124. A. D. Rees, 'Cenedl ddauddyblyg ei meddwil', *Barn*, 29 (March 1965), p. 129, trans. Martin Johnes, *Wales since 1939* (Manchester: Manchester University Press, 2012), p. 178.

125. Quoted in Siôn T. Jobbins, *The Phenomenon of Welshness II* (Llanrwst: Gwasg Carreg Gwalch, 2013), p. 249.

126. Wolfe, *Scotland Lives*, p. 91.

127. Quoted in Ellis, *Investiture*, p. 253.

128. Webb, *The Growth of Nationalism in Scotland*, p. 74.

15 'COSMOLOGIES OF OUR OWN': AFTER BRITAIN

1. Catherine Hall, *Macaulay and Son: Architects of Imperial Britain* (New Haven: Yale University Press, 2012), p. 195.

2. Thomas Babington Macaulay, *The History of England from the Accession of James II*, 5 vols. (New York: Harper & Brothers, 1856), vol. I, pp. 3, 5–6.

3. Macaulay also used 'aboriginal tribes' to refer to the 'wild and rugged' ways of the inhabitants of Scotland and especially Ireland.

4. Macaulay, *History*, vol. III, quoted in Theodore Koditschek, *Liberalism, Imperialism, and the Historical Imagination: Nineteenth-Century Visions of a Greater Britain* (Cambridge: Cambridge University Press, 2011), p. 144.

5. See David Skilton, 'Contemplating the Ruins of London: Macaulay's New Zealander and Others', *Literary London: Interdisciplinary Studies in the Representation of London*, 2:1 (March 2004), www.literarylondon.org/london-journal/march2004/skilton.html.

6. Quoted in Duncan Bell, *Reordering the World: Essays on Liberalism and Empire* (Princeton: Princeton University Press, 2016), p. 125.

7. Macaulay made a similar reference a few years later in the House of Commons, espousing education for 'the common people' while deploring the ignorance of a population permitted 'to grow up as rude and stupid as any tribe of tattooed cannibals in New Zealand'. This was the standardized image of a New Zealander in the 1840s – it would be years before settlers would buy in to the term as a self-designation. See Macaulay's 1847 speech: 'Education (April 19. 1847)' in Thomas Babington Macaulay, *The Works of Lord Macaulay*, vol. III, ed. Lady Trevelyan (London: Longmans, Green and Co., 1866), p. 388. See also Felicity Barnes, *New Zealand's London: A Colony and Its Metropolis* (Auckland: Auckland University Press, 2012).

8. Koditschek, *Liberalism, Imperialism*, p. 150.

9. J. G. A. Pocock, *The Discovery of Islands: Essays in British History* (Cambridge: Cambridge University Press, 2005), p. ix.

10. J. G. A. Pocock, 'British History: A Plea for a New Subject', *New Zealand Journal of History*, 8 (1974), pp. 3–21, 4–5.

11. J. G. A. Pocock, 'British History: A Plea for a New Subject: Reply', *Journal of Modern History*, 47:4 (December 1975), pp. 626–8, 626. For the influence of Pocock's reconceptualization of British history, see, for example, Hugh Kearney, *The British Isles: A History of Four Nations* (Cambridge: Cambridge University Press, 1989);

Alexander Grant and Keith J. Stringer (eds.), *Uniting the Kingdom: The Making of British History* (London: Routledge, 1995); Laurence Brockliss and David Eastwood (eds.), *A Union of Multiple Identities: The British Isles, c. 1750–1850* (Manchester: Manchester University Press, 1997).

12. J. G. A. Pocock, 'The Limits and Divisions of British History: In Search of the Unknown Subject', *American Historical Review*, 87:2 (1982), pp. 311–36, 311.

13. Pocock, 'British History', p. 21, emphasis added.

14. Pocock, *Discovery of Islands*, pp. 3–4.

15. This was the abiding theme of Pocock's magnum opus, *The Machiavellian Moment* (1975); on the thematic crossover between his prescription for a new British history and the wider optics of classical Republicanism, see Stuart Ward, 'Machiavellian Moments and the Exigencies of Leaving', *Historical Reflections*, 47:2 (Summer 2021), pp. 49–64.

16. Koditschek, *Liberalism, Imperialism*, p. 142.

17. See J. G. A. Pocock, 'Working on Ideas in Time', in L. P. Curtis (ed.), *The Historian's Workshop: Original Essays by Sixteen Historians* (New York: Knopf, 1970), pp. 153, 156.

18. Pocock, 'Reply', p. 626.

19. W. H. Oliver, *The Story of New Zealand* (London: Faber, 1960), p. 288.

20. Pocock, *Discovery of Islands*, p. 13.

21. Keith Sinclair, 'The Historian as Prophet', originally a 1963 public lecture subsequently published in Muriel F. Lloyd Pritchard (ed.), *The Future of New Zealand* (Christchurch: Whitcombe and Tombs, 1964), pp. 140–1. See also Giselle Byrnes, 'Introduction: Reframing New Zealand History', *The New Oxford History of New Zealand* (Melbourne: Oxford University Press, 2009).

22. W. H. Oliver, 'A Destiny at Home', *New Zealand Journal of History*, 19:1 (April 1985), pp. 9–15, 9–10.

23. For an archetypal example, see Russel Ward's, *The Australian Legend* (Melbourne: Oxford University Press, 1958). On the early take-up of the 'identity' trope in the context of the redundant 'Dominions', see Stuart Ward, 'The MacKenzian Moment in Retrospect (or How One Hundred Volumes Bloomed)', in Andrew S. Thompson (ed.), *Writing Imperial Histories* (Manchester: Manchester University Press, 2013), pp. 39–41.

24. Manning Clark, *The Quest for Grace* (Ringwood: Viking, 1990), p. 205.

25. The definitive biography is Mark McKenna's aptly titled, *An Eye for Eternity: The Life of Manning Clark* (Melbourne: Meigunyah Press, 2011), p. 558.

26. Jomo Kenyatta, *Facing Mount Kenya* (London: Secker and Warburg, 1938); Jawaharlal Nehru, *The Discovery of India* (New York: John Day, 1946); Eric Williams, *History of the People of Trinidad and Tobago* (London: Andre Deutsch, 1982, 1st ed. 1962).

27. The literature is vast, but for what is arguably the founding statement, see Ranajit Guha, 'On Some Aspects of the Historiography of Colonial India', in

Ranajit Guha and Gayatri Chakravorty Spivak (eds.), *Select Subaltern Studies* (Oxford: Oxford University Press, 1988), pp. 37–44.

28. A. G. Hopkins explores the intersections between the Afro-Asian experience of decolonization and the new nation-building effort in the former 'Dominions' in 'Rethinking Decolonization', *Past and Present*, 200 (2008), pp. 211–47.

29. W. H. Oliver, 'The Image of Europe in the New Zealand Experience', unpublished manuscript, 1970, PAM 327.930 4 OLI 1970, Alexander Turnbull Library, Wellington.

30. Pocock, *Discovery of Islands*, p. 22.

31. Ian McBride, 'J. G. A. Pocock and the Politics of British History', in Naomi Lloyd-Jones and Margaret M. Scully (eds.), *Four Nations Approaches to Modern 'British' History* (London: Palgrave, 2018), pp. 33–57, 44–5.

32. George Davie, *The Democratic Intellect* (Edinburgh: Edinburgh University Press, 2013, 1st ed. 1961), p. xxi.

33. The Church took a distinctly back seat to the Scottish universities in Davie's account, insisting that 'the secular component rather than the sacred … was chiefly responsible for the continuing foreignness of the Scottish ethos'. Or more precisely, he identified 'the distinctive life of the country not in its religion alone but in the mutual interaction of religion, law and education'. Davie, *Democratic Intellect*, pp. xviii, xxi.

34. Ben Jackson, *The Case for Scottish Independence: A History of Nationalist Political Thought in Modern Scotland* (Cambridge: Cambridge University Press, 2020), pp. 40, 47.

35. H. J. Hanham, *Scottish Nationalism* (Cambridge, MA: Harvard University Press, 1969), dustjacket.

36. Hanham, *Scottish Nationalism*, p. 162.

37. Hanham, *Scottish Nationalism*, p. 212. Hanham seemed initially unsure of the validity of the connection in H. J. Hanham, 'The Scottish Nation Faces the Post-Imperial World', *International Journal*, 23 (1968), p. 584.

38. Quoted in Camilla Schofield, *Enoch Powell and the Making of Post-Colonial Britain* (Cambridge: Cambridge University Press, 2013), p. 163.

39. See especially Chapter 12, pp. 372–5.

40. A. J. P. Taylor, *English History, 1914–1945: The Oxford History of England*, vol. XV (Oxford: Oxford University Press, 1965), p. v.

41. Taylor, *English History*, pp. v, 600.

42. Pocock, 'British History', pp. 3–4. Taylor responded with more of the same, dismissing out of hand Pocock's semantic tinkering with an imperious wave of the hand: 'Everyone knows what we mean whether we call our subject English history or British history. It is a fuss over names, not things.' A. J. P. Taylor, 'British History: A Plea for a New Subject: Comments', *Journal of Modern History*, 47:4 (1975), pp. 622–6, 622.

43. 'Lopsidedness' is Colin Kidd's term, quoted in Naomi Lloyd-Jones and Margaret M. Scull, 'A New Plea for an Old Subject? Four Nations History for the Modern Period', in Lloyd-Jones and Scull (eds.), *Four Nations Approaches to Modern 'British' History*, p. 5. See also Lloyd-Jones and Scull on the 'teleological tendency' whereby the New British History inadvertently 'shores up rather than dismantles the edifice of homogeneity' (p. 8).

44. Pocock, 'Limits and Divisions of British History', p. 318.

45. Pocock, 'British History', p. 6.

46. McBride, 'Pocock and the Politics of British History', p. 37.

47. Raphael Samuel, 'British Dimensions: "Four Nations History"', *History Workshop Journal*, 40 (Autumn, 1995), pp. iii–xxii, iv.

48. *The Press* (Christchurch), 'Nationalist Mood', 10 May 1973.

49. J. G. A. Pocock, 'Conclusion: Contingency, Identity, Sovereignty', in Grant and Stringer (eds.), *Uniting the Kingdom*, p. 297.

50. Ewan Morris, *Our Own Devices: National Symbols and Political Conflict in Twentieth-Century Ireland* (Dublin: Irish Academic Press, 2005), p. 220.

51. Morris, *Our Own Devices*, pp. 5, 219.

52. Quoted in Harry Saker, *The South African Flag Controversy, 1925–28* (Oxford: Oxford University Press, 1980), p. 164.

53. See H. Kumarasingham, 'The "Tropical Dominions": The Appeal of Dominion Status in the Decolonisation of India, Pakistan and Ceylon', *Transactions of the Royal Historical Society*, 23 (2013), pp. 223–45.

54. As Srirupa Roy notes, it was not enough simply to be anti-colonial: 'A positive specification of what the flag stood for was also required', which is where the contradictions 'began to emerge'. Srirupa Roy, '"A Symbol of Freedom": The Indian Flag and the Transformations of Nationalism, 1906–2002', *Journal of Asian Studies*, 65:3 (August 2006), pp. 495–527, 508, 511; see also Arundhati Virmani, 'National Symbols under Colonial Domination: The Nationalization of the Indian Flag, March–August 1923', *Past & Present*, 164 (August 1999), pp. 169–97.

55. *Daily Gleaner*, 'The Choice of National Emblems', 30 March 1962; *Sunday Gleaner*, 'Nationalism – What it Means', 15 April 1962; *Daily Gleaner*, 'Jamaican Identity', 19 April 1962.

56. See, generally, Gregory A. Johnson, 'The Last Gasp of Empire: The 1964 Flag Debate Revisited', in Phillip Buckner (ed.), *Canada and the End of Empire* (Vancouver: UBC Press, 2005), pp. 322–50; Lorraine Coops, '"One Flag, One Throne, One Empire"; The IODE, the Great Flag Debate, and the End of Empire', in Buckner (ed.), *Canada and the End of Empire*, pp. 251–71; see also José Igartua, *The Other Quiet Revolution: National Identities in English Canada, 1945–71* (Vancouver: UBC Press, 2006), ch. 7; C. P. Champion, *The Strange Demise of British Canada: The Liberals and Canadian Nationalism, 1964–68* (Montreal and Kingston: McGill-Queen's University Press, 2010).

57. Quoted in Rick Archbold, *I Stand for Canada: The Story of the Maple Leaf Flag* (Toronto: Macfarlane, Walter and Ross, 2002), p. 26.
58. Quoted in Champion, *Strange Demise*, pp. 161, 178.
59. See Igartua, *Other Quiet Revolution*, p. 185. Johnson quotes contemporary polling figures marking support for the Maple Leaf and the Red Ensign among English Canadians at 30 and 35 per cent, respectively, see 'Last Gasp', p. 246.
60. Minister for Internal Affairs Henry May, New Zealand Parliamentary Debates, Representatives, Vol. 385, 1 August 1973, 2886–7. The reference to 'Maori discontents' is from opposition spokesman Allan Highet in *New Zealand Parliamentary Debates*, 2898; see also notes of discussion: Meeting of New Zealand Day Celebrations Steering Committee, 2 October 1973, AAAC/7536 W5084, Box 231 CON/9/3/14, Archives New Zealand, Wellington (hereafter ANZ).
61. Submission by Maori Women's Welfare League to the Maori Affairs Committee, undated 1973, AAAC/7536, W5084, box 231 CON/9/1/5, ANZ; Margaret R. McCormick, honorary secretary of the Auckland Historical Society, to Henry May, 21 March 1975, AAAC/7536, W5084, box 227 CON/9/2/3, ANZ. See Stuart Ward, 'The "New Nationalism" in Australia, Canada and New Zealand: Civic Culture in the Wake of the British World', in Kate Darian-Smith, Stuart MacIntyre and Patricia Grimshaw (eds.), *Britishness Abroad: Transnational Movements and Imperial Cultures* (Melbourne: Melbourne University Press, 2007).
62. Editorial, *Age* (Melbourne) 24 January 1969; *Sydney Morning Herald*, 'Lord Mayor Asks Us for Aust Day Ideas', 27 January 1971.
63. See James Curran and Stuart Ward, *The Unknown Nation: Australia after Empire* (Melbourne: Melbourne University Press, 2010), ch. 5.
64. Wolfe to Arthur Donaldson, 16 January 1968, ACC 11987/110, Folder 4, SNP Archives, National Library of Scotland (hereafter SNPA).
65. See Stuart Ward, 'The Redundant "Dominion": Refitting the National Fabric at Empire's End', in Matthew Hayday and Raymond Blake (eds.), *Celebrating Canada*, vol. 1: *Holidays, National Days and the Crafting of Identities* (Toronto: Toronto University Press, 2016).
66. Memorandum by Dr Andrew W. Lees on Bannockburn Day, 7 January 1968, Arthur Donaldson Papers, Acc. 6038/6, Folder 4, SNPA. See also papers relating to the enhanced status of Bannockburn Day in Arthur Donaldson Papers, Folder 8.
67. David McCrone, 'Scotland Days: Evolving Nation and Icons', in David McCrone and Gayle McPherson (eds.), *National Days: Constructing and Mobilising National Identity* (London: Palgrave Macmillan, 2009), p. 31. On the more general reluctance among Scottish nationalists 'to mobilise simply around the signs and motifs bequeathed from the Scottish past' (as though these were a potential liability as much as an asset) see David McCrone, *Understanding Scotland: The Sociology of a Stateless Nation* (London: Routledge, 1992), p. 174.

68. See Jackson, *Case for Scottish Independence*, ch. 3. Nairn first lashed out at the SNP in the aftermath of Winifred Ewing's victory in Hamilton in 1968. See Tom Nairn, 'The Three Dreams of Scottish Nationalism', *New Left Review*, 49 (May–June 1968), pp. 3–18, 18.

69. The literature is vast but for a critical overview see Jeremi Suri, 'The Rise and Fall of an International Counterculture, 1960–75', *American Historical Review*, 114:1 (February 2009), pp. 45–68.

70. Donald Horne, *A Time of Hope: Australia, 1966–72* (Sydney: Angus & Robertson, 1980), p. 155.

71. Ezequiel Mercau, *The Falklands War: An Imperial History* (Cambridge: Cambridge University Press, 2019), p. 1.

72. Eric Hobsbawm, 'Falklands Fallout', *Marxism Today*, January 1983.

73. Anthony Barnett, 'Iron Britannia', *New Left Review*, 1:134 (1982), pp. 19–20.

74. 'settled like a sentiment' is from John M. MacKenzie, *Propaganda and Empire: The Manipulation of British Public Opinion, 1880–1960* (Manchester: Manchester University Press, 1984), p. 258.

75. Or a 'repeat of a repeat' as Barnett ventured, likening the Falklands to a re-enactment of Suez, which itself was a 'clownish attempt' to recreate the conditions of 'colonial domination'. 'Iron Britannia', p. 1.

76. *The Spectator*, quoted in Andrew S. Thompson, *The Empire Strikes Back?: The Impact of Imperialism on Britain from the Mid-Nineteenth Century* (Harlow: Longman, 2005), pp. 226, 344.

77. Quoted in Klaus Dodds, *Pink Ice: Britain and the South Atlantic Empire* (London: I. B. Tauris, 2002), p. 167.

78. Thompson, *Empire Strikes Back*, p. 226.

79. *The Guardian*, 'Myth Rules in Falklands', 3 May 1982, quoted in Mercau, *Falklands War*, p. 89. The SNP's Winifred Ewing similarly aired her disgust at hearing 'our British brothers prate so much support for self-determination'. Quoted in Mercau, *Falklands War*, p. 90.

80. Quoted in Mercau, *Falklands War*, p. 94.

81. Mercau, *Falklands War*, pp. 15, 89–98.

82. Willie Whitelaw, quoted in Chi-kwan Mark, 'Decolonising Britishness? The 1981 British Nationality Act and the Identity Crisis of Hong Kong Elites', *Journal of Imperial and Commonwealth History*, 48:3 (2019), pp. 565–90, 572.

83. Lord Boothby in Hansard (Lords), 5 July 1983, Vol. 443, cc. 504, 507.

84. Ezequiel Mercau, '"The Mouse that Roared": The Falklands and Gibraltar in Thatcher's (Greater) Britain', in Christian Damm Pedersen and Stuart Ward (eds.), *The Break-Up of Greater Britain* (Manchester: Manchester University Press, 2021).

85. John Flowerdew, *The Final Years of British Hong Kong: The Discourse of Colonial Withdrawal* (Basingstoke: Macmillan, 1998), p. 34.

86. Lord Kadoorie, the First Hong Kong-born member of the House of Lords, quoted in Mark, 'Decolonising Britishness', p. 578.

87. *South China Morning Post*, 16 October 1981.
88. *The Times*, quoted in Thompson, *Empire Strikes Back*, p. 228.
89. Quoted in Mark Hampton, *Hong Kong and British Culture, 1945–97* (Manchester: Manchester University Press, 2016), p. 2. The various headlines are cited in the footnotes on p. 11.
90. Loose ends nevertheless endured – with the British connection furnishing foggy memories of a more 'liberal' dispensation in the years ahead. With the help of selective memory, civil rights protesters still periodically revive the Union Flag as a symbol of their defiance of Beijing. See Hampton's discussion of these 'hangovers' in *Hong Kong and British Culture*, 'Epilogue'.
91. The two Quebec referendums were only indirectly concerned with the constitutional link with Britain (by way of severing ties to Canada) but it emerged out of the complex deliberations that attended the repatriation of the Constitution in 1980 and the attempt to forge a new constitutional pact in the form of the Charlottetown Accord – itself defeated at a Canada-wide referendum in 1992.
92. Ivor Jennings, *The Approach to Self-Government* (Cambridge: Cambridge University Press, 1956), pp. 55–6. Sincere thanks to H. Kumarasingham for sharing this reference.
93. Quoted in Richard Bourke, *Peace in Ireland: The War of Ideas* (London: Pimlico, 2012), p. 203.
94. Hansard, 21 November 1972, Vol. 846, cc. 1124–7.
95. Quoted in Simon C. Smith, 'Integration and Disintegration: The Attempted Incorporation of Malta into the United Kingdom in the 1950s', *Journal of Imperial and Commonwealth History*, 35:1 (2007), pp. 49–71.
96. Smith, 'Integration and Disintegration', p. 58.
97. Self-determination as such was not at issue; a Legislative Council had existed since 1950 with limited powers of self-government, soon to be replaced by the new House of Assembly in 1969, with British sovereignty retained in the executive authority of the governor – neither arrangement being affected by the 1967 poll.
98. *Economist*, 16 September 1967.
99. Government Secretariat Gibraltar to J. S. Bennett (Commonwealth Office), 5 July 1967, FCO 42/151, The National Archives, Kew.
100. As constitutional experts have argued, all referendums are inherently constitutive of the people they ostensibly consult. See Philippe Cauvet, 'A Democratic Critique of Referendums in France and in the United Kingdom: Convergence or Divergence?', in Géraldine Gadbin-George and Elizabeth Gibson-Morgan (eds.), *UK and France: Friends or Foes? (Trans)cultural and Legal Unions and Disunions* (Paris: Editions Le Manuscrit, 2019).
101. Robert Saunders, *Yes to Europe: The 1975 Referendum and Seventies Britain* (Cambridge: Cambridge University Press, 2018).

102. All three newspapers quoted respectively in Saunders, *Yes to Europe*, pp. 63–5.

103. Neil Marten, the Conservative anti-marketeer who first mooted the idea of a referendum on EEC membership in the Commons in March 1972, quoted in Saunders, *Yes to Europe*, p. 72; See also Robert Saunders, 'Brexit and Empire: "Global Britain" and the Myth of Imperial Nostalgia', *Journal of Imperial and Commonwealth History*, 48:6 (2020), pp. 1140–74.

104. Lewis Holden, 'This Flag Debate Has Only Just Begun', *RNZ*, 25 March 2016, www.rnz.co.nz/news/national/299907/this-flag-debate-has-only-just-begun.

105. J. G. A. Pocock, 'The Politics of the New British history" (2001) reprinted in *Discovery of Islands*, p. 290. The reference to self-harm is from the original Christchurch lecture, Pocock, 'British History', p. 14.

106. Ramsay Cook, 'Canadian Centennial Celebrations', *International Journal*, 22:4 (Autumn 1967), pp. 659–63, 663.

107. See also J. M. S. Careless, 'Limited Identities in Canada', *Canadian Historical Review*, 50:1 (March 1969), pp. 1–10. On the origins of Limited Identities see P. A. Buckner, '"Limited Identities" Revisited: Regionalism and Nationalism in Canadian History', *Acadiensis*, 30:1 (Autumn, 2000), pp. 4–15.

108. Richard Bourke, 'Pocock and the Presuppositions of the New British History', *Historical Journal*, 53:3 (2010), pp. 747–70, 747–8.

109. See, for example, Dane Kennedy, *The Imperial History Wars: Debating the British Empire* (London: Bloomsbury, 2018).

110. Miranda Johnson, *The Land is Our History: Indigeneity, Law, and the Settler State* (Oxford: Oxford University Press, 2016), pp. 9–10.

111. See *Sunday Times*, 'Minorities Feel More British than Whites', 18 February 2007; *Evening Standard*, 'Ethnic Minorities More Likely to Feel British than White People, Says Research', 13 April 2012.

112. Paul Gilroy, *There Ain't No Black in the Union Jack* (London: Routledge, 2013, 1st ed. 1987), p. 60.

113. Interview in *The Guardian*, 'The Last Humanist', 5 August 2021.

114. See Amelia Gentleman, *The Windrush Betrayal: Exposing the Hostile Environment* (London: Faber & Faber, 2019).

115. See, especially, Michael Kenny and Nick Pearce, *Shadows of Empire: The Anglosphere in British Politics* (Cambridge: Polity Press, 2018); Andrew Mycock and Ben Wellings (eds.), *The Anglosphere: Continuity, Dissonance and Location* (Oxford: Oxford University Press, 2019). On the more generalized resurgence of white nationalism in the English-speaking world, see Daniel Geary, Camilla Schofield and Jenny Sutton (eds.), *Global White Nationalism: From Apartheid to Trump* (Manchester: Manchester University Press, 2020).

116. Adam Ramsay, 'It's Time to Break Up Britain', *Open Democracy*, 11 December 2020, www.opendemocracy.net/en/opendemocracyuk/its-time-to-break-up-britain/.

CONCLUSION

1. In the influential formulation of Ernest Gellner, *Nations and Nationalism* (Ithaca: Cornell University Press, 1983), p. 1.
2. See discussion of Buchan in Chapter 2, pp. 69–70.
3. This is borne out by word searches in various data sets, such as Google Ngram, Hansard online and *The Times* digital archive, all of which register a rapid rise from the 1870s, peaking in the two decades either side of 1900, before tapering off after the First World War.
4. C. A. Bayly, *The Birth of the Modern World, 1780–1914* (Oxford: Blackwell, 2004), p. 12.
5. Reinhart Koselleck, quoted in Jürgen Osterhammel, *The Transformation of the World: A Global History of the Nineteenth Century* (Princeton: Princeton University Press, 2014), p. 77.
6. Duncan Bell, *The Idea of Greater Britain: Empire and the Future of World Order, 1860–1900* (Princeton: Princeton University Press, 2007), p. 119.
7. Charles W. Dilke, *Greater Britain: A Record of Travel in English-Speaking Countries during 1866 and 1867* (New York: Harper and Brothers, 1869, 1st ed. 1868), p. ix.
8. Onur Ulas Ince, *Colonial Capitalism and the Dilemmas of Liberalism* (Oxford: Oxford University Press, 2018), p. 2.
9. See discussion of John Darwin's thesis in Chapter 3. p. 97.
10. M. E. Farquhar, 'Candid Comments', *Trinidad Guardian Weekly*, 27 June 1948. See discussion in Chapter 6.
11. Richard Bourke, 'Pocock and the Presuppositions of the New British History', *Historical Journal*, 53:3 (2010), p. 762. See discussion in Introduction, pp. 11–12.
12. Frank Kermode, *The Sense of an Ending: Studies in the Theory of Fiction with a New Epilogue* (Oxford: Oxford University Press, 2000, 1st ed. 1967), pp. 4, 44.
13. See the national anthem entry of Bob Ellis in James Curran and Stuart Ward, *The Unknown Nation: Australia after Empire* (Melbourne: Melbourne University Press, 2010), ch. 5 and Humphries quote on p. 226.
14. See the discussion of J. G. A. Pocock's formulation in the Introduction, pp. 11–12.
15. Kermode, *Sense of an Ending*, pp. 181–2.
16. Ian Jack, *The Country Formerly Known as Great Britain: Writings, 1989–2009* (London: Jonathan Cape, 2009), pp. xi–xii.

Select Bibliography

ARCHIVE AND MANUSCRIPT COLLECTIONS

Alexander Turnbull Library, Wellington
  Alister McIntosh Papers, MS6759
Archives New Zealand, Wellington (ANZ)
  Department of External Affairs, Rhodesia, ABHS 950, W4627 Box 4171 245/8/3
  Suez Canal, Anglo-French Interventions, EA W2619, 217/1/12
  Department of Internal Affairs, New Zealand Day, AAAC/7536, W5084
  Imperial Affairs, Prime Ministers' Conference 1949, EA1 153/27/1
  United Kingdom Immigration, ABHS 7148, W4628 65/10/9
BBC Written Archives Centre, Caversham Park, Reading
Bodleian Library, Oxford
  Sir John Pestell Papers
British Columbia Archives, Victoria
  William McBride Papers
British Library India Office Collection
  Papers of Sir Olaf Kirkpatrick Caroe, Mss Eur. F203
Churchill Archives Centre, Cambridge (CAC)
  Dingle Foot Papers
  Duncan Sandys Papers
  Fenner Brockway Papers
Cory Library, Rhodes University, Grahamstown
  Ian Douglas Smith Papers
Gibraltar Archives, Gibraltar (GA)
Hatfield House, Archives and Collections
  5th Marquess of Salisbury Papers
Historical Archives of the European Union, Florence (HAEU)
Kenyan National Archives, Nairobi (KNA)
The Killie Campbell Africana Library, University of Kwa-Zulu Natal, Durban
  Black Sash Papers
  George Heaton Nicholls Papers
Library and Archives Canada, Ottawa (LAC)
  Diaries of William Lyon Mackenzie King, MG26–J13
  Escott Reid Papers, MG31

Records of the Department of External Affairs, RG25
Records of the Privy Council Office (Cabinet Conclusions), RG2
Sir Robert Borden Fonds, MG26–H
Linen Hall Library, Belfast (LHL)
Mitchell Library, Sydney
Donald Horne Papers, MSS3525
The National Archives, Kew (NA)
Cabinet Office Records (CAB)
Colonial Office (CO)
Department of Economic Affairs, Information Division (EW4)
Dominions Office (DO)
Foreign and Commonwealth Office (FO/FCO)
Home Office (HO)
Prime Minister's Office (PREM)
Treasury (T)
National Archives of Australia, Canberra (NAA)
Cabinet Submissions, Seventh and Eighth Menzies Ministry, A5819/A5827
Decisions of Cabinet Committees, Eighth Menzies Ministry, A5827
Department of External Affairs, A1838
Department of Prime Minister and Cabinet, A1209
Miscellaneous Items, Deputy Prime Minister John McEwen, M58
National Archives of Zimbabwe, Harare (NAZ)
CID File: Murder of Petrus Johannes Andries Oberholtzer, 4 July 1964, s. 3061
National Library of Australia, Canberra (NLA)
J. G. Crawford Papers, MS4514
R. G. Menzies Papers, MS4936
National Library of Wales, Aberystwyth (NLW)
Gwynfor Evans Papers (GEP)
Plaid Cymru Papers (PCP)
Nehru Memorial Library, New Delhi (NML)
Private Papers, Jawaharlal Nehru (post-1947)
V. L. Pandit Papers
Peterhouse College, Marondela, Zimbabwe
Sir Humphrey Gibbs Archive
Public Record Office of Northern Ireland (PRONI)
Queensland State Archives, Brisbane (QSA)
The Royal Archives, Windsor (RA)
Scottish National Party Archives, National Library of Scotland (SNPA)
Arthur Donaldson Papers, Acc 6038
Robert McIntrye Papers, Acc 10090
Minutes, Correspondence of the SNP, Acc 11987
Gordon Wilson Papers, Acc 13099
United Party Archives, UNISA, Pretoria (UPA)
Sir De Villiers Graaff Papers

NEWSPAPERS

Australia:
The Advertiser
The Age
The Argus
The Australian
Australian Financial Review
Australian Women's Weekly
The Canberra Times
The Courier Mail
The Daily Mercury
The Daily Mirror
The Goulbourne Evening Post
The Melbourne Herald
The Mercury
Nation
The North Queensland Register
The Sydney Morning Herald
The Telegraph
The Townsville Daily Bulletin
The West Australian
Canada:
The Calgary Herald
The Globe and Mail
The Ottawa Journal
The Toronto Daily Star
The Vancouver Sun
England:
The Daily Express
The Daily Graphic
The Daily Mail
The Daily Mirror
The Daily Sketch
The Daily Telegraph
The Economist
Encounter
The Evening News
The Evening Standard
The Guardian
(The Manchester Guardian until 1959)
Home Chat
The Lady
The Morning Telegraph
The New Statesman
The News Chronicle
The News of the World

The Nottingham Guardian
The Observer
The Spectator
The Sun
The Sunday Express
The Sunday Telegraph
The Sunday Times
The Times
The Western Gazette
Gibraltar:
The Gibraltar Chronicle
The Gibraltar Post
Hong Kong:
The South China Morning Post
Kenya:
The Daily Nation
The East African Standard
New Zealand:
The Auckland Star
The Christchurch Star
The Dominion
The New Zealand Herald
The New Zealand Truth
The Press
The Sunday News
The Sunday Times
Northern Ireland:
The Belfast Telegraph
The Irish News
The News Letter
The Protestant Telegraph
Republic of Ireland:
The Cork Examiner
The Irish Times
Rhodesia:
The Bulawayo Chronicle
The Bulawayo Citizen
The Rhodesia Herald
The Umtali Post
Scotland:
The Daily Record and Mail
The Glasgow Herald
The Hamilton Advertiser
The Press and Journal
The Scots Independent
The Scotsman

South Africa:
The Cape Times
The Natal Mercury
The Natal Witness
The Rand Daily Mail
The Star
The Sunday Times
Wales:
The Carmarthen Times
The Welsh Nation
The Western Mail
Y Cymro
Y Ddraig Goch
The West Indies:
The Advocate-News
Barbados Advocate
The Daily Gleaner
The Sunday Advocate
The Sunday Gleaner
The Trinidad Guardian

PUBLISHED COLLECTIONS OF SOURCES

Andre, Pamela (ed.), *Australia and the Postwar World: The Commonwealth and Asia, Documents 1948–49* (Canberra: Department of Foreign Affairs and Trade, 1998).

Ashton, S. R., Carl Bridge and Stuart Ward (eds.), *Australia and the United Kingdom, 1960–1975: Documents on Australian Foreign Policy* (Canberra: Dept of Foreign Affairs and Trade, 2010).

Ashton, S. R. and David Killingray (eds.), *The West Indies: British Documents on the End of Empire*, Series B, vol. 6 (London: The Stationary Office, 1999).

Ashton, S. R. and Wm Roger Louis (eds.), *East of Suez and the Commonwealth, 1964–71*, British Documents on the End of Empire, Part 1 (London: HMSO, 2004).

Boyle, Peter G. (ed.), *The Eden–Eisenhower Correspondence* (Chapel Hill: University of North Carolina Press, 2005).

Cobb, Daniel M. (ed.), *Say We Are Nations: Documents of Politics and Protest in Indigenous America since 1887* (Chapel Hill: University of North Carolina Press, 2015).

Das, Durga (ed.), *Sardar Patel's Correspondence, 1945–50*, vol. VIII (Ahmedabad: Navajivan Press, 1973).

Goldsworthy, David (ed.), *The Conservative Government and the End of Empire, 1951–57* (London: HMSO, 1994).

Gopal, Sarvepalli (ed.), *Selected Works of Jawaharlal Nehru*, 2nd ser, vol. 2 (New Delhi: Orient Longman, 1973).

Jordan, Matthew (ed.), *Australia and the Rhodesian Problem, 1961–1972: Documents on Australian Foreign Policy* (Canberra: Dept of Foreign Affairs and Trade, 2017).

Keith, Arthur Berriedale (ed.), *Speeches and Documents of the British Dominions, 1918–1931: From Self-Government to National Sovereignty* (Oxford: Oxford University Press, 1961, 1st ed. 1932).

McIntrye, W. David and W. J. Gardner (eds.), *Speeches and Documents on New Zealand History* (Oxford: Oxford University Press, 1971).

Mackenzie, Hector (ed.), *Documents on Canadian External Relations,* vol. 15: *1949* (Ottawa: DFAIT, 1995).

Mansergh, Nicholas (ed.), *Constitutional Relations between Britain and India: The Transfer of Power,* Vols. IX, X (London: HMSO, 1970–83).

Mansergh, Nicholas (ed.), *Documents and Speeches on British Commonwealth Affairs, 1931–52,* vol. 2 (Oxford: Oxford University Press, 1953).

Nettleford, Rex M. (ed.), *Norman Washington Manley and the New Jamaica: Selected Speeches and Writings, 1938–68* (Kingston: Longman Caribbean, 1971).

van der Poel, Jean (ed.), *Selections from the Smuts Papers,* vol. VII: *August 1945–October 1950* (Cambridge: Cambridge University Press, 1973).

OFFICIAL PUBLICATIONS

Commonwealth Parliamentary Debates
Fowlers Dictionary of Modern English Usage (2nd ed., Oxford University Press, 1965).
Hansard (UK)
New Zealand Parliamentary Debates
Rhodesian Law Reports

MEMOIRS AND DIARIES

Blundell, Michael. *So Rough a Wind* (London: Weidenfeld and Nicolson, 1964).

Butler, Lord. *The Art of the Possible* (London: Gambit, 1971).

Callaghan, James. *Time and Chance* (London: Collins, 1987).

Castle, Barbara. *The Castle Diaries: 1964–70* (London: Weidenfeld and Nicolson, 1984).

Catterall, Peter (ed.), *The Macmillan Diaries,* vol. II: *Prime Minister and After* (London: Macmillan, 2011).

Clark, Manning. *The Quest for Grace* (Ringwood: Viking, 1990).

Currie, Austin. *All Hell Will Break Loose* (Dublin: O'Brien, 2004).

Devlin, Bernadette. *The Price of My Soul* (London: Pan Books, 1969).

Dupont, Clifford. *The Reluctant President* (Bulawayo: Books of Rhodesia, 1978).

Eden, Anthony. *Full Circle* (London: Cassell, 1960).

Ewing, Winifred. *Stop the World: The Autobiography of Winnie Ewing* (Edinburgh: Birlinn, 2004).

Godwin, Peter. *Mukiwa: A White Boy in Africa* (London: Picador, 1996).

Greacen, Lavinia (ed.), *J.G. Farrell, In His Own Words: Selected Letters and Diaries* (Cork: Cork University Press, 2009).

Hall, Stuart with Bill Schwarz. *Familiar Stranger: A Life between Two Islands* (Durham, NC: Duke University Press, 2017).

Hamid, Shahid. *Disastrous Twilight: A Personal Record of the Partition of India* (Barnsley: Leo Cooper, 1986).

Horne, Donald. *Into the Open: Memoirs, 1955–99* (Sydney: Harper Collins, 2000).

Howard, Anthony (ed.), *The Crossman Diaries: A Selection from the Diaries of a Cabinet Minister 1964–1970* (London: Mandarin, 1991).

Inglis, Brian. *West Briton* (London: Faber & Faber, 1962).

James, C. L. R. *Beyond a Boundary* (Durham, NC: Duke University Press, 2013, 1st ed. 1963).

Lardner-Burke, Desmond. *Rhodesia: The Story of the Crisis* (London: Olbourne, 1966).

Lyttleton, Oliver. *The Memoirs of Lord Chandos* (New York: New American Library, 1963).

McCann, Eamonn. *War and an Irish Town* (London: Pluto, 1993, 1st ed. 1974).

Macmillan, Harold. *At the End of the Day* (London: Macmillan, 1973).

Martin, A. W. and Patsy Hardy (eds.), *Dark and Hurrying Days: Menzies' 1941 Diary* (Canberra: National Library of Australia, 1993).

O'Neill, Terrence. *The Autobiography of Terrence O'Neill* (London: Rupert Hart-Davis, 1983).

Payn, Graham and Sheridan Morley (eds.), *The Noel Coward Diaries* (London: Weidenfeld and Nicolson, 1982).

Reid, Escott. *Hungary and Suez 1956: A View from New Delhi* (Oakville, Ont.: Mosaic Press, 1986).

Smith, Ian. *The Great Betrayal: The Memoirs of Ian Douglas Smith* (London: Blake, 1997).

Thomas, George. *George Thomas, Mr Speaker: The Memoirs of Viscount Tonypandy* (London: Century, 1985).

Wilson, Gordon. *SNP: The Turbulent Years, 1960–1990* (Stirling: Scots Independent, 2009).

SECONDARY SOURCES

Affeldt, Stefanie. *Consuming Whiteness: Australian Racism and the 'White Sugar' Campaign* (Berlin: Lit Verlag, 2014).

Afshari, Reza. 'On Historiography of Human Rights: Reflections on Paul Gordon Lauren's *The Evolution of International Human Rights: Vision Seen*', *Human Rights Quarterly*, 29:1 (2007), pp. 1–67.

Ahmed, Sara. 'Affective Economies', *Social Text* 79, 22:2 (Summer 2004), pp. 117–39.

Aiyar, Sana. *Indians in Kenya: The Politics of Diaspora* (Cambridge: Cambridge University Press, 2015).

Anderson, Benedict. *Imagined Communities: Reflections on the Origins and Spread of Nationalism* (London: Verso, 2006, 1st ed. 1983).

Anderson, David. *Histories of the Hanged: Britain's Dirty War in Kenya and the End of Empire* (New York: W. W. Norton, 2005).

Anderson, David. 'Mau Mau at the Movies: Contemporary Representations of an Anti-colonial War', *South African Historical Journal*, 48:1 (2003), pp. 71–89.

Anderson, Kay. *Race and the Crisis of Humanism* (London: Routledge, 2007).

Anderson, Warwick. *The Cultivation of Whiteness: Science, Health and Racial Destiny in Australia* (New York: Basic Books, 2003).

Appadurai, Arjun. 'Introduction: Commodities and the Politics of Value', in Arjun Appadurai (ed.), *The Social Life of Things: Commodities in Cultural Perspective* (Cambridge: Cambridge University Press, 1986).

Aqui, Lindsay. 'Macmillan, Nkrumah and the 1961 Application for European Economic Community Membership', *International History Review*, 39:4 (2017), pp. 575–91.

Archbold, Rick. *I Stand for Canada: The Story of the Maple Leaf Flag* (Toronto: Macfarlane, Walter and Ross, 2002).

Armitage, David. *The Ideological Origins of the British Empire* (Cambridge: Cambridge University Press, 2000).

Armitage, David. 'Literature and Empire', in Nicholas Canny (ed.), *The Oxford History of the British Empire*, vol. 1: *The Origins of Empire* (Oxford: Oxford University Press, 1998).

Atkinson, Alan. 'Conquest', in Deryck M. Schreuder and Stuart Ward (eds.), *Australia's Empire* (Oxford: Oxford University Press, 2008).

Attwood, Bain. *Possession: Batman's Treaty and the Matter of History* (Melbourne: Miegunyah, 2009).

Attwood, Bain. *Rights for Aborigines* (Sydney: Allen & Unwin, 2003).

Attwood, Bain. *William Cooper: An Aboriginal Life Story* (Melbourne: Melbourne University Press, 2021).

Attwood, Bain and Andrew Markus. *Thinking Black: William Cooper and the Australian Aborigines League* (Canberra: Aboriginal Studies Press, 2004).

Bailkin, Jordanna. *The Afterlife of Empire* (Berkeley: University of California Press, 2012).

Banks, Margaret A. *Sir John George Bourinot: Victorian Canadian* (Montreal and Kingston: McGill-Queen's University Press, 2001).

Bar-On, Mordechai. 'David Ben Gurion and the Sèvres Collusion', in Wm Roger Louis and Roger Owen (eds.), *Suez 1956: The Crisis and its Consequences* (Oxford: Oxford University Press, 1989).

Barclay, Glen St J. *Commonwealth or Europe* (St. Lucia: University of Queensland Press, 1970).

Barczewski, Stephanie. *Heroic Failure and the British* (New Haven: Yale University Press, 2016).

Barnes, Felicity. 'Bringing Another Empire Alive? The Empire Marketing Board and the Construction of Dominion Identity, 1926–33', *Journal of Imperial and Commonwealth History*, 42:1 (2014), pp. 61–85.

Barnes, Felicity. '"Familiar London": New Zealand Travel Writing and the Imagined Metropolis, 1890–1940', *Studies in Travel Writing*, 14:4 (2010), pp. 397–409.

Barnes, Felicity. *New Zealand's London: A Colony and Its Metropolis* (Auckland: Auckland University Press, 2012).

Barnes, Juliet. *The Ghosts of Happy Valley: Searching for the Lost World of Africa's Infamous Aristocrats* (London: Aurum Press, 2013).

Barnett, Anthony. 'Iron Britannia', *New Left Review*, 1:134 (1982), pp. 19–20.

Bartlett, Thomas. *Ireland: A History* (Cambridge: Cambridge University Press, 2010).

Bashford, Alison. *Global Population: History, Geopolitics and Life on Earth* (New York: Columbia University Press, 2014).

Bateman, Anthony. *Cricket, Literature and Culture: Symbolising the Nation, Destabilising Empire* (London: Routledge, 2009).

Baxter, Beverley. 'The Passing of Bonar Law', *McLean's Magazine*, July 1921.

Bayly, C. A. *The Birth of the Modern World, 1780–1914* (Oxford: Blackwell, 2004).

Bayly, C. A. *Imperial Meridian: The British Empire and the World, 1780–1830* (London: Longman, 1989).

Bayly, Christopher and Tim Harper. *Forgotten Armies: Britain's Asian Empire & the War with Japan* (London: Penguin, 2005).

Beaglehole, J. C. 'The Development of New Zealand Nationality', *Journal of World History*, 2 (1954), pp. 106–23.

Behiels, Michael D. *Prelude to Quebec's Quiet Revolution: Liberalism Versus Neo-Nationalism, 1945–1960* (Kingston, Ont.: McGill-Queen's University Press, 1985).

Belgrave, Michael. '"We Rejoice to Honour the Queen, for She is a Good Woman, Who Cares for the Maori Race": Loyalty and Protest in Maori Politics in Nineteenth-Century New Zealand', in Sarah Carter and Maria Nugent (eds.), *Mistress of Everything: Queen Victoria in Indigenous Worlds* (Manchester: Manchester University Press, 2016).

Belich, James. 'How Much Did Institutions Matter? Cloning Britain in New Zealand', in Jack P. Greene (ed.), *Exclusionary Empire: English Liberties Overseas, 1600–1900* (Cambridge: Cambridge University Press, 2010).

Belich, James. *Paradise Reforged: A History of the New Zealanders from the 1880s to the Year 2000* (Auckland: Penguin, 2001).

Belich, James. *Replenishing the Earth: The Settler Revolution and the Rise of the Anglo-World, 1783–1939* (Oxford: Oxford University Press, 2009).

Bell, Duncan. *Dreamworlds of Race: Empire and the Utopian Destiny of Anglo-America* (Princeton: Princeton University Press, 2021).

Bell, Duncan. *The Idea of Greater Britain: Empire and the Future of World Order, 1860–1900* (Princeton: Princeton University Press, 2007).

Bell, Duncan. *Reordering the World: Essays on Liberalism and Empire* (Princeton: Princeton University Press, 2016).

Bell, Roger. *In Apartheid's Shadow: Australian Race Politics and South Africa, 1945–75* (Melbourne: Australian Scholarly Publishing, 2019).

Beloff, Max. 'Empire Reconsidered', *Journal of Imperial and Commonwealth History*, 27:2 (May 1999), pp. 13–26.

Beloff, Max. *Imperial Sunset,* vol. 1: *Britain's Liberal Empire, 1897–1921* (London: Methuen, 1969).

Bennett, Bridget and Hamilton Carroll. 'Imagining the Place of Home: Research Review', Arts and Humanities Research Council Report, 2014, http://www.leeds .ac.uk/arts/info/125130/imagining_the_place_of_home

Bennett, George and Alison Smith. 'Kenya from White Man's Country to Kenyatta's State, 1945–63', in D. A. Low and Alison Smith (eds.), *History of East Africa*, vol. 3 (Oxford: Clarendon Press, 1976).

Bennett, Tony and Janet Woollacott. *Bond and Beyond: The Political Career of a Popular Hero* (London: Routledge, 1987).

Benton, Lauren. *Law and Colonial Cultures: Legal Regimes in World History, 1400–1900* (Cambridge: Cambridge University Press, 2002).

Benvenuti, Andrea and Stuart Ward. 'Britain, Europe and the "Other Quiet Revolution" in Canada', in Phillip Buckner (ed.), *Canada and the End of Empire* (Vancouver: UBC Press, 2005).

Bhebe, Ngwabi and Terrence Ranger (eds.), *Soldiers in Zimbabwe's Liberation War* (London: James Currey, 1995).

Bickers, Robert. 'Cut Loose: The British in China and the Aftermath of Empire', in Christian D. Pedersen and Stuart Ward (eds.), *The Break-Up of Greater Britain* (Manchester: Manchester University Press, 2021).

Bidnall, Amanda M. 'West Indian Interventions at the Heart of the Cultural Establishment: Edric Connor, Pearl Connor, and the BBC', *Twentieth Century British History*, 24:1 (2013), pp. 58–83.

Biffen, John. *A Nation in Doubt* (London: Conservative Political Centre, 1976).

Blaazer, David. '"Devalued and Dejected Britons": The Pound in Public Discourse in the Mid 1960s', *History Workshop Journal*, 47 (Spring, 1999), pp. 121–40.

Black, Lawrence. *Redefining British Politics: Culture, Consumerism and Participation, 1954–70* (London: Palgrave, 2010).

Blackburn, Robin. 'Reclaiming Human Rights', *New Left Review*, 69 (May–June 2011), pp. 126–38.

Blake, Raymond B. 'From Dominion Day to Canada Day, 1946–82: History, Heritage and National Identity', *Asian Journal of Canadian Studies*, 17:2 (2001), pp. 1–32.

Blake, Robert. *The Unknown Prime Minister: The Life and Times of Andrew Bonar Law, 1858–1923* (London: Eyre & Spottiswoode, 1955).

Bleich, Erik. *Race Politics in Britain and France: Ideas and Policymaking since the 1960s* (Cambridge: Cambridge University Press, 2003).

Blunt, Alison. *Domicile and Diaspora: Anglo-Indian Women and the Spatial Politics of Home* (Oxford: Blackwell, 2005).

Blunt, Alison. 'Imperial Geographies of Home: British Domesticity in India', *Transactions of the Institute of British Geographers*, New Series, 24:4 (1999), pp. 421–40.

Blunt, Alison and Robyn M. Dowling. *Home* (New York: Routledge, 2006).

Boddice, Rob. *The History of Emotions* (Manchester: Manchester University Press, 2018).

Boehmer, Elleke. *Indian Arrivals: 1870–1915* (Oxford: Oxford University Press, 2015).

Bond, John. *They Were South Africans* (Cape Town: Oxford University Press, 1956).

Bongiorno, Frank. '"British to the Bootstraps? H. V. Evatt, J. B. Chifley and the Australian Policy on Indian Membership of the Commonwealth, 1947–49', *Australian Historical Studies*, 36:125 (2005), pp. 18–39.

Bongiorno, Frank. 'The New Progressivism: Anthony Crosland and the Coming of the Australian Sixties', in Shirleene Robinson and Julie Ustinoff (eds.), *The 1960s in Australia: People, Power and Politics* (Newcastle-upon-Tyne: Cambridge Scholars Publishing, 2012).

Booker, Christopher. *The Neophiliacs: The Revolution in English Life in the Fifties and Sixties* (London: Pimlico, 1969).

Borgwardt, Elizabeth. *A New Deal for the World: America's Vision for Human Rights* (Cambridge, MA: Harvard University Press, 2005).

Bourke, Richard. 'Languages of Conflict and the Northern Ireland Troubles', *Journal of Modern History*, 83 (September 2011), pp. 544–78.

Bourke, Richard. *Peace in Ireland: The War of Ideas* (London: Pimlico, 2012, 1st ed. 2003).

Bourke, Richard. 'Pocock and the Presuppositions of the New British History', *Historical Journal*, 53:3 (2010), pp. 747–70.

Bowie, Karin. *Public Opinion in Early Modern Scotland c. 1560–1707* (Cambridge: Cambridge University Press, 2020).

Branch, Daniel. *Defeating Mau Mau, Creating Kenya: Counterinsurgency, Civil War and Decolonization* (Cambridge: Cambridge University Press, 2009).

Brockliss, Laurence and David Eastwood (eds.), *A Union of Multiple Identities: The British Isles, c. 1750–1850* (Manchester: Manchester University Press, 1997).

Breen, T. H. '"Baubles of Britain": The American and Consumer Revolutions of the Eighteenth Century', *Past and Present*, 119 (May 1988), pp. 73–104.

Breen, T. H. 'An Empire of Goods: The Anglicization of Colonial America, 1690–1776', *Journal of British Studies*, 25:4 (October 1986), pp. 467–99.

Breen, T. H. 'Ideology and Nationalism on the Eve of the American Revolution: Revisions Once More in Need of Revising', *Journal of American History*, 84:1 (June 1997), pp. 13–39.

Brewer, John. *The Sinews of Power: War, Money and the English State 1688–1783* (London: Unwin Hyman, 1989).

Bridge, Carl. *Holding India to the Empire: The British Conservative Party and the 1935 Constitution* (New York: Envoy Press, 1986).

Bridge, Carl and Kent Fedorowich (eds.), *The British World: Diaspora, Culture and Identity* (London: Cass, 2003).

Bright, Rachel K. and Andrew R. Dilley, 'After the British World', *The Historical Journal*, 60:2 (2017) pp. 547–68.

Brivati, Brian. *Hugh Gaitskell* (London: Methuen, 2006).

Brooke, Peter. *Duncan Sandys and the Informal Politics of Britain's Late Decolonisation* (London: Palgrave, 2018).

Brown, Judith. *Global South Asians: Introducing the Modern Diaspora* (Cambridge: Cambridge University Press, 2006).

Brownell, Josiah. '"A Sordid Tussle on the Strand": Rhodesia House during the UDI Rebellion, 1965–80', *Journal of Imperial and Commonwealth History*, 38:3 (2010), pp. 471–99.

Bruce, Steve. *God Save Ulster! The Religion and Politics of Paisleyism* (Oxford: Oxford University Press, 1986).

Buckner, Philip A. '"Limited Identities" Revisited: Regionalism and Nationalism in Canadian History', *Acadiensis*, 30:1 (Autumn, 2000), pp. 4–15.

Buckner, Phillip A. 'The Long Goodbye: English Canadians and the British World', in Phillip A. Buckner and R. Douglas Francis (eds.), *Rediscovering the British World* (Calgary: University of Calgary Press, 2005).

Buckner, Phillip A. *The Transition to Responsible Government: British Policy in British North America, 1815–1850* (Westport: Greenwood Press, 1985).

Buckner, Phillip A. and R. Douglas Francis (eds.), *Rediscovering the British World* (Calgary: University of Calgary Press, 2005).

Buettner, Elizabeth. 'Cemeteries, Public Memory and Raj Nostalgia in Postcolonial Britain and India', *History and Memory*, 18:1 (Spring/Summer 2006), pp. 5–42.

Buettner, Elizabeth. *Empire Families: Britons and Late Imperial India* (Oxford: Oxford University Press, 2004).

Buettner, Elizabeth. *Europe after Empire: Decolonization. Society and Culture* (Cambridge: Cambridge University Press, 2016).

Buettner, Elizabeth. '"This is Staffordshire not Alabama": Racial Geographies of Commonwealth Immigration in Early 1960s Britain', *Journal of Imperial and Commonwealth History*, 42:2 (2014), pp. 710–40.

Burke, Edward. 'Counter-Insurgency against "Kith and Kin"? The British Army in Northern Ireland, 1970–76', *The Journal of Imperial and Commonwealth History*, 43:4 (2015), pp. 658–77.

Burke, Roland. *Decolonization and the Evolution of International Human Rights* (Philadelphia: University of Pennsylvania Press, 2010).

Burnard, Trevor. 'Harvest Years? Reconfigurations of Empire in Jamaica, 1756–1807', *Journal of Imperial and Commonwealth History*, 40:4 (2012), pp. 533–55.

Burton, Antoinette. *At the Heart of the Empire: Indians and the Colonial Encounter in Late-Victorian Britain* (Berkeley: University of California Press, 1999).

Burton, Antoinette. *Empire in Question: Reading, Writing and Teaching British Imperialism* (Durham, NC: Duke University Press, 2011).

Butler, L. J. and Sarah Stockwell (eds.), *The Wind of Change: Harold Macmillan and British Decolonization* (Basingstoke: Palgrave, 2013).

Butt Philip, Alan. *The Welsh Question: Nationalism in Welsh Politics, 1945–70* (Cardiff: University of Wales Press, 1975).

Byrnes, Giselle. 'Introduction: Reframing New Zealand History', in Giselle Byrnes (ed.), *The New Oxford History of New Zealand* (Melbourne: Oxford University Press, 2009).

Cain, P. J. and A. G. Hopkins, *British Imperialism: Crisis and Deconstruction* (London: Longman, 1993).

Cairncross, Alec and Barry Eichengreen, *Sterling in Decline: The Devaluations of 1931, 1949 and 1967* (Oxford: Basil Blackwell, 1983).

Callinicos, Luli. *Oliver Tambo: Beyond the Engeli Mountains* (Claremont: David Philip, 2004).

Calvocoressi, Peter. *The British Experience, 1945–75* (London: Bodley Head, 1978).

Camps, Miriam. *Britain and the European Community* (Princeton: Princeton University Press, 1964).

Cannadine, David. *Class in Britain* (London: Penguin, 2000).

Canny, Nicholas. *Making Ireland British, 1580–1650* (Oxford: Oxford University Press, 2001).

Careless, J. M. S. 'Limited Identities in Canada', *Canadian Historical Review*, 50:1 (March 1969), pp. 1–10.

Carlton, David. *Britain and the Suez Crisis* (Oxford: Blackwell, 1988).

Carothers, J. C. *The Psychology of Mau Mau* (Nairobi: Government Printer, 1954).

Carpenter, Humphrey. *That Was Satire That Was* (London: Victor Gollancz, 2001).

Carruthers, Susan. *Winning Hearts and Minds: British Governments, the Media and Colonial Counter-Insurgency, 1944–60* (London: Leicester University Press, 1995).

Carter, Sarah and Maria Nugent (eds.), *Mistress of Everything: Queen Victoria in Indigenous Worlds* (Manchester: Manchester University Press, 2016).

Caterall, Peter. '"Efficiency with Freedom"? Debates about the British Constitution in the Twentieth Century', in Peter Caterall, Wolfram Kaiser and Ulrike Walton-Jordan (eds.), *Reforming the Constitution: Debates in Twentieth-Century Britain* (London: Cass, 2000).

Cauvet, Philippe. 'A Democratic Critique of Referendums in France and in the United Kingdom: Convergence or Divergence?', in Géraldine Gadbin-George and Elizabeth Gibson-Morgan (eds.), *UK and France: Friends or Foes? (Trans) cultural and Legal Unions and Disunions* (Paris: Editions Le Manuscrit, 2019).

Chamberlain, Mary. *Empire and Nation-Building in the Caribbean: Barbados, 1937–66* (Manchester: Manchester University Press, 2010).

Champion, C. P. *The Strange Demise of British Canada: The Liberals and Canadian Nationalism, 1964–68* (Montreal and Kingston: McGill-Queen's University Press, 2010).

Chappell, Stephen. 'Air Power in the Mau Mau Conflict: The Government's Chief Weapon', *Rusi Journal*, 156:1 (2011), pp. 64–70.

Charlton, Michael. *The Price of Victory* (London: BBC, 1983).

Chester, Lucy P. *Borders and Conflict in South Asia: The Radcliffe Boundary Commission and the Partition of the Punjab* (Manchester: Manchester University Press, 2009).

Chisholm, Anne and Michael Davie. *Beaverbrook: A Life* (London: Pimlico, 1993).

Clausen, Mads. 'Donald Horne Finds Asia', in Agnieszka Sobocinska and David Walker (eds.), *Australia's Asia: From Yellow Peril to Asian Century* (Perth: UWA Publishing, 2012).

Clayton, Pamela. *Enemies and Passing Friends: Settler Ideologies in Twentieth Century Ulster* (London: Pluto Press, 1996).

Clendinning, Anne. 'Exhibiting a Nation: Canada at the British Empire Exhibition, 1924–1925', *Social History*, 39:77 (2006), pp. 79–107.

Clews, Roy. *To Dream of Freedom: The Story of the MAC and the Free Wales Army* (Talybont: Y Lolfa Cyf, 2001).

Cochrane, Peter. *Colonial Ambition: Foundations of Australian Democracy* (Melbourne: Melbourne University Press, 2006).

Coggins, Richard. 'Wilson and British Policy Towards Rhodesia', *Contemporary British History*, 20:3 (2006), pp. 363–81.

Cole, Douglas. '"The Crimson Thread of Kinship": Ethnic Ideas in Australia, 1870–1914', *Historical Studies*, 14:56 (April 1971), pp. 511–25.

Cole, Douglas. 'The Problem of "Nationalism" and "Imperialism" in British Settlement Colonies', *Journal of British Studies*, 10:2 (May 1971), pp. 160–82.

Colley, Linda. *Acts of Union and Disunion: What Has Held the UK Together – and What is Dividing It?* (London: Profile Books, 2014).

Colley, Linda. 'Britishness and Otherness: An Argument', *Journal of British Studies*, 31:4 (October 1992), pp. 309–29.

Colley, Linda. *Britons: Forging the Nation, 1707–1837* (London: Vintage, 1996, 1st ed. 1992).

Colley, Linda. *Captives: Britain, Empire and the World, 1600–1850* (London: Jonathan Cape, 2002).

Colquhoun, Archibald R. 'The Proposed British Zollverein', *North American Review*, 177: 561 (August 1903), pp. 172–182.

Conrad, Sebastian. *What is Global History?* (Princeton: Princeton University Press, 2016).

Constantine, Learie. *Colour Bar* (London: Stanley Paul, 1954).

Constantine, Stephen. '"Bringing the Empire Alive": The Empire Marketing Board and Imperial Propaganda', in John M. MacKenzie (ed.), *Imperialism and Popular Culture* (Manchester: Manchester University Press, 1986).

Constantine, Stephen. *Buy and Build: The Advertising Posters of the Empire Marketing Board* (London: Public Record Office, 1986).

Conway, Stephen. 'From Fellow-Nationals to Foreigners: British Perceptions of the Americans, circa 1739–1783', *The William and Mary Quarterly*, 59:1 (January 2002), pp. 65–100.

Cook, Ramsay. 'Canadian Centennial Celebrations', *International Journal*, 22:4 (Autumn 1967), pp. 659–63.

Cooper, Frederick. 'Afterword: Social Rights and Human Rights in the Time of Decolonization', *Humanity: An International Journal of Human Rights, Humanitarianism, and Development*, 3:3 (Winter 2012), pp. 473–92.

Cooper, Frederick. *Citizenship between Empire and Nation: Remaking France and French Africa, 1945–1960* (Princeton: Princeton University Press, 2014).

Cooper, Frederick. 'Reconstructing Empire in British and French Africa', *Past and Present*, 210 (2011) supplement 6, pp. 196–210.

Coops, Lorraine. '"One Flag, One Throne, One Empire": The IODE, the Great Flag Debate, and the End of Empire', in Phillip Buckner (ed.), *Canada and the End of Empire* (Vancouver: UBC Press, 2005).

Crosbie, Barry and Mark Hampton (eds.), *The Cultural Construction of the British World* (Manchester: Manchester University Press, 2015).

Csikszentmihalyi, Mihaly and Eugene Rochberg-Halton, *The Meaning of Things: Domestic Symbols and the Self* (Cambridge: Cambridge University Press, 1981).

Curran, James. *Curtin's Empire* (Cambridge: Cambridge University Press, 2011).

Curran, James. *The Power of Speech* (Melbourne: Melbourne University Press, 2004).

Curran, James and Stuart Ward, *The Unknown Nation: Australia After Empire* (Melbourne: Melbourne University Publishing, 2010).

Daly, Mary E. and Margaret O'Callaghan (eds.), *1916 in 1966: Commemorating the Easter Rising* (Dublin: Royal Irish Academy, 2007).

Dalyell, Tam. *Devolution: The End of Britain?* (London: Jonathan Cape, 1977).

Dalyell, Tam. *The Question of Scotland: Devolution and After* (Edinburgh: Birlinn, 2016).

Darby, Phillip. *British Defence Policy East of Suez* (London: Oxford University Press, 1973).

Darian-Smith, Kate, Stuart Macintyre and Patricia Grimshaw (eds.), *Britishness Abroad: Transnational Movements and Imperial Cultures* (Melbourne: Melbourne University Press, 2007).

Darwin, John. *After Tamerlane: The Global History of Empire* (London: Allen Lane, 2007).

Darwin, John. *Britain and Decolonisation: The Retreat from Empire in the Post-War World* (London: Macmillan, 1988).

Darwin, John. 'Decolonization and the End of Empire', in Robin Winks (ed.), *The Oxford History of the British Empire*, vol. V: *Historiography* (Oxford: Oxford University Press, 1999).

Darwin, John. *The Empire Project: The Rise and Fall of the British World-System, 1830–1970* (Cambridge: Cambridge University Press, 2009).

Darwin, John. *The End of the British Empire: The Historical Debate* (Oxford: Basil Blackwell, 1991).

Darwin, John. 'Fear of Falling: British Politics and Imperial Decline since 1900', *Transactions of the Royal Historical Society*, 36 (1986), pp. 27–43.

Darwin, John. *Unlocking the World: Port Cities and Globalization in the Age of Steam, 1830–1930* (London: Allen Lane, 2020).

Daunton, Martin and Rick Halpern (eds.), *Empire and Others: British Encounters with Indigenous Peoples, 1600–1850* (Philadelphia: University of Pennsylvania Press, 1999).

Davidson, Jim. 'The De-Dominionisation of Australia', *Meanjin*, 38 (1979), pp. 139–53.

Davidson, Jim. 'De-Dominionisation Revisited', *Australian Journal of Politics and History*, 51 (2005), pp. 108–13.

Davidson, Jim. *A Three-Cornered Life: The Historian, W. K. Hancock* (Sydney: UNSW Press, 2010).

Davie, George. *The Democratic Intellect* (Edinburgh: Edinburgh University Press, 2013, 1st ed. 1961).

Davies, John. *A History of Wales* (London: Penguin, 2007).

Davies, Norman. *The Isles: A History* (London: Macmillan, 1999).

Davis, N. Darnell. 'Mr. Froude's Negrophobia: or Don Quixote as Cook's Tourist', *Timehri: Journal of the Royal Agricultural and Commercial Society of British Guiana* 2, new series (1888), pp. 85–129.

de Costa, Ravi. 'Identity, Authority, and the Moral Worlds of Indigenous Petitions', *Comparative Studies in Society and History*, 48:3 (July 2006), pp. 669–98.

de Paor, Liam. *Divided Ulster* (Harmondsworth: Penguin, 1970).

Dedering, Tilman. 'Petitioning Geneva: Transnational Aspects of Protest and Resistance in South West Africa/Namibia after the First World War', *Journal of Southern African Studies*, 35:4 (December 2009), pp. 785–801.

Devine, T. M. 'The Break-Up of Britain? Scotland and the End of Empire', *Transactions of the Royal Historical Society*, 16 (2006), pp. 163–80.

Devine, T. M. 'The Challenge of Nationalism', in T. M. Devine (ed.), *Scotland and the Union, 1707–2007* (Edinburgh: Edinburgh University Press, 2008).

Devine, T. M. *To the Ends of the Earth: Scotland's Global Diaspora, 1750–2010* (London: Allen Lane, 2011).

Devine, T. M. *Independence or Union: Scotland's Past and Scotland's Present* (London: Allen Lane, 2016).

Dewar, Kenneth C. *Frank Underhill and the Politics of Ideas* (Montreal and Kingston: McGill-Queen's University Press, 2015).

Dewey, Robert Frank. *British National Identity and Opposition to Membership of Europe, 1961–63: The Anti-Marketeers* (Manchester: Manchester University Press, 2009).

Dhamoon, Rita Kaur, Davina Bhandar, Renisa Mawani and Satwinder Kaur Bains (eds.), *Unmooring the Komagata Maru: Charting Colonial Trajectories* (Vancouver: UBC Press, 2019).

Dilke, Charles W. *Greater Britain: A Record of Travel in English-Speaking Countries during 1866 and 1867* (New York: Harper and Brothers, 1869, 1st ed. 1868).

Dilke, Charles. *Problems of Greater Britain*, vol. I (London: Macmillan, 1890).

Dilley, Andrew. 'A Tale of Two Commonwealths? The (British) Commonwealth of Nations, Decolonisation and the Break-Up of Greater Britain', in Christian D. Pedersen and Stuart Ward (eds.), *The Break-Up of Greater Britain* (Manchester: Manchester University Press, 2021).

Dilley, Andrew. 'Un-Imagining Markets: Chambers of Commerce, Globalisation and the Political Economy of the Commonwealth of Nations, 1945–1975', in

David Thackeray, Andrew Thompson and Richard Toye (eds.), *Imagining Britain's Economic Future, c.1800–1975: Trade, Consumerism, and Global Markets* (London: Palgrave, 2018).

Dockrill, Saki. *Britain's Retreat from East of Suez: The Choice between Europe and the World?* (London: Palgrave Macmillan, 2002).

Dodds, Klaus. *Pink Ice: Britain and the South Atlantic Empire* (London: I. B. Tauris, 2002).

Dooley, Brian. *Black and Green: The Fight for Civil Rights in Northern Ireland and Black America* (London: Pluto, 1998).

Drayton, Michael. 'To the Virginian Voyage', in *Poems of Michael Drayton: Edited with an Introduction by John Buxton*, vol. 1 (Cambridge, MA: Harvard University Press, 1953).

Dubow, Saul. *Apartheid, 1948–1994* (Oxford: Oxford University Press, 2014).

Dubow, Saul. 'The Commonwealth and South Africa: From Smuts to Mandela', *Journal of Imperial and Commonwealth History*, 45:2 (2017), pp. 284–314.

Dubow, Saul. 'How British Was the British World? The Case of South Africa', *Journal of Imperial and Commonwealth History*, 37:1 (2009), pp. 1–27.

Dubow, Saul. 'Smuts, the United Nations and the Rhetoric of Race and Rights', *Journal of Contemporary History*, 43:1 (2008), pp. 45–74.

Dubow, Saul. 'South Africa and South Africans: Nationality, Belonging, Citizenship', in Robert Ross, Anne Kelk Mager and Bill Nasson (eds.), *The Cambridge History of South Africa*, vol. 2: *1885–1994* (Cambridge: Cambridge University Press, 2012).

Dubow, Saul. *South Africa's Struggle for Human Rights* (Athens: Ohio University Press, 2012).

Dubow, Saul. 'Were There Political Alternatives in the Wake of Sharpeville-Langa Violence in South Africa, 1960?', *Journal of African History*, 56:1 (2015), pp. 119–42.

Dummett, Ann and Andrew Nicol, *Subjects, Citizens, Aliens and Others. Nationality and Immigration Law* (London: Weidenfeld and Nicolson, 1990).

Dunn, J. S. *The Crowe Memorandum* (Newcastle upon Tyne: Cambridge Scholars, 2013).

Dutt, R. Palme. *Britain's Crisis of Empire* (London: Lawrence and Wishart, 1950).

Dutton, Geoffrey. *A Rare Bird: Penguin Books in Australia, 1946–96* (Ringwood: Penguin, 1996).

Dutton, Geoffrey (ed.), *Australia and the Monarchy: A Symposium* (Melbourne: Sun Books, 1966).

Eagleton, Terry. 'Afterword: Ireland and Colonialism', in Terrence McDonough (ed.), *Was Ireland a Colony: Economics, Politics and Culture in Nineteenth-Century Ireland* (Dublin: Irish Academic Press, 2005).

Easton, Brian. *In Stormy Seas: The Post-War New Zealand Economy* (Dunedin: University of Otago Press, 1997).

Eayrs, James. *The Commonwealth and Suez: A Documentary Survey* (London: Oxford University Press, 1964)

Eckel, Jan and Samuel Moyn (eds.), *The Breakthrough: Human Rights in the 1970s* (Philadelphia: University of Pennsylvania Press, 2015).

Edgerton, David. *The Rise and Fall of the British Nation: A Twentieth Century History* (London: Allen Lane, 2018).

Edgerton, David. *Science, Technology and British Industrial 'Decline', 1870–1970* (Cambridge: Cambridge University Press, 1996).

Edgerton, David. *Warfare State: Britain, 1920–70* (Cambridge: Cambridge University Press, 2006).

Egan, Bowes and Vincent McCormack. *Burntollet* (London: LRS Publishers, 1969).

Einzig, Paul. *Decline and Fall? Britain's Crisis in the Sixties* (London: Macmillan, 1969).

Elkins, Caroline. *Britain's Gulag: The Brutal End of Empire in Kenya* (London: Pimlico, 2005).

Elkins, Caroline. *Legacy of Violence: A History of the British Empire* (New York: Knopf, 2022).

Ellert, H. *The Rhodesian Front War: Counter-Insurgency and Guerrilla War in Rhodesia, 1962–80* (Gweru: Mambo Press, 1993).

Ellis, John S. *Investiture: Royal Ceremony and National Identity in Wales, 1911–69* (Cardiff: University of Wales Press, 2008).

Ellison, James. *Threatening Europe: Britain and the Creation of the European Community, 1955–1958* (Basingstoke: Macmillan, 2000).

England, Steve. *Magnificent Mercury: The First 125 Years of the Leicester Mercury* (Leicester: Kairos Press, 1999).

English, Richard. *Irish Freedom: The History of Nationalism in Ireland* (London: Macmillan, 2006).

Epstein, Leon D. *British Politics in the Suez Crisis* (London: Pall Mall Press, 1964).

Esler, Gavin. *How Britain Ends: English Nationalism and the Rebirth of Four Nations* (London: Head of Zeus, 2021).

Evans, Rhys. *Gwynfor Evans: Portrait of a Patriot* (Talybont: Y Lolfa Cyf, 2008).

Facchini, Manuele. 'The "Evil Genius": Sir Hugh Beadle and the Rhodesian Crisis, 1965–1972', *Journal of Southern African Studies*, 33:3 (September 2007), pp. 673–89.

Fairlie, Henry. 'On the Comforts of Anger', in Arthur Koestler (ed.), *Suicide of a Nation?* (London: Hutchinson, 1963).

Fanning, Ronan. *Fatal Path: British Government and Irish Revolution, 1910–22* (London: Faber & Faber, 2013).

Farrell, J. G. *Troubles* (London: Phoenix, 1993).

Fedorowich, Kent and Andrew S. Thompson (eds.), *Empire, Migration and Identity in the British World* (Manchester: Manchester University Press, 2013).

Finlay, Richard. 'For or against? Scottish Nationalists and the British Empire, 1919–1939', *Scottish Historical Review*, 71 (1992), pp. 184–206.

Fitzgibbon, Constantine. *Out of the Lion's Paw: Ireland Wins Her Freedom* (London: Macdonald, 1969).

Fitzmaurice, Andrew. *Humanism and America* (Cambridge: Cambridge University Press, 2003).

Fleming, Ian. *Casino Royale* (London: Jonathan Cape, 1953).

Flowerdew, John. *The Final Years of British Hong Kong: The Discourse of Colonial Withdrawal* (Basingstoke: Macmillan, 1998).

Foot, Paul. *The Rise of Enoch Powell* (Harmondsworth: Penguin, 1969).

Fowles, John. 'On Being English but Not British', *The Texas Quarterly*, 2:3 (Autumn 1964), pp. 154–70.

Frances, Martin. 'Tears, Tantrums and Bared Teeth: The Emotional Economy of Three Conservative Prime Ministers, 1951–63', *Journal of British Studies*, 41 (July 2002), pp. 354–87.

Francis, R. Douglas. 'Historical Perspectives on Britain: The Ideas of Canadian Historians Frank H. Underhill and Arthur R. M. Lower', in Philip P. Buckner and R. Douglas Francis (eds.), *Canada and the British World: Culture, Migration and Identity* (Vancouver: UBC Press, 2006).

Frankel, Philip. *An Ordinary Atrocity: Sharpeville and Its Massacre* (New Haven: Yale University Press, 2001).

Froude, James Anthony. *The English in the West Indies* (London: Longmans, Green, and Co., 1888).

Fryer, Peter. *Staying Power: The History of Black People in Britain* (London: Pluto, 1984).

Gamble, Andrew. 'A Union of Historic Compromise', in Mark Perryman (ed.), *Imagined Nation: England after Britain* (London: Lawrence and Wishart, 2008).

Gaskill, Malcolm. *Between Two Worlds: How the English Became Americans* (Oxford: Oxford University Press, 2014).

Geary, Daniel. 'From Belfast to Bob Jones: Ian Paisley, Protestant Fundamentalism, and the Transatlantic Right', in Daniel Geary, Camilla Schofield and Jennifer Sutton (eds.), *Global White Nationalism: From Apartheid to Trump* (Manchester: Manchester University Press, 2020).

Gellner, Ernest. *Nations and Nationalism* (Ithaca: Cornell University Press, 1983).

Gemmell, Jon. *The Politics of South African Cricket* (London: Routledge, 2004).

Gentleman, Amelia. *The Windrush Betrayal: Exposing the Hostile Environment* (London: Faber & Faber, 2019).

Geoghegan, Patrick M. *Liberator Daniel O'Connell: The Life and Death of Daniel O'Connell, 1830–1847* (Dublin: Gill and Macmillan, 2010).

Getachew, Adom. 'A Great Wall to Batter Down', *London Review of Books*, 22:10 (21 May 2020).

Getachew, Adom. *Worldmaking after Empire: The Rise and Fall of Self-Determination* (Princeton: Princeton University Press, 2019).

Gibbs, James. 'Uhuru na Kenyatta: White Settlers and the Symbolism of Kenya's Independence Day Events', *Journal of Imperial and Commonwealth History*, 42:3 (2014), pp. 503–29.

Gilroy, Paul. *There Ain't No Black in the Union Jack* (London: Routledge, 2013, 1st ed. 1987).

Girwar, S. Norman. 'The Future of Commonwealth Sugar in an Enlarged EEC', presented to the Eleventh AGM of the Caribbean Cane Farmers' Association, Kingston, Jamaica, 28 August 1972.

Godwin, Peter and Ian Hancock. *Rhodesians Never Die: The Impact of War and Political Change on White Rhodesia, 1970–1980* (Oxford: Oxford University Press, 1993).

Goldsworthy, David. *Colonial Issues in British Politics, 1945–61: From 'Colonial Development' to 'Wind of Change'* (Oxford: Oxford University Press, 1971).

Goldsworthy, David. 'Keeping Change within the Bounds: Aspects of Colonial Policy during the Churchill and Eden Governments, 1951–57', *Journal of Imperial and Commonwealth History*, 18:1 (1990), pp. 81–108.

Good, Robert C. *UDI: The International Politics of the Rhodesian Rebellion* (London: Faber, 1973).

Goodall, Heather. *Invasion to Embassy: Land in Aboriginal Politics in New South Wales, 1770–1922* (Sydney: Sydney University Press, 2008, 1st ed. 1996).

Goodman, Sam. *British Spy Fiction and the End of Empire* (London: Routledge, 2016).

Gopal, Priyamvada. *Insurgent Empire: Anticolonial Resistance and British Dissent* (London: Verso, 2019).

Gopal, Ram. *The Trials of Jawaharlal Nehru* (Bombay: The Book Centre, 1962).

Gopal, Saravelli. 'Churchill and India', in Robert Blake and Wm Roger Louis (eds.), *Churchill* (Oxford: Oxford University Press, 1993).

Gopal, Sarvepalli. 'India, the Crisis and the Non-Aligned Nations', in Wm Roger Louis and Roger Owen (eds.), *Suez 1956: The Crisis and its Consequences* (Oxford: Oxford University Press, 1989).

Gopal, Sarvepalli. *Jawaharlal Nehru: A Biography,* vol. 1: *1989–1947* (London: Jonathan Cape, 1975).

Gorman, Daniel. *The Emergence of International Society in the 1920s* (Cambridge: Cambridge University Press, 2012).

Gorman, Daniel. *Imperial Citizenship: Empire and the Question of Belonging* (Manchester: Manchester University Press, 2006).

Gosnell, R. E. 'A Greater Britain on the Pacific', *Westward Ho! Magazine*, 2:1 (January 1908), pp. 7–12.

Gottlieb, Evan. *Feeling British: Sympathy and National Identity in Scottish and English Writing, 1707–1832* (Lewisburg: Bucknell University Press, 2007).

Goulbourne, Harry. *Ethnicity and Nationalism in Post-War Britain* (Cambridge: Cambridge University Press, 1991).

Gould, Eliga H. *The Persistence of Empire: British Political Culture in the Age of the American Revolution* (Chapel Hill: University of North Carolina Press, 2000).

Gould, Eliga H. 'A Virtual Nation: Greater Britain and the Imperial Legacy of the American Revolution', *American Historical Review*, 104:2 (April 1999), pp. 476–89.

Granatstein, J. L. *Canada, 1957–67: The Years of Uncertainty and Innovation* (Toronto: McClelland and Stuart, 1986).

Grant, Alexander and Keith J. Stringer (eds.), *Uniting the Kingdom: The Making of British History* (London: Routledge, 1995).

Grant, George. *Lament for a Nation: The Defeat of Canadian Nationalism* (Ottawa: Carleton University Press, 1991, 1st ed. 1965).

Grant, Matthew. 'Historians, the Penguin Specials and the "State-of-the-Nation" Literature, 1958–64', *Contemporary British History*, 17:3 (2003), pp. 29–54.

Greacen, Lavinia. *J. G. Farrell: The Making of a Writer* (London: Bloomsbury, 1999).

Greene, Graham. *Ways of Escape* (London: Vintage, 1999, 1st ed. 1980).

Greene, Jack P. 'The American Revolution', *American Historical Review*, 105:1 (2000), pp. 93–102.

Greene, Jack P. 'Changing Identity in the British Caribbean: Barbados as a Case Study', in Nicholas Canny and Anthony Pagden (eds.), *Colonial Identity in the Atlantic World, 1500–1800* (Princeton: Princeton University Press, 1987).

Greene, Jack P. 'Empire and Identity', in P. J. Marshall (ed.), *The Oxford History of the British Empire*, vol. III: *The Eighteenth Century* (Oxford: Oxford University Press, 1998).

Greene, Jack P. *Evaluating Empire and Confronting Colonialism in Eighteenth-Century Britain* (Cambridge: Cambridge University Press, 2013).

Grob-Fitzgibbon, Benjamin. *Continental Drift: Britain and Europe from the End of Empire to the Rise of Euroscepticism* (Cambridge: Cambridge University Press, 2016).

Grob-Fitzgibbon, Benjamin. *Imperial Endgame: Britain's Dirty Wars and the End of Empire* (London: Palgrave Macmillan, 2011).

Guha, Ranajit. 'Not at Home in Empire', *Critical Inquiry*, 23:3 (Spring, 1997), pp. 482–93.

Guha, Ranajit. 'On Some Aspects of the Historiography of Colonial India', in Ranajit Guha and Gayatri Chakravorty Spivak (eds.), *Select Subaltern Studies* (Oxford: Oxford University Press, 1988).

Hadfield, Andrew. *Shakespeare, Spenser and the Matter of Britain* (London: Palgrave, 2004).

Haeussler, Mathias. 'The Popular Press and Ideas of Europe: The *Daily Mirror*, the *Daily Express*, and Britain's First Application to Join the EEC, 1961–63', *Twentieth Century British History*, 25:1 (2014), pp. 108–31.

Hall, Catherine. *Civilising Subjects: Metropole and Colony in the English Imagination, 1830–1867* (London: Polity, 2002).

Hall, Catherine. 'What is a West Indian?', in Bill Schwarz (ed.), *West Indian Intellectuals in Britain* (Manchester: Manchester University Press, 2003).

Hall, Catherine and Sonya O. Rose (eds.), *At Home with the Empire: Metropolitan Culture and the Imperial World* (Cambridge: Cambridge University Press, 2006).

Hall, Catherine. *Macaulay and Son: Architects of Imperial Britain* (New Haven: Yale University Press, 2012).

Hall, David. *Emerging from an Entrenched Colonial Economy: New Zealand Primary Production, Britain and the EEC, 1945–1975* (London: Palgrave, 2017).

Hall, H. Duncan. *Commonwealth: A History of the British Commonwealth of Nations* (London: Van Nostrand Rheinhold, 1971).

Hall, H. Duncan. 'The Genesis of the Balfour Declaration of 1926', *Journal of Commonwealth Political Studies*, 1:3 (1962), pp. 169–93.

Hammerton, A. James and Alistair Thomson, *Ten Pound Poms: Australia's Invisible Migrants* (Manchester: Manchester University Press, 2005).

Hampshire, Edward. *From East of Suez to the Eastern Atlantic: British Naval Policy 1964–70* (London: Routledge, 2016).

Hampshire, James. *Citizenship and Belonging: Immigration and the Politics of Demographic Governance in Postwar Britain* (Basingstoke: Palgrave, 2005).

Hampton, Mark. *Hong Kong and British Culture, 1945–97* (Manchester: Manchester University Press, 2016).

Hancock, W. K. *The Modern Map* (Oxford: Oxford University Press, 1941).

Hancock, W. K. *Survey of British Commonwealth Affairs*, vol. II: *Problems of Economic Policy, 1918–1939* (London: Oxford University Press, 1940).

Hanham, H. J. 'The Scottish Nation Faces the Post-Imperial World', *International Journal*, 23 (1968), p. 584.

Hanham, H. J. *Scottish Nationalism* (Cambridge, MA: Harvard University Press, 1969).

Hansen, Peter H. 'Confetti of Empire: The Conquest of Everest in Nepal, India, Britain and New Zealand', *Comparative Studies in Society and History*, 42:2 (2000), pp. 307–32.

Hansen, Peter H. 'Coronation Everest: The Empire and Commonwealth in the "Second Elizabethan Age"', in Stuart Ward (ed.), *British Culture and the End of Empire* (Manchester: Manchester University Press, 2001).

Hansen, Randall. *Citizenship and Immigration in Post-war Britain* (Oxford: Oxford University Press, 2000).

Hansen, Randall. 'The Kenyan Asians, British Politics, and the Commonwealth Immigrants Act, 1968', *The Historical Journal*, 42:3 (1999), pp. 809–34.

Harder, Peter. 'Cognitive Sociolinguistics, Language Systems and the Fall of Empires', in Jocelyne Daems, Eline Zenner, Kris Heylen, Dirk Speelman and Hubert Cuyckens (eds.) *Change of Paradigms – New Paradoxes* (Berlin: Mouton de Gruyter, 2015).

Hartley, Anthony. *A State of England* (London: Hutchinson, 1963).

Harvie, Christopher. *No Gods and Precious Few Heroes: Twentieth-Century Scotland* (Edinburgh: Edinburgh University Press, 2016, 1st ed. 1981).

Harvie, Christopher. *Scotland and Nationalism: Scottish Society and Politics, 1707 to the Present* (3rd ed., London: Routledge, 1998).

Hastings, Adrian. *The Construction of Nationhood: Ethnicity, Religion and Nationalism* (Cambridge: Cambridge University Press, 1997).

Hatton, Timothy J. 'Emigration from the UK, 1870–1913 and 1950–1998', *European Review of Economic History*, 8:2 (August 2004), pp. 149–71.

Hayday, Matthew and Raymond B. Blake, *Celebrating Canada*, vol. 1: *Holidays, National Days, and the Crafting of Identities* (Toronto: University of Toronto Press, 2016).

Hebert, Joel. '"Sacred Trust": Rethinking Late British Decolonization in Indigenous Canada', *Journal of British Studies*, 58:3 (2019), pp. 565–97.

Hechter, Michael. *Internal Colonialism: The Celtic Fringe in British National Development, 1536–1966* (London: Routledge & Kegan Paul, 1975).

Heffer, Simon. *Like the Roman: The Life of Enoch Powell* (London: Phoenix, 1999).

Heffer, Simon. *Nor Shall My Sword: The Reinvention of England* (London: Weidenfeld and Nicolson, 1999).

Henderson, Ailsa and Richard Wyn Jones, *Englishness: The Political Force Transforming Britain* (Oxford: Oxford University Press, 2021).

Hennessy, Peter. *Having It So Good: Britain in the Fifties* (London: Allen Lane, 2006).

Hennessy, Peter. *Never Again: Britain, 1945–51* (London: Jonathan Cape, 1992).

Hesse, Barnor. 'Diasporicity', in Barnor Hesse (ed.), *Un/settled Multiculturalisms* (London: Zed Books, 2000), pp. 97–9.

Hewitt, Christopher. 'The Roots of Violence: Catholic Grievances and Irish Nationalism during the Civil Rights Period', in Patrick J. Roche and Brian Barton (eds.), *The Northern Ireland Question: Myth and Reality* (2nd ed., Tonbridge: Wordzworth, 2013).

Hilton, Matthew. *Consumerism in Twentieth Century Britain: The Search for a Historical Movement* (Cambridge: Cambridge University Press, 2003).

Hinds, Donald. *Journey to an Illusion: The West Indian in Britain* (London: Bogle-L'Ouverture, 2001, 1st ed. 1966).

Hinds, Donald. *Mother Country: In the Wake of a Dream* (London: Hansib, 2014).

Hinds, Donald. 'The *West Indian Gazette*: Claudia Jones and the Black Press in Britain', *Race and Class*, 50:1 (2008), pp. 88–97.

Hiro, Dilip. *Black British, White British* (London: Eyre and Spottiswoode, 1971).

Hirschi, Caspar. *The Origins of Nationalism: An Alternative History from Ancient Rome to Early Modern Germany* (Cambridge: Cambridge University Press, 2012).

Hitchens, Peter. *The Abolition of Britain* (London: Quartet Books, 1999).

Hoare, Quintin and Geoffrey Nowell-Smith (eds.), *Selections from the Prison Notebooks of Antonio Gramsci* (London: Lawrence and Wishart, 1971).

Hobhouse, Hermione. *Lost London: A Century of Demolition and Decay* (London: Macmillan, 1971).

Hobsbawm, Eric. 'Falklands Fallout', *Marxism Today*, January 1983, pp. 13–19.

Holland, Alison. 'Does the British Flag Mean Nothing to Us?' British Democratic Traditions and Aboriginal Rights Claims in Interwar Australia, *Australian Historical Studies*, 50:3 (2019), pp. 321–38.

Holland, R. F. *Britain and the Commonwealth Alliance, 1918–1939* (London: Palgrave, 1981).

Hollen Lees, Lynn. *Planting Empire, Cultivating Subjects: British Malaya, 1786–1941* (Cambridge: Cambridge University Press, 2017).

Holt, Thomas. *The Problem of Freedom: Race. Labor, and Politics in Jamaica and Britain, 1832–1938* (Baltimore: Johns Hopkins University Press, 1992).

Hopkins, A. G. *American Empire: A Global History* (Princeton: Princeton University Press, 2018).

Hopkins, A. G. 'Rethinking Decolonization', *Past and Present*, 200 (2008), pp. 211–47.

Horne, Donald. *God is an Englishman* (Ringwood: Penguin, 1969).

Horne, Donald. *The Lucky Country: Australia in the Sixties* (Ringwood: Penguin, 1964).

Horne, Donald. *A Time of Hope: Australia, 1966–72* (Sydney: Angus & Robertson, 1980).

Horne, Nick (ed.), *Donald Horne: Selected Essays* (Melbourne: La Trobe University Press, 2017).

Horsman, Reginald. *Race and Manifest Destiny: The Origins of American Racial Anglo-Saxonism* (Cambridge, MA: Harvard University Press, 1981).

Howe, Stephen. *Anticolonialism in British Politics: The Left and the End of Empire* (Oxford: Oxford University Press, 1993).

Howe, Stephen. 'Internal Decolonization? British Politics since Thatcher as Post-colonial Trauma', *Twentieth Century British History*, 14:3 (2003), pp. 286–304.

Howe, Stephen. *Ireland and Empire: Colonial Legacies in Irish History and Culture* (Oxford: Oxford University Press, 2000).

Howe, Stephen. 'C. L. R. James: Visions of History, Visions of Britain', in Bill Schwarz (ed.), *West Indian Intellectuals in Britain* (Manchester: Manchester University Press, 2003).

Huddleston, Trevor. *Nought for Your Comfort* (New York: Doubleday, 1956).

Hudson, W. J. *Blind Loyalty: Australia and the Suez Crisis, 1956* (Melbourne: Melbourne University Press, 1989).

Hudson, W. J. and M. P. Sharp, *Australian Independence: Colony to Reluctant Kingdom* (Melbourne: Melbourne University Press, 1988).

Hunt, Lynn. *Inventing Human Rights: A History* (New York: Norton, 2007).

Hurwitz, Matthew. 'Relocating Englishness: The 1960s Postimperial Turn and National Identity in John Fowles *The Magnus*', *Modern Fiction Studies*, 61:3 (Fall 2015), pp. 446–68.

Hurwitz, Samuel J. 'The Federation of the West Indies: A Study in Nationalisms', *Journal of British Studies*, 6:1 (November 1966), pp. 158–9.

Huttenback, R. A. 'The British Empire as a "White Man's Country": Racial Attitudes and Immigration Legislation in the Colonies of White Settlement', *Journal of British Studies*, 13:1 (November 1973), pp. 108–37.

Huttenback, Robert A. 'Racism and Imperialism in the Antipodes', *Southeast Asia Series*, 19:2 (January 1971), pp. 1–15.

Huxley, Elspeth. *A Man from Nowhere* (London: Chatto & Windus, 1964).

Huxley, Elsbeth. *A Thing to Love* (London: Chatto and Windus, 1954).

Hyam, Ronald. *Britain's Declining Empire: The Road to Decolonisation, 1918–1968* (Cambridge: Cambridge University Press, 2006).

Hyam, Ronald and Peter Henshaw, *The Lion and the Springbok: Britain and South Africa Since the Boer War* (Cambridge: Cambridge University Press, 2003).

Hynd, Stacy. 'Killing the Condemned: The Practice and Process of Capital Punishment in British Africa, 1900–1950s', *Journal of African History*, 49 (2008), pp. 403–18.

Igartua, José. *The Other Quiet Revolution: National Identities in English Canada, 1945–71* (Vancouver: UBC Press, 2006).

Ilahi, Shereen. *Imperial Violence and the Path to Independence: India, Ireland and the Crisis of Empire* (London: I. B. Tauris, 2016).

Ince, Onur Ulas. *Colonial Capitalism and the Dilemmas of Liberalism* (Oxford: Oxford University Press, 2018).

Iriye, Akira. *Cultural Internationalism and World Order* (Baltimore: Johns Hopkins Press, 2000).

Jack, Ian. *The Country Formerly Known as Great Britain: Writings, 1989–2009* (London: Jonathan Cape, 2009), pp. xi–xii.

Jackson, Alvin. *Home Rule: An Irish History, 1800–2000* (Oxford: Oxford University Press, 2003).

Jackson, Alvin. *The Two Unions: Ireland, Scotland, and the Survival of the United Kingdom, 1707–2007* (Oxford: Oxford University Press, 2012).

Jackson, Ben. *The Case for Scottish Independence: A History of Nationalist Political Thought in Modern Scotland* (Cambridge: Cambridge University Press, 2020).

Jackson, Daniel. *Popular Opposition to Irish Home Rule in Edwardian Britain* (Liverpool: Liverpool University Press, 2009).

Jain, Rajendra K. 'Jawaharlal Nehru and the European Economic Community', *India Quarterly*, 71:1 (2015), pp. 1–15.

James, Robert Rhodes. *Anthony Eden* (London: Weidenfeld and Nicolson, 1986).

James, Winston. 'The Black Experience in Twentieth-Century Britain', in Philip D. Morgan and Sean Hawkins (eds.), *Black Experience and the Empire* (Oxford: Oxford University Press, 2004).

Jasanoff, Maya. *Edge of Empire: Lives, Culture, and Conquest in the East, 1750–1850* (New York: Alfred A. Knopf, 2005).

Jasanoff, Maya. *Liberty's Exiles: The Loss of America and the Remaking of the British Empire* (London: Harper Press, 2011).

Jebb, Richard. *The Britannic Question: A Survey of Alternatives* (London: Longmans, Green & Co., 1913).

Jeeves, Alan H. 'Arthur Keppel-Jones: Scholar, Teacher, Liberal Intellectual', *South African Historical Journal*, 32:1 (1995), pp. 24–33.

Jeeves, Alan H. 'Interview with Arthur Keppel-Jones', *South African Historical Journal*, 32:1 (1995), pp. 11–23.

Jeffreys, Kevin. *Retreat from the New Jerusalem: British Politics, 1951–64* (London: St Martin's Press, 1997).

Jenkins, Daniel Thomas. *The British, their Identity, and their Religion* (London: SCM Press, 1975).

Jennings, Ivor. *The Approach to Self-Government* (Cambridge: Cambridge University Press, 1956).

Jensen, Steven L. B. *The Making of International Human Rights: The 1960s, Decolonization and the Reconstruction of Global Values* (Cambridge: Cambridge University Press, 2016).

Jobbins, Siôn T. *The Phenomenon of Welshness II* (Llanrwst: Gwasg Carreg Gwalch, 2013).

Johnes, Martin. *Wales Since 1939* (Manchester: Manchester University Press, 2012).

Johnson, Gregory A. 'The Last Gasp of Empire: The 1964 Flag Debate Revisited', in Phillip Buckner (ed.), *Canada and the End of Empire* (Vancouver: UBC Press, 2005).

Johnson, Howard. 'The Black Experience in the British Caribbean in the Twentieth Century', in Philip D. Morgan and Sean Hawkins (eds.), *Black Experience and the Empire* (Oxford: Oxford University Press, 2004).

Johnson, Miranda. *The Land is Our History: Indigeneity, Law, and the Settler State* (Oxford: Oxford University Press, 2016).

Johnston, Hugh J. M. *The Voyage of the Komagata Maru: The Sikh Challenge to Canada's Colour Bar* (Vancouver: UBC Press, 2014, 1st ed. 1989).

Jones, Barry O. 'Pollard, Reginald Thomas (1894–1981)', in Melanie Nolan (gen. ed.), *Australian Dictionary of Biography,* vol. 18: *1981–1990, L–Z* (Melbourne: Melbourne University Publishing, 2012).

Jones, Craig Owen. '"Songs of Malice and Spite"? Wales, Prince Charles, and an Anti-investiture Ballad of Dafydd Iwan', *Music and Politics*, 7:2 (Summer 2013).

Jones, J. Mervyn. 'British Nationality Act, 1948', *British Yearbook of International Law*, 25 (1948), pp. 158–79.

Jordan, Matthew. '"Australia in this Matter is under Some Scrutiny": Early Australian Initiatives to the Rhodesian Problem, 1961–64', *International History Review*, 42:1 (2020), pp. 77–98.

Jordens, Ann-Mari. *Redefining Australians: Immigration, Citizenship and National Identity* (Sydney: Hale & Iremonger, 1995).

Kaiser, Wolfram. *Using Europe, Abusing the Europeans: Britain and European Integration, 1945–63* (London: Macmillan, 1996).

Kalusa, Walima T. 'The Killing of Lilian Margaret Burton and Black and White Nationalisms in Northern Rhodesia (Zambia) in the 1960s', *Journal of Southern African Studies*, 37:1 (March 2011), pp. 63–77.

Karatani, Rieko. *Defining British Citizenship: Empire, Commonwealth and Modern Britain* (London: Frank Cass, 2003).

Kaul, Chandrika. '"At the Stroke of the Midnight Hour": Lord Mountbatten and the British Media at Indian Independence', *The Round Table*, 97:398 (October 2008), pp. 677–93.

Kazimi, Ali. *Undesirables: White Canada and the Komagata Maru – An Illustrated History* (Vancouver: Douglas and McIntyre, 2012).

Kearney, Hugh. *The British Isles: A History of Four Nations* (Cambridge: Cambridge University Press, 1989).

Kelly, Matthew. 'Irish Nationalist Opinion and the British Empire in the 1850s and 1860s', *Past and Present*, 204 (August 2009), pp. 127–54.

Kendle, John. *Federal Britain: A History* (London: Routledge, 1997).

Kennedy, Dane. 'Constructing the Colonial Myth of Mau Mau', *International Journal of African Colonial Studies*, 25:2 (1992), pp. 241–60.

Kennedy, Dane. 'The Dream of Greater Britain', *Historical Reflections*, 47:2 (Summer 2021), pp. 105–17.

Kennedy, Dane. *The Imperial History Wars: Debating the British Empire* (London: Bloomsbury, 2018).

Kennedy, Paul. *The Rise and Fall of British Naval Mastery* (New York: Scribner, 1976).

Kennedy, Thomas C. 'Troubled Tories: Dissent and Confusion Concerning the Party's Ulster Policy, 1910–1914', *Journal of British Studies*, 46:3 (July 2007), pp. 570–93.

Kenny, Kevin (ed.), *Ireland and the British Empire* (Oxford: Oxford University Press, 2004).

Kenny, Mary. *Crown and Shamrock: Love and Hate between Ireland and the British Monarchy* (Dublin: New Island, 2009).

Kenny, Michael. *The Politics of English Nationhood* (Oxford: Oxford University Press, 2014).

Kenny, Michael and Nick Pearce, *Shadows of Empire: The Anglosphere in British Politics* (Cambridge: Polity Press, 2018).

Kenyatta, Jomo. *Facing Mount Kenya* (London: Secker and Warburg, 1938).

Keppel-Jones, Arthur. *When Smuts Goes: A History of South Africa from 1952–2010, First Published in 2015* (London: Victor Gollancz, 1947).

Kermode, Frank. *The Sense of an Ending: Studies in the Theory of Fiction with a New Epilogue* (Oxford: Oxford University Press, 2000, 1st ed. 1967).

Kidd, Colin. *Subverting Scotland's Past: Scottish Whig Historians and the Creation of an Anglo-British Identity, 1689–c. 1830* (Cambridge: Cambridge University Press, 1993).

Kidd, Colin. *Union and Unionisms: Political Thought in Scotland, 1500–2000* (Cambridge: Cambridge University Press, 2008).

Killingray, David. '"A Good West Indian, a Good African, and, in Short, a Good Britisher": Black and British in a Colour-Conscious Empire, 1760–1950', *Journal of Imperial and Commonwealth History*, 36:3 (2008), pp. 363–81.

Kinealy, Christine. *War and Peace: Ireland Since the 1960s* (London: Reaktion Books, 2010).

Kinealy, Christine. 'At Home with the Empire: The Example of Ireland', in Catherine Hall and Sonya O. Rose (eds.), *At Home with the Empire: Metropolitan Culture and the Imperial World* (Cambridge: Cambridge University Press, 2006).

Knowles, Valerie. *Forging Our Legacy: Canadian Citizenship and Immigration, 1900–1977* (Ottawa: Citizenship and Immigration Canada, 2000).

Koditschek, Theodore. *Liberalism, Imperialism, and the Historical Imagination: Nineteenth-Century Visions of a Greater Britain* (Cambridge: Cambridge University Press, 2011).

Koestler, Arthur (ed.), *Suicide of a Nation?* (London: Hutchinson, 1963).

Kong, Vivian. 'Multiracial Britons: Britishness, Diasporas, and Cosmopolitanism in Interwar Hong Kong', PhD Thesis, University of Bristol (March 2019).

Kostal, Rande W. *A Jurisprudence of Power: Victorian Empire and the Rule of Law* (Oxford: Oxford University Press, 2005).

Kumar, Krishan. *The Making of English National Identity* (Cambridge: Cambridge University Press, 2003).

Kumar, Krishan. *Visions of Empire: How Five Imperial Regimes Shaped the World* (Princeton: Princeton University Press, 2017).

Kumarasingham, H. 'The Historical Constitution', in Peter Cain and H. Kumarasingham (eds.), *The Cambridge Constitutional History of the United Kingdom*, vol. 1 (Cambridge: Cambridge University Press, 2023).

Kumarasingham, H. 'Constitution and Empire', in Peter Cain and H. Kumarasingham (eds.), *The Cambridge Constitutional History of the United Kingdom*, vol. 2 (Cambridge: Cambridge University Press, 2023).

Kumarasingham, H. 'The "New Commonwealth" 1947–49: A New Zealand Perspective on India Joining the Commonwealth', *The Round Table*, 95:385 (2006), pp. 441–54.

Kumarasingham, H. *Onward with Executive Power: Lessons from New Zealand, 1947–57* (Wellington: Institute of Policy Studies, 2010).

Kumarasingham, H. *A Political Legacy of the British Empire: Power and the Parliamentary System in Post-Colonial India and Sri Lanka* (London: I. B. Tauris, 2013).

Kumarasingham, H. 'The "Tropical Dominions": The Appeal of Dominion Status in the Decolonisation of India, Pakistan and Ceylon', *Transactions of the Royal Historical Society*, 23 (2013), pp. 223–45.

Kushner, Tony. *The Battle of Britishness: Migrant Journeys, 1685 to the Present* (Manchester: Manchester University Press, 2012).

Kyle, Keith. *Suez: Britain's End of Empire in the Middle East* (London: I. B. Tauris, 2011, 1st ed. 1991).

Laidlaw, Zoë and Alan Lester (eds.), *Indigenous Communities and Settler Colonialism: Land Holding, Loss and Survival in an Interconnected World* (London: Palgrave Macmillan, 2015).

Lake, Marilyn. *Progressive New World: How Settler Colonialism and Transpacific Change Shaped American Reform* (Cambridge, MA: Harvard University Press, 2019).

Lake, Marilyn and Henry Reynolds, *Drawing the Global Colour Line: White Men's Countries and the Question of Racial Equality* (Melbourne: Melbourne University Press, 2008).

Lamb, Richard. *The Failure of the Eden Government* (London: Sidwick and Jackson, 1987).

Lambert, John. 'An Unknown People: Reconstructing British South African Identity', *Journal of Imperial and Commonwealth History*, 37:4 (2009), pp. 599–617.

Lambert, John. '"Welcome Home": White English-speaking South Africans and the Royal Visit of 1947', *South African Historical Journal*, 69:1 (2017), pp. 101–12.

Lamming, George. *The Pleasures of Exile* (London: Michael Joseph, 1960).

Larkin, Philip. *High Windows* (London: Faber & Faber, 1974).

Lester, Alan. 'British Settler Discourse and the Circuits of Empire', *History Workshop Journal*, 54 (2002), pp. 25–48.

Lester, Alan. 'Humanism, Race and the Colonial Frontier', *Transactions of the Institute of British Geographers*, 37:1 (2012), pp. 132–48.

Lester, Alan. *Imperial Networks: Creating Identities in Nineteenth Century South Africa and Britain* (London: Routledge, 2001).

Levin, Bernard. *The Pendulum Years: Britain and the Sixties* (London: Jonathan Cape, 1970).

Levy, Andrea. *Small Island* (London: Headline, 2004).

Lewis, Joanna. '"Daddy Wouldn't Buy Me a Mau Mau": The British Popular Press and the Demoralization of Empire', in E. S. Atieno Odhiambo and John Lonsdale (eds.), *Mau Mau and Nationhood: Arms, Authority and Narration* (Oxford: James Currey, 2003).

Limb, Peter. 'Early ANC Leaders and the British World: Ambiguities and Identities', *Historia*, 47:1 (May 2002), pp. 56–82.

Limb, Peter. 'The Empire Writes Back: African Challenges to the Brutish (South African) Empire in the Early 20th Century', *Journal of Southern African Studies*, 41:3 (2015), pp. 599–616.

Linstrum, Erik. *Age of Emergency: Living with Violence at the End of the British Empire* (Oxford: Oxford University Press, 2023).

Linstrum, Erik. 'Facts about Atrocity: Reporting Colonial Violence in Postwar Britain', *History Workshop Journal*, 84 (Autumn 2017), pp. 108–27.

Linstrum, Erik. *Ruling Minds: Psychology in the British Empire* (Cambridge, MA: Harvard University Press, 2016).

Lloyd, Lorna. '"A Family Quarrel". The Development of the Dispute over Indians in South Africa', *The Historical Journal*, 34:3 (September 1991), pp. 703–25.

Lloyd, Lorna. '"A Most Auspicious Beginning": The 1946 United Nations General Assembly and the Question of the Treatment of Indians in South Africa', *Review of International Studies*, 16:2 (April 1990), pp. 131–53.

Lloyd-Jones, Naomi and Margaret M. Scull, 'A New Plea for an Old Subject? Four Nations History for the Modern Period', in Naomi Lloyd-Jones and Margaret M. Scull (eds.), *Four Nations Approaches to Modern 'British' History* (London: Palgrave Macmillan, 2018).

Longpré, Nicole. '"An Issue That Could Tear Us Apart": Race, Empire and Economy in the British (Welfare) State, 1968', *Canadian Journal of History*, XLVI (2011), pp. 63–95.

Lonsdale, John. 'Mau Maus of the Mind: Making Mau Mau and Remaking Kenya', *Journal of African History*, 31:3 (1990), pp. 393–421.

Louis, Wm Roger. 'American Anti-Colonialism, Suez, and the Special Relationship', *International Affairs*, 61:3 (1985), pp. 409–16.

Louis, Wm Roger. *The British Empire in the Middle East, 1945–51: Arab Nationalism, the United States and Postwar Imperialism* (Oxford: Oxford University Press, 1994).

Louis, Wm Roger. *Ends of British Imperialism: The Scramble for Empire, Suez and Decolonization* (London: I. B. Tauris, 2006).

Lower, Arthur R. M. *Canadians in the Making: A Social History of Canada* (Toronto: Longmans Green and Co., 1958).

Lowry, Donal. 'The Crown, Empire Loyalism and the Assimilation of non-British White Subjects in the British World: An Argument against "Ethnic Determinism"', in Carl Bridge and Kent Fedorowich (eds.), *The British World: Diaspora, Culture and Identity* (London: Cass, 2003).

Lowry, Donal. 'Rhodesia, 1890–1980', in Robert Bickers (ed.), *Settlers and Expatriates* (Oxford: Oxford University Press, 2010).

Lowry, Donal. 'Ulster Resistance and Loyalist Rebellion in the Empire', in Keith Jeffrey (ed.), *'An Irish Empire'? Aspects of Ireland and the British Empire* (Manchester: Manchester University Press, 1996).

Ludlow, Piers. 'Commercial Preferences: Economics and Britain's European Choices, 1945–2016', in David Thackeray, Andrew Thompson and Richard Toye (eds.), *Imagining Britain's Economic Future, c.1800–1975: Trade, Consumerism, and Global Markets* (London: Palgrave, 2018).

Ludlow, N. Piers. *Dealing with Britain: The Six and the First UK Application to the EEC* (Cambridge: Cambridge University Press, 1997).

Lustick, Ian S. *Unsettled States, Disputed Lands: Britain and Ireland, France and Algeria, Israel and the West Bank-Gaza* (Ithaca: Cornell University Press, 1993).

Lycett, Andrew. *Ian Fleming* (Phoenix: Turner Publishing, 1996).

Lyon, Peter. 'The Commonwealth and the Suez Crisis', in Wm Roger Louis and Roger Owen (eds.), *Suez 1956: The Crisis and its Consequences* (Oxford: Oxford University Press, 1989).

Macaulay, Thomas Babington. *The History of England from the Accession of James II, 5 vols.* (New York: Harper & Brothers, 1856).

MacDonald, Norbert. 'A Critical Growth Cycle for Vancouver, 1900–1914', *BC Studies*, 17 (Spring 1973), pp. 26–42.

MacDonald, Norbert. 'Population Growth and Change in Seattle and Vancouver, 1880–1960', *Pacific Historical Review*, 39:3 (August 1970), pp. 297–321.

Mackenzie, Francine. 'Trade, Dominance, Dependence and the End of the Settlement Era in Canada, Australia, New Zealand and South Africa, 1920–73', in Christopher Lloyd, Jacob Metzer and Richard Sutch (eds.), *Settler Economies in World History* (Leiden: Brill, 2013).

Mackenzie, Hector. 'An Old Dominion and the New Commonwealth: Canadian Policy on the Question of India's Membership', *Journal of Imperial and Commonwealth History*, 27:3 (September 1999), pp. 82–112.

MacKenzie, John M. 'Irish, Scottish, Welsh and English Worlds? The Historiography of a Four-Nations Approach to the History of the British Empire', in Catherine Hall and Keith McClelland (eds.), *Race, Nation and Empire: Making Histories, 1750 to the Present* (Manchester: Manchester University Press, 2010).

MacKenzie, John M. *Propaganda and Empire: The Manipulation of British Public Opinion, 1880–1960* (Manchester: Manchester University Press, 1984).

MacKenzie, John M. with Nigel Dalziel, *The Scots in South Africa: Ethnicity, Identity, Gender and Race, 1772–1914* (Manchester: Manchester University Press, 2012).

MacKenzie, John M. (ed.), *Imperialism and Popular Culture* (Manchester: Manchester University Press, 1986).

MacKenzie, John M. and Bryan Glass (eds.), *Scotland, Empire and Decolonisation in the Twentieth Century* (Manchester: Manchester University Press, 2015).

Mackey, Eva. 'Unsettling Expectations: (Un)certainty, Settler States of Feeling, Law, and Decolonization', *Canadian Journal of Law and Society / Revue Canadienne Droit et Société*, 29:2 (2014), pp. 235–52.

Mackinnon, Malcolm (ed.), *New Zealand in World Affairs*, vol. II: *1957–72* (Wellington: New Zealand Institute of International Affairs, 1991).

Magee, Gary B. 'The Importance of Being British? Imperial Factors and the Growth of British Imports, 1870–1960', *Journal of Interdisciplinary History*, xxxvii:3 (Winter 2007), pp. 341–69.

Magee, Gary B. and Andrew S. Thompson, *Empire and Globalisation: Networks of People, Goods and Capital in the British World, c. 1850–1914* (Cambridge: Cambridge University Press, 2010).

Magner, Brigid. 'Case Study: Anglo-Australian Relations and the Book Trade', in Craig Munro and Robyn Sheahan-Bright (eds.), *Paper Empires: A History of the Book in Australia, 1946–2005* (St Lucia: University of Queensland Press, 2006).

Mahone, Sloan. 'The Psychology of Rebellion: Colonial Medical Responses to Dissent in British East Africa', *Journal of African History*, 47 (2006), pp. 241–58.

Majdalany, Fred. *State of Emergency: The Full Story of Mau Mau* (London: Longmans, 1962).

Mann, Jatinder. 'The Evolution of Commonwealth Citizenship, 1945–48 in Canada, Britain and Australia', *Comparative Politics*, 50:3 (2012), pp. 293–313.

Mann, Jatinder. *The Search for a New Identity: The Rise of Multiculturalism in Canada and Australia, 1890s–1970s* (New York: Peter Lang, 2016).

Mansergh, Nicholas. *The Commonwealth Experience*, vol. 1: *The Durham Report to the Anglo-Irish Treaty* (London: Macmillan, 1982).

Mansergh, Nicholas. *The Commonwealth Experience*, vol. 2: *From British to Multiracial Commonwealth* (London: Macmillan, 1982).

Mansergh, Nicholas. *Survey of Commonwealth Affairs: Problems of Wartime Cooperation and Post-war Change* (London: Frank Cass, 1968).

Mansergh, Nicholas. *The Unresolved Question: The Anglo-Irish Settlement and Its Undoing, 1912–72* (New Haven: Yale University Press, 1991).

Mark, Chi-kwan. 'Decolonising Britishness? The 1981 British Nationality Act and the Identity Crisis of Hong Kong Elites', *Journal of Imperial and Commonwealth History*, 48:3 (2019), pp. 565–90.

Marks, Shula. *The Ambiguities of Dependence in South Africa: Class, Nationalism, and the State in Twentieth-Century Natal* (Baltimore: Johns Hopkins University Press, 1986).

Markus, Andrew. 'William Cooper and the 1937 Petition to the King', *Aboriginal History*, 7:1 (1983), pp. 46–60.

Marquand, David. *Britain since 1918: The Strange Career of British Democracy* (London: Phoenix, 2009).

Marquand, David. 'How United is the Modern United Kingdom?', in Alexander Grant and Keith J. Stringer (eds.), *Uniting the Kingdom? The Making of British History* (London: Routledge, 1995).

Marr, Andrew. *The Day Britain Died* (London: Profile Books, 2000).

Marshall, P. J. 'No fatal impact? The Elusive History of Imperial Britain', *Times Literary Supplement*, 12 March 1993.

Marshall, P. J. 'A Nation Defined by Empire, 1755–1776', in Alexander Grant and Keith J. Stringer (eds.), *Uniting the Kingdom? The Making of British History* (London: Routledge, 1995).

Marshall, P. J. '*A Free though Conquering People': Eighteenth-Century Britain and its Empire* (Aldershot: Ashgate, 2003).

Marston, Geoffrey. 'Armed Intervention in the 1956 Suez Canal Crisis: The Legal Advice Tendered to the British Government', *The International and Comparative Law Quarterly*, 37:4 (October 1988), pp. 773–817.

Maschler, Tom (ed.), *Declaration* (London: MacGibbon & Kee, 1957).

Matera, Marc. *Black London: The Imperial Metropolis and Decolonization in the Twentieth Century* (Berkeley: University of California Press, 2015).

Maugham, Somerset. *East of Suez: A Play in Seven Scenes* (New York: George H. Doran, 1922).

Mauss, Marcel. *The Gift* (London: Routledge, 1990).

Mawani, Renisa. *Across Oceans of Law: The Komagata Maru and Jurisdiction in the Time of Empire* (Durham, NC: Duke University Press, 2018).

Mawby, Spencer. 'Overwhelmed in a Very Small Place: The Wilson Government and the Crisis over Anguilla', *Twentieth Century British History*, 23:2 (2012), pp. 246–74.

May, Alex. 'Commonwealth or Europe?: Macmillan's Dilemma, 1961–63', in Alex May (ed.), *Britain, the Commonwealth and Europe: The Commonwealth and Britain's Applications to Join the European Communities* (Basingstoke: Palgrave, 2001).

Mazower, Mark. *No Enchanted Palace: The End of Empire and the Ideological Origins of the United Nations* (Princeton: Princeton University Press, 2009).

Mazrui, Ali A. 'African Attitudes to the European Economic Community', *International Affairs*, 39:1 (January 1963), pp. 24–36.

McAloon, Jim. *Judgements of All Kinds: Economic Policy-Making in New Zealand 1945–1984* (Wellington: Victoria University Press, 2013).

McBride, Ian. 'J. G. A. Pocock and the Politics of British History', in Naomi Lloyd-Jones and Margaret M. Scully (eds.), *Four Nations Approaches to Modern 'British' History* (London: Palgrave, 2018), pp. 33–57.

McBride, Ian. *The Siege of Derry in Ulster Protestant Mythology* (Dublin: Four Courts, 1997).

McBride, Ian. 'Ulster and the British Problem', in Richard English and Graham Walker (eds.), *Unionism in Modern Ireland* (Basingstoke: Macmillan, 1996).

McCourt, David M. 'What was Britain's "East of Suez Role"? Reassessing the Withdrawal, 1964–68', *Diplomacy and Statecraft*, 20:3 (2009), pp. 453–72.

McCrone, David. 'Scotland Days: Evolving Nation and Icons', in David McCrone and Gayle McPherson (eds.), *National Days: Constructing and Mobilising National Identity* (London: Palgrave Macmillan, 2009).

McCrone, David. *Understanding Scotland: The Sociology of a Stateless Nation* (London: Routledge, 1992).

McDermott, Harold N. 'Towards "That Republic in Which Complexions Do Not Matter": Derek Walcott's *Drums and Colours* Fifty Years On', *Anthurium: A Caribbean Studies Journal*, 11:2 (2014), doi:http://doi.org/10.33596/anth.269.

McDougall, Hamish. 'Buttering up: Britain, New Zealand and Negotiations for European Community Enlargement, 1970–71', *International History Review*, 43:2 (2021), pp. 333–47.

McGregor, Russell. 'Protest and Progress: Aboriginal Activism in the 1930s', *Australian Historical Studies*, 25:101 (October 1993), pp. 555–68.

McIntyre, W. David. 'The Strange Death of Dominion Status', *Journal of Imperial and Commonwealth History*, 27:2 (May 1999), pp. 193–212.

McKenna, Mark. *An Eye for Eternity: The Life of Manning Clark* (Melbourne: Meigunyah Press, 2011).

McKenna, Mark. '"An Audience with the Queen": Indigenous Australians and the Crown, 1954–2017', *Royal Studies Journal*, 5:1 (2018), pp. 157–67.

McKittrick, David and David McVea, *Making Sense of the Troubles* (London: Penguin, 2001).

McLaughlin, Malcolm. *The Long, Hot Summer of 1967: Urban Rebellion in America* (New York: Palgrave, 2014).

McLisky, Claire. 'The Emotional Economies of Protestant Missions to Aboriginal People in Nineteenth-Century Australia', in David Lemmings and Ann Brooks (eds.), *Emotions and Social Change: Historical and Sociological Perspectives* (New York: Routledge, 2014).

McNeil, Daniel. '"The Rivers of Zimbabwe will Run Red with Blood": Enoch Powell and the Post-Imperial Nostalgia of the Monday Club', *Journal of Southern African Studies*, 37:4 (December 2011), pp. 731–45.

McNeill, Ronald. *Ulster's Stand for the Union* (London: John Murray, 1922).

Mead, Matthew. '*Empire Windrush*: The Cultural Memory of an Imaginary Arrival', *Journal of Postcolonial Writing*, 45:2 (June 2009), pp. 137–8.

Meaney, Neville. 'Britishness and Australian Identity: The Problem of Nationalism in Australian History and Historiography', *Australian Historical Studies*, 32:116 (2001), pp. 76–90.

Meaney, Neville. 'Britishness and Australia: Some Reflections', in Carl Bridge and Kent Fedorowich (eds.), *The British World: Disapora, Culture, Identity* (London: Cass, 2003).

Meaney, Neville K. *A History of Australian Defence and Foreign Policy,* vol. I: *The Search for Security in the Pacific* (Sydney: Sydney University Press, 1976).

Meaney, Neville. 'The End of "White Australia" and Australia's Changing Perceptions of Asia, 1945–1990', *Australian Journal of International Affairs*, 49:2 (1995), pp. 171–89.

Megahey, Alan. *Humphrey Gibbs: Beleaguered Governor* (Basingstoke: Macmillan, 1998).

Mehrotra, S. R. 'On the Use of the Term "Commonwealth"', *Journal of Commonwealth Political Studies*, 2:1 (1963), pp. 1–16.

Mehta, Uday. *Liberalism and Empire: A Study in Nineteenth-Century British Liberal Thought* (Chicago: University of Chicago Press, 1999).

Meleady, Dermot. *Redmond: The Parnellite* (Cork: Cork University Press, 2008).

Mercau, Ezequiel. *The Falklands War: An Imperial History* (Cambridge: Cambridge University Press, 2019).

Mercau, Ezequiel. '"The Mouse That Roared": The Falklands and Gibraltar in Thatcher's (Greater) Britain', in Christian D. Pedersen and Stuart Ward (eds.), *The Break-Up of Greater Britain* (Manchester: Manchester University Press, 2021).

Metcalf, Thomas R. *Ideologies of the Raj* (Cambridge: Cambridge University Press, 1995).

Michelman, Cherry. *The Black Sash of South Africa: A Case Study in Liberalism* (London: Oxford University Press, 1975).

Milward, Alan S. *The UK and the European Community,* vol. 1: *The Rise and Fall of a National Strategy, 1945–1963* (London: Frank Cass, 2002).

Mintz, Sidney. *Sweetness and Power: The Place of Sugar in Modern History* (New York: Viking-Penguin, 1985).

Mishra, Pankaj. *From the Ruins of Empire: The Revolt against the West and the Remaking of Asia* (London: Allen Lane, 2012).

Mitcham, John C. *Race and Imperial Defence in the British World* (Cambridge: Cambridge University Press, 2016).

Mitchell, James. *Hamilton 1967: The By-Election That Transformed Scotland* (Edinburgh: Luath Press, 2017).

Mlambo, A. S. '"We Have Blood Relations over the Border": South Africa and Rhodesian Sanctions, 1965–1975', *African Historical Review*, 40:1 (2008), pp. 1–29.

Mokyr, Joel. *The Enlightened Economy: An Economic History of Britain, 1700–1850* (New Haven: Yale University Press, 2009).

Moore, R. J. *Making the New Commonwealth* (Oxford: Clarendon Press, 1987).

Morgan, Kenneth O. *Callaghan: A Life* (Oxford: Oxford University Press, 1999).

Morgan, Kenneth O. *Rebirth of a Nation: Wales 1880–1980* (Oxford: Oxford University Press, 1981).

Morris, Ewan. *Our Own Devices: National Symbols and Political Conflict in Twentieth-Century Ireland* (Dublin: Irish Academic Press, 2005).

Morris, James. 'The Popularisation of Imperial History: The Empire on Television', *Journal of Imperial and Commonwealth History*, 1 (1973), pp. 113–18.

Moyn, Samuel. *Human Rights and the Use of History* (London: Verso, 2017).

Moyn, Samuel. *The Last Utopia: Human Rights in History* (Cambridge, MA: Harvard University Press, 2010).

Mulholland, Marc. *Northern Ireland at the Crossroads: Ulster Unionism in the O'Neill Years* (London: Palgrave, 2000).

Murphy, Philip. 'Britain as a Global Power in the Twentieth Century', in Andrew Thompson (ed.), *Britain's Experience of Empire in the Twentieth Century* (Oxford: Oxford University Press, 2012).

Murphy, Philip. '"An Intricate and Distasteful Subject": British Planning for the Use of Force against the European Settlers of Central Africa, 1952–65', *English Historical Review*, cxxi:492 (June 2006), pp. 746–77.

Murphy, Philip. *Monarchy and the End of Empire* (Oxford: Oxford University Press, 2013).

Murphy, Philip. *Party Politics and Decolonisation: The Conservative Party and British Colonial Policy in Tropical Africa, 1951–1964* (Oxford: Oxford University Press, 1995).

Mycock, Andrew and Ben Wellings (eds.), *The Anglosphere: Continuity, Dissonance and Location* (Oxford: Oxford University Press, 2019).

Nairn, Tom. *After Britain: New Labour and the Return of Scotland* (London: Granta, 2000).

Nairn, Tom. *The Break-up of Britain: Crisis and Neo-Nationalism* (London: Verso, 1977).

Nairn, Tom. 'The Three Dreams of Scottish Nationalism', *New Left Review*, 49 (May–June 1968), pp. 3–18.

Natarajan, Kalathmika. 'Entangled Citizens: The Afterlives of Empire in the Indian Citizenship Act, 1947–55', in Christian D. Pedersen and Stuart Ward (eds.), *The Break-up of Greater Britain* (Manchester: Manchester University Press, 2021).

Negrine, Ralph. 'The Press and the Suez Crisis: A Myth Re-examined', *The Historical Journal*, 25:4 (1982), pp. 975–83.

Nehru, Jawaharlal. *The Discovery of India* (New York: John Day, 1946).

Newman, Keith. *Ratana the Prophet* (Rosedale: Raupo, 2009).

Newman, Peter C. *The Distemper of Our Times: Canadian Politics in Transition, 1963–68* (Toronto/Montreal: McClelland and Stuart, 1968).

Niergarth, Kirt. '"This Continent Must Belong to the White Races": William Lyon Mackenzie King, Canadian Diplomacy and Immigration Law, 1908', *International History Review*, 32:4 (December 2010), pp. 599–617.

Nutting, Anthony. *No End of a Lesson: The Story of Suez* (London: Constable, 1967).

O'Brien, Conor Cruise. *States of Ireland* (New York: Pantheon, 1972).

O'Callaghan, Margaret and Catherine O'Donnell, 'The Northern Ireland Government, the "Paisleyite Movement" and Ulster Unionism in 1966', *Irish Political Studies*, 21:2 (2006), pp. 203–22.

O'Connor, Kaori. 'The King's Christmas Pudding: Globalization, Recipes, and the Commodities of Empire', *Journal of Global History*, 4:1 (2009), pp. 127–55.

Ó Dochartaigh, Niall. *From Civil Rights to Armalites: Derry and the Birth of the Troubles* (New York: Palgrave Macmillan, 2005).

Ó Dochartaigh, Niall. 'Northern Ireland', in Martin Klimke and Joachim Scharloth (eds.), *1968 in Europe: A History of Protest and Activism, 1956–1977* (New York: Palgrave Macmillan, 2008).

O'Hara, Glen. 'Imagining New Zealand's Economy in the Mid-Twentieth Century', in David Thackeray, Andrew Thompson and Richard Toye (eds.), *Imagining Britain's Economic Future, c.1800–1975: Trade, Consumerism, and Global Markets* (London: Palgrave, 2018).

O'Malley, Kate. *Ireland, India and Empire: Indo-Irish Radical Connections, 1919–64* (Manchester: Manchester University Press, 2008).

O'Neill, Terrence. *Ulster at the Crossroads* (London: Faber & Faber, 1969).

O'Toole, Fintan. *Heroic Failure: Brexit and the Politics of Pain* (London: Head of Zeus, 2018).

Oliver, W. H. 'A Destiny at Home', *New Zealand Journal of History*, 19:1 (April 1985), pp. 9–15.

Oliver, W. H. *The Story of New Zealand* (London: Faber, 1960).

Olsen, Niklas. *The Sovereign Consumer: A New Intellectual History of Neoliberalism* (London: Palgrave Macmillan, 2019).

Onslow, Sue. *Backbench Debate within the Conservative Party and its Influence on British Foreign Policy, 1948–57* (Basingstoke: Palgrave Macmillan, 1997).

Onslow, Sue. '"Battlelines for Suez": The Abadan Crisis of 1951 and the Formation of the Suez Group', *Contemporary British History*, 17:2 (2003), pp. 1–28.

Onslow, Sue. 'Julian Amery and the Suez Operation', in Simon C. Smith (ed.), *Reassessing Suez 1956: New Perspectives on the Crisis and Its Aftermath* (Aldershot: Ashgate, 2008).

Ortolano, Guy. *The Two Cultures Controversy: Science, Literature and Cultural Politics in Postwar Britain* (Cambridge: Cambridge University Press, 2009).

Osborne, John. *West of Suez* (London: Faber, 1971).

Østergaard Nielsen, Jimmi and Stuart Ward, '"Cramped and Restricted at Home": Scottish Separatism at Empire's End', *Transactions of the Royal Historical Society*, 25 (2015), pp. 159–85.

Østergaard Nielsen, Jimmi and Stuart Ward, 'Three Referenda and a By-Election: The Shadow of Empire in Devolutionary Politics', in John M. MacKenzie and Bryan Glass (eds.), *Scotland, Empire and Decolonisation in the Twentieth Century* (Manchester: Manchester University Press, 2015).

Osterhammel, Jürgen. *The Transformation of the World: A Global History of the Nineteenth Century* (Princeton: Princeton University Press, 2014).

Owen, Lord. 'The Effect of Prime Minister Anthony Eden's Illness on his Decision-Making during the Suez Crisis', *QJM: An International Journal of Medicine*, 98:6 (2005), pp. 387–402.

Owen, Nicholas. 'Four Straws in the Wind: Metropolitan Anti-Imperialism, January-February 1960', in L. J. Butler and Sarah Stockwell (eds.), *The Wind of Change: Harold Macmillan and British Decolonization* (Basingtoke: Palgrave, 2013).

Owen, Nicholas. '"More Than a Transfer of Power": Independence Day Ceremonies in India, 15 August 1947', *Contemporary Record*, 6:3 (1992), pp. 415–51.

Pagden, Anthony. *Lords of All the World: Ideologies of Empire in Spain, Britain and France c.1500–c.1800* (New Haven: Yale University Press, 1995).

Paris, Michael. 'Africa in Post-1945 British Cinema', *South African Historical Journal*, 48:1 (2003), pp. 61–70.

Park, Bert E. *Ailing, Aging, Addicted: Studies of Compromised Leadership* (Lexington: University of Kentucky Press, 1993).

Parker, Matthew. *Goldeneye: Where Bond Was Born* (London: Hutchinson, 2014).

Parkinson, Alan F. *Ulster Loyalism and the British Media* (Dublin: Four Courts, 1998).

Patterson, Sheila. *Immigration and Race Relations in Britain, 1960–67* (New York: Oxford University Press, 1969).

Paul, Kathleen. '"British Subjects" and "British Stock": Labour's Postwar Imperialism', *Journal of British Studies*, 34:2 (1995), pp. 233–76.

Paul, Kathleen. *Whitewashing Britain: Race and Citizenship in the Postwar Era* (Ithaca: Cornell University Press, 1997).

Pearson, John. *The Life of Ian Fleming* (London: Bloomsbury, 2013, 1st ed. 1966).

Peden, G. C. 'Suez and Britain's Decline as a World Power', *The Historical Journal*, 55:4 (December 2012), pp. 1073–96.

Pedersen, Christian D. 'African Decolonisation and the Fate of Britishness, 1959–1965', PhD Thesis, University of Copenhagen (2016).

Pedersen, Christian D. and Stuart Ward (eds.), *The Break-up of Greater Britain* (Manchester: Manchester University Press, 2021).

Pedersen, Susan. *The Guardians: The League of Nations and the Crisis of Empire* (Oxford: Oxford University Press, 2015).

Pennybacker, Susan. *From Scottsboro to Munich: Race and Political Culture in 1930s Britain* (Princeton: Princeton University Press, 2009).

Perkins, John. *Geopolitics and Green Revolution: Wheat, Genes and the Cold War* (New York: Oxford University Press, 1997).

Perry, Kennetta Hammond. *London Is the Place for Me: Black Britons, Citizenship and the Politics of Race* (Oxford: Oxford University Press, 2016).

Pham, P. L. *Ending East of Suez: The British Decision to Withdraw from Malaysia and Singapore 1964–1968* (Oxford: Oxford University Press, 2010).

Phillips, Mike and Trevor Phillips, *Windrush: The Irresistible Rise of Multiracial Britain* (London: Harper Collins, 1998).

Pickering, Jeffrey. *Britain's Withdrawal from East of Suez: The Politics of Retrenchment* (London: Macmillan, 1997).

Pilkington, Edward. *Beyond the Mother Country: West Indians and the Notting Hill White Riots* (London: I. B. Tauris, 1988).

Pimlott, Ben. *Harold Wilson* (London: Harper Collins, 1992).

Pitts, Jennifer. *A Turn to Empire: The Rise of Imperial Liberalism in Britain and France* (Princeton: Princeton University Press, 2005).

Pocock, J. G. A. 'British History: A Plea for a New Subject', *New Zealand Journal of History*, 8 (1974), pp. 3–21.

Pocock, J. G. A. 'British History: A Plea for a New Subject: Reply', *Journal of Modern History*, 47:4 (December 1975), pp. 626–8.

Pocock, J. G. A. 'Conclusion: Contingency, Identity, Sovereignty', in Alexander Grant and Keith J. Stringer (eds.), *Uniting the Kingdom? The Making of British History* (London: Routledge, 1995).

Pocock, J. G. A. *The Discovery of Islands: Essays in British History* (Cambridge: Cambridge University Press, 2005).

Pocock, J. G. A. 'Empire, State and Confederation: The War of American Independence as a Crisis in Multiple Monarchy', in John Robertson (ed.), *A Union for Empire: Political Thought and the Union of 1707* (Cambridge: Cambridge University Press, 1995).

Pocock, J. G. A. 'The Limits and Divisions of British History: In Search of the Unknown Subject', *American Historical Review*, 87:2 (1982), pp. 311–36.

Pocock, J. G. A. 'Working on Ideas in Time', in L. P. Curtis (ed.), *The Historian's Workshop: Original Essays by Sixteen Historians* (New York: Knopf, 1970).

Poiner, Grechen and Sybil Jack (eds.), *Limits of Location: Creating a Colony* (Sydney: Sydney University Press, 2007).

Pooley, Colin and Jean Turnbull, *Migration and Mobility in Britain since the Eighteenth Century* (London: Routledge, 1998).

Porter, Bernard. *The Absent-Minded Imperialists: What the British Really Thought about Their Empire* (Oxford: Oxford University Press, 2004).

Potter, Robert B. and Mark Wilson. 'Barbados', in Robert B. Potter (ed.), *Urbanization, Planning and Development in the Caribbean* (London: Mansell, 1989).

Potter, Simon. *Broadcasting Empire: The BBC and the British World, 1922–1970* (Oxford: Oxford University Press, 2012).

Potter, Simon. *News and the British World: The Emergence of an Imperial Press System, 1876–1922* (Oxford: Oxford University Press, 2003).

Powell, Graeme. 'A Diarist in the Cabinet: Lord Derby and the Australian Colonies, 1882–85', *Australian Journal of Politics and History*, 51:4 (2005), pp. 489–90.

Price, John. *Orienting Canada: Race, Empire, and the Transpacific* (Vancouver: UBC Press, 2011).

Price, Richard. *An Imperial War and the English Working Class* (London: Routledge and Kegan Paul, 1972).

Prince, Simon. 'The Global Revolt of 1968 and Northern Ireland', *The Historical Journal*, 49:3 (September 2006), pp. 851–75.

Prince, Simon. *Northern Ireland's 1968: Civil Rights, Global Revolt and the Origins of the Troubles* (Dublin: Irish Academic Press, 2007).

Prince, Simon. '5 October 1968 and the Beginning of the Troubles: Flashpoints, Riots and Memory', *Irish Political Studies*, 27:3 (2012), pp. 394–410.

Prince, Simon and Geoffrey Warner. *Belfast and Derry in Revolt: A New History of the Start of the Troubles* (Dublin: Irish Academic Press, 2012).

Purdie, Bob. *Politics in the Streets: The Origins of the Civil Rights Movement in Northern Ireland* (Belfast: Blackstaff, 1990).

Putnam, Lara. 'Citizenship from the Margins: Vernacular Theories of Rights and the State from the Interwar Caribbean', *Journal of British Studies*, 53:1 (January 2014), pp. 162–91.

Raeburn, Michael. *Black Fire: Accounts of the Guerilla War in Zimbabwe* (London: Julian Friedmann, 1978).

Ranger, Terrence. 'Violence Variously Remembered: The Killing of Pieter Oberholtzer in July 1964', *History in Africa*, 24 (1997), pp. 273–86.

Rappaport, Erika. *A Thirst for Empire: How Tea Shaped the Modern World* (Princeton: Princeton University Press, 2017).

Rasch, Astrid. 'Autobiography after Empire: Individual and Collective Memory in Dialogue', PhD Thesis, University of Copenhagen (August 2016).

Rast, M. C. '"Ireland's Sister Nations": Internationalism and Sectarianism in the Irish Struggle for Independence, 1916–22', *Journal of Global History*, 10:3 (2015), pp. 479–501.

Reddy, William. *The Navigation of Feeling: A Framework for the History of Emotions* (Cambridge: Cambridge University Press, 2001).

Redwood, John. *The Death of Britain?* (London: Macmillan, 1999).

Reinecke, Carl. 'The Vanishing Point: The Story of the Publication of *The Lucky Country*', *Meanjin*, 75:2 (Winter 2016), pp. 42–54.

Reus-Smit, Christian. *Individual Rights and the Making of the International System* (Cambridge: Cambridge University Press, 2013).

Reynolds, Chris. *Sous les pavés . . . The Troubles: Northern Ireland, France and the European Collective Memory of 1968* (Bern: Peter Lang, 2014).

Reynolds, Z. Nia (ed.), *When I Came to England: An Oral History of Life in 1950s and 1960s Britain* (London: Black Stock, 2001).

Rich, Paul B. *White Power and the Liberal Conscience: Racial Segregation and South African Liberalism, 1921–60* (Manchester: Manchester University Press, 1984).

Richards, Eric. *Britannia's Children: Emigration from England, Scotland, Wales and Ireland Since 1600* (London: Hambledon & London, 2004).

Ridden, Jennifer. 'Britishness as an Imperial and Diasporic Identity: Irish Elite Perspectives, c. 1820–70s', in Peter Gray (ed.), *Victoria's Ireland?: Irishnesss and Britishness, 1837–1901* (Dublin: Four Courts Press, 2004).

Ritscherle, Alice. 'Disturbing the People's Peace: Patriotism and "Respectable" Racism in British Responses to Rhodesian Independence', in Philippa Levine and Susan Grayzel (eds.), *Gender, Labour, War and Empire* (London: Palgrave Macmillan, 2008).

Robbins, Keith. '"This Grubby Wreck of Old Glories": The United Kingdom and the End of the British Empire', *Journal of Contemporary History*, 15:1 (1980), pp. 81–95.

Robertson, John. 'Empire and Union: Two Concepts of the Early Modern European Political Order', in J. Robertson (ed.), *A Union for Empire: Political Thought and the Union of 1707* (Cambridge: Cambridge University Press, 1995).

Robertson, Paul and John Singleton, 'The Old Commonwealth and Britain's First Application to join the EEC: 1961–3', *Australian Economic History Review*, 40:2 (2000), pp. 159–77.

Robinson, Ronald. 'The Moral Disarmament of African Empire, 1919–1947', *Journal of Imperial and Commonwealth History*, 8:1 (1979), pp. 86–104.

Rollings, Neil. *British Business in the Formative Years of European Integration, 1945–73* (Cambridge: Cambridge University Press, 2007), pp. 129–37.

Roos, Neil. *Ordinary Springboks: White Servicemen and Social Justice in South Africa, 1939–1961* (Aldershot: Ashgate, 2005).

Rose, Peter. *How the Troubles Came to Northern Ireland* (Basingstoke: Palgrave, 2000).

Rose, Peter. 'Labour, Northern Ireland and the Decision to Send in the Troops', in Peter Caterall and Sean McDougall (eds.), *The Northern Ireland Question in British Politics* (London: Macmillan, 1996).

Rosenboim, Or. *The Emergence of Globalism: Visions of World Order in Britain and the United States, 1939–1950* (Princeton: Princeton University Press, 2017).

Rosenwein, Barbara. 'Worrying about Emotions in History', *American Historical Review*, 107 (2002), pp. 821–45.

Rowlands, E. 'The Politics of Regional Administration: The Establishment of the Welsh Office', *Public Administration*, 50 (Autumn 1972), pp. 333–51.

Rowley, C. D. *The Destruction of Aboriginal Society*, vol. 1: *Aboriginal Policy and Practice* (Canberra: Australian National University Press, 1970).

Rowse, Tim. 'The Identity of Indigenous Political Thought', in Lisa Ford and Tim Rowse (eds.), *Between Indigenous and Settler Governance* (Abingdon: Routledge, 2013).

Rowse, Tim. *Indigenous and Other Australians Since 1901* (Sydney: UNSW Press, 2017).

Roy, Anjali Gera. 'Making and Unmaking of Strangers: The *Komagata Maru* Episode and the Alienation of Sikhs as Undesirable Aliens', *Sikh Formations: Religion, Culture, Theory*, 12:1 (2016), pp. 67–86.

Roy, Srirupa. '"A Symbol of Freedom": The Indian Flag and the Transformations of Nationalism, 1906–2002', *Journal of Asian Studies*, 65:3 (August 2006), pp. 495–527.

Ruane, Joseph. 'Colonialism and the Interpretation of Irish Historical Development', in Marilyn Silverman and P. H. Gulliver (eds.), *Approaching the Past: Historical Anthropology through Irish Case Studies* (New York: Columbia University Press, 1992).

Rush, Anne Spry. *Bonds of Empire: West Indians and Britishness from Victoria to Decolonization* (Oxford: Oxford University Press, 2001).

Rush, Anne Spry. 'Imperial Identity in Colonial Minds: Harold Moody and the League of Coloured Peoples', *Twentieth Century British History*, 13:4 (2002), pp. 356–83.

Ryder, Sean. 'Defining Colony and Empire in Early Nineteenth-Century Irish Nationalism', in Terrence McDonough (ed.), *Was Ireland a Colony: Economics, Politics and Culture in Nineteenth-Century Ireland* (Dublin: Irish Academic Press, 2005).

Saker, Harry. *The South African Flag Controversy, 1925–28* (Oxford: Oxford University Press, 1980).

Sampson, Anthony. *Anatomy of Britain* (London: Hodder & Stoughton, 1962).

Samuel, Raphael. 'British Dimensions: "Four Nations History"', *History Workshop Journal*, 40 (Autumn, 1995), pp. iii–xxii.

Samuel, Raphael. 'Unravelling Britain', in *Island Stories*, vol. 2 (London: Verso, 1998).

Sandbrook, Dominic. *Never Had It So Good: A History of Britain from Suez to the Beatles* (London: Abacus, 2006).

Sandbrook, Dominic. *White Heat: A History of Britain in the Swinging Sixties* (London: Abacus, 2007).

Sanghera, Sathnam. *Empireland: How Imperialism Has Shaped Modern Britain* (London: Viking, 2021).

Sapire, Hilary. 'African Loyalism and Its Discontents: The Royal Tour of South Africa, 1947', *Historical Journal*, 54:1 (March 2011), pp. 215–40.

Sapire, Hilary. 'Ambiguities of Loyalism: The Prince of Wales in India and Africa, 1921–2 and 25', *History Workshop Journal*, 73 (Spring 2012), pp. 37–65.

Sapire, Hilary. '"We Have Seen the Son of Heaven/We Have Seen the Son of Our Queen": African Encounters with Prince Alfred on his Royal Tour, 1860', in Sarah Carter and Maria Nugent (eds.), *Mistress of Everything: Queen Victoria in Indigenous Worlds* (Manchester: Manchester University Press, 2016).

Sasson, Tehila. *The Solidarity Economy: Nonprofits and the Postimperial Origins of Neoliberalism* (forthcoming, Princeton University Press).

Sasson, Tehila, James Vernon, Miles Ogborn, Priya Satia and Catherine Hall, 'Britain and the World: A New Field?', *Journal of British Studies*, 57 (October 2018), pp. 677–708.

Saunders, Robert. 'Brexit and Empire: "Global Britain" and the Myth of Imperial Nostalgia', *Journal of Imperial and Commonwealth History*, 48:6 (2020), pp. 1140–74.

Saunders, Robert. *Yes to Europe: The 1975 Referendum and Seventies Britain* (Cambridge: Cambridge University Press, 2018).

Schaffer, Gavin. 'Legislating against Hatred: Meaning and Motive in Section Six of the Race Relations Act of 1965', *Twentieth Century British History*, 25:2 (2014), pp. 251–75.

Schenk, Catherine R. *The Decline of Sterling* (Cambridge: Cambridge University Press, 2010).

Schofield, Camilla. *Enoch Powell and the Making of Postcolonial Britain* (Cambridge: Cambridge University Press, 2013).

Schreuder, Deryck. 'The Making of the Idea of Colonial Nationalism', in John Eddy and Deryck Schreuder (eds.), *The Rise of Colonial Nationalism* (Oxford: Oxford University Press, 1988).

Schreuder, Deryck M. and Stuart Ward (eds.), *Australia's Empire* (Oxford: Oxford University Press, 2008).

Schrift, Alan D. (ed.), *The Logic of the Gift: Toward an Ethic of Generosity* (New York: Routledge, 1997).

Schwarz, Bill. 'Claudia Jones and *The West Indian Gazette*: Reflections on the Emergence of Post-colonial Britain', *Twentieth Century British History*, 14:3 (2003), pp. 264–85.

Schwarz, Bill. 'Forgetfulness: England's Discontinuous Histories', in Stuart Ward and Astrid Rasch (eds.), *Embers of Empire in Brexit Britain* (London: Bloomsbury, 2019).

Schwarz, Bill. '"The Only White Man in There": The Re-racialization of England, 1956–58', *Race and Class*, 38:1 (1996), pp. 65–78.

Schwarz, Bill. '"Shivering in the Noonday Sun": The British World and the Dynamics of "Nativisation"', in Kate Darian-Smith, Stuart Macintyre and Patricia Grimshaw (eds.), *Britishness Abroad: Transnational Movements and Imperial Cultures* (Melbourne: Melbourne University Press, 2007).

Schwarz, Bill. *The White Man's World: Memories of Empire*, vol. 1 (Oxford: Oxford University Press, 2011).

Schwarz, Bill (ed.), *West Indian Intellectuals in Britain* (Manchester: Manchester University Press, 2003).

Scott, Roger D. 'Ulster in Perspective: The Relevance of Non-European Experience', *Australian Outlook*, 23:3 (1969), pp. 246–57.

Seeley, J. R. *The Expansion of England: Two Courses of Lectures* (London: Macmillan, 1891, 1st ed. 1883).

Seldon, Arthur (ed.), *Rebirth of a Nation: A Symposium of Essays by Eighteen Writers* (London: Pan, 1964).

Selvon, Sam. *The Lonely Londoners* (London: Penguin, 2006, 1st ed. 1956).

Shanks, Michael. *The Stagnant Society: A Warning* (Harmondsworth: Penguin, 1961).

Shaw, Tony. *Eden, Suez and the Mass Media: Propaganda and Persuasion during the Suez Crisis* (London: I. B. Tauris, 1995).

Shuckburgh, Evelyn. *Descent to Suez* (London: Weidenfeld and Nicolson, 1986).

Shute, Neville. *In the Wet* (London: William Heinemann, 1953).

Simpson, A. W. Brian. *Human Rights and the End of Empire: Britain and the Genesis of the European Convention* (Oxford: Oxford University Press, 2001).

Simpson, Thula. *Umkhonto we Sizwe: The ANC's Armed Struggle* (London: Penguin, 2019).

Sinclair, Keith. *A Destiny Apart: New Zealand's Search for National Identity* (Wellington: Allen & Unwin, 1986).

Sinclair, Keith. 'The Historian as Prophet", in Muriel F. Lloyd Pritchard (ed.), *The Future of New Zealand* (Christchurch: Whitcombe and Tombs, 1964).

Singh, Anita Inder. 'Imperial Defence and the Transfer of Power in India', *International History Review*, 4:4 (November 1982), pp. 568–88.

Singh, Anita Inder. 'Keeping India in the Commonwealth: British Political and Military Aims, 1947–49', *Journal of Contemporary History*, 20:3 (July 1985), pp. 469–81.

Singh, Baba Gurdit. *Voyage of Komagatamaru or India's Slavery Abroad* (Calcutta: The Compiler, 1928).

Singh, R. P. 'The Irwin Declaration of 1929: Its Background and Implications', *Proceedings of the Indian History Congress*, 38 (1977), pp. 460–8.

Sithole, Ndabaningi. *Obed Mutezo: The Mudzimu Christian Nationalist* (Nairobi: Oxford University Press, 1970).

Skilton, David. 'Contemplating the Ruins of London: Macaulay's New Zealander and Others', *Literary London: Interdisciplinary Studies in the Representation of London*, 2:1 (March 2004), www.literarylondon.org/london-journal/march2004/skilton.html.

Skinner, Quentin. 'Some Problems in the Analysis of Political Thought and Action', *Political Theory*, 2 (1974), pp. 277–303.

Skinner, Rob. *The Foundations of Anti-Apartheid: Liberal Humanitarians and Transnational Activists in Britain and the United States, c.1919–64* (London: Palgrave, 2010).

Skinner, Rob. 'Humanitarianism and Human Rights in Global Anti-Apartheid', in Anna Konieczna and Rob Skinner (eds.), *A Global History of Anti-Apartheid: 'Forward to Freedom' in South Africa* (London: Palgrave, 2019).

Skinner, Rob. 'The Moral Foundations of British Anti-Apartheid Activism, 1946–1960', *Journal of Southern African Studies*, 35:2 (2009), pp. 399–416.

Sluga, Glenda. *Internationalism in the Age of Nationalism* (Philadelphia: University of Pennsylvania Press, 2013).

Sluga, Glenda. 'The Transnational History of International Institutions', *Journal of Global History*, 6 (2011), pp. 219–22.

Smith, Anthony D. *The Ethnic Origins of Nations* (Oxford: Blackwell, 1986).

Smith, Evan. 'The Pivot of Empire: Australia and the Imperial Fascism of the British Union of Fascists', *History Australia*, 14:3 (2017), pp. 378–94.

Smith, Howard. 'Apartheid, Sharpeville and "Impartiality": The Reporting of South Africa on BBC Television, 1948–61', *Historical Journal of Film, Radio and Television*, 13:3 (1993), pp. 251–8.

Smith, Jean P. 'Persistence and Privilege: Mass Migration from Britain to the Commonwealth, 1945–2000', in Christian D. Pedersen and Stuart Ward (eds.), *The Break-up of Greater Britain* (Manchester: Manchester University Press, 2021).

Smith, Simon C. 'Integration and Disintegration: The Attempted Incorporation of Malta into the United Kingdom in the 1950s', *Journal of Imperial and Commonwealth History*, 35:1 (2007), pp. 49–71.

Smith, Simon C. 'Prelude to the Suez Crisis", in Simon C. Smith (ed.), *Reassessing Suez 1956: New Perspectives on the Crisis and its Aftermath* (Aldershot: Ashgate, 2008).

Snow, C. P. *The Two Cultures and the Scientific Revolution* (Cambridge: Cambridge University Press, 1959).

Southgate, John. *The Commonwealth Sugar Agreement, 1951–74* (London: Czarnikow, 1984).

Spencer, Ian R. G. *British Immigration Policy Since 1939: The Making of Multi-Racial Britain* (London: Routledge, 1997).

Stamp, Gavin. *Lost Victorian Britain: How the Twentieth Century Destroyed the Nineteenth Century's Architectural Masterpieces* (London: Aurum Press, 2010).

Stearns, Peter and Carol Stearns. 'Emotionology: Clarifying the History of Emotions and Emotional Standards', *American Historical Review*, 90 (1985), pp. 813–36.

Steel, David. *No Entry: The Background and Implications of the Commonwealth Immigrants Act 1968* (London: C. Hurst, 1969).

Stewart, A. T. Q. *The Ulster Crisis: Resistance to Home Rule, 1912–14* (Belfast: Blackstaff Press, 1997).

Stewart, Gordon T. *Jute and Empire* (Manchester: Manchester University Press, 1998).

Stewart, Gordon T. 'The Strange Case of Jute', in John M. MacKenzie and Bryan Glass (eds.), *Scotland, Empire and Decolonisation in the Twentieth Century* (Manchester: Manchester University Press, 2015).

Stewart, Gordon T. 'Tenzing's Two Wrist Watches: The Conquest of Everest and Late Imperial Culture, 1921–1953', *Past and Present*, 149 (November 1995), pp. 170–97.

Stockwell, Sarah. *The British End of the British Empire* (Cambridge: Cambridge University Press, 2018).

Stoler, Ann Laura and Karen Strassler, 'Casting for the Colonial: Memory Work in "New Order" Java', *Comparative Studies in Society and History*, 42:1 (2000), pp. 4–48.

Strachey, John. *The End of Empire* (London: Victor Gollancz, 1959).

Strachey, Lytton. *Eminent Victorians* (London: Continuum, 2002, 1st ed. 1918).

Strachey, William. *The Historie of Travaile into Virginia Britannia* (London: Hakluyt Society, 1849).

Sutch, W. B. *Colony or Nation? Economic Crises in New Zealand from the 1860s to the 1960s* (Sydney: Sydney University Press, 1966).

Suri, Jeremi. 'The Rise and Fall of an International Counterculture, 1960–75', *American Historical Review*, 114:1 (February 2009), pp. 45–68.

Tait, Christopher. 'Brushes, Budgets and Butter: Canadian Culture and Identity at the British Empire Exhibition, 1924–25', in Philip P. Buckner and R. Douglas Francis (eds.), *Canada and the British World: Culture, Migration and Identity* (Vancouver: UBC Press, 2006).

Tanner, J. R. *Constitutional Documents on the Reign of James I, 1603–1625* (Cambridge: Cambridge University Press, 1960, 1st ed. 1930).

Tavuyanago, Baxter. 'The "Crocodile Gang" Operation: A Critical Reflection on the Genesis of the Second Chimurenga in Zimbabwe', *Global Journal of Human Social Science*, 13:4 (2013), pp. 1–10.

Tavuyanago, Baxter. 'Ndangana and the Crocodile Group Operation', History Honours dissertation, University of Zimbabwe (1985).

Taylor, A. J. P. 'British History: A Plea for a New Subject: Comments', *Journal of Modern History*, 47:4 (1975), pp. 622–6.

Taylor, A. J. P. *English History, 1914–1945: The Oxford History of England*, vol. XV (Oxford: Oxford University Press, 1965).

Taylor, Charles. *Multiculturalism: The Politics of Recognition* (Princeton: Princeton University Press, 1995).

Templeton, Malcolm. *Ties of Blood and Empire: New Zealand's Involvement in Middle East Defence and the Suez Crisis, 1947–57* (Auckland: Auckland University Press, 1994).

Thackeray, David. 'Buying for Britain, China, or India? Patriotic Trade, Ethnicity, and Market in the 1930s British Empire/Commonwealth', *Journal of Global History*, 12 (2017), pp. 386–409.

Thackeray, David. *Forging a British World of Trade: Culture, Ethnicity and Market in the Empire-Commonwealth, 1880–1975* (Oxford: Oxford University Press, 2019).

Thackeray, David and Richard Toye, 'What Was a British Buy? Empire, Europe and the Politics of Patriotic Trade in Britain, c.1945–1963', in David Thackeray, Andrew Thompson and Richard Toye (eds.), *Imagining Britain's Economic Future, c.1800–1975: Trade, Consumerism, and Global Markets* (London: Palgrave, 2018).

Thackeray, David, Andrew Thompson and Richard Toye (eds.), *Imagining Britain's Economic Future, c.1800–1975: Trade, Consumerism, and Global Markets* (London: Palgrave, 2018).

Thomas, Hugh. *The Suez Affair* (London: Weidenfeld and Nicolson, 1966).

Thomas, Hugh (ed.), *The Establishment: A Symposium* (London: Anthony Blond, 1959).

Thomas, J. J. *Froudacity: West Indian Fables by James Anthony Froude* (Philadelphia: Gebbie and Co, 1890).

Thomas, Martin. *Fight or Flight: Britain, France and Their Roads from Empire* (Oxford: Oxford University Press, 2014).

Thomas, Martin and Richard Toye (eds.), *Rhetorics of Empire: Languages of Colonial Conflict after 1900* (Manchester: Manchester University Press, 2017).

Thomas-Hope, Elizabeth. 'Hopes and Reality in the West Indian Migration to Britain', *Oral History*, 8:1 (Spring 1980), pp. 35–42.

Thompson, Andrew S. *The Empire Strikes Back?: The Impact of Imperialism on Britain from the Mid-Nineteenth Century* (Harlow: Longman, 2005).

Thompson, Andrew S. *Imperial Britain: The Empire in British Politics. c. 1880–1932* (Harlow: Pearson Education, 2000).

Thompson, Andrew S. 'The Languages of Loyalism in Southern Africa, c. 1870–1939', *English Historical Review*, cxviii (2003), pp. 617–50.

Thompson, Andrew S. 'Unravelling the Relationships between Humanitarianism, Human Rights, and Decolonization: Time for a Radical Rethink?', in Martin Thomas and Andrew S. Thompson (eds.), *The Oxford Handbook of the Ends of Empire* (Oxford: Oxford University Press, 2018).

Thompson, Andrew (ed.), *Britain's Experience of Empire in the Twentieth Century* (Oxford: Oxford University Press, 2012).

Thompson, Andrew and Martin Thomas (eds.), *The Oxford Handbook of the End of Empire* (Oxford: Oxford University Press, 2018).

Thompson, E. P. 'The Moral Economy of the English Crowd in the Eighteenth Century', *Past and Present*, 50 (February 1971), pp. 76–136.

Thompson, J. Lee. *A Wider Patriotism: Alfred Milner and the British Empire* (London: Pickering and Chatto, 2007).

Thompson, Noel. *John Strachey: An Intellectual Biography* (Basingstoke: Macmillan, 1993).

Thompson, P. S. *Natalians First: Separatism in South Africa, 1909–1961* (Johannesburg: Southern Book Publishers, 1990).

Thompson, Roger C. *Australian Imperialism in the Pacific: The Expansionist Era, 1820–1920* (Melbourne: Melbourne University Press, 1980).

Thörn, Håkon. *Anti-Apartheid and the Emergence of a Global Civil Society* (London: Palgrave, 2006).

Thornberry, Cedric. 'British Nationality Act', *The Modern Law Review*, 28 (March 1965), pp. 197–200.

Thornhill, Michael T. 'Britain, the United States and the Rise of an Egyptian Leader: The Politics and Diplomacy of Nasser's Consolidation of Power', *English Historical Review*, 119 (September 2004), pp. 892–921.

Thornton, A. P. 'Decolonisation', *International Journal*, 19:1 (Winter 1963/1964), pp. 7–29.

Tinker, Hugh. 'Jawaharlal Nehru at Simla, May 1949. A Moment of Truth?', *Modern Asian Studies*, 4:4 (1970), pp. 349–58.

Tomlinson, Jim. *Dundee and the Empire: Juteopolis 1850–1939* (Edinburgh: Edinburgh University Press, 2014).

Tomlinson, Jim. *The Politics of Decline: Understanding Post-War Britain* (Harlow: Longman, 2001).

Townend, Paul A. 'Between Two Worlds: Irish Nationalists and Imperial Crisis, 1878–1880', *Past and Present*, 194 (February 2007), pp. 139–74.

Toye, Richard. *Churchill's Empire* (London: Macmillan, 2010).

Toye, Richard. 'An Imperial Defeat? The Presentation and Reception of the Fall of Singapore', in Brian F. Farrell (ed.), *Churchill and the Lion City: Shaping Modern Singapore* (Singapore: NUS Press, 2011).

Toye, Richard. 'Words of Change: The Rhetoric of Commonwealth, Common Market and Cold War, 1961–63', in L. J. Butler and Sarah Stockwell (eds.), *The Wind of Change: Harold Macmillan and British Decolonization* (Basingstoke: Palgrave, 2013).

Trentmann, Frank. 'Before "Fair Trade": Empire, Free Trade, and the Moral Economies of Food in the Modern World', *Environment and Planning D: Society and Space*, 25 (2007), pp. 1079–102.

Trentmann, Frank. *Empire of Things: How We Became a World of Consumers, from the Fifteenth Century to the Twenty-first* (London: Allen Lane, 2016).

Trentmann, Frank. *Free Trade Nation: Commerce, Culture and Civil Society in Modern Britain* (Oxford: Oxford University Press, 2008).

Trollope, Anthony. *Tales of All Countries* (London: Chapman and Hall, 1867).

Tuson, Penelope. 'Mutiny Narratives and the Imperial Feminine', *Women's Studies International Forum*, 21:3 (1998), pp. 291–303.

Underhill, Frank. *In Search of Canadian Liberalism* (Toronto: Macmillan, 1960).

Vaisse, Maurice. 'France and the Suez Crisis', in Wm Roger Louis and Roger Owen (eds.), *Suez 1956: The Crisis and Its Consequences* (Oxford: Oxford University Press, 1989).

Varouxakis, Georgios. '"Great" Versus "Small" Nations: Size and National Greatness in Victorian Political Thought', in Duncan Bell (ed.), *Victorian Visions of Global Order: Empire and International Relations in Nineteenth-Century Political Thought* (Cambridge: Cambridge University Press, 2007).

Veracini, Lorenzo. 'Isopolitics, Deep Colonizing, Settler Colonialism', *Interventions*, 13:2 (2011), pp. 171–89.

Vernon, James. *Politics and the People: A Study in English Political Culture, c.1815–1867* (Cambridge: Cambridge University Press, 1993).

Viney, Graham. *The Last Hurrah: The 1947 Royal Tour of South Africa and the End of Empire* (London: Robinson, 2019).

Virmani, Arundhati. 'National Symbols under Colonial Domination: The Nationalization of the Indian Flag, March–August 1923', *Past & Present*, 164 (August 1999), pp. 169–97.

Von Tunzelmann, Alex. *Indian Summer: The Secret History of the End of an Empire* (London: Pocket Books, 2007).

Wagner, Kim A. *Amritsar 1919: An Empire of Fear & The Making of a Massacre* (New Haven: Yale University Press, 1919).

Walker, David. *Stranded Nation: White Australia in an Asian Region* (Perth: University of Western Australia Press, 2019).

Walker, Graham. *A History of the Ulster Unionist Party: Protest, Pragmatism and Pessimism* (Manchester: Manchester University Press, 2004).

Wallace, Elizabeth. *The British Caribbean: From the Decline of Colonialism to the End of Federation* (Toronto: University of Toronto Press, 1977).

Walsh, Maurice. *Bitter Freedom: Ireland in a Revolutionary World 1918–1923* (London: Faber & Faber, 2021).

Walshe, Peter. *The Rise of African Nationalism in South Africa: The African National Congress, 1912–52* (Berkeley: University of California Press, 1971).

Ward, Paul. *Britishness since 1870* (London: Routledge, 2004).

Ward, Russel. *The Australian Legend* (Melbourne: Oxford University Press, 1958).

Ward, Stuart. 'The Anatomy of Break-Up', in Christian D. Pedersen and Stuart Ward (eds.), *The Break-Up of Greater Britain* (Manchester: Manchester University Press, 2021).

Ward, Stuart. *Australia and the British Embrace: The Demise of the Imperial Ideal* (Melbourne: Melbourne University Press, 2001).

Ward, Stuart. 'Echoes of Empire', *History Workshop Journal*, 62 (2006), pp. 264–78.

Ward, Stuart. 'The European Provenance of Decolonization', *Past and Present*, 230 (2016), pp. 227–60.

Ward, Stuart. '"How Come England Did Not Know Me": The "Rude Awakenings" of the Windrush Era', in Christian D. Pedersen and Stuart Ward (eds.), *The Break-up of Greater Britain* (Manchester: Manchester University Press, 2021).

Ward, Stuart. 'Machiavellian Moments and the Exigencies of Leaving', *Historical Reflections*, 47:2 (Summer 2021), pp. 49–64.

Ward, Stuart. 'The MacKenzian Moment in Retrospect (or How One Hundred Volumes Bloomed)', in Andrew S. Thompson (ed.), *Writing Imperial Histories* (Manchester: Manchester University Press, 2013).

Ward, Stuart. 'A Matter of Preference: The EEC and the Erosion of the Old Commonwealth Relationship', in Alex May (ed.), *Britain, the Commonwealth and Europe: The Commonwealth and Britain's Applications to Join the European Communities* (Basingstoke: Palgrave, 2001).

Ward, Stuart. 'The "New Nationalism" in Australia, Canada and New Zealand: Civic Culture in the Wake of the British World', in Kate Darian-Smith, Stuart MacIntyre and Patricia Grimshaw (eds.), *Britishness Abroad: Transnational Movements and Imperial Cultures* (Melbourne: Melbourne University Press, 2007).

Ward, Stuart. '"No Nation Could Be Broker": The Satire Boom and the Demise of Britain's World Role', in Stuart Ward (ed.), *British Culture and the End of Empire* (Manchester: Manchester University Press, 2001).

Ward, Stuart. 'The Redundant "Dominion": Refitting the National Fabric at Empire's End', in Matthew Hayday and Raymond Blake (eds.), *Celebrating Canada*, vol. 1: *Holidays, National Days and the Crafting of Identities* (Toronto: Toronto University Press, 2016).

Ward, Stuart. 'Sir Alexander Downer and the Embers of British Australia', in Carl Bridge, Frank Bongiorno and David Lee (eds.), *The High Commissioners* (Canberra: Department of Foreign Affairs and Trade, 2010), pp. 145–63.

Ward, Stuart. 'Worlds Apart: Three "British" Prime Ministers at Empire's End', in Phillip Buckner and Doug Francis (eds.), *Rediscovering the British World* (Calgary: University of Calgary Press, 2005).

Ward, Stuart (ed.), *British Culture and the End of Empire* (Manchester: Manchester University Press, 2001).

Ward, Stuart and Astrid Rasch (eds.), *Embers of Empire in Brexit Britain* (London: Bloomsbury, 2019).

Ward, W. Peter. *White Canada Forever: Popular Attitudes and Public Policy Toward Orientals in British Columbia* (Montreal and Kingston: McGill-Queen's University Press, 2002, 1st ed. 1978).

Waters, Chris. '"Dark Strangers" in Our Midst: Discourses of Race and Nation in Britain, 1947–63', *Journal of British Studies*, 36:2 (April 1997), pp. 207–38.

Watts, Carl. 'Killing Kith and Kin: The Viability of British Military Intervention in Rhodesia, 1964–65', *Twentieth Century British History*, 16:4 (2005), pp. 382–415.

Webb, Keith. *The Growth of Nationalism in Scotland* (Glasgow: Molendinar Press, 1977).

Webster, Wendy. '"There'll Always Be an England": Representations of Colonial Wars and Immigration, 1948–68', *Journal of British Studies*, 40 (October 2001), pp. 557–84.

Webster, Wendy. *Englishness and Empire, 1939–65* (Oxford: Oxford University Press, 2005).

Webster, Wendy. *Mixing It: Diversity in World War Two Britain* (Oxford: Oxford University Press, 2018).

Wessell, Adele. 'There's No Taste Like Home: The Food of Empire', in Kate Darian-Smith, Patricia Grimshaw, Kiera Lindsey and Stuart Macintyre (eds.), *Exploring the British World: Identity, Cultural Production, Institutions* (Melbourne: RMIT Publishing, 2004).

White, Nicholas J. 'Reconstructing Europe through Rejuvenating Empire: The British, French and Dutch Experiences Compared', *Past and Present*, 210 (2011) supplement 6, pp. 211–36.

Wiener, Martin. *An Empire on Trial: Race, Murder, and Justice under British Rule, 1870–1935* (Cambridge: Cambridge University Press, 2009).

Wilgus, A. Curtis (ed.), *The Caribbean: Its Political Problems* (Gainesville: University of Florida, 1956).

Wilks, Terry. *The Biography of Douglas Mitchell* (Durban: King and Wilks, 1980).

Williams, Eric. *Capitalism and Slavery* (Chapel Hill: University of North Carolina Press, 1944).

Williams, Eric. *History of the People of Trinidad and Tobago* (London: Andre Deutsch, 1982, 1st ed. 1962).

Williams, Gwyn A. *The Welsh in Their History* (London: Croom Helm, 1982).

Williams, John. 'ANZUS: A Blow to Britain's Self-Esteem', *Review of International Studies*, 13:4 (October 1987), pp. 423–63.

Wilson, Kathleen. *The Sense of the People: Politics, Culture and Imperialism in England, 1715–1785* (Cambridge: Cambridge University Press, 1998).

Winchester, Simon. *In Holy Terror: Reporting the Ulster Troubles* (London: Faber, 1974).

Winder, Simon. *The Man Who Saved Britain* (London: Picador, 2006).

Windrich, Elaine. *Britain and the Politics of Rhodesian Independence* (London: Groom Helm, 1978).

Wolfe, Billy. *Scotland Lives: The Quest for Independence* (Edinburgh: Reprographia, 1973).

Wolpert, Stanley. *Shameful Flight: The Last Years of the British Empire in India* (Oxford: Oxford University Press, 2009).

Wood, Gordon S. *The Americanization of Benjamin Franklin* (New York: Penguin, 2004).

Wood, J. R. T. *A Matter of Weeks Rather than Months: The Impasse between Harold Wilson and Ian Smith, 1965–1969* (Bloomington: Trafford Publishing, 2008).

Wood, J. R. T. *So Far and No Further! Rhodesia's Bid for Independence during the Retreat from Empire, 1959–65* (Bloomington: Trafford Publishing, 2005).

Wormald, Jenny. 'The Creation of Britain: Multiple Kingdoms or Core and Colonies?', *Transactions of the Royal Historical Society*, 2 (1992), pp. 175–94.

Wright, Robert. 'From Liberalism to Nationalism: *Peter C. Newman's* Discovery of Canada', in Magda Fahrni and Robert Rutherdale (eds.), *Creating Postwar Canada: Community, Diversity and Dissent, 1945–75* (Vancouver: UBC Press, 2008).

Yapp, M. E. 'Suez Was Not the Turning Point', *Times Literary Supplement*, 16 July 1999.

Ziegler, Phillip. *The Authorised Life of Lord Wilson of Rievaulx* (London: Weidenfeld and Nicolson, 1993).

Ziegler, Philip. *Mountbatten: The Official Biography* (London: Collins, 1985).

Zuckerman, Michael. 'Identity in British America: Unease in Eden', in Nicholas Canny and Anthony Pagden (eds.), *Colonial Identity in the Atlantic World* (Princeton: Princeton University Press, 1987).

Zvogbo, Chengetai J. 'Church and State in Rhodesia: From the Unilateral Declaration of Independence to the Pearce Commission, 1965–72', *Journal of Southern African Studies*, 31:2 (June 2005), pp. 381–402.

Index